SECOND ED W9-BQM-736

Counseling Diverse Populations

Donald R. Atkinson
University of California—Santa Barbara

Gail Hackett
Arizona State University

Boston, Massachusetts   Burr Ridge, Illinois
Dubuque, Iowa   Madison, Wisconsin   New York, New York
San Francisco, California   St. Louis, Missouri

McGraw-Hill

A Division of The McGraw·Hill Companies

COUNSELING DIVERSE POPULATIONS. SECOND EDITION

Copyright 1998 by The McGraw-Hill Companies, Inc. All rights reserved. Previous edition 1995 by Brown & Benchmark Publishers, a Times Mirror Higher Education Group, Inc., company. Printed in the United States of America. Except as permitted under the United States Copyright Act of 1976, no part of this publication may be reproduced or distributed in any form or by any means, or stored in a data base or retrieval system, without the prior written permission of the publisher.

This book is printed on recycled, acid-free paper containing 10% postconsumer waste.

1 2 3 4 5 6 7 8 9 0 DOC/DOC 9 0 9 8 7

ISBN 0-697-25280-9

Publisher: Jane Vaicunas
Editor: Curtis M. McClay/Sharon Geary
Project manager: Jane C. Morgan
Production supervisor: Sandy Ludovissy
Cover design: David Arnold
Part Opener photo credits: 1 © Young-Wolff/Photo Edit. 2 © A. Boccaccio/The Image Bank. 3 © Stephen J. Wilkes/The Image Bank. 4 © Robert Ginn/Photo Edit. 5 © Marc Romanelli MCMXCV/The Image Bank. 6 © Barros and Barros/Image Bank
Compositor: ElectraGraphics, Inc.
Typeface: 10/12 Times Roman
Printer: R. R. Donnelley–Crawfordsville

Library of Congress Cataloging-in-Publication Data

Counseling diverse populations / [edited by] Donald R. Atkinson, Gail Hackett. — 2nd ed.
    p. cm.
    Includes bibliographical references and index.
    ISBN 0-697-25280-9
    1. Counseling. 2. Aged—Counseling of. 3. Women—Counseling of. 4. Handicapped—Counseling of. 5. Gays—Counseling of.
I. Atkinson, Donald R. II. Hackett, Gail.
BF637.C6C6372 1997
158´.3´08—dc21
                        97-8388
                        CIP

http://www.mhcollege.com

CONTENTS

PART 2
The Client with a Disability 137

PART 3
The Elderly Client 179

PREFACE

The purpose of this second edition of *Counseling Diverse Populations* is the same as the first edition, to call to the attention of mental health practitioners the unique experiences and needs of four groups within the American society that, along with ethnic and selected other groups, share the common experience of oppression. These four groups are people with disabilities, older people, women, and gay people. Each of these four groups has a common physical and/or behavioral characteristic that identifies individuals as members of the group and that has singled them out for differential and inferior treatment. Each of these groups has in the past experienced (and continues to experience) discrimination as a result of their physical and/or behavioral uniqueness. Discrimination for all four groups has ranged from negative stereotypes to physical violence. It is our thesis that mental health practitioners need to be aware of the unique experiences of these groups in order to effectively intervene on their behalf.

This edition represents a complete revision of the earlier edition. Part 1, which is written by the co-editors of the book, was completely reorganized and expanded from three chapters to five chapters. The first chapter describes how traditional psychotherapeutic approaches have ignored the experiences of, and failed to meet the needs of, people with disabilities, older people, women, and gay people. The first chapter also provides a rationale for identifying the four groups as minorities, as well as a brief profile of each group. In chapters 2 through 5, we review the past and present treatment of each group by society in general and mental health care providers in particular.

Part 2, which consists of three chapters on people with disabilities, is completely new to this edition. Part 3, "The Elderly Client," is also completely new to this edition. In part 4, we have retained two of three readings on the female client from the first edition, but chapter 14 is new to this second edition. Similarly, for part 5, "The Gay Client," we have retained two of the readings from the first edition but added a new reading for chapter 15. The last chapter (chapter 16), which examines the implications of diversity issues for counseling practice, counselor training, and counseling research, has been updated for the current edition.

This book is intended as a text for undergraduate and graduate courses in counseling psychology, clinical psychology, social work, and other mental health professions where human rights issues are discussed. The book might be used as a primary text in courses where diversity or human rights issues are the primary focus or as a supplemental text in counseling theory and technique courses. When used in conjunction with another McGraw-Hill publication, *Counseling American Minorities: A Cross-Cultural Perspective,* the book provides an excellent introduction to a broad range of diversity issues.

We hope the book will help mental health professionals look beyond the current *Diagnostic and Statistical Manual of Mental Disorders* and conventional psychotherapeutic strategies when diagnosing and treating clients. It is our belief that experiences, behaviors, attitudes, values, and needs based on membership in the groups discussed in this book must be taken into account as part of diagnosis and treatment. Furthermore, it is our hope that counselors and other mental health providers will reconceptualize their roles as facilitators of behavioral *and social* change when working with the diverse populations discussed in this book.

This book is dedicated to those individuals who, because of their physical ability, age, gender, or sexual orientation, have been singled out for differential and inferior treatment.
We would also like to dedicate this book to Gail's son, Ryan, and to the memory of Don's son, Jimmie.

D. R. A. and G. H.

PART 1

Counseling and Diverse Populations

1
Introduction

Traditional Approaches to Counseling and Psychotherapy

Most, if not all, mental health professions that practice counseling and psychotherapy can trace their roots to Freud and psychoanalysis; Shilling (1984) refers to Freud as "grandfather to all of us . . . who are psychologists and/or counselors" (p. 17). Many of the concepts and constructs developed by Freud are still perceived as necessary and sufficient conditions for psychotherapy. Indeed, Corey (1991) suggests that Freud's theory "is a benchmark against which many other theories are measured" (p. 96). While many of Freud's contributions to the mental health professions have been widely applauded, some of his ideas have been criticized as erroneous or even deleterious.

Two of the unfortunate legacies that Freud left to mental health professionals are the overemphasis on intrapsychic etiologies for mental health problems and the exclusive reliance on one-to-one psychotherapy for the treatment of psychological disturbances. Freud believed an individual's behavior was the result of instinctual, biological drives originating within the individual. While neo-Freudians and subsequent theorists have moved away from the heavy stress Freud placed on sexual instinct and aggression as determinants of behavior, they continue to emphasize an internal model of psychopathology, one which views the etiology of the client's problem (and the resources to resolve it) as residing within the client. Thus, for example, advocates of person-centered therapy believe that psychological maladjustment occurs when "the *organism denies* to awareness, or *distorts* in awareness, significant experiences" (italics added, Meador & Rogers, 1984, p. 159). Gestalt therapists believe that individuals are responsible for their own behavior and that "*People are responsible* for what they choose to do" (italics added, Simkin & Yontef, 1984, p. 291). Even behavior therapists, who eschew needs, drives, motives, traits, and conflicts as underlying causes of behavior, believe that "A crucial factor in therapy is the *client's motivation,* and *willingness to cooperate* in the arduous and challenging task of making significant changes in real-life behavior" (italics added, Wilson, 1984, p. 253).

If the primary mechanisms that shape and maintain affect, behavior, and cognition reside within the individual, then it follows that psychotherapy should focus attention on the individual. Freud's use of the psychoanalytic situation, a one-to-one therapeutic environment in which the analyst facilitates critical self-examination, had a significant and enduring impact on counseling and psychotherapy. This emphasis on intrapsychic pathology and psychotherapy is evident in the goals therapists have for counseling. Although the client may be encouraged to state therapeutic goals as part of the counseling process, therapists conventionally pursue metagoals of changing the client's affect, behavior, and/or cognitions. The therapist works on these metagoals by encouraging catharsis, interpreting feelings, challenging negative self-perceptions, assigning homework, and a myriad of other counseling strategies. Regardless of the counselor's material and the strategies employed to reach it, an underlying assumption of nearly all conventional counseling approaches is that some aspect of the client must change in order to resolve the problem. With the exception of embryonic group and family counseling efforts, counseling and psychotherapy prior to the 1950s involved a one-therapist, one-client model.

Family therapists were among the first to recognize the limitations of focusing therapy on the individual outside the context of the family. According to Nichols (1984), Freud actively discouraged psychotherapists from involving other family members when they were treating a patient. Involving other family members in therapy was discouraged because it would undermine the transference process, considered essential for treatment success. As a result, early attempts at interviewing with families were little more than individual psychotherapy for each family member. It was not until the early 1950s that researchers examining communication patterns in the families of schizophrenics developed a system theory approach to therapy and with it the concept that it is more effective to treat a family system conjointly than a single family member individually (Nichols, 1984).

The social conditions of the 1960s set the stage for a second, more disparate, group of mental health professionals to criticize the shortcomings of conventional psychopathology and psychotherapy theory. Civil rights, antiwar, feminist, and other human rights movements directly and indirectly motivated many disfranchised groups to seek (and in some cases demand) mental health services. Counselors and other mental health professionals soon discovered that their training did not prepare them to work with such issues as discrimination, alienation, and basic survival (Aubrey & Lewis, 1983). The result of pressure by disfranchised groups for counseling services has been referred to as a "fundamental if not revolutionary change" (Larson, 1982, p. 843) in counseling.

By the late 1960s, radical psychiatrists, social change psychologists, feminist counselors, and others were suggesting that psychological problems experienced by many clients were the result of oppressive environments, not intrapsychic pathology. Concurrently, a number of authors began criticizing the mental health professions for their neutral stance with respect to social issues. Seymour Halleck (1971) indicted psychotherapists for helping to maintain the status quo in social institutions that are oppressive. According to

Halleck, psychotherapists, whether they intend to or not, commit a political act every time they reinforce the positions of persons who hold power. Intrapsychic views of client problems were criticized for being shortsighted and for promoting institutional oppression through passive acceptance. This position is articulated in its extreme by Claude Steiner (1975) in his manifesto for psychiatrists:

> Extended individual psychotherapy is an elitist, outmoded, as well as nonproductive, form of psychiatric help. It concentrates the talents of a few on a few. It silently colludes with the notion that people's difficulties have their source within them while implying that everything is well with the world. It promotes oppression by shrouding its consequences with shame and secrecy . . . People's troubles have their source not within them but in their alienated relationships, in their exploitation in polluted environments, in war, and in the profit motive. (Steiner, 1975, pp. 3–4).

Sarason (1981) also chastised American psychology as "quintessentially a psychology of the individual organism, a characteristic that, however, it may have been and is productive has severely and adversely affected psychology's contribution to human welfare" (p. 827). In examining the social issues and counseling needs of the 1980s and 1990s, Aubrey and Lewis (1983) expressed concern that "counselors still tend to overlook the impact of environmental factors on individual functioning, to distrust the efficacy of preventative interventions, and to narrow the score of their attention to the individual psyche" (p. 10).

We share these concerns that counselors and psychologists ignore environmental sources of mental health problems and rely almost exclusively on an intrapsychic model of psychopathology. We believe that for some of the issues clients bring to counseling, particularly for clients from groups that are victims of oppression, counselors need to consider alternatives to the intrapsychic pathology and individual psychotherapy models. This book examines the experiences of four oppressed groups with the goal of sensitizing counselors to the external sources of the psychological problems and to the nontraditional interventions designed to assist them with these problems.

Defining Oppressed Groups as Minorities

The term *minority* has been widely used in the United States since the 1950s with reference to racial and ethnic groups, and more recently with respect to nonethnic groups. Based on Wirth's (1945) definition that minorities are groups who "because of physical or cultural characteristics, are singled out from the others in the society in which they live for differential and unequal treatment" (p. 347), the term has been generalized to any group oppressed by those in power. The concept of minorities being groups that are singled out for differential and unequal treatment allows us to expand the list of minorities beyond ethnic groups who are a numerical minority in the society. When applied to Blacks in South Africa and women in the United States, the term describes groups that are actually a numerical majority of the population. Gay men and lesbian women, young children and elders, to the extent they are oppressed by the social system in which they live, also can be identified as minorities.

Dworkin and Dworkin (1976) proposed that "a minority group is a group characterized by four qualities: identifiability, differential power, differential and pejorative treatment, and group awareness." (p. 17). Biological (skin color, eye shape and color, facial structure) and cultural (religion, dress, behavior) variables identify a minority group as does the position of inferior power relative to a power group (a group that uses power to influence and control others). When such differential power exists between two groups, it is probably inevitable that the dominant group exercise their power, resulting in differential and discriminatory treatment of the minority group. One effect of experiencing differential and discriminatory treatment is to make the minority group more aware of its common bond.

A definition offered by Kinloch (1979) also addresses the issue of power. Kinloch (1979) defines a minority as "any group that is defined by a power elite as different and/or inferior on the basis of certain perceived characteristics and is consequently treated in a negative fashion" (p. 7). Further, he identifies four types of minorities: those who are identified as different or inferior based on physiological criteria (e.g., non-White racial minorities, women, elders), cultural criteria (non–Anglo-Saxon ethnic groups), economic criteria (the poor and/or lower class), and behavioral criteria (e.g., gay men and lesbian women, persons with mental disabilities, persons with physical disabilities).

Similarly Larson (1982) identifies minorities as groups of people who are stigmatized by the majority group in some way. He refers to Goffman's (1963) classification system for identifying conditions subject to stigma. The system consists of three categories:

> (a) physical—for example, visible manifestations of disability; (b) blemishes of character, for example, conditions that are viewed as voluntary deviant choices such as political dissidents, alternate sexual orientations, criminals, some categories of mental illness, such as addictions; and (c) tribal—for example, racial, ethnic, linguistic, or religious groups. (Larson, 1982, p. 845)

These definitions by Dworkin and Dworkin (1976), Kinloch (1979), and Larson (1982) stipulate that oppressed individuals be recognized or perceived as a group sharing common characteristics in order to qualify as a minority. However, Pope (1995) makes the interesting point that even those individuals who attempt to "pass" as members of the dominant society (e. g., gay men or lesbian women who hid their sexual orientation, people of color who are not visibly identifiable and deny their ethnic heritage) experience oppression in the form of lower self-esteem, feelings of inferiority, and internalization of negative self-concepts (p. 303). Thus, the recognition or perception of membership in a minority group need not be public for a member of that group to experience the effects of oppression.

Not only are minority groups singled out for stigmatization and discrimination, they are placed in double jeopardy by a society that blames them for the social conditions they experience as a result of discrimination. This phenomenon, known as victim-blaming, "is the tendency when examining a social problem to attribute that problem to the characteristics of the people who are its victims" (Levin & Levin, 1980, p. 36). For example, early forms of victim-blaming of ethnic minorities were often racially based and usually cited assumed biological inferiorities as causes of the groups' social problems (e.g., Mexican-American assumed intellectual inferiority cited as a reason for Mexican-American underachievement in school). More recently, cultural deviance has been cited as a cause of social problems experienced by ethnic minorities (e.g., breakdown of the traditional two-parent family among Blacks cited as a reason for a myriad of problems experienced by that group). The argument that seductive behavior is the cause of child sexual abuse (Muller, Caldwell, & Hunter, 1995) and rape (Bell, Kuriloff, & Lottes, 1994) is another current example of blaming the victim. Thus, victim-blaming overlooks the societal and institutional causes of social problems experienced by minorities and blames the problem on assumed biological or cultural inferiority.

Victim-blaming is particularly insidious when the minority group toward which it is directed begins to accept the blame for problems caused by oppression:

> The ultimate personal consequence of victim-blaming occurs when victims come to see themselves as those who blame them do. Lower self-esteem, even self-hatred, are outcomes more likely to emerge for those who are already marginalized and devalued in society. One's adoption of negative images from others can be viewed as a form of auto-oppression which has within it the seeds of self-destruction. Tragically and ironically, self-destruction accomplishes for society what social isolation and genocide do, but without raising the spectre of rights violations. (Dressel, Carter, & Balachandran, 1995, p. 118)

A further negative effect of victim-blaming is to misdirect the resources expended to resolve the social problems faced by a minority. Ryan (1971) has suggested that once we identify a social problem, we study the group affected by it to determine how they are different from the rest of us. We next define those differences as the source of the problem and develop a bureaucratic program to correct the differences, not the social cause of the problem. Further, we often withhold resources from minorities needed to resolve the social sources of their problems because we assume they are incapable of resolving their own difficulties. The National Council on Aging has suggested that "The social and economic opportunities available to any group in this society depends not only on their own resources, capabilities and aspirations but, as importantly, on the resources, capabilities and aspirations that the public at large attribute to them" (Harris, 1975, p. i).

This book focuses on two groups who are perceived as different and treated in a negative fashion because of physical characteristics (women and elders), one group because of behavioral characteristics (gay men and lesbian women), and one group because of either physical or behavioral characteristics (people with disabilities). As we shall see in chapters 2 and 3, these four groups have experienced discrimination and victim-blaming much like ethnic minorities have.

Our readings relating to these four groups by necessity focus on the distinctiveness of each group and may reinforce the view that they are mutually exclusive populations. Nothing could be further from the truth. For example, the greater survival rate of Americans with lifelong disabilities and the growing number of elders with later-life disabilities (Ansello, 1991) means that there is considerable overlap between these two groups. Further, the fact that there are only 67 elderly men for every 100 elderly women in the United States suggests that there are a large number of elderly women with disabilities. Since some of those elderly women with disabilities are also Lesbians, the overlap of all four groups on which we have chosen to focus becomes obvious. The fact that the four groups are not mutually exclusive is significant because it suggests that many individuals in our society are subject to multiple layers of discrimination.

Brief profiles of these four groups, who were selected for the current discussion because they include substantial numbers of people who seek counseling services, are provided in the following section.

Profiles of Selected Minorities
Persons with Disabilities

Any discussion of persons with disabilities by necessity must begin with a discussion of the terms *handicap, handicapped, disability,* and *disabled.* Those who have followed the literature on people with disabilities have witnessed an evolution in terminology (not unlike the evolution in terminology used to designate members of racial/ethnic minority groups) applied to this population. Professional articles and federal laws in the 1970s followed the convention of referring to people with disabilities as "handicapped people" or "people with handicaps." During the 1970s, the terms *handicapped person* and *disabled person* were often used interchangeably. By the 1980s, however, advocates for people with disabilities began to make distinctions between handicap and disability. The term *disability* began to be used with reference to some physical or mental diagnosis, one which may or may not limit the individual's major life activities. The term *handicap* began to be used to indicate the restricting consequences of the diagnosed disability. Thus, a handicap was seen as more situationally defined than is a disability:

The disability may be considered as the persons' observable, measurable characteristic that is judged to be deviant or discrepant from some acceptable norm. In contrast, the handicap may be considered as the barriers, demands, and general environmental press placed on the person by various aspects of his or her environment, including other persons. (Fagan & Wallace, 1979, p. 216)

More recently, disability has been defined as "the functional limitation within the individual caused by physical, mental, or sensory impairments," while handicapped has been defined by Enns (1989) as "the loss or limitation of opportunities to take part in the normal life of the community on an equal level with others due to physical and social barriers" (cited in McNeil, 1993). Thus, an individual may have a disability (e.g., hearing loss) but may not define it as a handicap if he or she is not restricted from taking part in normal activities of life. On the other hand, people in the environment may create a handicap for the disabled person if they restrict the person from living a normal life.

By the mid-1980s, most health professionals had dropped the term *handicapped person* in favor of *disabled person,* and by the early 1990s, *person with a disability* became the more accepted terminology. According to Grealish and Salomone (1986), *disabled person* implies that the person is disabled in a total sense (physically, emotionally, intellectually). Although more cumbersome, *person with a disability* puts the emphasis on the whole person and recognizes that the disability is just one aspect of their personhood. In fact, some advocates for persons with disabilities prefer to use the expression *differently able* since it more accurately reflects the fact that we all have varying levels of mental and physical ability given the environmental conditions in which we happen to be (in the case of a blind and a sighted person in an unlighted room, being sightless may actually be an asset). However, some persons with disabilities object to this terminology since it tends to deny their impairment and their status as an oppressed person. At this point most professionals and advocates for people with disabilities have accepted the term *people with disabilities.*

The previous definitions of disability notwithstanding, there is some ambiguity about what constitutes an impairment or functional limitation; according to Kuehn (1991), "disability resists precise definition and measurement" (p. 8). One approach has been to identify specific mental or physical conditions that are medically or educationally diagnosable. The Education for All Handicapped Act (PL 94-142) includes the following categories of disabilities for children: (a) hearing impaired, (b) deaf-blind, (c) visually impaired, (d) speech impaired, (e) mentally retarded, (f) learning disabled, (g) emotionally disturbed, (h) orthopedically impaired, (i) other health impaired, and (j) multihandicapped (Fagan & Wallace, 1979). Disabling conditions in the "other health impaired" category range from asthma to lead poisoning and includes many chronic or acute health problems.

Another approach to defining disability is to identify the life activity affected. Thus, the Rehabilitation Act of 1973 defines an "individual with severe handicaps" as a person

1. who has a severe physical or mental disability which seriously limits one or more functional capacities (such as mobility, communication, self care, self-direction, interpersonal skills, work tolerance or work skills) in terms of employability;
2. whose vocational rehabilitation can be expected to require multiple vocational rehabilitation services over an extended period of time; and
3. who has one or more physical or mental disabilities resulting from a list of disorders/diseases or a combination of disabilities determined on the basis of an evaluation of rehabilitation potential to cause comparable substantial functional limitation. (Perlman & Kirk, 1991)

Ability to perform an activity or role is sometimes used to define disability. The U.S. Bureau of the Census has based their definition of a person with a *work disability* on the concept that "a person has a disability if he or she has a limitation in the ability to perform one or more of the life activities expected of an individual within a social environment" (U.S. Bureau of the Census, 1989, p. 1). The bureau defines a person with a work disability as someone for whom one or more of the following conditions are met

1. Identified by a question that asks "does anyone in this household have a health problem or disability which prevents them from working or which limits the kind or amount of work they can do?"

2. Identified by a question that asks "Is there anyone in this household who ever retired or left a job for health reasons?"

3. Did not work in the survey week because of a long term physical or mental illness or disability which prevents the performance of any kind of work (based on the "main activity last week" question on the basic CPS [Current Population Survey] questionnaire).

4. Did not work at all in previous year because ill or disabled (based on the "reason did not work last year" question on the March CPS supplement).

5. Under 65 years of age and covered by Medicare.

6. Under 65 years of age and a recipient of Supplemental Security Income (SSI). (U.S. Bureau of the Census, 1989, p. 1)

The person is considered to have a "severe" work disability if one or more of the final four conditions are met.

The Americans with Disabilities Act (ADA; P. L. 101-336) of 1990 defined disability very broadly, encompassing such chronic diseases as AIDS and diabetes:

Under the ADA, an individual is considered to have a disability if the person: (a) has a physical or mental impairment that substantially limits one or more of the major life activities; (b) has a record of such an impairment; or (c) is regarded as having such an impairment. (McNeil, 1993, p. 1)

More recently, the Census Bureau (McNeil, 1993) defined a person with a disability as someone with a limitation and a person with a severe disability as a person unable to perform one or more functional activities (seeing, hearing, speaking, lifting and carrying, climbing stairs, and walking) or one or more socially defined roles or tasks (getting around inside the home, getting in or out of bed, dressing, preparing meals).

Even when there is agreement about the categories of disabilities, there may be disagreement about whether an individual satisfies the criteria for the category. According to Bowe (1985), two trained observers may differ as to whether a person has a disability or not. Questions used by the Census Bureau to identify persons with a work disability "may screen out some legitimately disabled persons; less often, they may screen in some individuals who may not be disabled" (Bowe, 1985, p. 2). Clinical identification of people with disabilities may be improved with the revision of the International Classification of Impairments, Disabilities, and Handicaps. The first version of the ICIDH, which is published by the World Health Organization, appeared in 1980; revision of the ICIDH was initiated in 1994. The purpose of the ICIDH is to provide an international system for classifying disabilities (Burnette, 1995).

Perhaps because there is not a clear consensus on what constitutes a disability, even among U.S. governmental agencies, there are no clear-cut national estimates of the number of people with disabilities. The U.S. Bureau of the Census (1983) reported that over 6 million noninstitutionalized persons age 16 and over had a public transportation handicap in 1982. A person with a public transportation handicap is someone who, due to a mental or physical condition lasting over six months, cannot use buses, trains, subways, or other forms of public transportation.

These data on people with work and/or transportation disabilities are necessarily restrictive because they exclude persons under 16 and over 65, as well as those who have disabilities but who manage to work full-time and/or use public transportation. According to Tomes (1992), "14 percent of 231 million non-institutionalized U.S. residents were limited in ability to perform some normal activity" (p. 13), suggesting that there were over 32 million people with disabilities in the mid-1980s. According to the most recent estimate by the federal government published in the ADA, there were 43 million Americans with disabilities in 1990 (National Council on Disability, 1995).

Perhaps the most comprehensive and recent data on the numbers of people with disabilities are provided by the Survey of Income and Program Participation conducted the last three months of 1991 and the first month of 1992 and summarized in McNeil (1993) and U.S. Bureau of the Census (1995). According to this survey there were 48.9 million people "with a limitation in a functional activity or a social role" and 24.1 million "with a severe disability (unable to perform one or more activities or roles" (p. 32) at the time of the study. This study found a direct correlation between age and disability rate. Although the overall disability rate was 19.4 percent of the population, it increased steadily from a low of 5.8 percent for children under 18 years of age to 84.2 percent for persons 85 years of age and older. As might be expected, the likelihood that the disability will be severe increases with age. Within the age category of 15 to 64 years, the disability rate was slightly higher for women (20.2 percent) than men (18.7 percent) and somewhat higher for American Indians, Eskimos, and Aleuts (26.9 percent) than for Blacks (20.8 percent), Whites (17.7 percent), Hispanics (16.9 percent), and Asians/Pacific Islanders (9.6 percent). The broad definition of disability used in this survey identified a variety of conditions as the sources of disability:

> Among those 15 years old and over who had difficulty with a physical activity or an activity of daily living (ADL), the conditions most frequently cited as a cause of the difficulty were arthritis or rheumatism (mentioned by 7.2 million persons); back or spine problems (5.7 million); heart trouble (4.6 million); lung or respiratory trouble (2.8 million); high blood pressure (2.2 million); stiffness or deformity of the foot, leg, arm, or hand (2.0 million); diabetes (1.6 million); and blindness or vision problems (1.5 million). (U.S. Bureau of the Census, 1995)

There is every reason to believe that both the absolute number of people with disabilities and their proportion in the population will grow well into the twenty-first century. A sizable portion of the number of persons with disabilities are elderly, since the incidence of disability increases in old age. Van Hasselt, Strain, and Hersen (1988) cite evidence that as much as 46 percent of the persons 65 years of age and older have a serious and disabling health impairment. As the number and percentage of the U.S. population that are elderly increases (discussed in the next section), the number and percentage of people with disabilities will increase. It should be noted, however, that disabilities are a fact of life among a sizable number of young people as well. Van Hasselt et al. (1988) reported that as much as 10 percent of the children under 21 years of age in the United States have disabilities.

Citing World Health Organization data, Driedger (1989) estimates that 10 percent of the world's population or over 500 million people are persons with disabilities. Approximately 80 percent of these people live in the developing countries in Africa, Asia, the Middle East, Latin America, and the Caribbean. Regardless of the exact numbers and percentages, it is evident that people with disabilities make up a significant proportion of the population both in the United States and worldwide.

Elders

The determination of who is elderly and who is not is arbitrary at best. Although chronological age is frequently used for this purpose, it is often not an accurate indicator of biological age (measured by skin texture, hair color and thickness, reflex speed, etc.), psychological age (feelings, attitudes, way of looking at things, etc.), or social age (social roles and activities) (Aiken, 1995). Defining the term *aging* is also problematic. According to Griffiths and Meechan (1990), the definition of aging most widely accepted by biologists is one offered by Vander, Sherman, and Luciano (1985). These authors defined aging as a "progressive failure of the body's various homeostatic adaptive responses" (Griffiths & Meechan, 1990, p. 45).

> This definition has the advantage that it allows us to distinguish the aging process from degenerative changes that result from diseases. Although diseases such as cancer and atherosclerosis can interact and compound the aging process, they do not always accompany aging and therefore must be thought of as distinct processes. (Griffiths & Meechan, 1990, p. 45)

As we shall see in chapter 2, however, the disease model of aging was in vogue for the major part of the twentieth century, and only recently has functional capacity been used to assess the aging process.

Biologists, physicians, and chemists who have studied the physiological aging process (senescence) have long recognized that it occurs at varying rates among individuals (Strehler, 1962; Satlin, 1994). Various measures of physical aging have been employed; for example, hair color and loss, skin tone and texture, and muscle tone and flexibility have been examined as evidence of senescence. However, because individuals evidence changes in these physical attributes at widely varying chronological ages, physical standards of aging are averages for the population as a whole and are seldom useful in assessing the individual's status with respect to his or her own aging process. Increasingly, aging is being assessed in terms of functional capacity or the ability to engage in purposeful activity. Two types of activities, activities of daily living (ADLs) and instrumental activities of daily living (IADLs), are used to measure functional capacity. ADLs include getting in and out of a chair or bed, bathing, and using the toilet. IADLs include preparing meals, doing light housework, and shopping. Quite clearly, some individuals who are in their 40s have greatly restricted ADLs and IADLs, while others in their 70s and even 80s may have retained full functional capacity (Aiken, 1995).

The Social Security Act of 1935 had a major impact on our perceptions of who is an elder and who is not when it identified 65 as the magic age for determining who will receive full Social Security benefits. According to Achenbaum (1978), however, "The Committee on Economic Security determined that at least six other birthdays (60, 62, 68, 70, 72, and 75) were used as an eligibility criterion in public and private schemes operating in the 1930s" (p. 149). Legislators selected age 65 for Social Security purposes in the final analysis on the basis of cost estimates, actuarial data, and the spirit of compromise rather than on scientific information about the aging process. Recent discussions in Congress aimed at raising the age for full Social Security benefits also reflect economic and demographic pressures, not scientifically-based knowledge about aging.

Recent proposals to increase the age of qualification for full Social Security benefits are the result of people living longer than ever before and a shrinking number of people paying into Social Security.

> For the first time in history, most people can expect to live into the "long late afternoon of life." Whereas American life expectancy in 1900 was about forty-

nine, today's children will live an average of about seventy-five years (seventy-one for men, seventy-eight for women). This increase represents two-thirds of all the gains in life expectancy achieved since the emergence of the human species! (Cole, 1991, p. 25)

Due to an increasing life expectancy, the number of elderly people living in the United States has been increasing steadily since 1830, the first year for which census data are available. In 1830, there were less than one-half million White persons (non-Whites were not counted in the early reports) over 60 years of age. In 1870, the Census Bureau reported over 1.1 million citizens were age 65 or older. By 1900, that figure had more than doubled to just over 3 million. By 1940, the number of elderly had increased to 9 million, and by 1970, it had soared to over 20 million (Achenbaum, 1978). As of the 1990 census report, there were over 31 million Americans age 65 and over; of these, 13.1 million were age 75 and over, and 3 million were age 85 and over. By the year 2000, it is projected that the figure for persons 65 and over will increase to 35 million, and by 2050, it will have increased to almost 79 million (U. S. Bureau of the Census, 1992). Most of this growth in the first half of the twenty-first century will be due to the aging of the baby boomers. A rapid acceleration in the projected growth of the elderly population will occur between 2010 and 2020 as the peak of the baby boom generation turns 65 (Campbell, 1994).

Not only are elders increasing in absolute numbers, but they are increasing in proportion to the rest of the population. At the same time that life expectancy has been increasing, the birth rate has been declining steadily (since 1790 with the exception of the post World War II baby boom), causing the proportion of elders in the American population, as well as their absolute number, to increase dramatically. During the first nine decades of the twentieth century, the population in general tripled, while the population over age 65 increased tenfold (U.S. Bureau of the Census, 1992). In 1900, elders comprised about 4 percent of the U.S. population, but by 1990, they represented 12.5 percent. While the total U.S. population grew 13.5 percent from 1970 to 1982, the 65 and over age group grew 34.3 percent. This differential growth pattern is expected to accelerate as the baby boomers hit 65 years of age. Between 2010 and 2030, the elderly population is expected to grow by 76 percent, while the under age 65 population is expected to grow by only 6.5 percent. In 1990, 1 in 35 Americans were 80 years of age or older. By 2050, as many as 1 in 13 will be 80 years of age or older (U.S. Bureau of the Census, 1992).

As might be expected, the differing life expectancies for men and women noted earlier affects their representation in the elderly population. According to Hess (1980), the sex ratios of older men and women were approximately equal in 1930 but have changed dramatically since then. According to 1990 census data (U.S. Bureau of the Census, 1992), elderly women now outnumber elderly men 3 to 2. The differences between the number of elderly men and elderly women is most pronounced in the oldest age group. "At ages 65 to 69, women outnumber men 5 to 4; for those 85 years and over, women outnumber men 5 to

2" (U.S. Bureau of the Census, 1992, p. 2–8). It is important to note that life expectancy is a function of race/ethnicity as well as sex. For those persons born in 1989, the life expectancy is 79 years for White females, 74 years for Black females, 73 years for White males, and 65 years for Black males (U.S. Bureau of the Census, 1992). The elderly population is expected to become even more racially and ethnically diverse in the next half century:

> Hispanic elderly would increase from less than 4 percent of the total elderly population in 1990 to 16 percent by the middle of the next century. . . . The Black non-Hispanic proportion of the elderly population by the middle of the next century would be 10 percent, the White non-Hispanic proportion 67 percent, and the Asian and Pacific Islander proportion 7 percent. (U.S. Bureau of the Census, 1995)

Contrary to earlier generations, most of today's elderly men (comparable figures for women are not reported) retire before age 65:

> In 1950, two-thirds (68.6 percent) of men 55 or older, and nearly half (45.8 percent) of men 65 and older were in the labor force. In 1990, about 2 in 5 (39.3 percent) men 55 and over, and about 1 in 6 (16.4 percent) elderly men were in the labor force. (U.S. Bureau of the Census, 1992, p. 4–1)

This pattern is expected to reverse itself, however, due to increases in the qualifying age for Social Security benefits, less generous pension plans in the future, and the demand for elder workers. For those elderly who do retire early, the extra time has provided an opportunity to do volunteer work. According to Gerber, Wolff, Klores, and Brown (1989), 44 percent of the population between the ages of 50 and 74 do volunteer work.

A common misperception is that the majority (or at least a large percentage) of elders live in nursing homes. In reality, only 5 percent live in nursing homes, although the number does increase with advancing age. For elders aged 65 to 74, only about 1.5 percent lived in a nursing home in 1980 (the most recent date for which data are available). The percentage increases to 7 percent for ages 75 to 84 and 22 percent for ages 85 and above (U.S. Bureau of the Census, 1992). Almost 90 percent of all older couples (and 75 percent of all elderly persons) own and live in their own home. Of these older people who own their own home, almost 75 percent have paid off their mortgages. For most elderly householders, their home is their major asset. However, the property values of the homes owned by elders are lower than those owned by younger homeowners. In many cases, the homes of elderly persons are at least 40 years old and in need of structural repairs (Hess, 1991).

Another misperception is that most elderly need assistance with living (bathing, dressing, moving out of beds and chairs, toileting, and eating). Even among the oldest age group, less than half need this kind of assistance. Compared to the 2 percent of persons under age 65 who need assistance with living activities, "the proportion requiring assistance ranged from 9 percent for those aged 65 to 69 up to 45 percent for those aged 85 or older" (U.S. Bureau of the Census, 1992, p. 3–12). The need for assistance is also related to demographic variables. Elderly women are more likely to need assistance than are elderly men, and elderly Blacks are more likely to need assistance than are elderly Whites. "Those who needed assistance were more likely to live in households with lower income levels than persons who did not require assistance" (U.S. Bureau of the Census, 1992).

Contrary to still another common misperception, most noninstitutionalized elderly do not live with a relative. The majority (63 percent) of persons ages 65 to 74 were married and living with their spouse in 1992, while 25 percent lived alone, and 10 percent lived with relatives. However, the living arrangements of older people are, to some extent, a function of age, ethnicity, and sex. For persons 75 and over, the percent living with their spouses decreases (41 percent), the percent living alone increases (41 percent), and the percent living with other relatives increases (16 percent). Black elders compared to White elders are more likely to live alone (36 percent versus 31 percent), less likely to live with a spouse (37 percent versus 56 percent), and more likely to live with other relatives (25 percent versus 11 percent) than their White counterparts (U.S. Bureau of the Census, 1993). When adult children do provide care for their aging parents, it often occurs when the children themselves are elders. A recent survey of caregivers revealed that their mean age was 63.5, which meant that many of their aging parents were in their 80s and 90s (Schwiebert & Myers, 1994).

With women outliving men, it is not surprising that elderly women are more likely than elderly men to be living alone. Of 14.3 million persons aged 65 and older living alone in 1991, over 75 percent were women. One-third of the women ages 65 to 74 lived alone in 1991 compared to 13 percent of the men. More than half the women age 75 and older lived alone compared to 21 percent of the men. While three out of four elderly men were married and living with their wives, only two out of every five elderly women were married and living with their husbands in 1991. (U.S. Bureau of the Census, 1992).

According to Margolis (1990), about 1.5 million older Americans were housed in 16,000 nursing homes in 1989. Of those who live in nursing homes, almost all (93%) are White, and the majority (75 percent) are women (Hess, 1991). While it is a myth that most elderly people live in nursing homes, the percentage that do increases steadily with age. Of those aged 65 to 74 in 1982, only 1.5 percent lived in nursing homes. For persons aged 75 to 84, however, 6 percent lived in nursing homes in 1982, and this figure increased to 23 percent for those persons 85 and older. Because of this relationship between age and nursing home care, between one-third and two-fifths of persons 65 or older will spend some time in a nursing home during their lifetime. Due to the increasing numbers of elders, however, it is anticipated that those requiring long-term nursing care will rise from about seven million today to seventeen million by 2040 (Hess, 1991).

It is estimated that 5 million elderly who are ill or have severe disabilities live in the community, a figure that is almost four times the number living in nursing homes. Most of these elderly are women who are being cared for by a relative, usually a daughter; only 22 percent of the caregivers are husbands or sons. As we point out in chapter 3, caring for an elderly person with a severe disability places incredible stress on the caregiver and not infrequently leads to elder abuse. The strain on caregivers may become worse in the near future as the number of offspring available to provide the care decreases (due to smaller families) and the financial pressures on women in their middle years to work increases (Hess, 1991).

There is some evidence that "in terms of capacities, needs, and resources, we may be moving toward a two tiered old age" (Hess, 1980). Neugarten (1974) has identified these two tiers as the young-old and the old-old. The young-old are characterized by relatively good health and financial condition, while the old-old experience declining financial, physical, social, and psychological resources. To some extent this division between the young-old and the old-old is an artifact due to the varying economic, medical, and social opportunities available to different age cohorts and to the fact that more and more elderly are "aging successfully" (Satlin, 1994). Therefore, the reader is cautioned that the comprehensive data on age discrimination cited in chapter 3 will necessarily overstate the privations of the young-old while understating those of the old-old.

Women

Ostensibly the easiest of the four groups under discussion to define and identify, the issues related to women's status as an oppressed group are quite complex. Social scientists have had great difficulty clarifying the issues, much less reaching agreement; conflicting definitions of terms plague the field (Henley, 1985). We will employ descriptors in keeping with the consensus of opinion in the literature on the psychology of women, with the caveat that the usage of other writers may differ considerably.

Definitions

Ask anyone to describe the crucial differences between men and women and you will get a hodgepodge of physical, mental, behavioral, and characterological distinctions. However, contained within commonplace descriptions of sex differences are innumerable unfounded assumptions. There are some very real physical and genetic differences (e.g., average height, weight, muscle mass) between the sexes, but there are not the widespread intellectual, personality, and behavioral differences assumed by so many. In fact, there are *very few* sex differences that have been supported in the research literature; there are many more similarities than differences between boys and girls, men and women (Matlin, 1987). Why, then, are assumptions of significant sex differences so prevalent? The answer rests in society's gender-based norms and expectations (Gilbert, 1992).

Fundamental to this discussion of women and women's status in society is the crucial distinction between *sex* and *gender* (Unger, 1979). *Sex* refers to the biological condition of maleness or femaleness, the possession of the XY chromosomal configuration for men and boys, and the XX pattern for women and girls, along with the corresponding anatomical, hormonal, and physiological structures. In sociological parlance, sex is an *ascribed* status; we are assigned to a sex at birth (Richardson, 1981). *Gender,* on the other hand, is an *achieved* status, that is, one we learn. Gender refers to the psychological, social, and cultural aspects of being female or male within a particular social context (Richardson, 1981). Gender, therefore, is a social label describing the aspects of male and female behavior that are a result of socialization to the culturally prescribed norms for women and men. Gender *identity* is one's self-defined sex, male or female, which usually, but not always (in the case of transsexuals), corresponds with one's ascribed sex.

Far from semantic nitpicking, these distinctions reflect a crucial point: Most differences assumed to exist between the sexes have been found to be socially based rather than innate. Our language affects how we see the world, and the continuing use of the term *sex* differences to characterize observed differences in personality, cognitive functioning, interpersonal behavior, and vocational behavior only reinforces outdated notions of the biological source of such observed differences (Unger, 1979). Historically, observed or assumed sex differences have been employed to support arguments for the inferiority of women. Employing the term *gender* emphasizes the social construction of behavior and the existence of environmental causes for behavioral differences between women and men. To briefly illustrate, there do not seem to be any overall differences between men and women in the capacity to act assertively, yet in certain situations, women *do* act less assertively than men, because they have learned what is expected of them as women (Gilbert, 1992).

Gender-Role Socialization

Immediately upon sex assignment at birth, the process of differential socialization begins. Our society holds certain beliefs about personality differences between, and appropriate behavior for, boys and girls. These gender-role stereotypes (sometimes inaccurately referred to as sex-role stereotypes), or widely held but simplistic beliefs about the roles of women and men, influence how we act, what we see, how we interpret behavior, and how we respond to others. Studies have documented the content of the gender-role stereotypes commonly held within the mainstream American culture. Women are characteristically seen as expressive, that is, compassionate, tactful, emotional, nurturing, and dependent. Men are seen as instrumental, for example, objective, aggressive, independent, dominant, and competitive (Bem, 1974; Spence & Helmreich, 1978). Parents, family, the educational system, the media—all significant sources of influence on a growing child—communicate these expectations. As a result of gender-role socialization, we learn what behaviors and attitudes to exhibit according to our label, male or female. When men act in a culturally-approved, gender-appropriate way they are viewed as masculine; women are viewed as feminine when they act in ways considered appropriate for women in their culture.

The importance of understanding the social construction of gender lies in the consequent exposure of the political ideology underlying gender roles and the costs of adherence to this political ideology that result for both women and men. Margaret Mead's classic anthropological study (1935/1971) convincingly demonstrated the cultural relativity of gender roles and the place of social conditioning rather than biology in the development of gender differences in personality. She investigated three tribes in New Guinea, finding one in which both men and women displayed what our culture would consider feminine traits; another in which both sexes displayed the instrumental traits we usually describe as masculine; and a third in which adult males demonstrated expressive (feminine) characteristics while normal adult females displayed the aggressive, instrumental behaviors we label as masculine.

Despite Mead's research and other anthropological studies refuting the universality of the content of gender-role expectations, and thus their biological immutability, within a given culture people tend to assume that what they are used to is "normal" and therefore good, desirable, and natural. It has been argued that our culture (along with many others) is patriarchal, or male-dominated. The ideology underlying patriarchy is sexism, a political ideology resting squarely on the assumed inequality of women and men. As a consequence, our assumption that this culture's gender-role expectations for women are "normal" and our failure to question these stereotypical expectations produces a situation where society is training over half of its population to behave and think in ways detrimental to the achievement of gender equality. Further, as we shall see in chapter 3, many of the gender-appropriate feminine characteristics, traits, and behaviors adhered to in our society are devalued, and some are inherently harmful to the mental and physical health and well-being of women (Schaffer, 1981). Men, too, pay a price for strict adherence to the cultural masculine gender role (O'Neil, 1980).

Women as a Minority

Thus, gender stereotyping, the result of sexist ideology, maintains the status quo. The dominant group, men, are trained to behave in culturally-defined masculine ways that preserve the dominance of men as a group. It takes informed and concerted efforts on the part of men to circumvent their conditioning and societal pressures, even when they consciously ascribe to gender equality (O'Neil, 1980). Women, too, are socialized to think and behave in ways that preserve their relatively inferior status. The consequence is social and economic inequality, resulting in women's disadvantaged status in society. It is this inequitable situation, both a determinant and a result of long-standing and continuing sex discrimination, that defines women as a minority or oppressed group (Hacker, 1975).

The minority status of women, then, is due to their economic, legal, political, and social disadvantages rather than their numerical minority, as is the case with other minority groups. However, we must remember as we are discussing women's status throughout this book that gender combines with other minority statuses to produce multiple, often nonadditive, sources of oppression. For example, because of the gender differences in mortality rates, the ratio of women to men increases greatly with age (Collier, 1982); thus, most women experience at least a dual oppression as they grow older. Older women suffer differentially from problems of loneliness, isolation, and lack of potential partners (Collier, 1982). Different standards of physical attractiveness for the sexes produce a situation where women generally encounter a type of age discrimination that is much more profound than that encountered by men (Collier, 1982). Women of color experience the "double jeopardy" of sexism and racism; lesbian women encounter homophobia as well as sexism; and disabled women face similar double discrimination. We could continue indefinitely with the possibilities for multiplication of sources of discrimination and bias.

How can such a situation still exist in a country founded on the concepts of freedom and human equality? Are we exaggerating the scope of the problem? The answer is complicated but is intimately tied to the ideology of sexism, the oppression that is common to all women. As Amundsen (1971) states:

> Sexism, then, is an "ideology" in the sense that its beliefs and postulates are well-integrated, it functions to direct and guide social and political activity, and it rests on assumptions that are not reliably tested, but that to some degree are accepted on faith. (p. 108)

Feminism, defined simply as the advocacy of equality between men and women, has been a potent force in exposing unexamined sexist beliefs and behaviors.

Conversely, popular wisdom has it that we are now in a postfeminist era, where women have finally achieved equality and where sexism no longer holds sway. However, compelling evidence to the contrary exists, despite the real gains made by women on a variety of fronts. Faludi (1991), in particular, argued persuasively that we are now in a period of profound backlash against women's quest for equality. "The antifeminist backlash has been set off not by women's achievement of full equality but by the increased possibility that they might win it. It is a preemptive strike that stops women long before they reach the finish line" (Faludi, 1991, p. xx).

The history of sexism is long, and though its specific manifestations have changed over time, its potency as an ideology remains with us today. What is "normal" is seen as right and correct, and largely goes unquestioned. As John Stuart Mill, an early advocate of women's rights, so aptly stated, "So true is it that unnatural generally means only uncustomary and that everything which is usual appears natural. The subjection of women to men being a universal custom, any departure from it quite naturally appears unnatural" (1869/1970, p. 14). Women are surely in a better position than they were when Mill wrote these words, but equality in education, the work force, politics, and in the family is far from being achieved. In chapter 4, we will examine the status of women from a historical perspective, tracing the origin and development of sexism over time. As we will see, women's equality with men has not been one of linear, forward moving progress, but one of fits and starts, progression and regression. In chapter 5, we will discuss the legacy of sexism and its current manifestations in society, psychology, and the practice of counseling.

Gay Men and Lesbian Women

Descriptors

As is the case with labels employed for and by racial/ethnic minority groups, the nomenclature used when referring to gay people reveals strongly held assumptions about the group. *Homosexual* is the term often applied to individuals whose sexual preferences are predominantly for those of the same sex, yet the term *homosexuality* places primary emphasis on sexual preference, which is but one aspect of the life experience of the people so labeled (Clark, 1977).

An alternative term, *gay,* like the labels preferred by other minorities (e.g., African American, Chicano), emphasizes the positive and was developed within the homosexual community itself:

> Gay is a descriptive label we assign ourselves as a way of reminding ourselves and others that awareness of our sexuality facilitates a capacity rather than creating a restriction. It means that we are capable of fully loving a person of the same gender by involving ourselves emotionally, sexually, spiritually, and intellectually. (Clark, 1977, p. 73)

Thus, the term gay affirms all aspects of this orientation. Clark (1977) also explains that the designation *homosexual* is a clinical term with many negative associations, a term often used to separate gay people from the rest of society. The label *gay,* on the other hand, goes beyond a rigid classification of people into one group or the other:

> . . . It may even imply a frequent or nearly constant preference or attraction for people of the same gender, meaning I (as a Gay man) might notice more men than women on the street or might notice men before women. But the label does not limit us. We who are Gay can still love someone of the other gender. Homosexual and heterosexual when used as nouns are naive and destructive nonsense in the form of labels that limit. (Clark, 1977, p. 73)

In this book, we will generally use *gay,* although the term *homosexual* will be employed when referring strictly to sexual behavior or when it is most descriptive of the issue under discussion. As much as possible we will refer to gay women as lesbian women in order to make visible a group of people who are often relegated to invisibility (Faderman, 1991; Martin & Lyon, 1972).

Lesbian is an adjective that has been embraced by gay women because of the tendency of society to assume that gay people are exclusively male (Moses & Hawkins, 1982). Finally, we will avoid the use of the term *straight* to describe heterosexuals; if one is straight the implication is that the other is somehow crooked, deviant, or criminal (Woodman & Lenna, 1980). Gays often use the word *nongay* rather than either heterosexual or straight.

Sexual Orientation

Homosexuality has traditionally been viewed as a rare and deviant form of behavior, in contrast to the societal norm of heterosexuality. The two are often seen as mutually exclusive categories, yet in the landmark Kinsey Studies, researchers found that over 60 percent of male respondents had engaged in same-sex sexual behavior before the age of 16, and 30 percent had homosexual experiences in their early 20s (Kinsey, Pomeroy, & Martin, 1948). Findings for women were not as dramatic but were consistent with the data regarding men; homosexuality is far from rare, and homosexuality-heterosexuality is not, in the general population, a clear dichotomous classification (Kinsey et al., 1948; Kinsey, Pomeroy, Martin, & Gebhard, 1953).

The Kinsey reports (Kinsey et al., 1948; Kinsey et al., 1953) and subsequent research (Churchill, 1971; Kingdon, 1979) demonstrated that, conservatively, about 10 percent of the population are predominantly homosexual, and this figure appears to be fairly stable throughout history and across cultures. Although gay people are clearly a minority due to their oppressed status (which will be documented in chapter 4) and their numbers, they are a significant minority. Recently a "national survey" questioning this 10 percent figure has received considerable media attention (Cole, Gorman, Barrett, & Thompson, 1993). As of this writing, the actual research has not been made widely available, nor has the survey methodology been formally examined for scientific adequacy. However, the survey asked questions dealing only with sexual behavior within a relatively narrow age span, raising doubts about the accuracy of the statistics.

Kinsey and his associates (1948; 1953) argued that sexual preference should be viewed along a continuum. They developed a seven-point scale to measure the degree to which respondents in their studies were homosexual or heterosexual in their sexual behaviors. The 0 point on the Kinsey Scale means that a man or woman has never had *any* overt homosexual experience, while a 6 on the scale indicates no overt heterosexual experience. Moving up the scale from 0, a 1 means that an individual has some minimal amount of homosexual experience, but this is overshadowed by heterosexual experiences. A person scoring 2 on the Kinsey Scale has had significantly more homosexual experience but is still predominantly heterosexual. A Kinsey Scale 3 indicates a person with about equal experience of both a homosexual and heterosexual nature. A 4 on the Kinsey Scale describes a person who has had a great deal of heterosexual experience but is predominantly homosexual. A 5 on the Kinsey

Scale indicates some minimal heterosexual experience in a very dominantly homosexual individual; and as discussed before, a 6 on the Kinsey Scale is an exclusive homosexual.

In the Kinsey research, surprisingly few people fell on either end of the continuum, that is, exclusively heterosexual or homosexual. About half of all American men fell somewhere *between* the two end points. Women's responses were also distributed across the continuum, but as mentioned previously, fewer women than men indicated that their behavior was exclusively homosexual. Individuals falling at the midpoint of the Kinsey Scale sometimes describe themselves as "bisexual," but often have a preference for one sex or the other, in spite of their ability to relate to both (Moses & Hawkins, 1982).

We now see one way the issue of sexual orientation is more complex than it appears at first glance. However, Kinsey and his colleagues only addressed sexual *behavior*. Sexual preference is only one aspect of sexual orientation; affectional/emotional factors are, for many, far more important than the sexual attraction to a partner. Moses and Hawkins (1982) identify two of the major components of sexual orientation: "(1) the physical, which includes gender preference for sexual partners and sexual relationships, and (2) the affectional, which includes gender preference for primary emotional relationships" (p. 36). One's exploration of partners in fantasy and one's personal history must also be taken into account. A person may have had various types of sexual, affectional, or fantasy experiences in the past but have different types of experiences currently. If all components of an individual's sexual orientation are congruent, labeling is fairly easy. However, factors influencing sexual orientation may be inconsistent, defying simple categories.

Due to their unique status, gay people encounter barriers not experienced by other minority group members. First, gay people represent a statistically significant minority group in this country (i.e., well over 20 million individuals), and suffer from various forms of intolerance and oppression including lack of legal protection, harassment, loss of their jobs, and violence, all of which usually identify a minority group. However, many people still deny that gays are a true minority (Woodman & Lenna, 1980). Some of the arguments against affording minority status to gay people hinge on religious beliefs, others on the view that sexual orientation is a choice rather than a natural orientation (despite evidence to the contrary), and some of the arguments are reflective of ignorance and/or bias (Dworkin & Gutierrez, 1992a; Fassinger, 1991). Interestingly, virulently antigay statements routinely appear in the media, and these are accepted in due course in a way that would be considered unconscionable if such statements were directed at any other minority group.

Secondly, lesbian women and gay men grow up learning the same negative attitudes and hostility toward homosexuality that nongays do. *Homophobia* is the term used to describe ". . . the irrational fear of anyone gay or lesbian, or of anyone perceived to be gay or lesbian" (Dworkin & Gutierrez, 1992b, p. xx).

Although this definition is commonly used, some believe that the emphasis on fear alone (homo*phobia*) does not adequately impart the severity of responses, including violence, toward gays in this society. Other terms have been proposed as more adequate descriptors of antigay prejudice, for example, gay and lesbian hatred and heterosexism (Blumenfeld, 1992). *Heterosexism* refers not only to the belief that heterosexuality is the only acceptable sexual orientation, but also to the accompanying fear, disgust, and hatred of gay people, which results in discrimination (Blumenfeld, 1992). We will retain the term *homophobia,* but employ it in the expanded sense to indicate not only the fear of, but the prejudice and hatred toward, gay men and lesbian women.

Homophobic reactions are prevalent not only in society at large, but also characterize the responses of friends and family of gay people, as well as gays themselves (Dworkin & Gutierrez, 1992a; Weinberg, 1972). Gay people experience a unique situation among minority groups in that they are reared in heterosexual families which rarely provide the type of support needed in coping with a socially oppressed self-identity. Families of gays are, therefore, often an additional source of oppression (Beane, 1981). *Internalized* homophobia is also a major obstacle for lesbian women and gay men wrestling with their sexual orientation, further complicating an already complex process of self-definition. Heterosexuality is expected of everyone. When people begin to realize that they are not heterosexually oriented, they struggle with a highly charged and stigmatized self-label.

> "Coming out" or "coming out of the closet" is argot for acknowledging to self, being open about or asserting one's gay identify. Being "in the closet" is to conceal that identity. Among gays, the idea of coming out is more than just asserting a gay identity—it is a process by which an individual moves from the realization of homoerotic feelings to the acceptance of the sexual-affectional preference for people of the same sex. The next crucial step is to integrate those feelings positively into one's total self so that they can be asserted and to find affirmation in interactions with others. To use client's phraseology, the process involves a "coming out to self" and a "coming out to others." (Woodman & Lenna, 1980, p. 13)

Internalized homophobia and the coming out process are often major issues for gay men and lesbian women seeking counseling.

Gender Identity vs. Sexual Orientation

As discussed in the previous section, the term *gender identity* refers to one's self-identity as a male or female (Richardson, 1981). Sexual orientation should not be mistaken for gender identity. Gay men are men and lesbian women are women. The stereotype of the gay man as feminine equates sexual orientation with *gender-role,* not gender identity; and though the stereotypes do fit some gay men, they do not fit many others. Most gay men exhibit the same range of masculine gender-role behavior as heterosexual men. Likewise, lesbian women may act in feminine or masculine ways, just as nongay women do; their gender identity as women is not dependent on their sexual orientation (Richardson, 1981).

Neither should sexual orientation be confused with transexuality or transvestitism. Transsexuals are individuals whose gender identity is different from their sex assignment, for example, a man who feels he is a woman "trapped" in a man's body (Richardson, 1981). Some individuals who encounter such gender incongruence seek sex-reassignment surgery to resolve their dilemma, but transexuality is fundamentally different from sexual orientation.

Finally, transvestites are people who enjoy dressing in clothing considered socially inappropriate for their sex. Because of the more stringent sanctions for gender-inappropriate behavior for men in our society, cross-dressing appears to be much more of an issue for men than women. Despite the stereotypes, cross-dressing is unusual among gay men (Moses & Hawkins, 1982). Many men whose sexual orientation is predominantly or exclusively heterosexual cross-dress; gender identity and sexual orientation are often not an issue for transvestites (Moses & Hawkins, 1982).

In chapter 4, we will briefly describe the history of oppression of gay people. In chapter 5, we will explore current societal attitudes, along with the responses of the mental health establishment. Counseling issues related to the concepts introduced in this chapter will be expanded upon in later chapters.

References

Achenbaum, W. A. (1978). *Old age in the new land: The American experience since 1790.* Baltimore: The Johns Hopkins University Press.

Aiken, L. R. (1995). *Aging: An introduction to gerontology.* Thousand Oaks, CA: Sage Publications.

Amundsen, K. (1971). *The silenced majority.* Englewood Cliffs, NJ: Prentice Hall.

Ansello, E. F. (1991). The intersecting of aging and disabilities. In B. B. Hess & E. W. Markson (Eds.), *Growing old in America* (4th ed., pp. 207–218). New Brunswick, NJ: Transaction Books.

Aubrey, R. F., & Lewis, J. (1983). Social issues and the counseling profession in the 1980s and 1990s. *Counseling and Human Development, 15*(10), 1–15.

Beane, J. (1981). "I'd rather be dead than gay": Counseling gay men who are coming out. *Personnel and Guidance Journal, 60,* 222–226.

Bell, S. T., Kuriloff, P. J., & Lottes, I. (1994). Understanding attributions of blame in stranger rape and date rape situations: An examination of gender, race, identification, and students' social perceptions of rape victims. *Journal of Applied Social Psychology, 24,* 1719–1734.

Bem, S. L. (1974). The measurement of psychological androgyny. *Journal of Consulting and Clinical Psychology, 42,* 155–162.

Blumenfeld, W. J. (Ed.). (1992). *Homophobia: How we all pay the price.* Boston: Beacon Press.

Bowe, F. (1985). *Disabled adults in America: A statistical report drawn from census bureau data.* Washington, DC: U.S. Government Printing Office.

Burnette, E. (1995, October). Disabilities classification under revision. *APA Monitor, 26,* 46.

Campbell, P. R. (1994). *Population projections for states, by age, race, and sex: 1993 to 2020* (U.S. Bureau of the Census, Current Populations Reports, P25–111). Washington, DC: U.S. Government Printing Office.

Churchill, W. (1971). *Homosexual behavior among males: A cross-cultural and cross-species investigation.* Englewood Cliffs, NJ: Prentice Hall.

Clark, D. (1977). *Loving someone gay.* Millbrae, CA: Celestial Arts.

Cole, T. (1991). The specter of old age: History, politics, and culture in an aging America. In B. B. Hess & E. W. Markson (Eds.), *Growing old in America* (4th ed., pp. 23–37). New Brunswick, NJ: Transaction Books.

Cole, W., Gorman, C., Barrett, L. I., & Thompson, D. (1993, April 26). The shrinking ten percent. *Time, 27–29.*

Collier, H. V. (1982). *Counseling women.* New York: Free Press

Corey, G. (1991). *Theory and practice of counseling and psychotherapy.* Pacific Grove, CA: Brooks/Cole Publishing Company.

Dressel, P. L., Carter, V., & Balachandran, A. (1995). Second-order victim-blaming. *Journal of Sociology and Social Welfare, 22*(2), 107–122.

Driedger, D. (1989). *The last civil rights movement.* London: Hurst & Company.

Dworkin, A. G., & Dworkin, R. J. (1976). *The minority report.* New York: Praeger.

Dworkin, S. H., & Gutierrez, F. J. (Eds.). (1992a). *Counseling gay men and lesbians: Journey to the end of the rainbow.* Alexandria, VA: American Association of Counseling and Development.

Dworkin, S. H., & Gutierrez, F. J. (1992b). Introduction: Opening the closet door (pp. xvii–xxvii). In S. H. Dworkin & F. J. Gutierrez, (Eds.), *Counseling gay men and lesbians: Journey to the end of the rainbow.* Alexandria, VA: American Association of Counseling and Development.

Faderman, L. (1991). *Odd girls and twilight lovers.* New York: Penguin.

Fagan, T., & Wallace, A. (1979). Who are the handicapped? *Personnel and Guidance Journal, 58,* 215–220.

Faludi, S. (1991). *Backlash: The undeclared war against American women.* New York: Crown.

Fassinger, R. (1991). The hidden minority: Issues and challenges in working with lesbian women and gay men. *The Counseling Psychologist, 19,* 157–176.

Gerber, J., Wolff, J., Klores, W., & Brown, G. (1989). *Lifetrends: The future of baby boomers and other aging Americans.* New York: Macmillian Publishing Co.

Gilbert, L. A. (1992). Gender and counseling psychology: Current knowledge and directions for research and social action. In S. D. Brown & R. W. Lent (Eds.), *Handbook of Counseling Psychology* (2nd ed., pp. 383–416). New York: Wiley.

Goffman, D. (1963). *Stigma: Notes on the management of spoiled identity.* Englewood Cliffs, NJ: Prentice Hall.

Grealish, C. A., & Salomone, P. R. (1986). Devaluing those with disability: Take responsibility, take action. *The Vocational Guidance Quarterly, 34,* 147–150.

Griffiths, T. D., & Meechan, P. J. (1990). Biology of aging. In Kenneth F. Ferraro (Ed.), *Gerontology: Perspectives and Issues* (pp. 45–57). New York: Springer Publishing Company.

Hacker, H. M. (1975). Women as a minority group. In R. K. Unger & F. L. Denmark (Eds.), *Woman: Dependent or independent variable* (pp. 85–115). New York: Psychological Dimensions.

Halleck, S. L. (1971). Therapy is the handmaiden of the status quo. *Psychology Today, 4,* 30–34, 98–100.

Harris, L., and Associates (1975). *The myth and reality of aging in America.* Washington, DC: The National Council on Aging.

Henley, N. M. (1985). Psychology and gender. *Sign, 11,* 101–119.

Hess, B. B. (1980). *Growing old in America.* New Brunswick, NJ: Transaction Books.

Hess, B. B. (1991). Growing old in the 1990s. In B. B. Hess & E. W. Markson (Eds.), *Growing old in America* (4th ed., pp. 5–22). New Brunswick, NJ: Transaction Books.

Kingdon, M. A. (1979). Lesbians. *The Counseling Psychologist, 8,* 44–45.

Kinloch, G. C. (1979). *The sociology of minority group relations.* Englewood Cliffs, NJ: Prentice Hall.

Kinsey, A. C., Pomeroy, W. B., & Martin, C. E. (1948). *Sexual behavior in the human male.* Philadelphia: Saunders.

Kinsey, A. C., Pomeroy, W. B., Martin, C. E., & Gebhard, P. H. (1953). *Sexual behavior in the human female.* Philadelphia: Saunders.

Kuehn, M. D. (1991). Agenda for professional practice in the 1990s. *Journal of Applied Rehabilitation Counseling, 22,* 6–15.

Larson, P. C. (1982). Counseling special populations. *Professional Psychology, 13,* 843–858.

Levin, J., & Levin, W. C. (1980). *Ageism: Prejudice and discrimination against the elderly.* Belmont, CA: Wadsworth.

Margolis, R. J. (1990). *Risking old age in America.* Boulder, CO: Westview Press.

Martin, D., & Lyon, P. (1972). *Lesbian woman.* San Francisco: New Glide.

Matlin, M. W. (1987). *The psychology of women.* New York: CBS College Publishing.

McNeil, J. M. (1993). *Americans with disabilities: 1991–92 (Bureau of Census Current Populations Reports, P70-33).* Washington, DC: U. S. Government Printing Office.

Mead, M. (1935/1971). *Sex and temperament in three primitive societies.* New York: Dell.

Meador, B. D., & Rogers, C. R. (1984). Person-centered therapy. In R. J. Corsini (Ed.), *Current psychotherapies.* Itasca, IL: F. E. Peacock.

Mill, J. S. (1869/1970). *The subjection of women.* Cambridge, MA: M.I.T. Press.

Moses, A. E., & Hawkins. R. O. (1982). *Counseling lesbian women and gay men.* St. Louis: Mosby.

Muller, R. T., Caldwell, R. A., & Hunter, J. E. (1995). The construct dimensionality of victim blame: The situations of physical child abuse and rape. *Personality and Individual Differences, 19,* 21–31.

National Council on Disability. (1995). *The Americans with Disabilities Act: Ensuring equal access to the American dream.* Washington, DC: Author.

Neugarten, B. L. (1974). Age groups in American society and the rise of the young-old. *Annals of the American Academy, 415,* 187–198.

Nichols, M. P. (1984). *Family therapy: Concepts and methods.* New York: Gardner Press.

O'Neil, J. M. (1980). Male sex role conflicts, sexism, and masculinity: Psychological implications for men, women, and the counseling psychologist. *The Counseling Psychologist, 9,* 61–80.

Perlman, L. G., & Kirk, F. S. (1991). Key disability and rehabilitation legislation. *Journal of Applied Rehabilitation Counseling, 22,* 21–27.

Pope, M. (1995). The "salad bowl" is big enough for us all: An argument for the inclusion of lesbians and gay men in any definition of multiculturalism. *Journal of Counseling & Development, 73,* 301–304.

Richardson, L. W. (1981). *The dynamics of sex and gender: A sociological perspective* (2nd ed.). Boston: Houghton-Mifflin.

Ryan, W. (1971). *Blaming the victim.* New York: Vintage.

Sarason, S. B. (1981). An asocial psychology and a misdirected clinical psychology. *American Psychologist, 36,* 827–836.

Satlin, A. (1994). The psychology of successful aging. *Journal of Geriatric Psychiatry, 27,* 3–7.

Schaffer, K. F. (1981). *Sex roles and human behavior.* Cambridge, MA: Winthrop.

Schwiebert, V. L., & Myers, J. E. (1994). Midlife care givers: Effectiveness of a psychoeducational intervention for midlife adults with parent-care responsibilities. *Journal of Counseling & Development, 72,* 627–632.

Shilling, L. E. (1984). *Perspectives on counseling theories.* Englewood Cliffs, NJ: Prentice-Hall.

Simkin, J. S., & Yontef, G. M. (1984). Gestalt therapy. In R. J. Corsini (Ed.), *Current psychotherapies.* Itasca, IL: F. E. Peacock.

Spence, J. T., & Helmreich, R. L. (1978). *Masculinity and femininity: Their psychological dimensions, correlates, and antecedents.* Austin: University of Texas Press.

Steiner, C. (1975). Manifesto. In C. Steiner et al. (Eds.), *Readings in radical psychiatry.* New York: Grove.

Strehler, B. L. (1962). *Time, cells and aging.* New York: Academic.

Tomes, H. (March, 1992). Disabilities are major public interest issue. *APL Monitor,* p. 13.

Unger, R. K. (1979). Toward a redefinition of sex and gender. *American Psychologist, 34,* 1085–1094.

U.S. Bureau of the Census. (1983). *Labor force status and other characteristics of persons with a work disability: 1982 (Current Populations Reports, Series P-23, No. 127).* Washington, DC: U.S. Government Printing Office.

U.S. Bureau of the Census. (1989). *Labor force status and other characteristics of persons with a work disability: 1981 to 1988 (Current Population Reports, Series P-23, No. 160).* Washington, DC: U.S. Government Printing Office.

U.S. Bureau of the Census. (1992). *Sixty-five plus in America (Current Populations Reports, Special Studies, P23-178RV).* Washington, DC: U.S. Government Printing Office.

U.S. Bureau of the Census. (1993). *Marital status and living arrangements: March, 1992 (Current Population Reports, Series P-20, No. 468).* Washington, DC: U.S. Government Printing Office.

U.S. Bureau of the Census. (1995). *Population Profile of the United States (Current Population Reports, Series P23-189).* Washington, DC: U.S. Government Printing Office.

Vander, A. J., Sherman, J., & Luciano, D. (1985). Homeostatic mechanisms. In *Human physiology: The mechanisms of body function* (pp. 147–171). New York: McGraw-Hill.

Van Hasselt, V. B., Strain, P. S., & Hersen, M. (1988). *Handbook of developmental and physical disabilities*. New York: Pergamon Press.

Weinberg, G. H. (1972). *Society and the healthy homosexual*. New York: St. Martin's.

Wilson, G. T. (1984). Behavior therapy. In R. J. Corsini (Ed.), *Current psychotherapies*. Itasca, IL: F. E. Peacock.

Wirth, L. (1945). The problem of minority groups. In R. Linton (Ed.), *The science of man in the world crisis*. New York: Columbia University Press.

Woodman, N. J., & Lenna, H. R. (1980). *Counseling with gay men and women*. San Francisco: Jossey-Bass.

2
Oppression of People with Disabilities: Past and Present

Past Discrimination

Society's Treatment of People with Disabilities

Hohenshil and Humes (1979) summarized the treatment of persons with disabilities since prehistoric times as follows:

> Throughout the course of recorded human history, those persons who were different have often been destroyed, tortured, exorcised, sterilized, ignored, exiled, exploited, and even considered divine. Their problems have been crudely explained in terms of superstition and varying levels of scientific understanding. In the earliest primitive societies, physical abnormalities were not common beyond infancy because many tribes permitted the killing of such newborn children. . . . In more recent societies the handicapped have been pitied and cared for, and finally, they have been gradually accepted, educated, and often employed, with the same rights as those who are not handicapped. (p. 221)

As Hohenshil and Humes (1979) suggest, three views of persons with disabilities have been widely held from prehistoric through contemporary times in Western culture. Each is still present to some extent in modern society in the United States.

Burdensome View

The first view, that persons with disabilities are a burden on the community, originated with our first human ancestors. Early humans were almost certainly nomads, foraging for fruit, nuts, and plants and following game for food. Communities of humans presumably formed to enhance self-protection and food-gathering efficiency. Under these conditions, individuals who could not ambulate well enough to keep up with the group or who could not contribute to the food gathering activities were rejected, destroyed, or left to survive on their own (Obermann, 1965). In addition to the ability to ambulate, visual acuity, hearing ability, and other physical capabilities were presumably needed to contribute to group welfare. Limited mental ability was probably not viewed by the group as a burden, but no doubt it contributed to each individual's ability to survive in an environment in which humans were both predators and prey.

As agricultural societies developed, permanent villages began to appear. Although ambulation and other physical and mental abilities were still needed for farming activities, individuals no longer needed to keep up with the nomadic movements of the group. Persons with mild disabilities often were able to contribute to the welfare of the community and to maintain themselves to a degree not possible in earlier stages of human development. Some people with disabilities could plant fields, use hand tools, make pottery, and contribute to the commonweal in other ways. Severe physical disabilities were still viewed as "deformities," however, and the belief that disabilities were somehow supernaturally inspired, a belief dating back to prehistoric times, still persisted (Bowe, 1978):

> Lacking the technical means to find and demonstrate germs or histopathology, ancient doctors had to explain disease and physiological disorders in terms of evil spirits and cures had to be offered in terms of exorcism and magic. If the gods were smiling upon the well and the whole and the strong, the sick and the disabled and the weak must be the special property of demons. Thus the disadvantaged individual not only felt the frustrations resulting from lack of capability, he [*sic*] suffered social ostracism and personal feelings of unworthiness as well. (Obermann, 1965, p. 54)

Even in the golden era of Greek culture, it was common practice in Sparta, for example, to destroy babies and children with disabilities because they were viewed as a burden on their families and as a means of "upgrading" the race (Obermann, 1965; Rubin & Roessler, 1978). Although Aristotle and other Greek philosophers began to question negative societal attitudes toward persons with disabilities, the view that people with disabilities are a burden on society persisted, even as it does today in some circles. Centuries later, the Romans engaged in the same barbaric practice and were known to dispose of "some deformed and unwanted children . . . in sewers, located, ironically, outside the Temple of Mercy" (Garrett, 1969, p. 31).

Evidence that the burdensome view of persons with disabilities still exists in modern society is provided by studies of employment attitudes. In general, it can be concluded that negative attitudes toward persons with disabilities have severely limited their employment opportunities (Satcher & Hendren, 1991). This is particularly true of human services occupations, where employees have contact with consumers and the employees "appearance" presumably enters into hiring decisions. Businesses engaged in sales or service are less likely to hire persons with disabilities than manufacturing firms (Harris and Associates, 1986; Satcher & Hendren, 1991).

Charitable View

In Western society at least, a second view of persons with disabilities, that of charitable concern for their welfare, emerged as a forceful theme when Jesus

Christ drew attention to this population through his teachings. As a result, Christian churches accepted the plight of persons with disabilities as one of their charitable causes. This view of persons with disabilities held that they were among the "deserving poor." Providing food, shelter, and other services for people with disabilities became an important activity of the developing Church and other charitable organizations. Unfortunately, the provider-receiver relationship that was created as a result too often serves as a model for modern efforts to assist persons with disabilities. This second view of persons with disabilities, although motivated by sincere concern for their welfare, frequently translates into sympathy, pity, and a paternalistic attitude toward persons with disabilities (Bowe, 1978).

The charitable treatment of persons with disabilities received a setback in the Middle Ages, due in part to the poor economic conditions and the severe religious attitudes of the times (Rubin & Roessler, 1978). According to Scotch (1984), during the Middle Ages, persons with disabilities were often placed in institutions that offered little more than custodial care. The belief that disabilities were the result of supernaturalism returned in full force. "Disabled people were to be feared or ridiculed, objects of persecution on the one hand and court jesters on the other" (Bowe, 1978, pp. 7–8). Frequently, they were placed in asylums with "other individuals who did not play a productive role in the social and economic life of the community" (Scotch, 1984, p. 15). It was not until 1260 that one of the first separate institutions for persons with disabilities was established in Paris, an asylum for blind soldiers. Charitable treatment of persons with disabilities gained strength during the Renaissance and the Elizabethan English Poor Laws of 1597–1601 provided financial support to persons with disabilities who were living at home and unemployed (Rubin & Roessler, 1978).

One of the first institutions for persons with disabilities in the United States was a school for blind persons established in Baltimore, Maryland, in 1812. A school for the deaf was founded in Hartford, Connecticut, by 1817, and in 1893 the first school for children with physical disabilities was founded in Boston, Massachusetts (Obermann, 1965). By the late nineteenth century, a number of voluntary charitable organizations had been established in the United States that were concerned with the welfare of persons with disabilities. The Salvation Army, which organized in England, established an office in the United States in 1879. This was followed by the American Red Cross in 1881 and Goodwill Industries in 1902 (Scotch, 1984).

Although involved in establishing special schools for the blind, deaf, and mentally ill in the 1800s, state and federal governments did not become significantly involved with the needs of persons with disabilities until the twentieth century (Hohenshil & Humes, 1979). Then, "because of the negative by-products of industrialization, the tragedies of World War I, and a growing humanitarian philosophy, the United States government began to accept its responsibility for the vocational rehabilitation of both disabled veterans and the civilian disabled" (Rubin & Roessler, 1978, p. 44). State worker compensation laws providing medical treatment and financial compensation for injured workers were first passed in 1909, and by 1921, 45 states and territories had worker compensation laws. The first pillar of a federal vocational rehabilitation program was set in place when the Smith-Sears Veterans Rehabilitation Act was passed in 1918, mandating vocational training for veterans with disabilities. This was followed by the Smith-Fess Act of 1920, which provided limited services for people with physical disabilities (including vocational counseling). The Smith-Fess Act provided federal funding to participating states on a 50-50 basis. By 1935, all the states had vocational rehabilitation programs in operation. Also in 1935, passage of the Social Security Act gave the vocational rehabilitation program permanent authorization. In 1940, the program was expanded to include previously unserved populations, and the federal government's share of the funding was increased to 75 percent. Further expansion and strengthening of the federal rehabilitation program occurred in 1943 with the Barder-LaFollette Act and with the Vocational Rehabilitation Acts of 1954, 1965, and 1968 (Scotch, 1984).

Funk (1987) described the 40-year period from 1920 to 1960 as follows:

> From a broad disability/human rights perspective, the era reflects an increasing humanization of certain classes of disabled people based on qualities of "deservedness" and "normalcy" and "employability," and a move from total societal indifference to a recognition that the remaining "unfortunates" must receive some level of minimum care. However, the handicapped still retained their cast status in the public mind as dependent, unhealthy deviants, who would, in the great majority, always require segregated care and protection. (pp. 13–14)

Currently, about one-third of all adults with disabilities receive federal (Supplemental Security Income, Medicaid, Social Security Disability Insurance, Medicare) and state benefits because of their disabilities (Bowe, 1988).

Egalitarian View

While the concept of rehabilitation was an important step in the evolution of attitudes toward persons with disabilities, it was still based on a deficiency model and a view that society was performing a charitable act by providing services to deserving individuals. The focus of efforts by charitable organizations and governmental programs until the late 1960s was on rehabilitating persons with disabilities, not on adapting the environment to meet their needs. Furthermore, some rehabilitation statues actually operated to restrict the activities of persons with disabilities. According to Laski (1978), these statues

> reflected common stereotypes of disabled persons as dependent and inferior. Laws characteristically excluded handicapped persons from services, benefits and protections provided, as a matter-of-course, to all persons. Specialized legislation, enacted to protect the disabled was premised on notions of charity rather than enlightenment and implemented so as to segregate the disabled and suffocate their ability to participate in society. (p. 1)

By the late 1960s, a third view of persons with disabilities was emerging in the United States, a view that they are a disparate but identifiable group of individuals whose civil rights have been severely restricted, often through the efforts of well-meaning supporters. Central to this view was the philosophy that civil rights of persons with disabilities were being denied if government supported institutions were not architecturally designed to accommodate them.

> Advocates argued that disabled people should receive not special education at a special school, but supplemental services as part of a regular educational program in a regular classroom shared with able-bodied students; not sheltered workshops for the construction of handicrafts and the repair of discards, but participation in the mainstream labor market; not separate arrangements for transportation, recreation, and access to public facilities, but equal access to facilities and services used by the general public. By rejecting separate facilities, whether equal or unequal, disability rights advocates rejected the association of disabled persons with the "deserving poor" and launched a civil rights movement demanding full integration into the mainstream of American life, a movement parallel to those demanding equal rights without regard to race, gender, or age. (Scotch, 1984, pp. 10–11)

For many persons with disabilities, this civil rights movement is the most recent in a series of movements that have sought rights for laborers, people of color, women, and gay men and lesbian women (Driedger, 1989).

According to Scotch (1984), the groundwork for this egalitarian view of persons with disabilities was laid when the National Federation for the Blind and other groups lobbied state legislatures in the 1930s for guide dog and white cane laws. Guide dog and white cane laws were precedent-setting because they nullified restrictions placed on persons with disabilities by the larger society (e.g., allowing the use of guide dogs in public places where dogs are prohibited) and required able-bodied persons to adjust to their presence (e.g., drivers must take precautions upon seeing a white cane in use). The fact that young people who became disabled as the result of World War II were living longer and were more mobile than earlier generations of persons with disabilities also contributed to a climate for recognizing disability rights (Driedger, 1989). Further groundwork was laid with the Architectural Barriers Act of 1968, the first federal civil rights-oriented statute affecting persons with disabilities. This act required that a barrier-free design be employed in all new federal building construction.

For many years, the formation of a cohesive social or political group representing persons with disabilities was impeded by their diverse experiences and communication differences. With the social movements of the 1960s, however, came a recognition that they shared a common experience of oppression and exclusion, and a disability civil rights movement began to take form. Initially, informal and formal interaction took place among individuals sharing similar disabilities, and later interaction and political activity took place across disability lines (Scotch, 1984). The decade from 1965 to 1975 has been referred to by Abeson (1976) as the "era in which the battle cry for public policy advances changed from charitable solicitations to declarations of rights" (p. 5) on behalf of people with disabilities.

In 1972, the most comprehensive piece of legislature affecting people with disabilities to that date was signed into law by President Richard Nixon. It was entitled The Rehabilitation Act of 1973 and was intended to expand and improve the federal rehabilitation program. Section 504 of the act, however, included language borrowed from Title VI of the Civil Rights Acts of 1964 and has been referred to by Scotch (1984) as a civil rights law for persons with disabilities. The single sentence that constitutes Section 504 reads: "No otherwise qualified handicapped individual in the United States . . . shall, solely by reason of his [sic] handicap, be excluded from the participation in, be denied the benefits of, or be subjected to discrimination under any program or activity receiving Federal financial assistance." Bowe (1978), a leading disability rights activist, referred to Section 504 as "the single most important civil rights provision ever enacted on behalf of disabled citizens in this country" (p. 205). Unfortunately, however, the disability rights provided by the Rehabilitation Act of 1973 were limited to programs receiving federal assistance and did not apply to the private sector.

The Education of Handicapped Children Act (P. L. 94–142), which was signed into law by President Gerald Ford in November, 1975, also included important provisions for disability rights. This law stipulated that states must provide full educational opportunities to all children with disabilities and included federal funding toward this end. In addition to provisions for parents and child advocates to appeal educational decisions, the law mandated the concept of mainstreaming. In essence, this requirement stipulates that whenever possible children with disabilities must receive their education in regular classrooms with nondisabled students.

The list of rights won by people with disabilities through disability rights legislation during the period from 1965–1975 is indeed impressive. In addition to the right to public supported education, the list includes the following:

> The right of institutionalized handicapped persons to be free from unusual and cruel treatment; the right of institutionalized handicapped persons to be freed from employment without reimbursement and without rehabilitative purpose; the right to avoid involuntary institutionalization on the part of persons who represent neither a danger to society nor to themselves; the right of the handicapped to exercise the power to vote; the right of the handicapped both to marry and to procreate; the right of the handicapped to travel on the nation's public conveyances; and the right of the handicapped to access to America's buildings by means of removal of environmental barriers. (Abeson, 1976, p. 5)

For a period of time in the early 1980s, it appeared as if the disability rights movement in the United States had reached a plateau. According to Scotch (1984), the disability rights movement peaked in effectiveness in 1978, and he cited failure by Congress to pass an extension to the Civil Rights Act prohibiting discrimination on the basis of disability in all employment to support his position. He also suggested that many government officials sympathetic to disability rights had been removed from government agencies following the 1980 presidential election. By the end of the 1980s, however, a number of federal and state laws had been enacted that were designed to promote and enhance the career development of students with disabilities. Brolin and Gysbers (1989) listed the Job Training Partnership Act of 1982, the 1983 Amendments to the Education of the Handicapped Act of 1975, the Carl D. Perkins Vocational Education Act of 1984, the Developmental Disabilities Act Amendments of 1984, and the Rehabilitation Act Amendments of 1986 as evidence of continuing concern for the employment and civil rights of persons with disabilities. Unfortunately, although Brolin and Gysbers (1989) documented increased recognition by legislators throughout the 1970s and 1980s that better educational and rehabilitation services were needed for persons with disabilities, they also concluded that "students with disabilities are not attaining greater vocational and independent living success than they did in previous years" (p. 158).

Disability rights groups continued to lobby the Congress, and by the late 1980s, support for a comprehensive disabilities rights bill was gaining strength. In 1990, the Congress passed the Americans with Disabilities Act (ADA, Public Law 101-336), "the most sweeping civil-rights bill in more than 25 years" (Karr, 1990, p. B1). The ADA was signed into law by President Bush on July 26, 1990, and began to take effect two years later. The purposes of the ADA are

1. to provide a clear and comprehensive national mandate for the elimination of discrimination against individuals with disabilities;

2. to provide clear, strong, consistent, enforceable standards addressing discrimination against individuals with disabilities;

3. to ensure that the Federal Government plays a central role in enforcing the standards established in this Act on behalf of individuals with disabilities; and

4. to invoke the sweep of congressional authority, including the power to enforce the fourteenth amendment and to regulate commerce, in order to address the major areas of discrimination faced day-to-day by people with disabilities. (Karr, 1990, p. B1)

The ADA prohibits discrimination against persons with mental or physical disabilities in the private sector in four different areas: (1) employment, (2) telecommunications, (3) transportation, and (4) public services and accommodations. With respect to employment, the ADA specifies that employers with 15 or more employees have to "make reasonable accommodation to the known limitations of qualified persons with disabilities and to ensure that their hiring practices are nondiscriminatory" (Satcher & Hendren, 1991, p. 15). According to Youngstrom (1992), reasonable accommodations could include "hiring a reader for a blind employee; adjusting schedules so an employee can see a therapist in the middle of the day; and writing instructions for people who become anxious at oral directions" (p. 26).

The law also provides access to public buildings, telephone service, mass transportation, and government services for persons with disabilities.

This overview of laws pertaining to persons with disability is, by necessity, brief. For a readable, more extensive synopsis of 11 of the most important laws concerning rehabilitation and disability, including the ADA, we refer the reader to Perlman and Kirk (1991). For an even more comprehensive and detailed review of more than 50 laws related to this topic that were passed prior to the mid-1980s, we suggest obtaining the publication entitled *Summary of Existing Legislation Affecting Person with Disabilities* from the U.S. Department of Education (1988).

Three branches of the disability rights movement have emerged since the 1970s: (1) the independent living movement, (2) consumer organizations, and (3) self-help groups. The goal of the independent living movement is to mainstream living arrangements for persons with disabilities so that they are no longer segregated in special housing. The purpose of consumer organizations of persons with disabilities is to monitor rehabilitation, transportation, and housing services provided by the government and nonprofit rehabilitation organizations. Self-help organizations of persons with disabilities are designed to do just that, provide self-help services directly or by putting political pressure on the government (Driedger, 1989).

The disability rights movement has by no means been limited to the legislative action in the United States. According to Driedger (1989),

> Organizations composed entirely of persons with various disabilities—physical, mental and sensory—have sprung up in 100 countries since the mid-1970s. . . . One of the results of this recognition was a gathering of disabled people in Singapore in 1981 to form Disabled Peoples' International (DPI). DPI's mandate is to be the voice of disabled people and it believes that disabled people should be integrated into society and participate with the same rights as everyone else. With membership in sixty-nine countries, it is activist-oriented, it looks to lobby governments and the UN, and it educates the public about the aspirations and abilities of disabled people. (p. 1)

In March, 1988, a historic event occurred at Gallaudet University, the nation's only liberal arts college for the deaf, that provided evidence persons with disabilities could successfully organize to represent their own best interests. Drawing on the civil rights movement of the 1960s, protesting students at Gallaudet forced the resignation of a hearing campus president, who did not know sign language, and the appointment of a deaf replacement (Lewin, 1988).

Despite these successes by disability rights activists, it is important to recognize that all three views of persons with disabilities are represented in modern society. Further, there are those within the rehabilitation counseling profession that suggest securing rights for persons with disabilities has actually worked to the detriment of individuals in this group. For example, Nelson (1989) states that ". . . the perspective of justice has distorted our moral responsibility toward the disabled" (p. 228).

Psychology's Treatment of Persons with Disabilities

The counseling profession's involvement with persons with disabilities can be traced to the vocational rehabilitation movement, which emerged in the second decade of the twentieth century. The National Civilian Rehabilitation Conference first convened in 1924 and was renamed the National Rehabilitation Association (NRA) in 1927. Vocational rehabilitation over the next three decades moved from an educational emphasis, to a social work approach, to a vocational guidance approach (Cull & Hardy, 1972). The National Rehabilitation Counseling Association was established as a division of the NRA to meet the specialized needs of rehabilitation counselors, a profession struggling to identify itself. According to Rubin and Roessler (1978), the rehabilitation counseling profession is still attempting to define its role and function. The two major focuses of rehabilitation counselors to date have been on helping clients accept their disability and gain meaningful employment.

By the mid-1950s research psychologists began to take on interest in disabilities and their psychological impact, and rehabilitation psychology emerged as a specialization. Rehabilitation psychologists have focused their research on persons with disabilities and their self-perceptions, and on nondisabled individuals and their perceptions of persons with disabilities. Considerable research has also focused on the clinical process—developing a helping relationship, predicting work adjustment, promoting successful rehabilitation (Fenderson, 1984).

Rehabilitation psychology was not formally recognized as a division (Division 22) of the American Psychological Association (APA) until 1958 (at that time entitled the National Council on Psychological Aspects of Disability). However, while research psychologists formed a division to study the psychological effects of disabilities, the APA neglected to offer leadership in the area of disability rights. By the mid- to late-1970s, however, psychologists with disabilities within the APA began to lobby for greater access to APA conventions (i.e., to remove the architectural and communication barriers at convention centers). Their efforts resulted in the establishment of the Task Force on Psychology and the Handicapped by the APA Board of Social and Ethical Responsibility for Psychology in 1979. This task force attempted to draw the attention of psychologists to barriers faced by psychologists with disabilities. In their final report published in 1984 (Task Force, 1984), the Task Force recommended the establishment of a permanent Committee on Psychology and Handicaps. The committee was renamed the Committee on Disabilities and Handicaps in 1986 and was placed under the aegis of the APA Board of Social and Ethical Responsibility. In 1991, it was again renamed, this time as the Committee on Disability Issues in Psychology, with oversight by the Board for the Advancement of Psychology in the Public Interest. At that time, its responsibilities were broadened to include sensitizing and educating the APA membership about the role psychology can play to assist all persons with disabilities, not just psychologists with disabilities, to realize their potential (Tomes, 1992)

While a large number of helping professions (e.g., rehabilitation psychologists, rehabilitation counselors, occupational therapists, physical therapists, nurses, school psychologists, teachers) have focused their attention on people with disabilities, their efforts have primarily been to rehabilitate people with disabilities, not liberate them. According to Roberts (1989), the medical rehabilitation model that emerged in the 1940s actually contributed to negative images of persons with disabilities, even among members of this population themselves. Roberts (1989) suggests that millions of persons with disabilities who could not be rehabilitated to "normal" functioning have come to perceive themselves as rehabilitative failures (p. 233).

It seems ironic that a profession that prides itself in sensitivity to individual needs has been so slow to recognize disability rights and so ineffective in promoting them. Only recently have a few psychologists spoken out for disability rights, and the major profession representing psychologists has yet to take a strong, proactive stance on the issue. Rigler (1992) chastises the APA for failing to act ethically on behalf of both psychologists and clients with disabilities. With respect to psychologists with disabilities, she points out that

> Such people are often barred by attitudinal, architectural or communications barriers from making professional contributions to or attending APA-accredited or -sponsored programs, internships or conferences. Their employment prospects and post-hiring opportunities are dramatically limited. . . . If they have an interest in disability-related issues, they are often denied interviews in all but medically dominated, rehabilitation settings. . . . Even our vaunted new APA building contains barriers to people with disabilities, due to inadequate prior consultation with such people. (Rigler, 1992, p. 4)

Furthermore, as Bruce and Christiansen (1988) point out, even when some therapists do attempt to advocate on behalf of people with disabilities they can exacerbate prejudicial attitudes.

> They are largely unaware that in communicating their concerns they may inadvertently convey the prejudicial attitudes they are fighting and help reinforce the barriers they are trying to remove. . . . Even in the professional literature, problems with the pejorative use of language persist. (p. 190)

Writing in *The Vocational Guidance Quarterly,* a journal for professional vocational counselors, Grealish and Salomone (1986) charge counselors with responsibility for maintaining the status quo with respect to people with disabilities:

> Good intentions notwithstanding, however, as able-bodied citizens, you have tended to support (often by inaction) the attitude that an individual with a disability should be the object of sympathy and charity but not of equality and friendship. (p. 147)

The current emphasis within rehabilitation counseling to push for independent living (working) for people with disabilities often comes in conflict with earlier supported living (working) efforts. Szymanski, Johnston-Rodriguez, Millington, Rodriguez, and Lagergren (1995) point out that this is just one of many paradoxes within the rehabilitation counseling profession.

> Independence and community integration have been generally regarded as important rehabilitation goals. . . . However, it has been suggested that some disability services can isolate consumers from normal activities and supports . . . and that the financial policies related to disability can actually impede independence. (p. 17)

Thus, even with the best of intentions, rehabilitation services may impede the independence of people with disabilities. Furthermore, some psychologists and counselors share some of the same biases toward people with disabilities as are held by the lay public. Nathanson (1979) reviewed the research on attitudes that helping professionals, counselors in particular, have toward persons with disabilities. Some of the feelings he attributes to counselors of persons with disabilities include discomfort, fear, pity, guilt, frustration, and sorrow. Nathanson (1979) suggests that because counselors are human, their deeply held and often subconscious feelings and thoughts can have a profound effect on the counseling relationship with clients with disabilities.

According to the U.S. Bureau of the Census (1987), only about one in three persons with disabilities is employed. This low employment rate can be blamed in part on discrimination against people with disabilities by employers. May and Vieceli (1983) suggest, however, that employer attitudes will not change as long as counselors devote so little time and energy to job placement services and "counselors take the more comfortable path of delivering less threatening services to clients" (p. 45). They go on to suggest that the barriers to placing clients with disabilities in suitable occupations include counselor bias against job placement (considered unprofessional and "dirty work"), administrative pressure to increase the number of placements with little regard for their quality, and lack of placement training for rehabilitation counselors. Rigler (1992) points out that psychologists who work in inaccessible environments are discriminating against people with disabilities and are, therefore, acting unethically.

Many rehabilitation counselors share the biased attitudes toward people with disabilities that are held by employers. Several studies indicate that counselors feel people with disabilities are not motivated to work, they have little job training, and little or no work experience (Zadny, 1979; Zadny & James, 1978, 1979). Blaming people with disabilities for their lack of job training and work experience is an example of "blaming the victims" for the problems they face. The perception that people with disabilities are not motivated to work is simply not true for the majority. Harris (1986) found that although one-third of all adults with disabilities receive federal and state benefits due to their disabilities, 67 percent of these beneficiaries would rather work, even if they had to give up their government aid. Furthermore, when they are able to obtain employment, "handicapped workers' records on production, job performance, cost to employ, needs for job redesign, absenteeism, job turnover, and safety are as good, and in some cases, better than their nonhandicapped counterparts" (Mithaug, 1979).

The recently enacted ADA has implications for psychologists, particularly I/O psychologists who help select applicants for employment.

> Under the new law, psychologists will have to ensure that their employment and promotion tests don't unfairly screen out people because of their disabilities. They will have to demonstrate that tests measure "essential job functions"; disabled people can't be refused a position if they have trouble doing peripheral tasks or if they could perform core tasks with "reasonable accommodation." And psychologists will have to find alternate ways to give people with all kinds of physical and mental disabilities standardized tests and score them. (Youngstrom, 1992, p. 26)

Counselors and psychologists are also affected by the accessibility provisions of the law; those in private practice as well as public service have to make their services accessible to individuals with various types of disabilities. This includes the possibility of providing a sign language interpreter, as well as providing physical access to their office. It is clear that counselors and psychologists need to develop greater sensitivity to the experiences of persons with disabilities if they are to provide "equal opportunity" services and not just charitable assistance to this population.

Current Discrimination

Despite recent legislation on their behalf, discrimination against people with disabilities persists in the form of social, economic, and environmental discrimination and abuse.

Social Discrimination

As with all minority groups, discrimination against persons with disabilities has its roots in negative attitudes and stereotypes. Vargo (1989) reviewed the research on attitudes of the general public toward persons with disabilities and concluded that (a) these attitudes are generally negative; (b) some cultures are more accepting of persons with disabilities than others (in general, highly industrialized countries are more accepting than agrarian societies); and (c) in cultures where low social status is assigned to being female, women with disabilities must overcome more serious obstacles than men with disabilities. He also pointed to the Bible and the media as sources of negative attitude formation. With respect to the Bible, Vargo cited passages in both the Old and New Testaments implying that physical and mental disorders are punishments inflicted by God for not complying with religious laws. With respect to the media, he suggested that "disability as characterized in drama, literature, and movies is nearly always clothed in metaphor and that the metaphor most often used is symbolic of . . . 'monstrosity' " (Vargo, 1989, p. 283).

Livneh (1982) developed a system of 12 categories for classifying sources of negative attitudes toward persons with disabilities. According to Livneh (1982), people form negative attitudes due to sociocultural conditioning, childhood influences, psychodynamic mechanisms, perceptions of disabilities as punishment, image, marginality associated with a minority group, symbolic parallelism between disability and death, prejudice-provoking behaviors by people with disabilities, disability-related factors (levels of functionality severity), visibility, and observer-related factors (sex, age, ethnocentrism, authoritarianism). He concludes that attempts by researchers and clinicians to change negative attitudes toward people with disabilities have been unsuccessful because they have not addressed the multifarious and long-term nature of their source.

In addition to holding negative attitudes toward people with disabilities, there is some evidence that nondisabled people use different, sometimes discriminatory, interaction styles with people who have disabilities (Coon, Gouvier, Caldwell, & Hulse, 1991; Gouvier, Coon, Fuller, & Arnoldi, 1992; Gouvier, Coon, Todd, & Fuller, 1994). Gouvier et al. (1994) found that when asked for directions by someone in a wheelchair, nondisabled people used more redundant and concrete speech than they did when approached by someone not using a wheelchair. They found that people in general (but particularly women) were more likely to use "motherese," speech involving exaggerated prosodic inflections, diminutives in naming, and shortened phrase and sentence length, when addressing a person in a wheelchair than when speaking to a nondisabled person. They proposed that "prosodic variations constitute the key element that determines whether a speech pattern is perceived as discriminatory or not" (Gouvier et al., 1994, p. 267).

Mental health professionals are not immune to discrimination against people with disabilities. Several studies have found that counselors have significant biases against individuals with a variety of disabling conditions (Schofield & Kunce, 1971; Wicas & Carluccio, 1971). There is also some evidence that counselors who hold negative attitudes toward people with disabilities are, in general, less effective counselors than those who perceive people with disabilities more favorably (Cook, Kunce, & Getsinger, 1976).

A national survey cited by Bowe (1980) suggests most people support special efforts for people with disabilities, at least in the abstract. When asked if they supported special efforts (e.g., accessibility modifications, affirmative action in employment) on behalf of people with disabilities, 79 percent of the respondents answered yes. This figure was almost double the percentage responding affirmatively for special efforts on behalf of women (47 percent) and ethnic minorities (44 percent).

Social discrimination, however, continues to be problematic for people with disabilities. This suggests that Americans support a special effort for people with disabilities as long as it is in the abstract and they are not directly affected by it. Neighborhood resistance to the opening of group homes for the mentally retarded or mentally ill is a prime example of social discrimination. Bowe (1980) cites lack of knowledge about disabilities, stereotyping, and unnecessary selection requirements (for employment, membership, etc.) as other examples of social discrimination. Formal and informal labeling of people with mental disabilities is still another form of social discrimination (Lombana, 1982). Further, there is evidence that a social acceptability hierarchy exists for disabilities, with the more visible and functionally disabling conditions judged to be the least acceptable (Bruce & Christiansen, 1988).

Unfortunately, people with disabilities are subject to the same sources of attitude formation as are people who have no disabilities. As a result, some people with disabilities accept a number of intrapersonal and interpersonal misconceptions that seriously hamper their social and emotional development (Vargo, 1989). According to Vargo (1987), these misconceptions include the following:

1. My disability is a punishment.
2. All of my difficulties are caused by my disability.
3. Asking for help is a sign of personal weakness.
4. It is impossible for a disabled person to be happy.
5. I'm of less value as a person because I'm not able-bodied.
6. No one can possibly understand how I feel.
7. I can't continue to live like this.
8. I can't do things the way I used to, so why do anything at all?
9. I could never succeed in anything.
10. Life can't possibly be fulfilling for me. (p. 284)

There is fairly consistent evidence that people with chronic physical impairments rate their satisfaction with life lower than nondisabled people. However, research on life satisfaction suggests that it is the limitations in social-role performance, not the extent of the disability per se, that determines lower life satisfaction scores among people with disabilities (Nosek, Fuhrer, & Potter, 1995).

The effect of stereotypes that significant others hold of children with disabilities can be particularly pernicious and, combined with other factors, can contribute to a vicious cycle:

> A physical appearance that may alter initial reactions to the child, data on aptitudes and achievement that are not accurate, the assignment of benign academic tasks by those who plan for and work with the student, and the student's own sensitivity to his or her lack of acceptance and success may interact to produce behavior and performance that confirm the doubts of both the student and those who are closest to him or her. (Williams & Lair, 1991, p. 196)

Antonak and Livneh (1995) found evidence of a trend toward more positive attitudes toward people with disabilities in several recent reviews of research. This trend notwithstanding, these authors concluded that ". . . the acceptance and integration of persons with disabilities continue to be limited by the negative attitudes, misconceptions, and prejudicial stereotypes of health professionals, employers, coworkers, educators, peers, and neighbors" (Antonak & Livneh, 1995, p. 3).

Economic Discrimination

There is very clear evidence of a relationship between disability and education, unemployment, low earnings, and poverty. There is a strong correlation between years of school completed and likelihood of having a disability. "Among persons 25 to 64 years old, the proportion with a severe disability was 22.8 percent among persons who had not completed high school, 8.7 percent among high school graduates, 6.3 percent among persons who had completed some college but were not graduates, and 3.2 percent among college graduates" (McNeil, 1993, p. 11). Because the opportunity for education typically comes after people are identified as having a disability (except in cases of adventitious disability in young adulthood or later), it seems safe to conclude that people with disabilities do not have the opportunities to move up the educational ladder as do nondisabled people.

The unemployment rate for people with disabilities is somewhat deceiving because it does not include those people who have been out of work so long that they have given up looking for a job (according to Bowe, 1980, most people with disabilities have given up looking for jobs because they cannot obtain the education needed for employment, secure transportation to and from work, or obtain access to places of work). For both men and women ages 16 to 64 with a work disability, the unemployment rate in 1988 was 14.2 percent; for men with no work disability the unemployment rate was 6.2 percent, and for women with no work disability, the comparable figure was 5.2 percent. More telling figures are the data on full-time employment by work disability status. Only 23.4 percent of the men and 13.1 percent of the women with a work disability were employed full time in 1988. For men and women with no work disability, the respective figures were 74.8 percent and 47.1 percent (U.S. Bureau of the Census, 1989). The effect of a work disability on full-time employment is even more severe for individuals who are members of an ethnic minority group. Only 10.8 percent of Black persons with a work disability and 13.9 percent of those of Hispanic origin were employed full-time in 1988 compared to 26.2 percent of White persons with a work disability.

The data for work disabilities is also somewhat misleading because temporary work disabilities are included in these figures. Employment rates among people with severe disabilities, which are much lower than among people with no disability or a nonsevere disability, probably more accurately reflect the condition of the population we are discussing. Based on data gathered in late 1991 and early 1992, the employment rate for persons 21 to 64 years of age was 80.5 percent for the 117.2 million persons with no disability. By comparison, the employment rate was 76.0 percent for the 15.0 million persons with a nonsevere disability and 23.2 percent for the 12.6 million persons with a severe disability (U.S. Bureau of Census, 1995). Other recent surveys have also painted a disturbing view of the high rate of unemployment among people with disabilities. Harris and Associates (1986), for example, found in a survey of 1,000 people with disabilities that 66 percent were unemployed but wanted to work. Another study estimated that by the year 2000, 8 out of 18.3 million working-age Americans with any disability (44 percent) will be unemployed (Hearne, 1991, cited in Baesler, 1995).

Although the elimination of physical barriers is the focus of much of the legislation to create accommodation for people with disabilities, the high unemployment rates among persons with disabilities is more likely a function of the negative attitudes that employers have about them (Berry & Meyer, 1995; Satcher & Hendren, 1991), a spin-off of negative stereotypes held by the population at large. For example, employers frequently believe that persons with disabilities are accident-prone and will increase worker's compensation costs, are frequently absent from work, have low rates of productivity, and will not relate well with coworkers (Conti, 1995; Freedman & Keller, 1981). As might be expected, employers with the least exposure to people with disabilities have the most negative attitudes (McFarlin, Song, & Sonntag, 1991, cited in Berry & Meyer, 1995).

Although 26 states and the District of Columbia had laws barring discrimination against people with disabilities by employers prior to the recent enactment of the ADA of 1990 (as did the federal government for employers receiving federal funds), discrimination still occurred (LaFraniere, 1985). Discrimination against persons with disability also occurred despite Section 503 of the Rehabilitation Act of 1973, which has for the past 20 years required that any employer doing business with the federal government take affirmative action to hire persons with disabilities. It remains to be seen if the Americans with Disabilities Act of 1990, which extends nondiscrimination against persons with disabilities to employment in the private sector, can have an impact on these employment statistics.

Employers have been particularly reluctant to make adjustments to their work settings to accommodate people with disabilities because they assume it will be too expensive. By the mid-1980s, a legal precedent had been set requiring that an employer must make reasonable adjustments to minimize such dangers (Moskowitz, 1985). More recently, the ADA requires that "employers with more than 15 employees must make reasonable accommodation to the known limitations of qualified persons with disabilities and to ensure that their hiring practices are nondiscriminatory" (Satcher & Hendren, 1991). Karr (1990) cites the experiences of companies already in compliance with the disabilities-access rule as evidence that concerns about the cost of accommodating people with disabilities is overblown; a study at Syracuse University found that when access features are designed into new construction they add less than 1 percent, on average, to the total cost. Similarly, Noel (1990) reported that 51 percent of the companies using assistive accommodation were doing so at no cost, and for an additional 30 percent the cost was under $500.

Persons with disabilities who are able to secure employment earn average incomes that are considerably lower than average incomes for persons with no work disability. The average annual income in 1987 for men with a work disability was $15,497 compared to $24,095 for men with no work disability. For women with disabilities, the average annual income in 1987 was $8,075 compared to $13,000 for women with no work disability (U.S. Bureau of the Census, 1989). As might be expected due to the effects of double oppression, the mean earnings for Black persons with a work disability ($11,876) and persons of Hispanic origin who have a work disability ($12,213) are lower than White persons with a work disability ($15,869). More recent data from late 1991 and early 1992 indicates that the average monthly income for workers 35 to 54 years of age with no disability was $2,446. By comparison, those with a nonsevere disability earned $2,006 a month, while those with a severe disability earned only $1,562 (U.S. Bureau of Census, 1995).

As might be expected given these employment and income figures, the presence of a disability is associated with an increased probability of living in poverty. For people 15 years of age or older in late 1991 and early 1992, 12.2 percent of the population with no disability fall into the below-poverty category. By comparison, 14.1 percent of the population with a nonsevere disability and 24.3 percent of the population with a severe disability lived below the poverty level (U.S. Bureau of the Census, 1995). A 1992 U.S. Bureau of Census report focusing on work disabilities provides evidence that the economic impact is even more severe for women than for men. For persons with a severe work disability between 16 and 64 years of age, 29.7 percent of all men and 40.5 percent of all women lived below the poverty level in 1991. These figures compared to 9.4 percent of all men and 13.9 percent of all women between 16 and 64 in the general population living below the poverty level that same year.

In addition to increasing the probability of being unemployed, having a low income, and living in poverty, having a disability is also associated with a low probability of having private health insurance and high probability of having a government health plan or no health plan at all. Among people with a severe disability ages 15 to 64, 48.1 percent are covered by a private health insurance plan, 36.2 percent have no private coverage but are covered by a government plan, and 15.7 percent have no health insurance at all. This compares to 80 percent private insurance coverage, 5.2 percent government health coverage, and 14.8 no health insurance coverage for people without a disability (McNeil, 1993).

Bowe (1980) also cites evidence from Social Security Administration Surveys in 1965 and 1971 that indicate a worsening of the economic situation for people with disabilities. He points out, for example, that a smaller proportion of people with disabilities were employed in 1971 than in 1965.

The problems of economic discrimination are compounded for ethnic minorities with disabilities. For example, American Indian people with disabilities must live on reservations, primarily because state and federal agencies facing tight budgets often attempt to shift the responsibility for funding programs away from themselves. According to Joe (1988), "these jurisdictional questions and misinformation from service providers has and continues to plague the rights and accessibility to resources by disabled people in many American Indian communities" (p. 254). She points out that in addition to state-federal jurisdictional problems, American Indians with disabilities often do not receive mandated services due to inadequate financial resources, lack of culturally relevant programs, lack of public transportation, and the remoteness and isolation of most reservations. Small reservations are particularly affected by these barriers to services. Also, although children with moderate or mild disabilities have profited from the passage of P. L. 94-142, American Indian adults with disabilities and children with severe or multiple disabilities seldom receive any services unless they are institutionalized in state hospitals or nursing homes, often far from their families and cultural support systems (Joe, 1988).

Environmental Discrimination

> Some of the more glaring reflection of negative societal attitudes are seen in architectural designs. . . . Inaccessible housing, street corners without curb cuts, poor transportation services, signs and signals yielding only visual or only audio cues, and architectural designs that thwart an individual's full appreciation of societal membership in effect say to the individual with a disability: "you don't count," "you're not important to this society," and "you have little value."
> (Grealish & Salomone, 1986, p. 148)

In every community, there is evidence of continuing environmental discrimination (in the form of environmental barriers) against people with disabilities. Physical barriers exist in the form of rampless entry ways, steep flights of stairs, narrow or revolving doors, drinking fountains, elevator controls, telephones that are too high, and corridors that are too narrow. Communication barriers exist in the form of audio-only announcements (inaccessible to the deaf) and visual-only announcements (inaccessible to the blind) in stores, hotels, transportation centers, employment settings, and public buildings. Nor are personnel in these settings trained to assist deaf and blind people. Transportation barriers exist in subway, train, and bus systems that are inaccessible to the orthopedically disabled.

Although Section 504 of the Rehabilitation Act of 1973 required the removal of architectural, communication, and transportation barriers that affect people with disabilities in federal agencies and agencies supported by federal money, most of the mandated changes have yet to be achieved. Although enacted in 1973, the Department of Health, Education, and Welfare (DHEW) regulations for the Rehabilitation Act were not released until 1977. Because of the huge price tag alleged to be involved in making these accommodations, many state and local agencies have dragged their feet in implementing the regulations. Further, the regulations only apply to those agencies receiving assistance from the federal government (Bowe, 1980).

It is likely to be a long time before the accessibility mandates of the ADA will have an impact on some parts of the country, particularly on rural areas (Associated Press, 1992). Given the economic conditions of recent years, many small town governments and businesses are unwilling to make such changes as replacing street corner curbs with ramps, installing elevators, and providing wheelchair accessible buses. Also, the ADA requires only that existing services be brought into compliance with the law. Areas in which no public transportation is provided are not required to develop a new transportation service for people with disabilities.

Abuse

Ammerman, Van Hasselt, and Hersen (1988) reviewed the child abuse literature and found that children with disabilities were overrepresented among those physically abused. In addition to overrepresentation of children with disabilities among those who are abused, the Ammerman et al. (1988) review revealed an alarmingly high incidence rate of abuse among children with disabilities. They identified the following as characteristics of children with disabilities commonly associated with abuse: (a) prematurity, low birthweight, and medical complications; (b) disruption of mother-infant attachment; (c) parental stress; and (d) vulnerability in infancy. According to Blatt and Brown (1986), the abuse of children with disabilities in institutional settings is almost four times as high as it is in the community. Although no longitudinal, community-based studies have been conducted to date to determine if disabilities in children prompt abuse (Martin, 1995), there is obviously a relationship between disability and child abuse.

Persons with disabilities are also vulnerable to sexual abuse. Sullivan, Vernon, and Scanlan (1987) reviewed four studies of sexual abuse of children with a hearing disability and found that 54 percent of the boys and 50 percent of the girls had been sexually abused. Another study reported that an astonishing 96 percent of children with hearing impairments and other disabilities being evaluated at Boys Town's Center for Abused Handicapped Children had been sexually abused (Brookhouser, Sullivan, Scanlon, & Garbarino, 1986). Davis (1989) found that 75 to 80 percent of mentally retarded women living in various community residences had been sexually assaulted. The developmentally disabled are particularly vulnerable; the California Department of Developmental Services, Office of Human Rights, estimates that 50 to 90 percent of persons with developmental disabilities are sexually abused (Crossmaker, 1991). A survey of 245 women with disabilities revealed that 40 percent had experienced some form of abuse, including 12 percent who had been raped (Ridington, 1989). Mental illness is a disability that puts people at high risk for abuse. The U.S. Senate Subcommittee on the Handicapped (1985) examined 31 facilities for people with mental disabilities and found numerous cases of rape and sexual abuse and sexual harassment of patients by staff and other patients. These and other data clearly suggest that both children and adults with disabilities are at greater risk of sexual abuse and sexual assault than are those without disabilities (Sobsey & Mansell, 1990). Furthermore, Sobsey and Varnhagen (1991) concluded after reviewing previous research and conducting their own survey that "even when abuse is reported, police, courts, and social agencies are often unwilling to pursue charges when the victim is disabled" (p. 208).

When combined with the review that follows regarding abuse of elders, many of whom are persons with disabilities, these data provide strong documentation that persons with disabilities are at high risk of physical, sexual, and emotional abuse.

References

Abeson, A. (1976). Overview. In F. J. Weintraub, A. Abeson, J. Ballard, & M. L. LaVor (Eds.), *Public policy and the education of exceptional children*. Reston, VA: The Council for Exceptional Children.

Ammerman, R. T., Van Hasselt, B. B., & Hersen, M. (1988). Maltreatment of handicapped children: A critical review. *Journal of Family Violence, 3*, 53–72.

Antonak, R. F., & Livneh, H. (1995). Direct and indirect methods to measure attitudes toward persons with disabilities, with an exegesis of the error-choice test method. *Rehabilitation Psychology, 40*(1), 3–24.

Associated Press. (1992, October 6). Rural disabled find barriers slow to fall. *Santa Barbara New Press*, Section B, p. 1.

Baesler, E. S. (1995). Persuasive effects of an involving disability role play. *Journal of Applied Rehabilitation Counseling, 26*(2), 29–35.

Berry, J. O., & Meyer, J. A. (1995). Employing people with disabilities: Impact of attitude and situation. *Rehabilitation Psychology, 40*, 211–222.

Blatt, E. R., & Brown, S. W. (1986). Environmental influences on incidents of alleged child abuse and neglect in New York state psychiatric facilities: Toward an etiology of institutional child maltreatment. *Child Abuse and Neglect, 10*(2), 171–80.

Bowe, F. G. (1978). *Handicapping America: Barriers to disabled people*. New York: Harper & Row.

Bowe, F. (1980). *Rehabilitating America*. New York: Harper & Row.

Bowe, F. G. (1988). Recruiting workers with disabilities. *Employment Relations Today, 15*, 107–111.

Brolin, D. E., & Gysbers, N. C. (1989). Career education for students with disabilities. *Journal of Counseling & Development, 68*, 155–159.

Brookhouser, P. E., Sullivan, P., Scanlon, J. M., & Garbarino, J. (1986). Identifying the sexually abused deaf child: The otolaryngologist's role. *Laryngoscope, 96*, 152–158.

Bruce, M. A., & Christiansen, C. H. (1988). Advocacy in word as well as deed. *The American Journal of Occupational Therapy, 42*, 189–191.

Conti, J. V. (1995). Job discrimination against people with a cancer history. *Journal of Applied Rehabilitation Counseling, 26*(2), 12–16.

Cook, D. W., Kunce, J. T., & Getsinger, S. H. (1976). Perceptions of the disabled and counseling effectiveness. *Rehabilitation Counseling Bulletin, 19*, 470–475.

Coon, R. C., Gouvier, W. D., Caldwell, K., & Hulse, K. (1991). Perception of register variation in speech and its relation to differential judgements about handicapping conditions. *The Journal of Head Injury, 2*, 16–20.

Crossmaker, M. (1991). Behind locked doors—Institutional sexual abuse. *Sexuality and Disability, 9*, 201–219.

Cull, J. G., & Hardy, R. E. (1972). *Vocational rehabilitation: Profession and process*. Springfield, IL: Charles C Thomas.

Davis, M. (1989). Gender and sexual development of women with mental retardation. *The Disabilities Studies Quarterly, 9*(3), 19–20.

Driedger, D. (1989). *The last civil rights movement*. London: Hurst & Company.

Fenderson, D. A. (1984). Opportunities for psychologists in disability research. *American Psychologist, 39*, 524–528.

Freedman, S. M., & Keller, R. T. (1981). The handicapped in the work force. *Academy of Management Review, 6*, 449–458.

Funk, R. (1987). Disability rights: From cast to class in the context of civil rights. In Alan Gartner & Tom Joe (Eds.), *Images of the disabled, disabling images* (pp. 7–30). New York: Praeger Publishers.

Garrett, J. F. (1969). Historical background. In D. Malikin and H. Rusalem (Eds.), *Vocational rehabilitation of the disabled* (pp. 29–38). New York: New York University Press.

Gouvier, W. D., Coon, R. C., Fuller, K. H., & Arnoldi, K. R. (1992). Evaluation of linguistic variations by college students with and without head injuries. *Rehabilitation Psychology, 37*, 165–174.

Gouvier, W. D., Coon, R. C., Todd, M. E., & Fuller, K. H. (1994). Verbal interactions with individuals presenting with or without physical disability. *Rehabilitation Psychology, 39*, 263–268.

Grealish, C. A., & Salomone, P. R. (1986). Devaluing those with disability: Take responsibility, take action. *The Vocational Guidance Quarterly, 34*, 147–150.

Harris and Associates (1986). *The ICD survey of disabled Americans: Bringing disabled Americans into the mainstream. A nationwide survey of 1,000 disabled people.* New York: Author.

Hohenshil, T. H., & Humes, C. W. (1979). Roles of counseling in ensuring the rights of the handicapped. *Personnel and Guidance Journal, 58*, 221–227.

Joe, J. R. (1988). Government policies and disabled people in American Indian communities. *Disability, Handicap & Society, 3*, 253–262.

Karr, A. R. (1990, May 23). Disabled-rights bill inspires hopes, fears. *Wall Street Journal*, Section B, pp. 1–20.

LaFraniere, S. (January 27, 1985). Virginia's mentally ill caught in tug of war. *The Washington Post*, Section B, pp. 1–5.

Laski, F. (1978, May). *Legal strategies to secure entitlement to services for severely handicapped persons.* Paper presented at the Conference on Habilitation of Severely Handicapped Adults, Public Interest Law Center, Philadelphia, PA.

Lewin, T. (1988, March 13). Rights movement for disabled seen. *Santa Barbara News-Press*, p. 3.

Livneh, H. (1982). On the origins of negative attitudes toward people with disabilities. *Rehabilitation Literature, 43*, 338–347.

Lombana, J. H. (1982). Counseling handicapped children and youth. *Counseling and Human Development, 15*(4), 1–12.

Martin, S. (1995, October). Are children with disabilities more likely to be abused? *APA Monitor, 26*, 48.

May, V. R., & Vieceli, L. (1983). Barriers to placement: Strategies and resolution. *Journal of Rehabilitation, 49* (3), 43–46.

McNeil, J. (1993). Americans with disabilities: 1991–1992 (Bureau of Census, Currrent Population Reports, pp. 70–33). Washington, DC: US Government Printing Office.

Mithaug, D. E. (1979). Negative employer attitudes toward hiring the handicapped: Fact or fiction? *Journal of Contemporary Business, 8*(4), 19–26.

Moskowitz, D. B. (1985, September 16). Rights of handicapped expanded. *Washington Post.*

Nathanson, R. B. (1979). Counseling persons with disabilities: Are the feelings, thoughts and behaviors of helping professionals helpful? *Personnel and Guidance Journal, 58*, 233–237.

Nelson, R. M. (1989). Ethics and the physically disabled. In B. W. Heller, L. M. Flohr, & L. S. Zegans (Eds.), *Psychosocial interventions with physically disabled persons* (pp. 222–230). New Brunswick, NJ: Rutgers University Press.

Noel, R. T. (1990, August). Employing the disabled: A how and why approach. *Training and Development Journal*, 26–32.

Nosek, M. A., Fuhrer, M. J., & Potter, Carol. (1995). Life satisfaction of people with physical disabilities: Relationship to personal assistance, disability status, and handicap. *Rehabilitation Psychology, 40*, 191–202.

Obermann, C. E. (1965). *A history of vocational rehabilitation in America*. Minneapolis: Denison.

Perlman, L. G., & Kirk, F. S. (1991). Key disability and rehabilitation legislation. *Journal of Applied Rehabilitation Counseling, 22*, 21–27.

Ridington, J. (1989, March). *Beating the "odds": Violence and women with disabilities* (Position paper 2). Vancouver: DAWN (DisAbled Women's Network) Canada.

Rigler, A. L. (1992). Disability issues stance tests our ethical integrity. *APA Monitor, 23* (11), 4.

Roberts, E. V. (1989). A history of the independent living movement: A founder's perspective. In B. W. Heller, L. M. Flohr, & L. S. Zegans (Eds.), *Psychosocial interventions with physically disabled persons* (pp. 231–244). New Brunswick, NJ: Rutgers University Press.

Rubin, S. E., & Roessler, R. T. (1978). *Foundations of the vocational rehabilitation process.* Baltimore: University Park Press.

Satcher, J., & Hendren, G. R. (1991). Acceptance of the Americans with Disabilities Act of 1990 by persons preparing to enter the business field. *Journal of Applied Rehabilitation Counseling, 22* (2), 15–18.

Schofield, L. F., & Kunce, J. T. (1971). Client disability and counselor behavior. *Rehabilitation Counseling Bulletin, 14,* 158–165.

Scotch, R. K. (1984). *From good will to civil rights.* Philadelphia: Temple University Press.

Sobsey, D., & Mansell, S. (1990). The prevention of sexual abuse of people with developmental disabilities. *Developmental Disabilities Bulletin, 18,* 51–66.

Sobsey, D., & Varnhagen, C. (1991). Sexual abuse and exploitation of disabled individuals. In C. R. Bagley, & R. J. Thomlison (Eds.), *Child sexual abuse* (pp. 203–216). Toronto: Wall & Emerson, Inc.

Sullivan, P. M., Vernon, M., & Scanlan, J. M. (1987). Sexual abuse of deaf youth. *American Annals of the Deaf, 132,* 256–262.

Szymanski, E. M., Johnston-Rodriguez, S., Millington, M. J., Rodriguez, B. H., & Lagergren, J. (1995). The paradoxical nature of disability services: Illustrations from supported employment and implications for rehabilitation counseling. *Journal of Applied Rehabilitation Counseling, 26* (2), 17–21.

Task force on psychology and the handicapped (1984). Final report of the task force on psychology and the handicapped. *American Psychologist, 39,* 545–550.

Tomes, H. (March, 1992). Disabilities are major public interest issues. *APA Monitor.*

U.S. Department of Education (1988). *Summary of Existing Legislation Affecting Persons with Disabilities* (Publication No. E-88-22014). Washington, DC: U.S. Department of Education, Clearinghouse on the Handicapped.

U. S. Bureau of the Census. (1987). Unpublished tables from March 1987 Current Population Survey. *In Chartbook on disability in the United States.* Washington, DC: National Institute on Disability and Rehabilitation Research.

U. S. Bureau of the Census. (1989). *Labor force status and other characteristics of persons with a work disability: 1981 to 1988 (Current Population Reports, Series P-23, No. 160).* Washington, DC: U.S. Government Printing Office.

U. S. Bureau of the Census. (1995). *Population Profile of the United States (Current Population Reports, Series P23-189).* Washington, DC: U.S. Government Printing Office.

U. S. Senate Subcommittee on the Handicapped. (1985). Staff report on the institutionalized mentally disabled. *Joint Hearings of the Subcommittee on the handicapped.* Washington, DC: U.S. Government Printing Office.

Vargo, J. W. (1987, May). *'And sometimes I wonder about thee': A misconception hypothesis approach to viewing attitudes toward people with disabilities.* Paper presented at the meeting of the Canadian Guidance and Counselling Association, Toronto.

Vargo, J. W. (1989). 'In the house of my friend': Dealing with disability. *International Journal for the Advancement of Counselling, 12,* 281–287.

Wicas, C. A., & Carluccio, L. W. (1971). Attitudes of counselors toward three handicapped groups. *Rehabilitation Counseling Bulletin, 15,* 25–34.

Williams, W. C., & Lair, G. S. (1991). Using a person-centered approach with children who have a disability. *Elementary School Guidance & Counseling, 25,* 194–203.

Youngstrom, N. (1992). ADA is super advocate for those with disabilities. *Monitor, 23* (7), 26.

Zadny, J. J. (1979). Planning for job placement. In D. Vandergoot and J. D. Worrall (Eds.), *Placement in rehabilitation: A career development perspective.* Baltimore, MD: University Park Press.

Zadny, J. J., & James, L. F. (1978). A survey of job search patterns among state vocational rehabilitation clients. *Rehabilitation Counseling Bulletin, 22,* 60–65.

Zadny, J. J., & James, L. F. (1979). The problem with placement. *Rehabilitation Counseling Bulletin, 22,* 439–442.

3
Oppression of Elders: Past and Present

Past Discrimination

We ought not to heap reproaches on old age, seeing that we all hope to reach it. (Bion quoted in Diogenes Laertius' *Lives and Opinions of Eminent Philosophers.* Third century A.D.)

How good we all are, in theory, to the old; and how in fact we wish them to wander off like old dogs, die without bothering us, and bury themselves. (Edgar Watson Howe, *Ventures in Common Sense,* 1919)

Society's Treatment of Elders

According to Hendricks and Hendricks (1981), attitudes toward and treatment of older people have varied across the three major types of human societies, namely, nomadic, agricultural, and industrial. In hunting and gathering societies, life was precarious and marginal. Under such circumstances, elders were often left to die on their own when they could no longer contribute to the food supply or keep up with the nomadic movements of the group. However, some elderly persons who were a source of valued knowledge related to the group's physical and cultural survival were no doubt supported by other members of the group as long as possible.

In agricultural societies where property rights often became inherited and immutable, power and prestige were accorded elderly persons (usually men) who held these rights. Thus, the status of elders was generally much improved in agricultural societies over their status in nomadic tribes. However, sociologist Leo Simmons (1945), in his study of aging in 71 "primitive" nomadic and agricultural societies, found that although some degree of prestige for elders was prevalent in all societies, it applied to a "prime of life" old age and not to disability in old age. He also found that in all of the societies studied older people obtained support from others by rendering, in turn, essential services to the young and strong. In many of the societies studied, when elders could no longer contribute a valued service they were left to fend for themselves. It should be noted that the need to contribute to society did not necessarily work against older people in the ancient Greek and Roman societies. Kebric (1988) cites overwhelming evidence that many people lived active, productive lives into their 70s and 80s during the days of the Greek and Roman empires. In Greek society, men were expected to serve in the military until age 60.

Although earlier societies may have accorded elders a measure of prestige, there is also recorded evidence that negative stereotypes of older people have been with us since the pre-Christian era. According to Aiken (1995), ancient Romans considered old age a disease, and considerable energy was expended trying to find a "cure" for old age. Aristotle, in his *Treatise on Rhetoric*, describes old age as a time of conservatism and small-mindedness. Authors during the Middle Ages and the Renaissance reflected a similar theme. Pope Innocent III, in the thirteenth century, referred to old men as stingy, avaricious, sullen, and quarrelsome. Shakespeare's depiction of older people in his *Second Sonnet* is anything but flattering. He describes the end of a man's life as second childishness marked by loss of teeth, hearing, and virility (Hendricks & Hendricks, 1981). The negative stereotypes of elders were not restricted to men. In a review of terminology used historically to refer to older people, Covey (1988) found that gender was a critical factor in selecting terminology.

> The English language has a long history of separating old men from old women. Terms for old men tend to be focused on their being old-fashioned, uncouth, conservative, feeble, stingy, incompetent, narrow-minded, eccentric, or stupid. Terms for old women are focused on mysticism, bad temper, disagreeableness, spinsterhood, bossiness, unattractiveness, spitefulness, and repulsiveness. . . . Although women have longer lifespans than men, women are viewed as being old much earlier than men. Thus women have been subjected to old-age labels much earlier in life and for much longer periods during their life-spans. (pp. 291–292)

In the United States, elders commanded power and respect during the colonial period, due in part to their role as property owners. Fischer (1977) suggests respect for old age in colonial America also may have been due to the fact that it was comparatively rare (see data on changing American demographics in chapter 1). According to Fischer (1977), the undermining of the esteem with which older Americans were held began about the time of the American Revolution. He identifies 1770 to 1820 as a period of decline in hierarchically oriented institutions and a questioning of the hierarchies of sex, race, and age in particular. Furthermore, he cites the strong American cultural value of individualism as one of the forces that began to undermine the privileged status enjoyed by older people in the eighteenth century.

Historian Andrew Achenbaum (1978) examined experiences of elders from 1790 to 1970 and found marked differences between the way elders were perceived and treated in colonial and modern America. Prior to the Civil War, those elders who were physically able to work were expected to do so. They were also greatly valued for their moral wisdom and practical sagacity. After the Civil War, however, Americans

> began to challenge nearly every favorable belief about the usefulness and merits of age that had been set forth by republican and romantic writers and that still appeared

in contemporary literature. . . . By the outbreak of World War I, if not before, most Americans were affirming the obsolescence of old age. (Achenbaum, 1978, p. 39)

While there is disagreement about the factors that precipitated the decline in prestige accorded elders, most authors agree that the Industrial Revolution contributed significantly to the increasingly negative attitudes toward older people in the United States. In evolving from an agricultural to an industrial society, older people lost prestige as economic power moved from land to currency and greater emphasis was placed on change, mobility, and competition (Cowgill & Holmes, 1972; Hendricks & Hendricks, 1981). The shift from an economy based on agriculture to one based on production, service, and technology usurped the power that older family members held as property owners. The development of large-scale business and organizations had a profound effect on American values and lifestyles. Efficiency became the *sine qua non* of successful enterprise, and individuals within a corporate structure became dispensable (Achenbaum, 1978).

Perceptions of elders and their contribution to the labor force began to change. Businesses began discharging employees at a predetermined age rather than on the basis of their productivity. "Between 1861 and 1915, the federal government and especially private industry began to design and implement policies that discharged workers because they were considered too old to stay on the job" (Achenbaum, 1978, p. 48). The first federal retirement law was passed by Congress in 1861 when they mandated that naval officers must retire at age 62. The first private pension plan, motivated in part by a desire to remove older workers from the labor force, was implemented by the American Express Company in 1875. As a result of these subsequent laws and policies mandating a retirement age, the proportion of the labor force made up by persons over age 65 declined steadily from 1900 to 1970 (Achenbaum, 1978).

The rapid changes that accompanied the Industrial Revolution helped promote a valuing of youth. The young could better adapt to the many changes, it was assumed, and wisdom previously attributed to elders was supplanted in importance by intelligence attributed to the young. Advertisements that played upon a desire to appear and behave youthfully began to make their appearance after the Civil War (Achenbaum, 1978).

As U.S. society moved away from an agrarian base and the value of elderly parents began to decline, responsibility for caring for older people began to shift from the extended family to the government. Recognizing the need to provide medical care for elders, Presidential candidate Teddy Roosevelt in 1912 endorsed the Progressive Party's call for federal medical insurance. The concept of national medical insurance was dropped, however, when Woodrow Wilson won the election. The concept was reintroduced later in the decade by other Progressive reformers but was again opposed by medical societies and the American Federation of Labor (Fein, 1992). Thus, many elderly people who were forced to retire and whose families were no longer willing or capable of acting as a safety net, faced extended and sometimes terminal illness without adequate medical care.

Between World War I and World War II theories developed and were supported by circumscribed research that physical decay, mental decline, deviant psychological functioning, and personal isolation accompanied old age.

> Americans between 1914 and 1940 described the status of the aged more pessimistically than did their predecessors. . . . Americans after World War I perceived and voiced concern that current demographic and socioeconomic conditions were making old age per se a national problem as well as a personal misfortune. (Achenbaum, 1978, p. 109)

Levin and Levin (1980) suggest this developing view of older people as a societal "problem" is another example of victim-blaming. Thus, elders, who had mandatory retirement policies forced upon them by the federal government and private industry became a societal problem because they were not able to support themselves. Numerous surveys between 1914 and 1940 by civic groups, the U.S. Bureau of Labor, and state legislatures revealed that urbanization, industrialization, and the shortened working period of life were the real culprits of financial hardship experienced by elders (Achenbaum, 1978).

Initial efforts after World War I to cope with the economic insecurity of older people included the federal compulsory old age and disability insurance program for civil service employees enacted in 1920 and the expansion of retirement plans in the private sector at about the same time. Evidence that traditional solutions died hard can be found in the fact that five states enacted laws requiring children to support their indigent parents. Other states, however, began to pass old age assistance programs in the late 1920s, a trend that was accelerated by the Depression (Achenbaum, 1978).

The Great Depression of the 1930s was hard on many people, but it was particularly hard on the elders. Elders were the first to lose their jobs and the last to be hired. In addition, many lost life-long savings when banks were unable to fulfill their obligations to depositors. Several bills were introduced in Congress during the early 1930s aimed at meeting the economic needs of the older people, but they failed to become law, due in part to pressure from groups that perceived old-age pensions to be un-American. It is interesting to note, in fact, that the United States was one of the last Western industrialized nations to grant retirement pensions. The first was Germany in 1889. Most of the others passed such legislation in the next 25 years (Rich & Baum, 1984).

Finally, the Congress passed, and President Franklin Roosevelt signed into law (on August 14, 1935), the Social Security Act of 1935. Although Title I of the Act granted states considerable flexibility in determining the amounts of assistance elders would receive, it did include a provision with important ramification for the self-esteem of individuals receiving funds.

> By permitting applicants to appeal administrative decisions, the federal government made old-age assistance a right that could be legally enforced. Public relief in old age was no longer a gratuity. (Achenbaum, 1978, p. 135)

However, the Social Security Act did not include any provisions for medical benefits. Although Roosevelt originally envisioned national health insurance for elders as part of the Social Security bill, his Cabinet-level Committee on Economic Security convinced him that to include it could jeopardize any form of social assistance for older people. Once again, elders were left without a safety net for health problems. President Harry Truman took up the national health insurance banner when he proposed an economic bill of rights for all American citizens on September 6, 1945. However, the American Medical Association, invoking the fear of communism, successfully fought against the concept of national health insurance (Fein, 1992).

It should be noted that after 1941, elders began to organize to fight discrimination against them. Older citizens began to form lobby groups to push for legislation to assist the elders. Groups like the National Association of Retired Federal Employees, the National Retired Teachers Association, and The Gray Panthers became active lobbyists and played a major role in the establishment of a number of programs for elders. The American Association of Retired Persons (AARP) currently has a membership of over 27 million persons age 50 and over. "Originally formed to promote life insurance and other group benefits, AARP has slowly developed into a powerful political force" (Hess, 1991).

Since the passage of the Social Security Act, the federal government has evolved into a major clearinghouse for ideas related to aging. The first National Conference on Aging was held in 1950 with subsequent White House conferences on aging in 1961, 1971, and 1981. These conferences set forth recommendations concerning housing, nutrition, transportation, and other areas. Medicare and Medicaid, hospital insurance programs for older people, were passed in 1965, and Congress ensured all older people of a minimal income by passing the Supplementary Security Income program in 1972 (Achenbaum, 1978).

While Social Security and other programs have produced an overall improvement in the economic security of elderly citizens, the effects have not been evenly distributed across all groups of people. For example, people who supplement their benefits with income from savings or pension plans are better off than those on social security alone. Also, persons who minimally satisfy requirements for social security payments receive significantly lower retirement incomes than do those who made larger contributions to the system. As Margolis (1990) suggests,

> Social Security has never fulfilled its ample promise. From the working poor's perspective, the program's ideological reach has consistently exceeded its practical grasp. The reason is no secret: To the notion of equal entitlement, society has appended a typically American extenuation—the idea of just deserts, which tends to reward winners and penalize losers. (p. 23)

In linking benefits to a citizen's wage-based payments into the Social Security trust fund, the government has overlooked the contributions of the unpaid homemaker and the volunteer worker. This policy also overlooks the widespread employment discrimination experienced by women, people with disabilities, African Americans, Hispanics, and others that depress their wages and thus their Social Security benefits (Margolis, 1990). As a result, "old-age dependency remains a serious predicament, especially for minorities and women" (Achenbaum, 1978, p. 151).

It seems clear that since World War II, Americans have become increasingly sensitive to the plight of elders, yet a Louis Harris poll in 1975 revealed that most people still hold the images of older people that prevailed prior to World War II. "Americans continue to disparage the elderly's usefulness even though recent research lends substantial support for a concept of old age that recognizes the diversity in older person's abilities and conditions and that emphasizes positive as well as negative aspects of senescence" (Achenbaum, 1978 p. 163).

In summary, treatment of elders in Western society has been a function of their role in the economy. The most power and prestige were accorded elders in agricultural societies and the least in nomadic and industrial societies. The United States has responded more slowly than other nations to security problems of older people arising out of the Industrial Revolution. However, since the passage of the Social Security Act in 1934, a number of programs have been established to address these problems.

Negative stereotypes of elders are as old as human existence and persist despite recent research to the contrary. As we shall see, these stereotypes have often served as the rationale for discriminating against older people.

Psychology's Treatment of Elders

Although humans have probably been concerned about the aging process since prehistoric times, the formal study of aging by psychologists is relatively new. Aiken (1995) points out that Roger Bacon, Francis Bacon, Benjamin Franklin, and Francis Galton all wrote about aging during the thirteenth to nineteenth centuries, and an eighteenth-century British astronomer, Sir Edmund Halley, conducted the first scientific analysis of life expectancy. However, according to Birren (1964), "an empirically based psychology of aging did not appear until about 1835 with the work of Quetelet, and it showed a very slow growth in factual information until after World War II" (p. 9). In reviewing the history of the psychology of aging, Birren (1961) identifies three phases: Early Period (1835–1918); Beginning Systematic Studies (1918–1940); and Period of Expansion (1946–1960). The Early Period is typified by descriptive studies of human aging, descriptions of how human senses develop and change with advancing age. It was near the end of this period (1914) that an American, Ignaz Nascher, coined the term *geriatrics* to identify the branch of medicine that deals with the health problems of older people (Aiken, 1995). The Early Period was followed by the Beginning Systematic Studies during which numerous studies were conducted relating age to physical ability, reaction time, drive, mental ability, and other measures. Much of the research and writing of this period, as exemplified by G. Stanley Hall's (1923) *Senescence,* focused on the psychological decline of the aging individual.

The Period of Expansion was just that; more psychology of aging research was published in the 1950–1959 decade than had been published in the preceding 115 years (Birren, 1961, p. 127). It was also during this period (1945 to be exact) that the Division on Maturity and Old Age of the American Psychological Association was organized. Other significant events during this time included the convening of the National Conference on the Psychological Aspects of Aging (1953) and the publishing of the *Handbook of the Aging and the Individual.* The fields of gerontology and geriatrics grew rapidly during this time, but unfortunately, the declining ability of elders remained a central theme of the professional research and writing in these fields (Johnson, 1995). Similarly, a review of research on the psychology of aging by Levin and Levin (1980) revealed a continuing theme of decline in sensory and perceptual processes, psychomotor performance, cognitive processes, drives, and personality research. Similarly, a review of research on the creativity of artists and scientists leads to a rather pessimistic view of productivity in the later years.

> Beginning somewhere in the 20s, output first increases fairly rapidly until a peak is reached, usually sometime in the 30s or 40s, after which a gradual decline sets in. This age curve holds even after introducing all varieties of statistical controls for potential artifacts and spurious relationships. . . . Hence the age decrement in creativity after the mid-life optimum seems very real. Indeed, evidence strongly suggests that the longitudinal changes in creative achievement are cross-culturally and transhistorically invariant. (Simonton, 1990, p. 627)

These negative views of aging are now being challenged, and the majority of studies in recent years has documented that elders are aging well rather than aging ill. For example, Simonton (1990) identified a number of reasons why creative individuals can anticipate continued productivity during the latter part of their life and led him to conclude that "aging need not silence outstanding creativity in the last years" (p. 630). According to Johnson (1995), the White House Conference on Aging held in May, 1995, recognized the need to focus on positive aging rather than just looking for ways to respond to a dependent population. While applauding this shift from viewing aging as negative to viewing it as positive, Johnson (1995) adds a cautionary caveat:

> If we push the perception pendulum in the opposite direction in an effort to overcome the inaccurate exaggerations about negative views of aging from the past, we may produce an equally exaggerated image that older adults are all aging in health and wholeness. . . . Homogenizing older adults in this way could do as much harm as grouping them into the negative category. Both are unrepresentative. The reality is that older adults will not fit into a single profile. Some age in good health and some age ill, some are unremarkable either way, and some have varying experiences within their own particular life course. (pp. 124–125)

Although experimental psychologists have shown some interest in the effects of aging on mental capacities since the turn of the century, applied psychologists have only recently turned their attention to the psychological needs of elders. In a review of research on utilization of psychological services by elders, Gatz, Karel, and Wolkenstein (1991) found substantial evidence of underutilization despite the fact that mental health needs do not decrease with age and despite evidence that psychotherapy is effective with older people. Although some underutilization can be explained by the stigma older people attach to psychological services, another important factor is therapist resistance to working with older people (Kent, 1990). At an April, 1992 conference cosponsored by the APA's Practice Directorate, the National Institute of Mental Health, and the Retirement Research Foundation, several myths emerged as the reasons why psychologists have resisted serving the needs of elders (Moses, 1992). The prevailing myths or stereotypes held by psychologists are that "mental health issues disappear after mid-life, or that depression, anxiety and other problems are to be expected in the elderly and aren't worth treating" (p. 34). Related to this is the view that the mental health needs of elders have been neglected because it was assumed that the older people are developmentally static and coping mechanisms learned in their youth should suffice in old age (Mardoyan & Weis, 1981). Other reasons why psychologists have not addressed the needs of elders can be hypothesized. For example, applied psychologists traditionally have been more interested in the needs of children and young adults than in the needs of older adults (Piggrem & Schmidt, 1982). Also, in the absence of a national health insurance that guarantees remuneration for working with elders, many mental health practitioners have simply focused their services on more lucrative populations.

However, underutilization cannot be totally explained as resistance on the part of mental health workers. According to Raschko (cited in Cavaliere, 1995), "disjointed government programs, scarce funds, and the inherent difficulties in locating people who rarely seek help" (p. 11) contribute to underutilization of mental health services by elders. It is true that most elderly people are socialized to handle their own problems and to not be a burden on others; therefore, they are reluctant to request counseling and other mental health services (Atkinson, 1980). In a survey of 100 elderly persons, Kunkel and Williams (1991) found that

> recourse to a counselor or psychologist was considered to be neither relevant nor worthwhile except in the most extreme circumstances. The independence and guardedness themes suggested by other researchers among elderly persons were strongly present in this sample. . . . Few elderly persons in this sample thought that counselors were appropriate sources of help for retirement difficulties, fear of death, or sexual problems. . . . Many elderly persons may be part of a cohort that tends to view counseling services as irrelevant and even contrary to life experience. (p. 319)

However, there is reason to believe that this reluctance to use psychological services is changing with each new group of retiring cohorts and that future generations of elderly people will seek services on their own, rather than be referred by doctors, courts, home-health agencies, and adult children (Kent, 1990).

Notwithstanding the "reduced need" explanation for underutilization, there is a widely held belief among many mental health experts that psychological impairment increases with old age. Feinson (1991, p. 125) cited a number of quotes from policy-making individuals and commissions that document this belief. For example, The President's Commission on Mental Health concluded that "depression escalates decade by decade," the former director of the Center for the Study of Mental Health and Aging at the National Institute of Mental Health stated that "the prevalence of mental illness and emotional distress is higher among those over 65 than in the general population," and an official at the National Center for Health Statistics testified that "I have been told that depression is very prevalent among the elderly." However, after reviewing epidemiological studies conducted in the United States since 1950, Feinson (1991) concluded that

> The one consistent finding from all cross-sectional studies conducted during the past forty years is that, to the extent that a relationship exists between impairment and age, more disorders are found among younger, rather than older, age groups! (p. 133)

Due in part to the negative views about serving older people held by psychologists, training programs seldom provide course work on aging. Birren and Woodruff (1973) found that there was only one psychologist trained to work with older people for every 76,000 elderly persons; the ratio for the general population was one psychologist for every 3,400 people. Surveys of counselor education programs reveal that only a minority of them offer any course work on counseling older people (Myers, 1989; Salisbury, 1975). With respect to courses on aging and sexuality, there is actually evidence that health professionals in general are learning less than they did a decade ago. Karlen and Moglia (1995) surveyed sex educators in a variety of health professional programs and found "an overwhelmingly negative picture of what health professionals know, want to learn, and are taught about sex and aging" (p. 196). With respect to declining trainee interest in the topic, Karlen and Moglia (1995) concluded that their respondents' comments "underline the enduring strength of our society's traditional taboo against sex as a normal part of later life, and younger adults' emotional discomfort with seeing their elders as sexual beings" (Karlen & Moglia, 1995, p. 197). The respondents cited two reasons why less time and attention is being given to sexuality and aging in professional training than in the 1970s and 1980s: (a) the current important focus on problem areas of sex (HIV/AIDS, STDs, rape, sexual harassment, sexual abuse, unwanted pregnancies) takes time away from instruction about sex in middle and later life; and (b) classes on sexuality have never been incorporated as part of the mainstream of health education and as the generation of pioneering sexuality educators reach retirement, sexuality courses are being cut back or even dropped. Thus, although a substantial number of mental health practitioners have elderly clients among their caseload, few have had any training for working with this client population (Gatz et al., 1991).

Several conferences convened by the American Psychological Association have addressed the need for more training in this area. A conference was convened in 1981 in Boulder, Colorado, that resulted in a number of recommendations but no action plans. According to Dr. John Santos, a trustee of the Retirement Research Foundation, "APA just fell asleep at the wheel. . . . APA failed to set up mechanisms for helping psychologists develop curricula and service in this field" (quoted in Moses, 1992). An APA conference convened in Washington, D.C., in April, 1992, also resulted in a number of recommendations for training for gerontological practice, but it remains to be seen if the American Psychological Association puts them into action.

The American Counseling Association (ACA), on the other hand, has taken several steps to promote training of counselors who have at least a minimum competence in gerontological issues. According to Myers (1992), the ACA (or more accurately, its predecessor, the American Association for Counseling and Development) conducted five national projects on aging between 1977 and 1991 with total funding from the U.S. Administration on Aging for these projects exceeding $1 million. All five projects were focused on developing models and resources for preparing counselors to work with older persons. The most recent of the five projects identified "both generic competencies designed for training all counselors in gerontological issues and specialty competencies for training of gerontological counselors" (Myers, 1992, p. 37) and resulted in a proposal for a specialty credential in gerontological counseling that was accepted by the National Board for Certified Counselors (NBCC) in 1989. Gerontological competencies identified in these projects also contributed to the standards for training in gerontological counseling adopted by the Council for Accreditation of Counseling and Related Educational Programs (CACREP) in March, 1992. Further, the ACA has submitted standards to CACREP that were designed to infuse gerontological counseling into the common core preparation areas required for accreditation of counselor training programs. "This model would make it possible for all counselors (in accredited programs, at least) to graduate with some knowledge of the needs of older people and of ways to work successfully with them" (Myers, 1992, pp. 35–36).

With the aging of a significant proportion of our society and the lengthening of the life span has come a growing recognition by psychologists in the 1980s and 1990s that they must begin serving the elderly population. By sheer numbers, elders are making us increasingly aware of their special needs. Psychologists can make a significant contribution to their well being through both research and direct service efforts. Addressing researchers, Schaie (1993) points out that contemporary psychology should be concerned about ageism in contemporary psychology because: (a) the rapid growth of older people in the 1990s has focused considerable research attention on this population; (b) the increased funding for research in this area has attracted researchers with little previous experience with research on aging, researchers whose ageist language may reinforce societal stereotypes; and (c) psychological research is playing an increasingly important role in developing public policy. Similarly, direct service psychologists should be concerned about the impact their ageist attitudes and behavior may have on elders as more and more services are targeted for this age group.

> Ageism may be manifested by psychologists in many ways, including (a) assumptions of restrictions on behavior due to age, (b) positive or negative stereotypes about the elderly, (c) belief that age is usually or always a relevant dimension to variables under study, and (d) the untested assumption that data from one age group generalize to others. (Schaie, 1993, p. 49)

In chapter 18, we will discuss some of the steps that psychology must take to address the psychological needs of elders.

Current Discrimination
Social Discrimination

People continue to hold negative stereotypes about elders that are used to justify other forms of discrimination (i.e., if they are unproductive and inflexible, they should be forced to retire). A meta-analysis by Kite and Johnson (1988) of studies through 1985 revealed that attitudes toward older people were more negative than those toward younger people. Despite the increased publicity and concern over the rights of elders, Schwalb and Sedlacek (1990) surveyed college students in 1979 and again in 1988 and found that "the overall attitudes of college students toward older people were generally negative in both the 1979 and 1988 samples" (p. 129). They concluded that college students' attitudes toward older people do not seem to be changing. Chumbler (1995) reviewed the research on medical students' attitude and found that "many medical students are uncomfortable with elderly patients and their chronic health problems" (p. 39). Richman (1977) analyzed the content of 100 jokes about older people and 160 jokes about children and found that 66 percent of the former were negative while over 70 percent of the latter were positive. In a Louis Harris (1975) poll, adult Americans typically perceived persons over age 65 as not very sexually active, not very open-minded and adaptable, not very useful members of their community, and not very bright and alert. Johnson (1995) reported the results of a 1994 national telephone survey in which a random sample of adults overestimated the levels of poverty, isolation, poor health, and extent of serious problems experienced by older people.

Despite recent research that indicates elders are able to function physically and mentally longer and with much more capability than the pre-World War II research suggested, negative stereotypes persist among both the lay public and mental health professions. Butler (1979) identified a number of myths and stereotypes of unproductivity, disengagement, inflexibility, and senility, all of which he labeled as myths since they lack support from research findings. Levin and Levin (1980) reviewed two types of studies related to the functioning of elderly people. One set of studies examined the perceptions various age groups (children, college undergraduates, adults, older people) have of the sexual activity, job performance, intelligence, resistance to change, and disengagement from society of elderly persons. The other set of studies examined survey and behavioral indices of elderly functioning in these areas. In each area, the second set of studies refuted the stereotypes found in the first set. They concluded from this analysis that "images of the aged are based more on myth than reality, more on fiction than on fact" (p. 79) but that negative stereotypes are "passed from generation to generation through the process of socialization much like other cultural phenomena" (p. 85). Similarly, Hess (1980), reviewed hundreds of research reports and concluded that "many negative stereotypes are clearly not supported by the research data" (p. 532).

Nowhere are stereotypes of elders more extreme than in the arena of sexuality. Sexual stereotypes of older people include the perception that they are sexless, that their expressions of passion are gross and disgusting, that they are in danger of a heart attack when they engage in sex, and that sexually active elders are "dirty" old men and women. Stereotypes of older women are particularly negative and can have a devastating effect on an older woman's feelings of self-worth (Campbell & Huff, 1995). Sexual stereotypes, in turn, have an impact on how friends, relatives, and caregivers treat elders. Friends and relatives often directly and indirectly discourage elderly people from talking about sex or engaging in sexual behavior. According to Brown (1989), "nursing homes and institutions deny the elderly their rights to sexual relationships by segregating men from women, depriving them of the privacy necessary for intimacy, labeling sexual behavior as deviant and administering drugs as well as social pressure to prevent it" (p. 76).

Social discrimination against elders is not restricted to negative attitudes; it can also be observed in the form of overt behavior, as in the case of housing discrimination. Civic organizations and informal neighborhood groups often oppose housing developments for older people, ostensibly because they will alter the character of the community (Mitric, 1985) or detract from property value (McAllister, 1985).

Mental health practitioners also hold stereotypes of elders that cause them to discriminate against older clients with respect to the type of treatment they provide. According to Blank (1974), psychotherapy is the treatment of choice with depressed elders, yet "There are such negative feelings about the value of psychotherapy for aged persons that it is seldom used" (p. 148). Cohen (1990) points out that even the language of geriatric advocates tends to portray elders with disabilities as incapable of exercising control over their lives. Cohen (1990) surveyed numerous recent issues of the *Gerontologist, Generations,* and federal monographs and came up with the following terms used by mental health workers: "Elderly-at-risk, frail elderly, impaired elderly, institutionalized elderly, homebound elderly, chair-bound elderly, bedridden elderly, wheelchair bound elderly, vulnerable elderly, dependent elderly, patient [rather than consumer], and 'the Alzheimer' [referring to the person who has the disease]" (p. 14). He argues that terms like these rob older persons with disabilities of their motivation to assert themselves. Thus, even well-intentioned advocates may be contributing to a new ageism that restricts the capability of elders.

Economic Discrimination

Paradoxically, elders are currently among the most affluent and, at the same time, most poverty-stricken group in the United States. Due to rising salaries, the success of private and public pension plans, a growing economy, and the inflation of property values over the past five decades, many recent retirees are enjoying a higher standard of living than at any time in the history of the United States (Morris & Caro, 1995). Hess (1991) credits the decision by Congress to link changes in Social Security benefits to inflation and the introduction of health insurance for older people as reasons why "the incidence of poverty among America's aged has dropped from over one in three before 1960 to slightly under the national rate of 14 percent today" (p. 8). As a group, the median income for people over 65 rose 21 percent in inflation-adjusted dollars during the 1980s compared to 6 percent for all Americans.

These figures, plus the rapidly rising Medicare costs, have created a new stereotype of elders as "greedy geezers" (Holstein, 1995), "fat cats living the good life at the expense of everybody else" (Lewis, 1992b, p. 14). As a result, entitlements for older people are being blamed for the growing federal deficit, when "the major culprits are system-wide escalation of health costs and the 1981 tax cut" (AARP, 1992, p. 3). Furthermore, the rising federal deficit and the shrinking funds for programs that benefit children and adolescents are being blamed on the mandated increases in Social Security.

> Critics of Social Security and Medicare blamed the deteriorating condition of children and families on the "graying of the federal budget" (more than half of all federal domestic goes to the elderly) and raised the specter of intergenerational warfare between young and old. . . . The generational equity campaign continues to portray the elderly as selfish, politically powerful, and potentially dangerous. (Cole, 1991)

However, the view of elders as budgetary piranhas ignores the fact that the most costly entitlement programs are largely self-funded; many current retirees have been paying into Social Security since its inception. As Hess (1991) points out:

> It should also be realized that before the 1980s, the Social Security Trust Funds had never before been included in the regular federal budget, where they now serve to make the U.S. budget deficit appear *smaller* than it actually is. . . .
> If . . . one takes only the programs funded from general revenues (that is, excluding Medicare and Social Security), the elderly are not overly coddled, receiving a share of federal outlays considerably lower than their representation in the total population. The fact that assistance for poor children and their families is vastly under funded is an issue that should be addressed directly on its own merits and not made into a zero-sum situation in which the benefits available to one

group must come at the cost of reducing program for other needy populations. (p. 8)

According to Adams and Dominick (1995), "efforts in the United States to promote a politics of generational equity are best understood as part of a larger class struggle over the welfare state, an important aspect of which is the attempt to define the conflict in terms of age rather than class" (p. 41). As has been suggested by Holstein (1995), the debate about disproportionate resources going to the elderly has not lead to proposed programs that would redistribute these resources to children and other needy groups. Rather, the focus has been on budget reduction, a problem that could be addressed in other ways without denying dignity and health care to the current and future generations of elders.

Furthermore, the economic gains made by a minority of recently retired elders are in direct contrast to the experiences of many older persons, particularly single women, ethnic minorities, the seriously ill, and the "old old" (people over 85). Only 15.5 percent (3.2 million) of elderly households had annual incomes in 1990 that exceeded $40,000. By comparison, 28 percent (5.7 million) had incomes under $10,000 a year, and 3.7 million lived below the poverty level in 1990. Another 8.1 million have incomes no more than twice the poverty rate. The poverty and low income figures are particularly disturbing for women and ethnic minorities. Two million elderly women living alone (more than one in four) had incomes below the poverty level, and seven out of ten women aged 65 or older had incomes under $10,000 in 1988 (Hess, 1991). For older Hispanic and African American women, the poverty rate was 49 and 60 percent, respectively (Lewis, 1992b). According to the U.S. Bureau of the Census (1995), elderly women were more likely to live below the poverty level in 1992 (16 percent) than were elderly men (9 percent). Among elderly Blacks, 27 percent of the men and 38 percent of the women lived below the poverty level in 1992. Similar figures for elderly Hispanics were 17 percent for men and 25 percent for women.

Also, the federal figures on older people and poverty are misleading in that figures to compute the poverty level are adjusted by age.

> Because the elderly are considered to be relatively Spartan food consumers, the line for elderly poverty has been set below that for other age groups. Depending on which groups are being compared, the difference can run as high as 11 percent. To put it another way, it is possible for someone to live under the poverty line at age 64 and over it the following year, even if that person's income has not increased one cent beyond the cost-of-living index. (Margolis, 1990, p. 11)

Notwithstanding the large number of older people below or near the poverty level, the recent "fat cat" image of older people has been used as a rationale for proposals to reduce or eliminate entitlement programs that benefit elders. Americans for Generational Equality (AGE) was formed in 1985 to "promote greater public understanding of problems arising from the aging of the U.S. population and to foster increased public support for policies that will serve the economic interest of next century's elderly" (Gerber, Wolff, Klores, &

Brown 1989). The organization credits the entitlements received by the current generation for the ballooning federal deficit and argues that resources should be held in reserve for the future generation of elders. Thomasma (1989) points out that as the numbers of older people increase over the next 50 years, the United States will face a "tremendous economic and political crisis in providing health care and long-term care for the elderly" (p. 170). According to Cole (1991), the competition for limited federal resources has raised a number of moral questions, some of which could serve as the basis of future ageist social policies:

> Is it fair to spend such a large proportion of our health expenditures on the dying elderly? Do these expenditures actually benefit them? Should we be devoting so much of our biomedical research and technology to the diseases of aging? Questions of distributive justice inevitably lead to questions of social meaning. How do we justify funds spent on a population that is not economically productive? What "good" are old people anyway? (p. 27)

Ageist social policies are being proposed that basically would ration available resources by age; the impact of these proposals would include "a lack of respect for the aged in return for all they have done for the younger generations, the creation of institutional dumping grounds for elders, unjust decision-making for incompetent persons, and cutting off care for many elderly persons who could profit from it and return to a norm life" (Thomasma, 1989, p. 170). Proposals that seek to allocate health care on the basis of age are a form of economic discrimination that will reinforce (and be reinforced by) social discrimination against older people.

In addition to misperceptions that elders garner a disproportionate share of the country's wealth, concerns are being raised about their self-centered political activities. Rosenbaum and Button (1989) describe three hypotheses that have been raised about the impact of the growing elderly population on the politics of Sunbelt states. The "gray participation" hypothesis assumes that as the aging population increase, their political activism will increase. The "gray power" hypothesis assumes that the retirement community will form a voting bloc that supports services to older people. The "gray peril" hypothesis assumes that elders will resist local government taxing and spending programs other than those that provide immediate benefit to older people. In their survey of Florida's local public officials, however, Rosenbaum and Button (1989) found that although older persons are active in Florida's local politics, the retirement population is "far less organized and active in local political advocacy on its own behalf than either the gray power of gray peril hypotheses would assume" (p. 305).

Elders are often the first to lose their jobs in economic downswings. Although recent federal legislation increased the mandatory retirement age from 65 to 70, it did not eliminate occupational discrimination for those 70 and above, and people 65 to 70 are still pushed into retirement by unchallenging work (particularly among blue collar jobs), company pressure, self-fulfilling prophecy, and economic incentives provided, ironically, by the government (Levin & Levin, 1980).

> By no means are all labor force withdrawals voluntary, many coming for reasons of ill health or structural unemployment in different geographic settings and, most recently, as the result of the brutal "downsizing" of many American corporations, often accomplished through layoffs rather than early retirement incentives. . . . Older workers have greater difficulty in finding replacement jobs than do younger workers and may also have greater difficulty in changing fields. (Morris & Caro, 1995)

Older workers are often given the choice to retire early or take a drop in rank and pay. The Age Discrimination in Employment Act was supposed to eliminate or greatly reduce employment discrimination against older workers. According to Morris and Caro (1995), however, enforcement of the act "has been uneven over the years, and discrimination based on negative attitudes toward older workers continues" (p. 33). According to a survey by the Equal Employment Opportunity Commission Survey in 1983, most older people don't realize they can press age discrimination complaints. An increasing number do however. In 1983, 21,000 age discrimination suits were filed, a four-fold increase from 1979 (Morse, 1985). However, Caro and Motika (1992) found that only 15 percent of the discrimination cases filed in 1989 with the Massachusetts Commission Against Discrimination produced favorable outcomes for the worker. For older workers with complaints about hiring practices, the favorable outcome rate was even lower.

Once they lose their jobs, older workers find it difficult to obtain new employment (Morris & Caro, 1995). A survey by the U.S. Bureau of the Census found 5.1 million workers displaced in 1979, 750,000 of whom were between 55 and 64. Five years later in 1984, almost one-third of these 750,000 workers had still not found jobs, the highest rate of continued displacement for any age group (Rajeswary, 1985). Without jobs, many older people have to rely on Social Security benefits for their primary source of income. For a majority of the elderly population, Social Security benefits account for more than half of their income. Further, one in five of all older people (two in five Blacks) receive 90 percent or more of their income from Social Security.

Unemployment, low income, and poverty figures are most dismal for women and ethnic minorities as subgroups of the elderly population. Elders living alone (generally women) are among the very poor. According to the Council of Economic Advisers (Seaberry, 1985), women constituted 71.1 percent of the elderly poor but only 59.1 percent of the total elderly population. The death of a husband often marks the beginning of economic and social reversals for the surviving wife.

> The difference in age at marriage and the gap in life expectancy between men and women are related to the high proportion of women living alone, the earlier institutionalization of women than men, sharply reduced income and a disproportionally high level of poverty among women, and a need for special

support from family members or society. (U.S. Bureau of the Census, 1992, pp. 2–9)

The oldest of older people are also the poorest because they earned less than more recent retirees and often have used their savings for costly medical expenses, etc. In 1981, the poverty rates varied from 6 percent for White males living in families to 61 percent for Black females living alone (U.S. Bureau of the Census, 1983).

Although some elderly people retired in the 1980s and early 1990s with excellent pension plans that help account for the more affluent members of this population, the security of some of these pension plans is now threatened. According to Mayer (1993), the Pension Benefit Guaranty Corporation (a government agency), which insures 85,000 private defined-benefit pension plans covering over 40 million employees, will be as much as $19 billion in the red by 1997. There are other reasons to be concerned about the financial security of future retirees, even those who have lived relatively affluently most of their adult life. According to Rappaport (1995), the "old social contract" between employers and employee that provided health care and fixed income for former employees in retirement is being replaced by the "new social contract" that views health care and retirement income as the responsibility of the employee. Defined-benefit pension plans (where a level of income is guaranteed at retirement) increasingly are being phased out by many major companies in favor of defined-contribution plans (retirement income is based on how the employee invests his or her pension funds). Since most employees lack both the training and the time to properly manage their pension funds and consequently invest them in secure but low-interest portfolios, future retirees are likely to have even less expendable income than current retirees (Krain, 1995). Also, as more and more large companies downsize, move to other countries, or simply shut down, a greater percentage of the population is employed by small companies that do not offer pension plans of any kind (Rappaport, 1995). Smaller businesses (80 percent of all employees work for firms of 100 or fewer people) provide pension plans for only 43 percent of their full-time employees, while larger companies provide pension plans for 90 percent of their full-time employees (Gerber et al., 1989). Older workers who lose their jobs due to companies downsizing, leaving, or closing often use "contingent" jobs as an income bridge until they reach retirement (Lewis, 1992a). Contingent work consists of part-time, temporary, contract, and freelance jobs that pay less, provide fewer benefits, and offer less security than full-time jobs. According to Lewis (1992a),

> What is new about part-time, temporary and other contingent workers is the way they're being used by employers these days: as commodities to be plugged into the workplace on an "as-need" basis, and then to be dispensed with very much like water cooler refills or Dixie cups. . . . corporations are moving toward a new . . . job strategy that, in effect, cuts labor costs by converting full-time jobs to contingent jobs. (p. 2)

For workers over 50, this switch from full-time to contingent jobs means a loss of income, benefits, and security at a time in life when they should be most affluent and padding their pension funds for retirement years. The knowledge that they are "disposable" workers also threatens their self-esteem at a time when peers have moved to the top of their career ladders.

Unfortunately, Social Security and other federal and state programs for elders are also in trouble. The federal budget draft for fiscal 1986, for example, included proposed cuts in Medicare, Medicaid, food stamps, and federal retirement programs. While these cuts and those mandated for the Gramm-Rudman Act may have little effect on middle- and upper-class retirees, some lower income workers will be severely effected in old age (Marriott, 1984). A worst case scenario could place increasing numbers of elders below the poverty level for many years to come.

Victimization

Crimes Against Elders

Although recent research suggests violent crimes against elders are not as common as they were thought to be earlier, older persons often express a great deal of fear that they will be the victims of murder, rape, and other violent crimes. Although they may be more afraid of violent crime than victimization statistics appear to warrant, Aiken (1995) argues that

> there are reasons for their fears and for singling them out for special attention. One reason is that the effects of any economic loss on the elderly are, because of their lower average income, greater than for any age group over 30. Associated with diminished income is residence in high-crime, inner-city neighborhoods rather than more affluent suburbs. . . . Another reason why the elderly are more afraid of crime and deserve special consideration is their lesser physical strength and poorer health. Older adults are not able to defend themselves or escape from threatening situations. . . . [Also,] the emotional stress provoked by an attack tends to be greater in an elderly victim, who usually takes longer to recuperate psychologically. (pp. 345–346)

Older people are clearly the targets of criminals for selected types of crimes, particularly property crimes (Doyle, 1990; Aiken, 1995). Purse thieves often see elderly women as easy targets, and it is not uncommon that the victim is injured during the commission of the crime. Cashing a Social Security check can be a particularly dangerous time for an elderly person to be alone on a city street.

Nor are crimes against older people restricted to conventional criminal acts like robbery. Swindlers often prey upon elders, employing "pigeon drops" to filch their lifetime savings. Because of their strong desire to remain in their own home combined with their diminished ability to perform home maintenance and repair, older people may be particularly susceptible to home repair fraud. Older Americans may be the preferred targets of confidence men; according to Aiken (1995), "most of the victims of bunco and confidence games are elderly"

(p. 349). "The variety of schemes used is endless but often involves tricking the victim into handing over a large sum of cash—for example, to help a phony bank examiner catch a dishonest teller or to secure a share of some found money or a lost inheritance" (Doyle, 1990, p. 302). Hearing aid, insurance, medical, work-at-home, home improvement, investment, and postal fraud are all examples of swindles directed at older people (Aiken, 1995). Many such crimes go unreported due to the victim's embarrassment, and little solid information is available about their frequency.

Particularly pernicious is the health care fraud perpetuated by health care providers charged with looking after the physical well-being of elders. The House Select Committee on Aging concluded in 1984 that health fraud steals $10 billion a year from Americans 65 or older. Elders suffering chronic pain are a prime target (Colburn, 1985). Of 110,000 heart pacemakers implanted in elderly Americans in 1985, one in three may have been unnecessary according to the Senate Special Committee on Aging. While some of the unnecessary implants are due to incompetent doctors, the Senate Committee Chair, Senator John Heinz, is also quoted as saying "This committee's investigation, I'm sorry to say, reveals a Pandora's box full of crooked manufacturers, greedy doctors, and defective products" (UPI, 1985, A11). Although a law enacted by Congress in 1989 and effective January 1, 1991, limits doctors not participating in Medicare from charging patients more than 20 percent over the Medicare rate, "thousands of Medicare patients are being overcharged by their doctors" (McLeod, 1992). These excessive charges affect the elderly patient directly because he or she must make up the difference between what the doctor charges and what Medicare will pay; they also affect all Medicare patients and all taxpayers by draining Medicare resources.

Although elders may not experience more violent crimes than younger persons, fear of such crimes have a particularly debilitating effect on older people. While we all face the danger of criminal acts, the singling out of the older persons for certain criminal acts is a form of oppression of elders as a group (Butler, 1979).

Elder Abuse

Elder abuse has only recently been recognized as a form of oppression experienced by large numbers of older Americans. According to Myers and Shelton (1987), the public first became aware of child abuse in the 1960s and spouse abuse in the 1970s but did not become aware of elder abuse until the 1980s. Even then, it received little attention from mental health professionals, law enforcement officials, and legislators compared to the attention given to child abuse and spouse abuse. By the early 1980s, however, it became apparent that abuse of elders was common and widespread.

The House Select Committee on Aging, chaired by the late Representative Claude Pepper, began hearing testimony on abuse of older Americans by their family members and other caregivers in 1978. Since those initial hearings, the

Committee has issued three reports: (1) "Elder abuse: The hidden agenda" published in 1980; (2) "Elder abuse: A national disgrace" published in 1985; and (3) "Elder abuse: A decade of shame and inaction" published in 1990. (It should be noted that the U.S. House of Representatives allowed the House Select Committee on Aging to expire in 1993 after nearly two decades of serving as a forum for airing issues vital to older persons.) The first report revealed that elder abuse was not an isolated or localized problem involving a few frail older people. Instead, the Committee characterized it as a full-scale national problem that existed at a frequency and rate similar to that of child abuse. The second report revealed that instead of diminishing, elder abuse is increasing dramatically from year to year. The third and most recent report found further evidence that elder abuse is on the increase. While in 1980 they reported that 1 out of every 25 (roughly 1 million) older Americans were abused annually, in 1990 they found that 1 out of every 20 (about 1.5 million) older Americans are victims of abuse each year. Another estimate is that 1 in 10 elderly persons living with a family member is abused each year (Lau & Kosberg, 1978).

Abuse occurs in all types of settings, including domestic homes, private nursing facilities, and public hospitals. Abuse of elders also takes many different forms.

> The most shocking is the physical battering of an older person by the family member who is responsible for providing care. Less flagrant but perhaps equally devastating forms are threats of physical assault, verbal assaults, and financial exploitation. Prescription and over the counter drugs such as tranquilizers or sleeping pills that are given to older persons in order to make them more manageable are sources of potential abuse. Excessive alcohol consumption may be overlooked by family members or even encouraged for the same reason. Involuntary constriction—tying an older person to a bed or chair—is sometimes inappropriately used to maintain control. In some instances sexual abuse has been inflicted on older women. (King, 1984, p. 3)

Physical abuse is generally defined as assault, battery, assault with a deadly weapon or force, unreasonable physical constraint, sexual assault, or physical or chemical restraint under specified conditions. Other common types of elder abuse include neglect, abandonment, intimidation, and fiduciary abuse. The House Select Committee on Aging (1990) found that "physical violence, including negligence, and financial abuse appear to remain the most common forms of abuse, followed by abrogation of basic constitutional rights and psychological abuse" (p. XII). Abuse in institutional settings often takes the form of overmedication. "Older persons in institutions take an average of 10 to 12 drugs per day, in contrast to 4 to 7 per day for older persons living in communities" (Myers & Shelton, 1987). Cooper (1994) reported that a review of nursing home drug records by pharmacists revealed that medication errors or adverse drug reactions occurred each month for two out of three patients in surveyed nursing homes.

Most experts agree that reported cases are just the tip of the iceberg. Elder abuse is often ignored by third parties due to our negative stereotypes of aged people. Friends, relatives, and caretakers often ignore self-reports of violence and assume they are the result of a wandering mind. Bruises and cuts are often attributed to an aging body and ambulation problems (Kosberg, 1983). Also, elders are reluctant to report that their child is abusing them because of the shame it will bring to the family and because they are afraid of losing whatever support they do receive from the abusing child; over 70 percent of elder abuse cases are reported by third parties (Aiken, 1995). The House Select Committee on Aging (1990) found that elder abuse is less likely to be reported than is child abuse, perhaps due in part to the fact that there is no objective third party to report abuse of older people as there is with child abuse (Ifill, 1986). For child abuse, it is estimated that about one out of three cases is reported, while for elder abuse only one out of every eight cases was reported in 1990. The House Select Committee on Aging (1990) found the latter figures to be particularly alarming because in 1980 one out of every five cases was reported.

The decreasing proportion of reported cases suggests that elder abuse is becoming even more of a hidden problem at the same time that increased attention is focused on it. Prior to 1980, only 16 states had adult protective service laws mandating that elder abuse be reported. During the 10 year period from 1980 to 1990, mandatory reporting laws were passed in 26 additional states. Reporting of elder abuse is now mandatory for selected professionals in 42 states and the District of Columbia (Select Committee, 1990). The California mandatory reporting law is typical of that in many states. The California law stipulates that adult care custodians and health practitioners (including psychologists, psychiatrists, social workers, and marriage and family counselors) *must* report incidents of physical abuse and *may* report incidents of other types of abuse inflicted upon elderly or dependent adults. No one who is required to report known or suspected instances of abuse can be held liable for their report. Failure to report an instance of elder or dependent adult abuse can result in a fine of $1,000 or six months in jail or both. Individuals who make abuse reports even though they are not required to cannot be held liable unless it can be proven that they knowingly made a false report.

The victim of elder abuse is often physically or mentally impaired and frequently lives with the abuser (King, 1984). The House Select Committee on Aging (1990) found that most victims were age 75 or older and that women are more likely to be abused than men. According to Robert Butler (1983), "the most vulnerable elders seem to be poor frail women, unmarried or widowed" (p. x.1), but the victims of elder abuse can be male or female, rich or poor, married or unmarried, and from any ethnic or racial background.

Contrary to stereotype of the abusing institutional care provider, the abuser is often a spouse, adult child, or relative of the abused elder. Only about one out of every four abusers are care providers who are unrelated to the elderly victim

(Select Committee, 1990). Also contrary to stereotype, "rather than the victim being dependent on the abuser, in most instances the abused person describes the abuser as depending on him or her for finances, housing, transportation, cooking, cleaning, or other services" (Aiken, 1995).

A number of such factors combine to create the conditions under which an adult child will abuse their elderly parent.

> The likely abuser will usually be experiencing great stress. Alcoholism, drug addiction, marital problems and long-term financial difficulties all play a role in bringing a person to abuse his or her parents. The son of the victim is the most likely abuser, followed by the daughter of the victim. It is interesting to note that the abuser, in many cases, was abused by the parents as a child. (Select Committee, 1990, p. XII)

Furthermore, the adult child who is a caregiver for an aged parent is often facing problems associated with aging him- or herself (Schwiebert & Myers, 1994). As a result, the responsibilities of care providing often come at a time when the adult child is preparing for or entering retirement and beginning to experience a loss of resources.

It should be noted that identification of adult children as the typical abusers of older people has been challenged by recent research findings. Pillemer and Finkelhor (1988), cited in Aiken (1995), found that in the majority of cases of elder abuse, the victim's spouse (59 percent) was the abuser, followed by the victim's child (24 percent).

Giordano and Giordano (1984) reviewed the theoretical explanations for elder abuse and arrived at seven hypotheses. They were family dynamics, impairment and dependence, personality traits of the abuser, filial crisis, internal stress, and two particularly relevant to the thesis of this book, external stress and negative attitudes toward older people.

Perhaps even more insidious and more common than physical abuse is the psychological neglect and abuse suffered by many elderly people (Giordano & Giordano, 1984). Those living in nursing homes are often ignored and isolated by staff who have neither the time nor inclination to interact with their charges in a constructive way. Vladeck and Feuerberg (1995/1996) made the following observation about nursing homes as recently as 1980:

> While the care in many nursing homes had improved over the past, the odor of urine or disinfectant was frequently present, psychotrophic drugs were overprescribed, and residents were excessively restrained. Infections and bedsores were prevalent and the setting was drab. Most residents seldom left the institution and spent most of their time staring at the television doing nothing. (p. 9)

Vladeck and Feuerberg (1995/1996) conclude that although the quality of nursing home care has improved in recent years, "overall nursing home quality in 1995 still falls very short of what it should be" (p. 10). Furthermore, advocates for nursing homes point out that nursing home regulations that resulted in improvements in overall nursing home quality have come under siege from the current conservative Congress (Freeman, 1995/1996). Also, in recent years, there has been a tremendous expansion of community-based services, a change that carries with it problems of its own. Although it was generally assumed that any home- and community-based services for older people would be better than nursing home care, "the development of quality standards and enforcement mechanisms for these services has lagged considerably behind the movement on the nursing home front" (Vladeck & Feuerberg, 1995/1996, p. 12).

Those elders living with relatives are often treated as burdens on young families and made to feel guilty for their state of dependence (Kosberg, 1983). In recent years, the stress on family caregivers has led to "granny dumping," abandonment of elderly persons with disabilities on hospital emergency room doorsteps in desperation. According to Hey and Carlson (1991), such abandonment is much more routine than had been thought and provides graphic evidence that our long-term care policies in this country are inadequate.

Abuse of elders is a national disgrace, and responsibility for this growing problem rests at a number of different levels. At the national level, the 96th, 97th, 98th, 99th, 100th, and 101st session of Congress share in the blame for failing to pass the Prevention, Identification, and Treatment of Elder Abuse Act (or similar measure). Two bills that were enacted by the 98th Congress, The Child Abuse Amendments of 1984 (P. L. 98-457) and the Older Americans Act Amendments of 1987 (P. L. 98-459), which contained provisions for abused elders. Unfortunately, no appropriations were ever made available for the provisions relating to elder abuse. At the state level,

> each State in 1989 spent about $3.80 per elderly resident for protective services. The picture is a bit brighter for child abuse victims, for whom the States, on the average, spend about $45. Nearly one fourth (10 of 42) of States reporting spent less than a dollar per elderly resident for these services in 1989. (Select Committee, 1990, p. XIII)

Furthermore, "while the average amount per elderly resident for protective services has increased from $1.52 to $3.80 over the last 10 years, much of that has been eaten away by 62 percent increase in prices due to inflation over the same period" (Select Committee, 1990, p. XII).

At the local level, all of us can feel some share of the responsibility for ignoring the problem. In addition to the more obvious forms of discrimination against elders, benign neglect of our elders and their problems in living can be viewed as a form of discrimination and victimization (Atkinson, 1980). The United States clearly has the technology and resources to ease the life stresses placed upon older people due to failing health, loss of income, lack of transportation, difficulty living independently, isolation, victimization, and other problems. The fact that we are unwilling to prioritize the needs of elders over defense and space spending, for example, is evidence of discrimination by benign neglect. The fact that when we do respond to the needs of elders, it is often with high visibility material assistance rather than with low visibility social assistance (personal involvement, emotional nurturance, respect) provides further evidence of discrimination by benign neglect.

References

AARP (1992). New AARP study: Health costs, '81 tax cut fuel U. S. deficit. *AARP Bulletin, 33* (9), 3.

Achenbaum, W. A. (1978). *Old age in the new land: The American experience since 1790.* Baltimore: Johns Hopkins University Press.

Adams, P., & Dominick, G. L. (1995). The old, the young, and the welfare state. *Generations, 19,* 38–42.

Aiken, L. R. (1995). *Aging: An introduction to gerontology.* Thousand Oaks, CA: Sage Publications.

Atkinson, D. R. (1980). The elderly, oppression, and social-change counseling. *Counseling and Values, 24,* 86–96.

Birren, J. E. (1961). A brief history of the psychology of aging. *The Gerontologist, 1,* 69–77, 127–134.

Birren, J. E. (1964). *The psychology of aging.* Englewood Cliffs, NJ: Prentice Hall.

Birren, J. F., & Woodruff, D. S. (1973). Academic and professional training in the psychology of aging. In C. Eisdorfer & M. P. Lawton (Eds.), *The psychology of adult development and aging.* Washington, DC: American Psychological Association.

Blank, M. L. (1974). Raising the age barrier to psychotherapy. *Geriatrics, 29* (11), 141–144, 147–148.

Brown, L. K. (1989). Is there sexual freedom for our aging population in our long-term care institutions? *Journal of Gerontological Social Work, 13* (3), 75–93.

Butler, R. N. (1979). *Why survive? Being old in America.* New York: Harper & Row.

Butler, R. N. (1983). Foreword. In J. I. Kosberg (Ed.), *Abuse and maltreatment of the elderly: Causes and interventions.* Boston: John Wright.

Campbell, J. M., & Huff, M. S. (1995). Sexuality in the older woman. *Gerontology & Geriatrics Education, 16* (1), 71–81.

Caro, F. G., & Motika, S. (1992). *Age discrimination in employment: A review of cases filed in the Massachusetts Commission Against Discrimination.* Boston: Gerontological Institute, University of Massachusetts.

Cavaliere, F. (1995, December). Elderly deserve better mental health services. *APA Monitor, 26,* 11.

Chumbler, N. R. (1995). The development of a brief scale of attitudes toward treating elderly patients. *Gerontology & Geriatrics Education, 16,* 39–51.

Cohen, E. S. (1990). The elderly mystique: Impediment to advocacy and empowerment. *Generations, 14* (supp), 13–16.

Colburn, D. (1985. November 27). Pain, placebos, and profit. *The Washington Post,* HE9.

Cole, T. (1991). The specter of old age: History, politics, and culture in an aging America. In B. B. Hess & E. W. Markson (Eds.), *Growing old in America* (4th ed., pp. 23–37). New Brunswick, NJ: Transaction Books.

Cooper, J. L. W. (1994). Drug-related problems in the elderly patient. *Generations, 28* (2), 19–27.

Covey, H. C. (1988). Historical terminology used to represent older people. *The Gerontologist, 28,* 291–297.

Cowgill, D. O., & Holmes, L. (1972). *Aging and modernization.* New York: Appleton-Century-Crofts.

Doyle, D. P. (1990). Aging and crime. In Kenneth F. Ferraro (Ed.), *Gerontology: Perspectives and issues* (pp. 294–315). New York: Springer Publishing Company.

Fein, R. (1992). Prescription for change. *Modern Maturity, 35* (4), 22–35.

Feinson, M. C. (1991). Reexamining some common beliefs about mental health and aging. In B. B. Hess & E. W. Markson (Eds.), *Growing old in America* (4th ed., pp. 125–135). New Brunswick, NJ: Transaction Books.

Fischer, D. H. (1977). *Growing old in America.* New York: Oxford University Press.

Freeman, I. C. (1995/1996). A contemporary advocacy agenda for nursing home consumers. *Generations, 19,* 52–54.

Gatz, M., Karel, M. J., & Wolkenstein, B. (1991). Survey of providers of psychological services to older adults. *Professional Psychology: Research and Practice, 22,* 413–415.

Gerber, J., Wolff, J., Klores, W., & Brown (1989). *Lifetrends: The future of baby boomers and other aging Americans*. New York: McMillan Publishing Co.

Giordano, N. H., & Giordano, J. A. (1984). Elder abuse: A review of the literature. *Social Work, 29*, 232–236.

Hall, G. S. (1923). *Senescence: The last half of life*. New York: D. Appleton.

Harris, L. (1975). *The myth and reality of aging in America*. Washington, DC: The National Council on Aging.

Hendricks, J., & Hendricks, C. D. (1981). *Aging in mass society: Myths and realities*. Cambridge, MA: Winthrop.

Hess, B. B. (1980). Stereotypes of the aged. In B. B. Hess (Ed.), *Growing old in America*. New Brunswick, NJ: Transaction Books.

Hess, B. B. (1991). Growing old in the 1990s. In B. B. Hess & E. W. Markson (Eds.), *Growing old in America* (4th ed., pp. 5–22). New Brunswick, NJ: Transaction Books.

Hey, R. P., & Carlson, E. (1991). 'Granny dumping:' New pain for U.S. elders. *AARP Bulletin, 32* (8), 1, 16.

Holstein, M. (1995). The normative case: Chronological age and public policy. *Generations, 19*, 11–14.

Ifill, G. (1986, March 2). To millions of elderly Americans neglect is just one more form of abuse. *Washington Post*, Section B, pp. 1, 10.

Johnson, T. F. (1995). Aging well in contemporary society. *American Behavioral Scientist, 39*, 120–130.

Karlen, A., & Moglia, R. (1995). Sexuality, aging, and the education of health professionals. *Sexuality and Disability, 13*, 191–199.

Kebric, R. B. (1988). Old age, the ancient military, and Alexander's army: Positive examples for a graying American. *The Gerontologist, 28*, 298–302.

Kent, K. L. (1990). Elders and community mental health. *Generations, 14* (1), 19–21.

King, N. R. (1984). Exploitation and abuse of older family members: An overview of the problem. In J. J. Costa (Ed.), *Abuse of the elderly*. Lexington, MA: D. C. Heath.

Kite, M. E., & Johnson, B. T. (1988). Attitudes toward older and younger adults: A meta-analysis. *Psychology and Aging, 3*, 233–244.

Kosberg, J. I. (1983). *Abuse and maltreatment of the elderly: Causes and interventions*. Boston: John Wright.

Krain, M. A. (1995). Policy implications for a society aging well. *American Behavioral Scientist, 39*, 131–151.

Kunkel, M. A., & Williams, C. (1991). Age and expectations about counseling: Two methodological perspectives. *Journal of Counseling & Development, 70*, 314–320.

Lau, E., & Kosberg, J. (1978). Abuse of the elderly by informal care providers: Practice and research issues. Paper presented at the 31st Annual Meeting of the Gerontological Society, Dallas, Texas, November 20, 1978.

Levin, J., & Levin, W. C. (1980). *Ageism: Prejudice and discrimination against the elderly*. Belmont, CA: Wadsworth.

Lewis, R. (1992a). Disposable workers: New corporate policies put many older employees at risk. *AARP Bulletin, 33* (5), 2.

Lewis, R. (1992b). Ups and downs of the 1980s: New income data refutes "fat cat" age stereotype. *AARP Bulletin, 33* (2), 1, 14–16.

Mardoyan, J. L., & Weis, D. M. (1981). The efficacy of group counseling with older adults. *Personnel and Guidance Journal, 60*, 161–163.

Margolis, R. J. (1990). *Risking old age in America*. Boulder, CO: Westview Press.

Marriott, M. (1984, December 16). Plan to cut aid for aged draws fire. *Washington Post*, A16C.

Mayer, M. (1993). Pensions: The naked truth. *Modern Maturity, 36* (1), 40–44.

McAllister, M. (1985, March 16). McLean group opposes project for elderly. *Washington Post*, Section E, pp. 4, 5.

McLeod, D. (1992). Overcharge . . . Critics: Feds slighting Medicare patients. *AARP Bulletin, 33* (2), 1, 4–5.

Mitric, J. M. (1985, September 21). Housing for elderly opposed. *Washington Post*, Section E, pp. 37, 40.

Morris, R., & Caro, F. G. (1995). The young-old, productive aging, and public policy. *Generations*, Fall, 32-37.

Morse, S. (1985, August 13). Early retirement: Tarnishing the golden years. *The Washington Post*, Section C, p. 5.

Moses, S. (1992). More clinicians needed to help a graying America. *Monitor, 23* (8), 34.

Myers, J. E. (1989). *Infusing gerontological counseling into counselor preparation: Curriculum guide.* Alexandria, VA: American Association for Counseling and Development.

Myers, J. E. (1992). Competencies, credentialing, and standards for gerontological counselors: Implications for counselor education. *Counselor Education and Supervision, 32,* 34–42.

Myers, J. E., & Shelton, B. (1987). Abuse and older persons: Issues and implications for counselors. *Journal of Counseling and Development, 65,* 376–380.

Piggrem, G. W., & Schmidt, L. D. (1982). Counseling the elderly. *Counseling and Human Development, 14* (20), 1–12.

Pillemer, K., & Findelhor, D. (1988). The prevalence of elder abuse: A random sample survey. *Gerontologist, 28,* 51–57.

Rajeswary, I. (1985, July 27). Aging former steelworker recounts job-hunt plight. *The Washington Post,* Section A, p. 7.

Rappaport, A. M. (1995). Employer policy and the future of employee benefits for an older population. *Generations, 19,* 63–67.

Rich, B. M., & Baum, M. (1984). *The aging: A guide to public policy.* Pittsburgh: University of Pittsburgh Press.

Richman, J. (1977). The foolishness and wisdom of age: Attitudes toward the elderly as reflected in jokes. *Gerontologist, 17,* 210–219.

Rosenbaum, W. A., & Button, J. W. (1989). Is there a gray peril?: Retirement politics in Florida. *The Gerontologist, 29,* 300–306.

Salisbury, H. (1975). Counseling the elderly: A neglected area in counselor education and supervision. *Counselor Education and Supervision, 14,* 237–238.

Schaie, K. W. (1993). Ageist language in psychological research. *American Psychologist, 48,* 49–51.

Schwalb, S. J., & Sedlacek, W. E. (1990). Have college students' attitudes toward older people changed? *Journal of College Student Development, 31,* 127–132.

Schwiebert, V. L., & Myers, J. E. (1994). Midlife care givers: Effectiveness of a psychoeducational intervention for midlife adults with parent-care responsibilities. *Journal of Counseling & Development, 72,* 627–632.

Seaberry, J. (1985, February 7). Poverty still a problem for elderly. *Washington Post,* Elc, E2a.

Select Committee on Aging (1990). *Elder abuse: A decade of shame and inaction (Comm. Pub. No. 101-752).* Washington, DC: U.S. Government Printing Office.

Simmons, L. W. (1945). *The role of the aged in primitive society.* New Haven: Yale University Press.

Simonton, D. K. (1990). Creativity in the later years: Optimistic prospects for achievement. *The Gerontologist, 30,* 626–631.

Thomasma, D. C. (1989). Moving the aged into the house of the dead: A critique of ageist social policy. *Journal of the American Geriatrics Society, 37,* 169–172.

U.S. Bureau of the Census. (1983). *Population Profile of the United States: 1982 (Current Population Reports, Series P-23, No. 130).* Washington, DC: U.S. Government Printing Office.

U.S. Bureau of the Census. (1993). *Poverty in the United States (Current Population Reports, Series P60-185).* Washington, DC: U.S. Government Printing Office.

U.S. Bureau of the Census. (1995). *Population Profile of the United States (Current Population Reports, Series P23-189).* Washington, DC: U.S. Government Printing Office.

UPI. (1985, May 11). Fraud, abuse reported in pacemaker business. *Washington Post,* Section A, p. 11.

Vladeck, B. C., & Feuerberg, M. (1995/1996). Unloving care revisited. *Generations, 19* (4), 9–14.

4

Oppression of Women: Past and Present

Past Discrimination

Society's Treatment of Women

Women have been largely neglected in historical texts, existing mostly in passing references or as the wives, mothers, or lovers of great men. Only recently have historians begun to untangle the reality of women's lives throughout history from the fiction of myth and literature (Schulenburg, 1979). Virginia Woolf (1957) best summarized the problems in understanding women's place in history:

> If woman had no existence save in the fiction written by men, one would imagine her a person of utmost importance; very various; heroic and mean; splendid and sordid; infinitely beautiful and hideous in the extreme; as great as man, some think even greater. But this is woman in fiction. In fact, as Professor Trevelyan points out, she was locked up, beaten, and flung about the room. A very queer, composite being thus emerges. Imaginatively she is of the highest importance; practically she is completely insignificant. She pervades poetry from cover to cover; she is all but absent from history . . . Some of the most inspired words, some of the most profound thoughts in literature fall from her lips; in real life she could hardly read, could hardly spell, and was the property of her husband. . . . It was certainly an odd monster that one made up by reading the historians first and the poets afterward—a worm winged like an eagle; the spirit of life and beauty in a kitchen chopping up suet. But these monsters, however amusing to the imagination, have no existence in fact. (pp. 45–46)

Women's actual status in society has varied tremendously across time and across cultures (Leavitt, 1971). However, the generalization that must be derived from any study of women through the ages is that women's status has usually been inferior to men's (Nielsen, 1978).

Leavitt (1971) argued that the key to understanding women's status anywhere is her degree of participation in the economy of the society, as well as her control over the products she produces. Every known society employs some type of sexual division of labor, but this segregation of tasks per se is not the cause of the inferior status of women. Rather, it is the *nature* of the division of labor by sex that affects the relative status of men and women and that influences their relationships within each society (Nielsen, 1978).

Primitive Societies

In early hunting and gathering societies in the Old Stone Age and in the modern world where such societies still exist, women's status within the clan was roughly equal to men's (Leavitt, 1971). In primitive societies, the division of labor by sex originated because of women's limited mobility due to childbearing and rearing responsibilities. Men ranged widely as hunters, whereas women's responsibilities included gathering vegetables and grains. Women, however, contributed equally to the subsistence of the clan; their contribution to the food supply was stable and at least as important as men's. In fact, in some societies the clan depended primarily on the food gathered by women, with the meat provided by men being seen as a luxury (Martin & Voorhies, 1975).

With the domestication of animals and the agricultural advances in the New Stone Age, ten to twelve thousand years ago, came the beginnings of social changes that had a tremendous impact on women's status. Men are generally credited with the discovery of the domestication of animals, a development that evolved naturally from their earlier hunting activities (Deckard, 1983). Women's food gathering activities also subsequently led to important cultural advances:

> It is generally accepted that owing to her ancient role as the gatherer of vegetable foods, woman was responsible for the invention and development of agriculture. Modern analogies indicate that so long as the ground was prepared by hoeing and not by ploughing women remained the cultivator. (Hawkes & Woolley, 1963, p. 265)

Women are also credited with the invention of pottery, weaving and the loom, and various tools related to their work activities, such as tools for grinding wheat (Deckard, 1983). Most early horticultural and herding societies maintained their dependence on vegetables and grains as their primary food source, so women's status remained fairly high (Deckard, 1983).

In the clan societies of this time, women's status was probably the highest ever achieved. The existence of matrilineal clans, that is, communities in which kinship and descent were calculated through the women, were common in primitive agricultural societies (Deckard, 1983). More recent examples of this type of kinship system can be found among Native American tribes such as the Hopi (Leavitt, 1971).

Even in herding societies, where men's influence was greater and descent through the male line (i.e., patriliny) was typical, women were not necessarily demeaned or dominated in the ways they were later in history. Male dominance, or patriarchy, seems to have been stimulated by the increasing sexual division of labor and the decreasing importance of women's contribution to the economy of the community resulting from the invention of the plow (Leavitt, 1971). The plow changed agriculture from a female to a male occupation; women's hardest labor was ended, but women also lost control of the food supply. Consequently, their economic value diminished.

Increased agricultural productivity produced a situation where, for the first time in history, communities had surpluses of food and thus wealth. Accumulation of these surpluses were then consolidated by individual chiefs who sought ways to transfer their wealth and authority to their descendants. In clan societies, especially matrilineal societies, children were community property and paternity was unimportant. With the accumulation of private as opposed to community property, and the desire to preserve wealth through one's line, came the tendency to regard women as property and the necessity of secluding women to ensure legitimate sons (Gough, 1975).

It was not only women who were treated as property. The development of private property and surplus wealth also produced slave societies (Deckard, 1983). As slaves provided more and more of the productive work, women's value to the economy declined further; both slave and free women were used for sexual pleasure.

Ancient Greece and Rome

In Athenian Greece, 80 percent of women were slaves, sometimes performing the hardest work in the fields but more often employed in the household; however, even the wives of the ruling-class men were treated as property and had few rights (Childe, 1971). The golden era of Greek democracy applied only to the free male ruling-class. Ruling-class women were secluded, prohibited from participating in the political system, required to have a legal guardian, usually father or husband, and could not obtain a divorce except under extreme circumstances (Childe, 1971).

The great Greek philosophers and writers held that women were inherently inferior and evil. The Pandora legend exemplifies the woman-hatred (misogyny) that was widespread even among the intellectuals of ancient Greece. Aristotle, whose influence on religious and scientific thought, and on our culture generally, has been profound, felt that women were defective men. He classed women and children together, concluding that neither had a fully developed rationality; in his view, both women and children ought to be ruled by men (Schaffer, 1981). Women's status was slightly better within Roman culture; women were not excluded from political and social life, and their status was less obviously inferior (Hunter, 1976). However, women were still seen as the source of misery and suffering, and women's emancipation was viewed in Roman literature as a causal factor in the decline and fall of Rome (Hunter, 1976). These themes of women as inferior and woman as a source of evil and suffering appear throughout history in various forms.

Medieval Societies

In medieval times, slavery was replaced by systems of serfdom. Serfs were slightly better off than the slaves of ancient times but were still bound to the land and their masters. Society was ordered into classes: King, greater nobility, lesser nobility, and the serfs, with women varying in status according to their husband's or father's place in society. Christian doctrine was a strong source of support for the views on the inferiority of women at this time. Christ himself demonstrated a high regard for women and nothing appeared in his original teachings denigrating women. St. Paul was the major influence on the early and medieval church, and the Christian Church has historically held a low opinion of women as a result (Chafetz, 1978):

> The head of the woman is the man . . . . for a man is the image and glory of God . . . . I suffer not a woman to teach, nor to usurp authority over the man, but to be in silence. . . ." (St. Paul, quoted in Deckard, 1983, p. 197)

As in ancient Greece, medieval women of the nobility had little freedom. Nunneries were one of the few places where women could get an education and find respite from men's oppression. Despite the glorification of the "weaker sex" within the medieval code of chivalry, female serfs worked as hard as their male counterparts.

In the late medieval period, some women of the growing middle class achieved a measure of independence as merchants and as weavers and spinners (thus the term *spinster* for older, unmarried women) (Deckard, 1983). As capitalistic economies evolved, upper-class women's lives improved, although they were still regarded as inferior to men. Women generally had a more significant role in feudal societies than indicated in most historical texts, even though they were legally subjugated. For example, female serfs played a leading role in peasant uprisings and rebellions, perhaps because of their double oppression. Rebellious peasants often met at night and such night assemblies were claimed to be "witches' sabbaths" because of women's roles in them. Both men and women were tortured and burned as witches, but women were persecuted in greater numbers and with more vigor; the terms *woman* and *witch* became virtually equivalent (Nelson, 1979). Women's so-called "evil nature" was a source of both hatred and fear by the male rulers and nobility. Women who refused to accept their subordinate status or who obtained knowledge or power that was considered the domain of men (e.g., women who practiced the healing arts) were particularly vulnerable to charges of witchcraft and sorcery. Witch burnings were an effective means of social control (Nelson, 1979).

The Renaissance produced many advances in the status of upper-class women, including increased educational opportunities for women. Women of the lower classes did not fare as well. However, a considerable number of noblewomen of this time had a significant impact on history (e.g., Queen Isabella of Spain, Catherine de Medici, and Elizabeth I), and enlightened views on women were increasingly expressed. Thomas More, in his *Utopia,* specifically stated that women should receive an education equivalent to men's, adding the caveat that some books are more appropriate to one sex than another. The Protestant Reformation and the subsequent rise in religious bigotry cut short the progress stimulated by the Renaissance (Deckard, 1983).

The Enlightenment

The Age of Revolutions, generally regarded as a time when freedom and democracy began to flower in western Europe and the United States, was also a time of advances for women but not because the major philosophers of the time advocated that equality be extended to women. In fact, most liberal philosophers still held reactionary positions on women. Rousseau, one of the French Enlightenment's most important theorists said:

> Nature herself has decreed that woman, both for herself and her children, should be at the mercy of man's judgement. . . . When the Greek women married, they disappeared from public life; within the four walls of their home they devoted themselves to the care of their household and family. This is the mode of life prescribed for women alike by nature and reason. (Rousseau, quoted in Hunter College Women's Studies Collective, 1983, p. 71)

"Liberty, equality, and brotherhood" meant just that—liberty and equality for men, usually only property-owning men.

The Enlightenment did stimulate the writings of the first feminist philosophers. In 1792, Mary Wollstonecraft, in *A Vindication of the Rights of Woman,* spoke out against the oppression of women and argued for equal educational opportunities for upper-, middle-, and working-class women:

> Men, indeed, appear to me to act in a very unphilosophical manner when they try to secure the good conduct of women by attempting to keep them always in a state of childhood. . . . It is a farce to call any being virtuous whose virtues do not result from the exercise if its own reason. This was Rousseau's opinion respecting men: I extend it to women. (Quoted in Hunter's College Women's Studies Collective, 1983, p. 71)

One of the few male liberal philosophers who spoke out in support of the equality of women was John Stuart Mill. Mill and his wife, Harriet Taylor, collaborated on many works, including *On the Subjection of Women.* Mill argued that women were not innately inferior and ascribed women's inferior social status to environmental factors, such as lack of educational opportunities.

The Industrial era of the nineteenth and twentieth centuries was again a time of advances for women. The women's movement in the United States arose out of the abolitionist movement, and the history of both civil rights campaigns have been interconnected to the present day (Davis, 1981).

Women in America

Prior to the first women's movement, women in the United States had few rights; many women came to the United States as indentured slaves. White women were sold from London prisons or kidnaped from the streets; black women were kidnaped from Africa (Deckard, 1983). Married women did not "exist" legally apart from their husbands; they could not testify in court, their property belonged to their husbands, and they did not even have a right to their own children. In frontier settlements in early America, women enjoyed the rough "equality" borne of economic and social necessity:

> Women were just as indispensable as men, since a household which lacked their homemaking skills, as well as nursing, sharpshooting and hunting when needed, was not to be envied. As colonial society became more complex this tradition became obscured, but its roots remained in American life and thinking; as the frontier moved westward in a changing world, the idea that women were the equals of men traveled with it, with far-reaching results. (Flexner & Fitzpatrick, 1996, pp. 8–9).

Indeed, the western states have always been at the forefront of the fight for women's equality, with Wyoming the first state to give women the right to vote in 1869 (Flexner & Fitzpatrick, 1996).

Black female slaves in the southern states held a position very similar to the slaves in Athenian Greece. The same analogy could be extended to their White mistresses and the ruling-class women in Greece. The latter's status was higher but still subordinate to men. The paradox between the antebellum South's notions of chivalry and their beliefs about women's nature, the treatment of Black women in slavery, and the disadvantagement of free Black and poor and working-class White women, is captured in Sojourner Truth's famous statement. At a women's rights meeting in Ohio in 1851, a male clergy member ridiculed the demand for women's right to vote by arguing that women were weak, dependent, and helpless. Sojourner Truth responded:

> The man over there says women need to be helped into carriages and lifted over ditches, and to have the best place everywhere. Nobody ever helps me into carriages or over puddles, or gives me the best place—and ain't I a woman? Look at my arm! I have plowed and planted and gathered into barns and no man could lead me—and ain't I a woman? I could work as much and eat as much as a man—when I could get it—and bear the lash as well! And ain't I a woman? I have borne 13 children, and seen most of 'em sold into slavery, and when I cried out with my mother's grief, none but Jesus heard me—and ain't I a woman? (Quoted in Flexner & Fitzpatrick, 1996, p. 85)

The first Women's Rights Conference was held at Seneca Falls, New York, in 1848. The catalyst for this action was the refusal of male abolitionists to seat female delegates at the World Anti-Slavery Convention in London in 1840 (Flexner & Fitzpatrick, 1996). Although much disagreement arose over whether women should demand the right to vote (it was seen as too radical by many), the conference delegates did unanimously agree to use every means possible to end discrimination against women (Flexner & Fitzpatrick, 1996).

By the 1860's, women had made progress in certain areas, such as securing the right to control their own wages. Progress in education and work came more slowly, and women's right to vote was not won in the United States until the Nineteenth Amendment became law in 1920. Suffragists in the United States, after decades of work and continuing frustration, adopted some of the militant techniques of the British suffragists prior to the passage of the Nineteenth Amendment (Flexner & Fitzpatrick, 1996). The Equal Rights Amendment was originally brought before Congress in 1923 and then reintroduced every year until it passed in 1972, only to go down to defeat in 1982 (Deckard, 1983; Flexner & Fitzgerald, 1996).

Despite the advances made by women in the twentieth century in terms of their social roles, legal rights, and access to the political process, inequities persisted. The extreme disparity between what has been called the "happy housewife" myth and the reality of women's lives in the 1950s gave rise to the second women's movement (Amundsen, 1971). Betty Friedan, in her classic *The Feminine Mystique* (1963), gave voice to the dissatisfaction felt by many middle-class American women that reflected the gap between social ideology and social reality.

Dramatic legal progress was not obtained for women until the 1960s and 1970s. The Equal Pay Act of 1963, first introduced in 1945, required that women be paid at the same rate as men but did nothing to make job discrimination illegal (Deckard, 1983). Title VII of the comprehensive Civil Rights Bill of 1964 went much further and finally gave women legal recourse for discriminatory practices (Bird, 1971). Even though the sex discrimination section of this bill was introduced as a way to kill the bill (it was assumed by opponents of civil rights for minorities that the inclusion of women would cause the bill to be laughed off the floor), Title VII has had far-reaching effects (Deckard, 1983). Other legal "victories" for women's rights included the 1967 Executive Order 11246, prohibiting sex discrimination in employment by federal contractors and the passage of Title IX in 1972, prohibiting sex discrimination in educational institutions.

Psychology's Treatment of Women

The academic discipline of psychology was slow to attend seriously to female psychology and women's experiences, and the psychological literature was so full of blatant sexism that, in 1971, Naomi Weisstein was prompted to write of it: "Psychology has nothing to say about what women are really like, what they need and what they want, essentially because psychology does not know." (p. 209) Weisstein's central thesis, indicated by the title of her article "Psychology constructs the female or the fantasy life of the male psychologist" was that, due to the androcentric (i.e., male-centered) bias in the field, psychological research and theory had little connection to women's reality.

At the dawn of the discipline, usually traced to the late 1870s, psychologists were concerned with establishing a "scientific" field of study of the individual. The "woman question" was regarded as a social issue and, therefore, outside the purview of the nascent field (Shields, 1975).

> The business of psychology was the description of the "generalized adult mind," and it is not at all clear whether "adult" was meant to include both sexes. When the students of German psychology did venture outside of the laboratory, however, there is no evidence that they were sympathetic to those defending the equality of male and female ability. (Shields, 1975, p. 739)

The Search for Sex Differences

Although German psychology under Wundt chose to ignore women, the functionalist movement in the United States in the late nineteenth and early twentieth centuries stimulated a great deal of research on sex differences in human functioning. Functionalists, heavily influenced by evolutionary theory, sought mainly to establish the superiority of White males. Their attention was focused primarily on racial differences that supported White supremacy, but investigations of sex differences aimed at proving the subordinate role of women were a natural byproduct of such thinking (Shields, 1975).

Researchers in the functionalist tradition first began to search for the "proof" of women's inferiority by examining sex differences in cranial capacity (Gould, 1996). Women's heads are on the average smaller than men's, and this was originally thought to be the physiological mechanism of women's diminished capacity (Shields, 1975). Broca, an early researcher on brain functioning and cranial capacity, said the following:

> In general, the brain is larger in mature adults than in the elderly, in men than in women, in eminent men than in men of mediocre talent, in superior races than in inferior races. . . . Other things being equal, there is a remarkable relationship between the development of intelligence and the volume of the brain. (Broca, 1861; quoted in Gould 1996, p. 115)

This avenue of research came to a dead-end after several grand and notable failures: when adjusted for size of the body, women's brains were found to be *larger* than men's; no clear relationship could be established between achievement in life and cranial capacity after death; and repeatedly, the brains of highly eminent men (e.g., Walt Whitman and Anatole France) were found to be embarrassingly small (Gould, 1996).

Research on sex differences then proceeded through comparative examinations of whatever aspect of brain organization, structure, or functioning might provide the illusive evidence for the widely held and obvious conclusion of female intellectual inferiority. The legacy of this androcentric, biased approach to the scientific study of women is with us today, manifested in studies of sex differences in cerebral dominance and laterality (Unger, 1979).

Psychologists of the functionalist movement also focused their attention on the purported biological mechanisms of sex differences in temperament, including the presumed biological complementarity of the sexes and the effects of "maternal instinct" on women's "nature." As to the former, men were seen as having different metabolisms than women, resulting in two different and complementary natures:

> The feminine passivity is expressed in greater patience, more open-mindedness, greater appreciation of subtle details, and consequently what we call more rapid intuition. The masculine activity lends a greater power of maximum effort, of scientific insight, or cerebral experiment with impressions, and is associated with an unobservant or impatient disregard to minute details, but with a more stronger [*sic*] grasp of generalities. (Geddes & Thomson, 1890, quoted in Shields, 1975, p. 746)

These presuppositions about sex differences, though disproved repeatedly, continued to influence eminent psychological researchers, as did the concept of maternal instinct, an assumption strongly held in American society and predating the advent of formal psychology (Shields, 1975). In essence, ". . . women's emotional nature (including her tendency to nurturance) was a direct consequence of her reproductive physiology" (Shields, 1975, p. 749). This maternal tendency was seen as having a significant and detrimental impact on women's development. The long-standing impact of these sexist and unproven assumptions are illustrated in the comments made by Bruno Bettelheim, over 100 years after the ideas had first been introduced: ". . . as much as women want to be good scientists or engineers, they want first and foremost to be womanly companions of men and to be mothers" (Bettelheim, 1965, p. 15).

There was some oppositional voices "crying in the wilderness." In 1910, Helen Thompson Wooley characterized the extant research on sex differences as ". . . logic martyred in the cause of supporting a prejudice, unfounded assertions, and even sentimental rot and drivel . . ." (Quoted in Shields, 1975, p. 739). Leta S. Hollingworth effectively dismantled the carefully constructed arguments of that period on the intellectual inferiority of women in an article entitled "Social devices for impelling women to bear and rear children" (1916; Sherif, 1979). Nevertheless, the dominant sexist attitudes persisted within psychology.

The early functionalist influence on psychology, and the consequent search for the biological mechanisms of sex differences, was eventually supplanted by the behaviorist tradition in this country in the 1930s. Behaviorists, searching for the universal laws governing behavior, were not concerned with sex differences, so there came a hiatus in the study of female psychology in the United States (Shields, 1975). However, psychoanalytic theory was in ascendance in Europe, and eventually Freudian theory dominated the study of women.

Freud and His Followers

Although some of Freud's most famous clients were women, he was far less certain about female developmental processes than about male development. His theory of girls' development was presented fully 20 years after his more famous exposition of the Oedipal theory for boys. His writings on women reflect a trend common in psychological writings even today, that is, extending men's experiences to women's (Schaffer, 1981; Hare-Mustin, 1983). Psychoanalytic theory rests squarely on the dictum "anatomy is destiny" (for women but not men) and corresponding assumptions about the biological inferiority of women. Thus Freud, despite having written only three articles on women, has had a significant and negative impact on both past and contemporary psychological views of women (Rohrbaugh, 1979).

Freud's central thesis was that girls, lacking a penis, are never as motivated as boys by castration anxiety to resolve the central developmental dilemma of the Oedipal complex. Girls, therefore, tend to be more susceptible to psychological disturbances, as well as to lag behind boys developmentally (Rohrbaugh, 1979). On the consequences of these developmental differences, Freud had this to say:

> I cannot escape the notion (though I hesitate to give it expression) that for women the level of what is ethically normal is different from what it is in men. Their super-ego is never so inexorable, so impersonal, so independent of its emotional origins as we require it to be in men. (1925; Quoted in Rohrbaugh, 1979, p. 87)

In other words, women generally fail to develop a strong super-ego or conscience. Further, women are seen as developing various personality characteristics as a result of their differential development, penis envy in particular, and also including narcissism, vanity, jealousy, passivity, and masochism (Schaffer, 1981). Margaret Mead (1974) summarized one perspective on Freud when she commented that it was a pity that Freud, although contributing so much to psychology, understood so little about women (Mead, 1974).

Among Freud's followers were many critics: Helene Deutsch, Karen Horney, Alfred Adler, Clara Thompson, and Carl Jung all disagreed with various aspects of Freud's views on women (Schaffer, 1981). Adler, for example, posited that society requires men to assume positions of unnatural dominance over women. Karen Horney wrote extensively about the social and cultural biases in Freud's thinking and explicitly rejected the psychoanalytic notion of women as masochistic (Schaffer, 1981). In critiquing Freud, Horney also stressed his tendency to look at women from an exclusively male perspective; ". . . like all sciences and all valuations, the psychology of women has hitherto been considered only from the point of view of men" (1926; Quoted in Rohrbaugh, 1979, p. 108).

Such critiques of androcentric bias did not prevent later theorists, most notably Erik Erikson, from making the same mistakes. Erikson's (1968) schema outlining stages of identity development was developed out of boys' and mens' experiences. The theory was later expanded to account for women's development, but women received attention primarily in terms of their perceived deviance from the male model of development. Erikson (1968) hypothesized that a women's identity becomes clear only after her decision about a marriage partner; he saw a woman's role as a mother crucial to her development of an identity. Moreover, women were seen as becoming neurotic and feeling deprived, lonely, and unfulfilled unless their "inner space" (i.e., womb) was filled (via motherhood).

Bias in Psychology

Psychodynamic theory and its offshoots are not the only culprits behind the bias against women in psychology. Every research area within the field can be exposed in similar ways. One further example will suffice as an illustration of this "masculine bias" in scientific psychology. In the area of research on achievement motivation, elaborate theories evolved detailing the factors predictive of educational and vocational success (Atkinson & Feather, 1966; McClelland, Atkinson, Clark, & Lowell, 1953). These theories, as with many other theories in different domains, have been presented as equally applicable to men and women. Studies on achievement motivation, however, consistently yielded different results for women than men, and women's responses in such studies were not congruent with the hypothesized theories of achievement motivation (Rohrbaugh, 1979). Only upon careful reading of this literature can the reader determine the truth. The data on women were so confusing that they were consequently largely ignored by the major theorists and researchers.

We can identify four main themes characterizing psychology's historical treatment of women: (1) neglect of female psychology entirely; (2) blatant sexism, including searches for the presumed mechanisms of women's inferiority; (3) ignorance of women's unique experiences and the consequent unthinking extension of theories of male functioning and development to women; and (4) feminist analyses geared toward understanding women's personality patterns, behavior, and male-female relationships in social context. The latter theme, as we will see in the next section, is unfortunately still not in ascendance in mainstream psychology, despite the recent explosion of research and writing by feminist psychologists (Brown, 1994; Gilbert, 1992; Sherif, 1979; Worell & Remer, 1992).

Current Discrimination

"Americans are condescendingly sure that women in this country are much better off than women anywhere else" (Hewlett, 1986; p. 139). This statement probably best captures mainstream opinion in the United States today. It is *assumed* that women have achieved equality; women now have only to sort out the problems and responsibilities that have come with that success. Some writers have even referred to a "post-feminist era" (Faludi, 1991); nothing more need be done to advance women's rights. Unfortunately, the reality is far different from commonly held beliefs.

After the significant and far-reaching legal and social advances of the liberal 1960s and 1970s, we entered a regressive era in the 1980s and early 1990s. Conservative political groups became increasingly powerful politically, and some of the major goals of such groups were and are strongly antifeminist (Faludi, 1991). As a result of changes in the political climate, many of the advances in women's rights and civil rights programs were stalled or even reversed. For example, conservative forces successfully fought against the ratification of the Equal Rights Amendment (Deckard, 1983). Some conservative groups also oppose affirmative action, sex education, interference with the family in the form of programs combating child abuse, battered women's shelters, and funding for child care programs, all issues intimately related to women's social status (Faludi, 1991). The two Republican administrations in the 1980s consistently opposed most women's rights issues. The Equal Employment Opportunity Commission (EEOC), the agency responsible for enforcing antisex discrimination laws, was all but dismantled (Faludi, 1991), and Presidents Reagan and Bush had poor records of appointing women to influential offices, despite the appointment of the first female Supreme Court Justice by Reagan. President Reagan, in particular, had a record of appointing antifeminists when his appointments were female (Deckard, 1983). Although the Clinton administration has been strongly committed to women's issues, the problems and reverses in women's status require substantial and enduring redress. The following section documents the continuing problems faced by American women, despite the real and significant social advances that have been made in this century.

Social Inequality

As we have seen, attitudes towards women and women's relative status within a given society fluctuate over time in response to social and economic trends. The 1970s were a time when it became less socially acceptable to espouse the sexist notion of women's inherent biological inferiority; yet in the 1980s and 1990s, at least in some sectors of society, sexist thinking is actively promoted.

More commonly, people ascribe to the "different but equal" view. That is, women and men are social equals but have different roles, both equally valuable. On the surface this belief (and there are many variations of the theme) appears to be egalitarian. Upon closer inspection, another variant of sexist ideology is revealed. Women's special place and special roles invariably turn out to be inferior and devalued. For example, occupational segregation by sex is often justified on the basis of women's and men's different strengths, yet feminine characteristics are often reframed to encourage women to participate in low-paid drudge work. In American society, feminine characteristics lead women "naturally" to the "women's jobs" of beautician, secretary, child care worker, and waitress, and away from such masculine work as physician. Conversely, in Russia, feminine characteristics lead women "naturally" to predominate in the medical specialty of general practitioner (women account for 74 percent of all physicians in the former USSR), a relatively low-paid, low-status area of medicine, while masculine characteristics lead Russian men naturally to the higher-status specialties. In the United States, women remain underrepresented in the physical sciences.

> Cross-cultural evidence supports the view that the dearth of women in science is due to culture, not biology. In the United States, 15% of B.S. degrees go to women. Among tenure track faculty in physics, women are only about 3%. In contrast, in France 21% of Ph.D.s in physics go to women and 23% of university faculty in physics are women. In Italy, the figures are identical to those in France: 21% and 23%. Even in Turkey, 23% of physics faculty members are women. Cross-culturally, the percentage does not approach an equitable 50% except in Hungary, where 47% of physics faculty in universities are women. (Hyde, 1997, p. 286)

We will discuss occupational segregation in greater depth in the next section of this chapter. For now, it is important to note how social ideologies in the form of "women are not inferior, but . . ." are sexist at the core and promote and maintain women's inferior status (Deckard, 1983).

The ongoing subtle and often not-so-subtle sexism that prevails in American culture manifests itself in many forms. Research has repeatedly demonstrated that even very young children have already acquired stereotypical views of masculine and feminine characteristics, and the occupational choices open to each gender (Betz, 1994). Overall, some loosening in traditional gender-role stereotypes has been observed, but we are still far from equality.

Attitudes towards women's roles, especially work roles, have been changing markedly (Worell & Remer, 1992), but certain other fundamental assumptions remain largely unchanged. We shall see in the next section how traditional assumptions about women's gender-roles and responsibilities in the family continue to interact complexly with changing expectations for women, producing new problems for women, men, and society.

Economic Disadvantagement

A major cause of the economic disadvantages for women is the differential pay they receive for similar work. Although women accounted for 46 percent of the labor force in 1995, American women earn, on the average, 75 cents on the dollar compared to men (U.S. Women's Bureau, 1996). "Even in traditionally female occupations where women outnumber, women still earn less than men" (U.S. Women's Bureau, 1996, p. 3). The wage disparity is even more severe for racial/ethnic minority women and women who are disadvantaged in other ways, for example, the physically disabled (Faludi, 1991). "Earnings also vary by race and ethnicity, with white workers earning more, on average, than either black or Hispanic workers regardless of gender" (Herz & Wootton, 1996, p. 67). For example, in 1994, African-American women were earning 65 percent of what men on the average earned (Amparano, 1996). In 1994, Hispanic women were earning 57 cents on the dollar compared to men (Amparano, 1996). As of 1996, Hispanic women earned 78 percent of what non-Hispanic women earned (U.S. Women's Bureau, 1996). Even college educated women are not doing well; college-educated women continue to earn less than college-educated men (U.S. Women's Bureau, 1996).

On the positive side, between 1979 and 1994 the earnings gap between men and women narrowed considerably (13 percentage points). Conversely, although there has been some improvement in women's real earnings, this narrowing of the gender gap had more to do with men's real wages declining than dramatic improvements in women's circumstances (Herz & Wootton, 1996).

What are the reasons for the continuing disparity in earnings? A long-standing myth has been that women work for "pin money" (the term refers to extra pocket money for trinkets, e.g., pins, rather than earnings necessary for survival) and are not seriously attached to the work force (Farmer & Backer, 1977). In fact, most women work out of economic need, because they are single, divorced, or widowed, or if married because their earnings are required by the family for subsistence (Hewlett, 1986; U.S. Women's Bureau, 1996). Ongoing discrimination, even though illegal, continues. The reasons for the wage gap are complex and extend beyond overt discrimination to include inadequate maternity benefits and child care, occupational segregation by sex, devaluation of women's work, as well as outright pay inequities.

Maternity and Child Care Support

One of the most significant social changes in this century has been the increasing entry of married women and mothers into the paid labor force (Kahn-Hut, Daniels, & Colvard, 1982; U.S. Women's Bureau, 1996). Currently, nearly 59 percent of all women, that is, 6 out of 10, are in the labor force. Over 61 percent of married women and 70 percent of mothers with children under the age of 18 work outside the home (Betz, 1994; Galinsky & Bond, 1996; U.S. Women's Bureau, 1996). The overwhelming majority (nearly 95 percent) of all women will participate in the work force at some time in their lives (Betz, 1994). The failure of our society to provide adequate and affordable child care has been a significant drawback for working women and a formidable barrier to mothers of young children, often blocking participation in the paid labor force completely. Good high-quality private child care is very costly and can easily consume a substantial part of a working mother's earnings. Many single or divorced mothers of young children are virtually forced to go on welfare in order to survive, even when they would rather be working (Deckard, 1983). Employed women experience a double burden, working their paid jobs and also working as caretakers of spouses, children, and home.

Our country has an extremely poor record on the issues of maternity and child care:

> The United States is the only industrialized country that has no statutory maternity leave. One hundred and seventeen countries (including every industrialized nation and many developing countries) guarantee a women the following rights: leave from employment for childbirth, job protection while she is on leave, and the provision of a cash benefit, to replace all or most of her earnings. (Hewlett, 1986, p. 96)

Further, despite lip service given to Americans' priority on the family, all efforts at developing government programs for child care have failed. In 1971, President Nixon vetoed the Comprehensive Child Care Act, and subsequent administrations were unsupportive or even hostile toward any child care programs ("Adding Up the Victories," 1986; Faludi, 1991). Some businesses and major corporations are beginning to experiment with flex-time, parental leaves for fathers as well as pregnancy leaves for mothers, and child care programs for employees, but these efforts are scarce and totally inadequate to the scope of the problem (Hewlett, 1986).

In stark contrast, most European countries provide subsidized child care, child allowances, and other sources of support for women and their families, with consequent beneficial effects on women's economic status (Hewlett, 1986):

> It is also no coincidence that the country with the most developed benefits and services for working women—Sweden—is also the country with the smallest wage gap, while the country with the least developed benefits and services—the United States—is also the country with one of the largest wage gaps. (p. 99)

The consequence of this scarcity in support services is that women must bear the full burden of their double duty as worker and mother, and this double burden is then reflected in their earnings. Women are forced to go on welfare, take part-time instead of full-time work, and lose wages due to maternity or child care responsibilities, drastically lowering their earnings and future earning power.

Occupational Segregation and Comparable Worth

Although lack of adequate child care services is certainly one factor in the wage gap, occupational segregation by sex is clearly a more significant contributor (Hewlett, 1986). Faludi (1991) argued that occupational segregation by sex accounts for at least 45 percent of the wage gap. The extent of occupational segregation by sex has been dramatic in the past. For example, through the mid-1980s, the majority of employed women were still clustered into only 20 occupational areas (Faludi, 1991; Hewlett, 1986). Despite significant shifts in the gender composition of the entire range of occupations, in the 1990s ". . . women and men still tend to be concentrated in different occupations; women are highly over represented in clerical, sales, and services occupations, for example, while men are disproportionately employed in craft and laborer jobs" (Herz & Wootton, 1996, p. 56).

We have already seen in the historical overview that job segregation by sex is common to almost all societies, but we have also seen that such segregation need not necessarily lead to gender inequality in society. The current sex segregation in our economy, coupled with the denigration of "women's work," is both a consequence and continuing cause of the social and economic disadvantagement of women. Traditionally female jobs, that is, jobs where the majority of workers are women, are almost always lower paying and lower status occupational pursuits. Howe (1977) employed the term *pink collar* workers to characterize the dead-end, low-status nature of such women's jobs as beautician, waitress, and secretary. In 1980, 97.6 percent of all secretaries were women; in 1983, women comprised 70 percent of all retail and personal sales workers and 80 percent of all administrative support workers (Kahn-Hut, Daniels & Colvard, 1982). In 1994,

> . . . more than a quarter of employed women but only six percent of employed men worked in administrative support jobs. Women also were represented heavily in sales and service occupations. In fact, administrative support, sales, and service categories accounted for twice the share of employed women (57 percent) as employed men (28 percent). (Herz & Wootton, 1996, p. 57)

Women also continue to be overrepresented in traditional female professions. For example, in 1994, 85 percent of elementary school teachers were women (Herz & Wootton, 1996). In contrast, only 1 in every 10 women work in precision, craft, and repair jobs, whereas 4 in 10 men work in these generally higher paying areas (Herz & Wootton, 1996). In some cases, extreme job segregation by gender continues. For example, in 1994 only 10 percent of engineers, 7 percent of construction inspectors, 2 percent of electricians, and 1 percent of carpenters were female (Herz & Wootton, 1996).

Even where it appears that women are making significant inroads, the realities are discrepant with widely held perceptions. Despite dramatic increases in their absolute numbers in management positions in business and industry, White women and women and men of color have faced serious obstacles to advancement within the ranks of management (Morrison & Glinow, 1990). Overall, women comprise 50 percent of entry-level management, 25 percent of middle management, but only 1–2 percent of upper management positions (Hewlett, 1986).

There is considerable evidence that White women and people of color encounter a "glass ceiling" in management. The glass ceiling is a concept popularized in the 1980s to describe a barrier so subtle that it is transparent, yet so strong that it prevents women and minorities from moving up the management ladder. Only 2% of 1,362 senior executives were women . . . only 3.6% of board directorships and 1.7% of corporate officerships in the Fortune 500 were held by women; the Fortune 500 and the health industry indicated that 4.4% of board members were women and that 3.8% and 8.5% of their corporate officers, respectively, were women. (Morrison & Glinow, 1990, p. 200)

Recent research suggests that even the limited progress made by women in upper-level management positions is now eroding (Faludi, 1991).

Further compounding women's economic status is that the legal mandate of "equal pay for equal work," even if it were being enforced, would not resolve the economic problems encountered by women. In 1980, a registered nurse with over 14 years of education earned less than deliverymen; secretaries with 13+ years of education and comparably higher level job responsibilities earned less than truck drivers with an average of a ninth grade education (Kahn-Hut, Daniels, & Colvard, 1982). The concept of equal pay for *comparable* work was introduced as an attempt to resolve some of these discrepancies. Comparable work proponents advocated assessing the skills, education, and responsibilities required in various jobs and adjusting pay scales to reflect equal pay for work of comparable worth or social value (Kahn-Hut, Daniels, & Colvard, 1982), but they have made little progress in implementing this concept.

Wage Discrimination

Wage discrimination persists within fields as well. As indicated previously, women consistently earn less than men for the same work. In 1994, the average salary for men was $30,854, and the average salary for women was $22,205 (Amparano, 1996). As but a few specific examples, male computer scientists earned an average of $45,448 per year compared to female scientists' yearly earnings of $38,376; male internists earned $138,240, while female internists earned $119,258; and male retail cashiers took home $13,728, whereas female retail cashiers earned only $11,440 (Amparano, 1996). These wage differences are reflected in virtually all vocational areas, at all levels. In addition to being paid less than men for the same jobs, women also tend to be clustered in the lower levels of even traditionally female occupations. For example, although women predominate in elementary school teaching positions, in the mid-1980s only 26 percent of school administrators were female (Betz & Fitzgerald, 1987). Interestingly, men earn more than women even in female-dominated occupations; for example, in 1995, male elementary school teachers earned $713 per week, while female elementary teachers earned $627, and male registered nurses earned $715 per week compared to the $693 per week earned by female registered nurses (U.S. Women's Bureau, 1996).

Women are now receiving undergraduate degrees at overall parity with men, but despite clear progress, significant gender differences persist in a number of fields. For example, as of 1992, 28.7 percent of degrees in computer and information sciences, 14 percent of degrees in engineering, and 33 percent of degrees in the physical sciences were awarded to women (Costello & Krimgold, 1996). The most rapid progress has been made in areas traditional for women, whereas progress in highly nontraditional majors and career areas, although marked, is still fairly slow. Further, women receive only 7 percent of the engineering doctorates; fewer than 4 percent of engineers working in the field are women; and, although the wage gap between women and men is smaller in the scientific/technological fields than in other vocational areas, women engineers still earn less than men at comparable levels. The unemployment rate for female scientists and engineers is twice as high as men's (National Science Foundation, 1990). Again, racial/ethnic minority women and women with a disability experience a double or triple burden of disadvantagement; the wage gap and unemployment figures for these groups in the scientific/technical career areas is worse than for White women (National Science Foundation, 1990).

Statistics on female academics demonstrate the same pattern of wage discrimination and occupational segregation. Although 51 percent of instructors in institutions of higher education are women, most of these women are "ghettoized" in a limited number of fields and in unstable, lower paying positions, a situation that has not changed for years (Higher Education & National Affairs, 1986). At every level and in all fields, women earn less than their male counterparts, are less likely to be tenured, and the relatively few female administrators are most likely to be concentrated in traditionally female areas, such as home economics and nursing (Higher Education & National Affairs, 1986). "In 1992/93, as in 1980/81, the majority of men on the faculties of four-year colleges and universities had tenure and the majority of their female counterparts did not; in fact, the tenured proportions hardly changed for either sex between 1980/81 and 1992/93" (Costello & Krimgold, 1996, p. 280).

Economic Consequences of Unequal Treatment

An alarming development in recent years, an upshot of the wage gap and discriminatory practices, has long been termed "the feminization of poverty" (Pearce, 1979). When women combine their relatively lower earnings with a higher earning male, as in a marriage, their economic situation is markedly better than when they must survive independently. When women are the sole supporters of dependents, especially children, their economic situation is precarious. "The feminization of poverty" refers to the increasing percentage of women living below the poverty level due to their disadvantaged economic status. The major factors in this dramatic rise in the number of female-headed households subsisting below poverty level are occupational segregation and the wage gap. In 1994, over 34 percent of all families with female heads of the household were below the poverty level (U.S. Women's Bureau, 1996). For women of color, the statistics are even more alarming. For example, nearly half of families headed by Hispanic women are below the poverty level (U.S. Women's Bureau, 1996).

In addition to women's economic circumstances, changes in the divorce laws over the past two decades also seem to be contributing to the problem (Weitzman, 1985). The statistics on the effects of divorce on the economic status of husband and wife are striking: Divorced women (and their children) experience an immediate 73% drop in their standard of living after a divorce, while men experience a 42% gain in their economic status (Weitzman, 1985). Although Weitzman's (1985) statistics have been questioned (they are undoubtedly too high), the social, interpersonal, and personal consequences of this phenomenon remain and are as unsettling as the economic repercussions:

> When the downward change in the family standard of living followed the divorce and the discrepancy between the father's standard of living and that of the mother and children was striking, this discrepancy was often central to the life of the family and remained as a festering source of anger and bitter preoccupation. The continuation of this discrepancy over the years generated continuing bitterness between the parents. Mother and children were likely to share in their anger at the father and to experience a pervasive sense of deprivation, sometimes depression, accompanied by a feeling that life was unrewarding and unjust. (Wallerstein & Kelly, p. 231, 1980, quoted in Weitzman, 1985, p. 353)

Gender-Role Stereotyping

The point of this discussion thus far has been to highlight the continuing effects of past discrimination on women's social and economic status and to emphasize that women have not yet attained equality in employment. As previously discussed, however, the present state of affairs is not entirely due to overt sex discrimination; it will take many years for the recent female graduates pursuing traditionally male career areas to make an impact in the job market. Further, discrimination does not have to exist overtly to produce a situation where many women are still underutilizing their talents and abilities in career pursuits. As we have seen, there has been some loosening of the traditional gender-role stereotypes, and more female models in a wider range of occupational roles exist, but boys and girls continue to be trained in different ways (Worell & Remer, 1992). Although written long ago, Bem and Bem's (1970/1984) aptly articulated statement on the general issue remains compelling:

> Even if all discrimination were to end tomorrow, nothing very drastic would change. For job discrimination is only part of the problem . . . it does not, by itself, help us to understand why so many women "choose" to be

secretaries or nurses rather than executives or physicians. Discrimination frustrates choices already made. Something more pernicious perverts the motivation to choose. That "something" is an unconscious ideology about the nature of the female sex, an ideology which constricts the emerging self-image of the female child and the nature of her aspirations from the very beginning; an ideology which leads even those Americans who agree that a black skin should not uniquely qualify *its* owner for a janitorial or domestic service to act as if possession of a uterus uniquely qualifies *its* owner for precisely such service. (p. 12)

It is important to note, however, that because race/ethnicity and gender interact in complex ways, women of color experience sexism in its many forms differently than white women (Hays, 1996). For women of color, ". . . belonging to two groups whose positions are determined by oppression, her experience differs from that of her fellow victims, the man of color and the White woman, because her reality involves the dynamics of both racism and sexism." (Comas-Diaz & Greene, 1994, p.xi). "Women of color are not only exposed to oppression within the dominant group, but also experience sexism and oppression within their own ethnic and racial communities as well." (Comas-Diaz & Greene, 1994, p. 5)

Even when women of any racial/ethnic background are able to surmount their gender-role conditioning to enter challenging and demanding educational programs, they are still in need of additional support and encouragement. Freeman (1979) identified the "Null Environment" as a major problem for women in academic and vocational pursuits. This concept refers to the inherent discrimination against women and minorities that results, in academic situations when *neither* men nor women are actively encouraged or discouraged, from the differential socialization and external environments experienced by women and men. Freeman (1979) felt that women enter higher education with a "handicap" which a "null" academic environment does nothing to minimize or decrease, resulting in the inadvertent discouragement of women because of lack of *encouragement*. Thus, educators, and by extension counselors, may discriminate against women "without really trying." Women need active encouragement, not simply the absence of discrimination, to surmount the barriers posed by traditional feminine gender-role socialization.

Victimization

One of the most damaging manifestations of sexism in any society is the physical, sexual, and emotional abuse of women that results from virulent misogynist attitudes intertwined with women's relative powerlessness. The long-term emotional, interpersonal, and social costs of violence against women are considerable. Sexual assault is a constant (and statistically real) fear for most American women, regardless of age, physical attractiveness, race, or class (Enns, 1996). Some groups of women within society are more vulnerable to assault than others, but no women is "safe." Rape, sexual harassment, childhood sexual abuse, and other forms of violence against women have little to do with sexuality; sexual assault is motivated by domination and power.

Current statistics indicate the widespread nature of the problem: One in four women will be raped in her lifetime; one in two women will be physically battered by her spouse or significant other; conservatively, 25 percent of women experience some form of sexual harassment on the job—the figures are much higher for women in highly nontraditional occupations; and 10–30 percent of women are survivors of child sexual abuse, the perpetrator usually being male and someone close to the child (Courtois, 1986; Fitzgerald, 1993; Muehlenhard, Highby, Phelps, & Sympson, 1997). Countless other women have suffered emotional abuse, often for years. Because crimes of violence against women are grossly underreported, these statistics may very well be on the low side. While rape crisis centers, battered women's shelters, and support services for survivors of incest and child sexual abuse have done much to serve survivors of violence and inform the public, the root of the problem remains.

The social myths that exist about the seven areas of violence against women (i.e., battering, rape, girl child incest, pornography, prostitution, sexual harassment on the job, and sexual harassment between client and professional, e.g., doctor or therapist) reveal the underlying sexism behind these actions (Walker, 1979). One of the core myths about sexual and physical assaults on women is that the "victim" was responsible for the assault. With rape we often see the false and mistaken accusation of a seductive appearance on the part of the rape victim, an assumption also made about children victimized by sexual assault; and in the case of wife (woman) battering, we see the label "masochistic" placed on the victim to justify the assault (Collier, 1982; Martin, 1976). Victims (or, more positively, "survivors") of sexual harassment are accused of "sleeping their way to the top" or dressing too provocatively at work, and male therapists who sleep with their clients are often excused as having been "seduced" (Collier, 1982).

Another common myth (as false as the first) is that the abuser is mentally ill or, in the case of rape, has been overcome by a powerful sex drive (Collier, 1982). In fact, rapists have not been found to be different from nonrapists on measures of psychological functioning *except* in their tendency to act out their impulses via sexual assault; further, most rapes are premeditated (Collier, 1982). "The stereotype of the harasser is of the uneducated manual worker, the uncouth traveling salesman, the boorish office 'lech'. Professional individuals with impeccable credentials and multiple degrees are assumed to be beyond reproach, despite multiple examples to the contrary" (Fitzgerald, 1993). The common theme behind all of these forms of violence towards women and abuse of women is that they are methods of establishing dominance and control over women. Controversy exists in this area as to the exact reasons behind sexual and physical assaults. However, what can be said with some confidence is that women do not freely choose to be victimized, and women's and men's socialization, along with women's relative powerlessness in society, are central causative factors in violence towards women (Betz & Fitzgerald, 1993; Collier, 1982).

Interestingly, mental health professionals and the public at large have been bombarded in recent years with claims that statistics such as those cited above are grossly exaggerated (Enns, 1996). As part of the general social backlash against women over the past decade, two areas of research have been targeted: rape and sexual abuse statistics, relabeled "rape hype" and "false memory syndrome," respectively (Enns, 1996). The first series of claims, namely, that rape statistics have been inflated by feminists for political purposes, has ironically been aimed at a well conducted series of studies by Mary Koss and her colleagues (e.g., Koss, Gidycz, & Winsniewski, 1987), funded by the National Institute of Mental Health, wherein the authors reported the now well-known figure that one of four women reported being raped. In addition to various distortions that have appeared in the media, one of the crucial aspects of the debate is the finding by Koss and her colleagues (1987) that, although many women reported being treated in a manner that met the legal definition of rape,

> . . . 73% of the women who were survivors of rape did not label their experience as rape, and critics have contended that this statistic invalidates the research. [However,] although the Koss et al. (1987) study is most frequently cited and criticized, a substantial number of additional studies have examined rates of sexual assault and rape and have found similar prevalence rates. (Enns, 1996, p. 359)

It is common and solid scientific practice for researchers to develop operational definitions of the targeted behavior under study, in this case using the legal definition of rape. The fact that many women who have been raped do not recognize the experience as such is more a reflection of the status of women in our society than a negation of the one-in-four rape statistic (Muehlenhard, et al., 1997).

Another area of intense debate has been taking place around the issue of "recovered memories" of child sexual abuse (Enns, 1996). "Critics of therapy for adult sexual abuse survivors charge that therapists create false memories of abuse. Critics who focus on the 'epidemic' of false memory often use sensational language that resembles the rape hype literature" (Enns, 1996, pp. 73–74). Although there certainly may be cases of poorly trained or unethical therapists persuading clients to remember false details about sexual abuse, "false memory syndrome" (a popular, not a scientific term) movement advocates seek to deny that sexual abuse is a widespread problem. However, most of the evidence in support of therapists implanting memories is anecdotal and circumscribed (Enns, 1996).

On the other hand,

> During the past century, several cycles of awareness and denial of abuse have already occurred. Arguments that issues of abuse have been exaggerated are often

compelling to a society that prefers to believe that this is a just world. Within this climate, counselors may begin to question the perceptions and reality of their clients, or even avoid dealing with these issues for fear of creating an issue that does not really exist . . . To avoid the public amnesia that has already occurred several times in the past century, counselors must commit themselves to competent practice and outreach relevant to these issues. (Enns, 1996, p. 361)

Rather than embrace a reactionary standpoint, practitioners are advised: (1) to educate themselves on the issues, rather than rely on sensational media accounts; and (2) follow the various professional guidelines that have been developed for working with survivors of sexual abuse (Enns, 1996).

Women and the Mental Health System

As we have seen, the sexism embedded in society at large penetrated and influenced the development of scientific psychology. These biases within psychology have had profound consequences for the diagnosis and treatment of women by mental health practitioners.

Bias in Diagnosis

Women are much more likely than men to be treated for mental illness (Gove & Tudor, 1973; Williams, 1983); the sex ratio varies depending on the diagnosis and also on type of treatment facility, but women are clearly in the majority. Various explanations have been promulgated for this preponderance of women diagnosed as having mental problems: Women are weaker and therefore more susceptible to psychological disturbance than men; women's traditional gender roles are inherently mentally unhealthy; women are labeled as ill more often than men, but no genuine sex difference in the incidence of mental illness exists; and women subjected to excessive stress and tension manifest their disturbance via emotional symptoms congruent with their gender role, while men's disturbance is manifested in physical symptomology (Williams, 1983).

Phyllis Chesler (1972) in her classic book *Women and Madness* advanced the argument that mental illness in women is a result of underconformity or overconformity to the feminine sex role:

> Men do not usually seem as "sick" if they act out the male role fully—unless, of course, they are relatively powerless contenders for "masculinity." Women are seen as "sick" when they act out the female role (are depressed, incompetent, frigid, and anxious) and when they reject the female role (are hostile, successful, sexually active, and especially with other women). (p. 118)

A meta-analysis of 26 studies examining the relationships of gender roles to mental health produced results congruent with Chesler's thesis: "masculinity," as measured by various gender-role inventories, is more consistently and significantly associated with psychological measures of mental health than is "femininity" (Basoff & Glass, 1982).

A different but related argument has been advanced by writers who, taking note of the differences in rates of mental illness in married and unmarried men and women, have suggested that social roles are a significant factor in susceptibility to mental distress (Williams, 1983). Bernard (1971) demonstrated that men are happier when married than women; single women score higher than married women on various indices of psychological well-being than married women; and women make more adjustments in marriage than do men. These findings correspond with findings from psychological studies, indicating higher rates of mental illness for married women than single women or married men (Gove, 1980). Marriage seems to have a disadvantageous effect on women (Gove, 1973).

Arguments over the reasons for gender differences in the prevalence of mental illness may be moot; and in recent years, the literature has moved toward developing nonsexist and feminist approaches to therapy and counseling, rather than continue focusing on gender differences (e.g., Brown, 1994; Worell & Remer, 1992). As Johnson (1980) pointedly argues:

> To speak of the overall mental health of two sexes is too sweeping a generalization . . . diagnoses are frequently of questionable reliability . . . often based on ambiguous symptoms, subject to a variety of interpretation. . . . Furthermore, a report of symptoms is not synonymous with mental illness; a person can acknowledge symptoms, but be coping with them. (pp. 363–364)

Johnson goes on to argue that we must look at the complex confluence of female socialization, societal attitudes towards women and women's roles, and external stressors, including the treatment of women by clinicians, to understand and assist women therapeutically. The point here is not that sexism has waned in the 1990s; just that it is more productive to focus on what ought to be done rather than what is wrong.

Nevertheless, new controversies about gender bias have arisen over the past decade, revolving around two new diagnoses affecting women. In the revised third edition of the *Diagnostic and Statistical Manual of Mental Disorders (DSM-III-R)*, the standard guide for the diagnosis of mental problems, ". . . five areas of the *DSM* have been targeted as potentially harmful to women: Borderline Personality Disorder, Histrionic Personality Disorder, Dependent Personality Disorder, Self-Defeating Personality Disorder, and Premenstrual Dysphoria Disorder (Walsh, 1997, p. 338). Two gender-related diagnoses, "self-defeating personality disorder" (originally titled "masochistic personality disorder") and Premenstrual Dysphoria Disorder (i.e., premenstrual syndrome, originally labeled "late luteal phase disorder"), were included after considerable controversy, as unofficial diagnoses in the appendices of the *DSM-IIIR*. Many feminist psychologists viewed the attempts to officially sanction such diagnoses as a major step backwards for women:

> While the criteria for this diagnostic category [self-defeating personality disorder] are couched in non-sexist language, the behaviors described reflect the cultural conditioning experienced by females, hence labeling as masochistic the social and religious values taught women. Furthermore all the criteria reflect characteristics of women victims of violence. Therefore it is entirely possible that using such a diagnosis . . . will violate the civil rights of women by causing irreparable injury and undue hardship to women and victims of violence (most of whom are women). (Rosewater, 1985, p. 1)

To pathologize behaviors reflecting conformity to societal expectations and exhibited by a substantial majority of women, is clearly problematic. Caplan (1991) exposed the underlying sexism behind this diagnosis by proposing a parallel diagnosis pathologizing conformity to the traditional masculine gender role: the diagnosis of "delusional dominating personality disorder" (or the John Wayne syndrome) is no more scientifically supportable than the self-defeating personality disorder diagnosis. Serious charges about blaming the victim subsequently led to the withdrawal of the diagnosis "Self-defeating Personality Disorder" from the *DSM-IV* (American Psychiatric Association, 1994).

There were serious problems with the "Premenstrual Dysphoria Disorder" as well, among them that the diagnosis is not supported by research, symptoms associated with the premenstrual syndrome are adequately covered in existing diagnoses, and possible psychological and emotional effects of a medical condition experienced by women will be pathologized (Caplan, 1993; Kupers, 1997). However, that diagnosis was retained in the *DSM-IV* (Walsh, 1997). Kupers (1997) phrases her continuing objections to that inclusion in this manner:

> In regard to Late Luteal Phase Dysphoric Disorder, the question was why pathologize the women's natural cycles? Why not pathologize instead men's need to avoid all signs of emotion and dependency while maintaining an obsessively steady pace . . . ?" I coined the term 'pathological arrythmicity' for this disorder in men. . . . (p. 343)

Bias in Treatment

The classic study of bias on the part of mental health practitioners treating women was conducted by Broverman, Broverman, Clarkson, Rosenkrantz, and Vogel (1970). In this study, 79 clinicians were asked to rate the characteristics of mentally healthy adults, mentally healthy women, and mentally healthy men. Clinicians' ratings of the characteristics of mentally healthy men and adults were virtually identical; ratings of "mentally healthy" women were significantly different from the ratings of men, tending toward the stereotypical feminine gender-role traits held by the dominant culture. That is, healthy women, as compared to healthy men and adults, were characterized as being ". . . more submissive, less independent, less adventurous, more easily influenced, less aggressive, less competitive, more excitable in minor issues, having their feelings more easily hurt, being more emotional, more conceited about their appearance, less objective, and disliking math and science" (Broverman et al., 1970, p. 4). The Broverman et al. study has been interpreted to demonstrate a "double-standard" in mental health for women; masculine gender traits are more closely associated with depictions of mental health, yet women are socialized to display "feminine," less "healthy" characteristics, and may be deemed aberrant if they reject the feminine role (Collier, 1982; Sherman, 1980). A replication of the Broverman et al. (1970) research with a larger but similar sample yielded findings consistent with the earlier results; in 1985, males and females were still being described in gender-stereotypical ways (O'Malley & Richardson, 1985). However, O'Malley and Richardson also reported a "loosening" of stereotypes in that clinicians attributed *both* masculine and feminine traits to mentally healthy "adults."

The controversy stimulated by the landmark Broverman et al. (1970) study continues today. Although a number of investigations have yielded results supporting the contention that clinicians hold biased views toward women (e.g., Aslin, 1977; Dremen, 1978), are misinformed about women (e.g., Bingham & House, 1973), and actually respond in biased ways toward women (e.g., Abramowitz, 1977), other studies have failed to find such evidence of differential attitudes or treatment by gender (e.g., Davenport & Reims, 1978; Johnson, 1978). The two primary arguments against the existence of gender bias in counseling can be summarized as follows: (1) Some evidence for bias in attitudes may exist, but this is not evidence that these attitudes have a detrimental effect on women in counseling (e.g., Stricker, 1977); and (2) no empirical evidence of gender bias exists (e.g., Smith, 1980). Stricker (1977) argued that the research providing evidence for a double standard in mental health was itself biased, and the conclusions about such a double standard were based on questionable data, while Smith's (1980) metanalysis of the research literature revealed no demonstrable bias against women, or bias for stereotypical roles for women, on the part of counselors or psychotherapists.

One major problem with studies of gender bias is that, because the Broverman et al. (1970) study is so well-known, the validity of therapists' responses in studies of bias is questionable. It is, therefore, increasingly difficult to disentangle real changes in counselor attitudes toward women from possible experimental demands for social desirability. Further, problems abound in performing methodologically sound investigations in this area. Richardson and Johnson (1984) concluded that there *is* a basis in the empirical literature for claims of gender bias, but they recommended that the nature of such research be modified. Farmer (1982) also concluded that, although weak, there does exist evidence for gender bias in counseling. Other writers document instances of continuing, often subtle, biases against women in traditional forms of therapy (Brown, 1994; Worell & Remer, 1992) in developing arguments for adopting feminist perspectives in all aspects of counseling and therapy, beginning with assessment. Nevertheless, it will undoubtedly be far more productive if researchers focus attention on what *aspects* of counselor gender-role related attitudes and behaviors influence female (and male) clients negatively, rather than continue with the past preoccupation with demonstrating (or disproving) the overall existence of gender bias.

The articles in chapters 12 through 14 cover guidelines for counseling women and many of the newly evolving approaches to working with female clients in "sex-fair" ways. Suggestions for training and ongoing professional development in this area are outlined in chapter 18.

References

Abramowitz, C. V. (1977). Blaming the mother: An experimental investigation of sex-role bias in countertransference. *Psychology of Women Quarterly, 2,* 25–34.

Adding up the victories and defeats: A box score. (1986, November 23). *Los Angeles Times,* Section VI, p. 1.

American Psychiatric Association. (1994). *Diagnostic and statistical manual of mental disorders* (4th Ed.). Washington, DC: Author.

Amparano, J. (1996, August 4). Equal pay act didn't solve problem. *The Arizona Republic,* Section D, pp. 1–2.

Amundsen, K. (1971). *The silenced majority.* Englewood Cliffs, NJ: Prentice-Hall.

Aslin, A. L. (1977). Feminist and community mental health center psychotherapists' expectations of mental health for women. *Sex Roles, 3,* 537–544.

Atkinson, J. W., & Feather, N. T. (Eds.). (1966). *A theory of achievement motivation.* New York: Wiley.

Basoff, E. S., & Glass, G. V. (1982). The relationship between sex roles and mental health: A meta-analysis of twenty-six studies. *The Counseling Psychologist, 10,* 105-112.

Bem, S. L., & Bem, D. J. (1970/1984). Homogenizing the American women: The power of an unconscious ideology. Reprinted in A. M. Jaggar & P. S. Rothenberg (Eds.), *Feminist Frameworks* (2nd ed., pp.10–22). New York: McGraw-Hill (Originally published in 1970).

Bernard, J. (1971). The paradox of the happy marriage. In V. Gornick & B. K. Moran (Eds.), *Women in Sexist Society* (pp. 145–162). New York: New American Library.

Bettelheim, B. (1965). The commitment required of a woman entering a scientific profession in present-day American society. In J. A. Mattfield & C. G. Van Aken (Eds.), *Women and the scientific professions.* Cambridge, MA: M.I.T. Press.

Betz, N. E., & Fitzgerald, L. F. (1993). Individuality and diversity: Theory and research in counseling psychology. *Annual Review of Psychology, 44,* 343–381.

Betz, N. E., & Fitzgerald, L. F. (1987). *The career psychology of women.* New York: Academic Press.

Betz, N. E. (1994). Basic issues and concepts in career counseling for women. In W. B. Walsh & S. H. Osipow (Eds.), *Career counseling for women.* (pp. 1–42). Hillsdale, NJ: Erlbaum.

Bingham, W. C., & House, E. W. (1973). Counselors view women and work: Accuracy of information. *Vocational Guidance Quarterly, 21,* 262–268.

Bird, C. (1971). *Born female.* New York: Pocket Books.

Broverman, I. K., Broverman, D. M., Clarkson, F. E., Rosenkrantz, P. S., & Vogel, S. R. (1970). Sex-role stereotypes and clinical judgments of mental health. *Journal of Consulting and Clinical Psychology, 34,* 1–7.

Brown, L. S. (1994). *Subversive dialogues: Theory in feminist therapy.* New York: Basic Books.

Caplan, P. (1991). Delusional dominating personality disorder (DDPD). *Feminism and Psychology, 1,* 171–174.

Chafetz, J. (1978). *Masculine, feminine, or human?* Itasca, IL: Peacock.

Chesler, P. (1972). *Women and madness.* New York: Avon.

Childe, G. (1971). *What happened in history?* Baltimore: Penguin.

Collier, H. V. (1982). *Counseling Women.* New York: Free Press.

Comas-Diaz, L., & Greene, B. (Ed.). (1994). *Women of color.* New York: Guilford.

Costello, C., & Krimgold, B. K. (Ed.). (1996). *The American Woman, 1996–97.* New York: W. W. Norton.

Courtois, C. A. (1986, April). *The new scholarship on child sexual abuse: Counseling adult survivors.* Paper presented to the Annual Meeting of the American Educational Research Association, San Francisco.

Davenport, J., & Reims, N. (1978). Theoretical orientation and attitudes toward women. *Social Work, 23,* 306–309.

Davis, A. Y. (1981). *Women, race & class.* New York: Vintage Books.

Deckard, B. S. (1983). *The women's movement: Political, socioeconomic, and psychological issues* (3rd ed.). New York: Harper & Row.

Dremen, S. B. (1978). Sex-role stereotyping in mental health standards in Israel. *Journal of Clinical Psychology, 34,* 961–966.

Enns, C. Z. (1996). Counselors and the backlash: "Rape hype" and "false memory syndrome." *Journal of Counseling and Development, 74,* 358–631.

Erickson, E. H. (1968). *Identity, youth, and crisis.* New York: Norton.

Faludi, S. (1991). *Backlash: The undeclared war against American women.* New York: Crown.

Farmer, H. S. (1982). Empirical evidence for sex bias in counseling the weak. *The Counseling Psychologist, 10,* 87–88.

Farmer, H. S., & Backer, T. E. (1977). *New career options for women: A counselor's sourcebook.* New York: Human Science Press.

Fitzgerald, L. F. (1993). The last great open secret: The sexual harassment of women in the workplace and academia. *Federation of Behavioral, Psychological, and Cognitive Sciences.* Washington, DC: Author.

Flexner, E., & Fitzgerald, E. (1996). *Century of struggle: The women's rights movement in the United States.* Cambridge, MA: Belknap Press.

Freeman, J. (Ed.). (1979). *Women: A feminist perspective* (2nd ed.). Palo Alto, CA: Mayfield.

Galinsky, E., & Bond, J. T. (1996). Work and family: The experiences of mothers and fathers in the U.S. labor force. In C. Costello & B.K. Krimgold (Eds.), *The American Woman, 1996–97* (pp. 79–103). New York: W.W. Norton.

Gilbert, L. A. (1992). Gender and counseling psychology: Current knowledge and directions for research and social action. In S. D. Brown & R. W. Lent (Eds.), *Handbook of counseling psychology* (pp. 383–416). New York: Wiley.

Gough, K. (1975). The origin of the family. In R. R. Reither (Ed.), *Toward an anthropology of women.* New York: Monthly Review Press.

Gould, S. J. (1996). *The mismeasure of man* (Rev. ed.). New York: W.W. Norton.

Gove, W. R. (1973). Sex, marital status, and mortality. *American Journal of Sociology, 79,* 45–67.

Gove, W. R. (1980). Mental illness and psychiatric treatment among women. *Psychology of Women Quarterly, 4,* 345–362.

Gove, W. R., & Tudor, J. F. (1973). Adult sex roles and mental illness. *American Journal of Sociology, 78,* 812–835.

Hare-Mustin, R. T. (1983). An appraisal of the relationship between women and psychotherapy: 80 years after the case of Dora. *American Psychologist, 38,* 593–601.

Hawkes, J., & Woolley, L. (1963). *Prehistory and the beginning of civilization.* New York: Harper & Row.

Hays, P. A. (1996). Addressing the complexities of culture and gender in counseling. *Journal of Counseling and Development, 74,* 332–338.

Herz, D. E., & Wootton, B. H. (1996). Women in the workforce: An overview. In C. Costello & B.K. Krimgold (Eds.), *The American Woman, 1996–97* (pp. 44–78). New York: W.W. Norton.

Hewlett, S. A. (1986). *A lesser life: The myth of women's liberation in America.* New York: William Morrow.

Higher Education and National Affairs. (1986). *Women academics still experience discrimination.* Washington, DC: American Council on Education.

Howe, L. K. (1977). *Pink collar workers.* New York: Avon.

Hunter College Women's Studies Collective. (1983). *Women's realities, women's choices: An introduction to women's studies.* New York: Oxford University Press.

Hunter, J. (1976). Images of women. *Journal of Social Issues, 32,* 7–17.

Hyde, J. S. (1997). Gender difference in math performance. In M.R. Walsh (Ed.), *Women, men, and gender: Ongoing debates* (pp. 283–287). New Haven, CT: Yale University Press.

Johnson, M. (1978). Influence of counselor gender on reactivity to clients. *Journal of Counseling Psychology, 25,* 359–365.

Johnson, M. (1980). Mental illness and psychiatric treatment among women: A response. *Psychology of Women Quarterly, 4,* 363–371.

Kahn-Hut, R., Daniels, A. K., & Colvard, R. (1982). *Women and work: Problems and perspectives.* New York: Oxford University Press.

Koss, M. P., Gidycz, C. A., & Wisniewski, N. (1987). The scope of rape: Incidence and prevalence of sexual aggression and victimization in a national sample of higher education students. *Journal of Consulting and Clinical Psychology, 55,* 162–170.

Kupers, T. A. (1997). The politics of psychiatry: Gender and sexual preference in DSM-IV. In M. R. Walsh (Ed.), *Women, men, and gender: Ongoing debates* (pp. 340–347). New Haven, CT: Yale University Press.

Leavitt, R. R. (1971). Women in other cultures. In V. Gornick & B. K. Morgan (Eds.), *Woman in Sexist Society* (pp. 393–427). New York: New American Library.

Martin, D. (1976). *Battered wives.* New York: Pocket Books.

Martin, M. K., & Voorhies, B. (1975). *Female of the Species.* New York: Columbia University Press.

McClelland, D. C., Atkinson, J. W., Clark, R. A., & Lowell, E. L. (1953). *The achievement motive.* New York: Appleton-Century-Crofts.

Mead, M. (1974). On Freud's view of female psychology. In J. Strouse, (Ed.), *Women and analysis.* New York: Grossman.

Morrison, A. M., & Glinow, M. A. (1990). Women and minorities in management. *American Psychologist, 45,* 200–208.

Muehlenhard, C. L., Highby, B. J., Phelps, J. L., & Sympson, S. C. (1997). Rape statistics are not exaggerated (pp. 243–246). In M.R. Walsh (Ed.), *Women, men, and gender: Ongoing debates* New Haven, CT: Yale University Press.

National Science Foundation. (1990). *Women and minorities in science and engineering.* Washington, DC: Author.

Nelson, M. (1979). Why witches were women. In J. Freeman (Ed.), *Women: A feminist perspective* (2nd ed., pp. 451–468). Palo Alto, CA: Mayfield.

Nielsen, J. (1978). *Sex in society: Perspectives on stratification.* Belmont, CA: Wadsworth.

O'Malley, K. M., & Richardson, S. (1985). Sex bias in counseling: Have things changed? *Journal of Counseling and Development, 63,* 294–299.

Pearce, D. (1979). Women, work and welfare: The feminization of poverty. In K. W. Feinstein (Ed.), *Working women and families* (pp. 103–124). Beverly Hills, CA: Sage.

Richardson, M. A., & Johnson, M. (1984). Counseling women. In S. D. Brown & R. W. Lent (Eds.), *Handbook of Counseling Psychology* (pp. 832–877). New York: Wiley.

Rohrbaugh, J. B. (1979). *Women: Psychology's puzzle.* New York: Basic Books.

Rosewater, L. B. (1985). *A critical statement on the proposed diagnosis of masochistic personality disorder.* Unpublished manuscript.

Schaffer, K. F. (1981). *Sex roles and human behavior.* Cambridge, Mass.: Winthrop.

Schulenburg, J. T. (1979). Clio's European daughters: Myopic modes of perception. In J. A. Sherman & E. T. Beck (Eds.), *The prism of sex: Essays in the sociology of knowledge* (pp. 33–54). Madison, Wis.: University of Wisconsin Press.

Sherif, C. W. (1979). Bias in psychology. In J. A. Sherman & E. T. Beck (Eds.), *The prism of sex* (pp. 93–133). Madison, Wis.: University of Wisconsin Press.

Sherman, J. A. (1980). Therapist attitudes and sex-role stereotyping. In A. M. Brodsky & R. Hare-Mustin (Eds.), *Women and psychotherapy* (pp. 35–66). New York: Guilford.

Shields, S. (1975). Functionalism, Darwinism, and the psychology of women: A study in social myth. *American Psychologist, 30,* 739–754.

Smith, M. L. (1980). Sex bias in counseling. *Psychological Bulletin, 87,* 392–407.

Stricker, G. (1977). Implications of research for psychotherapeutic treatment of women. *American Psychologist, 32,* 14–22.

U.S. Women's Bureau. (1996, September). Fact sheet on women workers (No. 96-2). Washington, DC: U.S. Department of Labor.

Unger, R. K. (1979). Toward a redefinition of sex and gender. *American Psychologist, 34,* 1085–1094.

Walker, L. E. (1979). *The battered woman.* New York: Harper & Row.

Walsh, M. R. (Ed.) (1997). *Women, men, and gender: Ongoing debates.* New Haven, CT: Yale University Press

Weisstein, N. (1971). Psychology constructs the female, or the fantasy life of the male psychologist. In V. Gornick & B. K. Moran (Eds.), *Woman in sexist society* (pp. 207–224). New York: New American Library.

Weitzman, L. J. (1985). *The divorce revolution: The unexpected social and economic consequences for women and children in America*. New York: The Free Press.

Williams, J. H. (1983). *Psychology of women* (2nd ed.). New York: Norton.

Woolf, V. (1957). *A room of one's own*. New York: Harcourt, Brace Jovanovich. (Original work published 1929).

Worell, J., & Remer, P. (1992). *Feminist perspectives in therapy: An empowerment model for women*. New York: Wiley.

5
Oppression of Gay Men and Lesbian Women: Past and Present

Past Discrimination
Society's Treatment of Gays

> Attitudes toward gay people have varied considerably throughout the history of Western culture from the ancient civilizations of Greece and Rome, where homoeroticism was considered quite unremarkable, to the intolerance and persecution characteristic of both the Middle Ages and the Twentieth century. Regardless of opposition or tolerance, some group of people in every age turns out to be gay, the greatest difference between periods is not the proportion of the population that is gay, but in the way sexual preference is expressed. (Moses & Hawkins, 1982, p. 4)

Gay people, even more so than women, have been invisible in history. Most of what we know about homosexuality and attitudes toward homosexuality is derived from religious and legal sanctions against homosexual behavior (Bullough, 1976). We know very little, for example, about the everyday experience of gay people in different historical periods, and what evidence exists largely concerns gay men (Bullough, 1979). The attitudes of society, as illustrated in the preceding quote, have ranged the gamut from tolerance to harsh oppression; the norm in Western societies has been hostility and condemnation.

Gay people in the past (and, to a great degree, in the present) have kept their sexual orientation a secret. When gay people have surfaced in the historical record, it is often because of exposure and persecution, resulting in a distortion of the historical picture. For example, Oscar Wilde is one of the few "known" gay men in nineteenth century England because of his prosecution and imprisonment as a result of his liaison with Lord Alfred Douglas (Bullough, 1979). His name and lifestyle have been equated with homosexuality, yet his life is undoubtedly unrepresentative. In this chapter, therefore, we are largely confined to a discussion of broad societal attitudes because of the furtive nature of gay life and the relative neglect and active avoidance of the topic by past historians.

Although gay people have always been present as a significant minority and at certain times homosexual behavior has been viewed with tolerance or even as an acceptable developmental stage for men, at no time has exclusive homosexuality been acceptable for the majority of the population. Societal views towards gay people can be roughly categorized in terms of views of homosexual behavior as tolerable, as sin, as crime, and as sickness. The first three views will be addressed in this section, the last in the section on psychology's attitudes toward homosexuality.

Tolerant Attitudes Toward Homosexuality

Before detailing the overwhelmingly negative societal attitudes toward gay people, we will focus on some examples of societal views of homosexuality as a normal variant of sexual behavior. Plato was one of the first writers to propose an explanation of the origins of homosexuality. In his *Symposium*, Plato explained that people originally had four arms and four legs until the gods divided these individuals into two. The "double people" contained all male, all female, or both male and female elements, and sexual orientation could be explained in terms of "trying to find one's other half" (Bullough, 1976). Plato's attitudes are more a reflection than a cause of the tolerant attitudes of the Ancient Greeks toward gay people.

In classical Greek Society, homosexual or "homoerotic" attachments were viewed as a normal and acceptable stage of development, especially for men.

> Many Greeks represented gay love as the only form of eroticism which could be lasting, pure, and truly spiritual. The origin of the concept "Platonic Love" (which postdates Plato by centuries) was not Plato's belief that sex should be absent from gay affairs but his conviction that only love between persons of the same gender could transcend sex. The Attic lawgiver Solon considered homosexual eroticism too lofty for slaves and prohibited it to them. In the idealistic world of the Hellenistic romances, gay people figured prominently as star-crossed lovers whose passions were no less enduring or spiritual than those of their non-gay friends . . . Even among primitive peoples some connection is often assumed between spirituality or mysticism and homosexuality. Only in comparatively recent times have homosexual feelings came to be associated with moral looseness. (Boswell, 1980, p. 27)

Women in Ancient Greek society were not encouraged as men were to have homoerotic attachments; women of all classes led severely restricted lives. Very little solid evidence exists about female homosexuality. The scraps of information that survive about gay women take the form of the writings of Sappho, a sixth century B.C. poet from the Greek island of Lesbos (thus the term *lesbian* for gay women and *sapphic* as a description of love between women). Sappho was the head of a school for girls on Lesbos, and her poetry clearly praises love between women (Bullough, 1979). Bullough (1979) points out the fact that Sappho was married and describes the parallel to the lives of many women today who do not "come out" as gay until sometime after their marriage. One of the reasons for the paucity of information about Sappho appears to be the purposeful destruction of most of her poetry later, in the Christian era, because of the antigay attitudes of the Christian Church (Bullough, 1976).

The neglect of the topic of homosexuality throughout history, and especially the systematic erasure of evidence (e.g., Sappho's poems) about gay people's lives or positive attitudes toward homosexuality, makes the discussion of tolerant attitudes difficult. However, some evidence does exist from cross-cultural research performed on supposedly "inferior" people that helps to illuminate the topic. Discussions of the sexual customs of "heathens" or "primitive peoples" are very much more candid than Western observers' descriptions of their own cultures (Bullough, 1979).

Ford and Beach (1951) published a comprehensive survey of sexual activities across cultures and concluded that no absolute norms for sexual behavior could be identified; no one cultures' attitudes towards homosexuality can be viewed as representative. Even though their data probably suffered from underreporting of homosexual activity, they found that, of the societies where data existed about attitude toward homosexuality, fully 64 percent viewed it as normal, at least for some portion of the population (Ford & Beach, 1951). Some Native American subcultures, for example, fostered positive or tolerant attitudes towards gay men and lesbian women (Allen, 1989). "Many American Indian tribes had institutionalized homosexuality, at least of the male variety, into the role of the *berdache* (the male woman), while other primitive groups have chosen their Shamans from them" (Bullough, 1979, p. 2).

Finally, some idea can be gained of the pervasiveness of homosexual behavior across time and societies, of the neglect and active avoidance of the subject by mainstream historians, and of the contributions made by gay men and lesbian women to society, by examining the lives of eminent individuals in Western Civilization who were gay. Because the lives of prominent politicians, royalty, soldiers, artists, and writers have been open to a scrutiny not focused on the "average" person, eminent gay men and women are hardly representative. Their exposure by recent historical writings, however, allows gay men and lesbian women today to gain a sense of their own history that has previously been unavailable to them (Duberman, Vicinus, & Chauncey, 1989).

Rowse's (1977) book, *Homosexuals in history,* describes in some detail the lives of famous gay male artists, among them Leonardo da Vinci and Michelangelo; gay kings and other royalty, e.g., Richard the Lion Heart, Henri III of France, James I of England, Frederick the Great, and Ludwig II of

Bavaria; military commanders, such as Alexander the Great and Julius Caesar are also mentioned; scientists, such as Erasmus and Francis Bacon; musicians, e.g., Tchaikovsky; and other eminent gay men, e.g., T. E. Lawrence and John Maynard Keynes. Writers proliferate among known gay men and lesbian women, largely because their written work often contains references to or illuminates their personal lives. The philosophers George Santayana and Ludwig Wittgenstein, and the writers Cocteau, Oscar Wilde, Marcel Proust, Andre Gide, Lytton Strachey, E. M. Forster, Walt Whitman, Hart Crane, Herman Melville, and W. H. Auden were all gay (Bullough, 1979; Rowse, 1977). Prominent lesbian women in history are harder to identify and largely consist of writers and poets, for example, Virginia Woolfe, Collette, Elizabeth Bowen, Vita Sackville-West, Gertrude Stein and Alice B. Toklas, Willa Cather, and May Sarton (Foster, 1956; Rule 1975). One of the few examples in the older historical record of the daily existence of two lesbian women can be obtained from the intriguing story of "The Ladies of Llangollen," two Irish noble women who lived in Wales in the eighteenth century (Martin & Lyon, 1972).

Homosexuality as Sin

Some writers regard the Judeo-Christian religious tradition as the most significant force in determining Western attitudes toward gay people (Bullough, 1979). "The church bears heavy responsibility for our present attitudes toward sex deviates and their problems, and for the severe penalties with which the law has requited them for their offenses" (Wysor, 1974, p. 65). Boswell (1980), however, refutes this stance and argues persuasively that religious beliefs merely served to justify the oppression and persecution of groups, especially gays, who are held in contempt because of personal hostility and prejudice. Regardless of the exact role, cause, or justification of intolerance, Western religious views are an important factor to explore in any discussion of gays in history.

The interpretation of scriptural references to homosexuality has been a source of ongoing controversy (Baird & Baird, 1995). Wysor (1974) noted, from extensive research, that

> Exactly seven references in the entire Bible (refer) to what is interpreted by some as activity involving homosexuality. Six of these seem to refer to such activity among men, and one appears to refer to women. However, these have been quite sufficient to help generate over two thousand years of condemnation and judgment against persons who express their emotional and sexual natures man to man or woman to woman. (pp. 22–23)

The earliest reference in the Bible specifically condemning homosexuality (although not using the word) can be found in Leviticus: "Thou shalt not lie with mankind, as with womankind: it is an abomination" (quoted in Bullough, 1979, p. 19). However, it is the story of Sodom that has had the greatest influence on attitudes towards gays. The term *sodomy,* referring to anal intercourse, was derived from this biblical passage.

The destruction of Sodom and Gomorrah is commonly interpreted as resulting from the sin of homosexuality on the part of the townspeople, yet many scholars have pointed out that

> None of the biblical condemnations of homosexuality refer to Sodom, nor, more important, do any of the biblical references to Sodom explain just exactly what crimes the residents were guilty of having committed. In fact, when the Bible does spell out the sins for which Sodom (and Gomorrah, Admah, and Zeboin) were destroyed, they are listed as pride, unwillingness to aid the poor and needy, haughtiness, and the doing of abominable things, all actions and attitudes which many other biblical peoples and cities demonstrated. Though the doing of abominable things might refer to sexual activities, their greatest sin was clearly pride, contentment, and ignoring the needy, none of which was unforgivable. (Bullough, 1979, pp. 20–21)

Bailey (1955) argued that the antihomosexual aspects of the story of Sodom were added much later than the original writing, probably as part of an anti-Greek campaign by the Jews in Palestine (homosexuality being tolerated and even adulated in Greek culture). Evidence from early Talmudic writings indicates that the Jews, although hostile to homosexuality, were by no means actively and virulently antihomosexual (Bullough, 1979). Of course, there is no mention in any of the Christian scriptures of Christ saying anything about homosexuality (Bullough, 1979).

Nonetheless, various Christian theologians were virulently antigay, among them St. Paul, St. Augustine, and St. Thomas Aquinas. In the medieval period, it was Aquinas who originally proposed a separate category of "sins against nature," figuring homosexuality prominently in a list of such sins which also included bestiality, intercourse in an unnatural position, and masturbation (Bullough, 1979). Later, during the Reformation, Martin Luther and other Protestant theologians, while disagreeing with much of Catholic doctrine, continued the arguments of the early Church fathers against homosexuality (Bullough, 1979). Many of the same arguments, based on dubious scriptural interpretation, can still be heard today (e.g., Jones, 1995).

Boswell (1980), the author of the most complete scholarly analysis of religious views on homosexuality, summarized his views on the matter of scriptural justification of antigay sentiment:

> In the particular case at issue, the belief that the hostility of the Christian Scriptures to homosexuality caused Western society to turn against it should not require any elaborate refutation. The very same books which are thought to condemn homosexual acts condemn hypocrisy in the most strident terms, and on greater authority; and yet Western society did not create any social taboos against hypocrisy, did not claim hypocrites were 'unnatural,' did not segregate them into

an oppressed minority, did not enact laws punishing their sin with castration or death. No Christian State, in fact, passed laws against hypocrisy per se, despite its continual and explicit condemnation by Jesus and the church. In the very same list which has been claimed to exclude from the Kingdom of heaven those guilty of homosexual practices, the greedy are also excluded. And yet no medieval states burned the greedy at the stake. (p. 27)

Reverend Troy Perry, a gay activist, made a thought-provoking response to those who base anti-gay sentiments on the Bible. He felt that such persons:

. . . are exercising considerable judgment over which Biblical teachings to accept and which to disregard. Perry often refers to Leviticus, where the recommendation is made that two men who engage in a homosexual act should be stoned. He observes that in the same book of the Bible, it is said to be wrong for a woman to wear a scarlet dress or for anyone to eat shrimp. And yet people who wear scarlet and eat shrimp continue to cite Leviticus as their authority for condemning homosexuality. (Weinberg, 1972, p. 10)

Many other examples of selective reading of the scriptures to support personal attitudes are readily available.

Homosexuality as Crime

Religious views influenced legal codes throughout history, but laws against gays have also, in turn, influenced attitudes toward homosexuality. Modern American and European legal systems have been profoundly influenced by early Roman laws, especially the laws of Christian Rome (Bullough, 1979).

Bullough (1979) identifies the key Roman law about homosexuality affecting succeeding generations, and dating from about A.D. 390, as the law prescribing the death penalty for anal intercourse. The intention of this rarely enforced law was evidently to curb male prostitution. Later, this mandate became codified in the sixth-century collection of Roman laws sponsored by the Emperor Justinian, and the *corpus juris civilis* served as the foundation for the laws of the Christian Church (canon law), as well as European and English civil law (Bullough, 1979). A curious twist to the original condemnation of homosexuality was added by Justinian in the sixth century A.D., ". . . calling for repentance and confession by homosexuals, warning that God would condemn the sinner, and adding if they did not repent, society as a whole would be punished" (Bullough, 1979, p. 32). Such a warning naturally resulted in the scapegoating of gays; plagues, famines, and other disasters were commonly attributed to the "sin" of homosexuality, and gay people were sought out, castrated, and put to death in times of crisis.

Interestingly, the tendency to scapegoat gays is apparent throughout the historical record, from Ancient Roman times to today, and warrants a brief digression into the relationship between laws and social repression. Just as the emancipation of women was proposed as a cause for the decline and fall of

Rome, so too was homosexuality, despite the fact that homosexual behavior was outlawed and severely punished during Roman times.

> The civilization of the Roman Empire was vitiated by homosexuality from its earliest days. A question, uncomfortable to our contemporary lax moralists, may be raised: Is not the common practice of homosexuality a fundamental debilitating factor in any civilization where it is extensively practiced, as it is a wasting spiritual disease in the individual? (Cantor, 1963 quoted in Bullough, 1979, p. 89)

In the medieval period, accusations of witchcraft were often associated with claims of homosexual activity, and heretics were also usually charged with sodomy (Bullough, 1979). The term *faggot,* an epithet still employed for gay men, is derived from the term *fagot,* a bundle of twigs, sticks, or branches bound together; men accused of same-sex sexual activity were often used as kindling for burning witches (Grahn, 1984).

> Stigmatizing one's enemies with charges of homosexuality is a standard practice, and some in the past have raised it to great art. In his *Divine Comedy,* Dante describes many of the inhabitants of Hell as homosexual, most of them people who happened to be his political opponents. (Bullough, 1979, p. 92)

The Knights Templar, a powerful and wealthy organization in France in the fourteenth century, were destroyed primarily through accusations of homosexuality. This practice continued and more recently was evidenced in Nazi Germany and in the McCarthy era Red-baiting in the 1950s in this country (Bullough, 1979). In Nazi Germany, hundreds of thousands of homosexuals or men accused of homosexuality were incarcerated in the concentration camps and brutalized with special ferocity. Many of these homosexuals remained in jail after the war because West Germany did not eliminate antigay laws from the books until 1969 (Plant, 1986). Senator Joe McCarthy, in 1950, declared homosexuality as much of an issue as Communism, and initiated a campaign to get 3,500 "sex perverts" out of jobs in the federal government (Bullough, 1979).

The tradition of antihomosexual laws continued from Roman through medieval times in the form of legal prescriptions against "sodomy" and "crimes against nature." Although homosexual activity was one of the activities clearly indicted, the laws themselves were vague. Sodomy referred to a variety of sexual activities, including any form of heterosexual intercourse other than the position of a woman on her back. These ambiguities of language produce problems in deciphering the historical record. For example, Havelock Ellis, an early sex researcher, equated "buggery" and "sodomy" when he happened upon these terms. "Buggery" is currently employed as a derogatory term for anal intercourse, yet the word originally applied to members of a heretical group in the late medieval period who were often burnt at the stake for their heresy, not for homosexual activity (Bullough, 1979). Only later were the terms *buggery* and *sodomy* equated.

In the sixteenth century at the height of the Reformation and the resulting conflicts between Protestants and Catholics, negative attitudes about sexual activity in general, and homosexuality in particular, again resulted in sanctions appearing in the civil laws. Various cases of legal action against homosexual behavior appeared in England, but often antigay hostility was not the most prominent factor. For example, in the reign of Charles the First, the Earl of Castlehaven was charged with sodomy and rape and subsequently executed. The Earl was Catholic and anti-Catholic hostility on the part of the jurors was proposed as a more important reason for his conviction than the sodomy charges (Bullough, 1979).

The issue of homosexuality per se was revived in the seventeenth century. English legal commentators, for example, spent much time justifying antigay laws, usually drawing on biblical sources to support their views.

> Buggery is a detestable and abominable sin, amongst Christians not to be named, committed by carnal knowledge against the ordinance of the Creator, and order of nature, by mankind with mankind, or with brute beast, or by womankind with brute beast. (Bullough, 1979, p. 35)

This passage demonstrates the continuing view of homosexual behavior as a "crime against nature," the classification of homosexual behavior with various forms of "unnatural" heterosexual behavior, and also highlights the relative neglect of female homosexuality by the law. Women were, by definition, not considered capable of "buggery," except via anal intercourse with a man. The origins of this attitude seem to be the biblical injunction against a man "spilling his seed" except to procreate. Male semen, as the key to conception, was of vital importance; consequently, the sin was viewed as relatively minor when women engaged in lesbian activity (Bullough, 1979). Undoubtedly the low regard in which women were held also accounts for the lack of attention to lesbian activity (Deckard, 1983).

In France, with the introduction of the Napoleonic code came the view that any consenting sexual activity by adults in private was outside the purview of the law (Bullough, 1979). "Deviant sexual acts were treated as a crime only when they implied an outrage on public decency, when there was violence or absence of consent, or when one of the parties was under age or not regarded as able to give valid consent for one reason or another" (Bullough, 1979, p. 37). Despite the legal changes, public opinion in France and all of Europe remained hostile to gays. The Napoleonic code was adopted in whole or in part by many countries in Europe and in some Latin American countries. The one notable exception was Germany, long an active antagonist of France. Germany, under Prussian leadership in the nineteenth century, maintained the harsh Prussian laws against homosexuality; the death penalty was kept on the books until the twentieth century. By the late nineteenth century, only England and Germany retained their repressive laws against homosexual behavior, although the legal changes elsewhere in Europe often did not reduce the oppression experienced by gays.

In every country, there were some proponents of more liberal attitudes toward homosexuality. In England, for example, Jeremy Bentham, the founder of English utilitarianism, wrote extensively in the 1800s against regarding any kind of sexual activity as evil in and of itself and outlined guidelines for judging the morality of sexual activity. His central thesis was that public opinion should not be used as the final arbiter of sexual conduct, and he argued persuasively for changing the law (Bullough, 1979). Unfortunately, his writings were never published, probably due to the attitudes of the time.

In the late 1800s in England, Parliament hurriedly passed a series of laws originally designed to protect children from sexual abuse and prostitution. The wording of these laws inadvertently resulted in the prohibition of any sexual act between adult males, even if consenting and taking place in private. Oscar Wilde, as mentioned previously, was the first victim of this new act. Friedreich Krupp (1851–1902), the scion of the powerful armaments firm in Germany, also suffered because of his exposure as a homosexual at about the same time. Because accusations of sodomy were so difficult to prove, many gay men escaped legal prosecution. As in the case of Krupp, however, who committed suicide because of the scandal, many people were ruined by the accusation alone (Bullough, 1979).

In the United States, actual convictions for sodomy were rare but not unknown. Laws in the United States banning homosexual activity were largely instituted on the state or local level. In 1610, for example, the Virginia Colony passed the earliest sodomy law. The first recorded conviction for homosexual activities in the colonies occurred in 1637 in Plymouth, Massachusetts; the first execution for sodomy occurred several years later (Bullough, 1979; National Museum & Archive of Lesbian & Gay History, 1996). State courts often had difficulties defining the exact meaning of "crimes against nature." For example, the Texas courts in the 1860s judged that sodomy could not be punishable until it was defined. Thereafter, numerous court decisions in Texas and in other states were focused on identifying the various definitions of punishable crimes under the sodomy laws and eventually included oral intercourse and heterosexual and homosexual anal intercourse as crimes. Iowa only explicitly introduced sodomy as a crime in 1897; California finally passed laws clarifying what was meant by "crimes against nature" in 1915, including fellatio and cunnilingus, as well as anal intercourse (Bullough, 1979). California clearly prohibited lesbian activity as well as gay male activity but included heterosexual oral-genital contacts as well. These types of laws remained on the books in California into the 1970s and can still be found in other states in the 1990s.

Psychology's Treatment of Gay People

Thomas Szasz pointed out that ". . . what was defined as sin in the moral order became sickness in the evolution of the medical model and both definitions have equally destructive effects" (1979, quoted in Woodman & Lenna, 1980, p. 3). Essentially, the fields of psychology and psychiatry merely translated religious attitudes about homosexuality into medical terms, and these negative attitudes have long biased the "scientific" investigation of gay men and women.

Studies of Sexual "Degenerates"

The earliest social scientific studies of gay people were conducted by sociologists studying criminal behavior and "degeneracy." Many of the sociological writings of the nineteenth century attempted to explain the causes of homosexuality or, as it is sometimes still called, "sexual deviance," in an attempt to discern whether it was "curable" (Bullough, 1976; 1979).

> Most of the early students of sexual behavior believed that homoerotic behavior and other "perversions of nature" were biological in origin, stemming from such things as degeneration of genes, abnormal or incomplete embryonic development, incomplete social evolution, and disorders of the brain or sex glands or both. In order to determine what had gone wrong with these people and to be able to identify possible degenerates, there were a number of attempts to isolate their distinctive features. (Moses & Hawkins, 1982, p. 7)

Attempts to distinguish sexual deviates from "normal" people included a wide variety of what now seem amusing tests, including skull measurement and examination of distribution patterns of body hair (Moses & Hawkins, 1982). A sexual degenerate was seen, in the popular evolutionary terms of the time, as a "throw-back"—"degeneracy was a reversal of progressive evolution . . . a sexual degenerate was thus a primitive, animal-like person who might do anything" (Bullough, 1979, p. 9).

Some challenges to the prevailing views did appear. Karl Ulrichs, a gay man himself, argued that homosexual urges were inborn and therefore "natural" and posited a pattern of development for gay people whereby "inverts" as he called them (he created the term as a positive label for gays) had the physical features of one sex but were born with the sexual instincts of the other sex. He felt that the development of a "third sex" resulted in an "inversion" of sexual attraction for gay people but that gays were not "degenerates" as a result (Bullough, 1979).

Early Sex Researchers

The most important of the early social scientific and medical studies of gay people were conducted by Richard von Krafft-Ebing in the late nineteenth century (Bullough, 1979). Krafft-Ebing combined several prevailing views on "sexual inversion" and collected over 200 case studies in his famous

Psychopathia Sexualis of "abnormal" or "pathological" individuals to support his theses. He claimed that ". . . frequent abuses of the sexual organs (masturbation) or . . . an inherited abnormal constitution of the nervous system" (Bullough, 1979, p. 11) produced a perversion of the sexual instinct and "unnatural practices," such as homosexuality. His views on homosexuality were directly related to his religious view that the purpose of sex was reproduction; therefore, any other type of sexual activity was an "unnatural practice" (Bullough, 1979). Interestingly, the term *homo-sexuality* was first introduced to an English audience by one of Krafft-Ebing's translators, Charles Gilbert Chaddock (Halperin, 1989).

> Sexual inversion, the term used most commonly in the nineteenth century, did not denote the same conceptual phenomenon as homosexuality. "Sexual inversion" referred to a broad range of deviant gender behavior, of which homosexual desire was only a logical but indistinct aspect, while "homosexuality" focused on the narrower issue of sexual object choice. (Chauncey, 1982, quoted in Halperin, 1989, p. 38)

Havelock Ellis, the other prominent sex researcher of the period, worked from a premise very different from Krafft-Ebing's. Ellis, considered the forerunner of modern sex researchers, took a sympathetic and descriptive stance in relation to his subject. Ellis regarded homosexual behavior as a part of a spectrum of sexual activity and, although not a defender of gay people, he was a sex reformer who advocated repealing laws banning sexual activity between consenting adults in private (Bullough, 1979). Various other lesser-known sexologists of the nineteenth century also promoted the view that homosexuality was not a perversion, including John Addington Symonds and Magnus Hirschfeld (Bullough, 1979).

Freud and His Followers

Unlike his biased attitudes towards women and his subsequent negative impact on the psychology of women, Freud's views on homosexuality were fairly tolerant, and he had a mixed influence on attitudes toward gay people. Freud felt that homosexual behavior was a normal aspect of development, although he also thought that most people moved beyond it to heterosexuality in adulthood (Bullough, 1979). A letter he wrote to a distressed mother of a gay son illustrates his views:

> Homosexuality is assuredly no advantage, but it is nothing to be ashamed of, no vice, no degradation, it cannot be classified as an illness; we consider it to be a variation of the sexual function produced by certain arrest of sexual development. (Quoted in Moses & Hawkins, 1982, p. 8)

Freud demonstrated this same tolerance towards other variants of sexual behavior, but he actually paid little attention to homosexuality in his writings (Bullough, 1979).

It was Freud's followers who developed his preliminary ideas on the environmental rather than biological causes of variant sexual behavior which ultimately had a harmful effect on gays. The implication of the belief that gayness is environmentally caused and an immature stage of adult development led inevitably to attempts on the part of analytically trained psychiatrists and psychologists to "cure" gay people. The dynamic view, focused mostly on gay men, was that homosexuality was

> . . . a flight from incest. In the absence of a father, or in the presence of a weak one, a boy child who fell in love with his mother and sought to become her lover repressed his desire most effectively by suppressing sexual feeling toward all women. . . . The boy, suppressing his desires for the father, sought to be like the woman who accepted his father, but, unable to reconcile the incestuous sin of a father love, sought the father in other roles. (Bullough, 1979, pp. 13–14)

The psychoanalytic approach toward gays, promoted more by his followers than by Freud, has resulted in psychology's focus on curing rather than understanding gay women and men. Gay men and lesbian women were thus viewed, by different writers, as neurotic, mentally ill, ". . . egocentric, . . . lonely, unhappy, tormented, alienated, sadistic, masochistic, empty, bored, repressed, and neurotic" (Moses & Hawkins, 1982, p. 8).

Weinberg and Williams (1974), in their study of research on homosexuality, have pointed out the negative ramifications of the psychoanalytic case study approach to research on homosexuality. First, they criticized the psychoanalytic research as biased. Homosexual behavior was presumed from the start to be immature and productive of maladjustment, an assumption which was not subjected to empirical tests, at least by the psychoanalytically oriented psychiatrists and psychologists. Because pathology was presumed, only its possible causes were investigated. Second, the gay people who have been studied within this research tradition have been patients who cannot be assumed to be representative of all gays any more than nongay psychiatric patients can be presumed to be representative of all nongays. Finally, Weinberg and Williams (1974) criticized the literature on homosexuality as culture bound. As we have previously seen, cross-cultural studies cast grave doubt on the assumptions made about the pathology of homosexual behavior (Ford & Beach, 1951). Maladjustment among gay people is more likely caused by society's reactions to them than by inherent pathology. It was not until the Kinsey Studies (Kinsey, Pomeroy, & Martin, 1948; Kinsey, Pomeroy, Martin, & Gebhard, 1953) that homosexual behavior was examined from a descriptive viewpoint and more representative, nonclinical samples of gay people were obtained.

Heterosexuals vs. Homosexuals

When researchers within psychology and psychiatry finally approached the issue of *whether* gay people differed from nongay people on measures of pathology (rather than *presuming* pathology), interesting results emerged. Research findings have often been directly influenced by the preexisting assumptions of the investigators.

Bieber et al. (1962), for example, in a psychoanalytic study of gay men, found that a "close-binding intimate mother" was much more common for gay than nongay men. This retrospective case study is, of course, open to methodological critique. More important, however, are the criticisms of the conclusions derived from the data of Bieber et al. Because gay men were found to have come from homes differing in child-rearing practices, the assumption of the pathology of gay men was viewed as supported. Davison (1977), however, noted that ". . . one cannot attach a pathogenic label to a pattern of child-rearing unless one *a priori* labels the adult behavior pattern as pathological" (p. 198). This tautological thinking on the part of the researchers, that is, presuming pathology, looking for differences in early life experiences, and then using those demonstrated differences to support the original theory of pathology, is commonplace within the research literature on homosexual behavior.

Contrary to the above example, some psychologists conducted research on gay people from a nonpathological perspective, and their research has yielded results opposite of the views of the psychoanalysts. Evelyn Hooker (1957), in a landmark study, found no differences in mental health between gays and nongays. Hammersmith and Weinberg (1973) found positive correlations between an acceptance of a gay identity and mental health, while Weinberg (1970), Evans (1970), and Dean and Richardson (1964) also found no evidence of pathology on the part of gay men as compared to nongay men.

Current Discrimination

The long-standing historical pattern of social, legal, medical, psychological, and religious discrimination against gay people continues in various forms to this day. Many Americans still hold negative, homophobic attitudes toward gay people (Moses & Hawkins, 1982; National Museum & Archive of Lesbian & Gay History, 1996). Internalized homophobia remains with us, too. Nonetheless, research strongly suggests that the psychological problems experienced by gay people are profoundly influenced by the hostile and derogatory societal attitudes and the internalization of those homophobic attitudes Dworkin & Gutierrez, 1992).

Only relatively recently have social scientists moved from studying the presumed pathology of gay men and lesbian women and begun focusing on the correlates and precursors of homophobia in an attempt to understand the problems of gay people. Compared to those holding more favorable attitudes, people expressing negative attitudes toward gays generally (a) have had little personal contact with lesbians or gay men; (b) are less likely to have had any homosexual contact or label themselves as gay; (c) are more likely to see their peers as holding homophobic attitudes; (d) are more likely to live in areas of the country where homophobia flourishes, especially the Midwest and South, and rural areas and small towns; (e) are older and less educated; (f) are more likely to subscribe to a conservative religious ideology; (g) hold more restrictive views about gender roles; (h) have more negative views about sexuality in general; and (i) are more authoritarian (Herek, 1984; Melton, 1989).

In 1986, Herek reported that surveys showed that only 25 to 30 percent of Americans claimed to know a lesbian woman or gay man. A more recent *U.S. News & World Report* poll revised that figure upwards: 53 percent of respondents reported that they "Personally know someone who is gay and this familiarity makes them think more favorably about equal rights" (National Museum & Archive of Lesbian and Gay History, 1996, p. 104). Of course, given the large percentage of gay people in the population, it is safe to assume that *everyone* knows at least one or more gay people; the 53 percent figure undoubtedly represents those who are familiar with an *openly* gay man or woman. Further, in most surveys, the majority of respondents who knowingly have had contact with a gay person have positive attitudes about gays as a result of their contact (Herek, 1986; National Museum & Archive of Lesbian and Gay History, 1996). Conversely, in the *U.S. News & World Report* study, the 46 percent of respondents who did not know any gay people also opposed gay rights (National Museum & Archive of Lesbian and Gay History, 1996). Antigay sentiment is clearly based, to a large degree, on unfounded assumptions and untested stereotypes.

Homophobic individuals are more likely to hold racist and sexist attitudes, underscoring the common sources of all forms of oppression (Dunbar, Brown, & Amoroso, 1973). Some evidence also suggests that nongay men are more homophobic than nongay women (Morin & Garfinkle, 1978). It is unclear whether the issue has to do with fear of same-sex homosexuality (i.e., most research asks respondents for attitudes about homosexuality in general, which is usually taken as meaning gay males), or whether these findings are related to fear of femininity, violation of the male gender role, and/or other gender-role issues (Morin & Garfinkle, 1978).

Herek (1984), in a review of the research on homophobia, also pointed out that people hold positive and negative views about gays for different reasons. Understanding the complexity of these issues is important if efforts at attitude change are to be successful. Attitudes toward gays may develop out of personal experience with gay men or lesbian women and the resultant generalization of these experiences; because of defensiveness and the need to project some inner conflict or anxiety onto gays; or attitudes may be symbolic, representing firmly held beliefs or convictions (Herek, 1984).

Finally, in addition to outright homophobia, researchers have identified "heterosexual bias" as a problem for gay people. Even people who hold liberal attitudes about lesbian women and gay men may believe, either subtly or overtly, that heterosexuality is inherently superior to or more "natural" than homosexuality (Morin, 1977). This "heterosexual bias" precludes a true commitment to the validity of the gay lifestyle, and it represents at best tolerance toward, rather than a proactive affirmation of, gay people. Thus, homophobic attitudes may range from repulsion through pity to tolerance; only when public and personal attitudes are truly *accepting* will gay people attain equality in this society.

Social Discrimination

Surveys on public attitudes towards gays reveal both some trends toward tolerance combined with continuing negative attitudes. Levitt and Klassen (1974) conducted two attitude surveys in the early 1970s. In 1970, they found that over 75 percent of their sample of Americans believed that homosexual activity was wrong if no love was involved, and 70 percent felt homosexual activity was wrong even if the participants loved each other. The majority of the respondents felt that gays should not be allowed to hold positions of responsibility and authority, such as school teacher, minister, medical doctor, lawmaker, and judge (Levitt & Klassen, 1974). Other findings supported the existence of a hostile, destructive atmosphere for gay people in our society. The majority of people still believed that homosexuality was wrong and tended to agree with such statements as "Homosexuals are dangerous as teachers or youth leaders, because they try to get sexually involved with children"; and "Homosexuality is a social corruption that can cause the downfall of a civilization." Other widely held beliefs included the assumption that gay people act like members of the opposite sex, and gay men and lesbian women can be identified on the basis of their appearance (Levitt & Klassen, 1974).

Interestingly, this survey was conducted about the same time as the current gay liberation movement began (Bullough, 1979). Homosexual rights organizations are not a recent phenomenon; the first organized gay rights organization was formed by Magnus Hirschfield in 1897 in Germany (Lauritsen & Thorstad, 1974). However, the work of the early homosexual rights movements achieved no lasting effect on antihomosexual attitudes, and the movement was ended by the Nazis in the 1930s (Lauritsen & Thorstad, 1974).

Secret gay groups have existed in various countries and at different times most notably, in this country, the Mattachine Foundation, later the Mattachine Society, organized originally in 1950 (Bullough, 1979). The Daughters of Bilitis, a lesbian organization, was founded in 1955, published a magazine called the *Ladder,* and provided a beginning for much of the leadership of the lesbian movement of the 1970s (Bullough, 1979).

The contemporary gay rights movement grew out of the earlier secretive societies and was officially born in 1969 as a result of a spontaneous demonstration by gay men in reaction to police harassment at The Stonewall Inn, a popular gay men's bar in Greenwich Village (Bullough, 1979). Out of the "Stonewall riots" and succeeding demonstrations, the Gay Liberation Front, a civil rights organization, was formed (National Museum & Archive of Lesbian and Gay History, 1996; Teal, 1971). Although parallels can be found between the movement for the civil rights of gay people and other civil rights movements, the meaning of the Stonewall confrontation for gay men and lesbian women was also somewhat different than was, for example, the Watts riots of 1969 for Black people. Because of their stigmatized place in society and their ability to remain hidden, few gay men or lesbian women were willing to be public about their sexual orientation (Bullough, 1979). With the advent of the new wave of the gay rights movement and the resultant public support and affirmation of gays, many more gay people were willing to become visible, creating an overt, as opposed to the earlier covert, movement for social reform. However, as was the case with earlier movements, social progress has been slow (National Museum & Archive of Lesbian and Gay History, 1996).

The same authors of the aforementioned 1970 attitude survey conducted a follow-up survey on public attitudes about homosexuality in 1974 (Levitt & Klassen, 1974). The results of the two surveys are similar, revealing limited social progress in this period despite the active and public work on the part of the gay liberation movement. In 1974, the majority of Levitt and Klassen's sample still believed that homosexuality was wrong, and the majority tended to agree with such statements as "Homosexuals are dangerous as teachers or youth leaders, because they try to get sexually involved with children"; and "Homosexuality is a social corruption that can cause the downfall of a civilization." Other widely held beliefs included the assumption that gay people act like members of the opposite sex, and gay men and lesbian women can be identified on the basis of their appearance (Levitt & Klassen, 1974).

A 1977 Gallup poll revealed somewhat more positive attitudes, with 56 percent of Americans agreeing that gay people should have equal rights in job opportunities. These more accepting attitudes did not extend to the employment of gay people in certain types of positions; 65 percent of the sample believed that gays should not be allowed to be elementary teachers, 54 percent thought gay men and lesbian women should be denied jobs as members of the clergy, and 44 percent and 38 percent, respectively, agreed that gays should not be medical doctors or members of the armed forces (Gallup, 1977). Only 43 percent of this sample advocated legalization of homosexual activity, and 14 percent felt that gay people should be allowed to adopt children (Gallup, 1977). In a *Psychology Today* poll of a sample of liberals, 70 percent of the heterosexuals polled felt that "homosexual men are not fully masculine" (Tavris, 1977).

A national poll conducted in 1989 (reported in Fassinger, 1991) yielded even more evidence of positive changes in attitudes toward gays, although not widespread acceptance:

> The overwhelming majority of the nongay public, 81%, is opposed to discrimination based on sexual orientation, but 57% disapprove of gays living together as a married couple and 18% think homosexuality should be illegal. Two thirds believe discrimination has decreased during the past 10 years, but almost one fifth reported that they would withdraw support for a gay candidate for political office, even if they agreed with everything the individual said. Nongays would more easily accept a gay friend than a gay child, and one third would "try to change" a gay child. (p. 163)

The previously mentioned 1993 *U.S. News & World Report* poll (National Museum & Archive of Lesbian and Gay History, 1996) revealed some interesting inconsistencies in public attitudes towards gays. While 65 percent of respondents stated that they ". . . want to ensure equal rights for gay people," 50 percent opposed ". . . extending civil-rights laws to cover homosexuals" (National Museum & Archive of Lesbian and Gay History, 1996, p. 105).

Despite some encouraging results from public opinion polls, the overall climate in the United States is noticeably more antigay in the 1990s:

> Gay bashing is our new national pastime. From the Republican presidential campaign to the state of Oregon, homophobia has taken center stage. It is the last prejudice, a bias that public officials and everyday citizens are displaying without fear of instant condemnation or repudiation. . . . Imagine if a candidate for president or vice president said Jews or Catholics should not be in the cabinet, that women or African-Americans do not deserve rights. That candidate would be forced to withdraw. Not so when the prejudice is against lesbians or gay men. (Rothschild, 1992, p. A9)

Several notable reversals in civil rights for gays have occurred in the 1990s. Idaho and Oregon attempted to pass antigay measures in 1994, but the electorate voted both measures down (National Museum & Archive of Lesbian and Gay History, 1996). Similar laws have been proposed in other states, and in 1992 Colorado did, in fact, pass a statute forbidding gay antidiscrimination legislation. The statute has never been enforced, however, as the Colorado Supreme Court ruled that the measure violated the U.S. Constitution. It is virtually impossible to imagine any law *denying* basic civil rights to any other group in this society even being proposed, let alone passed. Furthermore, the antigay initiatives of the 1990s ". . . mimic a rash of ballot measures targeted at African-American civil rights in the 1960s and 1970s" (National Museum & Archive of Lesbian and Gay History, 1996, p. 252).

In 1992, Bill Clinton was the first presidential candidate to ever mention gays in an acceptance speech (National Museum & Archive of Lesbian and Gay History, 1996), and shortly after his inauguration, President Clinton proposed to end the ban on gays in the military, a move which was applauded by gays and civil rights groups. The consequent uproar in response to his proposal, however, is reflective of a retreat from tolerance. Despite overwhelming evidence to the contrary, the military and the majority of the public at large continue to argue against the suitability of gays for military service (Herek, 1993). One of the most dramatic episodes to date has been the opposing testimony to the Senate Armed Services Committee by Marine Colonel Fred Peck, testifying on behalf of the current ban, and his gay son, arguing for admitting gays into the military. The linchpin in Colonel Peck's reasoning for continuing discrimination was his concern for his son, and other gay people, who, he argued, would be in mortal danger from fellow military personnel (Smolowe, 1993). The question of whose problem it was, gays or the virulently homophobic armed forces, was evidently never considered. Research indicates, however, that ". . . lesbians and gay men are not inherently less capable of military service than are heterosexual women and men; that prejudice in the military can be overcome; that heterosexual personnel can adapt to living and working in close quarters with lesbian and gay male personnel; and that public opinion will be influenced by the way this issue is framed" (Herek, 1993).

The AIDs epidemic, too, has had a profound effect on attitudes toward gay people (Rudolph, 1989). AIDs has been identified as the "gay plague," has been labeled by some as punishment for immoral behavior, and has exacerbated already existing biases about gay people (Rudolph, 1989). Opposition to gay rights activities is also being justified by the AIDs crisis. Black (1986) reports graffiti highlighting this tendency: observed scrawled on a wall outside a New York University Conference on Gay/Lesbian Health was the slogan *Gay Rights = AIDS*.

Some methodological problems exist with both the research on correlates of homophobic attitudes and surveys about public attitudes toward gays. First, many surveys do not clearly differentiate between attitudes toward gay men and attitudes toward lesbian women. Second, questions are often phrased globally, reflecting general cultural beliefs and failing to reflect individual attitudes and the more specific ways gays are responded to negatively in everyday situations. Third, questions about the extent to which the survey data are representative abound (Morin, 1977; Morin & Garfinkle, 1978). Yet, some conclusions can be drawn. Widespread disapproval and stigmatization of lesbian women and gay men clearly exists in American society, and these negative attitudes are strong and persistent. The recent AIDs epidemic has undoubtedly contributed to justifying and maintaining such negative attitudes. Finally, cultural and social influences on the development of biased attitudes toward gays are as important to understanding the problems of gay men and lesbian women as is the study of gay adjustment, behavior, and reactions.

Legal Discrimination

The legal status of gay people in this country is largely dependent on local and state statutes, varying considerably depending on geographic location. No federal statutes exist protecting lesbian women and gay men from employment, housing, or child custody discrimination, and half of the states have laws on the books prohibiting various types of consensual sexual behavior, which are used largely against gay people (Hunter, Michaelson, & Stoddard, 1992). Although some employers have voluntarily implemented antidiscrimination policies, gays are rarely legally protected from employment discrimination.

Currently, 21 states still have sodomy statutes on the books (National Museum & Archive of Lesbian and Gay History, 1996). Periodic challenges to the so-called "sodomy" laws, which outlaw consensual same sex sexual relations whatever the actual behavior, have been made on a state-by-state basis with some successes, causing the elimination of these restrictions (National Museum & Archive of Lesbian and Gay History, 1996). However, a 1986 Supreme Court decision was a major setback for gay rights. In *Bowers v. Hardwick,* the Supreme Court made its first major ruling on a gay rights issue, overturning a federal appellate court decision in Georgia and refusing to extend constitutional protection to private homosexual acts between consenting adults (Jeffries, 1995). Essentially, this ruling denied the same protection enjoyed by nongays to gay people. The vote was close (5 to 4), and Justice Harry A. Blackmun vehemently chastised the Justices in the majority, calling the decision an opening for the state to ". . . invade the houses, hearts and minds of citizens who choose to live their lives differently" (Hager, 1986, pp. 1, 13).

Because lesbian women and gay men lack legal protection, gays are vulnerable to many other types of discriminatory behavior. For example, in *Gaylor v. Tacoma School District,* the Supreme Court refused to hear a case involving the dismissal, solely on the grounds of being gay, of a public school teacher who had years of outstanding work performance behind him (Moses & Hawkins, 1982). Only eight statewide laws protecting employment discrimination against gays exist (National Museum & Archive of Lesbian and Gay History, 1996). Though employment protection does exist for gay people in some cities (a full listing is available from the National Gay Task Force), most gays are economically vulnerable. Likewise, housing discrimination against gays is legal in most states and cities (National Museum & Archive of Lesbian and Gay History, 1996). Further, because many financial benefits accrue from legally sanctioned marriages, gay couples experience profound disadvantages.

> Some states have domestic partner laws, but most gay and lesbian couples cannot assume the basic rights of non-gay couples (e.g., insurance benefits, filing joint income tax returns, next-of-kin rights when a partner is hospitalized, and legal custody of children). The combination of the AIDS epidemic (prompting the need for legally sanctioned medical decisions and wills) and the "gayby boom" of

increasing numbers of gay and lesbian parents has led to a push for legal protection of family rights. (Fassinger, 1991, p. 162)

In 1993, the Hawaii Supreme Court ruled ". . . that the refusal to issue marriage licenses to same-sex couples appeared to violate the state constitutional right to equal protection, and ordered a trial in which the state would either have to present 'compelling' reasons for continuing to discriminate against gay and lesbian couples who want to marry, or stop discriminating." (National Museum & Archive of Lesbian and Gay History, 1996, p. 259). That ruling prompted a spate of activity aimed at passing laws against gay marriages in states across the country. Finally, gays have not had much success in court in attempts to retain custody of their children after a divorce. Because custody is decided on the basis of the "best interest of the child," and lesbianism or gayness is usually viewed as inherently unhealthy, gay people are vulnerable to losing their children solely on the basis of their sexual orientation (Falk, 1989).

Violence Against Gays

One of the alarming consequences of the rampant homophobia in our society is the relative impunity with which individuals can harass, assault, and persecute gay people. Herek (1986; 1989) documented the existence and prevalence of antigay violence and the particular ferocity and seriousness of these attacks. In statewide surveys, anywhere from 15 to 25 percent of the gays polled reported being survivors of physical violence directly related to their gayness (Herek, 1986); the majority of lesbian women and gay men have experienced antigay threats and verbal abuse (Herek, 1989).

The perpetrators of antigay violence are usually young men in groups; gay men are more likely to be the targets of physical assault, while lesbian women are more often sexually assaulted and harassed. The seriousness of the problem is highlighted by the following:

> Attacks against gay people often are characterized by an intense rage on the part of the attackers; thus there tends to be more violence than other physical assaults. Commenting on this phenomenon, sociologists Brian Miller and Laud Humphreys observed, "Seldom is a homosexual (murder) victim simply shot. He is more apt to be stabbed a dozen times, mutilated, *and* strangled." (Herek, 1986, p. 3)

Herek (1986) also notes that violence against lesbian women and gay men is increasing in frequency and attributes this increase to the public fears of gay people fueled by the AIDs crisis. Attacks on gay military personnel have received attention in tandem with the debates about gays in the military. In a 1993 incident, a U.S. Navy sailor was beaten to death by a shipmate because he was gay; he was bludgeoned so badly that his body could only be identified by his tattoos. On being sentenced, the murderer declared no remorse and said he would do it again because he was "disgusted by homosexuals" ("Sailor in beating death," 1993). The prevalence of attacks against gay men and lesbian women appears to be continuing to rise; for example, in 1994, antigay violence rose 2 percent around the country (National Museum & Archive of Lesbian and Gay History, 1996).

In addition to their susceptibility to senseless assaults and violence, gay *survivors* of violence must cope with the homophobic attitudes of medical personnel, police, and lawyers (Herek, 1989). The experience of these survivors is not unlike that of rape survivors. Often gay people are ". . . blamed by others for their assault, (and) accused of inviting the attack or deserving it" (Herek, 1986, p. 4). Because of their vulnerability to arbitrary dismissal from jobs or eviction from their residences, gay men and lesbian women who have been assaulted are unlikely to report their assault to law enforcement officials, fearing public exposure of their sexual orientation. As many as 80 percent of antigay assaults go unreported (Herek, 1986).

Gays and the Mental Health System

After decades of discriminatory treatment of gays by the mental health system, there have been some important changes in the "official" status of homosexuality within psychology and psychiatry. Generally, there has been a movement toward the treatment, in therapy and counseling, of the *problems* of lesbian women and gay men, rather than the condition of homosexuality (Stein & Cohen, 1986), and to gay-affirmative counseling (Hunt, 1993; Dworkin & Gutierrez, 1992). However, while this trend is positive, it does not necessarily reflect the attitudes and behaviors of all practitioners; gay clients are still often faced with subtle and even blatant homophobia, heterosexual bias, and misinformation about gays in counseling and therapy.

Bias in Diagnosis

A landmark in psychiatry's treatment of gay people occurred in 1973 when the American Psychiatric Association decided to remove homosexuality as a diagnosis from their *Diagnostic and Statistical Manual of Mental Disorders.* Although protesters of this decision accused the American Psychiatric Association of succumbing to political pressure by gay rights organizations, the reality was just the opposite (Krajeski, 1986). Bias in psychology and psychiatry had historically justified the assumption, never scientifically proven, that homosexuality per se was pathological. The 1973 decision to depathologize homosexuality, followed by a similar move on the part of the American Psychological Association in 1975, simply corrected a long-existing and unscientific injustice (Krajeski, 1986).

The diagnosis of homosexuality was replaced, in the *Diagnostic and Statistical Manual Disorders III* (American Psychiatric Association, 1980), with the diagnosis "ego-dystonic homosexuality." This diagnostic label has been employed with individuals who expressed dissatisfaction with their homosexual behavior and a desire to change their sexual orientation. It was grouped with other "Psychosexual Disorders," such as exhibitionism, masochism, and pedophilia in the *DSM-III*. Although an improvement over the previous diagnostic system, the inclusion of the diagnosis of ego-dystonic homosexuality in the *DSM-III* reinforced prevailing biases in society at large, shared by many mental health professionals. The emphasis on the individual rather than the social causes of distress remained, and gay people continued to be placed in a position inferior to that of nongays. An example of this perhaps subtle point is that there was never an official diagnosis of ego dystonic heterosexuality. The very idea appears absurd but only because of the cultural context of the stigmatization of gays.

The upshot of the ego-dystonic homosexuality diagnosis was that many professionals continued to "treat" gay clients for their gayness by promoting programs to change sexual orientation and thereby encourage gay people to personalize and internalize their oppression, rather than work through these issues with the goal of developing a positive gay identity. Ego-dystonic homosexuality was eliminated from the diagnostic nomenclature in the *DSM III-R* and the *DSM-IV*. However, this has not prevented practitioners from continuing to use the diagnosis unofficially. The ethical issues related to sexual orientation change programs will be discussed more fully in the following section on bias in treatment.

Bias in Treatment: Attitudes of Counselors and Therapists

The research on homophobia indicates that professionals, including mental health professionals, generally hold more positive attitudes about gay men and lesbian women than the public at large, but therapists' attitudes are not totally accepting (Moses & Hawkins, 1982). A large proportion of therapists and counselors appear to agree that homosexuality is not an illness; but attitude surveys also suggest that mental health professionals do see homosexuality and lesbianism as signs of some type of disturbance or developmental arrest, and many view the goal of changing sexual orientation as valid (Garfinkle & Morin, 1978; Martin, 1982). Therapists are generally uninformed about gay and lesbian lifestyles and issues (Graham, Rawlings, Halpern, & Hermes, 1984), tend to hold many of the societal stereotypes about lesbian women and gay men (Casas, Brady, & Ponterotto, 1983), and may exhibit distorted judgment about the clinical concerns of gay people (Davison & Friedman, 1981). Rudolph (1988) argued that inconsistency and ambivalence perhaps best describes the mental health establishment's perspective on counseling lesbians and gay men.

It is of vital importance to effective counseling and therapy for mental health professionals to work on their own attitudes and inform themselves about gay lifestyles and related information. In fact, our professional organizations and ethical guidelines expect a proactive stance of counselors. For example,

. . . in 1987 the American Counseling Association (ACA, formerly AACD) approved a Human Rights Position Paper stating that every member should 'engage in [an] ongoing examination of his/her own attitudes, feelings, stereotypic views, perceptions and behaviors that might have prejudicial or limiting impact on . . . gay/lesbian persons . . . [and] advocate equal rights for all individuals through concerted personal, professional, and political activity.' (Hunt, 1993, p. 2)

Gays seek counseling at a higher rate than nongays (Rudolph, 1988); therefore, some substantial percentage of any practitioner's client load will be gay, whether the counselor or therapist knows that those clients are gay or not. Paulsen (1983) reported that former gay clients of therapists perceived as holding negative views toward lesbians and gay men often experienced greater psychological distress after therapy. Further, in one study fully half of gay men and lesbian women preferred working with a gay counselor; this statistic is no doubt related at least to some extent to client fears of homophobic reactions from counselors (McDermott, Tyndall, & Lichtenberg, 1989). Nonetheless, there have been few research studies on therapist homophobia, and very little on the subject is available in the counseling and clinical literature; the topic is rarely addressed in training programs (Graham, Rawlings, Halpern, & Hermes, 1984) and is all but absent from the counseling literature (Betz & Fitzgerald, 1993). This lack of introspection on the part of counselors and therapists is particularly striking in the psychodynamic literature where Kwawer (1980) reported that not one article on "countertransference issues" with gay clients appeared.

Results of a survey of psychologists, presented in full in chapter 15, support the need for greater attention to therapist attitudes toward, and treatment of, gay men and lesbian women (Garnets, Hancock, Cochran, Goodchilds, & Peplau, 1991). Ninety-nine percent of the psychologists in the survey reported providing services to at least one lesbian or gay man; approximately 6 percent of the average caseload were gay men, while 7 percent were lesbian women (Garnets, et al., 1991). A majority of the respondents provided critical incidents illustrating the treatment of gay men and lesbian women in therapy. Examples of biased, inadequate, or inappropriate practice with gay clients included believing that homosexuality per se is pathological; attributing client problems to their sexual orientation; failing to recognize the effects of homophobia on gay clients; assuming that all clients are heterosexual; focusing on sexual orientation when it is not relevant; demanding that clients change their sexual orientation; trivializing or demeaning a client's gay identity; inappropriately terminating a client upon disclosure of the client's sexual orientation; lack of understanding about gay identity; gross insensitivity to the importance of a client's relationships; and numerous other examples of ignorance and bias.

In addition to misinformation, stereotyping, and homophobia, a more subtle but still more damaging and widespread therapist bias is "compulsory heterosexuality" (Rich, 1980); some of the negative examples provided previously reflect this prejudice. A form of heterosexual bias, Rich's concept of compulsory heterosexuality describes the implicit and unquestioned belief in the normality and inevitability of heterosexuality, resulting in the neglect in the literature, and by extension in the minds of mental health practitioners, of the very existence of gay people. Lesbian women have been more vulnerable to this lack of acknowledgment of their existence than gay men, as illustrated by an apocryphal tale about Queen Victoria. Upon being presented with a law criminalizing consenting adult homosexual activity, Victoria was unable to imagine that such a law had anything to do with "the ladies." She replied to her ministers, "Women don't do such things," and all references to lesbian women were expunged from the law (Weintraub, 1987).

Gay clients presenting themselves for counseling or therapy do not always reveal their sexual orientation to their therapists. "Compulsory heterosexuality" refers to the assumption on the part of the counselors, therapists, and society at large that everyone is heterosexual. Such an assumption can cause serious damage to gay clients who are still "in the closet" (Cohen & Stein, 1986).

Finally, some words about bisexuality. Although our emphasis has been specifically on gay men and lesbian women, much but not all of the discussion also applies to bisexuals. Bisexuality is not a well-understood phenomenon. On the one hand, bisexuality has been viewed as a state of confusion, or a transition from a heterosexual to a homosexual identity (Wolf, 1992). That is, bisexuals are simply gay men or lesbian women who have not yet accepted their identity. In fact, among the gay community, bisexuality is sometimes viewed as a betrayal, where the bisexual enjoys ". . . the privileges of heterosexual society while at the same time avoiding the stigma of homosexuality" (Zinik, 1985, p. 11).

On the other hand, going all the way back to Kinsey, human sexuality has been defined on a continuum, with very few at either "extreme" of heterosexuality or homosexuality. Thus, the bisexual can be viewed as flexible rather than confused; in this view, "bisexuality is characterized as the coexistence of heterosexual and homosexual feelings and behaviors, and an integration of homosexual and heterosexual identities" (Zinik, 1985, p. 11). Some of the confusion experienced by bisexuals may merely be the natural consequence of its "inherent complexity" (Wolf, 1992). Further, some authors believe that there may be some fundamental differences between homosexuality and bisexuality: ". . . exclusive homosexuality tends to emerge from a deep-seated predisposition, while bisexuality is more subject to influence and sexual learning" (Bell, Weinberg, & Hammersmith, 1981, quoted in Wolf, 1992, p. 176).

Thus, counseling issues of bisexuals ". . . are similar to those of gay and nongay people with the added stress that bisexuals feel 'caught between two worlds' and belonging to neither. . . . That all bisexuals are "just confused" or in the first stages of 'coming out' is a myth. Although research on bisexuals is sparse, some studies show that bisexuals become aware of their sexual orientation later than gay or nongay people. . . . People who later identify themselves as bisexual may come into counseling to sort out feelings of confusion and anxiety related to the dichotomous model of sexual orientation." (Hunt, 1993, p. 1).

Bias in Treatment: Ethical Issues

One of the overriding issues in the psychotherapeutic treatment of gay people concerns treatments designed to change sexual orientation. The controversy applies to therapists and counselors of *all* theoretical orientations but was particularly heated within the behavioral tradition. Therefore, the following discussion focuses mainly on behavioral interventions, but the reader should keep in mind the generalizability of the issues.

The behaviorists, while disagreeing vehemently with psychoanalytic views in general, did agree with the Freudians about the environmental origin of homosexuality (although the mechanisms theorized to cause homosexual behavior were thought about very differently) and also focused on curing rather than studying gay people (Bullough, 1979). The behaviorists have traditionally stated that they ascribe to a "value-free" stance and have focused on treating the client's presenting concern. Thus, the argument goes, the *client* has control over the goals of treatment, and the therapist or counselor is not passing judgment on the client's problem. Numerous behavioral sexual reorientation procedures have been developed, mostly for gay men (Adams & Sturgis, 1977). These behavioral treatments have taken the form of aversive techniques, including the use of chemicals to produce noxious reactions and electrical shocks, geared to reduce sexual responses to same-sex stimuli, and positive conditioning techniques designed to increase heterosexual arousal (Adams & Sturgis, 1977). Social skills training programs to enhance heterosexual dating skills are another example of behavioral approaches to the modification of homosexuality (Adams & Sturgis, 1977).

In the 1970s, some behaviorists raised serious questions about the behavioral treatment, or indeed any other treatment, of gays designed to change sexual orientation. Davison (1976; 1977) and Begelman (1975) were at the forefront of the debate over the ethics of behavioral reorientation treatment of gays.

> I believe that clinicians spend time developing and analyzing procedures only if they are concerned about a problem. This seems to be the case with homosexuality. And yet, consider our rhetoric that typically speaks of social labeling of behavior rather than viewing a given behavior as intrinsically normal or abnormal. Consider also the huge literature on helping homosexuals (at least males) change their sexual preference, and the paucity of literature aimed at helping the labelers change their prejudicial biases and encouraging the

homosexual to develop as a person without going the change route. (Davison, 1977, p. 199)

Thus, one criticism of sexual reorientation treatments is that there is no cure without a disease. Second, the availability of procedures encourages their use in treatment. Third, a charge of bias has been leveled (Davison, 1976; 1977; Begelman, 1975). "How can we honestly speak of non-prejudice when we participate in therapy regimes that by their very existence—and regardless of their efficacy—condone the current societal prejudice and perhaps also impede social change?" (Davison, 1977, p. 199)

Begelman (1975), arguing in much the same vein as Davison, has also pointed out the countertherapeutic effects of treating gay people *for their gayness:*

> . . . behavior therapists contribute significantly to preventing the exercise of any *real* option in decision-making about sexual identity, by further strengthening the prejudice that homosexuality is a "problem behavior," since treatment may be offered for it. As a consequence of this therapeutic stance, as well as a wider system of social and attitudinal pressures, homosexuals tend to seek treatment *for being homosexuals.* Heterosexuals, on the other hand, can scarcely be expected to seek voluntary treatment for being "heterosexual," especially since all the social forces arrayed—including the availability of behavior therapy for heterosexuality—attest to the acknowledgment of the idea that whatever "problems" heterosexuals experience are not due to their sexual orientation. (Begelman, 1975, p. 180)

Thus, despite the ostensibly "positive" view of behaviorally oriented therapists and counselors toward gay people, *in fact* gay men and lesbian women have been treated differently within this theoretical tradition. Gay-affirmative writers and researchers stress that individuals presenting themselves with the desire to change their sexual orientation are actually going through a stage in the "coming out" process in the development of a positive gay identity (Cass, 1979).

Gay adolescents are especially at risk of being damaged by efforts to change sexual orientation (Coleman & Remafedi, 1989). Intense homophobia, both external and internal, profoundly complicates the process of achieving a stable and mature personal and sexual identity on the part of teenagers; thus, gay teenagers may present with a desire "to be normal" (i. e., heterosexual). Lack of sensitivity and inappropriate treatment can be equally damaging. The gravity of the matter can be seen in recent statistics indicating that confusion over sexual orientation is a significant contributor to teenage suicide (Gibson, 1988). Working with adolescents grappling with issues of sexual orientation is challenging enough, but the process is further confounded by ethical issues, such as parental consent and confidentiality (Sobocinski, 1990). School counselors, who are the most likely mental health practitioners to be in a position to assist gay youths, may themselves be at risk of sanctions from school administrators for providing ethical, gay-affirmative counseling services. Readers are referred to Sobocinski's (1990) helpful overview of ethical issues and dilemmas in counseling gay and lesbian adolescents, and to Dworkin's (1992) general overview of ethical issues in treating gay, lesbian, and bisexual clients.

In conclusion, it can be seen that most of the problems experienced by lesbian women and gay men are a direct result of societal oppression and the internalization of homophobia, and homophobic attitudes have parallels with other prejudicial attitudes, such as sexism, racism, and ageism. Further, there is an intimate connection between antigay attitudes and gender-role beliefs, underscoring the relationship of homophobia and sexism. Finally, to be effective, counselors and therapists must not only inform themselves about gay lifestyles and treatment issues, but must also address their own homophobia and heterosexual biases in order to work therapeutically with gay clients.

Chapter 15 contains the previously mentioned survey of psychologists covering a range of issues that gay men and lesbian women experience in treatment, and chapters 16 and 17 specifically address some of the issues most relevant to counseling lesbian women and gay men, respectively.

References

Adams, H. E., & Sturgis, E. T. (1977). Status of behavioral reorientation techniques in the modification of homosexuality: A review. *Psychological Bulletin, 84,* 1171–1188.

American Psychiatric Association. (1980). *Diagnostic and statistical manual of mental disorders* (3rd ed.). Washington, DC: Author.

American Psychiatric Association. (1994). *Diagnostic and statistical manual of mental disorders* (4th ed.). Washington, DC: Author.

Bailey, D. S. (1955). *Homosexuality and the Western Christian tradition.* London: Longman's.

Baird, R. M., & Baird, M. K. (1995). *Homosexuality: Debating the issues.* Amherst, NY: Prometheus Books.

Begelman, D. A. (1975). Ethical and legal issues of behavior modification. In M. Hersen, R. Eisler, & P. M. Miller (Eds.), *Progress in behavior modification.* New York: Academic Press.

Bieber, I., Dain, H. J., Dince, P. R., Diellich, M. G., Grand, H. G., Gandlach, R. H., Kremer, M. W., Rifkin, A. H., Wilbur, C. G., & Bieber, T. B. (1962). *Homosexuality: A psychoanalytic study.* New York: Random House.

Black, D. (1986). *The plague years.* New York: Simon & Schuster.

Boswell, J. (1980). *Christianity, social tolerance, and homosexuality.* Chicago: University of Chicago Press.

Bullough, V. L. (1976). *Sexual variance in society and history.* New York: Wiley.

Bullough, V. L. (1979). *Homosexuality: A history.* New York: New American Library.

Casas, J. M., Brady, S., & Ponterotto, J. G. (1983). Sexual preference biases in counseling: An information processing approach. *Journal of Counseling Psychology, 30,* 139–145.

Cass, V. C. (1979). Homosexual identity formation: A theoretical model. *Journal of Homosexuality, 4,* 219–235.

Cohen, C. J., & Stein, T. S. (1986). Reconceptualizing individual psychotherapy with gay men and lesbians. In T. S. Stein & C. J. Cohen (Eds.), *Contemporary perspectives on psychotherapy with lesbians and gay men* (pp. 27–56). New York: Plenum.

Coleman, E., & Remafedi, G. (1989). Gay, lesbian, and bisexual adolescents: A critical challenge to counselors. *Journal of Counseling and Development, 68,* 36–40.

Davison, G. C. (1976). Homosexuality: The ethical challenge. *Journal of Consulting and Clinical Psychology, 44,* 157–162.

Davison, G. C. (1977). Homosexuality and the ethics of behavioral intervention. *Journal of Homosexuality, 2,* 195–204.

Davison, G., & Friedman, S. (1981). Sexual orientation stereotype in the distortion of clinical judgment. *Journal of Homosexuality, 6,* 37–44.

Dean, R. B., & Richardson, H. (1964). Analysis of MMPI profiles of 40 college-educated overt role homosexuals. *Journal of Consulting Psychology, 28,* 483–486.

Deckard, B. S. (1983). *The women's movement: Political, socioeconomic, and psychological issues* (3rd ed.). New York: Harper & Row.

Duberman, M. B., Vicinus, M., & Chauncey Jr., G. (Eds.). (1989). *Hidden from history: Reclaiming the gay and lesbian past.* New York: New American Library.

Dunbar, J., Brown, M., & Amoroso, D. (1973). Some correlates of attitudes toward homosexuality. *Journal of Social Psychology, 89,* 271–279.

Dworkin, S. H. (1992). Some ethical considerations when counseling gay, lesbian, and bisexual clients. In S. H. Dworkin & F. J. Gutierrez (Eds.), *Counseling gay men and lesbians: Journey to the end of the rainbow* (pp. 325–334). Alexandria, VA: American Association for Counseling and Development.

Dworkin, S. H., & Gutierrez, F. J. (Eds.). (1992). *Counseling gay men and lesbians: Journey to the end of the rainbow.* Alexandria, VA: American Association for Counseling and Development.

Evans, R. B. (1970). Sixteen personality factor questionnaire scores of homosexual men. *Journal of Consulting and Clinical Psychology, 34,* 212–215.

Falk, P. J. (1989). Lesbian mothers: Psychosocial assumptions in family law. *American Psychologist, 44,* 941–947.

Fassinger, R. E. (1991). The hidden minority: Issues and challenges in working with lesbian women and gay men. *The Counseling Psychologist, 19,* 157–176.

Ford, C. S., & Beach, F. A. (1951). *Patterns of sexual behavior.* New York: Harper.

Foster, J. H. (1956). *Sex variant women in literature.* New York: Vantage Press. [Reprinted: Baltimore: Diana Press, 1975]

Gallup, G. (1977, July 18). Gallup poll on gay rights: Approval with reservations. *San Francisco Chronicle,* July 18, pp. 1–18.

Garfinkle, E. M., & Morin, S. F. (1978). Psychologists' attitudes toward homosexual psychotherapy clients. *Journal of Social Issues, 34,* 101–112.

Garnets, L., Hancock, K. A., Cochran, S. D., Goodchilds, J., & Peplau, L. A. (1991). Issues in psychotherapy with lesbians and gay men. *American Psychologist, 46,* 964–972.

Gibson, P. (1988). Gay male and lesbian youth suicide. In *Report of the secretary's [Department of Health and Human Services] task force on youth suicide* (pp. 3-110 to 3-142). Washington, DC: U.S. Government Printing Office.

Graham, D. L. R., Rawlings, E. I., Halpern, H. S., & Hermes, J. (1984). Therapists' needs for training in counseling lesbians and gay men. *Professional Psychology, 15,* 482–496.

Grahn, J. (1984). *Another mother tongue: Gay words, gay worlds.* Boston: Beacon Press.

Hager, P. (1986, July 1). Ruling upholds ban on homosexual conduct. *Los Angeles Times,* pp. 1, 13.

Halperin, D. M. (1989). Sex before sexuality: Pederasty, politics, and power in classical Athens. In M. B. Duberman, M. Vicinus, & G. Chauncey Jr. (Eds.), *Hidden from history: Reclaiming the gay and lesbian past* (pp. 37–53). New York: New American Library.

Hammersmith, S. K., & Weinberg, M. S. (1973). Homosexual identity: Commitment, adjustment, and significant others. *Sociometry, 36,* 56–79.

Herek, G. M. (1989). Hate crimes against lesbians and gay men: Issues for research and policy. *American Psychologist, 44,* 948–955.

Herek, G. M. (1984). Beyond "homophobia": A social psychological perspective on attitudes toward lesbians and gay men. *Journal of Homosexuality, 10,* 1–21.

Herek, G. M. (1986, October 9). *Violence against lesbians and gay men.* Statement presented to the United States House of Representatives, Committee on the Judiciary, Subcommittee on Criminal Justice.

Herek, G. M. (1993). Sexual orientation and military service: A social science perspective. *American Psychologist, 48,* 538–549.

Hooker, E. (1957). The adjustment of the male homosexual. *Journal of Projective Techniques, 21*, 18–31.

Hunt, B. (1993). What counselors need to know about counseling gay men and lesbians. *Counseling and Human Development, 26*, 1–12.

Hunter, N. D., Michaelson, S. E., & Stoddard, T. B. (1992). *The rights of lesbians and gay men: The basic ACLU guide to a gay person's rights*. Carbondale, IL: Southern Illinois University Press.

Jeffries, J. C., Jr. (1995). Changing times: Gay rights. In R. M. Baird & M. K. Baird, *Homosexuality: Debating the issues* (pp. 103–118). Amherst, NY: Prometheus Books.

Jones, S. L. (1995). The loving opposition. In R. M. Baird & M. K. Baird, *Homosexuality: Debating the issues* (pp. 243–253). Amherst, NY: Prometheus Books.

Kinsey, A. C., Pomeroy, W. B., & Martin, C. E. (1948). *Sexual behavior in the human male*. Philadelphia: Saunders.

Kinsey, A. C., Pomeroy, W. B., Martin, C. E., & Gebhard, P. H. (1953). *Sexual behavior in the human female*. Philadelphia: Saunders.

Krajeski, J. P. (1986). Psychotherapy with gay men and lesbians. In T. S. Stein and C. J. Cohen (Eds.), *Contemporary perspectives on psychotherapy with lesbians and gay men* (pp. 9–26). New York: Plenum.

Kwawer, J. S. (1980). Transference and countertransference in homosexuality—Changing psychoanalytic views. *American Journal of Psychotherapy, 34*, 72–80.

Lauritsen, J., & Thorstad, D. (1974). *The early homosexual rights movement*. New York: Times Change Press.

Levitt, E., & Klassen, A., Jr. (1974). Public attitudes toward homosexuality: Part of a 1970 national survey by the Institute of Sex Research. *Journal of Homosexuality, 1*, 29–43

Martin, A. (1982). Some issues in the treatment of gay and lesbian patients. *Psychotherapy: Theory, research and practice, 19*, 341–348.

Martin, D., & Lyon, P. (1972). *Lesbian/woman*. New York: Bantam.

McDermott, D., Tyndall, L., & Lichtenberg, J. W. (1989). Factors related to counselor preference among gays and lesbians. *Journal of Counseling and Development, 68*, 31–35.

Melton, G. B. (1989). Public policy and private prejudice: Psychology and law on gay rights. *American Psychologist, 44*, 933–940.

Morin, S. F. (1977). Heterosexual bias in psychological research on lesbianism and male homosexuality. *American Psychologist, 32*, 629–637.

Morin, S. F., & Garfinkle, E. M. (1978). Male homophobia. *Journal of Social Issues, 34*, 2–47.

Moses, A. E., & Hawkins, R. O. (1982). *Counseling lesbian women and gay men*. St. Louis: Mosby.

National Museum & Archive of Lesbian and Gay History. (1996). *The gay almanac*. New York: Berkeley Books.

Paulsen, J. (1983, April). *Homophobia in American psychiatrists*. Paper presented to the Group for the Advancement of Psychiatry, Philadelphia.

Plant, R. (1986). *The pink triangle: The Nazi war against homosexuals*. New York: New Republic.

Rich, A. (1980). Compulsory heterosexuality and lesbian existence. Signs: *Journal of Women in Culture and Society, 5*, 631–660.

Rothschild, M. (1992, September 21). Gay bashing becomes new national pastime. *Arizona Republic*, Section A p. 9.

Rowse, A. L. (1977). *Homosexuals in history*. New York: Carroll & Graf.

Rudolph, J. (1988). Counselors' attitudes toward homosexuality: A selective review of the literature. *Journal of Counseling and Development, 67*, 165–168.

Rudolph, J. (1989). The impact of contemporary ideology and AIDS on the counseling of gay clients. *Counseling and Values, 33*, 96–108.

Rule, J. (1975). *Lesbian images*. New York: Doubleday.

Sailor in beating death of gay would "do it again." (1993, May 26). *Arizona Republic*, Section A p. 5.

Smolowe, J. (1993, May 24). Hearts and minefields. *Time*, pp. 41–42.

Sobocinski, M. R. (1990). Ethical principles in the counseling of gay and lesbian adolescents: Issues of autonomy, competence, confidentiality. *Professional Psychology: Research and Practice, 21*, 240–247.

Stein, T. S., & Cohen, C. J. (Eds.). (1986). *Contemporary perspectives on psychotherapy with gay men and lesbians*. New York: Plenum.

Teal, D. (1971). *The gay militants*. New York: Stein and Day.

Tavris, C. (1977, January). Men and women report their views on masculinity. *Psychology Today,* 35.

Weinberg, M. S. (1970). The male homosexual: Age-related variations in social and psychological characteristics. *Social Problems, 17,* 527–537.

Weinberg, M. S., & Williams, C. J. (1974). *Male homosexuals: Their problems and adaptations.* New York: Oxford University Press.

Weintraub, S. (1987). *Victoria: An intimate biography.* New York: E. P. Dutton.

Wolf, T. J. (1992). Bisexuality: A counseling perspective. In S. H. Dworkin & F. J. Gutierrez (Eds.), *Counseling gay men and lesbians: Journey to the end of the rainbow* (pp. 175–187). Alexandria, VA: American Association for Counseling and Development.

Woodman, N. J., & Lenna, H. R. (1980). *Counseling with gay men and women.* San Francisco: Jossey-Bass.

Wysor, B. (1974). *The lesbian myth.* New York: Random House.

Zinik, G. (1985). Identity conflict or adaptive flexibility: Bisexuality reconsidered. In F. Klein & T. Wolf (Eds.), *Bisexualities: Research and theory* (pp. 7–19). New York: Haworth.

PART 2
The Client with a Disability

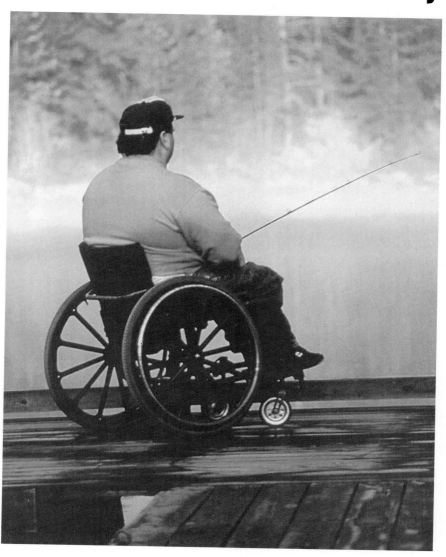

Members of an ethnic minority group, while often incorrectly treated as a homogeneous population, do share a common ethnic and cultural heritage. Women share the characteristics of sex, older people share the characteristic of longevity, and gay men and lesbian women share the characteristic of same-sex sexual orientation. People with disabilities, however, share no common physical or behavioral characteristic. They are an extremely diverse group, diverse in every way that humans can be different from each other. They come from different ethnicities, cultures, religions, and socioeconomic backgrounds, and include men and women across the full range of sexual orientation. Even the descriptor that unites them, disabilities, comes in many different types. As suggested in chapter 2, however, they do share the experience common to all minorities, the experience of oppression by the larger society.

They also share with all of us the desire to have their human needs fulfilled. As McDowell, Bills, and Eaton (1989) point out, "Persons with disabilities need what every individual needs—respect, encouragement, satisfying experiences, and the opportunity to develop his or her abilities" (p. 151). From chapters 1 and 2, however, we know that persons with disabilities are not treated the same as individuals without disabilities. This suggests that in addition to meeting the normal developmental needs experienced by all individuals, the counselor may need to address the influence of segregation and discrimination on their client when working with an individual with a disability.

In this part we present readings that examine the psychological and/or sociopolitical considerations relevant to counseling clients with disabilities. Living independently is a key component of meeting the psychological needs of, and achieving equal rights for, people with disabilities. In chapter 6, Nosek and Fuhrer define the concept of independence in terms of four major components: (1) perceived control of one's life, (2) physical functioning, (3) psychological self-reliance, and (4) environmental resources. They go on to examine the relationships among these components, citing examples of how important each is in the lives of people with disabilities and focusing on the need to feel in control of one's life. Reframing the four components as a needs hierarchy, the authors build a rationale for extending greater control over services that people with disabilities receive to the consumers of these services. They point out that contemporary medical and vocational rehabilitation are seldom under the control of the people they service. Furthermore, they suggest that research is needed to examine the effects of the four components of independence on the sense of autonomy experienced by people with disabilities.

In chapter 7, Steere, Gregory, Heiny, and Butterworth describe *lifestyle planning,* a planning approach that provides emotional and physical support for the client with a disability while empowering the client to make decisions on his/her own behalf. As these authors point out, the goal of lifestyle planning is to shift the focus of professional involvement away from planning *for* to planning *with* people with disabilities and their families. Written for rehabilitation specialists who may have been schooled in more directive forms of assistance, this chapter reminds all counselors that the client with a disability needs to be accorded the same respect and autonomy accorded any other client. Although generically trained counselors may already start with the assumption that their role is to facilitate client goal setting and attainment, professionals outside the rehabilitation specialty will find the specific suggestions for implementing lifestyle planning useful.

In chapter 8, Boyle points out the need for counselors to become more knowledgeable about, and sensitive to, issues of sexuality and disability. Although her suggestions for putting clients with disabilities at ease regarding the topic of sexuality is directed toward rehabilitation counselors, her recommendations are equally appropriate for "generalist" counselors who find themselves working with clients with disabilities. In particular, Boyle discusses the PLISSIT Model of sexuality counseling and how it can be a useful tool for the counselor who wants to assist a client with a disability who is dealing with the issue of sexuality.

References

McDowell, W. A., Bills, G. F., & Eaton, M. W. (1989). Extending psychotherapeutic strategies to people with disabilities. *Journal of Counseling & Development, 68,* 151–154.

6

Independence Among People with Disabilities: A Heuristic Model

Margaret A. Nosek and Marcus J. Fuhrer

Attempts to assess the independence of people with disabilities and to develop corresponding social service and rehabilitation programs that adequately address the need for independence have been hampered by the lack of a comprehensive definition of the term. This lack, in turn, has led to a proliferation of instruments focused mainly on physical and cognitive functioning and ignoring environmental barriers, managerial skills, and the individual's sense of control over acquiring services that enable meeting personal, self-selected goals. "By definition, a person with a physical disability lacks adequate tools for certain physical behaviors, but there is no necessary relationship between those missing or impaired physical tools and the ability to meet the demands of higher social, psychological, and cognitive tasks" (Kerr & Meyerson, 1987, p. 175). Corbett (1989) added that "a narrow focus upon basic skills impedes the quality of life and inhibits self-expression" (p. 159).

In response to the need to measure independence comprehensively in people with disabilities, this article presents a heuristic model of the construct of independence. The model identifies the elements that contribute to independence and examines their interrelationships according to a hierarchy of needs. Implications of this model for rehabilitation research and the development of a measurement instrument (Nosek, Fuhrer, & Howland, 1992) are also discussed.

Defining *independence* as embracing the ability for self-determinism, Price (1990) lamented that children with severe disabilities in special education programs have few opportunities to make choices that would prepare them for independent living in the community. These children "have very little control

Reprinted from *Rehabilitation Counseling Bulletin, 36,* 1992, pp. 6–20. Reprinted with permission. No further reproduction authorized without permission of the American Counseling Association.

over their lives. They are taught, transported, assessed, and evaluated with little possibility of input or understanding" (p. 16). As a result, studies have shown that special education graduates who did not fail in special education programs nevertheless did fail once they were on their own (Mithaug, Martin, Agran, & Rusch, 1988). Likewise, elderly residents of nursing homes who were no longer allowed to practice the independent behaviors they were accustomed to performing in the community soon lost these abilities (Avorn & Langer, 1982; Booth, 1986; Kiernat, 1987).

Rock (1988) believed that independence should not reflect any absolute measure of competence, but instead should concern control and choice. When she conducted in-depth, open-ended interviews of six people with physical disabilities, they expressed similar notions of independence that entailed risk taking, privacy, decision making, organization and control, and encouragement (Rock, 1988). For example, independence meant being able to go out alone; lock one's door; decide on what, how, and when money would be spent; determine how their own personal care tasks would be completed; and obtain encouragement to develop individual interests and talents. All five of these areas involved an element of choice, and all participants felt that independence implied choice and was meaningless without it. Despite the lack of control they had experienced while living at least 3 years in institutions, they were able to take and maintain control and choice in their lives once they had left institutional care. Brown and Lehr (1989) concurred that the emphasis needs to shift from merely increasing competence to increasing personal choice and self-control. They concluded, "Choosing how to live one's life is the 'catalytic trigger' of independence" (p. 269).

Mathews and Seekins (1987) incorporated interactions between personal and environmental characteristics into their interactional model of the determinants of independence. They discussed several components of independence as they apply to the needs of people with disabilities for achieving independence goals. Nevertheless, perceived control, perhaps the strongest component of independence, is mentioned only briefly as one aspect of the way individuals characteristically view their circumstances. Whereas people with disabilities classify social support as a personal characteristic, we consider it an environmental factor. Other investigators may overemphasize the role of environmental barriers but ignore the role of personal initiative (DeJong, 1979).

Kerr and Meyerson (1987) have questioned the value of independence as a goal of rehabilitation, stating that the mature person should be equally satisfied to be dependent, interdependent, independent, or dependable at various times in life. This "four-corner" rather than continuous model restricts the definition of independence to behavior, according to what one is doing at any given moment, thereby disregarding independence as a state of mind, attitude, trait, or general approach to life. The individual is relegated to the role of responder rather than initiator or controller. People with disabilities are not perceived as creating, altering, or controlling a situation; instead, they find themselves in a situation, then adapt by acting dependently, interdependently, independently, or dependably, as required by the circumstances. Independence is also expressed in terms of relationships with others, disregarding relationships with the environment and self-direction. Thus, the four-corner approach still does not assess independence beyond functioning and effectively skirts the need to operationally define independence and measure it in people with disabilities as an outcome variable. In general, previous notions of independence in people with disabilities, as discussed in the literature, tend to underestimate the importance of the degree of control they perceive they have over their lives.

Although the proposed model of independence is intended to be broadly applicable, it is analyzed in the context of disability and handicap (World Health Organization, 1980), circumstances that are generally acknowledged as significant impediments to independence. Indeed, the thinking that gave rise to this model originated with the definition of independent living for persons with severe disabilities presented by Frieden, Richards, Cole, and Bailey (1979). This definition focuses on controlling one's life, having options, making decisions, performing daily activities, and participating in the life of the community.

The Four Major Components

Diverse notions of independence can be distilled into four components: perceived control of one's life, physical functioning, psychological self-reliance, and environmental resources.

Perceived control is the expectation of being able to make decisions and engage in actions that will attain desirable consequences and avoid unfavorable ones (Baron & Rodin, 1978). It includes both self-control and control of the environment. Self-control is the ability to direct one's physical and mental abilities, emotions, and behavior, as embraced in Haworth's (1986) notion of competence. Perceived control also includes the belief that one can execute courses of actions required to deal with prospective situations, as in Bandura's (1982) concept of self-efficacy. Environmental control is the perception that one is able to exert power over human and material elements in the environment that particularly affect one's life. This is similar to the notion of internal locus of control presented by Rotter (1954) and others (e.g., Lefcourt, 1976; Phares, 1976). Control is enabled by predictability, which in turn is provided by education and informing people of what will happen to them in advance so that they can prepare for an event (Kiernat, 1987; Schultz, 1976). Adler (1930) described the need to control one's personal environment as inherent to life itself. A plethora of studies support his view with evidence associating lack of control with helplessness, declining health, and death (Seligman, 1975).

Physical functioning refers to basic survival abilities, such as moving about, dressing, eating, and processing sensory input. These are the activities of daily living that have been the subject of considerable analysis in the rehabilitation literature (Alexander & Fuhrer, 1984; Brown, Gordon, & Diller, 1983; Salkind, Beckwith, Nelson, & McGregor, 1982). To accomplish basic life tasks, individuals may elect to use equipment or assistance from another person (e.g., automobiles, eyeglasses, or someone to cook, clean, or maintain a checkbook). Persons with high autonomy in this area are capable of doing these things for themselves when necessary.

Psychological self-reliance is generally associated with the emotional autonomy, ego integrity, self-confidence, assertiveness, sense of purpose, cleverness, and decision-making skills necessary to judge effectively what actions must be taken to meet the demands of a situation and to initiate those actions. It includes coping, the capacity to handle stressful situations, and mastery, the ability to meet new challenges (Lowry, 1989). Whereas physical functioning has an instrumental, task-oriented character, psychological self-reliance includes managerial or executive functions. The person with high psychological self-reliance is emotionally stable, capable of functioning with little group support, and able to fulfill a range of social roles.

Environmental factors include all physical and social elements external to the individual that can either aid or obstruct the achievement of personal goals (Rice, Roessler, Greenwood, & Frieden, 1983). Factors such as family support, geographical location, terrain, economic situation, political climate, educational opportunities, architectural accessibility, support services, and cultural values are among the environmental elements relevant to developing independence. The perceived availability of resources in the environment is particularly crucial in considering independence. A resource is just as useless whether it is perceived to be unavailable or truly is unavailable.

Relationships among the Four Components

The components have a complex interrelationship that is frequently reciprocal in nature. The most obvious of these is between physical functioning and environmental resources. The less one is able to do for one's self, the more one must rely on other people or things in the environment. If, because of a disability, a person cannot dress himself or herself, some other person or device must be secured to compensate for this lack of ability so that the desired outcome, being dressed, can be accomplished. As the availability of environmental resources increases, demands on physical abilities decrease. Witness so-called modern conveniences. It is important to distinguish between reliance on conveniences, where the physical ability remains intact but is not used, and reliance on necessities, where environmental resources are used to substitute for an ability that does not exist. In other words, both a person with quadriplegia and a person without a disability may be able to drive a car out of the garage. If, however, the electric garage door opener malfunctions, the person without a disability may be able to accomplish the task adequately by opening the door manually, but the person with quadriplegia may be unable to accomplish the task at all. Thus, the compensatory relationship between ability and environment is largely a matter of convenience for the general population, but is more a matter of necessity for people with disabilities.

Psychological self-reliance is strongly influenced by physical abilities and environmental factors, especially during early development (Stendler, 1954; Troutt, 1980). The more one is able to understand and physically manage the environment, the greater the confidence and self-esteem one develops. Being able to physically explore the environment and learn from it provides an experience base on which to develop the executive abilities necessary to succeed in our society. The degree to which environmental resources are available to promote development strongly influences the manner in which genetic traits are expressed. For the child with spina bifida, an environment that provides opportunities and necessary support (e.g., personal assistance, mobility aides) for engaging in activities such as integrated play, music lessons, trips to museums, and the like can enable that child to express natural talents and interests. Psychological self-reliance is thus a product of genetics and environmental influences. Conversely, psychological elements are the catalysts for engaging environmental resources to compensate for physical inabilities. Resources may abound, but if the person is unable to recognize, access, or manage them, they are of little use. Once children with spina bifida grow up, they must be able to manage their own support systems, including people and material resources, in order to carry on effectively as independent persons.

The interrelationship of perceived control with physical, environmental, and psychological components is the most complex of all. It has already been said that the presence of physical abilities, environmental resources, and a sense of worth and competence enhances feelings of control over one's life (Perlmuter, Monty, & Chan, 1986). This feeling of control, however, may not have a direct effect on these three components; rather, it is probably a by-product of them. Persons feel in control when they believe they have value and the ability to deal effectively with their environment, that is, they have a high sense of self-efficacy (Bandura, 1989).

The strongest effect of perceived control is observed in the interaction of the three components. The more people sense that they have control, the more effective they can be in using resources to enhance their abilities. Studies done as early as 1967 have demonstrated that, after long periods of institutional care, people with physical or mental disabilities can successfully manage their own lives in the community, where they have more control (Edgerton, 1967; Rock, 1988). This can be seen even more clearly in reverse. When circumstances are such that persons feel they have little control, as under oppressive regimes or confinement, the incentive is reduced to enhance abilities or to better one's situation by more effective management of resources (White & Janson, 1986). In institutions, functioning may even deteriorate (Avorn & Langer, 1982), and dependency tends to increase. In a 3-year survey of 3,400 residents of 176 nursing homes, Booth (1986) found that even in homes with the highest standards of care, the less control residents had over their own lives, the more they lost control over the use of their faculties. Conversely, nursing home residents demonstrated enhanced alertness, active participation, and sense of well-being when allowed control over participation in social and leisure activities (Langer & Rodin, 1976). Several studies of elderly, chronically ill, and physically disabled populations have demonstrated the benefits of increasing perceived control over personal health and the environment (Avorn & Langer, 1982; Langer & Rodin, 1976; Schulz, 1976). Thus, according to Schulz (1976), "the fundamental issue is [no longer] whether patients should have options to exercise control, but under which conditions and in what form these options will prove decisive in relation to individual well-being" (p. 563). Of all the four components, control seems to be the least related to functioning, but the most strongly related to independence overall.

A Hierarchy of Needs

To understand more fully the interrelationships among the four components of independence, it is useful to consider them in reference to the demands of daily living and the fulfillment of fundamental human needs. The latter may be considered in a quasi-Maslovian hierarchy of four levels: basic survival, material well-being, productivity, and self-actualization needs. At the lowest level, basic survival requires adequate food, clothing, shelter, and safety to ensure maintenance of bodily functions and absence of serious illness. Material well-being demands a higher level of adequacy in meeting these basic needs and also requires mobility, communication, social interaction, and other elements of daily life that enable one to live comfortably. Productivity refers to the need to contribute something of value to oneself or others. It includes not only salaried employment and positive monetary balances, but also the sense that individuals are creating the maximum quality of life for themselves and society (National Council on the Handicapped, 1983). Self-actualization presumes commitment to individually established priorities and living in a way that allows pursuit of one's highest priorities. According to Maslow (1970), "self-actualization is [one's] desire for self-fulfillment, namely the tendency . . . to become actualized in what [one] is potentially . . . the desire to become more and more what one idiosyncratically is, to become everything that one is capable of becoming" (p. 46). To avoid imposing judgments about which pursuits constitute more valuable contributions to society, Maslow's criteria of altruistic behavior and intellectual pursuits are excluded from the current conception of self-actualization.

It is quite possible for an individual to be concerned with meeting needs at all four levels at once. During a particularly demanding day at work, for example, a person may be concerned 5% with survival, 1% with material well-being, 89% with productivity, and 5% with self-actualization. If that person has a severe physical disability and his or her attendant fails to show up, attention may shift to being 15% on survival, 75% on material well-being, 9% on productivity, and 1% on self-actualization.

Two key concepts have thus been presented: the components of independence and a hierarchy of needs. Next to be discussed is the manner in which the components of independence interrelate according to the level of need.

Interrelationship of Components in Relation to Needs
Basic Survival

Needs at the level of basic survival are fulfilled through a combination of physical functioning and perceived resources in the environment. Autonomous physical functioning here is what rehabilitation professionals refer to as independence in activities of daily living. At this level, psychological self-reliance may also serve a role in compensating for a lack of resources. Witness the example of street people who survive through cleverness despite being deprived of environmental resources. Perceived control is not substantially enhanced by mere survival, but when survival is threatened, feelings of control lower dramatically.

For persons with severe disabilities, additional resources may be necessary for survival, such as personal assistance, supervision, or certain medications. Certainly, such persons live with a much higher degree of threat to survival than do persons without disabilities. Loss of luggage containing life-sustaining medication or a late bus causing a missed meeting with an attendant could mean serious illness, not just inconvenience. People with these kinds of vulnerabilities must attend much more to meeting their needs for survival.

Although survival is generally considered prepotent for other levels of the hierarchy and not a terminal level unto itself, these needs are the primary area of concern for some people. It is an unfortunate fact of our society that some people with very severe disabilities are maintained at a mere level of survival in state institutions and boarding houses. They are, for the most part, fed, clothed, housed, and kept safe from illness or injury, but live far below any conscionable level of well-being and are allowed little opportunity for fulfillment of higher order needs. Melanson and Meagher (1986) compared nursing home residents to animals in a zoo; although basic survival needs are met, the environment fails to support individuality and autonomy. Having little opportunity to behave independently, residents often lose their ability to practice the behaviors necessary to meet higher order independence needs (Kiernat, 1987). When the National Citizens Coalition for Nursing Home Reform (1985) surveyed 457 residents of nursing homes, residents deplored their lack of input regarding basic daily routines such as what to eat, when to arise, when to go to bed, and how to obtain privacy. The dominant theme in their responses was lack of opportunity to exert some control over their own lives, even over basic survival functions.

Material Well-Being

To move from the level of survival to the level of material well-being, a higher order of environmental resources must be available and perceived. For a given individual, need fulfillment at this level results not so much from increases in physical and psychological capacity as from the increase of elements external to the individual, that is, environmental resources. The addition of these resources enables the individual to function more effectively and attend to higher pursuits. For example, a person with quadriplegia may not need an electric wheelchair to survive, but having one would increase independence by improving mobility both inside the home and in the community. Funding agencies, however, may not consider better mobility to be sufficient justification to provide an electric wheelchair, even if the individual's job does not pay enough to enable its purchase (Karr, 1983).

The role of the environment and available resources complicates the relationship between components at this level. Although available resources can compensate for limitations in physical functioning and enable basic survival and well-being, they also inextricably influence the development of psychological self-reliance. Psychological self-reliance is partly learned, partly inherited. Children are born egocentric, curious, and achievement oriented (Chapman, 1984). These natural tendencies can be suppressed by negative factors in their upbringing such as overprotective parents, medical professionals, or teachers; inaccessible environments; lack of educational opportunities; economic disadvantage; and societal discrimination. If positive influences are present, the psychological characteristics that contribute to independence can be enhanced. Also, on a day-to-day basis, persons are generally much better able to have strong feelings of self-worth, communicate assertively, and make rational judgments when their basic survival and well-being are not threatened. This is sufficient justification for placing considerable emphasis on environmental factors.

Although certainly not as heinous as the state institutions and boarding houses mentioned earlier, situations exist in our society that make material well-being a terminal level of need fulfillment for persons with disabilities. Some institutional and family environments manage to offer lives of considerable comfort to people with disabilities at the expense of control and opportunity for higher pursuit. Lowered expectations for productivity and self-actualization are often imposed by providers with good intentions. Also, an entrenched system of work disincentives inherent in some disability benefit programs ensures that recipients live comfortably in terms of material needs, but effectively discourages the pursuit of gainful employment. Until recently, a loss of Medicaid benefits resulted from even minimal earned income. Because of its threat to survival (not just well-being), this loss was avoided at all costs by many recipients. Recent congressional actions to amend the Social Security Act and remove this disincentive have enabled many people to progress from being maintained in a state of well-being to pursuing more productive endeavors and gaining more control of their lives.

Productivity

Productivity is our nation's most cherished indicator of independence. To enable productivity, needs at the level of survival and well-being generally must have been fulfilled and resources of acceptable quality and stability must be available. To achieve productivity, mere physical functioning is inadequate. Accomplishments attributable to physical prowess alone do not necessarily signify independence. The component of psychological self-reliance becomes more prominent here, with importance given to the ability to make effective judgments and decisions, to feel self-confident, to communicate needs and desires, and to perform managerial functions that ensure need fulfillment at lower levels. To the extent that persons are deficient in these abilities, they must have greater physical functioning; conversely, those who have limitations in physical functioning or environmental resources must be more resourceful, creative, assertive, and self-confident to achieve productivity.

A reciprocal relationship exists between productivity and the psychological and control components of independence. To the extent that productivity is achieved, psychological self-reliance is enhanced, thus enabling greater productivity (Hoff & Hohner, 1986). Similarly, perceived control is very much affected by the stability of one's survival and well-being and the degree to which one can be productive. When one is able to achieve a satisfactory level of productivity, feelings of control and self-esteem are enhanced. People who maintain their productivity for the sole purpose of meeting their needs for survival and minimal well-being can hardly be considered independent unless they are also engaged in humanitarian or other pursuits at the level of self-actualization that are unrelated to employment.

It is an anomaly of our society that independence is identified with productivity. People do not necessarily possess the psychological self-reliance necessary to be considered independent simply because they are productive. Quite to the contrary, for some people productivity may be a facade masking an extreme lack of independence. People with certain marketable skills can survive and achieve a high level of material well-being despite being emotionally insecure, unstable, and very dependent on others for direction. There are also situations in which people achieve productivity, but at such a low level that sufficient resources are not available to develop greater psychological self-reliance.

The importance and diversity of available resources should not be underestimated in addressing productivity, as is illustrated by the following two examples. A person with severe cerebral palsy and extensive speech impairment, but an IQ of 150, can be maintained in an institution and even achieve minimal productivity flipping levers on a machine with his feet in a sheltered workshop, yet never reach his potential for productivity as a computer scientist because of lack of environmental resources in personal assistance, equipment, education, and mobility. Conversely, a highly educated, well-employed person with a severe physical disability may have his or her entire productivity threatened because of lack of a competent, reliable, nonabusive personal assistant. Even when money, equipment, education, or mobility are not lacking, difficulty in finding an appropriate person to provide assistance can upset the entire balance of needs, particularly if family support systems are not available or functioning (Nosek, 1990).

Self-Actualization

Our model of independence includes the opportunity to function at the highest level of needs: self-actualization. At first glance, the minimum components of this level may seem to mimic those of productivity. Productivity, however, like basic survival and material well-being, can be attained without feeling self-directed, self-fulfilled, or in control of one's life—all integral components of self-actualization. Likewise, psychological self-reliance, though sometimes identified with the positive elements in self-actualization, does not necessarily include them. What then is the difference between the first three levels of needs and self-actualization?

Achieving self-actualization is a lifelong process requiring the stronger presence of psychological elements that go beyond self-reliance, such as a heightened sense of self-worth and self-understanding, greater powers of assertion, and broader and deeper wisdom in making judgments. Self-actualizing individuals have not only a more acute understanding of their life priorities, but also the ability to command resources to fulfill those priorities. They can attain this level of control over their lives only when the interrelationship of all psychological, physical, and environmental elements enables them to surpass basic survival needs and to transcend the level of productivity for its own sake. Once the capacity to meet these needs has been met, the self-actualizing person can voluntarily forsake stability at lower levels of survival, as seen, for example, in Zen Buddhists, Peace Corps volunteers, or missionaries. During the process of achieving self-actualization, one may even subordinate productivity to more personal goals.

Although independence is a prerequisite for self-actualization, self-actualization is not necessarily a prerequisite for independence; however, a close association between the two is predictable. The key difference is self-direction and voluntary choice, or the perceived control component of our model of independence. The self-actualizing person acts freely and willingly, without resentment or a sense of being forced to behave independently. Some people who find making decisions, being productive, and even surviving too burdensome seem to function independently, but against their will. Some would even prefer to sacrifice their independence by letting others take care of them on someone else's terms. When such a level of dependency is socially unacceptable or unavailable, they reluctantly grind on, tending to their own affairs, independent by all superficial indicators, yet resentful and miserable.

It is also controversial to consider independent behaviors self-actualizing without regard to social responsibility, in effect, to justify the means by the end.

What, indeed, is the difference between a person whose highest goal is to attain material wealth, but whose means are to swindle the public, and a person whose highest goal is to serve the public, but whose means is volunteer work? From the individual's perspective, both may believe they are using all their skills and talents to function at their highest potential. Nevertheless, when examined with reference to social mores, the first is condemned as a criminal but the second is praised as a saint. Given that our model of independence has been conceived in as value-free a manner as possible, it could not be used to distinguish between these two types of individuals without including Maslow's (1970) criteria for self-actualization of ethical behavior and *gemeinschaftsgefuhl*, "a genuine desire to help the human race."

Independence Needs and the Independent Living Movement

Meeting the self-actualization needs inherent to the independent living movement's model of independence requires greater control over the services consumers currently receive from medical and vocational rehabilitation establishments. Creating maximum control for an individual is rarely a concern of established institutions, because it is not essential to meet the levels of needs they try to address. Medical rehabilitation professionals tend to restrict their therapeutic goals of independence predominantly to the achievement of autonomous physical functioning for which, as discussed earlier, control is not a critical component. Vocational rehabilitation professionals are concerned solely with the development of physical and psychological abilities to achieve productivity. At the level of productivity, perceived control is only of secondary importance. One can survive, live comfortably, function autonomously, and be productive without necessarily feeling in control of one's life. Perceived control is essential only at the level of actualization. Unlike the staffs of most established institutions, people with disabilities and those working in the independent living movement are concerned primarily with the fulfillment of human potential, or self-actualization. Consequently, they define independence in terms of control and the ability and opportunity to make choices. This conflict in need priorities and interests between rehabilitation establishments and individuals has resulted in an ongoing struggle by consumers to persuade institutions to modify their policies and procedures, a struggle that has fueled the independent living movement.

As a result, persons with disabilities are often unable to obtain the services they need to achieve independence in terms of control over their lives. Some individuals might elect to forego independence in meeting some basic needs, such as certain activities of daily living skills, so that they can spend more time and effort attending to the higher needs of creativity and self-expression embodied in self-actualization. Such individuals may not be given the option to pursue these interests by rehabilitation establishments focused on improving physical functioning. Daniels (1988) and Corbett (1989) proposed that lower level needs in Maslow's hierarchy need not always be satisfied first to enable attention to higher levels of needs.

Efforts by consumers to increase their personal control and independence (Frieden & Cole, 1985), however, are beginning to have an impact on the thinking of medical institutions (Committee on Nursing Home Regulations, Institute of Medicine, 1986) and rehabilitation specialists (Kiernat, 1987) alike. Kiernat recommended that therapists providing rehabilitation services "serve as advocates for quality environments that support personal autonomy. Without the opportunity for self-determination, newly gained skills from rehabilitation are useless" (p. 3).

Implications for Research

The model of independence described here paves the way for developing an instrument to assess independence comprehensively along the four components of perceived control, physical functioning, psychological self-reliance, and characteristics of the physical and social environment. The ultimate goal is to integrate the assessment of these four components into a single holistic view of an individual's independence. This would take the form of a profile of an individual's status on each of the four dimensions of independence. Independence profile scores could then be applied to the development and evaluation of programs in physical medicine, rehabilitation, special education, and independent living. This information could be used to assist in planning services and in assessing the degree to which those services are meeting all aspects of independence needs. Once a comprehensive measure of independence has been developed, it would be a useful tool for researching the dynamics of independence. To what degree are each of the components amenable to change through service interventions? What factors contribute to effective change? Answers to these questions could influence needs assessment and service planning.

Independence profiles could be used for developing a predictive model of vocational rehabilitation outcomes. Rehabilitation counseling could then be directed toward helping individuals progress to a higher level of independence on each of the four components of their independence profiles as they relate to their vocational goals. Knowledge of where clients stand on each component would help counselors guide them in setting goals and in using the social services, medical modalities, rehabilitation programs, and independent living programs that would best enable them to meet these goals.

Studies are needed to determine the effects on autonomy of addressing previously ignored components of independence. For example, would persons with disabilities strive harder to regain lost functions if they had better control over their lives and the supportive services they received? Does improved access to personal assistance services make persons with disabilities more independent? In what ways could social services be delivered to create maximum individual control and minimal disincentives to independent living and productivity?

Responding to the perceived control component of independence would have a profound effect on service delivery systems. Traditional social services delivery practices of categorizing individuals and limiting their participation in programs based on restrictive criteria would have to be transformed to allow broader participation and a wider range of options in service delivery. The impact of such a transformation on systems operations, budgets, and individuals' lives warrant thorough study.

References

Adler, A. (1930). Individual psychology. In C. Murchison (Ed.), *Psychologies of 1930.* Worcester, MA: Clark University Press.

Alexander, J. L., & Fuhrer, M. J. (1984). Functional assessment of individuals with physical impairments. In A. S. Halpern & M. I. Fuhrer (Eds.), *Functional assessment in rehabilitation* (pp. 45–59). Baltimore: Paul H. Brookes.

Avorn, J., & Langer, E. (1982). Induced disability in nursing home patients: A controlled trial. *Journal of the American Geriatric Society, 30,* 397–400.

Bandura, A. (1982). Self-efficacy mechanism in human agency. *American Psychologist, 37,* 122–147.

Bandura, A. (1989). Human agency in social cognitive theory. *American Psychologist, 44,* 1175–1184.

Baron, R., & Rodin. J. (1978). Urban environment: Personal control as a mediator of crowding. In A. Baum, J. E. Singer, & S. Valins (Eds.), *The urban environment: Vol. 1. Advances in experimental psychology* (pp.145–192). Hillsdale, NJ: Erlbaum.

Booth, T. (1986). Institutional regimes and induced dependency in homes for the aged. *The Gerontologist, 26,* 418–423.

Brown, M., Gordon, W. A., & Diller, M. (1983). Functional assessment and outcome measurement: An integrative review. In E. L. Pan, T. Backer, & C. L. Vash (Eds.), *Annual review of rehabilitation* (Vol. 3, pp. 93–120). New York: Springer.

Brown, F., & Lehr, D. H. (1989). *Persons with profound disabilities: Issues and practices.* Baltimore: Paul H. Brookes.

Chapman, M. (Ed.). (1984). Intentional action as a paradigm for developmental psychology: A symposium. *Human Development, 27,* 113–144.

Committee on Nursing Home Regulations, Institute of Medicine. (1986). *Improving the quality of care in nursing homes.* Washington, DC: Academic Press.

Corbett, J. (1989). The quality of life in the 'independence' curriculum. *Disability, Handicap, & Society. 4,* 145–163.

Daniels, M. (1988). The myth of self-actualization. *Journal of Humanistic Psychology, 28,* 7–38.

DeJong, G. (1979). Independent living: From social movement to analytic paradigm. *Archives of Physical Medicine and Rehabilitation, 60,* 435–446.

Edgerton. R. B. (1967). *The cloak of independence: Stigma in the lives of the mentally retarded.* Berkeley: University of California Press.

Frieden, L., & Cole, J. A. (1985). Independence: The ultimate goal of rehabilitation for spinal cord-injured persons. *The American Journal of Occupational Therapy. 39,* 734–739.

Frieden, L., Richards, L., Cole, J., & Bailey, O. (1979). *ILRU source book: A technical assistance manual on independent living.* Houston: The Institute for Rehabilitation and Research.

Haworth, L. (1986). *Autonomy: An essay in philosophical psychology and ethics.* New Haven: Yale University Press.

Hoff, E. H., & Hohner, H. U. (1986). Occupational careers, work, and control. In M. M. Baltes & P. B. Baltes (Eds.), *The psychology of control and aging* (pp. 345–371). Hillsdale, NJ: Erlbaum.

Karr, W. (1983). The independent spirit as part of the rehabilitation process. *Rehabilitation Literature, 44,* 153–155.

Kerr, N., & Meyerson. L. (1987). Independence as a goal and a value of people with physical disabilities: Some caveats. *Rehabilitation Psychology, 32,* 173–180.

Kiernat, J. M. (1987). Promoting independence and autonomy through environmental approaches. *Topics in Geriatric Rehabilitation, 3,* 1–6.

Langer, E. J., & Rodin, J. (1976). The effects of choice and enhanced personal responsibility for the aged: A field experiment in an institutional setting. *Journal of Personality and Social Psychology, 34,* 191–198.

Lefcourt, H. M. (1976). *Locus of control: Current trends in theory and research.* New York: Wiley.

Lowry, L. (1989). Independence and dependence in aging: A new balance. *Journal of Gerontological Social Work, 13,* 133–146.

Maslow, E. (1970). *Motivation and personality* (2nd ed.). New York: Harper & Row.

Mathews, R. M., & Seekins, T. (1987). An interactional model of independence. *Rehabilitation Psychology, 32,* 165–180.

Melanson, P., & Meagher, D. (1986). Out of the jungle and into the zoo. *Gerontion, 1* (2), 26–30.

Mithaug, D. E., Martin, J. E., Agran, M., & Rusch, F. R. (1988). *Why special education graduates fail.* Colorado Springs, CO: Ascent Publications.

National Citizens Coalition for Nursing Home Reform. (1985, April 29). Report of a survey by the National Citizens Coalition for Nursing Home Reform. *Wisconsin State Journal,* p. 5.

National Council on the Handicapped. (1983). *National policy for persons with disabilities.* Washington, DC: Author.

Nosek, M. A. (1990). Personal assistance: Key to employability of persons with physical disabilities. *Journal of Applied Rehabilitation Counseling, 21,* 3–8.

Nosek, M. A., Fuhrer, M. J., & Howland, C. A. (1992). Independence among people with disabilities: II. Personal independence profile. *Rehabilitation Counseling Bulletin, 36,* 21–36.

Perlmuter, L. C., Monty, R. A., & Chan, F. (1986). Choice, control, and cognitive functioning. In M. M. Baltes & P. B. Baltes (Eds.), *The psychology of control and aging* (pp. 99–118). Hillsdale, NJ: Erlbaum.

Phares, E. J. (1976). *Locus of control in personality.* Morristown, NJ: General Learning Press.

Price, F. B. (1990). Independence and the individual with severe disabilities. *Journal of Rehabilitation, 56,* 15–18.

Rice, B. D., Roessler, R. T., Greenwood, R., & Frieden, L. (1983). *Independent living rehabilitation program development, management and evaluation.* Fayetteville, AK: Arkansas Rehabilitation Research and Training Center, University of Arkansas.

Rock, P. J. (1988). Independence: What it means to six disabled people living in the community. *Disability, Handicap, & Society, 3,* 27–35.

Rotter, J. B. (1954). *Social learning aud clinical psychology.* Englewood Cliffs, NJ: Prentice-Hall.

Salkind, N. J., Beckwith, R. M., Nelson, C. F., & McGregor, P. A. (1982). *A summary of instruments that assess independence* (Report No. 1). Lawrence, KS: Research and Training Center on Independent Living. University of Kansas.

Schultz, R. (1976). Effects of control and predictability on the physical and psychological well-being of the institutionalized aged. *Journal of Personal and Social Psychology. 33,* 563–573.

Seligman, M. (1975). *Helplessness.* San Francisco: Freeman.

Stendler, C. B. (1954). Possible causes of overdependency in young children. *Child Development, 25,* 125–146.

Troutt, B. (1980). Independence and ego identity reflected on minority students' utilization of the support services in an academic special program. *Dissertation Abstracts International, 41,* 2029A.

White, C. B., & Janson, P. (1986), Helplessness in institutional settings: Adaptation or iatrogenic disease? In M. M. Baltes & P. B. Baltes (Eds.), *The psychology of control and aging* (pp. 297–313). Hillsdale, NJ: Erlbaum.

World Health Organization. (1980). *International classification of impairments, disabilities, and handicaps: A manual of classification relating to the consequences of disease.* Geneva: Author.

7

Lifestyle Planning: Considerations for Use with People with Disabilities

Daniel E. Steere, Susan P. Gregory, Robert W. Heiny, and John Butterworth, Jr.

During the past decade, alternative approaches to planning that focus on a broadening view of lifestyle enhancement have emerged (Mount, 1986; O'Brien, 1987; Vandercook, York, & Forrest, 1989). A consistent message has been that traditional approaches to program planning for children, adolescents, and adults with disabilities have failed to capture and build on the dreams and aspirations of these people and their significant others. Instead of supporting individuals as they make decisions and plans for their own lifestyles, professionals have frequently identified needs, selected goals, and dictated plans (Mount et al., 1990; Racino, Walker, O'Connor, & Taylor, 1993).

In this article, we use the term *lifestyle planning* to describe a series of planning approaches that have been used to assist people with disabilities toward their making effective and informed decisions about their lives. These processes link current activities with anticipated events and living conditions. Lifestyle planning is in one sense a proactive way to lessen chances that people with disabilities will lead stereotypical, dependent, isolated lifestyles. The number and types of lifestyle planning approaches are expanding for people with disabilities. These approaches can enhance the roles that rehabilitation counselors and other professionals play in service planning. A fundamental change for professionals is a shift away from planning *for* to planning *with* people with disabilities and their families. Lifestyle planning enables an individual with a disability to explore options and to make choices. Because exploring options and making choices is integral to the process by which

Reprinted from *Rehabilitation Counseling Bulletin, 38,* 1995, pp. 207–223. Reprinted with permission. No further reproduction authorized without permission of the American Counseling Association.

individuals examine employment and other life activities, rehabilitation counselors should become knowledgeable about lifestyle planning.

This article describes lifestyle planning approaches that have been reported to date. We begin by reviewing the major features of approaches found in professional literature in the disability field. Next, we discuss areas in which lifestyle planning has been used, and then examine ways in which lifestyle planning can be used in the field of rehabilitation counseling. Finally, we discuss implications for changes in the system that may be necessary so that lifestyle planning can be more broadly implemented.

Approaches to Lifestyle Planning

Mount's *personal futures planning* process (1986) supports people as they make their own decisions. Plans are created by focusing on people with a disability, along with those who know them well and who agree to contribute to a shared vision of future lifestyle success. The atmosphere for discussion and planning is warm, supportive, and individually determined by the individual for whom the plan is created. Rather than notes and documentation traditionally used in team meetings, graphics are used, allowing all participants to take an active part in the meeting. The plan provides a rationale for individuals to support development of the person with a disability, so that person can enjoy the future of his or her dreams.

O'Brien (1987) described a lifestyle planning approach centering on the essential outcomes of consumer choice, community presence, community participation, competence, and respect. Planning efforts focus on arranging supports and services to increase the chance that these outcomes are realized. Functional, community-referenced activities are selected based on their potential to realize the outcomes.

The *McGill Action Planning System* (MAPS) is a mechanism for infusing lifestyle enhancement concerns into strategies for including students with disabilities in regular classrooms (Vandercook et al., 1989). Vandercook and her colleagues developed seven questions that guide a team of nondisabled peers, family members, and regular and special educators, in developing strategies intended to enhance the success of students in inclusive educational settings. The MAPS process provides a strong sense of collaboration among special and regular educators, as well as families and peers, and creates a sense of "mission" for lifestyle change efforts.

Powell et al. (1991) described a *career planning* process adapted from the lifestyle planning process of O'Brien (1987) to guide individuals entering community employment. This career planning process is used to identify individually selected quality of life outcomes for people with disabilities who are the focus of career planning meetings. Such outcomes include relationships, predictability, control, flexibility, and financial security. A six-step planning process includes the clarification of a personal profile, delineation and explanation of quality of life outcomes (given by priority of value), brainstorming of ways to address challenges to attainment of outcomes, and action planning. The career planning process was also adapted to refine transitions from school to adult life (Steere, Wood, Pancsofar, & Butterworth, 1990).

Butterworth et al. (1993) have expanded the career planning process to a broader *whole life planning* process. Their work has stressed the importance of settings and times of day that are convenient for the focus individual and that are conducive to their taking a lead role in developing their whole life plan. The authors also stress that whole life planning is an interactive process, not a product.

Circles of support is another term used to describe a team of concerned individuals who assist people with disabilities in making life decisions (Ludlum, 1993; Perske & Perske, 1992). Circles of support are organized by individuals (or their closest advocates) to help them evaluate life events and to make lifestyle decisions. A facilitator can be called on to assist team members in focusing on important lifestyle issues.

Numerous variations of these processes are being used, although many have not been widely disseminated. *Person-centered planning, person-driven planning,* and *life quilting* are among the terms that have been used for forms of lifestyle planning. Despite subtle variations among them, each of these approaches focuses on increasing personal life comfort and satisfaction through supports.

Appendix A summarizes and contrasts key information about the most frequently used approaches to lifestyle planning. Appendix B lists the steps used in conducting each of these different approaches. The appendixes provide more detailed background information about the lifestyle planning processes previously described. They also may be useful references as readers consider the elements that the lifestyle planning approaches have in common.

Common Elements of Approaches

Although numerous approaches to lifestyle planning have been described, they share several common elements. First, they are usually coordinated by a facilitator, a person who helps to establish the atmosphere for planning, records comments or uses graphics to depict ideas, and promotes productive discussion. Six additional elements are common to the approaches. They serve to (a) rely on a network of natural support resources; (b) create a positive, relaxed atmosphere for planning; (c) have the focus individual exert control over the planning process; (d) develop a positive personal profile; (e) create an unrestricted vision of success; and (f) initiate an ongoing action planning process. These six common elements are discussed as follows.

A Network of Natural Support Resources

A group of people who know the focus individual well and who have a vested interest in that person are assembled into an interacting, purposeful network without concern for profession or title. An atmosphere of creative collaboration on behalf of the individual allows full participation by all group members. A support network for a person with disabilities may include close family members, friends, peers, community members, neighbors, former teachers, and clergy. The focus person is the central member of the team, and extensive efforts are made to ensure that planning occurs with the focus person, not about him or her.

The reliance on a natural support network provides strength to the planning process. Recent research has highlighted the power of natural supports in obtaining and maintaining employment, as well as enhancing other life situations (Nisbet, 1992; Nisbet & Hagner, 1988; Silliker, 1993).

A Positive and Comfortable Working Atmosphere

To enhance the likelihood that the focus individuals have a positive experience of the planning process, those individuals would maintain control over the location of meetings, the time of day, refreshments, and other conveniences. The atmosphere is one of acceptance, comfort, support, and open and effective communication. Efforts are made to ensure that the focus person is most comfortable and feels acceptance by the group. Such meetings are typically held in people's homes, settings that are more conducive to person-centered meetings rather than meetings that center on the service provider. The atmosphere of a person-centered meeting is markedly different from most service planning meetings that are directed by professionals.

Control by the Focus Person

Because the various lifestyle planning approaches center on the person with a disability, everyone who makes up the group takes their direction from the needs and goals articulated by the person and his or her family, rather than what service providers may perceive as the needs and goals. The person with the disability is not only the focus of the discussion, but explicitly directs meetings pertaining to his or her own life.

Lifestyle planning emphasizes the individual's central role in the planning process in the following ways.

1. An external facilitator helps to ensure the focus person's role in the process.
2. Focus individuals exercise control over who will and will not be invited to planning meetings.
3. These planning approaches are unrestricted in content and what is considered relevant or important information.
4. Focus individuals often work with facilitators to prepare their own participation in meetings.

A Positive Personal Profile

Planning begins with a comprehensive profile that emphasizes capabilities and valued qualities of the focus person. This profile clarifies the rich fabric of the focus person's current lifestyle as a basis for increasing subsequent support for a future lifestyle. Each team member contributes a unique impression and knowledge of the focus person; the resulting profile provides a composite of that person from multiple viewpoints. More than one format may be used to create profiles, including timelines of significant factors or people in the focus person's life, photograph albums, or written lists of needed supports (Mount & Zwernik, 1988; Pancsofar, 1992).

An Unrestricted Vision of Success

A hallmark of these lifestyle planning processes is the result of a clear, unrestricted vision of success for the focus person. This vision is highly personal, centering on how the focus person wants to live. Such a vision of success may also be devised through multiple formats, including descriptions of desired quality of life outcomes, scenarios of desired future activity and attainment of new roles, and statements about desired environments as well as activities that occur in those environments. This vision sufficiently defines the desired lifestyle, so team members may assist the focus person in working toward its creation.

Ongoing Action Planning Based on Creative Solutions

Using the vision of success as a guide, the supporting team members implement action plans to enhance supports and services. This flexible implementation allows team members to meet the current interests of the focus person. Ideas for action planning are generated through open, creative brainstorming approaches to problem solving.

A high level of flexibility is possible with the six elements just described. Each element may be (and in many cases should be) implemented in multiple formats. Lifestyle planning holds great promise for creating services that directly support expressed wants and interests of people with disabilities. First, lifestyle planning approaches give the power for decision making to the focus person. This seat of power chiefly occurs because of a support team that represents the focus person's best interests and a format that responds to making life decisions with greater autonomy and independence. Second, lifestyle planning provides a context for linking plans and services to a person's daily community life. Third, lifestyle planning, because of the nature of the support groups, enlarges the number of connections to natural community supports. Finally, lifestyle planning provides a rational basis for evaluating services. Evaluation criteria may include lifestyle changes, not simply tracking of progress on formal program plans.

Uses of Lifestyle Planning

Because of its potential for getting to the heart of people's dreams and aspirations, lifestyle planning has been used successfully through a number of services. Such uses are summarized in Appendix C, along with references to which readers may refer for more detailed descriptions. The application of lifestyle planning approaches to the areas of curriculum development, transition from school to adult life, supported employment, community housing, positive behavioral supports, leisure, and service evaluation are briefly described as follows.

Curricular Content in Inclusive Education

It has long been established that people with disabilities must learn things they will need for success in their local communities. The focus is away from curricular prerequisites and toward direct teaching and support in activities that enhance inclusion in community life. Since the mid-1970s, this focus has been supported by legislative mandates for individualized educational planning. Despite the clarity of how we should choose what is taught to people, we often persist in selecting curricular content that lacks relevance to students' current or future lives. A persistent challenge, however, is the selection of curricular content that often lacks relevance to students' current or future lives.

Lifestyle planning can address such a persistent challenge. Indeed, the MAPS approach was developed specifically to resolve issues of curricular relevance and inclusion. In addition, O'Brien's (1987) approach to lifestyle planning has been described as an avenue for selecting community-referenced activities for youth and young adults with disabilities. In essence, if content is what we teach, then lifestyle planning processes help us decide why we should be teaching what we teach.

Transition from School to Adult Life

The Individuals With Disabilities Education Act of 1990 (P.L. 101-476) clearly establishes the mandate for effective transition services for all students with disabilities (Wehman, 1992). But the content of the transition cornponent of Individualized Education Programs (IEPs) sometimes continues to be established by professionals without careful consideration of a student's aspirations for lifestyle after graduation. The utility of lifestyle planning processes within transition planning is its clear rationale for the selection of goals the person sets for the period after graduation (Steere et al., 1990). This selection in turn helps to clarify the supports and services after graduation that have clear potential for contributing to lifestyle enhancement.

It is generally agreed that early transition planning (occurring no later than age 14) and early career education are needed for most students if they are to make informed choices upon graduation (Moore, Agran, & McSweyn, 1990; Szymanski, 1994; Wehman, 1992). It is also clear that parents play an essential role in the success of transition efforts (Stineman, Morningstar, Bishop, & Turnbull, 1993; Szymanski, 1994). A major challenge for professionals is to assist families in questioning the impact of educational services—as early as the primary grades—on their children's current and subsequent lifestyles. Along with questions of functionality and age appropriateness, questions that affect lifestyle should be asked frequently for students of all ages. For younger students, the primary question may be "What experiences has the child had that could help in making informed lifestyle choices later in life?"

Szymanski (1994) described transition planning as a longitudinal process that begins early in life. She portrayed fantasizing about careers, reinforcement of interests, and interaction with career role models as positive forces in career development. Lifestyle planning approaches, if used longitudinally throughout a child's educational experience can provide a structure for ensuring that essential aspects of early career development are realized. In particular, the close involvement of family members in lifestyle planning efforts may be enhanced as a result of the process.

Supported Employment

Despite the intent of supported employment to assist individuals in finding meaningful and fulfilling employment in their communities, many individuals are "placed" without careful attention to their lifestyle aspirations. But contemporary writings in supported employment indicate that placement in a job is not in and of itself a sufficient outcome. Rather, employment should be a vehicle to enhancement of an individual's overall quality of life (Fabian, 1992; Powell et al., 1991). The unmet challenge is to provide the necessary supports to individuals so they can participate in decisions about their own careers (Powell et al., 1991). When someone seems unable to make his or her own career decisions, support team members can play a larger role in helping that person make those decisions. For many an individual, support network members include not only parents but also siblings, friends, and other people who are closely concerned with the individual's well-being. The important point is that employment decisions, including career changes and advancements, are made by the focus person or people who know that person best.

A more longitudinal approach to services must be responsive to individuals' desires to make changes in their jobs, their homes, and their relationships. When support is needed for such decisions (and most people with or without disabilities do require support), lifestyle planning processes provide a structure for assisting people in evaluating and making major life changes.

Community Housing Decisions

Racino et al. (1993) argued convincingly for a separation of decisions about housing and support. These authors asserted that, too often, decisions about where people will live are made on the basis of the level of support that people require. Consequently, people who require more intense support to participate in the routine of daily community life tend to be relegated to more restrictive housing options in the continuum arrangement of residential services. (Taylor, 1988).

Racino et al. (1993) preferred lifestyle planning as the most meaningful approach toward assessing housing and support needs. They also alerted readers that lifestyle planning is no panacea to housing and support challenges, and that effective planning takes time and commitment from members of the support network. Despite these cautions, lifestyle planning is an effective strategy for addressing decisions pertaining to housing and support.

Positive Behavioral Supports

Lifestyle enhancement should be a driving force in the development of support services for people with challenging behavior (Horner et al., 1990). As with other traditional planning documents, "behavior management plans" have often been developed solely to reduce interfering behavior. Although it is critically important for some individuals that certain aspects of their behavior patterns be reduced, the success of such efforts should be measured by the impact that the reduced patterns have on one's lifestyle. This impact may be measured by a greater level of using adaptive skills, more rich and varied community activities, and more meaningful relationships. Thus, success in behavior intervention efforts is measured across many dimensions that document the positive effect of reduced interfering behavior on lifestyle.

Lifestyle planning is therefore an essential element in behavioral support plans. In essence, some form of lifestyle plan constitutes the rationale and basis for the rest of the plan. Without a lifestyle planning component, behavioral support plans must be considered incomplete.

Choice of Community Participation in Leisure Activities

A continuing challenge for professionals and others who support people with severe disabilities relates to the decisions about which activities will be most meaningful and beneficial (Pancsofar, 1992). Most people seek to attain a balance among work, personal management activities, and leisure activities. Leisure activities provide an outlet for stress, exercise, relaxation, an avenue for meeting people, and an opportunity for interests in areas other than vocation.

Too often, professionals who support individuals with disabilities are at a loss for what activities those individuals might engage in. Community outings can enhance an individual's presence in the community and participation, although the selection of activities is often determined by proximity to program sites. In contrast, the selection and implementation of leisure activities that are individually selected, based on the potential to enhance the lifestyle of an individual, is a new frontier. Although this area is still new, the use of a lifestyle planning process provides a grounding and rationale for planning and implementing leisure activities.

Evaluating Services Based on Lifestyle Change

A shift away from evaluating services based on their form or processes and toward an analysis of the outcomes of services is occurring (Fabian, 1991, 1992; Wood & Steere, 1992). But the professional community has yet to fully turn the corner to outcomes-based service evaluation. Although such an approach presents numerous challenges to implementation, this is clearly an area for continued collective effort in the profession.

In relation to longitudinal evaluation of services, lifestyle planning approaches could have applications for individuals as they reflect on their lives and the outcomes they have experienced. E. Pancsofar (personal communication, September 15, 1992) related the power of the use of lifestyle reflections by significant others in celebrating the life of a dying colleague. This is a little-explored area that could have significant potential in enhancing the quality of life for citizens with disabilities, as well as the quality of their dying experiences.

Lifestyle planning approaches provide a direction for the future. They provide an equally compelling view of one's past. Efforts to measure the impact of supports should therefore include retrospective analysis of what was decided with an individual, what occurred, and what the outcomes of the decisions were. In doing so, a rich personal history is chronicled.

Uses of Lifestyle Planning in Rehabilitation Counseling

The past 5 years have witnessed an increasing focus on consumer choice, empowerment, and self-determination in both legislation (Individuals With Disabilities Education Act of 1990; Rehabilitation Act Amendments of 1992) and professional literature (Parent, 1993; Szymanski, 1994). This focus increases the responsibility for rehabilitation counselors and other rehabilitation professionals to be responsive to individuals' aspirations and choices. Lifestyle planning approaches can substantially benefit the rehabilitation community in addressing this issue. In particular, the use of lifestyle planning approaches has specific implications for the processes of vocational assessment and job development. These potential uses of lifestyle planning are described in the remainder of this section.

Using Lifestyle Planning in Vocational Assessment

Lifestyle planning provides an alternative to traditional approaches to assessing the current abilities and interests of individuals who are entering the vocational rehabilitation system. With the input of support team members, lifestyle planning approaches can draw a rich picture of the person and his or her strengths on which to build a career. In addition, lifestyle planning processes can help substantially clarify individuals' aspirations for career development. Rehabilitation counselors now serve individuals with more significant disabilities who are eligible for supported employment services. The need to clarify vocational aspirations for these people is paramount. But for many individuals with severe disabilities who have a limited work history or none at all, this facet of counseling may be problematic. Lifestyle planning approaches directly address this challenge.

An innovative and beneficial use of lifestyle planning approaches in vocational assessment is to combine them with situational assessment strategies (Pancsofar, 1986) and job analysis and matching procedures (Moon, Inge, Wehman, Brooke, & Barcus, 1990). Although lifestyle planning processes alone may not yield sufficient information, they can provide a rationale and context for the use of specific community-based situational assessment sites.

Using Lifestyle Planning to Enhance Job Development and Retention

Successful job placement is usually the function of successful job matching and tailored, individualized support. Both components may be addressed in part through lifestyle planning. Job and worker compatibility is not merely a matter of physical characteristics such as strength and endurance, but is also a function of match between worker aspiration and career potential within a specific job. With more complete knowledge of the current aspirations of consumers, quality job matches that result in successful employment outcomes are more likely to occur.

Lifestyle planning approaches, by relying on support networks, can be powerful in organizing or refining support strategies to enhance job development and retention. This reliance can be of substantial benefit to rehabilitation counselors who not only seek to help consumers make a successful entry into a job, but also to help them maintain successful employment.

As lifestyle planning approaches are used more often by rehabilitation counselors, several systems considerations arise. These considerations are discussed in the remaining section of this article.

Systems Considerations

The use of lifestyle planning approaches raises questions about the relationship of these approaches to development of the service plan. It also prompts exploration of the role of the facilitator versus that of a counselor.

The Relationship of the Lifestyle Plan to the Service Plan

As lifestyle planning processes become more widely adopted, their relationship to service plans (Individualized Written Rehabilitation Plan [IWRP] or Individualized Education Program [IEP]) will be increasingly questioned. Is the essence of lifestyle planning only captured outside the traditional boundaries of the service plan? Are the two formats mutually exclusive or will lifestyle planning eventually replace traditional service plans and thereby become institutionalized? Debate over these questions has occurred and will continue as the use of lifestyle planning approaches expands.

We believe that service plans should be driven by a vision of lifestyle success (DiLeo, 1991; Steere et al., 1990). That is, no goal, objective, or activity of a service plan should be written without a clear relationship to the desired future that, if necessary, may be clarified through a lifestyle planning process. In essence, a service plan could be considered a component of the action plan step or element previously discussed.

The Role and Impact of a Facilitator

Most of the planning processes described in this article rely on an external facilitator to enhance positive and productive meetings. What is unclear is the impact of different facilitators on the outcomes of planning. Equally unclear is who should serve as facilitators, and what qualifies individuals to be facilitators of lifestyle planning meetings. This is an area that will require both continued research and careful consideration in terms of the rehabilitation planning system overall.

The use of a facilitator results in a different meeting format with which many rehabilitation counselors may be unfamiliar. In particular, the atmosphere of a lifestyle planning meeting is markedly different from more traditional, professionally driven meetings. This difference often necessitates a shift in the style of interaction during a meeting, whereby rehabilitation professionals hold a team-oriented discussion of ways to respond to consumer wishes.

The Role of the Rehabilitation Counselor

Rehabilitation counselors can play a pivotal role in planning and implementing lifestyle planning approaches. First, rehabilitation counselors must be knowledgeable about specific people who are adept at facilitating lifestyle planning meetings. In some situations, counselors may themselves develop the specific skills to facilitate lifestyle planning meetings (Ludlum, 1993). Counselors may be asked to participate in circles of support or lifestyle planning meetings. In addition, counselors may obtain information derived from lifestyle planning meetings about individuals who are requesting their services. Participation in lifestyle planning meetings may also help counselors to enhance their skills in asking relevant questions that assist all individuals they serve in making informed career decisions. Finally, as the lifestyle planning process becomes more widely used, individuals with disabilities may experience these processes early in school, toward developing transition plans. Such early experience will increase the likelihood that when individuals seek the services of a rehabilitation counselor they will be comparatively skilled at articulating their goals, thus enhancing the potential benefit of rehabilitation counseling services.

A concern for client choice continues to be an important issue for rehabilitation counselors. Counselors must balance attempts to enhance client choice with their own responsibility for the outcomes of service decisions. Lifestyle planning approaches provide a viable approach that can assist rehabilitation counselors with this issue. Because of the balance provided by support network members, a counselor can have greater confidence that clients' choices have been made with the support and assistance of caring people. This in turn allows greater confidence by the counselor that both client choice and responsible service decisions are enhanced.

Finally, training may be required by rehabilitation counselors and other rehabilitation professionals in the area of lifestyle planning. Such training should address approaches to lifestyle planning, essential common elements, and the potential roles of the counselor.

Summary

This article has reviewed current approaches to the emerging area of lifestyle planning. We have reviewed areas in which lifestyle planning approaches have been used and ways in which they can be used in the field of rehabilitation counseling. Finally, we have addressed key systems issues that will need to be considered in implementing lifestyle planning on a broader scale.

Lifestyle planning approaches do not solve all challenges faced in providing the best possible services to people with disabilities. Nevertheless, these planning approaches do help professionals focus on the right questions to ask in designing and implementing those services. In particular, they assist professionals and others who question the impact of services on individuals' lives. This article has reviewed a few of the areas in which such questioning should occur.

Many approaches exist for lifestyle planning. As rehabilitation counselors adapt and refine these approaches, they should continually strive to be flexible in their support. Many people obtain support in making career and other life decisions without assembling a formal team to meet. Instead, they may call on trusted supporters individually; family members and friends frequently give advice to one another. Others seek the formal assistance of life or career counselors to assist with major decisions. Similarly, individuals with disabilities should not be restricted to the lifestyle planning approaches described in this article. Instead, professionals should be versed in multiple avenues for addressing the important and relevant questions that are at the heart of quality services.

Finally, precaution should be taken to ensure that lifestyle planning approaches maintain their unique power, which could be done by keeping these approaches sufficiently separate from administrative planning processes. The reason is that there is a clear danger that lifestyle planning processes could be institutionalized. Thus, the approaches need protecting, as does the ability they afford people to focus clearly on real dreams and aspirations for an improved lifestyle. In that way, services may truly be enhancing for people with disabilities.

References

Butterworth, J., Hagner, D., Heikkinen, B., Farris, S., DeMello, S., & McDonough, K. (1993). *Whole life planning: A guide for organizers and facilitators.* Boston, MA: Institute for Community Inclusion.

DiLeo, D. (1991). *Reach for a dream! Developing individual service plans for persons with disabilities.* St. Augustine, FL: Training Resource Network.

Fabian, E. (1991). Using quality of life indicators in rehabilitation program evaluation. *Rehabilitation Counseling Bulletin, 34,* 344–356.

Fabian, E. (1992). Supported employment and the quality of life: Does a job make a difference? *Rehabilitation Counseling Bulletin, 36,* 84–97.

Hagner, D., & DiLeo, D. (1993). *Working together: Workplace culture, supported employment, and persons with disabilities.* Brookline, MA: Brookline Books.

Horner, R., Dunlap, G., Koegel, R., Carr, E., Sailor, W., Anderson, J., Albin, R., & O'Neill, R. (1990). Toward a technology of "nonaversive" positive behavioral support. *Journal of the Association for Persons with Severe Handicaps, 15,* 125–132.

Individuals With Disabilities Education Act of 1990, Public Law 101-476. (October 30, 1990).

Ludlum, C. (1993). *Tending the candle: A booklet for circle facilitators.* Manchester, CT: Communitas.

Malette, P., Mirenda, P., Kandborg, T., Jones, P., Burr, T., & Rogow, S. (1992). Application of a lifestyle development process for persons with severe intellectual disabilities: A case study report. *Journal of the Association for Persons With Severe Handicaps, 17,* 179–191.

Moon, S., Inge, K., Wehman, P., Brooke, V., & Barcus, M. (1990). *Helping persons with mental retardation get and keep employment: Supported employment issues and strategies.* Baltimore, MD: Brookes.

Moore, S., Agran, M., & McSweyn, C. (1990). Career education: Are we starting early enough? *Career Development for Exceptional Individuals, 13,* 129–134.

Mount, B. (1986). A choice of futures. Unpublished doctoral dissertation, University of Georgia.

Mount. B., Ducharme, G., & Beeman, P. (1991). *Person-centered development: A journey in learning to listen to penple with disabilities.* Manchester, CT: Communitas.

Mount, B., Ludlum, C., Beeman, P., Ducharme, G., Demarasse, R., Meadows, L., & Riley, E. (1990). *Imperfect change: Embracing the tensions of person-centered work.* Manchester, CT: Communitas.

Mount, B., & Zwernik, K. (1988). *It's never too early, it's never too late: A booklet about personal futures planning.* Mears Park Center, MN: Metropolitan Council.

Nisbet, J. (1992). *Natural supports in school, at work, and in the community for people with severe disabilities.* Baltimore, MD: Brookes.

Nisbet, J., & Hagner, D. (1988). Natural supports in the workplace: A reexamination of supported employment. *Journal of the Association for Persons With Severe Handicaps, 13,* 260–267.

O'Brien, J. (1987). A guide to lifestyle planning: Using the Activities Catalog to integrate services and natural support systems. In B. Wilcox and G. T. Bellamy (Eds.), *The activities catalog: An alternative curriculum design for youth and adults with severe disabilities* (pp. 175–189). Baltimore, MD: Brookes.

Pancsofar, E. (1986). Assessing work behavior. In F. R. Rusch (Ed.), *Competitive employment issues and strategies* (pp. 93~102). Baltimore, MD: Brookes.

Pancsofar, E. (Ed.). (1992). *Community connections.* Manchester, CT: Communitas.

Parent, W. (1993). Quality of life and consumer choice. In P. Wehman (Ed.), *The ADA mandate for social change* (pp. 19–44). Baltimore, MD: Brookes.

Perske, R., & Perske, M. (1992). *Circles of friends: People with disabilities and their friends enrich the lives of one another.* Nashville, TN: Abington.

Powell, T., Pancsofar, E., Steere, D., Butterworth, J., ltzkowitz, J., & Rainforth. B. (1991). *Supported employment: Developing integrated employment opportunities for people with disabilities.* White Plains, NY: Longman.

Racino, J., Walker, P., O'Connor, S., & Taylor, S. (1993). *Housing, support, and community: Choices and strategies for adults with disabilities*. Baltimore, MD: Brookes.

Rehabilitation Act Amendments of 1992, Public Law 102-569. (October 29, 1992).

Silliker, S. A. (1993). The role of social contacts in the successful job search. *Journal of Employment Counseling, 30,* 25–34.

Steere, D., Wood, R., Pancsofar, E., & Butterworth, J. (1990). Outcome-based school-to-work transition planning for students with severe disabilities. *Career Development for Exceptional Individuals, 13,* 57–69

Stineman, R., Morningstar, M., Bishop, B., & Turnbull, H. R. (1993). Role of families in transition planning for young adults with disabilities: Toward a method of person centered planning. *Journal of Vocational Rehabilitation, 3,* 52–61.

Szymanski, E. M. (1994). Transition: Life-span and life-space considerations for empowerment. *Exceptional Children, 60,* 402–410.

Taylor, S. (1988). Caught in the continuum: A critical analysis of the principle of least restrictive environment. *Journal of the Association for Persons With Severe Handicaps, 13,* 41–53.

Vandercook, T., York, J., & Forrest, M. (1989). The McGill Action Planning System (MAPS) A strategy for building the vision. *Journal of the Association for Persons With Severe Handicaps, 14,* 205–215.

Wehman, P. (1992). *Life beyond the classroom: Transition strategies for young people with disabilities*. Baltimore, MD: Brookes.

Wood, R., & Steere, D. (1992). Evaluating quality in supported employment: The standard of excellence for employment support services. *Journal of Vocational Rehabilitation, 2,* 35–45.

APPENDIX A

Comparison of Features of Lifestyle Planning Approaches

Approach	Purpose	Target Participants
Personal Futures Planning	Clarify services for transition to community life from restrictive environments	Children and adults with severe disabilities
MAPS	Clarify ways to enhance inclusion of students with disabilities	School-age-individuals with severe disabilities and their classmates
Career Planning	Clarify types of jobs searched for, entering, or changing employment	Individuals with severe disabilities
Lifestyle Planning	Clarify curricular content	Adolescents and young adults with severe disabilities
Whole Life Planning	Clarify educational and adult support	Adolescents and young adults with severe disabilities

APPENDIX B

Comparison of Steps of Lifestyle Planning Approaches

Approach	Steps
Personal Futures Planning (Mount Zwernik, 1988)	1. Develop a team or circle of support 2. Describe the quality of the person's present experiences 3. Describe changes in the person's environment or life circumstances that may influence the quality of their life 4. Describe a desirable future for the person 5. Describe threats and opportunities toward the desirable future 6. Describe barriers to the desirable future 7. Describe strategies for overcoming these barriers in order to move toward the desirable future 8. Describe changes that need to occur in the capabilities of the service system
MAPS (Vandercook, York, & Forrest, 1989	1. Determine the individual's history 2. Clarify team members' dreams for the individual 3. Clarify team members' nightmares for the individual 4. Develop team members' descriptions of the individual 5. Clarify the individual's strengths, gifts, and abilities 6. Clarify the individual's needs 7. Develop a description of an ideal day at school for the individual and the activities to be done to make it happen
Career Planning (Powell et al., 1991)	1. Form a career planning team 2. Develop a positive personal profile 3. Brainstorm quality of life outcomes 4. Conduct outcome compatibility analysis with specific work sites or types of work 5. Conduct analysis of challenges to optimal employment 6. Develop an action plan

Lifestyle Planning (O'Brien, 1987)	1. Convene the planning group
	2. Review the current lifestyle
	3. Conduct the planning meeting
	4. Follow up on the implementation of the plan
Whole Life Planning (Butterworth et al., (1993)	1. Organize the planning process
	2. Develop a personal profile
	3. Build a vision
	4. Develop an action plan
	5. Develop supports

APPENDIX C

References to Uses of Lifestyle Planning Approaches

Application to Lifestyle Planning Approach	References
Employment	Butterworth et al., 1993
	Hagner & DiLeo, 1993
	Powell et al., 1991
Transition from School to Adulthood	Steere et al., 1990
	Stineman et al., 1993
Community Housing	Racino et al., 1993
	Mount, Ducharme, & Beeman, 1991
Community Integration	Malette et al., 1992
Positive Behavioral Supports	Homer et al., 1990
School Curriculum and Inclusion	O'Brien, 1987
	Perske & Perske, 1992
	Vandercook, York, & Forrest, 1989

8

Rehabilitation Counselors as Providers: The Issue of Sexuality

Pamela S. Boyle

Sexuality can be defined as the integration of physical, social, emotional and intellectual aspects of an individual's personality which express maleness and femaleness (Chipouras, 1979). In American society, many of the messages we receive relate to physical aspects of sexuality, disregarding these other crucial components. Sexuality, in its broadest sense, is expressed in most circumstances in which an individual finds herself or himself daily: discussions of religion or politics, working, socializing, interacting with one's children or partner. It is a part of our identity and is as much a part of who we are as men and women as what we do. Typically, discussions about sexuality in our society focus on such topics as specific sexual acts, sexual function/dysfunction, size, satisfaction. These discussions are commonly performance oriented and focus on real or perceived deficits. Society's focus on beauty and perfection is undeniable. The notion that people with disabilities are sexual and have sexual feelings, needs and drives is frequently denied or at best, ignored.

Rehabilitation counselors and other human service providers are not necessarily exempt from these attitudes. Many professionals are, in general, uncomfortable with discussions of sexuality, having had little or no opportunity to become desensitized to the issue. The concept of "desensitization" is sometimes misinterpreted to mean that one becomes a blank slate, with no opinions or feelings about the issue. It actually means that one becomes more comfortable with sexual issues and more aware of his or her own attitudes, values and beliefs about sexuality. This comfort and awareness increases understanding not only of oneself but also of the attitudes, values and beliefs held by others.

It is not only essential that we adequately provide rehabilitation counseling

Reprinted from *Journal of Applied Rehabilitation Counseling* (1994), *25,* 6–9. Reprinted by permission of JARC Editor.

students with the skills, sensitivity and understanding to offer sexuality education and guidance to individuals with disabilities, but also that "seasoned veterans," those who have spent several years providing services in rehabilitation settings, be asked to include sexuality as one of many issues requiring time and attention. It seems far easier to do the former, in that one is dealing with a captive audience. Because sexuality and disability is ofen a "low priority" staff training or continuing education issue, the later group must become aware of the many print and audio-visual resources available to them to assist in their preparation to provide sexuality couseling and education. Also, they must examine the professional and personal qualities they already possess which give them a "leg up" in this effort.

There are many excellent resources available on issues of sexuality and disability. Numerous books have been published during the past few years and many regularly published journals include articles on this issue. The complete citations for those interested are provided in the references at the end of this article. Recommended reading for professionals interested in gaining factual information about sexuality and physical disability/chronic illness include those by Neistadt and Freda (1987), as well as Sadowski (1989) and an excellent book by Schover and Jensen (1988). Rehabilitation professionals wishing to increase their knowledge and understanding of sexuality and developmental disabilities would be wise to read publications by Kempton (1987), Monat (1982), in addition to Haavik and Menninger (1981). Counselors interested in a general textbook covering a multitude of issues related to human sexuality would be wise to obtain Francouer's (1991) publication. Given the dearth of professional training workshops and seminars, books and other publications have become important sources of knowledge for those with little background or exposure to sexuality and specifically to sexuality and disability. However, possessing factual information about sexuality and disability is only a part of what is necessary to assist rehabilitation clientele.

A rehabilitation counselor's professional training includes some of the very components which are necessary to effectively provide sexuality counseling and education to individuals with disabilities. Having factual information about the physical, emotional and psychological consequences of disability provides a firm foundation for examination of those which are sexual. Rehabilitation counselors are known for their ability to offer understanding, empathy and support to their clients. They develop helping relationships which provide the support and guidance an individual requires to realistically assess weaknesses and strengths, develop skills to manage significant life changes, deal with damage to one's self-concept and self-esteem and understand and work through issues with his or her significant others. They work to assist the individual to look forward to a full and productive life filled with possibilities. These professional skills will serve a client well in terms of acquiring sexuality and disability counseling and information from his or her rehabilitation counselor if that professional also has factual information to offer. Having information without also being a skillful, sensitive and non-judgmental counselor (and vice versa) will not be particularly effective in providing a client with satisfactory services related to sexuality and disability.

Even the most skilled rehabilitation counselor may feel that he or she is not the "right" or "best" person to provide sexuality related services to clients, citing the fact that they are not "sex counselors". One need not be a trained sexuality counselor to provide basic services to rehabilitation clients. The following listing, adapted from work by Kempton (1987) with additions by the author, should provide some common sense guidelines for rehabilitation professionals who wish to address sexuality:

1. The counselor should sincerely believe that sexuality is a valid rehabilitation issue, as important as any other which needs to be addressed in the rehabilitation process.
2. The professional should be an individual who has come to terms with his or her own sexuality and gained a fair degree of comfort with sexual language and behavior. Few rehabilitation professionals ever find complete comfort in this regard, but it is important to know where one's sensitivities lie and how they might interfere with a therapeutic relationship.
3. The counselor must also work to become accepting of individuals whose sexual lives are very different from their own. Gaining comfort and tolerance is a process which develops over time and with practice. One need not believe that he or she should simply feel this way in the early stages of working with the issue of sexuality.
4. Helping professionals should be sensitive but direct about issues of sexuality. This will set an example for the client that these matters can be freely discussed with the counselor and that he or she need not feel hesitant about raising them in the therapeutic setting. Often rehabilitation counselors are uncertain about how to raise the issue of sexuality with a client and instead waits for the client to take the lead. Individuals with disabilities commonly wait for the issue to be raised by the counselor. This "butting of heads" will not be productive. Instead, counselors must learn to take the initiative with the client, providing a "shopping list" of issues which can be discussed within the therapeutic relationship. The list should include sexuality and socialization. While clients may not wish to discuss these personal issues at that moment, the door has been opened for discussions in the future.
5. A healthy sense of humor about sexuality will serve both professional and client well. Sex and sexuality are not always serious, foreboding topics. It has been suggested that laughter is the best medicine and while sexuality is generally seen as quite a serious (if not grim) issue, sometimes a good laugh will help to put things in perspective.
6. Counselors should not expect their sexuality counseling efforts to be a "quick fix" for rehabilitation clients. It seems that counselors very often

expect that sexual concerns and problems should be resolved more quickly than other issues. Be patient and give people time to make changes, some of which are very difficult. Remember that at the core of this process of change is often a profound sense of pain, sadness and loss.

Rehabilitation counselors who decide that they have the professional and personal qualities necessary to provide basic sexuality guidance and who have done some reading about the issue may wonder what kinds of issues they will actually confront. Issues of concern to individuals with physical disabilities or chronic illnesses may be as "basic" as a discussion of body image and self-esteem or as technical as whether a woman with quadriplegia can become pregnant and have a normal pregnancy. Other issues may include resuming sexual activity after a stroke, the effects of multiple sclerosis on sexual functioning, socialization concerns, birth control and disability, physical and behavioral aspects of traumatic brain injury and concerns related to maintaining and strengthening an existing relationship. Professionals who strive to increase their knowledge will begin to understand that assisting rehabilitation clients with issues of sexuality may differ depending on whether the individual has a life-long or acquired disability and whether the disability is of a "static" (such as cerebral palsy and spinal cord injury) or "progressive" (multiple sclerosis, muscular dystrophy) nature.

Individuals with mental illness or recovering from substance abuse may need basic information about a variety of issues related to sexuality in order to assist them to make wise choices about sexual behavior and to safely enjoy this aspect of their lives. They may also need information about the kinds of medications they may be taking and how drugs can affect sexual functioning.

Rehabilitation counselors providing services to persons with mental retardation/developmental disabilities may address concerns of clients and their significant others related to informed consent, dating, the desire to marry/have children, appropriate public and private behavior, masturbation, protection against victimization and genetic issues among others. As in all areas of education and counseling provided to individuals with cognitive disabilities, sexuality education and counseling calls for repetition and reinforcement requiring a significant investment of time and energy.

In addition to drawing on one's skills and sensitivity to issues of sexuality and disability and to having basic information, a model of providing treatment for sexual problems and concerns has proven to be quite useful to helping professionals. The PLISSIT Model (Annon, 1974) of sexuality counseling offers professionals an opportunity to translate their sensitivity, information and desire to assist their clientele into the ability to provide concrete services. Despite the fact that it was developed twenty years ago, PLISSIT remains a valuable tool for counselors wishing to assist their clientele with issues concerning sexuality.

PLISSIT is an acronym which stands for Permission, Limited Information,

Specific Suggestion and Intensive Therapy. While the model was not specifically developed for use with people with disabilities, it offers rehabilitation professionals a very helpful framework. The PLISSIT Model, based on a behavioral approach to the treatment of sexual problems, has several strengths. First, it is useful in a variety of settings and can be adapted to whatever treatment time can be allotted. Each ascending level of this model requires a greater degree of comfort, skill, knowledge and training on the part of the rehabilitation counselor. This means that counselors are able to make decisions about how deeply they wish or are able to get involved in the sexual concerns of their clients. As professionals reach their limits in terms of level of comfort and competency, referrals to other professionals with more expertise can be made. It should be noted that a counselor's ability to provide intervention related to sexual issues may not remain constant given the wide variety of sexual concerns individuals with disabilities will have. All professionals, whatever their skills and comfort might be, should at the very least, be able to provide permission.

PERMISSION is offered through statements which provide reassurance to the individual that his or her concerns are legitimate and important. Statements of permission also give the message that the counselor is available to listen. A more relaxed therapeutic atmosphere can be created by offering permission-giving statements. Examples of this type of statements include:

- I'm glad you brought that up. I can see that it's really important to you.

- That's interesting—tell me more about that.

- Sounds like you have some legitimate questions about sexual matters. I'll be happy to tell you what I know.

A professional effectively opens the door to continued communication about sexual matters by offering permission-giving statements. If the rehabilitation counselor can do no more than listen and affirm the sexual concerns of the individual with a disability, he or she will have done a great deal. Ths initial discussion is the first step toward clarifying concerns and finding answers to questions. If the counselor finds that he or she is unable to offer any further assistance to the individual beyond Permission, an appropriate referral to a professional with additional skills and information is required.

LIMITED INFORMATION is the second level of the PLISSIT Model and requires increased competency and comfort on the part of the helper. At this level the counselor offers the client information directly related to his or her sexual concern. It is an excellent opportunity to dispel myths and fallacies related to issues of sexuality and disability. Examples of limited information counselors can provide include basic explanations of male and female anatomy, discussions of the effects of spinal cord injury on fertility, or the effects which some medications may have on the ability to function sexually. Provision of limited information may be enhanced by the use of appropriate visual materials, including pictures, diagrams or videos. Very often this factual information will be adequate to satisfy the concerns and questions of the individual. It is important to note that limited information is always offered in conjunction with an atmosphere of permission. Obviously, the counselor must possess accurate sexuality information to be able to offer it and have the time to do so. If the counselor is unable to provide the information requested by his or her client, it is once again essential that an appropriate referral be made to a more skilled and knowledgeable source of assistance.

SPECIFIC SUGGESTION, the third level of the PLISSIT Model, necessitates that the counselor obtain a basic sexual history. The rehabilitation counselor can gain a better understanding of the client's ideas and views about their difficulties or concerns, and what he or she has previously done in an attempt to resolve the problems. It is also important to determine what the individual's goals are in terms of problem resolution so that these goals can be clarified/altered and appropriate plans to intervene can be developed. For example, in counseling a person with chronic pain, the counselor may learn that the client's relationship with their spouse has suffered in that sexual relations have all but ceased due to the unrelenting pain. Brainstorming with the client possible suggestions to resolve or at least reduce the severity of the difficulty may include determining the time of day when pain medication is the most effective or exploring alternative positions for intimacy which won't exacerbate the pain. The use of pillows or soft wedges for support may also be suggested. Suggesting ways to open up communication with a partner may also be a strategy. Providing services at this level of the PLISSIT Model requires a fair investment of time, commitment, and comfort. It also requires that the counselor be quite knowledgeable about how a specific disability, whether it is physical, developmental or emotional, may impact on an individual and that he or she be able to speak about sexual matters with a fair amount of candor. Some rehabilitation counselors will not be willing or will feel they are not well enough informed to provide services at this level. If this is true, the greatest service one can offer is to make certain that an appropriate referral is made.

Significant levels of skill and knowledge are required to provide INTENSIVE THERAPY, the fourth level of the PLISSIT. Many rehabilitation counselors will not feel that they can offer services at this level. It should be noted that the majority of questions or concerns raised in counseling will be manageable at the first three levels of the model. For those individuals who have the need for ongoing, structured sexual counseling or therapy, the rehabilitation counselor must be prepared to make an appropriate referral to a therapist knowledgeable about both sexuality and about disability.

The PLISSIT Model combines counseling, education, helpful support and guidance in a structure which is useful by all levels of professionals and by a variety of disciplines, including rehabilitation counseling. Annon's (1974) book provides case examples and extensive commentary regarding use of this important therapeutic tool.

To use the PLISSIT Model as outlined, referral sources for rehabilitation clients in need of sexuality counseling or therapy which surpasses the skill or comfort level of the counselor must be located. These referrals may be difficult to find. It is wise to spend some time in staff or team meetings talking about sexuality. Not only might this help to increase comfort levels of all staff but it may help team members to identify co-workers who have well developed skills, knowledge or comfort levels, making them helpful referral sources.

It may also be possible to identify referral sources in one's community. Sometimes there are sexuality counselors, educators or therapists affiliated with large rehabilitation facilities. These specialists have skills and knowledge about sexual issues as well as about disability. Sometimes an individual sex educator, counselor, or therapist in private practice can be a referral source. Keep in mind that the majority of these practitioners will know very little about disability or about the sexual concerns of people with disabling conditions. While this doesn't necessarily predict an inability to provide services, it may mean that the rehabilitation professional must be prepared, with a client's permission, to offer information related to disability to this professional if there is no other referral option.

It may be possible to get referrals to qualified sources from organizations such as the American Association of Sex Educators, Counselors and Therapists, the American Board of Sexology, or The Sex Information and Education Council of the United States. Sometimes local affiliates of Planned Parenthood are helpful with finding community resources.

Many times the concerns and questions people with disabilities have about sexuality are able to be addressed within the rehabilitation counseling setting and do not require a referral to an outside source. Rehabilitation counselors bring to a therapeutic environment a special background of training, counseling skills and an understanding of the human condition. If they add to this foundation some basic information about sexuality, an understanding of the PLISSIT Model and a true willingness to look at the needs of the "whole person", the stage is set for providing truly comprehensive rehabilitation services. Rehabilitation counselors must keep in mind that a first unsuccessful attempt to get help with a sexual concern may mean that that individual never raises the issue again.

References

Annon, J. (1974). *The behavioral treatmemt of sexual problems.* Honolulu: Enabling Systems.

Chipouras, S., Cornelius, D., Daniels, S., & Makas, E. (1979). *Who cares? A handbook on sex education and counseling services for disabled people.* Washington, DC: George Washington University.

Francouer, R. (1991). *Becoming a sexual person.* New York: Macmillan Publishing Company.

Haavik, S., & Menninger, K. (1981). *Sexuality, law and the developmentally disabled person: Legal and clinical aspects of marriage, parenthood and sterilization.* Baltimore: Paul H. Brookes Publishing Company.

Kempton, W. (1987). *Sex education for persons with disabilities that hinder learning: A teacher's guide.* PA: The Amity Road Press.

Monat, R. (1992). *Understanding and expressing sexuality: Responsible choice for individuals with developmental disabilities.* Baltimore: Paul H. Brookes Publishing Company.

Neistadt, M., & Freda, M. (1987). *Choices: A guide to sex counseling with physically disabled adults.* Malabar, FL: Robert E. Krieger Publishing Company.

Sadowski, C. (1989). *Sexual concerns when illness or disability strikes.* Springfield, IL: Charles C Thomas.

Schover, L., & Jensen, S. (1988). *Sexuality and chronic illness: A comprehensive approach.* New York: The Guilford Press.

PART 3

The Elderly Client

In chapter 1, we presented data that document the aging of American society. Evidence was also presented in chapter 3 that suggests older people are at risk for psychological problems due to the losses they often experience following retirement. However, despite their growing representation in the general population and the increasing risk for psychological problems with aging, there is substantial evidence that elders are underserved by counselors and psychologists (Gatz, Karel, & Wolkenstein, 1991). Some of the underservice can be attributed to unwillingness on the part of older people to seek mental health services. However, a great deal of the blame must rest on the counseling profession, which has failed to properly address the needs of older people.

In the chapters that follow in part 3, the authors describe the experiences of older people and point out their counseling-related needs. They also discuss some specific counseling strategies that may be useful when working with elders. In chapter 9, Heller suggests a theme similar to that raised earlier by Nosek and Fuhrer in chapter 6 regarding people with disabilities, that mental health services for older people should be developed by the consumers of those services. Heller suggests that as counselors and mental health workers, we need to restructure our thinking from how to care for older people to how to prevent the loss of useful social roles for older people. He discusses how age-segregated housing has contributed to a sense of isolation and loss of rewarding social roles for some elders. In order to maintain older people in useful social roles and help society gain from their wisdom, Hiller suggests that counselors and other mental health workers encourage older people to integrate into ongoing family, neighborhood, and community activities. Counselors also can help promote the maintenance of useful social roles for elders by encouraging them to remain actively involved in self-help and advocacy organizations run for and by older people.

In chapter 10, Qualls alerts counselors to the stresses that occur for older couples after the children are gone and both spouses are retired. She points out that couples must adjust to increased time together, modified family roles, shifts in the balance of family power, changes in need for nurturance, and changing relationships with adult children. She also points out how specific later life events, such as retirement, impairment due to chronic illness, and disruptions in their children's lives, can have an impact on older couples. Qualls proposes that marital therapy with older couples begin with a marital assessment that examines how these processes and events are affecting the two partners. Intervention begins by "normalizing" the experiences of older couples. The counselor must also work through countertransference issues and deal with their own attitudes toward aging and loss.

In the final chapter in part 3, Kim and Atkinson examine some of the fiction and facts about aging and sexuality. Although they note that some men and women remain sexually active throughout their lifetime, there is some evidence of a gradual decline in sexual activity for most people beyond age 50.

The authors suggest that much of the decline in sexual activity can be attributed to societally imposed limitations, although some physiological changes due to aging do place limitations on some sexual activity. However, the need for intimacy remains constant across the lifetime, and there is some evidence that people who remain sexually active into old age gain some physical and emotional benefits from it. Kim and Atkinson offer a number of suggestions for addressing sexual concerns with older clients, with special attention to the needs of specific groups within the older population.

References

Gatz, M., Karel, M. J., & Wolkenstein, B. (1991). Survey of providers of psychological services to older adults. *Professional Psychology: Research and Practice, 22,* 413–415.

9

Prevention Activities for Older Adults: Social Structures and Personal Competencies That Maintain Useful Social Roles

Kenneth Heller

Current demographic trends are likely to present the mental health fields with a major dilemma in the years to come. The population of those older than 65 years of age has been steadily growing. Anticipated population changes through the year 2030 have been described graphically as "the graying of America" (Storandt, 1983). In the years ahead, there will he a sharp decline in the adult population that is younger than 35 years of age, while at the same time, the proportion of individuals older than 65 will be steadily increasing (Morrison, 1983). These changes have heen occurring throughout the world and reflect both reductions in birth rates and steep declines in mortality rates, particularly in the developing countries (Myers, 1990). In North America, 20% of the population will be older than 65 by the year 2025, as compared with fewer than 12% of the population in that age range in 1985. Given the increasing prevalence of older adults in the general population, however, it is odd that older adults typically have low rates of utilization of mental health services. In the 1970s and 1980s fewer than 4% of community mental health services were targeted to this group, and 70% of practicing psychologists and counselors reported never seeing older adults in their professional work (Santos & VandenBos, 1982; Smyer & Gatz, 1983). The most recent estimate of the proportion of older adults served by community mental health centers is 6%, still far below the proportion of older adults in the general population (Gatz & Smyer, 1992).

Reprinted from *Journal of Counseling and Development, 72,* 1993, 124–130. © ACA. Reprinted with permission. No further reproduction authorized without written permission of American Counseling.

There are several probable reasons for the underutilization of mental health services by older adults. Elderly persons generally report higher levels of life satisfaction and fewer worries and concerns than do younger individuals (Campbell, 1981). They also are more likely to conceptualize problems in terms of physical health and adverse life experiences rather than in terms of psychological deficits (Veroff, Kulka, & Douvan, 1981). Traditional counseling services that require potential clients to admit to psychological concerns before help can be offered are likely to find few takers among this age group. At the same time, there are professional barriers to involvement with elderly persons as well. Many service providers lack gerontological training and have negative expectations concerning treatment effectiveness with older adults (Gatz & Pearson, 1988; Smyer, Zarit, & Qualls, 1990). Despite their growing numbers, elderly persons continue to be the subject of negative societal and professional stereotypes.

The purpose of this article is to discuss the conceptual reorientation that will be needed if we are to provide more responsive psychological services to older adults. I will adopt a community-ecological perspective in that I argue that patterns of professional helping should be embedded in an ecological understanding of the role that significant others have in the lives of older adults and that existing social structures should be reinforced whenever possible. The solutions that professional counselors offer elderly persons should be congruent with their life-styles and values and should reflect their goals rather than being based on professional traditions and "wisdom" accumulated from practice with younger age groups.

The Heterogeneity of Old Age

There is a growing recognition that the aged population is a heterogeneous group. Age does not eradicate sex, race, or socioeconomic distinctions or differences in personality and temperament that occur among individuals. This diversity is often not appreciated when older adults are regarded as a single category of individuals older than 65 years of age (Myers, 1990). Besides individual personal characteristics, there can be major differences in the needs and capabilities of the "young-old" as compared with the "old-old." Thus, although only 5% of persons older than 65 years of age live in nursing homes, 22% of persons older than 85 live in such facilities, and this older group accounts for much of the increase in nursing home occupancy (Parmelee & Lawton, 1990). Even so, despite the popular stereotype of elderly persons as infirm and incapacitated, most older adults are not institutionalized and manage to live a meaningful and relatively independent existence.

Ageist stereotypes are fairly common in the popular press. They are not always negative (e.g., frail, forgetful), but increasingly, the problem of caring for chronically ill aged individuals is the focal point of much media attention (Gatz & Pearson, 1988). The focus is often on Alzheimer's disease, giving the impression to the public, as well as to elderly persons themselves, that aging means inevitable incompetence. In fact, moderate to severe dementia is found in only 4% to 6% of those 65 years of age and older (Gatz & Pearson, 1988); thus, the expectation of imminent senility with age is grossly exaggerated.

There are, of course, problems associated with increased age. A major problem is that individuals lose institutional roles with age (e.g., forced retirement at age 65) and find that their contribution to society is devalued not on the basis of personal attributes or behavior but because age has moved them to the role of a nonparticipant in society (Rosow, 1985). The loss of work roles and status, however, does not mean that elderly persons need to be socially nonproductive. Although people lose institutional roles with age, informal roles remain viable for a much longer period of time (Rosow, 1985). Informal roles depend on networks of friendships and voluntary activities that tie individuals to social institutions. Berger and Neuhaus (1977) referred to these as "mediating structures" that stand between the individual and the larger institutions of public life. The challenge for society will be to find ways for elderly citizens to perform useful social roles in mediating structures of neighborhood, family, and voluntary social organizations—roles that convey a continued sense of competence and esteem (Heller, Price, & Hogg, 1990).

Additional problems that can occur with age include declining health and losses in social networks resulting from death and migration of network members. Older adults typically have fewer choices available for the development of new social ties. Furthermore, when the mobility of citizens encourages the dispersion of kin, older adults often are cut off from useful social roles, as the bearers of traditional knowledge concerning family relations and child care. This is not to imply that most elderly citizens are cut off from family contact (Shanas, 1979), because technology can provide tools (e.g., telephones, airplanes) to bridge geographic isolation (Wellman, 1979). Still, there is cause for concern because recent evidence indicates that isolation and role loss are factors in the increased risk for morbidity and ultimate mortality among elderly persons. Studying an elderly population, Blazer (1982) found that decreased social interaction, impaired roles and attachments, and low perceived support were significant predictors of early mortality among the aged; the mortality rate among those with low perceived support was $3^{1}/_{2}$ times higher at a 30-month follow-up than for those with moderate-to-high perceived support.

Prevention Activities for and with Older Adults

Before 1970 there was unquestioned acceptance in the mental health fields of the proposition that psychotherapy was the only psychological method for helping people in distress (Cowen, 1973). The theories dominant in the mental health profession were largely psychiatric in origin, which meant that they were treatment and private practice oriented. Although public health concepts had always been a part of medicine, few physicians had ever taken seriously the public health mandate of promoting general health and well-being (Heller, Price, Reinharz, Riger, & Wandersman, 1984).

Two themes that community psychology brought to the mental health fields were a concern for prevention and a need to focus on broader ecological levels than just on the exclusive treatment of individuals. These themes can be found in modern public health theories in which disease is seen as an end product of an interaction between a host, a pathological agent, and conducive factors in the environment (Bloom, 1965). From this perspective, effective prevention can result from the modification of any of these factors (e.g., immunizing the host or modifying the environment). In a similar manner, prevention activities in the mental health sphere could involve community, organizational, or family-level programs to reduce the impact of environmental stress or efforts to strengthen the capacity of vulnerable individuals to deal with that stress (Heller, Price, & Sher, 1980).

Prevention programs for older adults can be built to emphasize the elements just described (e.g., environmental modification to reduce isolation and loneliness and to increase social usefulness, while at the same time providing help to maintain and improve older adult coping abilities; Kastenbaum, 1987). Although some negative environmental events are unavoidable, others may be more modifiable than we may realize. For example, although a decline in health or the death of a significant other may not be preventable, some of the risk factors associated with mortality and morbidity are modifiable so that deterioration in health can be slowed. What is important in any prevention program, however, is to provide realistic choices to older adults that they can access voluntarily. The heterogeneity of the older population means not only that no one program is likely to be suited to all older adults but also like any other segment of the population, many older adults continue to want to maintain control of important facets of their lives. Thus, community programs are best designed with the planning and participation of older adults themselves.

When psychologists and counselors think about "programs" for older adults, what usually comes to mind is some form of activity or companionship program to combat loneliness and keep older citizens occupied. Implicit in these endeavors is a view of older adults as individuals who are no longer likely to be active contributors to society. Reframing the question from "How should older adults be cared for?" to "Can we encourage the maintenance of useful social roles by older adults?" allows us to think of new possibilities (Heller, Price, Reinharz, Riger, & Wandersman, 1984).

In the past, little attention was given to the physical or social structures in which many older adults live and which, in part, determine their self-perception of social usefulness and integration. Three such factors are housing, employment, and the structure of social relationships. I turn to these next to demonstrate the importance of social settings and useful social roles in maintaining the psychological well-being of older adults.

Housing Alternatives and the Maintenance of Active Social Roles

Although the wide variety of housing alternatives discussed in the literature (Rowles, 1987) gives the impression of a plethora of choices, in fact, housing options for many older people turn out to be limited. Their choices may be constrained by growing physical incapacity, financial limitations, and the desire to maintain existing social ties and social routines. Although many older adults might prefer to remain in their existing residences, they are often forced by circumstances to consider relocation. Rowles (1987) distinguished between three overlapping categories of older adults and noted that each has distinct capabilities and needs. The "active old" are healthy and mobile individuals who require minimal assistance in maintaining an independent life-style. Most of these individuals do not relocate and when they do, their choices are usually voluntary, reflecting diminished household size and a desire to pursue leisure time pursuits. The "vulnerable old" are persons who require a supportive physical environment or some degree of practical help with everyday tasks. These individuals also might remain in their own homes with increasing use of supportive community services, but the greatest source of assistance is family members, particularly an adult daughter who emerges as the primary care giver. Because of increases in survival rates, it has been estimated that on average, women now spend more time as daughters to parents older than 65 than they spend as mothers of children under 18 years of age (Bengtson, Rosenthal, & Burton, 1990). Finally, the "frail elderly" are those who need constant care because of diminished health and competence. It is this last group for whom long-term hospital or institutional care becomes a necessity.

In discussing the planning of housing alternatives for aged persons, Parmelee and Lawton (1990) noted the constant dialectic between autonomy and security that is likely to occur. Recent gerontological theory has emphasized the desire of older adults to maintain independence regardless of whether they live in their own homes or move to special living arrangements. Autonomy means freedom of choice and action, and self-regulation of one's life space, with the minimal need to call for the assistance of others. At the same time, elderly persons and their family members have distinct concerns about safety and security. Physical and psychological security involve safety from environmental threats as well as easy access to health care and emergency services. Security can also be maintained by a sense of community and continuity with one's friends and neighbors. The problem is that gains in security are sometimes attained by sacrificing autonomy, as in the case of nursing homes that reward helplessness and dependence (Baltes & Reisenzein, 1986; Langer & Avorn, 1982; Piper & Langer, 1986). Overworked staff may find it easier to maintain institutional routines than to encourage initiative, particularly if they believe that rehabilitative attempts are futile in "curing" age-related decline (Parmelee & Lawton, 1990). What they miss is the importance of maintaining autonomy by reinforcing existing capabilities.

In an often-cited study by Langer and Rodin (1976), the researchers varied the feelings of control that residents had over events in a nursing home. Residents were randomly assigned to one of two floors that were brought together and were given a talk by the hospital administrator that either emphasized self-responsibility or benign care. The instructions to the self-responsibility group stated in part that "there are a lot of choices that you can make here." The emphasis for the benign care group was that "we want to take care of you." Although the hospital routine for both groups was essentially the same, the remarkable results of this study indicated that the groups encouraged to take more responsibility became more active, reported less unhappiness, showed better health for the 18-month follow-up period, and had lower mortality rates as compared with the benign-care group.

There is a long-standing debate in gerontology between the advocates and critics of age-segregated housing projects as appropriate settings for older adults. Advocates point to the advantages of a setting that can facilitate the replacement of lost friends with individuals of a similar age, an accepting and supportive peer group culture, the positive and nonstigmatizing benefits of mutual, reciprocal help that occurs among residents, and a sufficient population base to justify the provision of a wide array of supportive services (Feingold & Werby, 1990). Critics of segregated housing for elderly persons note the isolation of such settings from mainstream community activities and concerns, the conflict and gossiping that can occur in small, tight-knit communities, and the depressing effect of "waiting for death" as one's friends and neighbors pass away with increasing frequency (Keith, 1990; Rowles, 1987).

Can the benefits of supportive structures present in age-segregated housing be obtained without the negative effects of isolation from useful social roles that can be a too frequent concomitant of such projects? Multigenerational housing, in which older adults live with members of their extended families, is one such possibility. In this pattern, older adults live with younger family members sharing some common living space while performing needed household tasks. It is a fairly common housing arrangement in many nonindustrialized countries and can still be found in more rural areas of this country (Kendig, 1990). Urbanization and geographic mobility, however, have changed traditional housing patterns and have decreased the availability of useful family roles for older adults. For example, it is difficult to help with child care or be involved in other household tasks in families that no longer live in close proximity.

Home sharing, in which older adults take others into their homes as "boarders" or move into the home of another family, also can provide an opportunity for companionship and sharing of household chores (Pynoos, Hamburger, & June, 1990), but it is not an option favored by many older adults (Jaffee & Wellin, 1989; Parmelee & Lawton, 1990; Pritchard & Perkocha,

1989). A home and its possessions often provide a sense of identity and connection to life experience that may be disrupted by others who move in with different routines and possessions of their own. Security is enhanced in such an arrangement, but with the potential for loss of autonomy. Although home sharing is generally seen as a positive experience by those who participate, shared housing matches among nonrelated adults do not last long. The average length of a house-sharing arrangement is 3 to 4 months, with few lasting longer than 1 year (Thuras, 1989).

Age-integrated cooperative housing projects are a more promising alternative. Cooperative living arrangements and planned communities have traditionally been available to those with resources, but these often involve hiring a management team to perform common maintenance tasks for residents, as in the condominium model. In some cases, tenants themselves manage their own buildings, hiring others to perform only the most technical services, but even here, resources are needed to purchase services and so are rarely available to those with limited incomes. One exception is the cooperative housing movement in Canada, which is supported by the national government to provide housing options for citizens of all income brackets (Hulchanski, 1987). Another interesting example is the tenant cooperatives that developed in this country in response to inner-city building abandonment. Leavitt and Saegert (1990) interviewed residents of apartment buildings in Harlem that had been abandoned by their landlords and compared those that had been taken over by tenant cooperative associations with those that had not. One of the surprises in their data was that many of the leaders of the building cooperatives were older women. The older residents were likely to have a longer tenure in the building and to have more to lose through forced relocation, but they also were active and vital women accustomed to managing household affairs. Rather than sitting by passively waiting for what seemed to be inevitable neighborhood deterioration, they took charge of revitalization efforts within their buildings, which, in turn, helped stabilize neighborhood conditions.

Given the dispersion of the nuclear family in the United States, it is unlikely that we will return to an earlier norm in which older adults live with family members, performing useful household tasks. Our social stereotypes of older adults as irritable and interfering individuals also make it unlikely that they will be often chosen voluntarily as members of housing cooperatives. After all, why choose to live with an older person if that individual is unlikely to contribute to your well-being? Older adults, however, do have the maturity and experience that make them valuable contributors to society. For example, note the number of older world leaders and the number of older citizens in other cultures who are regularly turned to for advice and help. The purpose of discussing housing alternatives is to note that we probably pay a price for our youth-oriented, mobile society. It isn't just that older adults are unnecessarily disenfranchised from useful social roles but also that the rest of us are deprived of their wisdom and counsel. What is needed for change to occur are attitude shifts and social structures that would allow the positive characteristics of older adults to be more highly utilized. In this regard, counselors and other mental health specialists can play a useful role in helping to integrate older adults into ongoing family, neighborhood, and community activities.

Retirement Transitions and the Maintenance of Active Social Roles

Work is one of the major ways that individuals define themselves as persons. As Price (1985) noted, "For many of us, the kind of work we have—or don't have—is an eloquent, if silent, statement of who we think we are and what is meaningful to us" (p. 2). Although the workplace can be an important source of identity maintenance, in actuality labor force participation by older adults in this country has been declining steadily over the last 40 years. This decline is associated with the financial incentives for retirement that can be found in Social Security and other pension plans. Even though mandatory retirement before the age of 70 has been legally eliminated from most occupations, there are major financial disincentives in these plans for staying on the job. The net result is that in practice, retirement at age 65, or between 62 and 65, is now the norm. It is not that most U.S. workers choose this option voluntarily—some would prefer staying on beyond age 65, while others would be content to retire much earlier. In fact, research indicates that most older employed men would prefer part-time work instead of complete retirement. This alternative, however, is generally not available. Movement to part-time work, especially if it involves a change in employer, usually involves a significantly lower wage rate. Thus, American workers who would like to continue working at some level are often faced with two relatively unattractive alternatives. Continued full-time work beyond the age of 65 usually involves significant losses in retirement income provided by pension plans. On the other hand, a switch to part-time work means a lower wage rate. Given these alternatives, it is not surprising that most workers choose full retirement by age 65 (Quinn & Burkhauser, 1990).

An attractive alternative is phased retirement, which is much more common in European countries than it is in the United States (Casey & Bruche, 1983; Swank, 1982). There is a wide variety of phased retirement plans, but their essential elements involve some degree of progressive reduction in time on the job while maintaining full employee salary and benefits.

Phased retirement plans have several advantages for employers. They are attractive to employees and can be a factor in retaining skilled workers and reducing training costs associated with worker turnover and the need to train new employees. Worker morale and productivity can be maintained as new employees are introduced working alongside older workers, learning some of their skills and responsible work ethic. The advantage of phased retirement for employees is that it allows for a gradual adaptation to retirement and the development of interests outside of the regular work environment. In the United States, it is more typical to terminate older employees than it is to plan for their phased retirement. This practice, however, may change given the anticipated shifts in the demographic composition of the work force. It is expected that there will be fewer individuals in the active work force in the next several decades; thus, there may be incentives to keep older workers on the job for a longer period.

It is important to recognize that retirement is not a major stressor for all workers because individuals vary in their attachment to the work role. Many low-skill blue-collar workers have dull and monotonous jobs that are not particularly meaningful or important (Kasl & Cobb, 1979); thus, their primary adjustment to retirement is economic. On the other hand, there are others for whom work provides a sense of identity and support that is not available in other aspects of their lives. Thus, what is needed most is a flexible policy that allows for part-time employment for those who choose to continue in this role. Although it is difficult to argue for the continued employment of older adults in a tight job market, future upturns in the economy will again require a well-trained and stable labor force, characteristics that are often found among older adults.

Variations in the Supportiveness of Social Relationships

Research indicates that friends and family members often perform different functions for older adults. Friends are more likely to provide outlets for socializing, thus moderating feelings of loneliness, whereas family members are more likely to provide both emergency and long-term care (Gottlieb, 1983). Litwak (1989) further distinguished between long-term, intermediate, and short-term friends. Long-term friends, those known for more than 10 years, are more likely to live at some distance, but these friendships are likely to be maintained through a set of common values, life-styles, and experiences. Long-term friends help define normative behaviors around slowly changing roles such as dealing with retirement issues, changing parental demands, or failing health. Long-term friends who are contacted periodically through in-person or telephone contacts reaffirm one's sense of self by their continued affectional commitment and by their reinforcement of basic life-style choices that have been made over the years. Short-term friends are more likely to provide companionship for free-time activities and share and help with daily tasks. Thus, a move to an age-segregated housing unit may provide an increase in short-term friends who can help with daily tasks (Allan & Adams, 1989), but is less likely to have a positive influence on self-identity and self-esteem.

There is a great deal of evidence that supportive networks reduce both morbidity and mortality (Berkman, 1985; Minkler, 1985), but the basic processes involved are still unknown. The sources of support that are most likely to bolster a sense of morale and well-being still remain unanswered questions in the research literature. As social networks shrink with age, family members become increasingly relied on for both physical care and emotional support, yet it has been argued that active friendship ties, particularly with long-term friends, have a stronger relationship to subjective well-being than do family ties (Arling, 1976; Larson, Mannell, & Zuzanek, 1986; Lee & Ishii-Kuntz, 1988; Spakes, (1979). Larson and his colleagues (1986) suggested that although family members are increasingly relied upon for social contact, active leisure occurs more frequently among friends and is more likely to involve reciprocity, a sharing of interests, and positive affect. Even so, there are several conditions in which family support may be equally important. The inability to maintain short-term, temporal reciprocity in relationships (because of poor health) and loss of economic resources are particular impediments to the continuance of peer friendships. On the other hand, family relationships are more likely to be governed by a more long-term sense of reciprocity (Antonucci & Jackson, 1987), with a concomitant expectation that in times of need older adults will be cared for by their children. As Antonucci (1985) noted, many elderly individuals have higher expectations of support from family members than from friends because they themselves had been earlier support providers to family members.

Although family support may be of value, there are several reasons why family members may withdraw from frequent contact with elderly persons. Our own previous research has found that elderly women vary in their relational competence skills; thus, it is possible that some elderly women may lack the skills needed for maintaining supportive family ties (Hogg & Heller, 1990). Furthermore, with technological advancement and the fragmentation of the nuclear family, many older adults no longer serve a useful role in society as transmitters of cultural knowledge. There is less reason to contact elderly persons about work assignments or child rearing if much of their knowledge is considered obsolete. At the same time, their own withdrawal from work and child care roles means that older adults may have less interesting things to say about daily events. With much time on their hands and little to do, elderly persons are more likely to attend to problems of declining health and physical symptomatology. Discussions of chronic health problems can be frustrating and anxiety arousing to family members, because they can do little to change declining health and may, at the same time, be reminded of their own vulnerability to similar problems. Thus, there are several reasons why family members may withdraw from contact and the conflicting demands created by the support role.

The dilemma, then, for older adults is that while friendship networks become increasingly constricted with age because of declining health and death of network members, relying on family members exclusively for support can also pose problems. It would not make sense simply to attempt to increase support from family members if the individuals involved did not have the skills to manage the negative aspects of such relationships. For example, rather than encourage family members to increase their contacts with an elderly parent or grandparent, a prior step might involve discussion and training concerning how to manage the anxiety that might occur in such interactions (Gottlieb, 1988).

Still, it is important to recognize that there are many older adults who maintain active lives and rich and fulfilling relationships with friends and family members. Thus, the heterogeneity of the older adult population means that care must be taken in planning social or psychological intervention. Some individuals might not need extensive programs, whereas others who do may not be in a position to take advantage of help that is offered without prior training.

The discussion thus far has focused on the impact of social structures and social relationships in facilitating the adjustment of older adults. Skill, however, is needed to develop and maintain social networks, particularly as family members and friends move away or die. I turn now to a discussion of the personal competencies that are needed to maintain social relationships.

The Role of Personal Competencies in Enhancing Social Participation

There has been a general neglect of research focused on the social competence of community-dwelling older adults, perhaps because of an age stereotype among researchers that leads them to expect that friendship development and maintenance is less important to elderly persons than to a younger cohort (Hogg & Heller, 1990). For the most part, social competence research with elderly persons has focused on the skills needed for adjusting to a nursing home environment (e.g., Berger & Rose, 1977; Carstensen, 1983). Measures of social competence related to nursing home adjustment, however, may tap different skills from those that may be important for more interactive social participation. Thus, for example, research with young adults has suggested that the components of social competence that are related to friendship development include assertion, empathy, and role-taking skills (Davis, 1983; Riggio, 1986). Persons low in self-perceived assertiveness were found to initiate fewer interactions and to respond less effectively to the social invitations of others (Jones, Chernovetz, & Hansson, 1978). Assertion has been found to be related to the ability to access friendships, whereas empathy and role taking have been found to be related to the maintenance of friendships (Hansson, Jones, & Carpenter, 1984). Hansson et al. (1984) discussed empathy and role taking as attributes that enable persons to find ways to contribute to the maintenance of a friendship. They further argued that the converse of empathy and role taking (insensitivity to the viewpoints of others and social imperceptiveness) should lead to frustrating and stressful relationships.

There are many life stressors facing older adults that challenge existing competencies. The shrinking of social networks of many older adults means that extra effort will be needed to make new contacts or maintain existing ties. The loss of loved ones also presents a need to manage grief, chronic feelings of loneliness, and conflicts that may arise with existing network members. Declining health and financial resources mean that assistance may be required to manage basic activities of daily living, such as shopping or housework. Each of these spheres (e.g., initiating social contacts, managing instrumental needs, coping with negative emotion, managing interpersonal conflict) requires competencies that may never have been adequately learned or may have been learned at one time only to fall into disuse under the routine of married life. For example, many older widows may never have made important decisions without first consulting their husbands. With a husband's death, many may find it extremely difficult to initiate independent action.

Implications for Intervention

The conceptual orientation of policymakers and practitioners toward older adults is to view them as a problem population who must be protected and cared for, but not as functioning members of society whose skills and expertise should be maximized. To be sure, declines in functional abilities continually occur with age. For example, research indicates that the practical problem-solving ability of adults peaks in middle age and then declines thereafter, even in problems that are fequently encountered by elderly persons (Denney & Pearce, 1989). In this study, however, the problem-solving ability of 60- and 70-year olds was almost identical to the performance of 2-year olds. Thus, decline does not always mean loss of function. Indeed, despite our youth-oriented society, in some performance situations we will do as well, or better, with older rather than with younger participants. That is not how society views older adults, however, and ultimately how a problem is viewed determines the solutions that are attempted (Cowen, 1973; Heller et al., 1984).

By calling for a focus on prevention, rather than a continued emphasis on counseling and psychotherapy, we are not implying that older adults are poor candidates for psychotherapy, and we certainly do not want to reinforce the continued neglect of this population by mental health specialists. Indeed, innovative therapeutic work with older adults and their families is being done (Herr & Weakland, 1979; Knight, 1986; Santos, Hubbard, McIntosh, & Eisner, 1984; Smyer, 1984; Smyer et al., 1990; Thompson, Gallagher, & Breckenridge, 1987). A theme in much of the newer therapeutic work is to help older adults rediscover and expand on existing competencies and improve their sense of perceived efficacy rather than the more traditional stance of having clients review their feelings about past negative events and relationships (Lewinsohn, Antonuccio, Steinmetz, & Teri, 1984; Rodin, Cashman, & Desiderato, 1987; Shostak, 1988). Rodin et al. (1987) concluded their review of intervention programs for older adults by noting that regardless of focus, the most effective therapeutic approaches are those that successfully combat helplessness and demoralization.

The prevention orientation we advocate involves a double-pronged emphasis. The first focuses on attempts to allay hopelessness and improve motivation and problem solving as suggested earlier. The second involves an examination of the ecological niche within which older adults live. One cannot expect much enthusiasm for life among those who are lonely and isolated and who no longer have valued roles in society. We used the examples of housing and employment patterns to illustrate some of the environmental presses impinging on older adults and to suggest that current policies are not immutable. Promising alternatives include a return to multigenerational housing, but now for unrelated individuals who, along with sharing some common living space, also share household duties. The part-time employment of older adults also can be an attractive option in situations in which technical skill, precision, and experience are valued more than is speed of performance. Older workers also are a benefit in transmitting stable work habits and positive employment values.

Mental health professionals may feel uneasy considering these suggestions because housing and labor policies are certainly not under their control. The typical mental health specialist is usually far removed from policymakers and so may feel impotent about influencing national or even local policies toward the elderly. Policies, however, reflect public attitudes and traditions, and although these change slowly, shifts in public beliefs do occur over time. Although there are many factors associated with changes in community beliefs and practices (Heller, 1992; Heller et al., 1984), a primary ingredient is education in problem awareness. One need only see the changes that have occurred in public attitudes toward AIDS, for example, to understand the power of public education and discussion.

Israel (1988) described a variety of community-based interventions that have received some empirical support. These include programs aimed at strengthening existing social ties by education and consultation to family members of the elderly; various kinds of support groups and support services for older adults that facilitate independent living; training older adults in the role of natural helpers (e.g., health aides and school tutors); and participation in self-help and advocacy organizations run by and for older adults (e.g., the Gray Panther organization). Participating in and consulting with members of any of these groups is a useful way for mental health specialists to engage in active prevention programming.

The overarching theme in these activities involves helping the public to understand the social dilemmas that older adults face and the value of their continued integration as useful citizens. Public education is the major first step for policy changes to occur. Furthermore, it is not a message that will be hard for people to understand. After all, we are talking about our own self-interest, because those of us who live that long will be the major beneficiaries of any policy changes that occur.

References

Allan, G. A., & Adams, R. G. (1989). Aging and the structure of friendship. In R. G. Adams & R. Blieszner (Eds.), *Older adult friendship: Structure and process* (pp.45–64). Newbury Park, CA: Sage.

Antonucci, T. C. (1985). Personal characteristics, social support, and social behavior. In R. H. Binstock & E. Shanas (Eds.), *Handbook of aging and the social sciences* (2nd ed., pp. 9–128). New York: Van Nostrand Reinhold.

Antonucci, T. C., & Jackson, J. S. (1987). Social support, interpersonal efficacy, and health: A life course perspective. In L. L. Carstensen & B. A. Edelstein (Eds.), *Handbook of clinical gerontology* (pp. 291–311). New York: Pergamon Press.

Arling, B. (1976). The elderly widow and her family, neighbors, and friends. *Journal of Marriage and the Family, 38,* 757–768.

Baltes, M. M., & Reisenzein, R. (1986). The social world in long-term care institutions: Psychosocial control toward dependency? In M. M. Baltes & P. B. Baltes (Eds.), *The psychology of control and aging* (pp. 315–343). Hillsdale, NJ: Erlbaum.

Bengtson, V., Rosenthal, C., & Burton, L. (1990). Families and aging: Diversity and heterogeneity. In R. H. Binstock & L. K. George (Eds.), *Handbook of aging and the social sciences* (3rd ed., pp. 263–287). San Diego, CA: Academic Press.

Berger, P. L., & Neuhaus, R. J. (1977). *To empower people:The role of mediating structures in public policy.* Washington, DC: American Enterprise Institute for Public Policy Research.

Berger, R., & Rose, S. (1977). Interpersonal skill training with institutionalized patients. *Journal of Gerontology, 32,* 346–353.

Berkman, L. F. (1985). The relationship of social networks and social support to morbidity and mortality. In S. Cohen & S. L. Syme (Eds.), *Social support and health* (pp. 241–263). Orlando, FL: Academic Press.

Blazer, D. G. (1982). Social support and mortality in an elderly community population. *American Journal of Epidemiology, 115,* 684–694.

Bloom, B. L. (1965). The "medical model," miasma theory, and community mental health. *Community Mental Health Journal, 7,* 333–338.

Campbell, A. (1981). *The sense of well-being in America.* New York: McGraw-Hill.

Carstensen, L. (1983). *Assessing social isolation among elderly nursing home residents.* Unpublished doctoral dissertation, West Virginia University, Morgantown.

Casey, B., & Bruche, G. (1983). *Work or retirement?* Hants, England: Gower Publishing.

Cowen, E. L. (1973). Social and community interventions. *Annual Review of Psychology, 24,* 423–472.

Davis, M. (1983). Measuring individual differences in empathy: Evidence for a multidimensional approach. *Journal of Personality and Social Psychology, 44,* 113–126.

Denney, N. W., & Pearce, K. A. (1989). A developmental study of practical problem solving in adults. *Psychology and Aging, 4,* 438–442.

Feingold, E., & Werby, E. (1990). Supporting the independence of elderly residents through control over their environment. In L. A. Pastalan (Ed.), *Aging in place: The role of housing and social supports* (pp. 25–32). New York: Haworth Press.

Gatz, M., & Pearson, C. G. (1988). Ageism revised and the provision of psychological services. *American Psychologist, 43,* 184–188.

Gatz, M., & Smyer, M. A. (1992). The mental health system and older adults in the 1990s. *American Psychologist, 47,* 741–751.

Gottlieb, B. H. (1983). *Social support strategies: Guidelines for mental health practice.* Beverly Hills, CA: Sage.

Gottlieb, B. H. (1988). Support interventions: A typology and agenda for research. In S. W. Duck (Ed.), *Handbook of personal relationships* (pp. 519–541). New York: Wiley.

Hansson. R., Jones, W., & Carpenter, B. (1984). Relational competence and social support. In P. Shaver (Ed.), *Review of personality and social psychology: Emotions, relationships. and health* (pp. 265–284). Beverly Hills, CA: Sage.

Heller, K. (1992). Ingredients for effective community change: Some field observations. *American Journal of Community Psychology, 20,* 143–163.

Heller, K., Price, R. H., & Hogg, J. R. (1990). The role of social support in community and clinical intervention. In I. G. Sarason, B. R. Sarason, & G. R. Pierce (Eds.), *Social support: An interactional view* (pp. 482–507). New York: Wiley.

Heller, K., Price, R. H., Reinharz, S., Riger, S., & Wandersman, A. (1984). *Psychology and community change: Challenges of the future* (2nd ed.). Homewood, IL: The Dorsey Press.

Heller, K., Price, R. H., & Sher, K. J. (1980). Research and evaluation in primary prevention: Issues and guidelines. In R. H. Price, R. F. Ketterer, B. C. Bader, & J. Monahan (Eds.), *Prevention in mental health: Research, policy and practice* (pp. 285–313). Beverly Hills. CA: Sage.

Herr, J. J., & Weakland, J. H. (1979). *Counseling elders and their families.* New York: Springer.

Hogg, J. R., & Heller, K. (1990). A measure of relational competence for community-dwelling elderly. *Psychology and Aging, 5,* 580–588.

Hulchanski, J. D. (1987). *Cooperative housing in Canada* (CPI Bibliography No. 191). Chicago, IL: Council of Planning Librarians.

Israel, B. A. (1988). Community-based social network interventions: Meeting the needs of the elderly. *Danish Medical Bulletin* (Special supplement, Series 6), 36–44.

Jaffee, D. J., & Wellin, C. (1989). The nature of problematic homesharing matches: The case of Share-A-Home of Milwaukee. In D. J. Jaffe (Ed.), *Shared housing for the elderly* (pp. 181–193). New York: Greenwood Press.

Jones, W., Chernovetz, M., & Hansson, R. (1978). The enigma of androgyny: Differential implications for males and females. *Journal of Consulting and Clinical Psychology, 46,* 298–313.

Kasl, S. V., & Cobb. S. (1979). Some mental health consequences of plant closing and job loss. In L. A. Ferman & J. P. Gordus (Eds.), *Mental health and the economy* (pp. 255–299). Kalamazoo, MI: Upjohn Institute for Employment Research.

Kastenbaum, R. (1987). Prevention of age-related problems. In L. L. Carstensen & B. A. Edelstein (Eds.), *Handbook of clinical gerontology* (pp. 322–334). New York: Pergamon Press.

Keith, J. (1990). Age in social and cultural context: Anthropological perspectives. In R. H. Binstock & L. K. George (Eds.), *Handbook of aging and the social sciences* (3rd ed., pp. 91–111). San Diego, CA: Academic Press.

Kendig, H. L. (1990). Comparative perspectives on housing, aging, and social structure. In R. H. Binstock & L. K. George (Eds.), *Handbook of aging and the social sciences* (3rd ed., pp. 288–307). San Diego, CA: Academic Press.

Knight, B. (1986). *Psychotherapy with older adults.* Beverly Hills, CA: Sage.

Langer, E. J., & Avorn, J. (1982). Impact of the psychosocial environment of the elderly on behavioral and health outcomes. In R. D. Chellis, J. F. Seagle, Jr., & B. M. Seagle (Eds.), *Congregate housing for older people* (pp. 15–25). Lexington, MA: Heath.

Langer, E. J., & Rodin, J. (1976). The effects of choice and enhanced personal responsibility: A field experiment in an institutional setting. *Journal of Personality and Social Psychology, 34,* 191–198.

Larson, R., Mannell, R., & Zuzanek, J. (1986). Daily well~being of older adults with friends and family. *Psychology and Aging, 1,* 117–126.

Leavitt, J., & Saegert, S. (1990). *From abandonment to hope: Community-households in Harlem.* New York: Columbia University Press.

Lee, G. R., & Ishii-Kuntz, M. (1988). Social interaction, loneliness, and emotional well~being among the elderly. *Research on Aging, 9,* 459–482.

Lewinsohn, P. M., Antonuccio, D. O., Steinmetz, J. L., & Teri, L. (1984). *The coping with depression course: A psychoeducational intervention for unipolar depression.* Eugene, OR: Castalia Publishing Co.

Litwak, E. (1989). Forms of friendships among older people in an industrial society. In R. G. Adams & R. Blieszner (Eds.), *Older adult friendship: Structure and process* (pp. 65–88). Newbury Park, CA: Sage.

Minkler, M. (1985). Social support and health of the elderly. In S. Cohen & S. L Syme (Eds.), *Social support and health* (pp. 199–216). Orlando, FL: Academic Press.

Morrison, M. H. (1983, May). The aging of the U.S. population: Human resource implications. *Monthly Labor Review,* pp. 13–19.

Myers, G. C. (1990). Demography of aging. In R. H. Binstock & L. K. George (Eds.), *Handbook of aging and the social sciences* (3rd ed., pp. 19–44). San Diego, CA: Academic Press.

Parmelee, P. A., & Lawton, M. P. (1990). The design of special environments for the aged. In J. E. Birren & W. Schaie (Eds.), *Handbook of the psychology of aging* (3rd ed., pp. 465–489). San Diego, CA: Academic Press.

Piper, A. I., & Langer, E. J. (1986). Aging and mindful control. In M. M. Baltes & P. B. Baltes (Eds.), *The psychology of control and aging* (pp. 71–89). Hillsdale, NJ: Erlbaum.

Price, R. H. (1985). Work and community. *American Journal of Community Psychology, 13,* 1–12.

Pritchard, D. C., & Perkocha, J. (1989). Shared housing in California: A regional perspective. In D. J. Jaffe (Ed.), *Shared housing for the elderly* (pp. 49–66). New York: Greenwood Press.

Pynoos, J., Hamburger, L., & June, A. (1990). Supportive relationships in shared housing. In L. A. Pastalan (Ed.), *Aging in place: The role of housing and social supports* (pp. 1–24). New York: Haworth Press.

Quinn, J. F., & Burkhauser, R. V. (1990). Work and retirement. In R. H. Binstock & L. K. George (Eds.), *Handbook of aging and the social sciences* (3rd ed., pp. 308–327). San Diego, CA: Academic Press.

Riggio, R. E. (1986). Assessment of basic social skills. *Journal of Personality and Social Psychology, 51,* 649–660.

Rodin, J., Cashman, C., & Desiderato, L. (1987). Intervention and aging: Enrichment and prevention. In M. W. Riley, J. D. Matarazzo, & A. Baum (Eds.), *Perspectives in behavioral medicine: The aging dimension.* Hillsdale, NJ: Erlbaum.

Rosow, I. (1985). Status and role change through the life cycle. In R. Binstock & E. Shanas (Eds.). *Handbook of aging and the social sciences* (pp. 62–93). New York: Van Nostrand Reinhold.

Rowles. G. D. (1987). A place to call home. In L. L. Carstensen & B. A. Edelstein (Eds.), *Handbook of clinical gerontology* (pp. 335–353). New York: Pergamon Press.

Santos, J. F., Hubbard, R. W., McIntosh, J. L., & Eisner, H. R. (1984). Community mental health and the elderly: Service and training approaches. *Journal of Community Psychology, 12,* 359–368.

Santos, J. F., & VandenBos, G. R. (Eds.). (1982). *Psychology and the older adult: Challenges for training in the 1980s.* Washington, DC: American Psychological Association.

Shanas, E. (1979). Social myth as hypothesis: The case of the family relations of old people. *Gerontologist, 19,* 3–9.

Shostak, A. B. (1988). Retirees and technology assessment: The case for serving as a technoguide. In G. Lesnoff-Caravaglia (Ed.), *Aging in a technological society* (pp. 259–271). New York: Human Sciences Press.

Smyer, M. A. (1984). Working with families of impaired elderly. *Journal of Community Psychology, 12,* 323–333.

Smyer, M. A., & Gatz, M. (Eds.). (1983). *Mental health and aging: Programs and evaluations.* Beverly Hills, CA: Sage.

Smyer, M. A., Zarit, S. H., & Qualls, S. H. (1990). Psychological intervention with the aging individual. In J. E. Birren & W. Schaie (Eds.), *Handbook of the psychology of aging* (3rd ed., pp. 375–404). San Diego, CA: Academic Press.

Spakes, P. R. (1979). Family, friendship, and community interaction as related to life satisfaction of the elderly. *Journal of Gerontological Social Work, 1,* 279–293.

Storandt, M. (1983). Psychology's response to the graying of America. *American Psychologist, 38,* 323–326

Swank, C. (1982). *Phased retirement: The European experience.* Washington, DC: National Council for Alternative Work Patterns.

Thompson, L. W., Gallagher, D., & Breckenridge, J. S. (1987). Comparative effectiveness of psychotherapies for depressed elders. *Journal of Consulting and Clinical Psychology, 55,* 385–390.

Thuras, P. D. (1989). Habits of living and match success: Shared housing in Southern California. In D. J. Jaffe (Ed.), *Shared housing for the elderly* (pp. 159–172). New York: Greenwood Press.

Veroff, J., Kulka, R. A., & Douvan, E. (1981). *Mental health in America: Patterns of health-seeking from 1957–1976.* New York: Basic Books.

Wellman, B. (1979). The community question: The intimate networks of East Yorkers. *American Journal of Sociology, 84,* 1201–1231.

10

Marital Therapy with Later Life Couples

Sara Honn Qualls, Ph.D.

David Collier (1993) opens his documentary film, *"For Better or For Worse,"* featuring five couples married longer than fifty years, with a scene depicting spontaneous bickering between Dan and Sophie, a couple we later appreciate for their spunky, outspoken style of commitment. Their initial spat is about whether Collier should be allowed to film Sophie as she finishes fussing with her hair before the formal interview begins. As they finish the exchange, Dan rolls his eyes and says privately to the camera, "This is after nearly sixty years, you can imagine what it was like after two!" In this brief comment, Dan captures a key issue in marital development: marital relationships both change and remain the same. Threaded throughout the documentary, Dan and Sophie describe how their marriage has enduring patterns overlaid with adaptations and changes brought about by life experiences, including those related to aging.

Long-married older couples' marital stories typically reflect the overlapping patterns of continuity and change. The main thesis of this paper is that the major normative and nonnormative events of later life are sufficient to perturb the structure and function of even long-term, stable marriages. Older couples seen in marital therapy are those who have not been able to accommodate the potentially dramatic transitions required of them. My intent is to engender respect for the amount of marital adjustment required in later life, to provide a map for identifying what provokes change and where it occurs in marriage, and to describe key aspects of assessment and treatment that address the content as well as the context of later life marital difficulties.

What Provokes a Marital Transition in Later Life?

A developmental approach to marriage implies that there are periods in life when certain activities are more likely to occur than at other times. For example, early

Reprinted from *Journal of Geriatric Psychiatry* (1995), *28*, 139–163. Reprinted with permission of Publisher.

in marriage couples negotiate strategies for accomplishing basic marital tasks (e.g., how to fight, how to show affection, how to define household roles). Other transitions occur when the entry or exit of children forces alterations in those initial patterns, or when work roles intrude on family life in significant ways.

The last period of the family life cycle includes several events whose impact on marriage can be dramatic. The phase is foreshadowed by the exit of children from the home. At this point, the couple shifts into a new phase of the family life cycle, the final couple phase. This period is likely to be four to five times longer than the prechildren couple phase (Brubaker, 1985a). For many, the first significant event of this phase is the retirement of the couple from their jobs. At some point, most couples experience the onset of impairment from illness in at least one spouse. Less normative, but moderately probable, are events caused by disruption in the lives of adult children. The death of one spouse is another significant event in the life of a marriage, provoking a final transition to "marriage by memory." Each of these events has profound psychological impact on the individual spouses, and, consequently, requires some degree of adjustment in the marriage.

What aspects of the marriage must accommodate to the effects of later life events? In the section that follows, I describe briefly what I consider to be several key functions that are accomplished in all marriages in a more or less effective or satisfying manner. As discussed in more detail below, these functions are inevitably influenced by any major transition in the marriage.

What Aspects of Marital Stucture Are Altered?

Time Structure

Throughout the marriage, couples must negotiate issues regarding time spent alone and together. The structuring of time is a major factor which influences the most concrete aspect of this issue: time spent together. In young and middle adulthood, employment typically structures many hours of separateness several days each week. The crunch of task demands during child-rearing years also encourages a division of labor that structures nonwork family time. Couples during the child-rearing years typically complain about not having enough time together as a couple to nurture the marriage, and not having enough time separately to nurture each of them as individuals. In other words, young and middle adulthood are characterized by major overload of demands on time.

Empty nest and retirement initiate a phase in which time is increasingly less structured by external social roles, and must be structured internally within the relationship. Arguments over recreation become more common (Levenson, Carstensen, & Gottman, 1993). Couples may find themselves with too much couple time, and no "legitimate" reasons for creating separateness. The struggle over management of time reflects a broader psychological struggle to maintain a separate identity and self in later life when formal roles are stripped away.

Within the marriage, this struggle is often enacted through conflict about togetherness and separateness in space and time. Most marriages negotiate the transition well, taking advantage of the new freedom of choice about how to use time and space.

Roles

Roles are a major conceptual structure used to understand marriage. The diversity of marital roles include, among others, household task roles, financial management, and maintenance of family relationships. Young and middle adulthood are characterized by the addition and establishment of societal and familial roles. Negotiation of role assignments is expected early in a relationship, while conflict over competence of performance in roles may continue throughout a marriage. Beginning with the end of active parenting, marital roles become more salient as the parenting roles diminish. Furthermore, marital roles gain flexibility as a consequence of the increasing opportunities for personality flexibility (Gutmann, 1987). Most of the normative and nonnormative events characteristic of later life are likely to stimulate some role transition. For example, either the onset of an illness in one spouse that limits his or her capability to enact familiar roles or the loss of a formal occupational role may stimulate a shakeup in marital roles. Role transitions may generate opportunities for more creative structuring of the relationship, or may be experienced as a period of chaos when familiar interaction patterns are strained, awkward, or unpredictable.

Communication

Early in a relationship, couples develop routine strategies for showing affection, signaling interest in sex, fighting, and communicating impersonal as well as sensitive information. Observational researchers have identified particular patterns of communication that are repeated in the experience of particular couples, as well as more general patterns that characterize distressed and nondistressed couples (Gottman, 1979). Zeitlow and Sillars (1988) examined differences in patterns of conflict resolution between younger and older couples. They found that in comparison with younger couples, older couples identified fewer topics worthy of argument. Unfortunately, many of the couples sampled had difficulty ending a fight sequence once it had begun. Other research affirms that older couples report a lessened probability of conflict (Levenson et al., 1993). Perhaps over the decades of marriage couples determine which issues are salient enough in their relationship to warrant resistance to compromise. They draw their battle lines on those particular issues. Other areas of disagreement are avoided, or treated as a routine, predictable difference that is not allowed to generate much conflict energy. More observational research is needed to test these and other hypotheses about how older couples' communication patterns may differ from younger couples.

After years of interaction, communication regarding familiar activities may become very routine, perhaps relying more on nonverbal signals than verbal description once the behavior pattern has become familiar. However, during periods of change, couples are faced with novel situations to which they must respond and adjust. Routine, nonverbal communication is seldom sufficient to negotiate adequately the changes needed to adapt to the transitions. More explicit, verbal communication is likely to be needed. Couples who have relied on routine patterns may be frustrated by the inadequacy of their previous communication methods to meet the needs of the new situation. Under certain conditions couples need to expand their communication repertoire. If they lack the skills to recognize or implement a broader array of communication mechanisms, they will experience conflict and dissatisfaction with the marriage. The extent to which older couples experience this is unknown, nor is it clear that the events of later life are unique in provoking the need for a wider repertoire of communication tools. Likely, the shifts in level and type of communication needed during transitions occur throughout the life course with variation primarily in the details of the transition. Later life may be unique only to the extent that the marriage structure may have been stable for decades prior to the events of later life.

Power Balance

Power is distributed in a marriage according to resources controlled, both perceived and real. Spouses share power in some domains, and apportion power in others. Throughout marriage, role transitions can provoke shifts in the balance of marital power. Feminist family therapists have emphasized the role of control over money as a major determinant of marital power (Walters, Carter, Papp, & Silverstein, 1988). Women whose husbands are the sole source of family income lack the financial resources to have realistic power in negotiating autonomy. Power can also he influenced by the strength of "presence" of the spouses in a marriage. For example, one spouse's ability to "out-talk" another may create power differences. Capability to function also determines power in a relationship. Skills, abilities, and intelligence can be used to enhance the power of resources under one spouse's control.

Some events of later life affect the balance of marital power by altering resource control; for example, illness may alter capacity to use resources. Changes in occupational roles may alter not only availability of resources, but patterns of control over them. Marital power may also be affected by the involvement of adult children in decision making regarding health, housing, or services for an ill or frail couple (Barusch, 1987).

Nurturance

Marriage is a primary source of emotional support for most married persons (Weiss, 1974). Spouses often serve as primary attachment figures for each other, offering basic support of the self. Expressions of affection, sexuality, and direct caregiving can all be experienced as nurturant and affirming of the self. As Carstensen's Social Selectivity Theory argues, spouses take on even more importance in later life when older adults usually choose to shrink their network and rely more heavily on a select set of people (Carstensen, 1992). Certainly, the caregiving literature repeatedly affirms that spouses are the most preferred and most likely care providers (Horowitz, 1985).

Events of later life often change the patterns of nurturance. Retirement usually increases the amount of time available for affection and caregiving. The amount of time and energy available for nurturance may decrease if an adult child requires care. The balance of reciprocal nurturance may be altered when one spouse becomes severely impaired. The effects of such changes on the marital dyad are explored below.

Relationships with Children

Whether in the active period of parenting or post empty nest, married persons who are parents must negotiate relationships with children. Women tend to carry primary responsibility for that task through the parenting years, although men's interest and involvement may increase in late midlife (Gutmann, 1987). Beginning with the adolescent transition toward autonomy for the children, parenting roles are altered to allow children to mature into adults. Although less active than earlier in the family's life cycle, parents continue to be involved and helpful to their adult children. When the children mature appropriately, they claim their personal authority as separate adults who share adulthood status as peers of their parents (Williamson, 1991). Although the intergenerational dyads are always parent and child (history cannot be erased), the two generations share the same levels of autonomy and personal responsibility. When the autonomy of either generation is threatened, the other generation tends to supply considerable assistance; for example, when aging parents' health declines, or a middle-aged child experiences a financial reversal (Johnson, 1983).

Negotiating the transition to their children's autonomy challenges the marital relationship for some couples. Marriages that routinely involve others to absorb their conflicts are likely to catch adult children in their triangular web. The child's autonomy may be threatened and marital functioning undermined. The transition toward decreasing autonomy for frail elderly parents may also challenge the marriage. Marital partners often find that the boundaries around decision making must shift when either a child's or a spouse's capacity for autonomy is altered.

Impact of Specific Later Life Events on Marital Structure

Some effects of the major events of later life on these basic marital processes are summarized in Table 1. The matrix depicted in this table illustrates the broad ripple effect of an event on the major functions of a marriage. Note that

Table 1

Impact of Events of Later Life on Marital Processes

Events	Marital Processes					
	Time Structure	Roles	Communication	Power Balance	Nurturance	Relationships with Children
Retirement	End of work-structured separateness Increase in togetherness at home	Dedifferentiation (decreased uniqueness, increased overlap) Potential to decrease gender typing	Need strategies to negotiate separateness and role transition More shared experience decreases need for oral reporting	Role transition provokes shift in power balance Power from previous domain may be altered Potential of egalitarianism increased in traditional couples	Increased opportunity for small daily expressions	Opportunity for increased contact and more directly involved roles Visits with children often occur on distant turf
Onset of Impairment from Chronic Illness	Usually increased portion of time devoted to basic care Health constrains activity options	Ill spouse experiences role loss Well spouse experiences role gain	Anger expressions are more threatening or complicated Impairment may constrain ill spouse's capacity to communicate (e.g., stroke, cognitive impairment, decreased initiation)	Sources of power for ill spouse decreases Well spouse's increase in responsibility brings increased power	Ill spouse's opportunity to nurture may be constrained Well spouse's caregiving role creates imbalance in time spent nurturing	Children may be more "inside" the marriage than previously (boundary issues salient) Children's role in supporting primary caregiver or ill parent may threaten spouse

Disruptions in Children's Lives					
Increased time spent experiencing and expressing concern as coparents Potential for increase in responsibility and decrease in leisure time	Ambiguity in parenting roles increases May provoke increase in financial, childcare, or other support responsibilities	Need for problem-solving communications may increase Negotiating support within appropriate boundaries challenges communication patterns	Boundary around marital dyad may be stretched Can triangulate the marriage	Nurturance often needs to be redirected outside marriage again (increased strain on marital satisfaction)	Complex roles salient as aging parents again are giving Opportunity for reciprocity

the three events chosen include family events as well as individuals' life events. Typically, retirement and illness occur primarily in the life of one spouse. However, when a major event is experienced by one spouse, the marriage inevitably experiences reverberations. Married partners' lives are inextricably webbed together such that a life event experienced by one spouse will almost certainly affect the other (Pruchno, Blow, & Smyer, 1984). Occasionally, both spouses will experience the events simultaneously, generating more rapid change. Presumably, disruptions in the children's lives affect both spouses, although one spouse may become more involved with the child's needs than the other.

Retirement

With retirement, a couple's time is no longer structured by work schedules, and their roles are no longer constrained by the division of labor created by work and child-rearing demands. For many, this is a welcome relief; for some it is an ambiguous problem to be solved (Lipman, 1980). The cessation of externally structured time and roles places a responsibility on the couple to determine their own structure and negotiate their needs to be apart and together. Roles are often simplified, leading to increasing overlap. Role differentiation based on gender thus decreases, although it is still evident in the allocation of traditionally feminine tasks (Hill & Dorfman, 1982; Brubaker, 1985b).

Role shifts may affect many aspects of marital functioning: balance of power, amount of time spent together, patterns of task allocation and leisure, patterns of nurturance and affection, and relationships with children. Retired spouses who obtained significant self-esteem through their work may seek more affirmation of their personal worth from their spouses. Cole (1986) suggests that learning to affirm one's spouse for who that person is rather than what he or she *does* is a normal marital development transition in later life.

Many of these changes occur subtly over time and are not the subject of a formal conversation about the changes. However, there are occasions in therapy with troubled couples when it becomes evident that the current conflict is rooted in the unsuccessful transition following retirement. In later life, maturity of personality predicts satisfaction in marriage more than it does in earlier life, perhaps because of the subtle but dramatic impact of this transition (Swensen, Eskew, & Kohlhepp, 1981).

As noted above, alterations in life structure put pressure on couples to communicate their preferences and discomforts. Communication skills for negotiating new life structures are needed, but may be rusty because couples have often been maintaining roles rather than creating new ones.

> When Johnny O'Leary retired last year, he and Maeve planned to spend their first year traveling to visit their children who are scattered up and down the East coast. Their first visit was so miserable that they returned home angry and unwilling to even consider continuing their journey. Maeve complains that Johnny has turned

into a silly little boy when they are in public, and has invaded her house when they are at home. She says he makes constant demands that she reorganize things to suit him. He responds that she has become a bitter old woman who doesn't know how to have any fun or make any changes. He was very upset that she was so critical of the children they visited. She accuses him of finding ways to get in her way because he has nothing better to do. She also hints that he embarrassed her horribly when he drank too much at their daughter's home. They both acknowledge readily that this is not the first serious fight in their lives. But this is the time they had looked forward to enjoying when they finally had time to be together.

Onset of Impairment from Chronic Illness

When one spouse becomes impaired, the other spouse typically becomes the caregiver (Johnson, 1983). In younger-old adults, the caregiving is likely to be subtle or mutual, whereas in later old age one spouse is more likely to be the primary dependent one (Cole, 1986). Roles and time are increasingly structured around the delivery of basic care which may include help with dressing and ambulation, cleanliness, toileting, eating, and taking medication. The adjustment process typically results in the ill spouse experiencing role loss while the caregiving spouse experiences role gain. Consequent to role shifts are shifts in power and opportunities to nurture. The caregiving spouse usually gains in power and opportunities to nurture (whether acknowledged or not) while the ill spouse loses in both areas. These shifts are often reflected in an awkwardness in communicating caring and anger. The ill spouse is obligated to be appreciative (because of being dependent) and to limit expressions of anger. The caregiving spouse is obligated to be gracious because the power potential could demoralize or psychologically destroy the other spouse. How does a caregiver vent anger at a "helpless" spouse? How does an ill spouse experience or offer an expression of affection that is not tainted with his or her dependency? Cognitive impairment in one spouse creates a particularly complex caregiving context because of the severity of behavior problems that often result, the ambiguity of the transition from shared to caregiver-focused responsibility, legal and financial complications, and the misunderstanding of the support network.

While spouses usually try to maintain the caregiving responsibility, children may take on roles as secondary caregivers or critical onlookers. In many families these roles are not familiar or comfortable for any of the players. With serious impairment, a caregiving spouse may look to members of other generations to join with him or her in decision making. This bending of generational boundaries is likely to be fraught with awkwardness and meaning that may generate unpleasant levels of anxiety.

Jeffrey and Edith have modeled perfectly the "united front" style of parenting. Their children have never seen them disagree. Both were immigrants from Poland in the late 1930s with the remnant of their families who survived. They have always referred to themselves as the "lucky ones" and demanded that the family live in harmony because "nothing is worth fighting about among ourselves." The children have long believed that Jeffrey simply deferred to Edith, but he never seemed to complain. Recently, however, Jeffrey has become very belligerent over small daily concerns (e.g., when to go shopping or where to have lunch). Their family doctor tells them that Jeffrey has early stage dementia, but offers little guidance about how to handle the behavioral outbursts. Their oldest daughter, who lives nearby, has tried in several ways to talk to her father about backing off, but has become convinced that he is tired of playing second fiddle and is finally asserting himself. She tells her mother to give her Dad more control. Edith is baffled about how to handle his tantrums, and often calls her son who lives 2000 miles away for advice. This son, a physician, has insisted that they put Dad on Haldol to reduce his outbursts. Neither Edith nor her daughter believe medication is the right thing to do. Edith is growing more depressed as she feels helpless to fix Jeffrey's behavior, yet feels lonely and isolated without him as her confidant. The children's disagreement upsets her very much.

Disruptions in Children's Lives

In later life, most adult children live apart from their parents. Despite being separated in household (and perhaps by thousands of miles), adult children's lives can have a profound impact on their parents, especially when the children experience major disruptions. Two types of disruption in children's lives can affect parents in particular. Any change in an adult child's capacity to be autonomous (e.g., due to major illness or financial loss) is likely to reawaken active parenting concerns and behaviors in the older generation. Parents may take on direct caregiving roles, lend money, or sponsor a business loan. Changes in children's family stability may also generate concern or active intervention from aging parents. For example, midlife divorce is almost always experienced by the divorcing couple's parents as a major event. Parents become more involved in a variety of significant ways and styles (Lesser & Comet, 1987; Johnson, 1988). The regression of roles that characterizes the parent-child relationship when the adult child needs assistance can strain the relationship and interrupt normal developmental tasks for both generations.

Role changes vi-à-vis the children may provoke role changes in the aging couple's relationship. For example, the emergence of a significant parenting role may diminish the time available for marital affection and play, or it may generate conflict. Parenting roles may also fill a gap left by loss of work roles, a change that could he very relieving to a couple who had not made the transition into retirement successfully. Or reactivation of parenting roles could represent a loss for a couple who were delighted with the freedom and leisure focus of retirement. In essence, the renewal of an active parenting role has the inherent potential for marital conflict or enhanced marital satisfaction depending on the capacity to accommodate the transition.

George and Irene have an on-going battle over how much help to give their daughter, Judy. Judy divorced her husband two years ago, and hasn't quite gotten on her feet yet. She and her two boys (ages 7 and 9) lived with her parents for the first year. George finally put his foot down and demanded that she get a place of her own. Judy's earnings are adequate to pay for a small apartment, but without the amenities to which the boys grew accustomed during her marriage. Irene feels that Judy's job takes her away from the boys too much, and has tried to step in as a surrogate mother. George is angry because this is the time in their lives when they expected to enjoy life without so many schedules to meet, and particularly without a house full of active, noisy boys. Irene goes over to Judy's house every morning to get the boys ready for school, and stays with them after school. George has to get his own breakfast for the first time in his life, and has a lot of long hours to fill during the day. When Irene returns home for dinner, George refuses to hear any discussion of the activities of her day. He wants them to do something pleasant for the evening, just the two of them. Irene resents his unhelpful, selfish attitudes, and generally spends the evening sewing for Judy and the boys.

The matrix in Table 1 could be expanded to include many other normative and nonnormative events of later life, and several other marital functions. For example, the effects of relocating or deciding not to drive could be examined. Other marital functions might include the sexual relationship or conflict resolution patterns. The intent of this exploration is to focus attention on the significant effects of the events of later life on the most basic domains of marital functioning.

Marital Assessment in Therapy

My model of marital assessment follows directly from this developmental perspective on relationships, with one important caveat. A subset of older couples comes to therapy because of interpersonal distress that is caused by new, difficult behaviors produced by one or both spouses. In this subgroup these behaviors are caused by cognitive impairment due to delirium or dementia, but are attributed to personality or marital difficulties rather than to the true organic disease. Thus, it is imperative that clinicians perform initial screening of each spouse's cognitive functioning. If there is any suggestion of organic disease a thorough gerontopsychological assessment should be done. Guidelines for this are offered elsewhere in the literature (Lawton, 1986). Generally, they include evaluation of basic mental status, depression, daily life structure, Activities of Daily Living and Instrumental Activities of Daily Living, and a complete medical examination with appraisal of medication usage. The initial assessment can be done in an unstructured interview format, without appearing to perform a formal assessment, or in a more structured intake evaluation format. Regardless, it is critical to know the level of functioning of each spouse individually before considering the interpersonal dynamics.

Assessment of the primary marital complaints can proceed straightforwardly. Older couples tend to appreciate a problem-focused evaluation. The primary differences in assessing older versus younger couples' marital problems lie in the context of the problem within the marital, family, and societal histories. While taking the marital and family history, the therapist gathers information on how the couple has handled previous marital transitions. In the marital history, couples usually describe the chronology of significant events, such as dates of marriage, births of children, household relocations, significant historical events that affected them, unexpected challenges. Clinicians familiar with marital development can help the couple fill in details of their marital story by interviewing them about the psychological and relational effects of major transitions. For example, how did you as a couple handle your children's difficulty with the move from the East to West coasts? What did you as a couple do with all of the home together time that you gained when the children left home? Questions of this type give the therapist rich information about how the basic developmental tasks of adulthood have been handled. Through this marital life review, couples reveal their accumulated strengths and limitations in handling interpersonal transitions. They also inform the therapist of their shared (and unshared!) story or interpretation of themes from their life. Such information is invaluable in deciding how to frame the current dilemma and what resources are available to draw on during interventions. It is important to identify the societal context of the marriage. Many factors influence the norms and mores for marriage and for aging. Among the relevant societal contexts to explore are ethnicity, race, social class, birth cohort, geographic region, and religious involvement. A respectful questioning stance leads the couple to describe the important cultural factors that helped shape their choices, reactions to stress, and present difficulties.

In the course of the marital review, the question, "Why now?" should be addressed clearly. The therapist with a view of the marital history can establish a richer (and more accurate) frame for what brought the couple to seek help at this point. Florsheim and Herr (1990) distinguish between couples with long-term histories of marital conflict and those whose conflict has emerged as a response to challenges of later life. For couples with a long history of conflict, there is likely to be a special provocative event or process that has brought them to a therapist at this particular point. Couples with no history of serious conflict may have sought help to manage a developmental transition of later life that, while normative, may be sufficiently novel to have confused them. Many couples will seek a comforting explanation of how so much distress could arise this late in life. Family members who helped the couple seek assistance may supply essential information and may need to be included in the therapy if the family members have the primary motive for seeking help.

In addition to the historical context of the marriage, the couples' current skill in accomplishing basic tasks of the marriage should be evaluated. The components of marriage described in Table 1 provide a framework for assessing a couple's skills and style of accomplishing basic marital tasks. How is their time structured? What roles have they defined? How do they communicate feelings, problems, requests, beliefs? How is power divided? Who nurtures whom and how? What is their relationship with children, if any? What changes have occurred recently in any of these areas? How have the spouses been trying to solve their problem? Systems theorists emphasize that a couple's effort to cope with the changes caused by a life event may actually produce the problem for which they seek help (Herr & Weakland, 1979). For example, the classic story of a spouse whose territory has been invaded by a recent retiree illustrates how the retiree's efforts to restructure time by assisting the spouse has produced another problem, conflict over territory.

One way to integrate the preceding detailed assessment of marital history, skills, and basic structure and function, is to look for marital themes. There are four basic themes I use to examine important interpersonal relationships across the lifespan. Family relationships will almost always illustrate these themes because it is in families that the most basic interpersonal processes are negotiated. For married older persons, the marriage is a primary context in which such basic interpersonal processes are played out.

The first three themes are described by Bengtson and Kuypers (1985) as a set of polarities: autonomy-dependency, connectedness-separateness, and continuity-dislocation. Humans move back and forth along the continuum throughout their lifespan. For example, early in the lifespan, children struggle to move from dependency toward autonomy (the "terrible twos" and adolescence). Throughout much of adulthood humans function as if they are essentially autonomous, denying their dependency on other people and institutions as much as possible. In later life, we are again confronted with the dependency end of the continuum. The three themes identified by Bengtson and Kuypers capture core interpersonal dynamics centering around autonomy, intimacy (connectedness-separateness), and tolerance of change (continuity-dislocation).

A fourth polarity to consider is that of idealization-disappointment. The narcissistic self continues throughout the lifespan to attempt to idealize the world and self, only to be confronted by reality, with the consequent experience of disappointment. Spouses usually engage, to some degree, in a similar vacillation between idealization of their relationship and disappointment. Their ability to incorporate reality into their self-protective visions is a skill that warrants assessment. Some of the difficulties encountered in adjusting to events of later life arise from rigidity of movement along this continuum.

These themes are worthy of exploration in any careful examination of later life marriage. How has the couple handled them during past marital transitions? What are the couple's values regarding these processes, their skill in negotiating them? Many of the problems later life couples encounter will relate directly to their ways of handling the basic processes underlying these themes.

Therapeutic Intervention

Following directly from the thesis that marital developmental transitions are often the cause of marital distress in later life, an initial step in therapy is to define as normally expected any developmental transition currently being experienced. Many couples are caught by surprise at the impact on the marriage of a life event or individual developmental transition. Once the event or transition is labeled and viewed as normal, it loses some of its anxiety-provoking power. Couples often can address the transition directly once they view it appropriately.

When "normalizing" their distress from the event is not sufficient assistance, I follow the principle of proceeding from the least to most intensive forms of intervention as necessary. The PLISSIT model of sex therapy intervention (Annon, 1975) uses the acronym to summarize a sequence of increasingly involved interventions progressing from Permission, to Limited Intervention, Specific Suggestion, and finally Intensive Therapy. Couples who can benefit from simply labeling and describing the expected distress they might experience from a developmental transition are benefiting from the Permission level of intervention. Some couples need more assistance figuring out how to apply that information to their benefit in what might be called a Limited Intervention. Couples who need assistance in identifying a specific strategy for altering their behavior (e.g., restructuring their relationship with a problematic adult child) would need a Specific Suggestion. Intensive Therapy would be reserved for couples whose basic relationship structure or processes need to be renovated.

An additional focus for intervention with later life couples is their place within the broader family system. For example, with increasing frailty, couples may find themselves losing power within the family structure. Accordingly, therapists will need to evaluate the interplay between the couple and the family to determine whether empowerment oriented interventions are indicated to help the couple assert their needs within the family.

Unique Aspects of Work with Elderly Couples

Knight (1986) suggests that two unique aspects of clinical work with older persons are the countertransference issues and the salience of physical health concerns to mental health. The same argument could be made with regard to marital therapy.

Countertransference issues in marital therapy can be at least as complex as those in individual therapy. Work with older adults inevitably requires therapists to reexperience their own responses to profound loss (Knight, 1986). Therapists are also challenged psychologically to work with their parents' (or grandparents') generation regarding issues typically not revealed to someone of the therapist's generation (e.g., intimacy or sexuality). Finally, therapists must be aware of the differences between the values and role expectations typical of their own cohort and those of their elderly clients. Cohort differences can be handled easily once the therapist is educated about them. The other countertransference issues require more constant monitoring because they represent basic emotional responses from the therapist's own personal experience.

The lifespan context of work with older couples sometimes shapes the focus of therapy. Each partner brings a particularly long history (whether married for decades to this spouse or not), and a particularly short future. The long history contains a wealth of experiences that can serve as reference points for framing the current problem and possible intervention strategies. These events usually include successful experiences of coping that can be a great resource for therapy. Also, every couple has a few unresolvable issues that are either accepted like a long-term achy joint, or serve as a constant reminder of the couple's inability to resolve something important. The sense of resignation some couples display regarding what is and is not changeable may be difficult for a younger therapist to understand because of the difference in cohort values and lifespan perspective.

Therapists need to keep in mind the shorter future for the marriage as well as its long history. Couples are sometimes willing to try something new simply because they are aware that every day counts. Young couples sometimes experience their long potential future as a fearful trap into which they do not wish to become snared. The young spouse may feel a tremendous urgency to change the other because he or she cannot imagine living with a particular habit or behavior for thirty or forty years. Most older couples know they have lived with difficult behaviors for a long time, and have survived. They show more commitment to the marriage and less urgency about changing their spouse. However, some younger-old couples (in their sixties) see immediate divorce as their last opportunity for freedom to be alone or with a more compatible spouse before they are trapped by the frailty of old age.

Couples seeking therapy after years of living in relationships usually want to focus their work on the particular problem that brought them in. They seldom come to therapy for the purpose of generally improving their relationship. This may reflect the values of a particular aged cohort who has reserved its use of mental health services for problem resolution rather than using it for prevention or mental health promotion. Sexuality is often a hidden dimension of marriage in this cohort. Although sensuality and sexual behavior are part of most marriages, they may not be discussed unless the therapist asks. Sexuality may offer a positive resource to the marriage or be a source of serious distress. The majority of aging-related sexual difficulties are associated with changes in physical health status, and many can be addressed successfully. As is true with all ages, however, older couples can experience sexual difficulties because of intimacy-related problems.

The theme of loss that the therapist must monitor in counter-transference relationships is a key theme for most older couples. Whether articulated or not, the issue of progressive losses looms large in the present or on the horizon of older marriages. How will they handle their physical deterioration when it affects daily functioning? How will they manage the transition to caregiver being the one who receives care? How can they prepare for widowhood? These questions, while often unspoken, are powerful and usually very salient within the relationship.

Many later life couples seen in therapy are in a caregiver-receiver relationship. Daily life for many of these couples is extraordinarily taxing of basic resources of energy, time, and finances. Caring for a chronically ill spouse is often highly demanding, placing an exceptional burden on the caregiver, and creating an exceptional lack of an active role for the recipient. Research has documented the heavy burden experienced by caregivers, and their consequent vulnerability to physical and mental health problems. Caregiver burnout has important consequences for the well-being of both parties. Assessment of the level of burden and future planning by the couple for caregiver support are very important.

Married couples in which one spouse is seriously ill, whether a major physical or cognitive impairment, have significant marital adjustments to make. Therapists who come to know a couple only in this later stage of deterioration may be tempted to view them as if they are in some sort of a paraprofessional "arrangement" to provide care for a sick person, hardly married. Indeed, many such couples feel as if they are unmarried in a marriage; in a sort of marital purgatory. I find that couples are greatly relieved when I acknowledge the ambiguity of their roles and the dimensions of their relationship that have been severely altered by their transition experience (e.g., time, nurturance, power).

Many of the caregiving spouses need to be prodded to anticipate their future as widow(er)s, and to begin planning to meet their social, intellectual, and physical needs that are no longer shared by their spouses. Prevention of caregiver burnout and consequent premature placement of the ill spouse in a nursing home is the rationale that can stimulate caregivers to begin taking better care of their own needs even if it means having separate time away from the ill spouse. Note, however, that these spouses often want their loyalty to their care receiving spouses understood and respected. They are still married, feel married, and want there to be no misunderstanding of their commitment. A therapist can help them identify the challenge of being happily committed to the spouse even when they are aware that their needs for companionship and intimacy are no longer being met within the marriage.

Reassurance that the marriage continues to be meaningful to a widow long after the spouse has died is often comforting. Marriage as memory is still a meaningful marriage to the survivor, but seldom is respected by the social network. The therapist's validation helps a widow(er) reintegrate an important part of her or his identity and social network.

Summary

The major events of later life are sufficiently powerful to disrupt the patterns by which couples had been accomplishing basic marital functions. A careful examination of the course of events in later life, and the influences of these events on specific marital functions, is a useful approach to assessing late life marriages and guiding therapeutic interventions. Proceeding from a developmental perspective, causes of marital change and perturbation, and areas of marital functioning in which change occurs are identified. Key aspects of assessment and treatment of late life marital problems are described. Among precipitating causes of change are the exit of children from the home, retirement of one or both spouses from occupation, physical illness or impairment, problems of the couple's adult children, and the final transition to marriage by memory with the death of a spouse. Important functions of marriage that are impacted by these transitions and events are time spent together or apart, the allocation of marital roles, the form and content of the couple's communications, the balance of power in the marriage, emotional nurturance, and relationships with children.

Assessment is made of marital complaints and the strengths and limitations of the couple in handling their interpersonal transitions. Due to their long personal and marital histories, older couples' distress during later life must be examined in the context of an entire lifetime of interpersonal experience. Four basic themes which help to integrate the marital assessment are expressed in the polarities of autonomy-dependency, connectedness-separation, continuity-discontinuity, and idealization-disappointment. Therapeutic intervention ranges from the reassurance of identifying as such normal, expected marital developmental transitions, to intensive therapy. The couple's place within the family system is an important focus of treatment. Because illness and impairment are more prevalent with age, the health status of each spouse needs to be identified in order to specify the problem accurately and to work realistically with the couple's potential for growth and development. The therapist must track closely his or her countertransference reactions to working with clients who are likely to be in another generation, and whose experiences are usually deeply influenced by loss.

References

Annon, J. F. (1975), *The Behavioral Treatment of Sexual Problems*. Honolulu, HI: Enabling Systems.

Barusch, A. S. (1987). Power dynamics in the aging family: A preliminary statement. *J. Gerontol. Soc. Work*, 11:43–56.

Bengtson, V. L., & Kuypers, J. A. (1985). The family support cycle: Psychosocial issues in the aging family. In: *Life-Span and Change in a Gerontological Perspective*. In J. M. A. Munnichs, P. Mussen, E. Olbrich, & P. G. Coleman (Eds.). Orlando, FL: Academic Press, pp. 257–273.

Brubaker, T. H. (1985a). *Later Life Families*. Beverly Hills, CA: Sage.

———— (1985b). Responsibility for household tasks: A look at golden anniversary couples aged 75 years and older. In: *Social Bonds in Later Life: Aging and Interdependence*. In W. A. Peterson & J. Quadagno (Eds.). Beverly Hills, GA: Sage.

Carstensen, L. L. (1992). Social and emotional patterns in adulthood: Support for socioemotional selectivity theory. *Psychol. & Aging*, 7:331–338.

Cole, C. L. (1986). Developmental tasks affecting the marital relationship in later life. *Amer. Behav. Scient.*, 29:389–403.

Collier, D. (Director, Producer). (1993). *For Better or For Worse*. [Film]. Berkeley, CA: Studio B. (Available from D. Collier, 2121 Bonar Sr., Studio B, Berkeley, CA 94702).

Florsheim, M. J., & Herr, J. J. (1990). Family counseling with elders. *Generations,* 14:40–42.

Gottman, J. M. (1979). *Marital Interaction: Experimental Investigations.* New York: Academic.

Gutmann, D. (1987). *Reclaimed Powers: Toward a New Psychology of Men and Women in Later Life.* New York: Basic Books.

Herr, J. J., & Weakland, J. H. (1979). *Counseling Elders and Their Families.* New York: Springer.

Hill, E. A., & Dorfman, L. T. (1982). Reaction of housewives to the retirement of their husbands. *Fam. Rel.,* 31:195–200.

Horowitz, A. (1985). Family caregiving to the elderly. *Ann. Rev. Gerontol. & Geriatrics,* 5: 194–246.

Johnson, C. L. (1983). Dyadic family relations and social support. *Gerontologist,* 23:377–383.

——— (1988). Active and latent functions of grandparenting during the divorce process. *Gerontologist,* 28:185–191.

Knight, B. (1986). *Psychotherapy with Older Adults.* Beverly Hills, CA: Sage.

Lawton, M. P. (1986). Functional assessment. *Geropsychological Assessment and Treatment.* In L. Teri & P. M. Lewinsohn (Eds.), pp. 39–84. New York: Springer.

Lesser, E. K., & Comet, J. J. (1987). Help and hindrance: Parents of divorcing children. *J. Marit. & Fam. Therapy,* 13:197–202.

Levenson, R. W., Carstensen, L. L., & Gottman, J. M. (1993). Long-term marriage: Age. gender, and satisfaction. *Psychol. & Aging,* 8:301–313.

Lipman, A. (1980). Role conceptions of couples in retirement. In: *Social and Psychological Aspects of Aging.* C. Tibbits & W. Donahue (Eds.). New York: Arno Press.

Pruchno, R. A., Blow, F. C., & Smyer, M. A. (1984). Life events and interdependent lives: Implications for research and intervention. *Hum. Develop.,* 27:31–41.

Swensen, C. H., Eskew, R. W., & Kohlhepp, K. A. (1981). Stage of family life cycle, ego development, and the marriage relationship. *J. Marr. & Family,* 43:841–853.

Walters, M., Carter, B., Papp, P., & Silverstein, O. (1988). *The Invisible Web: Gender Patterns in Family Relationships.* New York: Guilford Press.

Weiss, R. S. (1974). The provisions of social relationships. *Doing Unto Others.* In Z. Rubin (Ed.). Englewood Cliffs, NJ: Prentice-Hall.

Williamson, D. S. (1991). *Intimacy Paradox: Personal Authority in the Family System.* New York: Guilford Press.

Zeitlow, P. H., & Sillars, A. L. (1988). Life-stage differences in communication during marital conflicts. *J. Soc. & Pers. Rel.,* 5:223–245.

11

What Counselors Need to Know About Aging and Sexuality

Audrey U. Kim and Donald R. Atkinson

Discussion of aging and sexuality among elders is a relatively recent phenomenon in the professional counseling literature. In part, this is due to the negative attitudes associated with both sexuality and older people in our society. Although idealized and exaggerated images of sexuality abound in the media and popular culture, sex remains a taboo topic in most families, schools, churches, and other socializing institutions. Moreover, the youth cult in Western society dictates that sex is appropriate only for the young, healthy, and physically attractive, and as a result, elders are treated as neuters (Gochros, Gochros, & Fisher, 1986; Kellett, 1993). Thus, until recently, the subject of aging and sexuality has largely been overlooked by counselors and other professionals working with older adults. The purpose of this chapter is to provide counselors with information about aging and sexuality and to suggest ways counselors might address sexual problems among the elderly.

Before examining some of the facts about aging and sexuality, it is instructive to look at common perceptions regarding the intersection of these two human qualities. Historically, sexuality for men and women over age sixty-five has been considered inappropriate and immoral and a foolish attempt to regain lost youth (Covey, 1989). Common myths about seniors are that they are not interested in sex (and judged to be "dirty" if they do express such interest), not able to feel sexual, not sexually desirable, and not physically capable of engaging in sexual behavior (Hall, Selby, & Vanclay, 1982; McDougall, 1993). The research literature, however, indicates that elders do continue to engage in sexual behaviors throughout their lifetime and that sex continues to maintain importance in their lives (e.g., Kaplan, 1990; Starr & Weiner, 1981).

Several authors have speculated about the roots of these negative attitudes about aging and sexuality. Hodson and Skeen (1994) suggest that by ignoring the sexuality of the elderly, younger people are trying to avoid the inevitability of their own aging. Adult children may also be reluctant to think of their parents as sexual creatures because they are uncomfortable with the thought of their parents having sex (Foster, 1996; Rose & Soares, 1993). In addition, cultural attitudes that revere reproductiveness and youth contribute to the expectation that seniors are, or should be, asexual (Deacon, Minichiello, & Plummer, 1995).

However, the reality is that sexuality is not just for the youthful nor is it exclusively about human reproduction. Sexual expression and physical contact satisfy important human needs for intimacy, love, and pleasure that persist throughout the life span (Deacon et al., 1995; Nay, 1992). As the population lives to an older age, the capacity to engage in sexual behavior for nonreproductive purposes becomes a quality of life issue for a major portion of our society (Sherwin, 1990). Since sexuality is among the last of the biological functions to deteriorate with age, sex may, in fact, become more important for older adults (Kaplan, 1990). In recent years, as more people live to an older age and as attitudes toward sexuality become more enlightened, more elderly are seeking sexual counseling (Schiavi, 1990), and it becomes increasingly important for counselors to become knowledgeable about this issue.

At the same time, counselors working with the elderly should be aware of the physiological and psychological changes that occur with age and be careful not to promote unrealistic expectations (Segraves & Segraves, 1995). Professionals who work with the elderly may be overly optimistic about aging and sexuality, perhaps in an effort to appease their own fears of aging (Rose & Soares, 1993). However, overly optimistic attitudes may promote unrealistic standards and gloss over important realities that have a direct impact on sexuality among the elderly (Rose & Soares, 1993). For example, older adults are more likely than young adults to experience chronic illness and disability, and as a result, they may become more dependent on others (Rose & Soares, 1993). In addition, seniors typically require increased time for arousal, longer refractory periods, and reduced intensity of sexual arousal response (Spence, 1992). Thus, although it is important for counselors to counteract the common misperceptions that desexualize seniors, they also should educate themselves and older adults about the realities of sexuality and the aging process.

Research on Aging and Sexuality

The body of research on aging and sexuality has grown steadily since the seminal work of Kinsey and his colleagues (1948, 1953) and Masters and Johnson (1966). However, it is important to recognize the methodological limitations inherent in many of these studies so as not to misinterpret the data derived from them. For one, many studies have utilized cross-sectional rather than longitudinal designs. Cross-sectional studies that attribute variations in sexual attitudes and behavior solely to age, while ignoring such factors as cohort experience and generational differences, are problematic (Hendricks & Hendricks, 1986; Schiavi, 1990). For example, Allgeier and Allgeier (1984) note that previous studies reporting decreased sexual interest and activity with age are more attributable to generational differences than to the aging process.

Moreover, many of these studies contained limited samples of older adults; thus, any conclusions drawn from the results must be interpreted with caution (Kellett [1991] points out that Kinsey et al. [1948] concluded 75 percent of men over the age of 80 were impotent based on a sample size of four). It is also important to consider that research is embedded in conceptual frameworks about sexuality that are biased by the preconceived ideas of younger researchers, who are, themselves, influenced by cultural standards that are largely insensitive to the older person's sexual needs (Deacon et al., 1995). Finally, it should be noted that most of the limited research on sexuality and aging has been conducted on heterosexual European Americans. As such, the results may have limited application to gay and bisexual elders and to older adults from ethnic minority cultures. Although we will attempt to address these groups in this chapter, it should be recognized that much of what follows is based on research with heterosexual European Americans.

Sexual behavior

In contrast to common perceptions, research indicates that seniors maintain an interest in sex and continue to engage in sexual activities throughout their life. In one of the few longitudinal studies of sexual behavior among aging adults, Pfeiffer and Davis (1972) found that interest in coital activity was common among older adults aged 60 to 94. Starr and Weiner (1981) surveyed 800 men and women between the ages of 60 and 91 and found that 99 percent of the respondents expressed a desire for a sexual relationship, and 80 percent stated that they were still sexually active. In a review of several studies of aging and sexuality, Kaplan (1990) concluded that 70 percent of healthy 70 years olds remain sexually active and are having sex at least once a week.

However, researchers have also documented a decline in sexual activity among the elderly. Kinsey and his colleagues (1948, 1953), in their cross-sectional survey, were the first to document a gradual decline in all measures of sexual activity. Although Schiavi (1990) noted that men over age 60 were underrepresented in the Kinsey et al. (1948) sample, subsequent studies conducted at Duke University (Pfeiffer, Verwoerdt, & Wang, 1968) confirmed and extended Kinsey's results. Pfeiffer et al. concluded that there was a gradual decline in the frequency of intercourse, as well as a decrease in the intensity of sexual interest with age. Martin (1977, 1981) also found an age-related decrease in frequency of intercourse in his longitudinal study of older men. More recent studies have concluded that there is a decline in sexual interest and frequency with age for both men and women (Mulligan, Retchin, Chinchilli, & Bettinger, 1988; Roughan, Kaiser, & Morley, 1993; Schiavi, 1990). Even when controlling for the respondent's and partner's health status, Marsiglio and Donnelly (1991) noted that age was a significant predictor of sexual activity. However, a key point to consider is that much of the research to date has restricted the definition of sexual activity to heterosexual intercourse; thus, the results may be misleading. Adams (1980) found that when sexual activity was defined to include activities other than heterosexual intercourse, the results actually indicated an increase in sexual functioning among elders.

A variety of factors may contribute to the decline in sexual activity among older adults. Lack of a partner or the illness of a spouse are commonly cited reasons (Crose & Drake, 1993; Roughan et. al., 1993). A number of studies have also indicated that the male partner's attitudes or physical condition is often responsible for the cessation of sexual activity among older women (Kaiser, 1991; Palmore, 1981). Similarly, Bachman et al. (1984) found that 32 percent of postmenopausal women cited their partner's disinterest as the reason for celibacy, while 25 percent acknowledged their own disinterest as a factor. Another interesting research finding is that previous sexual interest and activity is predictive of sexual behavior in later years (George & Weiler, 1981; Persson, 1990; White, 1982), reinforcing the long-standing adage to "use it or lose it." Although sex may not be important to some older people, for those who have been sexually active in their youth, sex will most likely continue to play an important role as they age (Hodson & Skeen, 1994).

Negative stereotypes and lack of education also may be related to the decline in sexual activity among some elderly. In addition to citing ill health and absence of a functional partner, women in the Roughan et al. (1993) study attributed decline in sexual activity to negative societal stereotypes about elderly female sexuality. Thus, a senior's own internalized societal proscriptions about aging and sexuality may play a role in his or her declining level of sexual behavior. In support of this hypothesis, Persson (1990) found that the more sexually active elders in his study had more positive attitudes toward sex, indicating that for some older people, fear of disapproval may be a reason for the cessation of sexual activity. Bachmann and his colleagues (1984) found that sexually inactive postmenopausal women tended to be from lower socioeconomic status groups, suggesting that those who are more educated may be freer from cultural inhibitions and sexual stereotypes.

Although the frequency of sexual behavior may decrease with age, sex can still remain a satisfying and enjoyable experience throughout the life span (Segraves & Segraves, 1995). Crose and Drake (1993) concluded that even though the incidence of sexual activity declined for older women, their overall satisfaction with sex remained the same or even increased with age. Likewise, Schiavi, Mandeli, and Schreiner-Engel (1994) found no age differences in terms of sexual enjoyment and satisfaction among older men, even though they showed a decline in sexual desire, arousal, and activity.

In summary, a review of the literature indicates that there may be a decline in the frequency of sexual behavior and some decrease in sexual interest with age. In general, although some elderly remain sexually active into their 80s or even their 90s, most will experience a gradual decline in sexual activity after age 50 and a more marked decline after age 70 (Segraves & Segraves, 1995). At the same time, it is noteworthy to consider that sexual functioning is quite variable among all age groups and thus it is misleading to generalize research results to all older adults (Segraves & Segraves, 1995). Furthermore, those who remain sexually active may enjoy sex as much or more in old age as they did when they were younger.

Physiological Factors

Notwithstanding the studies that point to the decline in sexual activity among older adults, many researchers have emphasized that there is no physiological reason why a healthy man or woman cannot continue to engage in and enjoy sexual activity throughout the entire life span (Spence, 1992). Although the average person over the age of 50 may have some degree of physical impairment that may have an impact on sexual activity, the importance of physical limitations is typically exacerbated by a variety of cultural, intrapsychic, and relationship stressors, transforming minor limitations into full-fledged sexual disability (Kaplan, 1990). Aging is accompanied by physiological changes that may affect sexual functioning, but the aging process itself does not abolish the need or capacity for sexual activity (Kaye, 1993; Kellet, 1991).

However, it is important for counselors to be knowledgeable about the physiological changes that do occur with age and which may affect the sexual experience. As they age, many men experience changes in erectile and ejaculatory functions (Schiavi, 1990). While younger men are able to achieve and maintain an erection through either physical or psychological stimulation, older men often need continuous physical stimulation to achieve an erection (Kellett, 1993; Wagner & Green, 1983). However, most older men find that once an erection is achieved, it can be maintained for an extended period of time without ejaculation (Steinke, 1991). Moreover, the older male may not always experience a demand for orgasm and ejaculation during intercourse (Masters & Johnson, 1981). Although older men produce less semen and expel it with less force during ejaculation than when they were younger, for most healthy men, the pressure within the penis remains sufficient for sexual intercourse (Kaplan, 1990). As men age, the orgasm is of shorter duration (Whitbourne, 1990) and the refractory period (time between ejaculation and next erection) increases substantially; at age 17, the refractory period may be just a few minutes but at age 70, it can be as long as 48 hours (Kaplan, 1990; Turnbull, 1990). Although these physiological changes do not necessarily affect the subjective enjoyment of the sexual experience, it is important for counselors to educate elders about them. Otherwise, the older man and his partner may become disturbed by these normal changes and dysfunction and performance anxiety may result (Whitbourne, 1990).

For women, the onset of menopause is a marking point in physiological changes related to sexuality. After menopause, women experience a decline in the circulating levels of estrogen and progesterone. As a result, the rate and amount of vaginal lubrication are decreased, and there is a general atrophying of vaginal tissue, making the vagina more sensitive (Thienhaus, Conter, & Bosmann, 1986). Reduced sexual activity in older women is often erroneously attributed to these endocrinal changes (Sherwin, 1990). However, Segraves and Segraves (1995) note that the decrease in levels of estrogen and progesterone levels are not a major factor in predicting sexual interest and activity after menopause, and that sociocultural factors and the meanings assigned to menopause may be more salient explanations for the decline in sexual activity for many women. Nonetheless, there is some evidence that estrogen replacement can be beneficial for postmenopausal women. Walling, Anderson, and Johnson (1990), in their review of research on replacement therapies, concluded that estrogen replacement seems to have a beneficial effect on the libido, although the mechanism behind this is unclear. On a positive note, menopause may allow the woman to feel freer to explore and enjoy sex without the fear of pregnancy (Whitbourne, 1990).

Other physiological changes experienced by older women include a reduced size of the cervix, uterus, and ovaries, as well as some loss of elasticity and thinning of the vaginal wall (Weg, 1983). As they age, some women may also experience pain during intercourse (dyspareunia) or involuntary spasms of the outer third of the vagina that interfere with intercourse (Masters & Johnson, 1981). The response of the older woman's clitoris, however, remains generally the same as that of the younger woman, and women are able to enjoy orgasms throughout their lifetime (Steinke, 1991). Counselors may want to suggest Kegel exercises (Roughan & Kunst, 1981), contraction and relaxation of the pubococcygeal muscles, for older women in order to restore tone to vaginal muscles and tissue.

Hormonal changes also occur in the older man; specifically, there is a decrease in the levels of testosterone. Because many people associate testosterone with virility and masculinity, the older man's decline in testosterone may affect how he and others feel about his sexuality (Whitbourne, 1990). However, the relationship between testosterone levels and sexual arousal has yet to be proven (Schiavi, 1990). Moreover, when health levels and living status are controlled, age differences in testosterone levels for men are virtually eliminated (Harman & Tsitouras, 1980).

A sexual problem experienced by many older men is impotence. Slag et al. (cited in Morley & Kaiser, 1992) reported that one-third of males over age 40 will be impotent at some point in their lives. The causes of impotence are usually multifactorial, but the most common cause is vascular disease involving penile arteries (Morley & Kaiser, 1992). Counselors also should be aware that medications, especially antihypertensives, are a factor in impotence in up to 25 percent of older males (Slag et al., cited in Morley & Kaiser, 1992). In addition, approximately 10 percent of impotence in older men is related to psychological causes (Slag et al., cited in Morley & Kaiser, 1992). For example, Widower's syndrome describes the temporary impotence some men experience after the death of their first wife; it is often attributed to feelings of guilt for betraying the deceased partner (Levy, 1994; Morley & Kaiser, 1992).

When considering the effects of aging on sexuality, it is crucial not to confuse the aging process with the illnesses that often accompany old age.

Although there is a rise in the incidence of sexual dysfunction with age, age is also associated with an increase in medical problems and the use of medications. Thus, it is often difficult to determine whether sexual problems are attributable to age or to specific diseases or to medications used to treat the diseases (Schiavi, 1990; Spence, 1992).

Alzheimer's and other forms of dementia associated with advanced age may affect sexual activity. Patients with dementia may behave in sexually inappropriate ways and make inappropriate sexual demands due to cognitive deficits (Morley & Kaiser, 1992; Spence, 1992). Dementia is also associated with the loss of libido (Kellett, 1991), which may lead the patient with dementia to lose interest in sex. In such cases, the partner may need to be more assertive in initiating and maintaining the sexual relationship (Turnbull, 1990). However, other problems may arise in the relationship. For example, the caretaking partner may begin to find the partner with dementia sexually unattractive; others may regard sex as inappropriate to their caretaking role (Litz, Zeiss, & Davis, 1990). Fortunately, only a minority of seniors suffer from dementia.

In working with elderly clients, counselors need to be aware of other physical ailments and medical conditions related to aging that may affect sexual functioning. Diabetes is common among older people and is the most common organic cause of impotence (Deacon et al., 1995). Diabetes also can result in ejaculatory problems for men. For women, diabetes may lead to the atrophying of the uterine and ovarian tissue, but this should have little overall impact on sexual functioning (Golan & Chong, 1992; Kellett, 1991).

There is a common perception that after a stroke or cardiac arrest, patients should abstain from sexual intercourse. The misguided fear that sex will lead to another, possibly fatal, incident may inhibit the patient and his or her partner from engaging in sex. However, the anxiety and tension related to the restriction of sex pose greater risks than the physical risk associated with intercourse (Butler & Lewis, 1988). Contrary to common perceptions that stroke sufferers may not be interested in sex, most people who have suffered a stroke experience only a slight and temporary decreased interest in sex (Kellett, 1991; Thienhaus et al., 1986). However, disabilities resulting from the stroke may affect sexual expression, such as hugging, embracing, fondling, and intercourse, as well as verbal communication (Deacon et al., 1995). Damage to neural pathways may also inhibit the feeling of erotic sensations. Many people erroneously interpret the breathlessness of orgasm as a strain on the cardiorespiratory system when it is induced by central stimulation (Kellett, 1991). In fact, the danger of a coronary attack during sex is slight and can be minimized among those predisposed to heart attacks by taking nitroglycerin tablets prior to sex (Hodson & Skeen, 1994).

Many older adults suffer from some form of arthritis. Arthritis may negatively affect sexual functioning by causing pain in movement and restricting certain movements necessary to intercourse (Turnbull, 1990). For heterosexual elders who have severe arthritis, intercourse from the vaginal rear entry position is often more comfortable than the traditional missionary position. Sexual intercourse in the morning after a period of rest may also be preferable to nighttime activity (Turnbull, 1990).

A large number of seniors also undergo surgery. Some surgeries, such as prostratic surgery, may damage parasympathetic nerves, thus inhibiting physiological arousal (Kellett, 1991). After a prostatectomy, the volume of ejaculate is often reduced substantially. Moreover, surgeries that involve extensive physical change or bodily scarring may have a negative impact on the individual's self-image (Golan & Chong, 1992; Kellett, 1991). Also, any disease that results in malaise or depression may be a cause for decreased libido (Kellett, 1991).

On a positive note, research indicates that sexual activity may actually provide physiological benefits that counteract the effects of aging. For example, intercourse lubricates the atrophic vagina by stimulating blood flow (Lewis, 1986) and helps to lessen the shrinkage of the vagina (Masters & Johnson, 1966). The exercise associated with sex may also be beneficial for those suffering from arthritis (Robinson, 1983).

Finally, in addition to being knowledgeable about the natural physiological changes that occur with aging, counselors should be aware of the effects commonly prescribed medications and habituating drugs can have on sexual functioning. Specifically, antihypertensives, tranquilizers, and antidepressants can adversely affect erectile function, as well as the libido (Kellett, 1991; Turnbull, 1990). Many drugs given to heart disease patients affect erections in men and lubrication in women (Turnbull, 1990). However, the most common causes of sexual failure for older adults are alcohol and tobacco (Kellett, 1991).

Psychological Issues

It is important to consider psychological as well as physiological factors in looking at the sexual functioning of elders. Research indicates that there is a significant relationship between knowledge about sexual issues, positive attitudes about sexuality, and sexual behavior in later years (Hillman & Stricker, 1994; White, 1982). Accordingly, negative attitudes toward sex learned at a young age may impact a person's ability to enjoy sex as an older adult (Deacon et al., 1995). These results suggest that psychological and attitudinal factors are just as important, if not more important, than physiological ones in explaining the decline in sexual activity among the elderly. Thus, it is critical for counselors to educate elders about sexual issues, although changing such beliefs, which are often linked with values, morals, and religious beliefs developed over a lifetime, may not be an easy task (Steinke, 1988). Without education, elders may internalize the ageist stereotypes that prevail in our society, leading them to believe that they should not feel sexual or act in a sexual manner (Deacon et al., 1995). For some older adults, such stereotypes can become a self-fulfilling prophecy and influence sexual behavior (Steinke, 1991).

A variety of psychological issues related to aging may affect an elder's sexual functioning. For example, relationship issues may be exacerbated in old age and manifest themselves in sexual problems (Deacon et al., 1995; Kaplan, 1990). Couples who have been together for a long time may be dealing with problems of boredom in their relationship (Spence, 1992). In addition, issues related to performance and self-esteem may be salient for older adults. Masters and Johnson (1966) reported that the decline in male sexual activity was more the result of fear of failure than any physiological effects of aging. For example, an older man's fears about performance anxiety may prevent him from achieving an erection. As men age, many become increasingly vulnerable to the psychological effects of performance anxiety; this anxiety is heightened for those who already feel insecure about their sexuality (Kaplan, 1990). Moreover, retirement may lower self-esteem for some men, which may, in turn, have an impact on their sexual performance (Deacon et al., 1995).

While older men may have to deal with issues of performance, older women must combat traditional gender roles that proscribe their sexuality. Women's sexuality has been associated with reproduction, marriage, or prostitution, and dependent on beauty and youthfulness (Nay, 1992). Although mature men are still perceived as being sexually attractive, older women are generally not considered to be attractive and sexual beings (Sherwin, 1990). Thus, an older woman may fear that she is no longer physically attractive to her partner (Spence, 1992). However, one interesting finding from Starr and Weiner's (1981) research was that both men and women preferred sexual partners their own age.

On a positive note, for some elders, the sexual experience may actually improve with age. The majority of women in Crose and Drake's (1993) study noted that their attitudes toward sex had become more positive over time; they felt less pressured and were more aware of their own needs. Similarly, women in another study reported that they believed that sex had become better with age and that they associated sex in later life with pleasure and release of tension (Nay, 1992). For older men, the changes in erectile functioning enable them to gain ejaculatory control and maintain erection for longer periods than in their youth (Heiman, Lopiccolo, & Lopiccolo, 1976). The increased time needed to achieve sexual arousal can prolong the period of sensual enjoyment prior to orgasm, and in heterosexual couples, the man is more able to coordinate his pleasure cycle with his female partner (Whitbourne, 1990). Research points to the emotional as well as the physical benefits of sex. For example, Brecher (1984) reported that those who enjoyed an active sex life and intimate relationships were more likely to state a higher level of life satisfaction. In contrast, repressing sexuality can lead to problems, such as emotional distress (Starr & Weiner, 1981).

Implications for Practice

Because it is hard for many older clients to broach the topic of sexuality, the counselor may want to initiate such a discussion. The counselor's mere acknowledgment of an elderly client's sexuality may be a relief to the client and open the door for a frank discussion of sexual issues (Rose & Soares, 1993). To begin, the counselor can educate the older adult about sexual issues (Steinke, 1991). Many older adults were raised in an era when accurate information about sex was not widely available.

Programs geared toward providing sex education to older adults and their care providers have been successful in positively changing and enhancing their attitudes about sex, sexuality, and aging (Levy, 1994). For example, White and Catania (1982) implemented a sex education program in a nursing home for staff, elderly residents, and residents' families; afterward, sexual intercourse increased by 400 percent among residents. Rowland and Haynes (1978) also implemented a six-week sex enhancement program for elderly couples in which they provided subjects with information on human sexual functioning and instruction on communication exercises and sexual techniques. An evaluation of this program documented significant increases in sexual satisfaction, frequency of certain sexual activities, and positive attitudes about marital and life satisfaction. The authors noted that their program was geared toward sex enhancement (increasing the enjoyment and satisfaction of sexual interactions) rather than sex therapy (focusing on treating specific sexual dysfunctions). However, the majority of the couples in this study did complain of specific sexual dysfunctions, and the authors acknowledged that the program could have been even more effective if it had included sex therapy sessions tailored to treat the couples' specific sexual problems. In designing programs for elders, counselors may want to consider combining components of sexual enhancement and sex therapy. At the same time, emphasizing sex education and enhancement may be more effective in drawing in older adults who are uncomfortable with the idea of therapy and sexual dysfunction.

As part of the education process, counselors should broaden the definition of sexuality to encompass all forms of intimacy, such as touching, caressing, and kissing, as well as masturbation (Hodson & Skeen, 1994). Our society largely equates sex with genital contact, and many elders grew up in a time when being sexual meant having intercourse (Shaw, 1994). However, this provides a very limited view of sexual expression. Although noncoital activities can provide an important source of sexual expression and may provide more comfortable ways of meeting intimacy needs for elders, these expressions of sexuality are not as valued in our society as intercourse (Crooks & Baur, 1980). It is important for counselors to validate alternative expressions of sexuality and educate elders about the options available. Fortunately, research suggests that as people age, their expressions of sexuality become more varied and less emphasis is placed on coitus. Starr and Weiner (1981) found in their survey of 800 respondents that older people defined and expressed sexuality in more diffuse and varied ways than did younger cohorts, indicating that modifications in sexual expression and preferred sexual activity may be prevalent with advanced age. Similarly, Bretschneider and McCoy (1988) found that the most common forms of sexual activity among healthy, upper middle-class residents in retirement facilities were (a) touching and caressing without sexual intercourse, (b) masturbation, and (c) intercourse.

In general, counselors may want to advise older couples to shift their lovemaking from lengthy intercourse toward experimentation with alternate forms of sexual gratification (Kaplan, 1990). For example, couples may be encouraged to extend the use of mutual masturbation (Kellett, 1991), or explore their sexual fantasies and share erotica with each other (Kaplan, 1990). Counselors may also suggest that couples engage in more tender and gentler lovemaking and use lubricants for the benefit of the postmenopausal woman who has more fragile genitalia. In order to diminish performance anxiety, couples may be instructed to use sensate-focus methods (Masters & Johnson, 1970).

Finally, it is important that in addressing sexual issues, counselors also educate older adults about AIDS and HIV. Along with the assumption that elders do not engage in sexual behavior follows the supposition that older adults are not affected by AIDS. In fact, a substantial and increasing number of elderly individuals have developed AIDS (Gutheil & Chichin, 1991; Linsk, 1994). Although most cases of infection have been associated with blood transfusions or IV drug use, elders have also contracted the AIDS virus through unsafe sexual practices (Linsk, 1994). Thus, it is important that counselors not neglect older adults when educating the general population about AIDS and HIV.

The following are specific groups within the elderly population that may require special attention by counselors.

Single Older Adults

Another important point to keep in mind when working with seniors is that there are significantly more older women than men (Minichiello, Alexander, & Jones, 1992). This has implications for heterosexual women's opportunities for relationships and sexual activity in later years. One of the most common reasons cited by older women as the cause of decline in sexual intercourse was the unavailability of a suitable partner (Morley, cited in Morley & Kaiser, 1992). Since women typically live to an older age than men and often marry men who are older than they, many women are left without partners in their later years (Kaplan, 1990). Older men are more likely than older women to be married and to remarry if divorced or widowed (Crose & Drake, 1993: Minichiello et al., 1992). The phenomenon of single older adults is even more marked among African Americans, who are twice as likely to be divorced and separated, and proportionately more likely to be widowed as compared to European Americans (AARP, 1986).

Thus, counselors may want to suggest alternative ways single older people, both men and women, might meet their sexual needs, including sexual activities and expressions that do not require a partner (Levy, 1994). However, seniors may be averse to alternative expressions of sexuality, such as sexual fantasizing, masturbation, sex outside marriage, polygamy, or sexual relations with a person of the same sex, because of their historically and culturally influenced lifelong beliefs and values (Thienhaus et al., 1986). Although masturbation remains an important sexual outlet (Bretschneider & McCoy, 1988), many elders may have negative feelings about masturbation because of the stigma against this activity when they were growing up. At the same time, there is evidence that more older people are using masturbation for sexual release now than in the past (Hodson & Skeen, 1994). Older heterosexual women, for whom the issue of partner availability is most pressing, may find that they can meet their intimacy needs through an attachment to or living arrangement with another older woman. Although these relationships are not sexual in the conventional sense, they can still provide an important source of support and emotional intimacy (Capuzzi & Friel, 1995).

Older Gay, Lesbian, and Bisexual Men and Women

In working with elders, counselors need to be sensitive to the needs of older gay men, lesbian women, and bisexual individuals. The first step for most counselors is to address and overcome their own biases about homosexuality and bisexuality. In addition, it is important to keep in mind that sexual function and dysfunction have largely been defined from a heterosexual and masculine perspective that focuses on the achievement of coitus (Deacon et al., 1995). Furthermore, the research to date on bisexuality and homosexuality has largely ignored older populations, and studies on older ethnic minority gays and bisexuals are virtually nonexistent (Jacobson & Grossman, 1996). Although in recent years there has been a growing interest in studying the sexual expression of older gays and lesbians (Fortunato, 1994), the needs of bisexual individuals has yet to be adequately addressed. In part, this is related to society's discomfort with bisexuality because it does not fit the traditional tendency to categorize individuals as either homosexual or heterosexual. Bisexual persons have, as a result, been marginalized by both the gay and lesbian communities and by a predominantly heterosexual society (Paul, 1996).

Just as there are myths about elders and sexuality, there are inaccurate perceptions about older homosexuals and bisexuals. Although there are common notions that older gay men are lonely, depressed, and unattractive to each other, and that older lesbian women are unemotional, lonely, and unattractive to each other, these myths have not been supported by empirical research (Berger, 1980; Fortunato, 1994; Reid, 1995).

In order to survive in a world that is generally hostile and oppressive toward homosexuality and sexual minorities, older lesbian, gay, and bisexual persons have had to develop a variety of coping mechanisms (Jacobson & Grossman, 1996). It is important to remember that the difficulties experienced by homosexual and bisexual elders have more to do with society's negative attitudes than to being gay or bisexual (Berger, 1984). Some authors have hypothesized that the aging process may compound the feelings of stigmatization already present for sexual minorities (e.g., Kimmel, 1978). However, it has also been suggested that older adults who are homosexual may, in some respects, find the adjustment to old age easier than their heterosexual counterparts, because they have had experience dealing with the stigma of being gay (Berger & Kelly, 1986; Vacha, 1985; Wolf, 1982); the same principle may also apply to bisexual persons. Heterosexual elders, by comparison, may be less prepared to deal with society's ageist biases. The literature, in fact, indicates that adjustment to aging varies according to the individual, depending on the person's satisfaction with being gay and the pattern of early gay developmental events (Aldeman, 1991). For an elder who is still struggling with issues about his or her own sexual orientation, such difficulties may become exacerbated with old age. At the same time, Hodson and Skeen (1994) point out that, in some cases, the death of the heterosexual partner may allow the surviving partner to acknowledge his or her own homosexuality.

In working with seniors, it is important to also remember that gay and lesbian elders may have values and beliefs that are very different from their younger counterparts, since they grew up before the sexual revolution and Gay Liberation (McDougall, 1993). At the same time, many authors have noted that bisexual and homosexual elders deal largely with the same issues of sexuality faced by heterosexuals (Berger, 1984; Paul, Weinrich, Gonssiorek, & Hotvedt, 1982). Thus, many of the issues addressed throughout this chapter also apply to bisexual and homosexual clients.

Elders in Institutions

Another population that requires special attention is elders who are residents of nursing homes and other institutions. Some institutions and institutional staff in such settings harbor the biases against elderly sexuality evidenced in our society at large; they do not provide for, and may even inhibit, the sexual expression of elderly residents. Most facilities do not provide adequate privacy for residents, so residents have little opportunity to experience sexual intimacy (Nay, 1992). Moreover, many facilities segregate men and women and do not accommodate even married couples by allowing them to share a room, let alone a bed (Brown, 1989). Normal expressions of sexuality are often considered to be the result of age-related behavioral problems or senility; a resident who behaves in a sexual manner may even be reprimanded (Brown, 1989; Hodson & Skeen, 1994).

Counselors who work in nursing homes can educate staff and residents that elderly expression of sexuality is normal and to be expected. Counselors can also ensure that these facilities provide some privacy for residents to facilitate sexual activities among elders.

Ethnic Minority Elders

To date, there has been virtually nothing written about the sexuality of elders from diverse cultures. The research on elderly sexuality has focused almost exclusively on European American samples. The cross-cultural research on sexuality that has been conducted with ethnic minorities has concentrated on teenagers, and the findings of younger populations may not be generalizable to older adults. In order to fully understand how older adults deal with sexual issues, counselors must consider the variables of race, ethnicity, and culture, because sexual behavior is the product of social norms and some of the variability manifested in sexual behavior is the result of cultural differences among people (Abramson & Imai-Marquez, 1982). In their review of the research on women, ethnicity, and sex, Rushton and Bogaert (1987) noted a number of differences in sexual behavior and attitudes based on race and ethnicity, especially in terms of sexual restraint and precocity. Although it is impossible to sufficiently address the sexuality of ethnic minority elders due to the lack of relevant research, the following is a discussion of some of the limited research conducted to date on sexual attitudes and behavior among ethnic minority elders.

In their analysis of Japanese Americans, Hirayama and Hirayama (1986) noted that compared to non-Asians, Japanese Americans are less physically demonstrative. However, they cited ethnographic evidence indicating that traditional Japanese society was relatively uninhibited about sexual matters and that Japanese-Americans have overaccommodated to more inhibited Judeo-Christian attitudes about sex prevalent in mainstream American society. Along these lines, Abramson and Imai-Marquez (1982) found that in a comparison study of Japanese Americans and European Americans, Japanese Americans evidenced more sex guilt. This finding was true even for highly acculturated Japanese American subjects and even more pronounced for Japanese American women. The authors noted that this was in keeping with the tendency of Japanese American families to de-emphasize and suppress sexuality (Connor, 1976). More generally, the Abramson and Imai-Marquez (1982) study suggests that there may be an interaction between sex and ethnicity in determining sexual attitudes.

In contrast, the literature seems to indicate that African Americans may be less constricted in terms of sexual attitudes and behavior when compared to European Americans. For example, Weinberg and Williams (1988) found that both African American men and women reported more liberal attitudes about pre- and extramarital sex, thought about sex more often, and had fewer sexual problems than the European Americans sampled. Houston's (1981) study of college students revealed that African American men and women reported looking at erotic materials more than their European American counterparts. However, Wyatt and Dunn's (1991) study of women found that African American participants evidenced higher levels of sex guilt than did their European American peers. A more recent study conducted by Oggins, Leber, and Veroff (1993) of African American and European American newlyweds found that sexual enjoyment had different meanings for African American and European American men and women but also noted that socioeconomic class may be a mediating variable.

It is important to point out that none of the studies previously mentioned was conducted on an elderly population. However, the research cited does indicate that ethnic minority adults may exhibit different sexual attitudes and behaviors compared to European Americans, on whom most of the sex research has been conducted. In their study of adolescents, Davis and Harris (1982) found that ethnicity was significantly related to subjects' sexual knowledge, sexual interests, and sources of information, and the authors noted the importance of considering ethnicity in planning a sex education program. The same suggestion can be applied to counselors working with elders. At the same time, counselors should keep in mind that although ethnicity may be an important factor in understanding an individual's sexuality, there are diverse attitudes about sexuality and other topics *within* various cultural groups.

Conclusion

While it is important for counselors to educate seniors, it is also important for them to understand that elders may have values regarding sexuality different from their own and to respect those differences (Spence, 1992). For one, counselors should be sensitive to the fact that elders from various ethnic, cultural, and religious backgrounds may have different views of sexuality and appropriate sexual behavior. In general, today's elderly were raised in a milieu when discussion of sexuality was highly inhibited and sexual practices were generally defined by male superior marital intercourse (Hodson & Skeen, 1994). Thus, counselors can provide a valuable service by providing accurate information regarding sexuality and aging to elders. Moreover, many elders seem receptive to educational programs (Smith & Schmall, 1983). At the same time, counselors must be careful not to impose their own views of sexuality onto older clients. It is important to recognize that although alternative expressions of sexuality, such as masturbation, provide an important sexual outlet, some elders may be averse to such practices (Hodson & Skeen, 1994; Thienhaus et al., 1986). However, there are some indications that older adults are more comfortable with masturbation and other alternative forms of sexual expression now than in the past. It is likely that as the middle aged of today grow older, elders' attitudes toward nontraditional concepts of sexuality will become more enlightened (Hodson & Skeen, 1994).

References

Abramson, P. R., & Imai-Marquez, J. (1982). The Japanese-American: A cross-cultural, cross-sectional study of sex guilt. *Journal of Research in Personality, 16,* 227–237.

Adams, C. (1980). *Sexuality and the older adult.* Unpublished doctoral dissertation, University of Massachusetts.

Aldeman, M. (1991). Stigma, gay lifestyles and adjustment to aging: A study of later life gay men and lesbians. In J. Lee (Ed.), *Gay midlife and maturity* (pp. 7–32). New York: Haworth Press.

Allgeier, E., & Allgeier, A. (1984). *Sexual Interactions.* Lexington, MA: D. C. Heath.

American Association of Retired Persons. (1986). *A portrait of older minorities.* Washington, DC: American Association for Retired Persons.

Bachmann, G., Leiblum, S. R., Kemmann, E., Colburn, D. W., Swartzman, L., & Shelden, R. (1984). Sexual expression and its determinants in the post-menopausal woman. *Maturitas, 6,* 19–26.

Berger, R. M. (1980). Psychological adaptation of the older homosexual male. *Journal of Homosexuality, 5* (3), 161–175.

Berger, R. M. (1984). Realities of gay and lesbian aging. *Social Work,* Jan-Feb, 57–62.

Berger, R. M., & Kelly, J. J. (1986). Working with homosexuals of the older population. *Social Casework: The Journal of Contemporary Social Work, 67,* 203–210.

Brecher, E. M. (1984). *Love, Sex, and Aging.* Boston: Little, Brown.

Bretschneider, J. G., & McCoy, N. L. (1988). Sexual interest and behaviour in healthy 80- to 102-year olds. *Archives of Sexual Behaviour, 17,* 109–129.

Brown, L. (1989). Is there sexual freedom for our aging population in long-term care institutions? *Journal of Gerontological Social Work, 13,* 75–93.

Butler, R. N., & Lewis, M. I. (1988). *Love and Sex After 60.* New York: Harper & Row.

Capuzzi, D., & Friel, S. E. (1995). Current trends in sexuality and aging: An update for counselors. In D. R. Atkinson & G. Hackett (Eds.), *Counseling Diverse Populations* (pp. 207–216). Dubuque, IA: Wm. C. Brown Communications, Inc.

Connor, J. W. (1976). Family bonds, maternal closeness and suppression of sexuality in three generations of Japanese Americans, *Ethos, 4,* 189–221.

Covey, H. (1989). Perceptions and attitudes toward sexuality of the elderly during the Middle Ages. *Gerontologist, 29,* 93–100.

Crooks, R., & Baur, K. (1980). *Our Sexuality.* Menlo Park, CA: Benjamin Cummings.

Crose, R., & Drake, L. K. (1993). Older women's sexuality. *Clinical Gerontologist, 12,* 51–56.

Davis, S. M., & Harris, M. B. (1982). Sexual knowledge, sexual interests, and sources of sexual information of rural and urban adolescents from three cultures. *Adolescence, 17,* 471–492.

Deacon, S., Minichiello, V., & Plummer, D. (1995). Sexuality and older people: Revisiting the assumptions. *Educational Gerontology, 21,* 497–513.

Fortunato, V. (1994). *Homosexuality, aging and social support.* Unpublished master's thesis, La Trobe University, Melbourne, Victoria, Australia.

Foster, S. (1996). Sexual health in later life. *Counseling Today, 38* (11), 14.

George, L. K., & Weiler, S. J. (1981). Sexuality in middle and late life. *Archives of General Psychiatry, 38,* 919–923.

Gochros, H., Gochros, J., & Fisher, J. (Eds.). (1986). *Helping the sexually oppressed.* Englewood Cliffs, NJ: Prentice Hall.

Golan, O., & Chong, B. (1992). Sexuality and ageing: Some physical aspects. *Geriaction, 11,* 10–11.

Gutheil, I. A., & Chichin, E. R. (1991). AIDS, older people, and social work. *Health & Social Work, 16,* 237–244.

Hall, A., Selby, J., & Vanclay, F. M. (1982). Sexual ageism. *Australian Journal on Ageing, 1,* 29–34.

Harman, S. M., & Tsitouras, P. D. (1980). Reproductive hormones in aging men: Measurement of sex steroids, basal luteinizing hormone and leydig cell response to human chorionic gonadotropin. *Journal of Clinical Endocrinology and Metabolism, 51,* 35–40.

Heiman, J., Lopiccolo, L., & Lopiccolo, J. (1976). *Becoming orgasmic: A sexual growth program for women.* Englewood Cliffs, NJ: Prentice-Hall.

Hendricks, J., & Hendricks, C. (1986). *Aging in mass society: Myths and realities.* Boston, MA: Little, Brown.

Hillman, J. L., & Stricker, G. (1994). A linkage of knowledge and attitudes toward elderly sexuality: Not necessarily a uniform relationship. *The Gerontologist, 34,* 256–260.

Hirayama, H., & Hirayama, K. K. (1986). The sexuality of Japanese Americans. *Journal of Social Work & Human Sexuality, 4,* 81–98.

Hodson, D. S., & Skeen, P. (1994). Sexuality and aging: The hammerlock of myths. *The Journal of Applied Gerontology, 13,* 219–235.

Houston, L. N. (1981). Romanticism and eroticism among Black and White college students. *Adolescence, 16,* 263–272.

Jacobson, S., & Grossman, A. H. (1996). Older lesbians and gay men: Old myths, new images, and future directions. In R. C. Savin-Williams & K. M. Cohen (Eds.), *The Lives of Lesbians, Gays, and Bisexuals* (pp. 345–367). Fort Worth, TX: Harcourt Brace & Company.

Kaiser, F. E. (1991). Sexuality and impotence in the aging man. *Clinical Geriatric Medicine, 7,* 63–71.

Kaplan, H. S. (1990). Sex, intimacy, and the aging process. *Journal of the American Academy of Psychoanalysis, 18,* 185–205.

Kaye, R. A. (1993). Sexuality in the later years. *Ageing and Society, 13,* 415–426.

Kellett, J. M. (1991). Sexuality of the elderly. *Sexual and Marital Therapy, 6,* 147–155.

Kellett, J. M. (1993). Sexuality in later life. *Reviews in Clinical Gerontology, 3,* 309–314.

Kimmel, D. C. (1978). Adult development and aging: A gay perspective. *Journal of Social Issues, 34,* 113–130.

Kinsey, A. C., Pomeroy, W. B., & Martin, C. E. (1948). *Sexual behavior in the human male.* Philadelphia: W. B. Saunders.

Kinsey, A. C., Pomeroy, W. B., Martin, C. E., & Gebhard, P. H. (1953). *Sexual behavior in the human female.* Philadelphia: W. B. Saunders.

Lewis, A. P. (1986). Keeping menopausal women healthy. *Medical Aspects of Human Sexuality, 20,* 70–76.

Levy, J. A. (1994). Sexuality in later life stages. In A. S. Rossi (Ed.), *Sexuality across the life span* (pp. 287–309). Chicago: The University of Chicago Press.

Linsk, N. L. (1994). HIV and the elderly. *Families in Society, 75,* 362–372.

Litz, B. T., Zeiss, A. M., & Davis, H. D. (1990). Sexual concerns of male spouses of female Alzheimer's disease patients. *The Gerontologist, 30,* 113–116.

Marsiglio, W., & Donnelly, D. (1991). Sexual relations in later life: A national study of married persons. *Journal of Gerontology, 46,* 338–344.

Martin, C. E. (1977). Sexual activity in the aging male. In J. Money & H. Maraph (Eds.), *Handbook of sexology* (pp. 815–824). New York: Excerpta Medica.

Martin, C. E. (1981). Factors affecting sexual functioning in 60–79 year old married males. *Archives of Sexual Behavior, 10,* 399–420.

Masters, W. H., & Johnson, V. E. (1966). *Human Sexual Response.* Boston: Little, Brown.

Masters, W. H., & Johnson, V. E. (1970). *Human Sexual Inadequacy.* Boston: Little, Brown.

Masters, W. H., & Johnson, V. E. (1981). Sex and the aging process. *Journal of the American Geriatrics Society, 29* (9), 385–390.

McDougall, G. J. (1993). Therapeutic issues with gay and lesbian elders. *Clinical Gerontologist, 14,* 45–57.

Minichiello, V., Alexander, L., & Jones, D. (1992). *Gerontology: A multidisciplinary approach.* Englewood Cliffs, NJ: Prentice Hall.

Morley, J. E., & Kaiser, F. E. (1992). Aging and sexuality. In J. L. Albarede, A. J. Campbell, J. Grimley Evans, D. Guez, F. Jimenez Herrero, L. Rubenstein, L. G. Serro-Azul, H. Werner, et al. (Eds.), *Facts and Research in Gerontology* (pp. 157–165). New York: Springer Publishing Co.

Mulligan, T., Retchin, S. M., Chinchilli, V. M., & Bettinger, C. B. (1988). The role of aging and chronic disease in sexual dysfunction. *Journal of the American Geriatrics Society, 36,* 520–524.

Nay, R. (1992). Sexuality and aged women in nursing homes. *Geriatric Nursing, 13,* 312–314.

Oggins, J., Leber, D., & Veroff, J. (1993). Race and gender differences in Black and White newlyweds' perceptions of sexual and marital relations. *The Journal of Sex Research, 30,* 152–160.

Palmore, E. (1981). *Social patterns in normal aging: Reports from the Duke longitudinal study.* Durham, NC: Duke University Press.

Paul, J. P. (1996). Bisexuality: Exploring/Exploding the boundaries. In R. C. Savin-Williams & K. M. Cohen (Eds.), *The lives of lesbians, gays, and bisexuals* (pp. 436–461). Fort Worth, TX: Harcourt Brace & Company.

Paul, W., Weinrich, J. D., Gonsiorek, J. C., & Hotvedt, M. E. (1982). *Homosexuality.* Beverly Hills, CA: Sage.

Persson, G. (1990). Sexuality in a 70-year-old urban population. *Journal of Psychosomatic Research, 24,* 335–342.

Pfeiffer, E., & Davis, G. C. (1972). Determinants of sexual behavior in middle and old age. *Journal of the American Geriatrics Society, 20,* 151–158.

Pfeiffer, E., Verwoerdt, A., & Wang, H. S. (1968). Sexual behavior in aged men and women. *Archives of General Psychiatry, 19,* 753–758.

Reid, J. D. (1995). Development in late life: Older lesbian and gay lives. In A. R. D'Augelli & C. J. Patterson (Eds.), *Lesbian, gay, and bisexual identities over the lifespan* (pp. 215–242). New York: Oxford University Press.

Robinson, P. K. (1983). The sociological perspective. In R. Weg (Ed.), *Sexuality in the later years: Roles and behavior* (pp. 81–103). San Diego, CA: Academic Press.

Rose, M. K., & Soares, H. H. (1993). Sexual adaptations of the frail elderly: A realistic approach. *Journal of Gerontological Social Work, 19,* 167–178.

Roughan, P. A., Kaiser, F. E., & Morley, J. E. (1993). Sexuality and the older woman. *Clinics in Geriatric Medicine, 9,* 87–106.

Roughan, P. A., & Kunst, L. (1981). Do pelvic floor exercises really improve orgasmic potential? *Journal of Sex and Marital Therapy, 7,* 223–229.

Rowland, K. F., & Haynes, S. (1978). A sexual enhancement program for elderly couples. *Journal of Sex & Marital Therapy, 4,* 91–113.

Rushton, J. P., & Bogaert, A. F. (1987). Race differences in sexual behavior: Testing an evolutionary hypothesis. *Journal of Research in Personality, 21,* 529–551.

Schiavi, R. C. (1990). Sexuality and aging in men. *Annual Review of Sex Research, 1,* 227–249.

Schiavi, R. C., Mandeli, J., & Schreiner-Engel, P. (1994). Sexual satisfaction in healthy aging men. *Journal of Sex & Marital Therapy, 20,* 3–13.

Segraves, R. T., & Segraves, K. B. (1995). Human sexuality and aging. *Journal of Sex Education and Therapy, 21,* 88–102.

Shaw, J. (1994). Aging and sexual potential. *Journal of Sex Education and Therapy, 20,* 134–139.

Sherwin, B. B. (1990). The psychoendocrinology of aging and female sexuality. *Annual Review of Sex Research, 1,* 227–249.

Smith, M., & Schmall, V. L. (1983). Knowledge and attitudes toward sexuality and sex education of a select group of older people. *Gerontology and Geriatrics Education, 3,* 259–269.

Spence, S. H. (1992). Psychosexual dysfunction in the elderly. *Behaviour Change, 9,* 55–64.

Starr, B. D., & Weiner, M. B. (1981). *The Starr-Weiner report on sex and sexuality in the mature years.* New York: Stein and Day.

Steinke, E. E. (1988). Older adults' knowledge and attitudes about sexuality and aging. *Journal of Nursing Scholarship, 20,* 93–95.

Steinke, E. E. (1991). Sexuality in aging. In E. M. Baines (Ed.), *Perspectives on gerontological nursing* (pp. 78–93). Newbury Park, CA: Sage Publications, Inc.

Thienhaus, O. J., Conter, E. A., & Bosmann, H. B. (1986). Sexuality and ageing. *Ageing and Society, 6,* 39–53.

Turnbull, J. (1990). Sex and Alzheimer's disease. In R. C. Hamdy et al. (Eds.), *Alzheimer's disease: A handbook for caregivers* (pp. 78–84), St. Louis, MO: C. V. Mosby Co.

Vacha, K. (1985). *Quiet fire: Memoirs of older gay men.* Trumansburg, NY: Crossing Press.

Wagner, G., & Green, R. (1983). *Impotence.* New York: Plenum Press.

Walling, M., Anderson, B. L., & Johnson, S. R. (1990). Hormonal replacement therapy for postmenopausal women: A review of sexual outcomes and related gynecological effects. *Archives of Sexual Behavior, 19,* 119–137.

Weg, R. B. (1983). Beyond intercourse and orgasm. In R. B. Weg (Ed.), *Sexuality in the later years: Roles and behaviour* (pp. 163–174). New York: Academic Press.

Weinberg, M. S., & Williams, C. J. (1988). Black sexuality: A test of two theories. *The Journal of Sex Research, 25,* 197–218.

Whitbourne, S. K. (1990). Sexuality in the aging male. *Gender & Aging, 14,* 28–30.

White, C. B. (1982). Sexual interest, attitudes, knowledge and sexual history in relation to sexual behaviour in the institutionalized aged. *Archives of Sexual Behaviour, 11,* 11–21.

White, C. B., & Catania, J. A. (1982). Psychoeducational intervention for sexuality with the aged, family members of the aged and people who work with the aged. *International Journal of Aging and Human Development, 15,* 121–138.

Wolf, D. G. (1982). *Growing older: Lesbians and gay men.* California: University of California Press.

Wyatt, G. E., & Dunn, K. R. (1991). Examining predictors of sex guilt in multiethnic samples of women. *Archives of Sexual Behavior, 20,* 471–485.

PART 4

The Female Client

Psychology's treatment of women has been marred by sexism and discrimination in the past, and that legacy continues to influence the field to some extent. Nevertheless, over the past two decades there has been an explosion of research on the psychology of women, with consequent advances in the counseling and psychotherapy literature (Worell & Remer, 1992). Our knowledge of the psychology of gender and gender issues in counseling has progressed markedly (Betz & Fitzgerald, 1993). Unfortunately, many counselors remain uninformed about women's issues, gender influences on psychological distress, and the special techniques necessary for ethical and effective counseling with female clients.

In the late 1970s, Division 17, the Division of Counseling Psychology of the American Psychological Association, passed a set of guidelines for counseling women. Fitzgerald and Nutt (1986) expanded on these principles, clarified their rationale, presented extensive documentation in support of each principle from the literature on the psychology of women, and provided guidance for their implementation in counseling. These principles, presented in chapter 12, represent the essential minimal competencies for counseling women. Although some updating of the supporting literature is in order, the principles themselves remain current despite the publication date.

Beginning with a solid grounding in the literature on the psychology of women, counselors must then go on to develop a thorough understanding of the impact of gender on psychological theory and practice, the needs of special subgroups of women, the effects of sexism on women's and men's lives, and the influence of gender on the counseling process (Fitzgerald & Nutt, 1986). The counselor's gender-related attitudes and biases must continually be examined and confronted; sexism can easily creep into counseling, to the detriment of the client. Only after working on their attitudes and acquiring the requisite knowledge can counselors effectively employ some of the singular skills useful in counseling women (Fitzgerald & Nutt, 1986).

Implicit within the principles for counseling women is the assumption that counselors must, at the very least, adopt a nonsexist approach with their female clients. Many counselors believe that counseling should be neutral or value-free and that avoiding explicitly sexist attitudes, remarks, and behavior results in nonsexist counseling. However, attempts to adopt a "neutral" stance very often result in inadvertent sexism. The next chapter covers one approach to feminist counseling. The term *feminist* as used herein simply refers to an advocate of equality between the sexes, but feminist therapy has been concerned primarily with women's issues (Worell & Remer, 1992).

In chapter 13, McNamara and Rickard (1989) explore an important dimension of feminist counseling, that is, adapting one's counseling approach to the stage of feminist identity development of the client. Feminist identity development refers to the process of coming to terms with sexism and gender-related influences on women's lives. Female clients vary considerably in their views of the world, their awareness of sexism, and their perspectives on the issues that bring them to counseling. McNamara and Rickard (1989) describe an existing model of feminist identity development; discuss how this model can be an aid to the counselor in understanding the client; suggest how the feminist counselor may respond differently to clients at different stages of awareness; and provide some suggestions for future research on the topic. Throughout their article, McNamara and Rickard (1989) emphasize how the counselor may effectively address gender issues in a manner respectful of the client's beliefs and needs.

The article by DeVoe (1990) in chapter 14 delineates guidelines for male counselors working with female clients. Feminist counseling is clearly "not for women only," but male counselors need to take special care in working with women. DeVoe (1990) addresses some of the core issues of female clients for which male counselors might need to take special steps to be aware and knowledgeable, for example, anger, autonomy, power, and gender role stereotyping. DeVoe (1990) also discusses how men can be supportive of feminism, follow feminist principles in their counseling, and also addresses instances in which men might want to refer the female client to a female counselor. Finally, DeVoe (1990) reminds us that feminist counseling benefits male as well as female clients.

References

Betz, N. E., & Fitzgerald, L. F. (1993). Individuality and diversity: Theory and research in counseling psychology. *Annual Review of Psychology, 44,* 343–381.

DeVoe, D. (1990). Feminist and nonsexist counseling: Implications for the male counselor. *Journal of Counseling and Development, 69,* 33–36.

Fitzgerald, L. F., & Nutt, R. (1986). The Division 17 principles concerning the counseling/psychotherapy of women: Rationale and implementation. *The Counseling Psychologist, 14,* 180–216.

McNamara, K., & Rickard, K. M. (1989). Feminist identity development: Implications for feminist therapy with women. *Journal of Counseling and Development, 68,* 184–189.

Worell, J., & Remer, P. (1992). *Feminist perspectives in therapy: An empowerment model for women.* New York: Wiley.

12

The Division 17 Principles Concerning the Counseling/Psychotherapy of Women: Rationale and Implementation

Louise F. Fitzgerald and Roberta Nutt

In 1978 the Division of Counseling Psychology of the American Psychological Association (APA) approved the *Principles Concerning the Counseling and Psychotherapy of Women* as an official policy statement for the Division. These Principles, subsequently endorsed by Divisions 16, 29, and 35, have also served as a general resource document for the APA, and are cited as a resource in the *Guidelines for the Provision of Counseling Psychological Services* (APA, 1983).

Almost from the inception of the *Principles,* the Division 17 Committee on Women, which authored them, had anticipated the need for an extensive exposition of each principle, to guide psychologists seeking to implement both their spirit and their content. Thus, the present document, which presents the background and rationale for each principle as well as suggestions for implementation, was born. The result of over 5 years of work, the document has been extensively reviewed, revised, and again reviewed—not only by the committee and its various resource and support persons but also by psychologists from all across the country, both within and without Division 17. The process of cooperation, incorporation, and revision has been both frustrating and inspiring, as we worked to produce a document that could stand as a guide to our science and our profession for at least a decade. The final version was approved by the Division 17 Executive Committee at its 1984 midyear meeting.

This document is the product of literally hundreds of women (and men) who have contributed time, thought, and effort over nearly half a decade to bring this project to fruition, and thus, to contribute to the welfare of women everywhere. Although it bears our names, we are intensely aware that it is truly a cooperative product of the committee, the division, and ultimately, our profession as a whole.

PRINCIPLE I. Counselors/therapists should be knowledgeable about women, particularly with regard to biological, psychological, and social issues which have impact on women in general or on particular groups of women in our society.

Historically, the discipline of psychology has been male-defined and male-oriented (Unger & Denmark, 1975). O'Leary (1977) notes that theories of human behavior were advanced mostly by male psychologists, who investigated and attempted to verify their formulations through empirical investigations of male subjects (Carlson & Carlson, 1961; Dan & Beekman, 1972; Weisstein, 1971). She points out that female subjects were excluded from research on a variety of grounds, including the greater variability of female response, the practical difficulties involved in obtaining sufficient numbers of subjects for analysis of sex differences, and the researchers' lack of interest in such differences in areas in which they had been demonstrated to exist (Prescott & Foster, 1974). The most dramatic example of such male bias in psychology is that of achievement motivation research, in which the existence of sex differences has long been recognized (McClelland, Atkinson, Clark, & Lowell, 1953) but ignored. Only recently have (female) researchers begun to explore such differences (Farmer, 1976; Helmreich & Spence, 1978; Mednick, Tangri, Hoffman, 1975). Tellingly, O'Leary writes, "As a traditionally trained social psychologist, I was taught to view sex differences as a nuisance variable to be controlled, not investigated" (p. 3).

Although there are, no doubt, many psychologists who still subscribe to this position, believing the study of women to be of only peripheral interest, knowledge about, and interest in, women has virtually exploded in the last decade. The study of women has attained scientific respectability, as formally recognized by the American Psychological Association's (APA) formation of a Division of the Psychology of Women. Despite such advances, many counselors/therapists have little or no knowledge of the various biological, psychological, and social issues that have such great impact on their women clients. Counselors sampled by Bingham and House (1973) were misinformed on over 50% of the material presented them concerning women and work, and a recent replication (Pope, 1982) showed only minimal change. In this same vein, Birk and Fitzgerald's (1979) survey of APA-approved counseling psychology training programs indicated that only 56% of the respondents offered a course in the psychology of women on an annual basis.

It is difficult to conceive of a counselor/therapist functioning effectively with women clients unless that counselor or therapist has been, in some fashion, trained in the psychology, biology, and sociology of women. Although few of us would still subscribe to the psychoanalytical dictum that biology is destiny, few would deny that biology is basic—that it exerts an enormous effect on women's lives, both as an organismic variable and as a stimulus variable (Unger, 1979). Not only does the natural functioning of biological processes, such as menstruation, pregnancy, parturition, and menopause, affect the experience of every woman; but disruptions in these processes, such as premenstrual syndrome, infertility, miscarriage, and stillbirth, have tremendous physiological, psychological, and social impact. Familiarity with this body of knowledge is prerequisite for therapeutic work with women. The counselor/therapist must also be prepared with knowledge concerning the determinants of sexual differentiation, both genetic and hormonal. Because of the widespread misconceptions concerning the link between hormones and behavior, it is vital that the professional be familiar with research in this area. Similarly, Money and Ehrhardt (1972) provide data helpful to the understanding of the acquisition of gender identity. And, the therapist should understand the menstrual cycle and the climacterium. Finally, it should be noted that natural processes, such as aging and illness, as well as conditions of physiological and emotional disability have particular impact on women in a society that values them most highly for their conformity to a youthful, physically perfect, and sexually appealing stereotype. Knowledge of the physiological and psychological correlates of disability is essential to working with handicapped women (Dailey, 1979, 1982).

Maccoby and Jacklin (1974) review the literature on psychological sex differences and note four such differences that appear to be reliable— differences in verbal ability, visual-spatial ability, mathematical performance, and aggression. Work in this area of differential psychology is proceeding very rapidly, requiring that counselors and therapists stay abreast of current research. Other psychological factors—such as possible differences in achievement motivation (Helmreich & Spence, 1978), sex-role bias in various theories of personality development (Williams, 1977), and the emerging career psychology of women (Fitzgerald & Betz, 1983; Fitzgerald & Crites, 1980; Hansen & Rapoza, 1978)—are an indispensable component of the knowledge base for counseling women. Similarly, Gilligan (1982), in a landmark volume, demonstrates that previous theories of moral development, based exclusively on studies of male subjects, have resulted in formulations in which women are usually characterized as morally unevolved, and their thinking as an irrational, illogical, and underdeveloped form of thought. Her work forms the basis for a new formulation concerning the dimensions of moral thought that appears to characterize more accurately and completely the development of women. Familiarity with these and similar findings provides a richer and more balanced context within which counselors and therapists may comprehend more accurately the experience of their women clients.

Sociological issues are also of great importance here. Even if some underlying biological predisposition for sex-typed behavior were to be established, the role of socialization and role prescription would retain its enormous significance in women's lives. Familiarity with the work of sociologists (Skolnick & Skolnick, 1971) and social psychologists (O'Leary, 1977) is necessary for an understanding of the social context of women's behavior.

Finally, it should be pointed out that, above all, counselors and therapists deal with problems—emotional, psychological, and social problems—as well as with the developmental issues of everyday living. Whatever the final biological and/or environmental underpinnings of such problems may turn out to be, it is clear that certain of them are more common to the experience of women (e.g., eating disorders, depression, agoraphobia). Similarly, women more often experience certain "shaping" conditions (e.g., incest) that may predispose them to certain kinds of psychological vulnerability. It is critical for counselors/therapists to know these pathologic/pathogenic areas, as well as the normal areas of differences, if they are to function effectively with female clients.

Principle I requires that counselors/therapists be knowledgeable about women, particularly in the biological, psychological, and social areas outlined above. Such knowledge presupposes, at a minimum, formal coursework in these areas, preferably supplemented by advanced seminars, continuing education courses, and so forth. Further, training programs are encouraged to include modules in core courses (e.g., developmental psychology, personality theory, career psychology) relating their content to women's issues.

PRINCIPLE II. Counselors/therapists are aware that the assumptions and precepts of theories relevant to their practice may apply differently to men and women. Counselors/therapists are aware of those theories and models that prescribe or limit the potential of women clients, as well as those that may have particular usefulness for women clients.

Psychological theory, developed and investigated largely through the study of men, has often had little to offer that is useful for predicting and explaining the behavior of women. One of the major reasons for this has been the assumption, largely implicit, of an androcentric (male-centered) model of behavior (Rawlings & Carter, 1977). That is, theories have been constructed that have attempted to explain human behavior largely in terms of masculine behavior. Female behavior patterns have been (1) assumed to be similar; (2) assumed to be the opposite (Broverman, Broverman, Clarkson, Rosenkrantz, & Vogel, 1970); or (3) more generally, simply ignored.

Fitzgerald and Crites (1980) note that it has become commonplace among career psychologists to suggest that current theories of career choice cannot adequately explain the vocational behavior of women. Osipow (1975) suggested that career development theory is based on several implicit assumptions (e.g., a choice supply, motivation to choose) that women, as a group, often cannot meet. Thus is the explanatory power of the theories attenuated for women. For example, the developmental stages of exploration and specification postulated by Super (Super, Starishevsky, Matlin, & Jordaan, 1963) may not accurately describe women's development, suggesting that female adolescent exploration may well be pseudo-exploration pending marriage plans . . . more significant exploration may actually occur later, when the major duties of child rearing have been completed. Thus, the establishment and maintenance stages are correspondingly delayed. (Fitzgerald & Crites, 1980, p. 46)

Osipow (1975) further points out that the concept of occupational environments is problematic for predicting women's behavior, as the Realistic environment of Holland's (1973) classification has been essentially closed to them. And, the idea of personality types is similarly problematic, as sex-role prescriptions inhibit the implementation of a full range of role types of women. Thus, the assumptions and precepts of these theories clearly apply differently to men and women.

In addition, it is obvious that some theories and models have a clearly limiting effect on women's options. "Shields (1975) and other historians have suggested that psychology and science in general have replaced religion as the justifier of women's inferior position in society" (Grady, 1979, p. 172). She notes that the most damaging assertions are in the area of personality: "It is in the field of personality that women are labeled 'field dependent' or [as] having an 'external locus of control' and the inferior position of women is subtly supported" (Grady, 1979, p. 176). In general, however, feminist psychologists agree that it is classical psychoanalytic personality theory and some of its offshoots (e.g., Deutsch, 1944, 1945; Erikson, 1964, 1975) that have been most damaging to women. With its strong androcentric bias and focus on biological determinism, this model has become a symbol of everything women have found wrong with psychology—as well as of everything that psychology has found wrong with women.

Vaughter (1976) suggests that our theoretical models be analyzed from a social-political perspective and notes certain theoretical positions that may be helpful in explaining women's behavior.

Though the inadequacies of naive behaviorism are apparent (Sutherland, 1974), behavioristic models do encourage us to assume that woman is sane, not crazy; that she is bright and reasonable, not hysterical; and that ill-advised behavior patterns may not be ill advised at all, given the nature of the environment in which her behaviors take place. (p. 132)

Vaughter continues her analysis by suggesting that ethological approaches can enhance our understanding of the development of women's behavior patterns. In this vein, probably the most obvious example is that provided by the experiences of battered women. Whereas traditional models address the (to some) inexplicable behavior of such women (self-reproach, assumption of responsibility for the battering, and staying in the battering relationship) in terms of the women's personality dynamics (e.g., masochism), an ethological analysis outlines the *context* of the behavior, both proximate and in the larger society, and comes to entirely different conclusions.

Theories based on biological determinism have been criticized repeatedly by feminist and nonfeminist writers alike. In this context, it seems important to point out the subtle, but critical, distinction between those formulations dictating that behavior is biologically *determined* and those suggesting that it may be biologically *influenced*. The ways in which biology influences women's behavior are extensively discussed under Principle I; review of this material suggests that it would be naive to state that biology has no impact on women's lives. There is, however, a great difference between suggesting that biology *influences* women's behavior and stating that it *determines* such behavior.

Additionally, although there is obviously nothing inherently negative or repressive in the suggestion of a partial biological basis for behavior, such notions can certainly be used inappropriately and have often been applied unthinkingly. It seems reasonable to suggest that, rather than shy away from such theories, effort be put into accurately elaborating their applicability to women.

In addition to social learning theory, ethological analysis, and recapitulation of biological approaches, script analysis (Steiner, 1972; Wyckoff, 1977)—which has developed out of the radical psychiatry movement—also provides a helpful framework for describing, predicting, and altering what Vaughter labeled "ill-advised behavior patterns." Finally, feminist analysis and therapy (Brodsky, 1977; Brodsky & Hare-Mustin, 1980; Gilbert, 1980; Rawlings & Carter, 1977) is the example of *par excellence* of a psychological model that has particular usefulness for women clients.

Specific suggestions for implementation of Principle II are difficult to formulate; compliance with its spirit requires an awareness that is difficult to operationalize. Until research provides us with a firmer base, counselors/therapists are reminded

1. The great body of psychological theory is constructed on an androcentric model, with a concomitant masculine bias. This is particularly true of personality theory. It is necessary to examine continually our theoretical bases to identify androcentric assumptions that are, at best, unhelpful, and more usually, damaging.

2. Certain theoretical models are, by their nature, facilitative of women's growth. In general, those models that emphasize the influence of social learning are to be preferred to those that are committed to biological determinism. However, Principle II encourages, above all, critical thinking and attempts at understanding the meaning of all existing theories for women, including those that have not dealt with women in full or helpful ways in the past.

PRINCIPLE III. After formal training, counselors/therapists continue to explore and learn of issues related to women, including the special problems of female subgroups, throughout their professional careers.

Research has thoroughly documented the role that counselors/therapists have played in the imposition and perpetuation of sex-role stereotypes (Abramowitz,

Abramowitz, Jackson, & Gomes, 1973; Broverman et al., 1970; Chesler, 1972; Fabrikant, 1974; Maslin & Davis, 1975; Neulinger, 1968; Steinmann, 1975). Arguably, much, if not most, of this research has investigated the attitudes and behavior of counselors/therapists trained before the advent of the women's movement. Thus, their training and professional socialization were not informed by recent developments in the psychology of women, nor did they (and their clients) benefit from the more liberal attitudes stimulated by these developments. Such an argument would suggest that therapeutic repression of women is a phenomenon of the past, not to be found among younger practitioners.

It is true that the classic studies of counselor bias investigated, for the most part, a population trained before the advent of modern psychology of women, although it should be pointed out that the research of Maslin and Davis (1975)—among others—studied counselors who were in training in the mid-1970s. Still, it is likely that current graduate students in counseling and clinical psychology are receiving better training for working with women than did their predecessors. Although Birk and Fitzgerald (1979) found that only 56% of those responding to their informal survey of APA-approved counseling psychology training programs were offering a yearly course in the psychology of women in 1979, it seems reasonable to assume that this represents an almost 100% increase over, say, 1969.

However, given that current students are indeed receiving better training in this area than before, at least two issues remain to be addressed: First, what is the responsibility of professionals who completed their training without exposure to current theory and research in the psychology and counseling/ psychotherapy of women; and second, what is the responsibility of any professional—whenever and however trained—for incorporating the almost explosive expansion of knowledge currently taking place in this area?

It seems almost unnecessary to observe that the more senior counselors/ therapists have the same responsibility for equipping themselves with basic theory, knowledge, and skills for working with women as do current trainees. To do otherwise would appear to be in violation of ethical codes and licensing laws that require that one not practice outside one's area of competence. Postgraduate courses in the psychology and counseling of women, seminars, and continuing education workshops are currently widely available. Division 35 of the APA and the journal, *Psychology of Women Quarterly,* are completely devoted to the study and counseling of women, as is the Association of Women in Psychology (AWP) and its annual conference. The Committee on Women of the Division of Counseling Psychology is actively developing training guidelines, synthesizing various knowledge bases, and creating and documenting resource materials for counseling women. Other APA and AACD (American Association for Counseling and Development) divisions have also developed similar groups concerned with these issues. For example, Division 12 (Clinical Psychology) of the APA has a Committee on Equal Opportunity and

Affirmative Action, as well as a section on Clinical Psychology of Women; and Division 29 (Psychotherapy) has developed a Committee on Women. Thus, senior counselors and therapists should have little difficulty meeting their training needs in this area.

In a similar vein, it is incumbent upon all mental health professionals to keep abreast of the rapidly expanding knowledge concerning women. Recent research concerning sex differences, brain lateralization, female occupational stress, and sex restrictiveness in interest inventories are only some of the more obvious examples. In particular, work concerning the special needs and problems of diverse subgroups of the female population is proceeding quite rapidly. For example, knowledge concerning gay women (Escamilla-Mandanaro, 1977), female prison inmates (Giallombardo, 1966; Heffernan, 1972), and female members of racial minorities (Helms, 1979; Lerner, 1973) is becoming increasingly available. Again, there is no lack of training and resource materials for the counselor who wishes to stay abreast of current developments affecting his or her practice with women. Counselors and therapists can grow in understanding of self and others through facilitating or participating in sex-role awareness groups or specific program groups (e.g., returning women's groups) and so forth.

In summary, review of the above discussion suggests the following guidelines for complying with Principle III:

1. Counselors/therapists whose training did not include basic material concerning women (outlined in Principle I) should equip themselves appropriately for working with women through postgraduate study, continuing education courses and workshops, and acquaintance with the various professional groups and materials devoted to the psychology and counseling of women.

2. Similarly, all counselors/therapists should continue to keep abreast of developments in this rapidly expanding area of knowledge. Effective practice with female clients requires continuing education for all practitioners.

PRINCIPLE IV. Counselors/therapists recognize and are aware of all forms of oppression and how these interact with sexism.

Prejudice has been defined as

> an antipathy based upon a faulty and inflexible generalization. It may be felt or expressed. It may be directed toward a group as a whole, or toward an individual because he [*sic*] is a member of that group. . . . The net effect of prejudice, thus defined, is to place the object of prejudice at some disadvantage not merited by his own misconduct. (Allport, 1954)

Various forms of prejudice, with their consequent oppression, operate more or less openly in Western society, and in fact, have been—at least until quite recently—institutionalized in many of the legal statutes of this country. Probably the most obvious example is that of racial prejudice; however, prejudice against the so-called lower classes, the elderly, and homosexual persons is also widespread.

Race and social class intertwine with sex to form an interlocking structure that is particularly oppressive to minority group women. Socialized from birth into a society that devalues females and severely limits their choice of roles and rewards, no woman remains untouched by sexism. However, the oppression experienced by Third World (i.e., minority) women and lower-class women is compounded by the force of racism and classism. The life experiences of minority women and poor women have largely been omitted from formulations of the psychology of women, as well as from traditional psychology (Griscom, 1979). The theories that are only now being constructed about female psychology are often, ironically, as irrelevant to the description and explanation of the experience and behavior of black, Chicano, poor, elderly, and gay women as were the androcentric formulations of mainstream psychology to the behavior of white, middle-class women a decade ago. Frieze, Parsons, Johnson, Ruble, and Zellman (1978) point out the differences between the black and white female experience. They note that the women's liberation movement has been largely a white, middle-class phenomenon and that black women have generally not played a prominent role. Suggesting that black women may feel that they must take a supportive role vis-à-vis black men who have been psychologically scarred by racism (Hare & Hare, 1970), they indicate that the whole issue of differential treatment on the basis of sex may be of less concern to black women. Some data suggest that black women may not be as discriminated against on the basis of sex as are white women, that they are less likely to derogate other women, and are more self-confident than their white counterparts (Frieze et al., 1978). Ironically, however, black women suffer more economically from a system that incorporates both sexism and racism. And, in fact, they earn, on the average, less than any other group with the same education. It would appear that work with black women, and other Third World female clients, requires different knowledge, skills, and abilities than does work with female clients in general. For example, counselors/therapists would need familiarity with the ways in which racial attitudes and political or institutional policies have restricted the lives of minority persons; an awareness of myths and stereotypes of Third World women to understand their harmful impact on clients; sensitivity to and acceptance of nontraditional (and possibly nonfeminist) cultural values; special knowledge of subgroups (e.g., the high rate of suicide among black female adolescents); a willingness to examine their own racial attitudes; and finally, flexible basic counseling skills that are sensitive to individual differences while taking into account discrimination based on group membership (Helms, 1979; McDavis, 1978). Additionally, it is important to recognize the strengths of minority women (e.g., self-reliance and independence) that can be utilized effectively in counseling (Ford, 1978).

Lower-class women, like minority women, traditionally have been thought neither to need nor to be able to profit from counseling and psychotherapy.

Untrained to address the unique needs of the lower classes, mental health professionals have often abandoned poor women to the least trained professionals, frequently substituting medication for psychotherapy. Poverty narrows not only the realistic choices available to many women, but also limits their sense of control over their lives; insensitivity to a woman's struggle to manage multiple life stresses related to insufficient resources can reduce the effectiveness of therapeutic interventions. Still, it is important to remember that although economic and social problems may be a priority for lower-income women, mental health problems, for which counseling or psychotherapy *is* appropriate, afflict poor no less than middle-class women (Siassi, 1974).

Prejudice against lesbian women has been particularly virulent, possibly because it is these women who are seen as being the most deviant in terms of traditional female role prescriptions. Lesbian mothers have repeatedly had to defend their fitness for motherhood. In Seattle, one lesbian couple won custody of their children, but were forced to establish separate residences; whereas in Santa Cruz, a lesbian mother maintained custody of her children only under the condition that she live separately from her lover (Rawlings & Carter, 1977). In addition, lesbian women have unique problems relating to the lack of sufficient support systems. Fear of being labeled "gay," and the resulting social ostracism, operates to isolate lesbian women from one another. Further, such social isolation often results in the continuation of incompatible or destructive relationships, because of fear of loneliness, lack of comfort and support (Zaller, 1982). Although there is a rapidly growing network of gay counselors/therapists, which is becoming increasingly active in professional organizations and affairs, and whose members possess the particular skills and expertise to work with lesbian women, it is incumbent upon all counselors/therapists who work with female clients to acquaint themselves with this most critical area.

Finally, Frieze et al. (1978) point out that "statistics on psychological disorders consistently show that women over 40 have a higher incidence of disorders than men of the same age or younger women. Among the many possible reasons for this disparity, two seem crucial: loss of self-esteem due to the physical effects of aging, and role loss associated with children's departure from the home" (p. 268). These authors suggest resources and strategies for counselors/therapists who work with women facing the aging process in our youth-oriented society. For example, many writers have suggested that the negative consequences of children leaving home have been overemphasized, pointing out that this can be a time of freedom, relief, peace, and a time to do things for oneself.

In reviewing the discussion above, it would appear that the prerequisites for effective counseling with women are complicated almost to the point of being unmanageable. However, the complexity of the issue must not be taken as grounds for avoiding it. As a beginning, it is important to note that no one person, obviously, can be expert in all areas. Rather, compliance with this Principle requires an acquaintance with and sensitivity to the various issues raised, and a willingness to refer appropriately to those with special expertise in the appropriate area.

PRINCIPLE V. Counselors/therapists are knowledgeable and aware of verbal and nonverbal process variables (particularly with regard to power in the relationship) as these affect women in counseling/therapy so that the counselor/therapist interactions are not adversely affected. The need for shared responsibility between clients and counselors/ therapists is acknowledged and implemented.

Counseling/psychotherapy traditionally has implied an unequal power relationship between the therapist and the client. Although the degree of this power differential varies, depending on the theoretical orientation of the counselor, only feminist therapy (Rawlings & Carter, 1977) and radical psychiatry approaches (Steiner, 1972; Wyckoff, 1977) specifically abjure this differential as being destructive to the client.

The unequal distribution of power in the counseling relationship has been recognized and discussed by many writers, many of whom see such a distribution as inherent in the process, and not necessarily unfortunate. Strong (1968), for example, sees counseling as a process of interpersonal influence and discusses the three counselor power bases of expertness, attractiveness, and trustworthiness that facilitate counselor influence attempts. The APA explicitly recognizes the client-counselor power inequality when it states in its ethical code, "Psychologists are continually cognizant of their own needs and of *their inherently powerful position vis-à-vis clients* [emphasis added] in order to avoid exploiting their trust and dependency" (APA, 1981). Halleck (1971), in his analysis of the politics of psychotherapy, discussed the significance of power in the therapeutic relationship, particularly with respect to symptomatology, therapeutic intervention, and societal focus.

It is probably true that all therapeutic encounters are inherently and unavoidably characterized by the power inequality described above. The counselor/therapist in his or her role as expert caregiver can probably not avoid being seen by the client—who has come to the encounter because of a perceived need for assistance—as a potent, powerful individual. Even feminist and radical therapists, with their explicit disclaimer of the power role, and a strong commitment to joint client-counselor responsibility, can probably not avoid such client perceptions, at least in the early stages of the process. Thus, sensitivity to the issue and use of power and influence variables is necessary for the counselor who does not wish to exploit client trust.

This issue is all the more salient for women clients. Chesler (1972) has stated, "For women, the psychotherapeutic encounter is just one more instance of an unequal relationship, just one more opportunity to be rewarded for expressing distress and to be helped by being expertly dominated" (p. 373). Symonds (1973) discusses the psychology of submission, which affects women's sense of adequacy and immobilizes them. The typical patriarchal model encourages women to be helpless and dependent; counselors/therapists must ensure that they do not reinforce and perpetuate such dynamics through their interventions.

This is particularly true when the counselor/therapist is a male. The power differential between counselor and client is paralleled by the corresponding male/female power differential. When both sets of dynamics are operative, as they are when a woman is being seen by a male counselor/therapist, the power inequality is exacerbated.

Frieze et al. (1978) discuss how dominance and status are communicated nonverbally. They note that nonverbal channels of communication are of major importance for perceiving emotion (Auger, 1969), and conclude that the two major types of nonverbal messages are those indicating dominance or status, and those communicating warmth and expressiveness. They state that men are generally more dominant and display higher status on a nonverbal level, whereas women show more liking and warmth. They then proceed to discuss the role of such indicators as dress, use of space, body position and gesture, touching, eye contact, and smiling in sending dominance messages. Even a cursory reading of their analysis leads to the conclusion that many of the nonverbal variables that characterize male dominance behaviors also characterize therapist status behaviors.

Although it is difficult, and some would say undesirable, to eliminate all power differential in the counseling relationship, counselors/therapists can and should ensure that their power is used in therapeutic ways for their clients' benefit, and not to maintain stereotypic dependency behaviors. A good beginning for ensuring shared responsibility between counselors/therapists and clients can be found in Rawlings and Carter (1977). In discussing client safeguards against the misuse of influence by therapists, they note the parallels between feminist therapy and Argyris's (1975) model of reciprocal influence. Such strategies as contract setting, explication of counselor values, encouraging autonomy, nonuse of diagnostic labels, and cautious use of diagnostic testing are not unique to feminist therapy; however, they take on a powerful role in equalizing the power differential when used in this context, whereas the use of videotape emerges as a powerful training tool for assisting counselors and therapists to identify and modify nonverbal behaviors. Counselors/therapists are referred to Rawlings and Carter (1977) for a complete discussion of these and other strategies for ensuring joint counselor/client responsibility for change.

Finally, it is important to educate the client concerning her rights and responsibilities in the therapy relationship, either through discussion or the use of written materials. The Association for Women in Psychology and Division 35 of the APA have developed a booklet that provides an excellent example of such material.

PRINCIPLE VI. Counselors/therapists have the capability of utilizing skills that are particularly facilitative to women in general and to particular subgroups of women.

Given that the nature of women's existential position leads to the exacerbation and complication of the wide range of concerns brought to the counseling process, as well as to many problems unique to their sex, it seems reasonable to propose that counselors/therapists need to review and add to their skills in order to better facilitate the growth of their women clients. Although it is probably true that there are few, if any, skills and techniques that are *uniquely* necessary for working with women, it is also true that there *are* specific techniques that have been developed in response to women's problems, and that are critically necessary and particularly facilitative for such work.

One of the most well-known of these techniques is assertion training. Although criticized by some as a focus on technique rather than on attitude change (Collier, 1982), assertiveness training has emerged as a preeminent method for assisting women to deal with a wide variety of life problems. In the context of his theory of learned helplessness, Seligman (1973) draws a connection between lack of assertiveness and women's depression. He suggests that because women are socialized to be more passive and dependent than are men, they are more likely to learn to depend on others to take care of them, and therefore, do not acquire a wide repertoire of coping skills. According to Seligman's theory, this would explain why women are more likely than men to become depressed. It also suggests that assertion training would be a powerful treatment for the depression, as well as a preventative of depression (Jakubowski-Spector, 1973). Case studies have been reported that provide suggestive evidence that assertion training can be helpful in treating depression (Bean, 1970; Cameron, 1951; Fensterheim, 1972; Katz, 1971; Lazarus & Serber, 1968; Stevenson & Wolpe, 1960). In addition, it is reasonable to suggest that such training would produce positive effects in treatment of role conflict, dual-career problems, and issues of discrimination, sexual harassment, and response to similar sexist behaviors of others.

A second technique that seems quite promising is the sex-role analysis (Brodsky, 1977). This technique consists of a structured comparison of the positive and negative consequences of traditional and nontraditional sex-role behaviors. It can be used with groups as well as with individual clients, and can be made as individualized or generic as the situation calls for. Such analysis can identify (unconscious) sex-role expectations, bringing these expectations into awareness for client exploration. As women clients become aware of sex-role constrictions in their behavior, they discover strengths in themselves that had previously been unknown, or regarded negatively. Rawlings and Carter (1977) also suggest that this technique can lessen the feelings of discouragement and depression that are sometimes experienced in the initial stages of therapy through inducing a change of frame in which responsibility for the woman's failure to act in desired ways is partially shifted to societal conditions, thus allowing her a rationale that does not threaten self-esteem. In addition, sex-role analysis explores the consequences of nontraditional behavior and explains why it is sometimes unacceptable to others.

A third technique that has had promising results with women is the use of consciousness-raising groups (Brodsky, 1977). Although traditionally leaderless groups, and thus not amenable to counselor/therapist facilitation, these groups constitute powerful referral resources and therapeutic adjuncts. They are particularly suited to the exploration of personal identity issues and the heightening of self-awareness that results from the comparing of personal experiences. Consciousness-raising groups help to develop awareness of shared frustrations, anger, and self-doubt, and the structure of the group provides peer support for the process of growth. The process of modeling (Bandura, 1965, 1969) assists group members to learn new roles and behaviors from other members.

There are many other techniques and processes particularly suited to working with women clients. Wyckoff (1977) describes the application of script analysis to solving women's problems; Zaller (1982) suggests the unique suitability of Gestalt techniques for women. Dewey (1974) proposes the Nonsexist Vocational Card Sort as an alternative to traditional interest inventories; whereas Fitzgerald and Crites (1980) and Harmon (1977) point to the positive benefits of career counseling for women. And, these are only a few.

PRINCIPLE VII. Counselors/therapists ascribe no preconceived limitations on the direction or nature of potential changes or goals in counseling/ therapy for women.

Role possibilities for women traditionally have been defined in terms of what is considered appropriate for a female. In effect, choices in life-styles and career opportunities have been constrained, because the only acceptable female roles were those of wife and mother (Weisstein, 1977). Psychological theories that have formed the base for counseling and psychotherapy have incorporated and institutionalized such role definitions and set them as the criteria against which female mental health was evaluated, as well as postulating them as the (only) desirable outcomes of the counseling process. Classical psychoanalytic theory is the most obvious example, but there are others. For example, Bettleheim (1965) proposed that, other considerations aside, women "want first and foremost to be womanly companions of men and to be mothers," whereas neo-Freudian psychologist Erik Erikson (1964, 1975), in discussing women's "inner space," stated that women had a biological, psychological, and ethical commitment to take care of human infancy. Erikson (1981) has recently softened this position somewhat, noting that issues of identity are affected by changing cultural norms and that women have a "right to postpone both marriage and motherhood and first care for things men have traditionally cared for—productivity in business, and creativity, from art to politics" (p. 255). This statement, however, still carries the notion of the eventual inevitability of the traditional role functions. Thus does the sociological status quo become reified into the psychological ideal.

During the last two decades, critics of the mental health professions began to suggest that these professions were functioning as agents of social control by relying on an adjustment model of mental health that requires acceptance of biologically based traditional roles and behaviors as the criterion for psychological and emotional well-being. Evidence began to accumulate indicating strongly that when traditional role behavior was used as a *predictor* of mental health, rather than as a *criterion* of mental health, the correlation was strongly and consistently negative. Such data as Rice and Rice's (1973) finding that femininity in females is associated with poor adjustment and Bernard's (1971) famous study of marriage, which found married women to be less well-adjusted than single women on a variety of indicators, suggested that female clients might be well served by counselors/therapists who assist them to exercise more freedom in choosing satisfying roles. Yet, studies—such as those by Broverman et al. (1970), Maslin and Davis (1975), and others—indicate that therapists have often demonstrated a "double standard" of mental health, which operates to stigmatize women who deviate from the feminine stereotype.

Similarly, the literature in career psychology has consistently shown that when women do work outside the home (and most of them do, or will, at some point), they are overwhelmingly overrepresented in the lower-level "traditionally female" occupations, in which the job duties and tasks parallel the helping, nurturing, and serving aspects of the traditional female sex role (Fitzgerald & Betz, 1983; Fitzgerald & Crites, 1980). Moveover, it has been demonstrated repeatedly that career counselors encourage and approve such gender-appropriate occupational involvement and negatively evaluate clients who wish to pursue nontraditional occupations (Bingham & House, 1973; Fitzgerald & Cherpas, 1985; Pope, 1982; Thomas & Stewart, 1971) despite a veritable explosion of materials designed to educate counselors concerning vocational counseling for women (e.g., Farmer & Backer, 1977; Hansen & Rapoza, 1978). Such data suggest that counselors/therapists have often set preconceived limits on the direction or nature of therapeutic and counseling goals for women, such limits being defined by the traditional dimensions of the female gender role. It is to such a priori limitations that this principle speaks.

It is important to note that counselors'/therapists' insistence on *nontraditional* goals or changes for all women clients is equally in violation of this principle. For example, Harmon (1977) notes that, traditionally, career counseling has dealt mainly with the gratification of higher-level psychological needs of the individual, and that many women may not be prepared for such career counseling. Counselor insistence on career goals that hold the promise of self-actualization may be very threatening to traditional women who have yet to meet their lower-order needs for safety and self-esteem (Maslow, 1970) or to work through adequately the conflict posed by combining work and family roles. Clearly, "no preconceived limitations" means just that and is applicable whether those limitations are conservative or radical in nature. The critical consideration is acknowledgement of a respect for individual differences and client responsibility for choice. In that spirit, counselors/therapists are reminded:

1. Marriage, singleness, parenting, or choosing to remain child free, and/or gay relationships are all viable life choices. They are each capable of being healthy and growth-producing conditions, or being damaging and exploitative, depending on the characteristics and dynamics of each situation. Counselors/therapists encourage their clients to explore themselves, their values, and their options.

2. Realistic career choice consists of obtaining the best possible match between a woman's abilities, interests, and values, and those which are required and rewarded by the occupation. Many women require a great deal of encouragement and permission to explore beyond the traditional boundaries, even when interest and aptitude data indicate that this is appropriate.

3. Differential psychology, as one of the traditional foundations of counseling psychology, carries a philosophical commitment to the value of individual differences, on which Principle VII is based.

PRINCIPLE VIII. Counselors/therapists are sensitive to circumstances where it is more desirable for a woman client to be seen by a female or male counselor/therapist.

Many writers have suggested that it is advisable for women clients to be seen, not by the traditionally male counselor or therapist, but rather by a female who presumably possesses heightened sensitivity to a woman's experiences (Chesler, 1972; Rice & Rice, 1973). For example, Radov et al. (1977) write that in the current climate of social change, "it is especially necessary for women to have therapists who are sensitive to issues highlighted by the women's liberation movement" (p. 508). Rice and Rice (1973) note

> Advantages of pairing a female therapist with a female patient struggling with conflictual role demands in a changing society include a greater sensitivity to issues and an ability to empathize with feelings; the provision of a role identification model; and the offer of potentially important solutions that may stem from the therapists's own personal experience. (p. 195)

Thomas (1982) indicates that women are more likely to seek female therapists during crises such as rape, pregnancy, or domestic violence.

These prescriptions of female counselors for female clients contain two assumptions: first, that female counselors are likely to be more effective with female clients, presumably because they will be more sympathetic to women's concerns; and second, that female clients *prefer* female counselors, which preference is further assumed to have impact on the progress of the subsequent therapeutic relationship. These assumptions have gone largely unexamined and, despite their logical appeal, may not be completely well founded. Orlinsky and Howard (1966, 1980) in a reanalysis of their original process study (Howard, Orlinsky, & Hill, 1970) found that female therapists were, overall, more effective with female clients than were male therapists, particularly with schizophrenic women or women with an anxiety reaction. Female therapists were also found to be more effective with every type of woman client (e.g., single, married, mothers) except one—the male therapists were more effective with female single parents. However, when therapist experience was examined, highly experienced male therapists were as effective as the female therapists, demonstrating that male therapists can learn to work effectively with women. Therefore, the general assumption that a female counselor is de facto more effective with women clients than is her male colleague is not always justified. In particular, research concerning sex bias in psychotherapy suggests that at least some female therapists share with their male colleagues a separate standard of mental health for female clients (Abramowitz et al., 1973; Broverman et al., 1970). Likewise, bias in career counseling has been demonstrated in female as well as male counselors (Scholssberg & Pietrofessa, 1973; Thomas & Stewart, 1971). Such studies present strong evidence against equating "female" with "feminist" or even "nonsexist," despite the commonsense appeal of such an equation. Frieze (1975) has pointed out, in another context, that women are often mistakenly treated as a homogeneous group. This process is probably responsible for the fallacy inherent in the present case. It should, however, be obvious that femaleness is neither a necessary nor a sufficient qualification for feminism.

Research on female client preference for male and female counselors is sparse and inconclusive (Tanney & Birk, 1973). Although some studies have found that women prefer same-sex therapists (Howard et al., 1970; Koile & Bird, 1956), others have reported that women prefer male counselors (Fuller, 1964; Mezzans, 1971), whereas still others report no gender effect (Heppner & Pew, 1977). Other variables, such as type of problems, counselor age, race, and level of experience, no doubt overdetermine or interact with counselor gender in studies of counselor preference. For example, Fuller (1964) found that female college clients with personal-social problems expressed a preference for female counselors. Similarly, Brodsky (1977) writes that retrospective reports indicate that there are two answers to the question, "Should women clients see male therapists?"

1. "No," for young, single women, uncertain as to their direction in life, or in their relationships with men, or both; and

2. "Yes," if the client is older or married. *We do not, however, know what other factors, yet to be studied, may also have a bearing on the answer.* (p. 335; emphasis added)

These prescriptions receive support from Orlinsky and Howard (1980), who write, "Those women who most clearly benefited from having a female therapist were the single women and the young, single women" (p. 27).

It appears that at the present time, research is not completely adequate as a base for recommendations concerning the advisability of women clients seeing male or female therapists. Yet, such recommendations must be made, and indeed, are being made every day. On what basis, then, should this be done?

Principle VIII requires that counselors/therapists be sensitive to circumstances in which it is more desirable for a woman client to be seen by a female or male counselor/therapist. As a beginning, it seems reasonable to suspect that the sex of the therapist may take on added salience in working with special subgroups of female clients. For instance, the victims of rape, incest, and domestic violence may respond in a more trusting and open manner to women therapists than to males. Similarly, women with sexual concerns and those seeking abortion counseling may feel more comfortable working with female counselors.

Highly vulnerable in the one-down power relationship between the sexes that is exemplified by the traditional male therapist-female client dyad, submissive female clients may benefit greatly from working with a woman therapist who effectively models assertiveness and appropriately shares responsibility for the counseling process with the client. The use of a male cotherapist in marital counseling may be effective in modeling an egalitarian male-female relationship for the couple and a wide range of affect for both partners. Finally, it is likely that issues of job discrimination and sexual harassment would warrant working with a female therapist.

Until research provides the basis for formulating more than the most tentative of guidelines, counselors and therapists are reminded

1. There appears to be no firm basis for assuming a priori that all female counselors/therapists are more effective and less sex-biased than their male counterparts when working with female clients.

2. The research on client preference for a same- or opposite-sex counselor is inconclusive. Open discussion with the client regarding her preferences, combined with professional judgement, appears to be the most appropriate course at present.

3. It is assumed that the sex of the counselor becomes particularly salient in certain situations. Rape, incest, abortion counseling, domestic violence, and other, mostly sexual, concerns are assumed, at present, to be more appropriately assigned to a female therapist. Similarly, young, single women are likely to benefit most from treatment by a female counselor.

PRINCIPLE IX. Counselors/therapists use nonsexist language in counseling/ therapy, supervision, teaching, and journal publication.

Contemporary linguistic theory points out that the language one speaks not only *reflects* one's view of the world, but also *determines* one's view of it (Bolinger, 1968). As Cormican (1977) states

> Whatever a particular culture considers to be the "real world" is really constructed, unconsciously for the most part, by the language spoken in that culture (Barnouw, 1963). The language one speaks, then, will both inculcate and reflect the cultural belief about, among other things, women and men. (p. 1)

Feminists have asserted that the use of male terms as generic or gender neutral reflects bias against women. In the last century, Elizabeth Cady Stanton

(1895) recognized the relationship between language and sexism and criticized the use of *he, his,* and *man* in the Bible. More recently, Christ (1980) notes that although sophisticated religious thinkers "would deny that they think of God as an old white man in the sky, the unconscious association of deity with maleness is perpetuated by language and symbol" (p. 117). In an empirical investigation of the hypothesis that the generic masculine is gender neutral, Moulton, Robinson, and Elias (1978) demonstrated that the use of male terms in a generic sense induces people to think of males, even in contexts that are specifically gender neutral. In other words, when the generic masculine was used, Moulton et al.'s subjects thought of males. Persons who are unimpressed by the logic or evidence in this argument, who maintain that attention to language is a trivial matter and that the generic use of masculine terminology is indeed gender neutral, are invited to test this hypothesis by suggesting that the use of the generic *feminine* is equally gender neutral.

The *Publication Manual of the American Psychological Association* (1974) first addressed this issue in its second edition by suggesting that journal authors "be aware of the current move to avoid generic use of male nouns and pronouns when content refers to both sexes" (p. 28). This position was strengthened and elaborated in 1977 through the publication of "Guidelines for Nonsexist Language in APA Journals" (APA, 1977) and again in 1983 with the third edition of the *Publication Manual of the American Psychological Association* (APA, 1983), which require that authors exercise care in choosing nouns, pronouns, and adjectives that minimize or eliminate ambiguity in sex role or sex identity and that writing be free of implied or irrelevant evaluation of the sexes.

Commitment to nonsexist language, however, requires more than the elimination of generic masculine forms. This usage, which Graham (1975) labels as *exclusion,* has been merely the most obvious form of linguistic sexism, not the only one. In an extensive analysis of this phenomenon, Graham identifies a number of socialization mechanisms that operate to linguistically distort gender-specific words:

1. Labeling the supposed "exception to the rule" (e.g., woman doctor, male nurse, lady lawyer). Unger (1979) notes that the term "feminine logic" is a particularly sexist example of this usage.

2. Trivializing female gender forms (e.g., poetess, suffragette, and—lately—libber).

Unger (1979) points out that terminology referring to women resembles that referring to children to a surprising extent. For example,

> excluding any negative connotations, words like doll, honey, pussycat, and baby can apply equally well to women or children (particularly girl children). Our language, like our culture, equates adulthood with manhood (Graham, 1975). There is a clear demarcation between the words boy and man that does not exist between girl and woman. (Unger, 1979, p. 41)

Greer (1970) has noted a parallel similarity between the terminology referring to women and that referring to food, suggesting that the use of words such as honey, tomato, sugar, cupcake, and so forth perpetuate the stereotyping of women as consumable objects.

The third form of sexist language to which this principle calls attention is that often found in the resource materials related to counseling women. In particular, career information is often not sex-fair, perpetuating through exclusion and other stereotyping mechanisms the notions that some careers are, or are not, appropriate for women (Fitzgerald & Crites, 1980). Although some progress is being made in this area, much remains to be done. Counselors/ therapists are referred to the *Guidelines for the Preparation and Evaluation of Non-print Career Media* recently published by the National Vocational Guidance Association (National Vocational Guidance Association, 1977) and, more generally, to the list of sources on nondiscriminatory language (particularly Bass, 1979) in the APA *Publication Manual* (American Psychological Association, 1983) and similar documents.

Finally, a related issue is that of the desirability of sensitivity to all generic labels of women, including *blind, deaf, epileptic,* and so forth. Such labels focus attention on the disability as the defining aspect of the woman's existence and encourage stereotyping of the most undesirable sort. The use of descriptive phrases (e.g., women with visual handicaps, women with hearing problems) is much preferred to the more generic adjectives.

In summary, this principle requires

1. Counselors/therapists avoid the use of the generic masculine form in all professional activities (counseling/therapy, supervision, teaching, and journal publications).

2. Counselors/therapists avoid other forms of sexist language (e.g., trivializing, labeling "exceptions") in all professional activities.

3. Counselors/therapists ensure that resource materials related to counseling women are adequate, complete, and sex-fair. If sex-stereotypic career information is retained because it is otherwise accurate and the best available, it should be clearly labeled with the caution that it is, indeed, sex-stereotypic.

4. Counselors/therapists avoid the use of generic adjectives describing women with handicaps, in order to avoid excessive focus on the disability.

PRINCIPLE X. Counselors/therapists do not engage in sexual activity with their women clients under any circumstances.

One of the most basic issues that arises concerning women is that of actual emotional, physical, and/or sexual exploitation. For many years, professionals and laypeople alike have heard "horror stories" of women who sought psychological assistance, but were sexually and emotionally exploited by their counselor/therapist. Evidence provided by Holroyd and Brodsky (1977) indicates that such stories have a foundation in fact. Surveying licensed Ph.D. psychologists, they found that 5.5% of male and 0.6% of female respondents reported having had sexual intercourse with clients. Bouhoutsos, Holroyd, Lerman, Forer, and Greenberg (1983) report similar figures (4.8% and 0.8% for males and females, respectively).

Although sexual activity with either male or female clients is clearly unethical under any circumstances, it is emphasized here as a particular problem for female clients. Karasu (1980) has argued that the dyadic relationship in traditional counseling/psychotherapy replicates the "one-down" position in which women are frequently placed.

> This may encourage the fantasy that an idealized relationship with a powerful other is a more desirable solution to life's problems than taking autonomous action. Such a posture, in fact, may set the stage for the kind of sexual exploitation that occurs in instances of therapist-patient sex. (Karasu, 1980, p. 1510)

It should be pointed out that these comments are equally applicable to homosexual, as well as to heterosexual liaisons, although there is currently little, if any, data on this phenomenon in gay therapy. Bouhoutsos et al. (1983) state that, in their study of 559 patients who were sexually intimate with their therapists, the overwhelming majority of the cases (92%) occurred between female clients and male therapists. Interestingly, the majority of sexual relationships with male clients (58%) also involved male therapists.

The American Psychological Association Task Force on Sex Bias and Psychotherapy describes three ways in which sexual relations between client and counselor/therapist reflect sex bias:

1. nearly all complaints are from women patients regarding male therapists;
2. stereotypic feminine qualities, especially passive dependence, are exploited; and
3. the male therapist has considerably more power in the therapy situation than the female patient, a classic situation for the operation of sexual politics. (APA, 1975, p. 1170)

It should be gratuitous to point out that erotic contact with clients is based on the counselor/therapist's need for power, reassurance, or sexual gratification and is not an activity that is engaged in for the benefit of the client. Holroyd and Brodsky (1977) discuss the results of Butler's (1975) study in which psychologists and psychiatrists who had had sexual relations with clients were interviewed. Of this sample 90% of the therapists said they were vulnerable, needy, or lonely when the relationship began; 55% admitted they were frightened of intimacy; 70% said they maintained a dominant position in the relationship; and 60% saw themselves in a fatherly role with the client.

Bouhoutsos et al. (1983) present powerful evidence that such conduct is not only self-serving and unethical but results in damage to the client. In their sample, ill effects included depression, loss of motivation, impaired social or marital adjustment, significant emotional disturbance, suicidal feelings or behavior, and increased drug and alcohol use. Of those surveyed, 48% had difficulty recommencing therapy, and 64% experienced ill effects on their personal adjustment; overall, 90% of the clients suffered negative effects. These authors suggest that their data provide a rationale for enacting legislation proscribing sexual conduct between therapist and patient. Such prohibitions against client-counselor sexual relationships are consistent with the ethical formulations of all traditional mental health professions (American Psychiatric Association, 1973; American Psychological Association, 1981; National Association of Social Workers, 1980). In this context, the Ethical Standards of the American Psychological Association state:

> Psychologists are continually cognizant of their own needs and of their potentially influential position vis-à-vis persons such as clients, students, and subordinates. They avoid exploiting the trust and dependency of such persons. Psychologists make every effort to avoid dual relationships that could impair their professional judgment or increase the risk of exploitation. . . . Sexual intimacies with clients are unethical. (APA, 1981, p. 636)

PRINCIPLE XI. Counselors/therapists are aware of and continually review their own values and biases and the effects of these on their women clients. Counselors/therapists understand the effects of sex-role socialization upon their own development and functioning and the consequent values and attitudes they hold for themselves and others. They recognize that behaviors and roles need not be sex-based.

Frieze et al. (1978) have written, "Most types of psychotherapy rely upon a fairly long-term relationship between the therapist and the client, during which the client's actions, feelings, and attitudes are discussed and interpreted *according to the training and biases of the therapist*" (p. 274; emphasis added). Bart (1971) states directly that value-free counseling/psychotherapy is a myth, whereas Halleck (1971) maintains that all systems of psychotherapy contain implicit value systems, and Strong (1968) describes counseling as a process of interpersonal influence. According to Rawlings and Carter (1977), "In deciding who to treat, what diagnostic categories to assign, which treatment goals to set, and which techniques or strategies to employ, therapists are exercising value judgments" (p. 5).

Agreement on the point is widespread (London, 1964; Pepinsky & Karst, 1964; Rosenthal, 1955). Although some writers demur (e.g., Harkness, 1976; Kremer, 1973), most counselors/therapists have accepted the evidence that indicates that it is not possible for the counselor to be value-free during the therapeutic interaction. Rosenthal (1955), for example, has demonstrated that it was the clients who modified their values to resemble more clearly those of their therapists who were judged to be most improved in therapy.

Given that counselors'/therapists' values powerfully influence both process and outcome, it becomes important to examine those values and the implications they have for women clients. Rawlings and Carter (1977) agree with Halleck (1971), who suggests that psychotherapy ordinarily operates "to conceal the existence of social conflict and to preserve the *status quo*" (Halleck, 1971, p. 30). Thus, women, who constitute the majority of clients (Chesler, 1972), are the largest consumers of a service that may work against their best interests.

Rawlings and Carter (1977) discuss the personal sources of therapist/counselor values that work against women clients' interests, such as personality traits of dogmatism and authoritarianism, as well as stereotypic views of masculinity and femininity. They further note three *professional* sources of counselor/therapist values about women: first, the personality theories they adopt, which shape their view of human nature; second, their models of psychopathology, which determine which problems get treated; and third, their models of mental health, which determine the goals of treatment. As has been pointed out in earlier sections of these guidelines (see, for example, Principle II), models of both personality and psychopathology that are guided by the principles of biological determinism tend to be both limiting and damaging to women clients, whereas models emphasizing cultural determinism and social learning help women to locate the causes of their problems *outside of themselves* and to suggest corrective actions.

Rawlings and Carter (1977) identify three models of mental health that shape the goals of treatment: the *normative* model, which prescribes conformity to sex-stereotypic patterns of behavior; the *androcentric* model, which values male-associated characteristics and behaviors for *both* sexes; and the *androgynous* model, which emphasizes a blend or balance of both male-associated and female-associated behaviors for both sexes. Rawlings and Carter (1977) cite extensive evidence of benefits to be derived from the androgynous model, including higher levels of moral judgment (Block, 1973); ego maturity (Block, 1973); cognitive functioning (Maccoby, 1966); creativity (Hammer, 1964; Helson, 1966); and sex-role adaptability (Bem, 1975).

Review of the foregoing discussion gives rise to two conclusions, on which Principle XI is based: first, the counselor/therapist's value system plays an important role in the therapeutic process; and second, some value systems, as guided by various theoretical models of personality, psychopathology, and mental health, are limiting and damaging to women clients, whereas others are facilitative. In complying with Principle XI, counselors/therapists are reminded:

1. We are all products of our culture, and therefore, subject to the influences of sex-role socialization. We, like other people, have been taught the "normative model" of sex-role behavior and must work to develop unbiased attitudes and values so that clients are neither covertly nor overtly forced into sex-based behaviors or roles (Nutt, 1979). Suggested methods of

self-examination and development include personal counseling/therapy, independent study, workshop attendance, and experiments in personal life styles.

2. Samler (1960) has written, "Drawing upon models of the healthy personality, it should be possible to develop testable hypotheses relative to the values to be supported (in counseling)" (p. 37). The evidence at present suggest adherence to personality models which emphasize cultural determinism and the influence of social learning, as well as acceptance of psychological androgyny as a viable model of mental health.

3. Self-disclosure by the counselor/therapist of relevant personal values is not only appropriate for a relationship for which the counselor and client are mutually responsible, but may facilitate therapeutic change.

PRINCIPLE XII. Counselors/therapists are aware of how their personal functioning may influence their effectiveness in counseling/therapy with women clients. They monitor their functioning through consultation, supervision, or therapy so that it does not adversely affect their work with women clients.

It is imperative for counselors/therapists to be aware of their own psychological functioning so that it does not interfere with their work with clients. Corey (1977) states that it is the therapists' responsibility to themselves and to their clients to work actively toward expanding their own areas of distortion, bias, prejudices, and vulnerability.

Counselors whose personal needs are not being met outside of the counseling relationship may possibly set a course of work that is more appropriate to their own needs than to those of their clients. Butler's (1975) investigation of therapists who had engaged in sexual relations with clients indicated that these psychologists and psychiatrists reported themselves as vulnerable, needy, or lonely when the relationship began.

Other research points to a relationship between counselor needs and client treatment. For example, therapist scores on the Machiavellianism Scale, which measures willingness to manipulate others, appears related to attitudes about clients and therapy (Maracek, 1975). In a small sample of clinicians who were members of the American Psychological Association (N = 55; 43 males and 12 females), Machiavellianism in male therapists was linked to a preference for treating women clients. This relationship was not found for female therapists, but this may be due to the extremely small sample size. Machiavellian therapists of both sexes were more likely to favor the use of placebo drug treatments and the coercion of individuals into treatment, as well as to place importance on control over their clients. Those therapists with a strong control orientation were more likely to feel that sex was permitted in therapy in more circumstances than therapists who were less concerned about control. Unger (1979) interprets Maracek's data to mean that some power-oriented therapists may seek female clients and may respond to them in a not altogether therapeutic way.

Issues in counselors'/therapists' personal lives may have great impact on their work. For example, Aslin (1978) points out, with reference to working with divorced women, that the counseling psychologist's attitudes are particularly important in dealing with women who have lost the wife role. A therapist who supports the normative expectation that a female be primarily wife and mother will at least subtly communicate this attitude to her. Thus, the therapist may reinforce the client's sense of failure and lost identity and even encourage her to desperately find another mate rather than to be assertive and develop herself socially and intellectually. Although Aslin does not point it out, this may also be true for a counselor who is herself in the process of giving up the wife role. The point here is that personal issues often become therapeutic issues—our own, not our clients'. In the event that the counselor/therapist feels that his or her effectiveness is threatened in establishing or maintaining a healthy therapeutic relationship, he or she is reminded of the ethical guideline of the American Psychological Association that states:

> Psychologists recognize that personal problems and conflicts may interfere with professional effectiveness. Accordingly, they refrain from undertaking any activity in which their personal problems are likely to lead to inadequate performance or harm to a client, colleague, student, or research participant. If engaged in such activity when they become aware of their personal problems, they seek competent professional assistance to determine whether they should suspend, terminate, or limit the scope of their professional and/or scientific activities. (APA, 1981, p. 634)

In addition, this principle addresses the need for adequate consultation and supervision, a need often neglected once the neophyte counselor/therapist attains full professional status. In addition to the formal consultation suggested by the APA guidelines, the formation of ongoing peer supervision groups is encouraged, to assist in increasing early awareness of issues that may have a damaging effect on therapeutic effectiveness and client welfare.

PRINCIPLE XIII. Counselors/therapists support the elimination of sex bias within institutions and individuals.

According to Rice and Rice (1973), the increasing efforts of women to reexamine their personal, social and sexual roles have had important implications for many social institutions, such as work, marriage, religion, and education. Because it is the nature of institutions to resist change, great tension often exists, not only in the relationship between individual women and such societal institutions but also in the relationship of counselors and therapists to the institutions in which they live and work. Thus, it is not unusual to find mental health professionals who are committed to eliminating sexist treatment of women employed by institutions and surrounded by colleagues who perpetuate such treatment. Similarly, many find themselves in institutions or situations in which sexist treatment of individual clients, or students, would not be tolerated; and yet paternalistic, stereotyped, and often, degrading treatment of *groups* of women, or women as a group, is the warp and woof of everyday life.

The issue implicit in this situation can be framed as follows: Is it sufficient for counselors/therapists to attempt to change the behavior of individuals (e.g., clients, students) or does nonsexist treatment of women imply the necessity of working for institutional and social change? And, if so, how?

For many feminist counselors/therapists, the choice is clear. Agel (1971) writes, "Feminist therapy is opposed to personal adjustment to social conditions. The goal is social and political change." Similarly, Rice and Rice (1973) tell us:

> Aiding a handful of individuals to paths of greater self esteem and personal fulfillment within one's lifetime can, of course, be personally rewarding and meaningful, but if our goal is to achieve a truly egalitarian society, we must do more. The provision of community, consultative, and political experience for trainees is one solution. (p. 193)

It seems reasonable to suggest that it is difficult for the counselor who maintains a placid view regarding social and political change to encourage action in his or her client—or, to serve as a role model for his or her students and trainees. It seems even more difficult to attempt to change the behavior of large numbers of people without changing the organizations and institutions that influence the behaviors of those people.

Despite such considerations, many counselors/therapists have adopted a passive stance towards individual and institutional practices that have a detrimental effect on women, although such practices may be inimical to their own personal value system. Gluckstern (1977) has suggested that this passivity may result partially from the nature of counselor training that militates against being effective activists in the social arena. Noting that "our training encourages us to look for and focus on factors *within* the individual which restrict growth" (p. 443), she suggests that the person-centered explanations of problem behavior learned in training inhibit the search for structural change. Gluckstern presents a model for personal and institutional change interaction that demonstrates that involvement in the process of institutional change produces therapeutic personal change.

Rawlings and Carter (1977) suggest further ways that counselors/therapists can become involved in social action, either personally or through encouraging client activism. They note the training of paraprofessionals, both as clinicians (Sobey, 1969) and as client advocates (Felton, Wallach, & Gallo, 1974) and the sharing of expert knowledge that allows the development of what Iscoe (1974) has called a *competent community;* and they remind us that the 1973 Vail Conference (Ivey & Leptaluoto, 1975) of professional psychology clearly supported the advocacy of social change as an appropriate and necessary professional responsibility.

The notion of working for social change, or intervening at levels beyond the individual, is a difficult one for many professionals. Some are clearly uninterested, according to Halpern (cited in Roe, 1959), whereas others fear a backlash effect, either for themselves or for women in general. In this context, it is helpful to review Freeman's (1975) concept of the "null environment." Speaking specifically to academic environments, but with implications for all institutions, Freeman notes that a null environment (i.e., one lacking in support and encouragement) has effects on women similar to those of overt discrimination, due to the nature of previous socialization and experience. She argues that unless we make special efforts to create institutional support for women, we are—by accepting the status quo—continuing to place women at a disadvantage.

Obviously, there are as many methods and levels of involvement as there are persons; each must determine the nature of his or her own commitment. What is required by Principle XIII is that individuals not *ignore* sex bias, sex discrimination, and the like, on the part of individuals and institutions with whom we work. Samler wrote, almost 20 years ago,

> It is important that we do not be above it all, that we not be dispassionate and neutral. Apart from the abnegation of moral responsibility, if we are so impossibly dispassionate, time and events will shunt us aside. Let us decide that we will be part of the events that move and determine our collective fate. We are each part of one another, and we must act so. (1969, p. 22)

It is difficult to offer practical guidelines for counselors/therapists supporting the elimination of sex bias within institutions and individuals. Each situation is unique and requires its own response. At the very least, it would seem necessary that we avoid working in and for organizations that discriminate against women, either formally or informally. When this is not possible, this principle suggests the necessity of using all feasible means to confront such discrimination and to ensure its elimination. As Vetter (1973) has written,

> Counselors must not continue to perpetuate such a situation. . . . It seems time for counseling psychology to pick up the challenge, rather hesitantly offered by Samler (1964) to become involved in social action; to make it a definite part of our professional task to set out to affect the status quo. (p. 64)

References

Abramowitz, S. I., Abramowitz, C. V., Jackson, C., & Gomes, B. (1973). The politics of clinical judgment: What nonliberal examiners infer about women who don't stifle themselves. *Journal of Consulting and Clinical Psychology, 41*, 385–391.

Agel, J. (Ed.) (1971). *The radical therapist.* New York: Ballantine Books.

Allport, G. W. (1954). *The nature of prejudice.* Cambridge, MA: Addison-Wesley.

American Psychiatric Association. (1973). The principles of medical ethics with annotations especially applicable to psychiatry. *American Journal of Psychiatry, 130,* 1057–1064.

American Psychological Association. (1974). *Publication manual* (2nd ed.). Washington, DC: Author.

American Psychological Association. (1975). Report of the task force on sex bias and sex-role stereotyping in psychotherapeutic practice. *American Psychologist, 30,* 1170–1178.

American Psychological Association. (1981). Ethical principles of psychologists. *American Psychologist, 36,* 633–638.

American Psychological Association. (1983). *Publication manual* (3rd ed.). Washington, DC: Author.

American Psychological Association Publication Manual Task Force. (1977). Guidelines for nonsexist language in APA journals: Publication manual change sheet 2. *American Psychologist, 32,* 487–494.

Argyris, C. (1975). Dangers in applying results from experimental social psychology. *American Psychologist, 30,* 469–475.

Aslin, A. L. (1978). Counseling "single-again" (divorced and widowed) women. In L. W. Harmon, J. M Birk, & M. F. Tanney (Eds.), *Counseling women.* Monterey, CA: Brooks/Cole.

Auger, E. R. (1969). *Nonverbal communication of normal individuals and schizophrenic patients in the psychology interview.* Unpublished doctoral dissertation, University of California, Los Angeles.

Bandura, A. (1965). Influence of models' reinforcement contingencies on the acquisition of imitative responses. *Journal of Personality and Social Psychology, 1,* 589–595.

Bandura, A. (1969). Social learning theory of identification processes. In D. A. Goslin (Ed.), *Handbook of socialization theory and research.* Chicago: Rand McNally.

Barnouw, V. (1963). *Culture and personality.* Homewood, IL: Dorsey Press.

Bart, P. (1971). Depression in middle-aged women. In V. Gornick & B. K. Moran (Eds.), *Women in sexist society.* New York: Basic Books.

Bass, B. M. (1979). Confessions of a former male chauvinist. *American Psychologist, 34,* 194–195.

Bean, K. (1970). Desensitization, behavior rehearsal, then reality: A preliminary report on a new procedure. *Behavior Therapy, 1,* 542.

Bem, S. L. (1975). Sex-role adaptability: One consequence of psychological androgyny. *Journal of Personality and Social Psychology, 31,* 634–643.

Bernard, J. (1971). The paradox of the happy marriage. In V. Gornick & B. K. Moran (Eds.), *Women in sexist society.* New York: Basic Books.

Bettleheim, B. (1965). The commitment required of a woman entering a scientific profession in present-day American society. In J. A. Mattfield & C. G. Van Aken (Eds.), *Women and the scientific professions.* Cambridge, MA: MIT Press.

Bingham, W. C., & House, E. W. (1973). Counselors' attitudes toward women and work. *Vocational Guidance Quarterly, 22,* 16–32.

Birk, J., & Fitzgerald, L. F. (1979). Survey of APA-approved counseling psychology training programs concerning preparation for counseling women. Unpublished survey.

Block, J. H. (1973). Conceptions of sex-role: Some cross-cultural and longitudinal perspectives. *American Psychologist, 28,* 512–526.

Bolinger, D. (1968). *Aspects of languages.* New York: Harcourt Brace Jovanovich.

Bouhoutsos, J., Holroyd, J., Lerman, H., Forer, B. R., & Greenberg, M. (1983). Sexual intimacy between psychotherapists and patients. *Professional Psychology: Research and Practice, 14,* 185–196.

Brodsky, A. M. (1975, March). *Is there feminist therapy?* Paper presented at the Southeastern Psychological Association Symposium, Atlanta.

Brodsky, A. M. (1977). Therapeutic aspects of consciousness-raising groups. In E. I. Rawlings & D. K. Carter (Eds.), *Psychotherapy for women: Treatment toward equality.* Springfield, IL: Charles C Thomas.

Brodsky, A. M., & Hare-Mustin, R. T. (1980). *Women and psychotherapy.* New York: The Guilford Press.

Broverman, I. K., Broverman, D. M., Clarkson, F. E., Rosenkrantz, P. S., & Vogel, S. R. (1970). Sex-role stereotypes and clinical judgments of mental health. *Journal of Consulting and Clinical Psychology, 34,* 1–7.

Butler, S. (1975). *Sexual contact between therapists and patients.* Unpublished doctoral dissertation, California School of Professional Psychology, Los Angeles.

Cameron, D. E. (1951). The conversion of passivity into normal self-assertion. *American Journal of Psychiatry, 98.*

Carlson, E. R., & Carlson, R. (1961). Male and female subjects in personality research. *Journal of Abnormal and Social Psychology, 61,* 482–483.

Chesler, P. (1972). *Women and madness.* Garden City, NY: Doubleday.

Christ, C. (1980). *Diving deep and surfacing.* Boston: Beacon Press.

Collier, H. (1982). *Counseling women: A guide for therapists.* New York: Free Press.

Corey, G. (1977). *Theory and practice of counseling and psychotherapy.* Monterey, CA: Brooks/Cole.

Cormican, J. D. (1977). *How the English language distorts the psychology of women.* Unpublished manuscript, Syracuse University, Syracuse, NY.

Dailey, A. I. (1979). Physically handicapped women. *The Counseling Psychologist, 8,* 41–42.

Dailey, A. L. (1982). Sexuality in spinal cord injured high school students. *The School Counselor, 29,* 213–219.

Dan, A. J., & Beekman, S. (1972). Male versus female representation in psychological research. *American Psychologist, 27,* 1078.

Deutsch, H. (1944). *The psychology of women* (Vol. 1). New York: Grune & Stratton.

Deutsch, H. (1945). *The psychology of women* (Vol. 2). New York: Grune & Stratton.

Dewey, C. R. (1974). Exploring interests: A nonsexist method. *Personnel and Guidance Journal, 52,* 311–315.

Erikson, E. (1968). *Identity: Youth and crisis.* New York: Norton.

Erikson, E. H. (1964). The inner and outer space: Reflections on womanhood. *Daedalus, 92,* 582–606.

Erikson, E. H. (1975). Once more the inner space. In *Life and history and the historical moment.* New York: Norton.

Escamilla-Mondanaro, J. (1977). Lesbians and therapy. In E. I. Rawlings & D. K. Carter (Eds.), *Psychotherapy for women: Treatment toward equality.* Springfield, IL: Charles C Thomas.

Fabrikant, B. (1974). The psychotherapist and the female patient: Perceptions, misperceptions and change. In V. Franks and V. Burtle (Eds.), *Women and therapy.* New York: Bruner/Mazel.

Farmer, H S. (1976). What inhibits achievement and career motivation in women? *The Counseling Psychologist, 6,* 12–14.

Farmer, H., & Backer, T. (1977). *New career options for women: A counselor's sourcebook.* New York: Human Science Press.

Felton, G. S., Wallach, H. F., & Gallo, C. L. (1974). Training mental health workers to better meet patient needs. *Hospital and Community Psychiatry, 25,* 299–302.

Fensterheim, H. (1972). Assertive methods and marital problems. In Ruben, R. D., Kinsterheim, H., Henderson, G. D., & Ullman, L. P. (Eds.). *Advances in behavior therapy.* New York: Academic Press.

Fitzgerald, L. F., & Betz, N. E. (1983). Issues in the vocational psychology of women. In W. B. Walsh & S. H. Osipow (Eds.), *Handbook of vocational psychology* (Vol. 1). Hillsdale, NJ: Lawrence Erlbaum.

Fitzgerald, L. F., & Cherpas, C. (1985). On the reciprocal relationship between gender and occupation: Rethinking the assumptions concerning masculine career development. *Journal of Vocational Behavior, 27,* 109–122.

Fitzgerald, L. F., & Crites, J. O. (1980). Toward a career psychology of women: What do we know? What do we need to know? *Journal of Counseling Psychology, 27,* 44–62.

Ford, D. J. (1978). Counseling for the strengths of the black woman. In L. W. Harmon, J. M. Birk, & M. F. Tanney (Eds.), *Counseling women.* Monterey, CA: Brooks/Cole.

Freeman, J. (1975). *Women: A feminist perspective.* Palo Alto, CA: Mayfield.

Frieze, I. H. (1975). Women's expectations for and causal attributions of success and failure. In M. T. S. Mednick, S. S. Tangri, & L. W. Hoffman (Eds.), *Women and achievement.* New York: John Wiley.

Frieze, I. H., Parsons, J. E., Johnson, P. B., Ruble, D. N., & Zellman, T. L. (1978). *Women and sex roles: A social psychological perspective.* New York: W. W. Norton.

Fuller, F. F. (1964). Preference for female and male counselors. *Personnel and Guidance Journal, 42,* 463–467.

Giallombardo, R. (1966). *Society of women: A study of a women's prison.* New York: John Wiley.

Gilbert, L. A. (1980). Feminist therapy. In A. M. Brodsky & R. T. Hare-Mustin (Eds.), *Women and psychotherapy.* New York: The Guilford Press.

Gilligan, C. (1982). *In a different voice.* Cambridge, MA: Harvard University Press.

Gluckstern, N. B. (1977). Beyond therapy: Personal and institutional change. In E. Rawlings & D. Carter (Eds.), *Psychotherapy for women: Treatment toward equality.* Springfield, IL: Charles C Thomas.

Grady, K. E. (1979). Androgyny reconsidered. In J. H. Williams (Ed.), *Psychology of women: Selected readings*. New York: W. W. Norton.

Graham, A. (1975). The making of a nonsexist dictionary. In B. Thorne & N. Henley (Eds.), *Language and sex: Difference and dominance*. Rowley, MA: Newbury House.

Greer, G. (1970). *The female eunuch*. London: Paladin.

Griscom, J. L. (1979). Sex, race, and class: Three dimensions of women's experience. *The Counseling Psychologist, 9*, 10–11.

Halleck, S. L. (1971). *The politics of therapy*. New York: Science House.

Hammer, E. (1964). Creativity and feminine ingredients in young male artists. *Perceptual and Motor Skills, 19*, 414.

Hansen, L. S., & Rapoza, R. S. (Eds.). (1978). *Career development and counseling of women*. Springfield, IL: Charles C Thomas.

Hare, N., & Hare, J. (1970). Black women 1970. *Transaction, 8*, 65–68.

Harkness, C. C. (1976). Career counseling: Dreams and reality. Springfield, IL: Charles C Thomas.

Harmon, L. W. (1977). Career counseling for women. In E. I. Rawlings & D. K. Carter (Eds.), *Psychotherapy for women*. Springfield, IL: Charles C Thomas.

Heffernan, E. (1972). *Making it in prison: The square, the cool, and the life*. New York: John Wiley.

Helmreich, R., & Spence, J. T. (1978). The Work and Family Orientation Questionnaire: An objective instrument to assess components of achievement motivation and attitudes toward family and career (Ms. No. 1677). *JSAS Catalog of Selected Documents in Psychology, 8*, 35.

Helms, J. E. (1979). Black women. *The Counseling Psychologist, 8*, 40–41.

Helson, R. (1966). Personality of women with imaginative and artistic interests: The role of masculinity, originality, and other characteristics in their creativity. *Journal of Personality, 34*, 1–25.

Heppner, P. P., & Pew, B. (1977). Effects of diplomas, awards, and counselor sex on perceived expertness. *Journal of Counseling Psychology, 24*, 147–149.

Holland, J. L. (1973). *Making vocational choices: A theory of careers*. Englewood Cliffs, NJ: Prentice-Hall.

Holroyd, J. C., & Brodsky, A. M. (1977). Psychologists' attitudes and practices regarding erotic and non-erotic physical contact with patients. *American Psychologist, 32*, 843–849.

Horner, M. S. (1968). *Sex differences in achievement motivation and performance in competitive and noncompetitive situations*. Unpublished doctoral dissertation, University of Michigan, Ann Arbor.

Horner, M. S. (1972). The motive to avoid success and changing aspirations of women. In J. M. Bardwick (Ed.), *Readings on the psychology of women*. New York: Harper & Row.

Howard, K. I., Orlinsky, D. E., & Hill, J. A. (1970). Patients' satisfaction in psychotherapy as a function of patient-therapist pairing. *Psychotherapy: Theory, Research and Practice, 7*, 130–134.

Iscoe, I. (1974). Is clinical child psychology obsolete? Some observations on the current scene. In G. J. Williams & S. Gordon (Eds.), *Clinical child psychology: Current practices and future perspectives*. New York: Behavioral Publications.

Ivey, A. E., & Leptaluoto, J. R. (1975). Changes ahead: Implications of the Vail Conference. *Personnel and Guidance Journal, 53*, 747–752.

Jakubowski-Spector, P. (1973). Facilitating the growth of women through assertiveness training. *The Counseling Psychologist, 4*, 75.

Karasu, T. B. (1980). The ethics of psychotherapy. *American Journal of Psychiatry, 137*, 1510.

Katz, R. (1971). Case conference: Rapid development of activity in a case of chronic passivity. *Journal of Behavior Therapy and Experimental Psychiatry, 2*, 187–193.

Koile, E. A., & Bird, D. J. (1956). Preferences for counselor help on freshman problems. *Journal of Counseling Psychology, 3*, 97–106.

Kremer, B. J. (1973). What the hell are counselors for? Literary perceptions. *Personnel and Guidance Journal, 51*, 706–710.

Lazarus, A. A., & Serber, M. (1968). Is systematic desensitization being misapplied? *Psychological Reports, 23*, 215–218.

Lerner, G. (1973). *Black women in white America: A documentary history*. New York: Vintage Books.

London, P. (1964). *The models and morals of psychotherapy*. New York: Holt, Rinehart & Winston.

Maccoby, E. E. (1966). Sex differences in intellectual functioning. In E. E. Maccoby (Ed.), *The development of sex differences*. Stanford, CA: Stanford University Press.

Maccoby, E. M., & Jacklin, C. N. (1974). *The psychology of sex differences.* Stanford, CA: Stanford University Press.

Maracek, J. (1975, April). *Power and women's psychological disorders: Preliminary observations.* Paper presented at the meeting of the Eastern Psychological Association, New York.

Maslin, A., & Davis, J. L. (1975). Sex-role stereotyping as a factor in mental health standards among counselors-in-training. *Journal of Counseling Psychology, 22,* 87–91.

Maslow, A. (1970). Motivation and personality (2nd ed.). New York: Harper & Row.

McClelland, D. C., Atkinson, J. W., Clark, R. A., & Lowell, E. L. (1953). *The achievement motive.* New York: Appleton-Century-Crofts.

McDavis, R. J. (1978). Counseling Black clients effectively: The eclectic approach. *Journal of Non-White Concerns in Personnel and Guidance, 7,* 41–47.

Mednick, M. T. S., Tangri, S. S., & Hoffman, L. W. (Eds.). (1975). *Women and achievement.* New York: John Wiley.

Mezzans, J. (1971). Concerns of students and preference for male and female counselors. *Vocational Guidance Quarterly, 20,* 42–47.

Money, J., & Ehrhardt, A. A. (1972). *Man and woman, boy and girl: Differentiation and dimorphism of gender identity.* Baltimore: Johns Hopkins University Press.

Moulton, J., Robinson, G. M., & Elias, C. (1975). Sex bias in language use: Neutral pronouns that aren't. *American Psychologist, 33,* 1032–1036.

National Association of Social Workers. (1980). *Code of ethics.* Washington, DC: Author.

National Vocational Guidance Association. (1977). *Guidelines for the preparation and evaluation of nonprint career media.* Author.

Neulinger, J. (1968). Perceptions of the optimally integrated person: A redefinition of mental health. *Proceedings of the 76th Annual Convention of the American Psychological Association, 3,* 553–554.

Nutt, R. L. (1979). Review and preview of attitudes and values of counselors of women. *The Counseling Psychologist, 8,* 18–20.

O'Leary, V. E. (1977). *Toward understanding women.* Monterey, CA: Brooks/Cole.

Orlinsky, D. E., & Howard, K. I. (1976). The affect of sex of therapist on the therapeutic experiences of women. *Psychotherapy: Theory, Research and Practice, 13,* 82–88.

Orlinsky, D. E., & Howard, K. I. (1980). Gender and psychotherapeutic outcome. In A. M. Brodsky & R. T. Hare-Mustin (Eds.), *Women and psychotherapy.* New York: The Guilford Press.

Osipow, S. H. (1975). The relevance of theories of career development to special groups: Problems, needed data, and implications. In S. Picou & R. Campbell (Eds.), *Career behavior of special groups.* Columbus, OH: Charles E. Merrill.

Pepinsky, H. H., & Karst, T. O. (1964). Convergence: A phenomenon in counseling and in psychotherapy. *American Psychologist, 19,* 333–338.

Pope, D. J. (1982). *Women and work: A comparison of graduate students in counseling and business on attitudes, factual knowledge, and androgyny.* Unpublished doctoral dissertation, Kent State University, Kent, OH.

Prescott, S., & Foster, K. (1974, September). *Why researchers don't study women: The responses of 67 researchers.* Paper presented at the annual convention of the American Psychological Association, New Orleans.

Radov, C. G., Masnick, B. B., & Hauser, B. B. (1977). Issues in feminist therapy: The work of a women's study group. *Social Work, 22,* 507–509.

Rawlings, E., & Carter, D. (Eds.). (1977). *Psychotherapy for women: Treatment toward equality.* Springfield, IL: Charles C Thomas.

Rice, J. K., & Rice, D. G. (1973). Implications of the women's liberation movement for psychotherapy. *American Journal of Psychiatry, 30,* 191–196.

Roe, A. (1956). *The psychology of occupation.* New York: John Wiley.

Rosenthal, D. (1955). Changes in some moral values following psychotherapy. *Journal of Consulting Psychology, 19,* 431–436.

Samler, J. (1960). Change in values: A goal in counseling. *Journal of Counseling Psychology, 7,* 32–39.

Samler, J. (1969). *The vocational counselor and social action.* Washington, DC: National Vocational Guidance Association.

Schlossberg, N. K., & Pietrofessa, J. J. (1973). Perspectives on counseling bias: Implications for counselor education. *The Counseling Psychologist, 4,* 44–54.

Seligman, M. E. P. (1973). Fall into helplessness. *Psychology Today, 6,* 43.

Shields, S. A. (1975). Functionalism, Darwinism, and the psychology of women: A study in social myth. *American Psychologist, 30,* 739–754.

Siassi, I. (1974). Psychotherapy with women and men of lower classes. In V. Franks & V. Burtle (Eds.), *Women in therapy.* New York: Bruner/Mazel.

Skolnick, A. S., & Skolnick, J. H. (Eds.). (1971). *Family in transition: Rethinking marriage, sexuality, childrearing, and family organization.* Boston: Little, Brown.

Sobey, F. (1969). Volunteer services in mental health: An annotated bibliography 1955–1969. *National Clearing House for Mental Health Information,* p. 1002.

Stanton, E. C. (1895). *The woman's Bible.* New York: European.

Steiner, C. (1972). *Scripts people live.* New York: Grove Press.

Steinmann, A. (1975, September). *Male-female concepts of sex roles: Twenty years of cross-cultural research.* Paper presented at the annual convention of the American Psychological Association, Chicago.

Stevenson, I., & Wolpe, J. (1960). Recovery from sexual deviation through overcoming non-sexual neurotic responses. *American Journal of Psychology, 116,* 737–742.

Strong, S. R. (1968). Counseling: An interpersonal influence process. *Journal of Counseling Psychology, 15,* 215–224.

Super, D. E., Stariskevsky, R., Matlin, N., Jordaan, J. P. (1963). *Career development: Self-concept theory.* Princeton, NJ: College Entrance Exam Board.

Sutherland, J. W. (1974). Beyond behaviorism and determinism. *Fields within fields, Winter,* 32–46.

Symonds, A. (1973, October). *The liberated woman: Healthy and neurotic.* Paper presented at the meeting of the Association for the Advancement of Psychoanalysis.

Tanney, M. F., & Birk, J. M. (1973). Women counselors for women clients? A review of the research. In L. W. Harmon, J. M. Birk, L. E. Fitzgerald, & M. F. Tanney (Eds.), *Counseling women.* Monterey, CA: Brooks/Cole.

Thomas, A. H., & Stewart, N. R. (1971). Counselor response to female clients with deviate and conforming career goals. *Journal of Counseling Psychology, 18,* 352–357.

Thomas, B. (1982). Unpublished paper, Kent State University, Kent, OH.

Unger, R. K. (1979). *Female and male: Psychological perspectives.* New York: Harper & Row.

Unger, R. K., & Denmark, F. L. (Eds.). (1975). *Woman: Dependent or independent variable?* New York: Psychological Dimensions.

Vaughter, R. M. (1976). Review essay: Psychology. *Signs, 2,* 120–146.

Vetter, L. (1973). Career counseling for women. *The Counseling Psychologist, 4,* 54–66.

Weisstein, N. (1971). Psychology constructs the female, or the fantasy life of the male psychologist. In M. H. Garskof (Ed.), *Roles women play: Readings toward women's liberation* (pp. 68–83). Monterey, CA: Brooks/Cole.

Williams, J. H. (1977). *The psychology of women: Behavior in a biosocial context.* New York: W. W. Norton.

Wyckoff, H. (1977). *Solving women's problems.* New York: Grove Press.

Zaller, S. (1982). Unpublished paper, Kent State University, Kent, OH.

13

Feminist Identity Development: Implications for Feminist Therapy with Women

Kathleen McNamara and Kathryn M. Rickard

Downing and Roush (1985) proposed a model of feminist identity development based, in part, on Cross's (1971) model of Black identity development. The model provides a framework for understanding the developmental process women go through in confronting sexism in contemporary society and coming to terms with the personal meaning sexism has in their lives. The model proposes a five-stage theory: (1) passive-acceptance, (2) revelation, (3) embeddedness-emanation, (4) synthesis, and (5) active commitment.

The Downing and Roush (1985) model has significant implications for feminist psychotherapy with women. Feminist therapists come from diverse schools of psychotherapy; however, there are certain inherent values and beliefs that distinguish feminist therapy from other brands of psychotherapy (Rawlings & Carter, 1977). In feminist therapy, the sociopolitical roots of women's problems are emphasized in conceptualizing the etiology and maintenance of clinical problems. There is a fundamental assumption that women have less political and economic power than men do and that the patriarchal structure of society is detrimental to women's mental health. Feminist therapy involves a process of helping the woman explore the extent to which her difficulties may be social (external) in origin. The presenting clinical problem itself may be depression, anxiety, an eating disorder, or a relationship issue. However, rather than focusing predominantly on psychodynamics or behavioral contingencies, as the psychoanalyst or behavior therapist might do, the feminist therapist focuses on how being female in a patriarchal society contributes to the development and maintenance of the

Reprinted from the *Journal of Counseling & Development, 68,* 1989, pp. 184–189. Reprinted by permission. No further reproduction authorized without written permission of the American Counseling Association.

problem. Although feminist therapists use a variety of therapeutic techniques, there is a common emphasis placed on assisting clients in developing their autonomy, their self-sufficiency, and ultimately effecting sociopolitical change to benefit women. *Nonsexist therapy* is distinguished from *feminist therapy* in that it typically functions from a humanistic-egalitarian model and does not emphasize sociopolitical explanations of mental health problems among women (Rawlings & Carter, 1977).

The Downing and Roush (1985) model of feminist identity development offers a framework for viewing the developmental process that is likely to take place in successful feminist therapy. Furthermore, the model provides insight into the potential issues that are likely to emerge as women go through the therapeutic change process. Finally, it can be logically inferred from the model what the pitfalls of feminist psychotherapy might be if the client's developmental level is not considered.

Following a summary of the model, this article will explore the process of feminist psychotherapy at each stage of a client's feminist identity development. The potential pitfalls of feminist therapy, particularly with the passive-acceptant woman, are discussed and suggestions are made regarding how to facilitate the client's movement to higher levels of development. These suggestions are based on the work of Greenspan (1983), who has outlined a unified feminist approach to therapy with women that integrates the useful aspects of the traditional therapies with the tenets of feminism.

A second purpose of this article is to offer hypotheses for future research into the issues raised by the model. Although there has been some research conducted to validate the Downing and Roush model (Rickard, 1988a; Rickard, 1988b), the usefulness of applying the model to an understanding of the therapeutic change process, as described here, remains to be tested.

The Downing and Roush Model

In Stage 1, *passive-acceptance,* the woman accepts traditional sex roles, seeing them as advantageous to her, and she considers men to be superior to women. She is either unaware of or denies prejudice and discrimination against women, and she unquestioningly accepts the "white male system" (Schaef, 1985). She carefully selects her peers in order to maintain her equilibrium.

In Stage 2, *revelation,* a crisis, or series of crises or contradictions occur that cannot be ignored or denied. These experiences might include participation in a consciousness-raising group, discrimination against female children, divorce, denial of credit or job application, and so forth. For a woman in this stage, anger, and secondarily, guilt, are intensely felt over oppression experienced in the past and her participation in that oppression. Intense self-examination and questioning of previous roles occur. This stage is also characterized by dualistic thinking regarding male-female relationships, where all men are seen as negative and all women as positive.

In Stage 3, *embeddedness-emanation,* a woman develops close emotional connections with other similar women, which provides her with the opportunity to discharge her anger in a supportive environment. Carefully chosen other women also provide affirmation and strength in her new identity. Much like the immersion of Blacks in the "Black is Beautiful" culture, women become embedded in a "Sisterhood is Beautiful" culture during Stage 3. Emanation occurs as more relativistic thinking replaces dualism, and men are interacted with cautiously.

Stage 4, *synthesis,* is characterized by the development of a positive feminist identity, where both oppression-related explanations for events and other causal factors can be considered in making attributions. No longer does the woman see sexism as the cause for all social and personal ills. She is able to take a stand that may separate her from many other feminists and yet still maintain her identity as a feminist. There is an integration of personal and feminist values that result in an authentic feminist identity.

Stage 5, *active commitment,* is characterized by translation of the consolidated feminist identity of stage four into meaningful and effective action. Women in this stage set personal priorities, based on their unique talents, for effecting societal change.

Recently, data were reported that provide empirical support for the validity of the Downing and Roush (1985) model. Rickard (1987) developed an inventory (Feminist Identity Scale, FIS) to measure level of feminist identity. A factor analysis of that measure supported the stages as proposed. A significant positive relationship was found between self-esteem and level of identity development, indicating that the higher the level of feminist identity development, the higher the self-esteem score. Ascending positive correlations between stage of feminist identity and positive attitudes toward working women were also found. Individuals categorized as highly passive-acceptant had significantly lower androgyny scores than low passive-acceptant individuals and high synthesis level individuals. Groups hypothesized to score higher on passive-acceptance (Right to Life, College Textiles & Clothing organizations) had significantly higher passive-acceptance scores and lower revelation, embeddedness, and synthesis scores than did groups expected to score low on passive-acceptance (Gay/Lesbian Alliance, NOW organization) (Rickard, 1987). Dating behaviors displayed by women at different FIS levels were consistent with differing sex role behaviors hypothesized to accompany feminist identity development (Rickard, in review). Finally, quality ratings of slides attributed to either a male or female artist were significantly different for women in varying levels of feminist identity development. Passive-acceptance level women valued the work of male artists more than identical work attributed to a female artist. The effect was reversed for revelation level women, and synthesis level women did not preferentially rate the work of one gender over that of another (Rickard, in press).

The Downing and Roush (1985) model probably relates to women's cognitive-developmental levels. Specifically, Perry's (1970) theory of intellectual-ethical development, and the ego and moral developmental theories of Kohlberg (1981), Loevinger and Wessler (1970), and Gilligan (1982) are relevant to this model. An individual's experiences, and his or her cognitive-developmental understanding of those experiences, interact in a reciprocally facilitative manner, and behaviors are reorganized at successive developmental stages. It is believed that identity is one central schema through which experience is approached and integrated. Although not all women use feminist identity as a developmental blueprint, the model is useful for those women who do.

Feminist Therapy and the Stage 1 Client

Typically, feminist therapists begin their work with clients by attempting to establish an equal relationship and demystifying the therapeutic process (Rawlings & Carter, 1977). This might be done by encouraging the client to ask the therapist questions, not for diagnostic reasons, but to encourage the client to raise legitimate concerns about the therapist and the therapeutic process. Demystifying the therapeutic process also usually involves assisting the client in naming a therapeutic goal in concrete terms and deciding together what the "treatment plan" will be. Questioning the therapist and setting clear goals are designed to encourage the client to take responsibility for the selection of her therapist and for evaluating the progress of her own therapy (Greenspan, 1983).

Early on in feminist therapy the therapist often encourages the client to trust herself as a person who is knowledgeable and powerful in her own right, and the feminist therapist resists forming roles of "expert" and "subordinate." The feminist therapist attempts to uncover the social etiology of her client's problems and uses her own personal experience as a woman in a male-dominated culture to identify with the client. Identification with the client and self-disclosure are strategies commonly employed by feminist therapists (Greenspan, 1983) and are designed to help convey to the client the common social condition that women share. These strategies are also designed to achieve one of the primary goals of feminist therapy: to help a woman see how her power as an individual is inextricably bound to the collective power of women as a group (Greenspan, 1983).

This seemingly positive and egalitarian approach to working therapeutically with women may be experienced adversely by the passive-acceptant woman entering therapy. According to the model, the passive-acceptant woman accepts the patriarchal structure of society without question or scrutiny and sees her role in society as advantageous. Given her worldview, she is likely to be searching for an expert who will tell her what to do and she is likely to be uncomfortable with the feminist therapist's attempt to equalize the relationship. She is likely to see herself as the "patient" or "victim" and see the therapist as "the doctor" or "rescuer" who will have solutions to her problems.

Naming a therapeutic goal may be exceedingly difficult for the Stage 1 woman. Her goal may be "to be happier," "not to nag her husband so much," or "not to be so needy." Turning these global concerns into concrete goals can be difficult. The woman in passive-acceptance tends to rely on the therapist to tell her what to do to feel better rather than explore the source of her difficulties.

As the feminist therapist conveys the idea that the client's problems may stem from social roots, the client may feel misunderstood and may lose confidence in her therapist's ability to help her. The Stage 1 client is likely to believe the problem is her problem, not due to the social conditions women face. For example, a Stage 1 woman who is attempting to work full time and simultaneously fulfill the traditional role of wife and mother may come to therapy with the goal of being less irritable, more easygoing, and less "stressed-out." The Stage 1 client is likely to see her situation as a personal one and have difficulty viewing her situation as part of a larger dilemma that women face in this culture. If the therapist self-discloses in order to convey the commonalities that women share, the client may wonder how the therapist can help if she too struggles with similar issues.

These possible reactions to and experiences of feminist therapy stem, in part, from the Stage 1 client's view of herself as a subordinate to the therapist, and her passive acceptance of the patriarchal structure of society as the way it is and the way it should be. However, these possible reactions may also occur when the feminist therapist fails to consider the developmental aspects of feminist identity and the world and self view of the Stage 1 client.

Avoiding the Pitfalls

There are some key issues that might be addressed, and a process that might take place in Stage 1, that would help the client remain in therapy and move past the first stage in her feminist identity development.

First, it would seem to be important to be explicit with the client about the attempts that are made to equalize the relationship and demystify the process. The therapist might elicit the client's feelings about efforts made to engage in a therapeutic relationship that is nonhierarchical. Responding to the client's fears and skepticism about the process and emphasizing the benefits the therapist believes she stands to gain are more direct ways of meeting the client at her developmental level. Greenspan (1983) emphasizes the importance of avoiding heavy social interpretations of client problems, and instead, asking the right questions and empathetically listening to what the client says. It would seem to be crucial with the Stage 1 client to move at the client's pace in order to help her discover for herself the role sexism plays in her problems.

With respect to therapist self-disclosures, it would seem especially important at Stage 1 to check out how the client feels when the therapist discloses. It is important not to assume that the client feels warmly toward the therapist just because she acts warmly in response to self-disclosures. The

Stage 1 woman has likely been conditioned to respond this way, and her actual feelings may or may not be congruent with her behavior.

A discussion of how she feels about therapist disclosures may provide the inroad for discussing the "rescue fantasy" that Greenspan (1983) has noted is common in many female clients. This fantasy involves the woman viewing herself as a victim and the therapist as a rescuer. A discussion of this possible fantasy can lead into a discussion of her historic reliance on a male provider for sustenance and status. Movement might then take place into an analysis of the benefits that are derived from maintaining her worldview: factors such as economic security and less pressure to achieve. A key question might be: *What does your reliance on a male provider cost you?* These costs may include her tentative self-esteem, lack of autonomy, lack of skills and training, and lack of self-sufficiency.

Focusing on these kinds of issues and using this kind of process are potential ways of avoiding the pitfalls of feminist therapy with the Stage 1 woman and facilitating her movement to Stage 2, revelation.

Feminist Therapy and the Stage 2 Client

Several therapeutic issues might be considered when working with the Stage 2 client, whether she has entered the revelation stage as part of the therapeutic process or entered therapy as a result of a revelation experience in her life. There is likely to be a shift in terms of the client-therapist dependency issue. The client may be less likely to depend on the therapist to give her solutions but instead depend on her to affirm her anger and dualistic thinking about male-female relationships. Anger is a key characteristic of this stage, as is dualistic thinking, and the client may openly question herself and her roles. She may be more open to the change process at this point, given the flux she is likely to be experiencing.

At this point in therapy, the dependency between the client and therapist can be viewed as a "legitimate dependency," in that her need for affirmation and the therapist's willingness to provide it may facilitate her movement on to Stage 3, embeddedness. At this stage of development, the client is likely to be ready to be mobilized. Additionally, feminist therapists are noted for being particularly effective at legitimizing and validating angry feelings and using anger to combat feelings of helplessness, powerlessness, and low self-esteem (Rawlings & Carter, 1977). Due to the openness to change at this stage, clients would likely be receptive to interventions aimed at helping them to use straight communication and possibly dropping covert, manipulative behaviors. While it may be difficult to point out contradictions between the client's newly formed ideas about herself and her behaviors (because she wants affirmation), clients are likely to be energized at this stage to try new behaviors (e.g., assertion skills) that enable them to test their autonomy and independence.

Stage 2 would seem to be the ideal time to encourage the client to participate in some form of group work. During Stage 1, individual psychotherapy can be more efficient in helping the client move past passive-acceptance, because the therapist can focus exclusively on the woman's own sex-role history and help her examine the price she pays for remaining passive. However, in Stage 2, the client most likely needs to begin to form connections with other women, besides the therapist, in order to move on to Stage 3. The therapist may wish to make referrals to existing community groups or she may be able to refer to her own ongoing women's group.

The goal of therapy during Stage 2 is to "use" the anger and "work" the client's self-questioning to encourage identification with other women. This would seem to be crucial to her continued movement. If the connection with other women is not achieved, Stage 3 is not possible.

Feminist Therapy and the Stage 3 Client

Stage 3 involves an embeddedness in the female culture and valuing what is uniquely female. Connection with other women provides a safe environment to discharge anger and receive affirmation of one's new identity. However, a barrier to Stage 3 may be feelings of fear and competition with other women. For clients who experience these feelings, it would seem important to explore how these feelings may stem from a view of women as "products" to be either selected or rejected by men. If the client gives up this view of herself as an object or product, she is likely to shift to a view that women must bind together against messages that perpetuate this view of women.

A client may become "embedded" in feminism as she matures through the developmental process in therapy or she may enter therapy at this point in her feminist identity development. Typically, women in this stage of development will want to remain in the "safety" of an all-female culture and may shy away from or be hostile toward men. There is a dualistic mode of thinking that views males as "bad" and females as "good." Women at this stage will tend to be hypervigilant of sexism in their lives and view all problems in their lives as stemming from sexism. Relationships with male superiors, co-workers, spouses, and even acquaintances may become strained.

In therapy, the affirmation a client receives from her therapist and other women in her therapy group may serve to reinforce her anger, and if the client's relationships with men are not examined, she may become stuck at this stage of her development, remain angry, and have difficulty reaching synthesis. In order to move on to synthesis, the client must begin to separate her anger toward a male system that perpetuates discrimination against women from her anger against individual men in her life.

Although the men in her life are indeed part of the system she rejects, and may in fact benefit from it, the individual male is not the system itself. The process of combining and separating causal attributions for events in her life is necessary for her to make accurate attributions and take personal responsibility for her part in the conflict and problems in her life. For example, a woman struggling with an eating disorder and low body esteem might benefit from acknowledging the research that has revealed that women are more critical of their bodies and desire lower body weights than men expect or desire for women (Fallon & Rozin, 1985). These are attitudes some women have internalized from a system that objectifies women's bodies but which individual men do not by and large support.

As the client begins to view men more as individuals with their own problems and issues, "emanation" occurs and the client can move on to the next stage.

Feminist Therapy and Stages 4 and 5

The next step, labeled *synthesis* in the model, is really a process of differentiating the self from the feminist "party line" in which she is embedded. Again, the dependency issues may emerge in the form of questions regarding how her feminist friends will view her if she decides she does not fully adhere to the typical feminist perspective on a particular issue. For example, the client may be opposed to abortion but feels this is not "the feminist" perspective. The client is faced with the task of integrating her personal beliefs with her feminist convictions. Here the struggle is to be authentic within her feminist identity and break out of playing a role that is not truly genuine or carefully self-examined.

It would seem that the therapist needs to validate the feelings of confusion and questioning and facilitate the differentiation process that allows synthesis to occur. In addition, the therapist might want to guard against viewing the client as backsliding or regressing if she struggles with traditional versus "liberated" attitudes. Allowing the client to fully explore her genuine beliefs and opinions is necessary for her to achieve an authentic feminist identity.

From this process it would seem that Stage 5 would naturally follow; here the process reaches a culmination in active commitment. At this stage the therapist would facilitate the prioritizing and decision-making process. The client is now faced with how she will implement her feminist identity via commitment to carefully selected personal and political goals. Her goal may be to strive toward an egalitarian marriage or raise her children as freely as possible from sex-role constraints. She may choose to commit to local political action on behalf of women or to promote feminism in her line of work. She may initially wrestle with what the "correct" feminist commitments might be—signs that she is still struggling at Stage 4, but as she lets go of an externally defined identity and truly makes a personal commitment, she will begin functioning at Stage 5.

Therapist Level of Feminist Identity

The model, as proposed by Downing and Roush (1985), is considered to be recyclical in nature. Therefore, therapists themselves may be at different points in their development on different issues in their lives and thus able to help some clients better than others. For example, a therapist who has cycled through the stages regarding career/professional issues, but finds she is recycling again as she re-experiences revelation (Stage 2) regarding issues in her marriage, may work very effectively with a woman dealing with discrimination on the job but not so effectively with a woman going through a divorce. It would seem important for feminist therapists to be vigilant of their own process with respect to their feminist identities and clarify for themselves how their own developmental level of functioning may help or hinder their work with clients at any given time. Seeking supervision from a colleague on such cases where the therapist's developmental process may interfere with the facilitation of the client's growth would certainly be a responsible way of dealing with these kinds of client-therapist developmental interactions. In addition to supervision and case consultation for feminist therapists working through their own "stuck points" as they relate to their clinical work, training programs on developmental theory for feminist therapists-in-training would promote self-examination and self-monitoring of new therapists.

Future Research

Rationally and experientially, we have found the model to have significant implications for understanding the developmental issues of some female clients. However, research has not directly addressed the application of the model to the therapy process. Therefore, the purpose of this section is to briefly delineate research hypotheses derived directly from the model, from previous writings on feminist therapy, and from our work with clients. The research hypotheses will be presented in three sections:

1. Hypotheses relating to client developmental level
2. Hypotheses involving therapist factors that may impinge on therapy
3. The issues posed by the interaction of clients and therapists of differing feminist identity levels

It would be expected that clients at varying feminist identity levels would differ in their ability to label emotional states and to link them to specific environmental antecedents. For instance, passive-acceptant level women should experience more global, undifferentiated emotional responses, such as depression, shame, or diffuse anxiety, than women at subsequent levels. They might present to the therapist more frequently with vague complaints of feeling down, tired, or nervous, or with frequent headaches. Since negative affect is not viewed as appropriate female behavior, it may be internalized or somaticized. It is believed that women who have managed to work through to subsequent feminist identity level 5 would have recognized and legitimized such anger and fear. They should be acutely aware of examples of the series of losses often involved in relinquishing past ways of coping and giving up illusions of safety and certainty. Therefore, more specific labeling of emotional responses (sadness and pain, loss, resentment) and greater facility in linking affect to environmental antecedents would be expected.

It would also be hypothesized that clients at synthesis and active commitment levels would have higher self-esteem and experience greater personal responsibility for therapy gains (perhaps exhibited through self-efficacy measures). The synthesis level woman's broader understanding of the societal forces from which she has struggled to be free would suggest a greater ability to integrate personal problems within a societal context and more appropriate selection of internal or external attributions for her difficulties. She would not be expected to view the self-focus often required to work through issues as "selfish," but to view it as necessary to her ability to fully function with others.

It would be anticipated that clients at differing levels would vary in their willingness to join support groups, with embeddedness level women being most responsive to these alternatives. Embeddedness level women would be expected to respond less positively to bibliotherapy than clients at other levels for the same reasons. Passive-acceptant level clients would be most likely to request concrete, specific interventions for targeted behaviors, since they often view the therapist as "the doctor."

Therapist variables center on the therapist's ability to understand these clients, and, therefore, their ability to facilitate growth. It is hypothesized that therapists at passive-acceptance and revelation levels would experience stronger countertransference issues yet be less aware of their potential influence on the client. Anger and urgency often felt by revelation level women might cause these therapists to be most directive and least tolerant with their clients' issues. It would be expected that revelation level therapists as a group would be least interested in, and less effective with, clients desiring to resolve heterosexual relationship problems or clients experiencing difficult authority-individuation issues.

The manner in which therapists conceptualize presenting problems should reflect their level of feminist identity development. The degree to which therapists view issues within a societal context should influence their assessments and interventions with clients. Systems assessments would be expected in therapists at higher feminist identity levels. Therapists at embeddedness, synthesis, and active commitment levels would be expected to value and utilize available resources outside of therapy, to encourage feminist support groups when appropriate, and to be most aware of available community resources.

Mismatches in the client-therapist dyad may lead to clients dropping out of therapy. It would be hypothesized that passive-acceptance level clients would be more likely to drop out of therapy with a revelation level therapist than with synthesis or active commitment level therapists. The passive-acceptant therapist might mislabel the revelation level client's anger, perhaps as hostility, with clients at higher developmental levels eventually dropping out of therapy.

Clients at synthesis or active commitment levels would be unlikely to remain in therapy with therapists in earlier identity levels. Generally, it would be anticipated that synthesis or active commitment level therapists would be most prepared to understand the developmental issues, the affect, and the fear regarding developmental progression in clients at all feminist identity levels, and to validate and assist the client in working through the process.

Finally, one note on therapist-client gender match seems relevant. When Cross's (1971) developmental racial identity model was tested on Black college students seeking therapy (Parham & Helms, 1981) a significant preference for Black versus White counselors was found. Specifically, pro-White, anti-Black therapist preference was found for individuals in Stage 1. During Stages 2 and 3 (resembling revelation and embeddedness level feminist development), pro-Black, anti-White counselor preferences emerged. Finally, latter stage attitudes were not associated with preference for either Black or White counselors. The authors concluded that increasing comfort with one's own racial identity facilitated comfort with therapists regardless of race. This conceptualization and the findings of Parham and Helms (1981) parallel that expected to account for differences in therapist preference by feminist identity level. Passive-acceptance women would be expected to prefer male therapists, while revelation and embeddedness women should prefer female therapists. Synthesis level and active commitment level women would not be expected to prefer therapists of one gender over another.

Recent research has suggested that, under certain circumstances, female clients benefit from female therapists more than male therapists (Howard & Orlinsky, 1979; Kaplan, 1979; Kirshner, Genak, & Hauser, 1978; Mogul, 1982), particularly with less experienced therapists. The authors suggest that the positive quality of the relational bond between female therapists and clients, the female therapist's sensitivity to inherent power differences, and the willingness of women to use themselves as vehicles for reaching empathic understanding may account for these effects. Within this developmental model, it would be predicted that women entering therapy in revelation and embeddedness, particularly, might experience greater satisfaction and a more positive therapeutic outcome when working with female therapists rather than male therapists.

References

Cross, W. E. (1971). Negro-to-Black conversion experience: Toward a psychology of black liberation. *Black World, 20*(9), 13–27.

Downing, N. E., & Roush, K. L. (1985). From passive-acceptance to active commitment: A model of feminist identity development for women. *The Counseling Psychologist, 13*(4), 695–709.

Fallon, A. E., & Rozin, P. (1985). Sex differences in perceptions of desirable body shape. *Journal of Abnormal Psychology, 94*, 102–105.

Gilligan, C. (1982). *In a different voice.* Cambridge, MA: Harvard University Press.

Greenspan, M. (1983). *A new approach to women and therapy.* New York: McGraw-Hill.

Howard, K. I., & Orlinsky, P. E. (1979). *What effect does therapist gender have on outcome for women in psychotherapy?* Paper presented at The American Psychological Association, New York.

Kaplan, A. G. (1979). Toward an analysis of sex-role related issues in the therapeutic relationship. *Psychiatry, 42,* 112–120.

Kirshner, L. A., Genak, A., & Hauser, S. T. (1978). Effects of gender on short-term psychotherapy. *Psychotherapy: Theory, Research, and Practice, 15,* 158–167.

Kohlberg, L. (1981). *The philosophy of moral development.* San Francisco: Harper & Row.

Loevinger, S., & Wessler, R. (1970). *Measuring ego development.* San Francisco: Jossey-Bass.

Mogul, K. M. (1982). Overview: The sex of the therapist. *American Journal of Psychiatry, 139,* 1–11.

Parham, T. A., & Helms, J. E. (1981). The influence of Black students' racial identity on preferences for counselor race. *Journal of Counseling Psychology, 82,* 250–257.

Perry, W. (1970). *Forms of ethical and intellectual development in the college years.* New York: Holt, Rinehart and Winston.

Rawlings, E. I., & Carter, D. K. (1977). *Psychotherapy for women.* Springfield, IL: Charles C Thomas.

Rickard, K. (1987, March). *A model of feminist identity development.* Paper presented at the annual meeting of the Association for Women in Psychology, Denver, Colorado.

Rickard, K. (in review). The effect of feminist identity level on gender prejudice toward artists' illustrations. Manuscript submitted for publication.

Rickard, K. (in press). The relationship of self-monitored dating behaviors to level of feminist identity on the FIS. Manuscript submitted for publication. *Sex Roles.*

Schaef, A. W. (1985). *Women's realities: An emerging female system in a white male society.* New York: Winston Press.

14

Feminist and Nonsexist Counseling: Implications for the Male Counselor

Doug DeVoe

As the modern feminist movement enters its third decade, progress continues to be made toward the attainment of equal political, social, and economic status for women. Progress, however, has been slow, and a number of institutions still maintain sexist socialization practices that threaten the progress that has been made during the last 30 years.

The role of counselors is becoming increasingly important as a potential way to eliminate sexism. Women are seeking help through counseling and therapy, and that process should provide a safe means for producing change. It is critical that counselors understand that all women have in some way been negatively affected by political, economic, and social forces. Male counselors and therapists, in particular, need to be aware of the impact of those forces on women as well as the diverse and complex lives that women lead.

The literature concerning feminist issues has focused attention on this important topic of sexism. The literature has been somewhat negligent, however, in emphasizing the critical role that counselors play in facilitating social change toward a more egalitarian view of the world. The literature has been especially negligent in emphasizing the role that male counselors might play in facilitating that social change. The purpose of this article is to reacquaint the counselor with the tenets of feminist and nonsexist therapies and focus specifically on the role of male counselors in eliminating social, economic, and political inequality.

Reprinted from the *Journal of Counseling & Development, 69,* 1990, pp. 33–36. Reprinted by permission. No further reproduction authorized without written permission of the American Counseling Association.

The Nature of Feminist and Nonsexist Therapy

Both feminist and nonsexist therapies are particularly useful for women clients; each, however, has a slightly different focus. According to Rawlings and Carter (1977), the major difference is that "feminist therapy incorporates the political values and philosophy of feminism from the women's movement in its therapeutic values and strategies while nonsexist therapy does not" (p. 50). Nonsexist therapy is generally used with traditional women clients who may find the tenets of feminism threatening. Feminist therapy is used with women clients who are not satisfied with the constricting, culturally defined roles for women and are seeking other alternatives (Rawlings & Carter, 1977).

Feminist therapy emphasizes the need for social change by improving the lives of women rather than by helping them adjust to traditional roles in society (Dworkin, 1984; Gilbert, 1980; Kaschak, 1981; Rawlings & Carter, 1977; Sherman, Koufacos, & Kenworthy, 1978; Thomas, 1977). Feminist counselors typically perceive women's problems as being caused by cultural, social, and political forces rather than by internal states (Epperson & Lewis, 1987).

In reviewing the literature on feminist therapy (Gilbert, 1980; Kaschak, 1981; Mowbray, Lanir, & Hulce, 1984; Rawlings & Carter, 1977; Russell, 1984), two main principles are emphasized: (a) "The personal is political" and (b) Therapist-client interactions are seen as egalitarian. Concerning the first principle, "The personal is political," Gilbert (1980) suggested that women clients need to become aware of how their lives have become influenced by society's expectations and roles. Therefore, one of the goals of therapy is to help women receive validation for their unique experience as women and change society rather than be molded by society. Concerning the second principle in which therapist-client interactions are seen as egalitarian, Gilbert (1980) recommended that clients be encouraged to counsel with therapists who will view them as equals. Furthermore, therapists can help clients increase autonomous behavior and become more self-confident and self-directed. Women need to be made aware of the importance of self-nurturance and learn to value themselves as women as well as value other women (Gilbert, 1980; Thomas, 1977). The personal power between the client and therapist should be equal whenever possible, and explanations within the counseling session should be in concepts and words that the client can easily understand (Rawlings & Carter, 1977).

Implications for the Male Counselor

Men may need to pay particular attention to certain issues when counseling with women. The issues of anger, autonomy, power, and stereotypical roles have great impact on women clients and are extremely important issues for women in therapy. For some women, because of previous dependence on men, their emotional responses to anger are more likely to be repressed and viewed as unacceptable. For other women, autonomy and power are often seen as masculine traits and inappropriate for women. Men's greater, or perhaps different, familiarity with anger, autonomy, and power can potentially provide therapeutic benefit for their women clients.

Anger

For many feminists anger is perceived as the major issue for women and as an appropriate response to oppression. Anger may also be a reaction to unresolved individual conflicts (Kaschak, 1981). Russell (1984) stated that anger targeted at producing social change may be very positive but can also be detrimental, and can even create retaliation if used against individuals close to the client. Gilbert (1980) summarized a feminist view of the expression of anger as "essential to the establishment of women's personal power" (p. 259).

Counselors who are tuned in to their women clients may sense an unwillingness to express anger. It is imperative that these counselors work toward providing a safe environment for the expression of anger. Men who are effective in expressing anger in constructive ways can serve as important role models for women. Counselors can point out the potential benefits of venting repressed rage and perhaps suggest the use of techniques appropriate for the situation (such as Gestalt techniques). Therapists must ideally help clients turn anger toward socially applicable action (Russell, 1984).

Autonomy

Women's ego identity is often based on a concern for others and what pleases men. Counseling and therapy should concentrate on shifting women's focus from others to self for their own survival as strong individuals (Chesler, 1972). By shifting the focus from others to self, women increase their autonomy. Women also increase autonomy by developing power to "carry things through and stop expecting that they will need to be rescued by a person wiser and stronger" (Rawlings & Carter, 1977, p. 59). Autonomy can be improved when women take responsibility for their own behavior. Deciding what they want out of life and what they want for themselves will also help them achieve autonomy (Rawlings & Carter, 1977).

It has been suggested that male counselors can keep women dependent through extended nonessential therapy, and care must be taken to avoid this situation (Chesler, 1971, 1972; Fabrikant, 1974). When clients are continually encouraged to decide for themselves and continually reinforced for taking independent action, autonomy is fostered, and the therapeutic outcome is more successful for the client (Gilbert, 1980).

Male counselors must certainly be sensitive to a client's need for approval and work to diminish that need through development of self-determination and an independent self-identity (Brodsky, 1980). This may be facilitated by helping the client focus on herself in the present and focus on successes with independent behavior and action. Much time should be spent on client self-exploration to gain insight and awareness of behaviors and emotions that are unique to the individual.

Power

According to Kaschak (1981), the feminist view of the power differential between client and therapist is that any difference in the counseling relationship is considered inappropriate and is a reflection of exploitative patriarchal relationships. Rawlings and Carter (1977) supported the idea that the power differential between men and women is a central problem. Women are often viewed as masculine and somehow less healthy by both society and clinicians when they show assertiveness or power in their personalities. These women run serious risks by acting like "males" and are more likely to be referred to a therapist to reassert their "femininity" (Chesler, 1972).

The role of the counselor is critical to ameliorate the power differential between men and women. Counselors must approach the relationship with the client as an equal; the relationship is nonexploitative and the client is seen as the best expert on her own processes (Kaschak, 1981). Feminist therapists typically perceive themselves as having certain skills and expertise to help their clients. Such therapists view self-disclosure as necessary for the emergence of an equal client-counselor relationship and for the elimination of any exploitative aspects of power. Male counselors and therapists often view power differently. For example, Polk (1974) identified six sources of perceived male power such as the following:

1. Psychological
2. Institutional
3. Expert
4. Reward
6. Brute force
7. Normative

Psychological power, for example, gives men the advantage of social conditioning that helps them fit the value structure of institutions better than does women's social conditioning. Men control the basic institutions of socialization such as educational institutions, the media, and religion, giving them institutional power. Men act as gatekeepers of knowledge, regarding themselves as experts in every field and possessing expert power. Men reward women for conforming to traditional gender roles and withhold reward for not conforming. Because men are physically stronger than women and more confident in their strength, they have social control over women shown by demonstrations of masculine strength such as beatings and rape. Normative power is dominated by men because they control gender role definitions in society. Male counselors can help empower women clients to deal more effectively with these sources of perceived power by first recognizing their own identification with these power sources and resolving any intrapersonal disputes about them. Specifically, counselors can help clients understand that these sources of power are, in part, responsible for women's perceptions of male domination.

While helping women break down these power differentials, male counselors can help women empower themselves through involvement in consciousness-raising groups and organizations that effect social change. Women can effect social change through demonstrations and political action.

Gender Role Stereotyping

For some feminists gender roles are viewed as negative and should be completely abolished in favor of an androgynous model of mental health. At the very minimum therapists should value gender specific differences in behavior (Kaschak, 1981). Feminists are aware of the existence of gender role stereotyping and oppression and the effects of social influence on women's personal experience (Thomas, 1977).

Bem (1987) studied the effects of a gender-typed individual performance and found that traditional gender roles produce unnecessary and possibly even dysfunctional patterns of avoidance restricting simple everyday behaviors. Bem summed up her study by saying that behavior should have no gender and gave a prescription for a liberated sexual identity: "Let sexual preference be ignored; Let sex roles be abolished and; Let gender move from figure to ground" (p. 223).

Counselors must firmly believe that anatomy does not determine what roles men and women should play in society. Women should be encouraged to explore nontraditional behaviors and free themselves from roles that restrict their opportunities. Women can be comfortable with the use of power; they can be assertive and decisive and also be sensitive, nurturing, and emotionally expressive. Men can be emotionally responsive and tender as well as analytical and competent (Rawlings & Carter, 1977).

Counselors should also be aware of possible gender role stereotyping in career exploration counseling. Women need to first explore their fears of success and failure, their internal issues of ambivalence and commitment, and their current self-image. After examining these aspects of herself as a woman, the woman client can build a positive self-image necessary in a career decision making (Washor-Liebhaber, 1982) that is free of culturally imposed definitions of masculinity and femininity (Bem, 1987).

Characteristics of the Effective Feminist Counselor

Counselors who intend to adopt a feminist approach to therapy are challenged to a difficult task, because feminist therapy requires changing one's value system and not mastering new techniques (Chambless & Wenk, 1982). An awareness of one's own values is important for effective counseling when using any nonsexist therapy. In feminist counseling, values are communicated to the client and must be shared openly, because feminist therapy is considered to be value based (Kaschak, 1981). The personal values of a counselor can influence which behaviors a client values in herself (Rawlings & Carter, 1977). Client attributes that have been influenced by her socialization may elicit value biases in the counselor. For example, the social class, race, sex, and values of the client can result in clinical judgment bias (Abramowitz & Dokecki, 1977). On the other hand, client-counselor values that converge during therapy result in positive improvement in the client (Thomas, 1977). Thomas has also pointed out that the value system of a feminist therapist must include the belief in the potential of women and how their potential is blocked by society's stereotyping of gender roles. Feminist therapists encourage clients to ignore traditional gender roles and be assertive, make nonstereotypic life decisions, develop equality in the assigning of tasks in their relationships, feel their power and strength, and become their own person (Thomas, 1977).

It is also important for a counselor to know what sexist issues women face in society, and this can be accomplished by participating in feminist consciousness-raising or support groups that have the effect of raising awarenesses of a woman's experiences (Rawlings & Carter, 1977). Feminist counselors serve as role models moving clients toward social, economic, and political action. A male therapist who shares his feminist values openly and honestly can be a model for women (or men) clients. This type of modeling can help clients question and explore any unexamined values or assumptions that they may have (Thomas, 1977). Men can also serve as role models by disclosing involvement in consciousness-raising groups and in social, economic, and political actions that support feminism. This modeling can be especially effective if the relationship between the therapist and client is such that the client does not feel that the counselor is "a special male who will treat her differently than other males" (Hare-Mustin, 1981, p. 566).

For one to consider oneself as possessing the characteristics of a feminist, three criteria must be met, according to Offen (1988):

1. When assessing a woman's status in society relative to men, counselors must acknowledge women's values as their own rather than think of them as the aesthetic ideal of womanhood invented by men, and they must recognize the validity of a woman's own interpretation of her lived experience.

2. When experiencing institutionalized injustice or inequity toward women by men as a group, women should exhibit a consciousness of it, discomfort, or even anger over its existence.

3. Women challenge the coercive power, force, or authority that upholds male prerogatives in a culture and advocate the elimination of injustice. Feminists must necessarily be at odds with male dominated culture and society (Offen, 1988).

The effective feminist counselor is aware that the "personal is political"; the oppression of women must be eliminated by altering society at its roots (Kaschak, 1981). The counselor must view the client as an equal both in and out of the counseling relationship. Feminist counselors must help clients become aware of the importance of self-nurturance and learn to value themselves as women and also value other women (Gilbert, 1980; Thomas, 1977). As stated earlier, the personal power between the client and counselor should be equal whenever possible, and explanations within the counseling session should be in words and concepts that the client can easily understand (Kaschak, 1981; Rawlings & Carter, 1977).

Recommendations for Training Feminist and Nonsexist Therapists

There are many ways that men can support feminism and be a part of the solution to the problem of sexism. As feminists, we need to be aware of the experience of women and increase our consciousness as well as our training efforts to prepare new therapists for counseling with women.

Feminist therapy is not just a method that can be taught and used if appropriate, but is a way of life for the therapist and the client (Thomas, 1977). Teaching counselors a new way of life involves connecting feminism with therapy to remove abuses of power and sexism from therapy. As counselors meet in peer consultations, publish articles and books, and develop training and systems of referral, more becomes clear about feminist therapy (Thomas, 1977).

There is a need to continue to motivate both women and men toward feminist political change. This may be accomplished through men's studies programs (Brod, 1987a, 1987b) and/or women's studies programs (Libertin, 1987) as a more formal way of studying feminist issues. But there are a number of different ways to increase awareness of the limitations that society and gender role stereotyping place on both women and men. Lectures and providing inservice training workshops for students and professional staff, consulting with feminist colleagues, exchanging ideas and feelings about certain cases, reading feminist literature or books on the psychology of women, and joining consciousness-raising groups (which may require a great deal of time but offer a much deeper emotional investment in understanding feminist issues) are all ways to train new or experienced counselors on the issues facing women (Chambless & Wenk, 1982).

Russell (1986) evaluated a 5-week microtraining program in feminist counseling skills and found an increase in the skill of self-disclosure and increasing liberalism in attitudes toward women. Sherman, Koufacos, and Kenworthy (1978) found that 70% of the therapists in their study perceived a need for special training at the postgraduate, graduate, and undergraduate levels to work with women clients. These researchers also found male therapists to be less informed than female therapists especially in the areas of female sexuality, menstruation, pregnancy, childbirth, and menopause. Worell (1981) listed four criteria she believes would help to develop specialists in counseling women:

1. Cognitive and experiential courses related to gender role concerns
2. Commitment to research on the development, psychology, and counseling of women
3. Community action through workshops, consultation, and program development with community agencies
4. Practicum and internship experiences in different settings concerned directly with counseling women

When Men May Not Be Appropriate Counselors for Women Clients

Rawlings and Carter (1977) raised doubts about men's contributing to changing the social role system. They suggested that women cannot count on men in this regard because men benefit more from sexism than women do and men are reluctant to give up their position of privilege. Men who take this position should not counsel women. Men who have rescue fantasies about women should not counsel with dependent women whose husbands mistreat them. Men should avoid counseling women who are hostile toward men or with women who relate to men in a seductive manner. Women should avoid male counselors when they are in the crisis of divorce. Men should refer women who are extremely dependent and are inhibited and who equate femininity with passivity and docility (Rawlings & Carter, 1977).

Orlinsky and Howard (1980) reported that women with depressive reactions, anxiety reactions, and schizophrenia had more positive experiences with female therapists. They also found that single women and especially young single women benefited more from female counselors. Brodsky (1980) discovered that women seek other women counselors for treatment of specific crises affecting women such as rape, pregnancy, and domestic violence. Russell (1984) summarized the results of various studies and concluded that young women who are still in the process of defining their roles are best served by female therapists with an awareness of gender role issues.

Hope for the Future

Although the focus of this article was on the male therapist, feminist therapy does not apply only to women. Men can benefit from feminist counseling in important ways. For example, exposure to the tenets of feminism can increase awareness of the damaging effects of sexist values on relationships and begin to change the inappropriate power differential that exists between men and women. The difficult part for men may be in sharing their power or authority with women so that an equal balance of power can prevail in society. Men *can* change their behaviors to reflect a more feminist or at least nonsexist orientation.

Feminist values have begun to have an impact on family, school, and other socializing institutions. The time is long overdue for those principles and values to permeate the counseling relationship.

References

Abramowitz, C. V., & Dokecki, P. R. (1977). The politics of clinical judgment: Early empirical returns. *Psychological Bulletin, 84,* 460–476.

Bem, S. L. (1987). Probing the promise of androgyny. In M. R. Walsh (Ed.), *The psychology of women* (pp. 206–225). New Haven, CT: Yale University Press.

Brod, H. (1987a). The new men's studies: From feminist theory to gender scholarship. *Hypatia, 2,* 179–196.

Brod, H. (1987b). Does manning men's studies emasculate women's studies? *Hypatia, 2,* 153–157.

Brodsky, A. M. (1980). A decade of feminist influence on psychotherapy. *Psychology of Women Quarterly, 4,* 331–343.

Chambless, D. L., & Wenk, N. M. (1982). Feminist vs. nonfeminist therapy: The client's perspective. *Women and Therapy, 1,* 57–65.

Chesler, P. (1971). Women as psychiatric and psychotherapeutic patients. *Journal of Marriage and the Family, 33,* 746–759.

Chesler, P. (1972). *Women and madness.* New York: Doubleday.

Dworkin, S. (1984). Traditionally defined client, meet feminist therapist: Feminist therapy as attitude change. *The Personnel and Guidance Journal, 62,* 301–305.

Epperson, D. L., & Lewis, K. N. (1987). Issues of informed entry into counseling: Perceptions and preferences resulting from different types and amounts of pretherapy information. *Journal of Counseling Psychology, 34,* 266–275.

Fabrikant, B. (1974). Psychotherapist and the female patient: Perceptions, misperceptions, and change. In V. Franks & V. Burtle (Eds.), *Women in therapy.* New York: Brunner/Mazel.

Gilbert, L. (1980). Feminist therapy. In A. M. Brodsky & R. Hare-Mustin (Eds.), *Women and psychotherapy: An assessment of research and practice* (pp. 245–265). New York: Guilford.

Hare-Mustin, R. T. (1981). A feminist approach to family therapy. In E. Howell & M. Bayes (Eds.), *Women and mental health* (pp. 553–571). New York: Basic Books.

Kaschak, E. (1981). Feminist therapy: The first decade. In S. Cox (Ed.), *Female psychology: The emerging self* (pp. 387–401). New York: St. Martin's Press.

Libertin, M. (1987). The politics of women's studies and men's studies. *Hypatia, 1,* 51–58.

Mowbray, C. T., Lanir, S., & Hulce, M. (1984). Feminist therapy. *Women and Therapy, 1,* 89–96.

Offen, K (1988). Defining feminism: A comparative historical approach. *Signs: Journal of Women in Culture and Society, 14,* 119–157.

Orlinsky, D. E., & Howard, K. I. (1980). Gender and psychotherapeutic outcome. In A. M. Brodsky & R. Hare-Mustin (Eds.), *Women and psychotherapy: An assessment of research and practice* (pp. 3–34). New York: Guilford.

Polk, B. B. (1974). Male power and the women's movement. *Journal of Applied Behavioral Psychology, 10,* 410.

Rawlings, E., & Carter, D. (1977). (Eds.). *Psychotherapy for women.* Springfield, IL: Charles C Thomas.

Russell, M. N. (1984). *Skills in counseling women.* Springfield, IL: Charles C Thomas.

Russell, M. N. (1986). Teaching feminist counseling skills: An evaluation. *Counselor Education and Supervision, 25,* 320–331.

Sherman, J., Koufacos, C., & Kenworthy, J. A. (1978). Therapists: Their attitudes and information about women. *Psychology of Women Quarterly, 2,* 299–313.

Thomas, S. A. (1977). Theory and practice in feminist therapy. *Social Work, 22,* 447–454.

Washor-Liebhaber, G. (1982). Women's career decision making process: A feminist perspective. *Women and Therapy, 1,* 51–58.

Worell, J. (1981). New directions in counseling women. In E. Howell & M. Bayes (Eds.), *Women and mental health* (pp. 620–637). New York: Basic Books.

PART 5
The Gay Client

Although the psychological literature on gays has moved from a focus on pathology to an emphasis on diversity and affirmation, practicing counselors and therapists have not necessarily changed their views to the same extent (Dworkin & Gutierrez, 1992). As we saw in chapter 5, many counselors and therapists remain misinformed and continue to hold negative attitudes about gays (Betz & Fitzgerald, 1993). Despite ethical guidelines mandating egalitarian treatment of gay men and lesbian women, not all counselors have taken the necessary steps to address their homophobic attitudes and increase their knowledge and awareness of lesbian women and gay men. Further, although gay men and lesbian women have many concerns in common, each group faces unique issues (Dworkin & Gutierrez, 1992). In chapter 15, the results of a survey on bias and sensitive practice with gay and lesbian clients is presented; in chapters 16 and 17, the essential attitudes, knowledge, and skills necessary for gay-affirmative counseling are explored in some depth.

Garnets, Hancock, Cochran, Goodchilds, and Peplau (1991) report on a survey of psychologists that was designed to elicit cases of "good practice," as well as bias in the treatment of gay men and lesbian women. Their specific illustrations of biased, inadequate, or inappropriate practice on the one hand, and exemplary practices on the other, provide concrete guidance and a wealth of information for counselors working with gay clients. The illustrations should also assist counselors in examining their own attitudes and behaviors in counseling.

Browning, Reynolds, and Dworkin (1991), in chapter 16, address a range of issues and concerns confronting lesbian women, with special attention to those that may arise in counseling. Important aspects of the lesbian experience, all of which counselors must understand in order to work effectively with lesbian clients, are discussed: the coming out process, career development, aging, the problems and prospects of lesbian couples, and lesbian parenting. The special issues related to counseling concerns of lesbians are also covered, e.g., substance abuse, domestic violence, and sexual abuse. Some attention is devoted to the concerns of lesbian women of color. The article ends with a series of recommendations for counseling, including a discussion of the need for feminist counseling with lesbian clients.

Finally, in their article "Affirmative psychotherapy for gay men," Shannon and Wood (1991) cover many of the same issues, e.g., the coming out process, career issues, aging, gay couples and gay parenting, and cultural influences, describing some of the unique ways these issues are played out in the experiences of gay men in our society. Shannon and Wood (1991) also address concerns of particular importance to gay men, e.g., antigay violence and AIDS. This article, too, ends with a series of recommendations for counselors.

References

Betz, N. E., & Fitzgerald, L. F. (1993). Individuality and diversity: Theory and research in counseling psychology. *Annual Review of Psychology, 44,* 343–381.

Browning, C., Reynolds, A. L., & Dworkin, S. H. (1991). Affirmative psychotherapy for lesbian women. *The Counseling Psychologist, 19,* 197–215.

Dworkin, S. H., & Gutierrez, F. J. (Eds.). (1992). *Counseling gay men and lesbians: Journey to the end of the rainbow.* Alexandria, VA: American Association for Counseling and Development.

Garnets, L., Hancock, K. A., Cochran, S. D., Goodchilds, J., & Peplau, L. A. (1991). Issues in psychotherapy with lesbians and gay men: A survey of psychologists. *American Psychologist, 46,* 964–972.

Shannon, J. W., & Woods, W. J. (1991). Affirmative psychotherapy for gay men. *The Counseling Psychologist, 19,* 197–215.

15

Issues in Psychotherapy with Lesbians and Gay Men

A Survey of Psychologists

Linda Garnets, Kristin A. Hancock, Susan D. Cochran, Jacqueline Goodchilds, and Letitia Anne Peplau

In 1975, the American Psychological Association (APA) took a strong stance regarding bias toward lesbians and gay men, resolving that 'homosexuality per se implies no impairment in judgment, reliability or general social and vocational abilities" (see Appendix A for the full text of the resolution). The APA urged psychologists "to take the lead in removing the stigma of mental illness long associated with homosexual orientations" (Conger, 1975). In recent years, attention has been drawn to ways in which a client's ethnicity, gender, sexual orientation, or physical disability can affect clinical judgment and treatment strategies. There has been a corresponding effort to develop guidelines to help practitioners avoid bias in psychotherapy (APA, 1975). Recognizing that practice does not spontaneously or quickly follow policy changes, the Committee on Lesbian and Gay Concerns (CLGC), sponsored

Garnets, L., Hancock, K. A., Cochran, S. D., Goodchilds, J., & Peplau, L. A. (1991). Issues in psychotherapy with lesbians and gay men. *American Psychologist, 46,* 964–972. Copyright © 1991 by the American Psychological Association. Reprinted with permission.

jointly by the Board of Social and Ethical Responsibility in Psychology (BSERP) and the Board of Professional Affairs (BPA),[1] formed a task force in 1984 to investigate the range of bias that may occur in psychotherapy with lesbians and gay men. This article is an abridged report of the task force's research, findings, and recommendations.[2]

The therapeutic process is inevitably affected by the values and biases of therapists (Lopez, 1989; Murray & Abramson, 1983). The mission of CLGC's Task Force on Bias in Psychotherapy with Lesbians and Gay Men was to describe the range of problems that gay male and lesbian clients can face in psychotherapy and to provide an empirical basis for the development of guidelines and suggestions for practice. In addition to those relatively few psychologists who choose to specialize in working with lesbians and gay men, most nonspecialist therapists will also see gay male and lesbian clients. There are many ways, subtle and obvious, in which bias can occur, and issues inherent in treating these populations competently are complex. The data obtained by this survey should be used as a starting point for the development of educational materials and model curricula for graduate and professional training.[3] There is a growing body of literature on sexual orientation that should be more widely disseminated to practicing psychologists. Suggested readings regarding bias in therapy with lesbians and gay men as well as gay-affirmative therapy are listed in Appendix B.

This article is an abridged report of the results of a survey conducted in 1986. It relies on methodology adapted from similar work done by the BPA Task Force on Sex Bias and Sex-Role Stereotyping in Psychotherapeutic Practice (APA, 1975). Three major limitations of the survey are acknowledged. First, practitioners may not always be aware of a client's sexual orientation. Unlike gender or race, or frequently, ethnicity, the sexual orientation of a client may or may not be obvious or revealed to a therapist. A client may never disclose his or her sexual orientation or may disclose it at any point during the course of the treatment. The invisibility of sexual orientation raises complex therapy issues that we do not address in this article. Second, when the survey was conducted in 1986, there was much less public awareness of acquired immunodeficiency syndrome (AIDS), few respondents mentioned AIDS issues, and we therefore do not deal with the serious

---

[1] The Committee on Lesbian and Gay Concerns has been a standing committee of APA since 1980. At the time this report was completed it reported to the Board of Social and Ethical Responsibility in Psychology (BSERP), and it now reports to the Board for Psychology in the Public Interest (BAPPI), which superseded BSERP in 1990. The Board of Professional Affairs falls under the auspices of the Practice Directorate.

[2] The full report is available from CLGC. APA, 1200 17th Street, N.W., Washington, DC 20036.

[3] On May 10, 1991, the Arizona State Psychological Association formally adopted a standard of practice with lesbian and gay male clients based on the results of this survey.

therapeutic and ethical issues in that area. Third, we do not address gender differences in the therapy experiences of lesbians and gay men. Although the task force decided to approach issues of sexual orientation as a generic category, there are doubtless many ways in which the gender of a gay male or lesbian client and the gender of the therapist may combine to affect the psychotherapy experience. A full exploration of this complex issue would require a careful comparison of the therapy experiences of lesbians versus gay men with male versus female therapists, an undertaking beyond the scope of this article.

Method

The survey was developed to elicit instances of biased care as well as examples of beneficial care provided to gay male and lesbian clients. The four-page survey also contained questions that elicited demographic data and information about the respondents' professional background and provision of psychotherapy. Respondents were asked whether they knew of "any specific experiences of lesbian or gay clients in psychotherapy" from friends or colleagues, from their own professional practice, or from their own experiences as a client in psychotherapy. Those who knew of incidents were asked to respond to the following four critical incident questions:

1. Describe any incident where a therapist provided biased, inadequate, or inappropriate care to a gay or lesbian client in psychotherapy. For each incident, indicate your source of information (e.g., "A friend or colleague told me about it." "I was the client." "My client told me." "I observed it.")
2. Describe any incidents where a therapist provided care demonstrating special sensitivity to a gay or lesbian client in psychotherapy. For each example, indicate your source of information.
3. In your opinion, what professional practices are especially *harmful* in psychotherapy with lesbian and gay clients?
4. In your opinion, what professional practices are especially *beneficial* in psychotherapy with lesbian and gay clients?

Data Collection

To obtain a large and diverse sample of critical incidents involving both lesbian and gay male clients in psychotherapy, we solicited opinions from a broad group of psychologists. The goal was to include psychologists who, regardless of their own sexual orientation, would be likely to have knowledge of the provision of psychotherapeutic services to gay male and lesbian clients, as well as gay male and lesbian psychologists who may themselves have received psychotherapeutic services. We were also interested in the knowledge that psychologists may have from observations or conversations with colleagues, students, or friends. To ensure a response rate adequate for analysis, we used

1986 APA membership rolls to survey all members, fellows, and associates of Divisions 44 (Society for the Psychological Study of Gay and Lesbian Issues) and 35 (Psychology of Women), and a random sample of 4,000 licensed members of APA (balanced by gender) who were not members of either of those divisions. The anonymous questionnaire, accompanied by an explanatory cover letter and a postage-paid envelope, addressed to APA Central Office, was fielded in November 1986 to a target sample of 6,580 psychologists. The cover letter explained that

> This survey is designed to collect information about the experiences of lesbians and gay men in psychotherapy. You may know about this topic from friends or colleagues, from experiences you may have had as a client, or—if you have engaged in practice—in your role as therapist. Our goal is to obtain a wide range of information from diverse sources.

Of the 6,580 questionnaires mailed, 45 were returned undeliverable. From the remaining 6,535 questionnaires, 2,544 were completed and returned. This is a response rate of 38.9%.

Results

The survey succeeded in obtaining information from a diverse sample of psychologists. The 2,544 respondents ranged in age from 26 to 86 years (mean = 46.5 years, median = 44 years). Reflecting the oversampling of women in the sampling frame, 69% of respondents were women. Nearly all participants were White (96%), with only 2% Black, 1% Hispanic, and less than 1% Asian. Respondents came from all areas of the United States, with a scattering (1%) from Canada. Eighty-five percent self-identified as heterosexual, 11% as gay male or lesbian, and 4% as bisexual. Among women, 87% self-identified as heterosexual, 9% as lesbian, and 5% as bisexual. Among men, 81% self-identified as heterosexual, 15% as gay, and 4% as bisexual.

Of the total sample, 1,481 respondents (58.2%) indicated that they knew of psychotherapy experiences of gay and lesbian clients and provided critical incident material. This subgroup (hereafter referred to as "the sample") is the focus of the report. These individuals also constitute a diverse sample, differing from the entire group of respondents only in that a somewhat larger percentage (23% vs. 15%) self-identified as gay male, lesbian, or bisexual.

The majority (93%) of the sample were licensed psychologists. The median year of licensure was 1978. About 87% were currently providing psychotherapy services. Among providers, more than one third had been in practice less than seven years.

Reflecting the diversity of the psychotherapy field, respondents reported varied theoretical orientations to the practice of psychotherapy, with 85% of the sample reporting both a primary and secondary theoretical orientation. Of the options provided, an eclectic orientation was most frequently cited. Sizeable percentages also indicated analytic-psychodynamic, relationship, cognitive, and behavioral orientations as either primary or secondary. Only 5% reported a gay-affirmative orientation to therapy. Of those respondents who were lesbians or gay men, 29% reported a gay-affirmative orientation. This contrasts with 2% of bisexual providers and less than 1% of heterosexual practitioners.

Nearly all of the psychotherapy providers (99%), regardless of sexual orientation, reported that they had seen at least one gay male or lesbian client in psychotherapy at some point during their careers. The average respondent reported that 6% of their current clients were gay men and 7% were lesbians. Only 1% of service providers had never worked with gay male or lesbian clients, and 38% had seen more than 20 such individuals in their careers. Twenty-two percent of the practitioners in this sample specialized in providing services to gay men or lesbians. Among lesbians and gay male practitioners, 71% specialized in treating homosexual clients, compared with 42% of the bisexual providers and only 9% of the heterosexual providers.

It should be noted that these materials are not based on or intended to be a representative sample of APA members. The sample is neither representative of psychologists in general (as 95% of the sample were practitioners), nor of practitioners (as 67% of the sample were women, compared with 31% of practitioners in APA who are women).

Analysis of Open-Ended Responses

For each of the four open-ended questions, a work group was formed, consisting of task force members (one of whom served as leader of each group) and additional psychologist volunteers from the Los Angeles and San Francisco areas. Group members, working individually with typed copies of verbatim responses, identified specific themes in the responses. Each group then discussed and revised the wording of themes and selected illustrative responses for each. Task force members consolidated the results from the four separate work groups and organized all materials into three broad categories: strategies of intervention, issues of special relevance to lesbian and gay male populations, and issues about therapists' expertise and training.

In the search for major themes, it was decided to combine responses to the two negative questions and to the two positive questions. Each pair of questions addressed two convergent sources of information about the same general issues (e.g., specific examples of biased practice and more abstract statements about the nature of biased practice). Finally, task force members reviewed the thousands of open-ended responses to select examples that most clearly reflected the meaning of each theme and the range of comments provided by respondents.

The goal was not to chart the frequency of particular types of bias or to identify the most common types of beneficial or harmful practices. Rather, we sought to identify the full range of possibilities, to categorize both harmful and beneficial practices, and to illustrate these with concrete examples. In the following section, we first present 17 themes illustrating biased, inadequate, or inappropriate practice in three major areas. Next, we present 14 themes that illustrate exemplary practice in the same areas. Each theme is accompanied by verbatim examples from open-ended responses. In some instances, the biased and beneficial themes represent opposite sides of the same issue—for example, contrasting a therapist's lack of knowledge about social prejudice against gay men and lesbians with a therapist's special sensitivity to social prejudice. In other cases, somewhat different issues emerged in the negative and positive descriptions, and these are reflected in our reporting somewhat different themes.

Biased, Inadequate, or Inappropriate Practice: Key Themes and Illustrations

Assessment

1. A therapist believes that homosexuality per se is a form of psychopathology, developmental arrest, or other psychological disorder:

> I'm convinced that homosexuality is a genuine personality disorder and not merely a different way of life. Everyone that I have known socially or as a client has been a complete mess psychologically. I think they are simply narcissistic personality disorders—see the description in the *DSM-III*—that's what they have looked and acted like—all of them.

2. A therapist automatically attributes a client's problems to her or his sexual orientation without evidence that this is so:

> A client sought treatment for depression because of job loss and physical disability. Client was told by a therapist that the latter would only help client if the client was willing to consider "dealing with the client's sexual orientation"— meaning changing it—as part of the treatment process.

3. A therapist fails to recognize that a client's psychological symptoms or distress can be influenced by the client's own negative attitudes or ideas about homosexuality:

> I have had clients describe . . . therapists' outright denial that a client has experienced societal homophobia or therapists' failure to recognize internalized homophobia as a source of depression and low self-esteem.

4. A therapist automatically assumes a client is heterosexual or discounts a client's self-identification as gay or lesbian:

> The therapists I have seen have either avoided talking about sexuality all together or when they have talked about it, have assumed me to be heterosexual, making it harder for me to bring up the issue.

My client indicated another therapist told her she "wasn't really gay" and was acting out problems related to her father. This woman consistently self-identified over the years (she was mid-thirties) as lesbian in sexual orientation.

Intervention

5. A therapist focuses on sexual orientation as a therapeutic issue when it is not relevant:

> I have seen several gay patients and in each case the person reported that even though their previous therapist said that he or she accepted their homosexuality; the therapist continued to focus upon their being "gay" as "the problem" rather than upon what the person sought help for such as relationship problems, trouble handling guilt about it with family or work, general social anxiety, or other problems totally unrelated to being gay.

6. A therapist discourages a client from having or adopting a lesbian or gay orientation, makes the renunciation of one's homosexuality a condition of treatment, or in the absence of a request by the client seeks to change the sexual orientation of the client:

> A therapist kept insisting that a client had latent heterosexual orientation which should be brought out instead of accepting the client's stated preference for homosexual relations.

> A client was pressured to become "normal," to change conscious sexual fantasies (daydreams) to heterosexual ones.

> A lesbian told me about her first therapist who encouraged her to date men and give up her ideas and feelings regarding women as intimate partners.

7. A therapist expresses beliefs that trivialize or demean homosexuality and gay male and lesbian orientation or experience:

> A lesbian struggling with her sexual identity was challenged by her therapist, "If you have a uterus, don't you think you should use it?"

> A colleague told me she "couldn't help" expressing astonishment and disgust to a male client who "confessed homosexuality."

> A lesbian client dropped her male therapist who said in vengeance to her disclosure that she was "into women" that I don't care, I have a client who is "into dogs."

8. Upon disclosure of homosexuality, a therapist abruptly transfers a client without the provision of appropriate referrals to the client or assistance with the emotional difficulties associated with the transfer:

> A 19 year old male client . . . had been receiving therapy from a University athletic department's sports psychologist. . . . The student-client developed transference toward the psychologist and in the seventh session shared with the psychologist his affection/positive feelings—referring to being "surprised that he could feel love for a man that way." The psychologist became angry, immediately terminated the session and all therapy.

Identity

9. A therapist lacks understanding of the nature of lesbian and gay male identity development, for example by considering a gay male or lesbian identity possible only for adults, by viewing lesbian or gay male identity solely in terms of sexual behavior, or by interpreting a client's gay male or lesbian identity as a "phase" that will be outgrown:

> My therapist treated being gay only as a sexual activity, not as a way of viewing life or my self-concept or identity.

> I was a client in first year grad school. The psychologist I was seeing insisted I was not gay, only going through an identity crisis. I was gay since age 12 or 13. It was my first experience in therapy and it only served to continue my confusion for several more years. I discontinued therapy after 4 sessions and was seriously depressed.

10. A therapist does not sufficiently take into account the extent to which lesbian or gay male identity development is complicated by the client's own negative attitudes toward homosexuality:

> My partner went to a heterosexual female therapist. She consistently minimized "coming out" fears and homophobia in the culture. She may have had therapeutic reasons for doing so, but my lover felt misunderstood and her struggles unappreciated.

11. A therapist underestimates the possible consequences of a gay male or lesbian client's disclosure of his or her homosexuality to others, for example to relatives or employers:

> A lesbian friend told me about a male therapist who tried to convince a young gay man (18–20) to come out to his parents—even though his parents were likely to be abusive. The therapist seemed unaffected by knowledge of society's or parents' homophobia.

Relationships

12. A therapist underestimates the importance of intimate relationships for gay men and lesbians, for example by failing to support the maintenance of or encouraging dissolution of a client's relationship solely because it is a homosexual relationship, or by failing to provide or recommend couples or family therapy when it would be the most appropriate intervention:

> A friend told me of a lesbian, dying of cancer, being advised by her therapist to cut off all relationships and contact with lesbian friends in order to reconcile with her religion and find peace in herself.

> A gay male couple seeking assistance with inhibited sexual desire on the part of one partner . . . were told the problem indicated the one partner probably really wasn't gay and that the recommended intervention was to break up their relationship.

A lesbian couple, seeking relationship therapy, was advised that such therapy was not applicable to their "type" of relationship, that it should not be considered a permanent relationship, and that they might consider going to "gay bars" to meet other people like themselves.

13. A therapist is insensitive to the nature and diversity of lesbian and gay male relationships and inappropriately uses a heterosexual frame of reference:

A lesbian [client was] told to read a book about heterosexual marriage problems because they were "the same" as the issues in her lesbian relationship.

A therapist dealt with gay clients, explicitly, stating that all gays played either "butch" or "fem" roles—for both women and men.

Family

14. A therapist presumes a client is a poor or inappropriate parent solely on the basis of a gay or lesbian sexual orientation, for example by automatically attributing a child's problems to his or her parent(s) being lesbian or gay without evidence that this is so, or by opposing child custody to such parents on the grounds that their sexual orientation in itself makes them unfit:

In the agency in which I formerly worked, a lesbian client whose son was the identified patient was told to move her "friend" out of her home because it was harmful to her son's sexual identity.

A lesbian client related to me that a psychologist seeing her, her lover and two grammar school aged boys for family therapy related to child behavior problems/child management concerns, told her that if her boys were to see her dating a man at least once, they would "mind" better and would comply with her more frequently. The psychologist continued that if she were to have the male date spend the night and have breakfast with her and the boys the next morning, he was sure that their "masculinity crisis" would be cured.

15. A therapist is insensitive to or underestimates the effects of prejudice and discrimination on lesbian and gay male parents and their children:

I explained to my therapist that my son was being teased in school because I am gay. The therapist told me that all kids get teased and that I should just ignore it.

Therapist Expertise and Education

16. A therapist lacks knowledge or expertise, or relies unduly on the client to educate the therapist about gay male and lesbian issues:

I have heard from clients of inadequate care from therapists who claim understanding of the problems that are faced but who, in fact, are quite naive about the problems and offer rather sophomoric solutions applicable to heterosexual situations. Some have been so poorly informed about the lifestyle that in their dismay of the way in which gays/lesbians are treated, they have "bent" confidences and come dangerously close to exposing their clients.

My client told me of a male therapist (heterosexual) who treated her by mainly asking questions about her lifestyle. She felt this was inappropriate and that he didn't know enough.

17. In an educational context, a therapist teaches information about lesbians or gay men that is inaccurate or prejudiced, or actively discriminates against gay male and lesbian students or colleagues:

In a clinical case presentation by a psychology intern who was providing appropriate treatment to a gay client, a senior psychology faculty member stated "this guy is a faggot—don't you have any reaction to that?"

A [gay] clinical psychology student was required to get aversion therapy from a professor as a condition of his remaining in the program once he was discovered.

Exemplary Practice: Key Themes and Illustrations

Assessment

1. A therapist understands that homosexuality, in and of itself, is neither a form of psychopathology nor is necessarily evidence of psychopathology or developmental arrest, and recognizes that gay men and lesbians can live fulfilling lives:

In my own experience as a client, I have felt that my lesbianism has been treated with respect, as a key part of my identity, but never as a sign of psychopathology per se.

My therapist encouraged me to read a book on gay couples to help me see how many gay men have long term satisfying relationships. She helped me to work through my own biases which assumed that gay men could not have happy lives.

2. A therapist recognizes the multiple ways that societal prejudice and discrimination can create problems that lesbians and gay men may seek to address in therapy:

A therapist asked a client questions about discrimination and harassment and believed the client that some problems were external (and real) to her.

I worked with a therapist once who really looked at the different problems I had as a lesbian. These problems were viewed as stemming from society's alienation of us, not as something inherent with homosexuality.

3. A therapist considers sexual orientation as one of many important attributes that characterize a client and does not assume that it is necessarily relevant to the client's problems:

I have had clients tell me they feel a special sensitivity from me in dealing with this issue because I don't treat them as if their sexual orientation is the distinguishing characteristic about them to the exclusion of all others.

I worked with a depressed patient who had, among other things, relationship problems. She told me after quite some months of therapy that a comment of mine, early in the therapy, helped her feel safe and that she could trust me. Apparently I had asked her whether being lesbian was currently an issue for her and "believed her" when she said "no".

4. A therapist recognizes the possible synergistic effects of multiple social statuses experienced by ethnic minority gay men and lesbians:

I know of therapists who clarify the racism that exists within the gay community and how it affects the development of a positive self-image among ethnic minority lesbians and gay men.

Many ethnic minority gay and lesbian clients have expressed much frustration and feelings of isolation in the gay community and tend to [attribute to themselves feelings that] it is related to [their] being gay rather than the racism they experience.

Intervention

5 A therapist uses an understanding of the societal prejudice and discrimination experienced by lesbians and gay men to guide therapy and to help gay male or lesbian clients overcome negative attitudes or ideas about homosexuality:

A male client I worked with came to therapy expressing dissatisfaction with his heterosexual relationships. During the course of therapy it became apparent that this young man was fearful and ashamed of his attraction to men. The patient was able to deal with this in the supportive therapeutic context and later was able to express and accept his homosexuality.

6. A therapist recognizes that his or her own sexual orientation, attitudes, or lack of knowledge may be relevant to the therapy and tries to recognize these limitations, seeking consultation or making appropriate referral when indicated:

When a lesbian client says "I am a lesbian, is that all right with you?" or "Is that a problem for you?" (or in some other way tells me she is gay), I am aware that my "straightness" is part of what that question's all about, and I talk about it directly: "I am straight and that may be a problem for you. I trust myself to be a gay-affirmative therapist, but it will probably take a while for you to test that out and trust me." I find this is very helpful because it communicates my understanding . . . of what it's like for a gay person to open up to a straight person in our homophobic society.

As a therapist who is straight working on occasion with lesbian women, I allow myself to ask questions when I don't understand, rather than mask my inadequacy, and to use a network of lesbian colleagues and friends as resources when I need information, i.e. books, referrals or consultations to be an appropriate therapist for my lesbian clients.

I have personally sought out specific training in counseling gay/lesbian clients, becoming aware of my own homophobic attitudes/practices, which has led to greater effectiveness on my part.

7. A therapist does not attempt to change the sexual orientation of the client without strong evidence that this is the appropriate course of action and that change is desired by the client:

> In my own private practice, I had a male client who expressed a strong desire to "go straight." After a careful psychological assessment, his wish to become heterosexual seemed to be clearly indicated and I assisted him in that process.

> My therapist has been very sensitive to this issue of "going straight as the solution for a gay patient." She has consistently portrayed the attitude that being gay is ok and not something that is sinful, awful, etc. She has very sensitively maintained that there are societal hassles associated with being gay.

Identity

8. A therapist assists a client with the development of a positive gay male or lesbian identity and understands how the client's negative attitudes toward homosexuality may complicate this process:

> One client of mine went into therapy in his early 20s to confess his sudden realization that he was gay. The heterosexual therapist was immensely supportive of his coming out and encouraged him to make contact with the gay community.

> I have a patient whose identity and negative self-esteem were developed very early in response to feeling bad/wrong about being lesbian. I have helped her integrate this as one aspect of growing up lesbian in an anti-lesbian family and society as well as looking at her specific early family developmental concerns that weren't related to her being lesbian.

Relationships

9. A therapist is knowledgeable about the diverse nature of lesbian and gay male relationships and supports and validates their potential importance for the client:

> My therapist understood that although many gay men have open relationships, it was important for me and my partner to have a monogamous one.

> My lover and I saw a therapist who explained to us that there were a variety of different models possible in establishing gay relationships. The therapist encouraged us to work out our own relationship, rather than to live up to someone else's standards.

10. A therapist recognizes the potential importance of extended and alternative families for gay men and lesbians:

> A friend told me how when she was coming out her therapist suggested family therapy for her and her lover and her lover's children together and facilitated creating the new family unit.

11. A therapist recognizes the effects of societal prejudice and discrimination on lesbian and gay relationships and parenting:

I worked with a long-term therapy case of an older gay male whose long-time (20+ years) partner was admitted to a nursing home for terminal care of cancer. Issues of privacy and expression of caring and grief in the presence of primarily heterosexual men were especially salient. The patient's dealing with the burial arrangements while not being recognized as a legal spouse or family member were particularly stressful.

I take care to validate the pressures on gay and lesbian parents due to their lifestyle. For example, I helped a lesbian couple develop strategies to deal with the ostracism they were experiencing from other parents at the child's school because they were gay.

I wanted children, but doubted that this was a wise decision, because I am a lesbian and couldn't provide a traditional home environment. My therapist helped me to understand that I could be a good parent, and that I had bought into societal attitudes about lesbians raising children.

A gay parent came in to see me about a problem with his son. He felt that if he weren't gay, his son would not be having these problems. After assessing the situation, it became clear that his son did have some difficulties, but they were unrelated to the father's gayness. I helped the client to address his own attitudes that contributed to his blaming his son's problems on his homosexuality.

12. A therapist understands that the family of origin of a lesbian or gay male client may need education and support:

A colleague (a heterosexual male) discussed with me that when he was seeing a family disturbed by the disclosure that their 17 year old son was gay, he corrected the parents' misinformation, gave them accurate information about sexual preference. Then he assisted the family in maintaining close contact/involvement with their gay son, and assisted the 17 year old in developing a positive image of himself as a gay man.

Therapist Expertise and Education

13. A therapist is familiar with the needs and treatment issues of gay male and lesbian clients, and uses relevant mental health, educational, and gay male and lesbian community resources:

A gay man, a client of mine, age 20, told me he particularly appreciated my willingness to gather information about coming out, including meeting with campus representatives, which he was not yet ready to do, having just concluded in therapy he was gay.

14. A therapist recognizes the importance of educating professionals, students, supervisees, and others about gay male and lesbian issues and actively counters misinformation or bias about lesbians and gay men:

A colleague told me of how they changed the intake forms at the agency to include gay/lesbian and space for "significant other" identification instead of spouse.

I observed a colleague, at a case conference, ask the presenter if he had asked his single male patient about homosexual experience. The presenter had assumed that because he had never had a girlfriend or been married, he was asexual.

Recommendations

The task force identified and categorized a broad range of harmful practices in the provision of psychotherapy to gay male and lesbian clients. Some of these biased, inadequate, or inappropriate practices are already proscribed under existing APA ethical guidelines (e.g., APA, 1981, Principle 2, Competence; Principle 7, Welfare of Client). Unfortunately, many other practices that the task force found to be both questionable and disturbing are not covered. Greater awareness of the potential problems and difficulties encountered by lesbian and gay male clients identified in this survey may help clinicians to avoid bias.

Problems with biased, inadequate, or inappropriate care are common. Fifty eight percent of the psychologists surveyed knew of negative incidents, including cases in which practitioners defined lesbians or gay men as "sick" and in need of change, and instances in which a client's sexual orientation distracted a therapist from treating the person's central problem. The provision of responsive psychotherapy services to all lesbian and gay male clients remains a challenge, but a challenge the profession can meet. A key step is to develop guidelines for appropriate psychotherapy with gay male and lesbian clients and to ensure that all psychologists receive adequate training.

The results also show that psychologists, regardless of their own sexual orientation, can provide appropriate and sensitive care to lesbians and gay men. The beneficial practices identified in this survey suggest issues and strategies that may help therapists provide ethical and competent care and that may point the way toward the development of lesbian- and gay-affirmative practice.

The issues identified by this survey do not fully exhaust the range of concerns about bias in the psychotherapeutic treatment of gay male and lesbian clients. Important issues not addressed in this study include AIDS; the potential invisibility and complex disclosure issues of gay male and lesbian clients during therapy; gender differences in the therapy experiences of gay men and lesbians; the possible relevance of the therapist's own sexual orientation; specific issues for gay and lesbian therapists (e.g., multiple roles in small communities); and issues that are covered in other APA ethical guidelines (e.g., sex between therapist and client).

Despite APA's 15-year-old nondiscrimination policy regarding lesbians and gay men, bias and misinformation persist among some psychologists. In this survey, 99% of the psychotherapy service providers reported having at least one lesbian or gay male client. It is therefore vital that the profession take the additional steps necessary to make the policy a reality. This can be achieved through education and training, expanded ethical and professional guidelines, and research. There is a clear need for further education to provide accurate information and to train psychologists to be sensitive to bias based on sexual orientation. Such training should be undertaken in every setting in which therapists are trained: graduate school (courses and supervision), professional in-service training, and continuing education programs. Graduate professional education must include instruction in this area for all new psychologists, not only for those who will specialize in the provision of psychotherapy to lesbians and gay men.

The results of this survey provide a starting point for the development of educational materials and model curricula for graduate and professional training, There is a growing research literature on sexual orientation (Garnets & Kimmel, 1991). This work should be disseminated widely to practicing psychologists. Some suggested readings regarding bias in therapy with lesbian and gay men as well as gay affirmative therapy are presented in Appendix B.

Moreover, the survey results raise new and challenging ethical issues. Some of these may not be addressed by existing ethical guidelines and must be discussed within the profession in terms of their implications for practice. Further research is needed to identify when bias based on sexual orientation occurs, to increase understanding of the processes through which biased judgements develop, and to test models to reduce bias.

The task force was impressed by the high response rate, by the high proportion of respondents who knew of incidents, and by the thousands of detailed responses and opinions provided in respondents' replies. We were also dismayed and disheartened at the evidence that, despite APA's formal, repeatedly stated nondiscriminatory policies, understanding, acceptance, and adherence to those goals are seriously lacking.

The APA must continue to promote its nondiscriminatory policies about homosexuality. New ways to enforce these policies among its members and to help practitioners achieve goals of nondiscriminatory, gay-affirmative practice must be found. For two decades, APA has taken the lead in encouraging mental health professionals to remove the stigma of mental illness from homosexuality and to provide unbiased and appropriate services to lesbians and gay men. The 1990s should be a time for renewed commitment to this important principle.

References

American Psychological Association. (1974). *Ethical standards for providers of psychological services.* Washington, DC: Author.

American Psychological Association. (1975). Report of the task force on sex bias and sex-role stereotyping in psychotherapeutic practice. *American Psychologist, 30,* 1169–1175.

American Psychological Association. (1977). Standards for providers of psychological services. *American Psychologist, 32,* 495–505.

American Psychological Association. (1981). Ethical principles of psychologists. *American Psychologist, 36,* 633–638.

Conger, J. (1975). Proceedings of the American Psychological Association, for the year 1974: Minutes of the annual meeting of Council of Representatives. *American Psychologist, 30,* 620–651.

Garnets, L., & Kimmel, D. (1991). Lesbian and gay male dimensions in the psychological study of human diversity. In J. Goodchilds (Ed.), *Psychological perspectives on human diversity in America* (pp. 137–192). Washington, DC: American Psychological Association.

Lopez, S. R. (1989). Patient variable biases in clinical judgement: Conceptual overview and methodological considerations. *Psychological Bulletin, 106,* 184–203.

Murray, J., & Abramson, P. R. (1983). *Bias in psychotherapy.* New York: Praeger.

APPENDIX A

Resolution Passed January, 1975, by American Psychological Association the Council of Representatives

The American Psychological Association supports the action taken on December 15, 1973 by the American Psychiatric Association, removing homosexuality from that Association's official list of mental disorders. The American Psychological Association therefore adopts the following resolution:

> Homosexuality, per se, implies no impairment in judgment, stability, reliability, or general social or vocational capabilities: Further, the American Psychological Association urges all mental health professionals to take the lead in removing the stigma of mental illness that has long been associated with homosexual orientations.

Regarding discrimination against homosexuals, the American Psychological Association adopts the following resolution concerning their civil and legal rights:

> The American Psychological Association deplores all public and private discrimination in such areas as employment, housing, public accommodation, and licensing against those who engage in or who have engaged in homosexual activities and declares that no burden of such judgment, capacity, or reliability shall be placed upon these individuals greater than that imposed on any other persons. Further, the American Psychological Association supports and urges the enactment of civil rights legislation at the local, state, and federal level that would offer citizens who engage in acts of homosexuality the same protections now guaranteed to others on the basis of race, creed. color, etc. Further, the American Psychological Association supports and urges the repeal of all discriminatory legislation singling out homosexual acts by consenting adults in private.

APPENDIX B

Bias in Therapy and Gay Male and Lesbian Affirmative Therapy
Suggested Readings

Bias in Therapy with Lesbians and Gay Men

Buhrke, R. A. (1989). Female student perspectives on training in lesbian and gay issues. *The Counseling Psychologist, 17,* 629–636.

Casas, J. M., Brady, S., & Ponterotti, J. G. (1983). Sexual preference biases in counseling: An information processing approach. *Journal of Counseling Psychology, 30,* 139–145.

Dardick, L., & Grady, K. E. (1981). Openness between gay persons and health professionals. *Annals of Internal Medicine, 93*(Part 1), 115–119.

Davison, G., & Friedman, S. (1981). Sexual orientation stereotyping in the distortion of clinical judgement. *Journal of Homosexuality, 6*(3), 37–44.

Davison, G., & Wilson, T. G. (1973). Attitudes of behavior therapists toward homosexuality. *Behavior Therapy, 4,* 686–696.

DeCrescenzo, T. (1983/1984). Homophobia: A study of the attitudes of mental health professionals toward homosexuality. *Journal of Social Work and Human Sexuality, 2*(2/3) 115–136.

Fort, J., Steiner, C. M., & Conrad, F. (1971). Attitudes of mental health professionals toward homosexuality and its treatments. *Psychological Reports, 29,* 347–350.

Gambrill, E., Stein, T., & Brown, C. (1983/1984). Social services use and need among gay/lesbian residents of the San Francisco Bay area. *Journal of Social Work and Human Sexuality, 3,* 51–68.

Garfinkle, E., & Morin, S. (1978). Psychotherapists' attitudes toward homosexual psychotherapy clients. *Journal of Social Issues, 34,* 101–112.

Gartrell, N., Kraemer, H., & Brodie, H. K. (1974). Psychiatrists' attitudes toward female homosexuality. *Journal of Nervous and Mental Disease, 159,* 141–144.

Glenn, A., & Russell, R. (1986). Heterosexual bias among counselor trainees. *Counselor Education and Supervision, 25,* 222–229.

Lief, H. (1977). Sexual survey #4: Current thinking on homosexuality. *Medical Aspects of Human Sexuality, 11,* 110–111.

Messing, A., Schoenberg, R., & Stephens, R. (1983/1984). Confronting homophobia in health care settings: Guidelines for social work practice. *Journal of Social Work and Human Sexuality, 2*(2/3). 65–74.

Morin, S. (1977). Heterosexual bias in psychological research on lesbianism and male homosexuality. *American Psychologist, 32,* 629–637.

Morin, S., & Charles, K. (1983). Heterosexual bias in psychotherapy. In J. Murray & P. R. Abramson (Eds.), *Bias in psychotherapy* (pp. 309–338). New York: Praeger.

Nuehring, E. M., Freinm, S. B., & Tyler, M. (1974). The gay college student: Perspectives for mental health professionals. *The Counseling Psychologist, 4*(4), 64–72.

Schwanberg, S. L. (1985). Changes in labeling homosexuality in health sciences literature: A preliminary investigation. *Journal of Homosexuality, 12*(1), 51–73.

Thompson, G. H., & Fishburn, W. R. (1977). Attitudes toward homosexuality among graduate counseling students. *Counselor Education and Supervision, 17,* 121–130.

Watters, A. (1986). Heterosexual bias in psychological research on lesbianism and male homosexuality (1979–1983): Utilizing the bibliographic and taxonomic system of Morin. *Journal of Homosexuality, 13,* 35–58.

Gay Male and Lesbian Affirmative Models of Therapy

Berzon, B. (1988). *Permanent partners: Building gay and lesbian relationships that last.* New York: E. P. Dutton.

Boston Lesbian Psychologies Collective (Eds.). (1987). *Lesbian psychologies: Explorations and challenges.* Urbana: University of Illinois Press.

Bozett, F. W. (Ed.). (1987). *Gay and lesbian parents.* New York: Praeger.

Bradford, J., & Ryan, C. (1987). *National lesbian health care survey: Mental health implications.* Washington, DC: National Lesbian–Gay Health Foundation.

Brown, L. S. (1989). New voices, new visions: Toward a lesbian/gay paradigm for psychology. *Psychology of Women Quarterly, 13,* 445–458.

Cabaj, R. (1988). Homosexuality and neurosis: Considerations for psychotherapy. *Journal of Homosexuality, 15*(1/2), 13–23.

Chan, C. S. (1989). Issues of identity development among Asian-American lesbians and gay men. *Journal of Counseling and Development, 68,* 16–20.

Coleman, E. (Ed.). (1987). Integrated identity for gay men and lesbians: Psychotherapeutic approaches for emotional well-being. *Journal of Homosexuality, 14*(1/2).

Collett, B. (Ed.). (1982). Psychotherapy with lesbians. *Women and Therapy, 1*(4).

Garnets, L., Herek, G. M., & Levy, B. (1990). Violence and victimization of lesbians and gay men: Mental health consequences. *Journal of Interpersonal Violence, 5,* 366–383.

Gartrell, N. (1984). Combatting homophobia in the psychotherapy of lesbians. *Women and Therapy, 3,* 13–29.

Gochros, H. (1983/1984). Teaching social workers to meet the needs of the homosexually oriented. *Journal of Social Work and Human Sexuality, 2*(2/3), 137–156.

Gonsiorek, J. (Ed.). (1982). *Homosexuality and psychotherapy: A practitioner's handbook of affirmative models.* New York: Haworth Press.

Gonsiorek, J. C. (1982). Homosexuality: The end of an illness. *American Behavioral Scientist, 25*(4).

Gonsiorek, J. C. (1988). Current and future directions in gay/lesbian affirmative mental health practice. In M. Shernoff & W. Scott (Eds.), *The sourcebook on lesbian/gay health care* (2nd ed., pp. 107–113). Washington, DC: National Lesbian–Gay Health Foundation.

Graham, D., Rawlings, E., Halpern, H., & Hermes, J. (1984). Therapists needs for training in counseling lesbians and gay men. *Professional Psychology: Research and Practice, 15,* 482–496

Harrison, J. (1987). Counseling gay men. In M. Scher, M. Stevens, G. Good, & G. Eichenfield (Eds.), *Handbook of counseling and psychotherapy with men* (pp 220–231). Newbury Park, CA: Sage.

Hetrick, E. S., & Stein, T. S. (Eds.). (1984). *Innovations in psychotherapy with homosexuals.* Washington, DC: American Psychiatric Press.

Hidalgo, H., Peterson, T. L., & Woodman, N. J. (Eds.). (1985). *Lesbian and gay issues: A resource manual for social workers.* Silver Spring, MD: National Association of Social Workers.

Isay, R. (1985). On the analytic therapy of homosexual men. In A. Solnit, P. Eissler, & P. Neubarger (Eds.). *Psychoanalytic Study of the Child* (pp. 234–255). New Haven, CT: Yale University Press.

Kingdon, M. A. (1979). Lesbians. *Thc Counseling Psychologist, 8,* 44–45.

Krajeski, J. (1986). Psychotherapy with gay men and lesbians: A history of controversy. In C. Cohen & T. Stein (Eds.). *Contemporary perspectives on psychotherapy with lesbians and gay men* (pp. 9–26). New York: Plenum.

Loiacano, D. K. (1989). Gay identity issues among Black Americans: Racism, homophobia, and the need for validation. *Journal of Counseling and Development, 68,* 21–25.

Malyon, A. (1982). Biphasic aspects of homosexual identity formation. *Psychotherapy: Theory, Research and Practice, 19,* 335–340.

Martin, A. (1982). Some issues in the treatment of gay and lesbian patients. *Psychotherapy: Theory, Research, and Practice, 19,* 341–348

McWhirter, D. P., & Mattison, A. M. (1984). *Male couples: A study of how relationships develop.* Englewood Cliffs, NJ: Prentice Hall.

Moses, A. E., & Hawkins, R. O. (1982). *Counseling lesbian women and gay men: A life issues approach.* St. Louis, MO: Mosby.

Rabin, J., Keefe, K., & Burton, M. (1986). Enhancing services for sexual-minority clients: A community mental health approach. *Social Work, 31*(4), 294–298.

Riddle, D., & Sang, B. (1978). Psychotherapy with lesbians. *Journal of Social Issues, 34*(3), 84–100.

Rothblum, E. D., & Cole, E. (Eds.). (1989). Lesbianism: Affirming nontraditional roles. *Women and Therapy, 8*(1/2).

Scasta, D. L. (1989 & 1990). *Journal of Gay and Lesbian Psychotherapy,* all volumes.

Schoenberg, R., & Goldberg, R. S. (1985). *With compassion toward some: Homosexuality and social work in America.* New York: Haworth.

Stein, T. (1988). Theoretical considerations in psychotherapy with gay men and lesbians. *Journal of Homosexuality, 15,* 75–95,

Stein, T., & Cohen, C. (Eds.). (1986). *Psychotherapy with lesbians and gay men.* New York: Plenum.

Winkelpleck, J. M., & Westfeld, J. S. (1982). Counseling considerations with gay couples. *The Personnel and Guidance Journal, 60,* 294–296.

Woodman, N. J., & Lenna, H. R. (1980). *Counseling with gay men and women.* San Francisco: Jossey-Bass.

16

Affirmative Psychotherapy for Lesbian Women

Christine Browning, Amy L. Reynolds,
and Sari H. Dworkin

There is a full range of psychological issues within the lesbian community, as in all communities, which may be addressed within a therapeutic context. Lesbians struggle with the same intra- and interpersonal issues that nongays experience. Yet lesbians also experience concerns that are uniquely related to surviving in a world that is heterosexist and homophobic.

As psychologists, we must be willing and able to offer affirmative psychotherapy for lesbian women and work to educate the nongay community to accept and celebrate lesbian relationships and communities. We must seek out information and experiences that will educate us about the unique concerns that lesbian women face, and we must learn about the theories and therapeutic strategies necessary for effective therapy with lesbian clients.

This article presents a theoretical overview of issues in counseling lesbian women, as well as offering suggestions for effective therapeutic interventions with lesbian clients. Sections of this article include identity development, identity management, interpersonal issues, and special issues germane to counseling lesbians such as substance abuse, domestic violence, and sexual abuse. We conclude with recommendations for treatment and suggestions for research.

Identity Development

In the broadest sense, "coming out" as a lesbian is "adopting a nontraditional identity [and] involves restructuring one's self-concept, reorganizing one's personal sense of history, and altering one's relations with others and with society" (DeMonteflores & Schultz, 1978, p. 61). Many psychological models

From C. Browning, A. L. Reynolds, and S. H. Dworkin, "Affirmative Psychotherapy for Lesbian Women" in *The Counseling Psychologist, 19,* 177–196, 1991. Copyright © 1991. Reprinted by permission of Sage Publications, Inc., Newbury Park, CA.

of identity formation have examined how lesbian women and gay men experience the lifelong process of coming out to themselves and others (Fassinger, this issue). Here we highlight those aspects of the identity development process unique to lesbians.

The issues affecting lesbians can be best understood by examining the situation of many women in U.S. culture. Growing up in a sexist culture creates a double bind for women and, therefore, lesbians (Vargo, 1987). If women fulfill their traditional socialized roles and behaviors (e.g., caregiver, dependent), then they are seen as unhealthy. Yet if women step outside their prescribed gender-role expectations and take on behaviors and roles ascribed to men (e.g., provider, instrumentality), they are often seen as inappropriate (Vargo, 1987). By choosing to be woman-identified, lesbians construct their self-image differently from heterosexual women (Vargo, 1987). Research suggests that some lesbians may reject a stereotypic female role early in their development (Groves, 1985); however, even lesbians characterized by the stereotypic female role will encounter homophobia in their daily lives.

The lesbian community provides a social context in which a woman can define herself as lesbian (Groves, 1985) and has helped women to develop an awareness of the dynamics of being female and lesbian. Because the boundaries of acceptable role behavior are often different within the lesbian community, lesbians may find support there for aspects of their identity as women that are not traditionally accepted by the nongay community (Moses & Hawkins, 1982). According to DeMonteflores and Schultz (1978), feminism and the women's movement facilitated the coming-out process for many lesbians by providing a sense of solidarity, community, and positive role models, which are vital to the formation of a positive lesbian identity (Sophie, 1988). Despite homophobia within the feminist community, many lesbians have felt safer coming out within the women's movement rather than in the male-dominated gay movement (Clinton, 1989).

Women may also develop their lesbian identity by a different route than gay men, because of the influence of feminist culture. Faderman (1984) identifies three phases of self-definition for lesbians, which she believes may be reversed for gay men: (a) critical evaluation of dominant social norms, (b) encounters with stigma and internalized homophobia, and (c) sexual experiences. Faderman's work, though controversial, suggests that for at least some lesbians, the feminist community provides a facilitative sociopolitical context for the development of erotic preferences. Therapists can help clients in all phases of the identity development process to participate in lesbian or feminist communities, thereby using the potentially facilitative environment for the development of a positive lesbian identity.

Identity Management

The process of identity management is an ongoing, ever-changing process through which one defines and redefines what it means to be lesbian or gay (Cass, 1979). As has been suggested, increased contact with the lesbian community, as well as a broadening definition of what it means to be a lesbian, creates an opportunity for a positive identity even within a homophobic culture.

Coming Out to Others

Coming out to friends and family is an important step in the process of claiming a positive and integrated identity and is crucial for self-acceptance and self-esteem (Murphy, 1989). Unlike nongays or members of particular racial groups, lesbian women are usually part of a culture to which their parents do not belong (Zitter, 1987). Lesbians may come out to family or friends in order to decrease feelings of isolation and to maintain a sense of personal integrity. As women, lesbians are often relationship-oriented; as a result, coming out to others may be especially stressful (Zitter, 1987).

Regardless of preparation, a family's response to self-disclosure often is unpredictable (Griffin, Wirth, & Wirth, 1986). Families may need time to unlearn negative messages about lesbians and to grieve the loss of expectations and hopes. Families may respond in many ways. They may be immediately accepting, they may try to ignore or deny the new information, or they may reject the family member temporarily or permanently. The process of coming out to one's family is also affected by long-standing family patterns and dysfunctions. Old family wounds, such as alcoholism and sexual abuse, may be reopened while the family is in conflict, which further complicates this process and creates additional pain, vulnerability, and confusion (Brown, 1988).

Nongay friends may have less difficulty accepting a friend's self-disclosure because they have less at stake in her identity and less involvement in her future life (Moses & Hawkins, 1982). Both families and close friends have their own coming out to do and may also become targets of homophobia and discrimination. In fact, families often have limited support systems, and this isolation makes their process of acceptance more difficult (Brown, 1988). Thus the adjustment and acceptance of families is often determined by the availability of resources and social support (Neisen, 1988).

Therapists can aid a lesbian woman in her decision-making process about how to come out and with whom to share her identity. By examining her motivations, goals, and the potential costs and benefits of sharing her lesbian identity with others, she will be able to make the most positive decision. Therapists must help ensure that alternative social supports are available and that different methods (by letter, in person) have been explored (see Berzon [1988] for a thorough discussion of coming out issues).

Occupational/Career Issues

Coming out as a lesbian has implications for choosing a career and managing one's identity within a career. A lesbian woman may realize at an early age that she will never depend on a man's salary (Hetherington & Orzek, 1989) and may, therefore, choose a male-dominated occupation in order to maximize her earning potential. Because women, however, are still not widely supported in pursuing nontraditional occupations (Wilcox-Matthew & Minor, 1989), lesbians who have chosen these occupations may experience discrimination and other difficulties. A lesbian will need to decide if she wants to work in an occupation in which her sexual orientation need not be hidden, because self-disclosure in many occupations will result in overt or covert discrimination (Hetherington & Orzek, 1989). For example, many lesbians in such fields as teaching, child care, and child psychology remain "closeted" because of the myth that they recruit children to the gay life-style. A lesbian woman may choose to live in a large city or become involved in national gay/lesbian professional organizations in order to decrease feelings of isolation.

The interdependence of careers and relationships is also important for many lesbians (Berzon, 1988). Lesbian couples face the same dual-career issues as nongay couples, but because their relationship is not validated by society, they usually cannot get support or assistance in dealing with these issues (Hetherington & Orzek, 1989). Therapists can help clients explore occupational options and distinguish between realistic and unrealistic fears; they can also provide information and support, as the following case example illustrates:

> Kay is a 22-year-old confident, assertive lesbian woman. She enjoys working outdoors with her hands and wants to earn a good salary, so she decided to become a construction worker. She recently enrolled in a local community college's 2-year program. Kay decided to see a counselor when the sexist remarks of the male students and teachers began affecting her self-esteem. Kay was one of only two women in the program. Some of the male students frequently alluded to the fact that women do not belong in the construction trades and that any woman who is interested in this field must be "queer." Kay was terrified that they would discover that she was a lesbian.
>
> When Kay entered therapy she was depressed, and not eating or sleeping well. She did not want to give up the program and yet was unsure if she could continue to handle the hostile climate. Kay was very involved in the lesbian community and had a good support system. Her friends supported her interest in construction, which increased Kay's concern that she might betray the community if she left the program. Therapy consisted of providing a safe environment to express her anger and frustration, cognitive disputations of irrational beliefs, role-playing ways to approach male instructors and students, assertiveness training to express discomfort with community expectations for her, and rehearsal of behavioral responses to potential problems.

Race, Ethnicity, Class, Locale

The development of a lesbian identity does not occur in a vacuum. Intrapsychic dimensions play a part in identity development, as well as factors such as race, ethnicity, class, and locale. For women of some racial and ethnic groups, acceptance of a lesbian identity means violating the role expectations of the culture (Chan, 1989; Espin, 1987; Loiacano, 1989). Women of such groups are polycultural and multiply oppressed (Espin, 1987), identified as a woman in patriarchal culture, as a minority in a culture that is racist and anti-Semitic, and as a lesbian in a homophobic culture.

Lesbian women who are members of certain racial and ethnic groups need to balance their identities within the lesbian/gay culture and within their racial/ethnic communities. The limited research available suggests that developing a lesbian identity may be the more salient process (Chan, 1989; Espin, 1987; Loiacano, 1989). Research suggests (e.g., Chan, 1989) that more social interaction as an ethnic woman or woman of color takes place within the lesbian community than interaction as a lesbian within her racial/ethnic communities. This often creates problems because the lesbian community itself is permeated by racism (Chan, 1989; Espin, 1987) and anti-Semitism (Beck, 1982). Because coming out to families within racial/ethnic communities often means rejection and loss of support, survival in a racist culture becomes more difficult. Larger urban areas may offer opportunities for women to more effectively integrate both aspects of their identity because of the availability of a wider variety of racial/ethnic lesbian organizations.

There has been little research on rural lesbian women or research examining the impact of class or socioeconomic status on the development of a lesbian identity. Many authors believe that the isolation of rural lesbians, the lack of information about lesbians, the lack of role models, and the homophobia present in rural communities affect the coming-out process (D'Augelli, 1989; Moses & Buckner, 1986). The key to managing a lesbian identity in rural areas is discretion (D'Augelli, 1989); thus a major challenge for the rural lesbian is meeting other lesbians. Sometimes the anxiety over being discovered is so severe that rural lesbians isolate themselves from most social situations (Moses & Buckner, 1986). Isolated from other lesbians and in need of social support, rural lesbians are less likely to self-disclose to their families because they fear the loss of family contact. One major consequence of isolation is the difficulty in meeting potential partners; thus rural lesbians often resign themselves to being single and lonely, or they may stay in long-term relationships that are dysfunctional (Moses & Buckner, 1986). The difficulties of rural life for lesbians often lead to low self-esteem and offer a special challenge to therapists working in these geographical areas.

Age-Related Issues

There are two areas on the aging continuum which are frequently neglected in research on lesbian lives: the young and the old. Each has unique needs and issues which are not always captured by our current generic models of lesbian identity development. Coming out for the adolescent lesbian is generally more difficult than for the adult lesbian (Schneider, 1989). The adolescent generally is more dependent (economically and emotionally) on her family, which intensifies her fear of parental rejection. She also has more restricted access to the lesbian/gay community for support and guidance. The young lesbian does not typically have adult lesbian role models available to help her develop a positive lesbian identity. Because most lesbians are raised in nongay households, they do not learn how to cope with societal discrimination. Lesbians of some racial/ethnic groups may learn from parents how to deal with racism, but they will not learn coping strategies to deal with the heterosexism and homophobia within their own culture as well as the dominant culture.

There are two major areas in which lesbian adolescents may need assistance: (a) making decisions about coming out to family, and (b) developing a social support network. If a lesbian adolescent chooses to come out to her parents, the therapist can identify resources to help parents (e.g., Griffin et al., 1986). Frequently the young lesbian feels as though she is the "only one." Gibson (1988) found that of suicide attempts among adolescents, approximately one third are thought to be related to concerns about sexual orientation. Therapists should help young lesbians identify resources that will reduce isolation and facilitate the development of a social support network (see Gerstel, Feraiso, & Herdt, 1989, for a description of a lesbian and gay youth program in a lesbian/gay community). Books, newsletters, films, and lesbian and woman-identified music may help the young lesbian feel connected to the larger lesbian and gay community.

At the other end of the age continuum are older lesbians. Most of the research on the aged ignores issues of sexual orientation or focuses on relationship issues within traditional heterosexual marriages (Fassinger & Schlossberg, in press). In addition to the era and chronological age at which a woman came out, other variables such as ethnicity/race, health status, economic resources, and strength of her social support system must also be considered. As lesbians age, they become aware of the potential need to interact with professional caregivers. However, in her study on midlife (over 50) lesbian women, Tully (1989) found reluctance to be completely open about sexual orientation with caregivers and unwillingness to trust caregiving systems and the legal system. Kehoe (1988), in her study of 100 lesbians over 60, found that the most serious problems expressed by old lesbian women were loneliness and economic worries. As therapists, we must be sensitive to the needs of the older lesbian by recognizing the impact on identity of coming out during an era when lesbians were viewed as sick or sinful. Health-care institutions, as well as senior-services centers, must be monitored for systematic discrimination or ignorance of the needs of the older lesbian, and advocacy interventions must be implemented as needed.

Interpersonal Issues

No matter how well integrated into the nongay culture or how supported one feels by a lesbian community, being a lesbian creates a feeling of alienation and marginality. Even in supportive settings, there is always the experience of being "other" (Brown, 1989), which affects one's identity and self-esteem, as well as having pervasive impact on interpersonal relationships.

Lesbian Couples

All romantic relationships have certain qualities in common, yet lesbian couples can never be viewed separate from their socialization as women or their experience of living and loving in a homophobic culture. Because the heterosexual world does not honor lesbian relationships and offers little institutional or personal support for them, lesbians often see their relationships as temporary or unimportant (Pharr, 1988). Few role models exist for lesbians to learn how to maintain long-term relationships. Public affection, relationship rituals (such as weddings and bridal showers), and legal benefits represent several examples of social support to which most lesbian couples do not have access. Berzon (1988) outlines three factors that block long-term lesbian relationships: (a) expectation of failure, (b) lack of legal and social supports, and (c) invisibility of long-term relationships. These factors exacerbate many of the conflict areas experienced by lesbian couples, such as power, autonomy and intimacy, sex, monogamy versus nonmonogamy, stages in the coming-out process, role-playing, differences of race and culture, political and class differences, and money and family conflicts (Berzon, 1988; Clunis & Green, 1988). Many of these issues are common in nongay relationships as well, but several deserve discussion, as they affect lesbian couples in unique ways.

Nonmonogamy is a major area of ongoing attention within the lesbian community. Often monogamy is seen as a patriarchal value (Toder, 1979), and nonmonogamy is seen as a political statement about disclaiming ownership of one's partner. Lesbian nonmonogamy is often open and consciously planned and consists of ongoing, rather than casual, sexual affairs (Kassoff, 1989). Lesbians also express a strong desire for equality and shared power within relationships (Peplau, Cochran, Rook, & Padesky, 1978), and often dislike conventional relational roles (Clunis & Green, 1988). Although these relationship values may be strongly espoused by some lesbian couples, there are often many differences in each partner's expectations, confounded by the reality of trying to maintain a relationship within a nonsupportive context.

When a couple's differences threaten the relationship, therapists can help partners learn to negotiate. The female socialization process may create a tendency in lesbians to listen to each other intensely but to have difficulty in asserting their own needs, thereby blocking the resolution of issues (Roth, 1989). Traditional female gender-role socialization also has encouraged women to value a high degree of emotional intimacy in relationships. As a result, when two women form a relationship, there is a tremendous potential for emotional closeness between partners (McCandlish, 1982). In addition, there are elements of lesbian relationships that support the value of women's individual independence. When individuals are able to achieve a balance between the need for autonomy and the need for intimacy, the relationship will frequently be perceived as satisfying. When this balance is not present, couples frequently experience conflicts over power, dependency, and nurturing within the relationship (Burch, 1987).

Many authors have discussed the issue of fusion in lesbian relationships, that is, the difficulty of maintaining separate identities within the relationship, and a tendency for merging in thoughts, actions, or feelings (Burch, 1982; Kresten & Bepko, 1980; Pearlman, 1989). For some, this merger or fusion is a more pervasive state, in which excessive dependency leads to tension and anxiety when there is emotional and/or physical distance between partners. Sometimes couples find themselves merged when there is a perceived threat to either the relationship or a member of the couple; given societal homophobia and heterosexism, there is always an underlying threat to lesbian couples, and additional energy must be put into defining and affirming relationship boundaries. For example, during holiday times, the parents of a lesbian woman may ignore her relationship by expecting their daughter to come home without her partner, forcing the daughter to assert more adamantly her commitment to her partner, or to capitulate to family demands and later make up for the denial by increased attention to her partner and by self-imposed social isolation. Hence societal homophobia reinforces a propensity for merging.

Helping couples achieve balance between intimacy and autonomy requires that therapists not impose their own ideas of appropriate balance (McCandlish, 1982), and couples groups may be especially helpful to lesbian couples for support in maintaining healthy relationships. Therapists can also facilitate an understanding of the role that heterosexist culture plays in creating relationship stress, which can result in either emotional distance or enmeshment.

Because lesbian communities are often small, interracial couples are fairly common and the impact of racial/cultural differences must be addressed because each partner will experience the relationship differently based on her race (Garcia, Kennedy, Pearlman, & Perez, 1987). A Caucasian woman, for example, may experience extreme guilt and pain when she hurts her partner in an intended or unintended way; her partner, on the other hand, may experience pain, hurt, and rage when the woman closest to her appears to be "the enemy" (Garcia et al., 1987). Many women of color or ethnic women have experienced multiple interracial friendships or relationships, whereas Caucasian women often have little history of significant interracial relationships. Interracial relationships create risks for both women, including loss of support from family or racial/ethnic community, daily stresses of dealing with racism as a couple, and misunderstanding and miscommunication, as the following case example illustrates:

> When Toni and Megan entered therapy, they had been in a relationship for 2 years. Toni was a 32-year-old African-American woman who worked as an

attorney for a local firm. Megan was a 29-year-old Caucasian woman who was completing a doctorate in women's studies and sociology. Megan was very active and "out" in the women's community and had an open relationship with her family while Toni was more cautious with whom she disclosed their relationship. Megan resented how Toni's decision to be closeted was beginning to affect their relationship and their social support networks. Toni was angered by Megan's inability to understand the complexities of being an African-American lesbian.

Couples therapy began with an emphasis on listening to and expressing feelings, and discussing the dynamics of being an interracial couple. Their social group was mostly Caucasian women, which made Toni feel like an outsider. Megan began to realize that she had never examined her privilege as a Caucasian woman and how those dynamics affected their relationship. Using a conflict resolution and negotiation model allowed each woman to express her feelings and feel heard. Therapy created more empathy in their relationship and improved their communication skills, especially with angry feelings. They made some agreements about changes they both wanted in the relationship including broadening their social group, making initial introductions between Megan and Toni's family, and deciding to join an interracial couples' support group.

Sexual issues are another area of potential difficulty in lesbian relationships. Loulan (1984) describes lesbian sex as "anything that two lesbians do together," implying that lesbian sexuality and its importance to individual women cannot be described simply. Not all lesbians engage in all forms of sexual behaviors, and there are very few studies that have examined what actually constitutes sex for lesbians (Loulan, 1987). The definition of lesbian sex is important primarily in its meaning for the couple; thus the focus should be on the individual's and couple's perceptions of what constitutes sex rather than societal or therapists' definitions. According to Berzon (1988), women are programmed to prefer a loving context for their sexual expression, and the type of sexual contact commonly expressed by lesbian couples may emphasize cuddling or passionate kissing, in addition to genital contact (Clunis & Green, 1988).

Discrepancy in sexual desire and absence of sexual desire are the most frequent problems reported by lesbian couples (Hall, 1987). Blumstein and Schwartz (1983) report that the decrease in sexual frequency sometimes experienced by lesbian couples is related to lack of time, lack of physical energy, and becoming accustomed to one's partner. Hall (1987) suggests that although the initial merging between partners is experienced as highly erotic, after time it becomes necessary for individuality to emerge in order to reactivate erotic interest. Therapists can help clients negotiate intimacy and autonomy as a way to increase sexual satisfaction.

Absence of sexual desire may be related to the mixed messages about sexuality given to women in our culture (see Loulan, 1984). These messages about female sexuality are combined with negative messages about lesbians and can be powerful inhibitors toward the positive expression of lesbian sexuality (Loulan, 1987). When these negative messages are internalized, they may become manifested in shame, anxiety, guilt, or avoidance of sex. Also the process of recovery influences lesbian sexuality, whether the recovery is from chemical dependency, eating disorders, emotional/physical illness, or sexual abuse (discussed later in this article). It should be noted that although lesbian women are in the lowest risk category for the transmission of sexually transmitted diseases (STDs) and AIDS, they should give full consideration to the precautions for safer sex (Loulan, 1987); also, lesbians who are seeking to become pregnant through insemination may be at risk for AIDS if the donor has engaged in high-risk behavior, and appropriate caution should be exercised.

Increasing numbers of lesbians are choosing to parent (see Fassinger, this issue). There have always been lesbian mothers and families; in the past, however, most children of lesbian families were conceived in the context of a nongay relationship and later the mother came out as a lesbian. Today many lesbian women are choosing to have children, either within a relationship or as single parents (Clunis & Green, 1988).

There are several excellent resource books available for lesbians contemplating parenthood (Alpert, 1988; Pies, 1985). Deciding to become a lesbian mother requires a great deal of planning and decision making, with attention to issues such as deciding how to get pregnant or adopt a child; coming out (to children, child-care and school personnel); the role of the nonbiological mother and the impact of having two mothers; and concerns about the child's reactions and welfare in a context of societal prejudice. Where children are already present, the loss of custody becomes an important issue because the legal system rests on homophobic and sexist assumptions that question the fitness of a lesbian mother. Despite prejudice, studies that have examined these issues have not found any deleterious effects on children raised by lesbian mothers (Falk, 1989).

A final parenting issue to consider is the impact of children on the couple's relationship. One major stress for lesbian couples is the invisibility of the nonbiological parent and the lack of legal rights for the nonbiological parent in the event of the mother's death or the dissolution of the relationship. When a couple decides to have children or begin a relationship in which there are already children, there may also be changes in the couple's support system. These reactions are important because for many lesbians, friendships serve as alternative families. Lesbian mothers need to learn how to renegotiate their relationships with friends and/or develop new support groups that provide such opportunities.

Despite the large number of enduring lesbian relationships, many relationships between women end, whether by choice, illness, death, or other means. The lack of legal and social support can contribute to the dissolution of the relationship, and it also makes the parting more difficult (Becker, 1988). Engelhardt and Triantafillou (1987) discuss the viability of a lesbian/feminist mediation process as a method for dealing with both legal and emotional ramifications created by the ending of relationships. Lesbians ending relationships may need to come out publicly in order to receive the support they need. Also, because many lesbians come out in the context of a relationship, the loss of that relationship may threaten their lesbian identity. However, Becker (1988) has pointed out that because women have traditionally been socialized to put others' needs first, the end of a relationship can be an opportunity to redefine priorities that reflect her emerging needs.

Research indicates that most lesbians report friends as their primary source of support during a relationship termination (Becker, 1988). However, lesbian couples need to negotiate how to communicate with friends and establish separate spaces for themselves with friends within the context of small communities and overlapping social networks. In fact, one of the unique elements of lesbian relationships is that many ex-lovers continue to be friends and maintain close ties with each other (Becker, 1988). Thus the need to negotiate the ex-lover relationship may reflect not only the previous level of emotional bonding between partners, but also the reality of lesbian communities, where women may continue to socialize, attend cultural events, and work on political activities together. Therapists can help their lesbian clients by identifying strategies to facilitate the transition between ending a partner relationship and developing a friendship relationship with an ex-lover.

Special Issues in Counseling Lesbians
Substance Abuse

An issue of special concern to the lesbian community is substance abuse. Research indicates that the rates of substance abuse are higher for lesbians than for nongay women and that lesbians are more likely to be children of an alcoholic parent (Glaus, 1989). As members of an oppressed group, lesbians experience ongoing discrimination, and some authors point to a connection between oppression and addiction (Nicoloff & Stiglitz, 1987). A confounding factor is that, historically, bars were often the only place where lesbian women could meet one another. Even today, for many lesbians, the bar continues to be the first place to explore one's sexual identity. In order to access alternatives to the bar culture, a lesbian must be at the point in her identity development where she is comfortable enough to participate in community-oriented groups and activities that may require a greater degree of self-disclosure and identity acceptance (Glaus, 1989).

Internalized homophobia is thought by some authors to influence the use of drugs and alcohol (Glaus, 1989). In the early stages of the coming-out process, a woman may experience conflict between the emerging awareness of her lesbian sexual orientation and the social prejudices she has internalized. Using drugs/alcohol may be an attempt to numb herself to her emotions and to avoid accepting herself as a lesbian. Glaus (1989) notes that the chemically dependent lesbian may also use denial to protect herself from an unsupportive social environment.

Unique factors experienced by lesbians must be incorporated within treatment approaches. Some of these issues involve whether or not to come out to staff while in treatment; the involvement of the lesbian's partner and friendship network in her recovery; and the difficulty some lesbian clients have with the Alcoholic Anonymous (AA) model, as well as group members who might express homophobic and sexist attitudes. Lesbians who are involved with recovering substance abusers or who grew up in alcoholic homes may utilize the resources of Al-Anon or Adult Children of Alcoholics (ACOA) groups, with attention to the issues already noted. The therapist who is knowledgeable about lesbian and gay community resources that address chemical dependency will be better able to assist her/his client in achieving and maintaining sobriety in the context of an affirming social environment.

Domestic Violence

Since the early 1980s, domestic-violence service providers have been witnessing physical abuse within lesbian relationships and describing intervention strategies for both mental health providers and the lesbian community (e.g., Hart, 1986). Despite the minimal empirical data regarding the frequency of abuse in lesbian couples, abusive relationships occur across all socioeconomic classes, ages, and ethnicities/races (Hart, 1986). There is a myth that lesbians, because of their socialization as women and commitment to egalitarian relationships, do not encounter domestic violence. Lesbians, however, do engage in physical abuse and the reasons are similar to those of male abusers: the belief that others exist for the abuser's well-being, possessiveness, the need to dominate, and often abuse of alcohol and drugs (Hart, 1986). It is important for therapists to recognize, however, that although chemical abuse may be a factor, women may remain abusive even after recovery from their addiction (Morrow & Hawkhurst, 1989).

There are some significant issues about lesbian violence that are critical for understanding the lesbian survivor's experience. These issues relate to (a) the denial of the existence of lesbian violence within the lesbian community; (b) the victim's difficulty in identifying the abuse (often because the victim has exercised self-defense); (c) the lack of adequately trained service providers; and (d) the difficulties domestic violence shelters experience in providing services to lesbians because of the fear that funding sources will be cut. Effective intervention strategies must focus not only on individual treatment for the victim and abuser but also on education about domestic violence within the lesbian community.

Sexual Abuse

A survey by Loulan (1987) found that 38% of lesbians had experienced sexual abuse from a family member or stranger before the age of 18, which is similar to the proportion of nongay women who have experienced abuse. The high proportion of women who have experienced sexual abuse suggests that there is a high probability in lesbian couples that one or both of the partners will be survivors of abuse. This poses some unique challenges for the lesbian couple because they may be at different stages of the recovery process or have different needs. Frequently a survivor may experience flashbacks of the abuse during sex or be unable to engage in sex, which may anger, frustrate, or even trigger a flashback for the partner.

In addition, clients may believe that their lesbian identity results from prior sexual abuse. Information about the prevalence of abuse among nongay women, with an emphasis on sexual orientation as an attraction to women rather than a rejection of men, may help clients separate feelings about sexual abuse from concerns about sexual orientation. Many communities have incest/sexual abuse groups and services for survivors and their partners; these groups, however, are not always inclusive of lesbians or their partners, or designed to meet their unique needs, and therapists may be needed to advocate for such services. The following case example illustrates some of the issues related to sexual abuse:

> Terry, a 45-year-old, Caucasian lesbian, sought therapy after the ending of her 2-year relationship. This had been her first long-term relationship and was the first time Terry had experienced any sadness when a relationship had ended. The relationship ended in a familiar way when Terry initiated an affair with a mutual friend. Terry grew up in a chaotic family system. Her alcoholic father spent time in prison and her mother was chronically ill and died when Terry was a young teenager. When Terry was 10 and her parents were unavailable, she was molested daily by her uncle. She reported that this was the only time she remembered feeling loved.
>
> As an adult she always conveyed a strong, independent image to others while feeling very vulnerable and scared. Terry coped with these feelings by frequent casual sex, binge eating, and compulsive shopping. She had previously abused drugs and alcohol but had been sober for 5 years prior to beginning therapy. Insight-oriented therapy focused on increasing Terry's self-esteem by developing self-nurturing behaviors and restructuring self-perceptions. Terry gained insight regarding how she had connected sex with affection and attention. She also recognized how her mistrust of women and difficulty in establishing nonsexual friendships was related to her experiences of sexual abuse and inadequate parenting. The breakup had given her "permission" to grieve for years of unmet emotional needs and begin to change her pattern of controlling her level of emotional involvement in relationships. In therapy she was able to begin to develop stronger personal boundaries and relate more honestly with others.

Spiritual and Existential Issues

Rainone (1987) defines spirituality as compassion for self and for others. Prior to the women's movement, the lesbian social scene consisted of bars, softball, and secret organizations (DeCrescenzo & Fifield, 1979). Although these outlets still exist, the feminist movement gave rise to a politically active community that created a political analysis of the oppression of lesbians (Pearlman, 1987). Lesbians may create meaning in their lives by working to end oppression while at the same time developing friendship networks and creating alternative families.

Traditionally, people have met their spiritual needs through caring for others and through religion. The Western Judeo-Christian tradition has not been kind to lesbian women, with scriptural interpretations, customs, and religious doctrine used to create shame (Ritter & O'Neill, 1989). Thus many lesbians have left the church and others have joined groups such as Metropolitan Community Church and gay/lesbian synagogues within the Reform Jewish Movement in order to meet spiritual needs within an accepting context (Ritter & O'Neill, 1989). Still others have recreated witchcraft or the goddess movement, where women and those who are not bound by rigid gender roles are esteemed and valued (Adler, 1986).

Therapists can help lesbians recognize and validate needs for spiritual community and discover how to fulfill them. Awareness of gay/lesbian organizations within existing religions and alternatives to traditional religion will help therapists provide these resources for clients seeking to meet their spiritual needs.

Conclusions and Recommendations

In this article, we have provided a broad overview of many of the issues that challenge lesbians in contemporary living, including some suggestions for therapeutic interventions. The other articles in this issue articulate many of the specific guidelines critical in working effectively with lesbian and gay clients (i.e., confidentiality, therapist attitudes incorporating diversity, and the impact of societal oppression on identity). The following are recommendations that we would like to add, pertaining to therapeutic and research work with lesbian women:

1. *Feminist therapy.* The recognition that the personal is political is a basic tenet of feminist therapy. Working with lesbian clients requires that the therapist acknowledge the influence that heterosexism and sexism have on lesbian women and the concerns that they bring to therapy. Feminist therapy incorporates the reality of societal oppression into the therapeutic work, recognizes the role of power differences within the therapist/client relationship, and recognizes the impact that gender, ethnicity/race, and sexual orientation have on the experience of both the client and therapist.

     Therapists can help empower the lesbian client by acknowledging that she is the expert about her life, by demystifying the process of therapy, by making relevant self-disclosures to facilitate client growth, and by collaboratively negotiating the goals of therapy. Therapists must ensure that they are aware of any biases that might impair their ability to respect the lesbian client's life experience.

2. *Advocacy.* As Fassinger (this issue) notes, the field of psychology does not have a long history of providing affirmative psychotherapy to lesbian and gay people and has been used as an instrument of social control to label difference as deviance. As gay and lesbian people assert their right to exist and to access the rights and privileges accorded to nongay people, there are growing efforts to criminalize and label lesbians and gays as mentally ill. The current resurgence, for example, of the "reparative therapies" to "convert" lesbians and gays to heterosexuality is one area in which psychology is again being used as an agent of social control (Welch, 1990). Although the American Psychological Association (APA) has made several policy statements that a person's sexual orientation is not indicative of psychological impairment, psychologists must do more. Psychologists (including nongay psychologists) can be in very powerful positions to serve as advocates for lesbian and gay people, and they have the expertise and credibility to educate society about these issues. With specific training, as described in more detail by Buhrke and Douce (this issue), psychologists can serve as expert witnesses in child-custody cases; help to organize services in communities where none exist; and provide sensitivity training in hospitals, police departments, community agencies, schools, churches, and mental-health training programs.

3. *Research implications.* The literature that has been published on lesbian women has primarily presented survey research, theoretical articles, and clinical observations. More empirical research needs to be done in a number of areas that involve the daily life challenges faced by lesbians and ways to change social attitudes to eliminate homophobia and heterosexism. The following are areas in which research is critically needed:

1. The coming-out process for lesbians and how the process is affected by variables of race/ethnicity, age, physical ability, and sociopolitical climate.

2. The effect of gender, race, and sexual orientation on career decisions and employment discrimination.

3. The emergence of the lesbian "baby boom" and the definition of family, as well as longitudinal studies on the experiences of the children of lesbians.

4. Process and outcome studies on effective psychotherapy for lesbians, particularly in areas such as sexual abuse, substance abuse, and domestic violence.

5. How AIDS is affecting lesbians in their roles as caregivers to persons with AIDS, and other health-care issues for lesbians (including AIDS).

6. Process and outcome studies on the influence of training in lesbian/gay psychology for providers of mental health services.

These recommendations represent a first step toward developing a professional response to the needs of lesbians. Historically, women, and lesbians in particular, have been ignored in the historical and psychological literature. As we enter the 1990s, we have a great deal of work to do to make psychology reflective of and responsive to the needs of diverse human populations. In our roles as educators, investigators, healers, and advocates, psychologists can influence society to become a more supportive environment for lesbian women to grow and develop to their full capacities.

References

Adler, M. (1986). *Drawing down the moon*. Boston, MA: Beacon.

Alpert, H. (Ed.). (1988). *We are everywhere: Writings by and about lesbian parents*. Freedom, CA: Crossing Press.

Beck, E. T. (Ed.). (1982). *Nice Jewish girls: A lesbian anthology.* Watertown, MA: Persephone.

Becker, C. S. (1988). *Unbroken ties: Lesbian ex-lovers.* Boston: Alyson.

Berzon, B. (1988). *Permanent partners.* New York: Dutton.

Blumstein, P., & Schwartz, P. (1983). *American couples.* New York: Morrow.

Brown, L. S. (1988). Lesbians, gay men and their families: Common clinical issues. *Journal of Gay and Lesbian Psychotherapy, 1,* 65–78.

Brown, L. (1989). New voices, new visions: Toward a lesbian/gay paradigm for psychology. *Psychology of Women Quarterly, 13,* 445–458.

Burch, B. (1982). Psychological merger in lesbian couples: A joint psychology and systems approach. *Family Therapy, 9* (3), 201–208.

Burch, B. (1987). Barriers to intimacy: Conflicts over power, dependency, and nurturing in lesbian relationships. In Boston Lesbian Psychologies Collective (Eds.), *Lesbian psychologies* (pp. 126–141). Chicago: University of Illinois Press.

Cass, V. C. (1979). Homosexual identity formation: A theoretical model. *Journal of Homosexuality, 4,* 219–235.

Chan, C. S. (1989). Issues of identity development among Asian-American lesbians and gay men. *Journal of Counseling and Development, 68,* 16–20.

Clinton, K. (1989, June 25). Kate Clinton: The gay '90s. *San Francisco Examiner,* p. 63.

Clunis, D. M., & Green, G. D. (1988). *Lesbian couples.* Seattle: Seal Press.

D'Augelli, A. R. (1989). Lesbian women in a rural helping network: Exploring informal helping resources. *Women and Therapy, 8,* 119–130.

DeCrescenzo, T., & Fifield, L. (1979). The changing lesbian social scene. In B. Berzon (Ed.), *Positively gay* (pp. 15–23). Los Angeles: Mediamix.

DeMonteflores, C., & Schultz, S. (1978). Coming out: Similarities and differences for lesbians and gay men. *Journal of Social Issues, 34,* 59–72.

Engelhardt, B. J., & Triantafillou, K. (1987). Mediation for lesbians. In Boston Lesbian Psychologies Collective (Ed.), *Lesbian psychologies* (pp. 327–343). Chicago: University of Illinois Press.

Espin, O. (1987). Latina lesbian women. In Boston Lesbian Psychologies Collective (Ed.), *Lesbian psychologies* (pp. 35–55). Chicago: University of Illinois Press.

Faderman, L. (1984). The "new gay" lesbians. *Journal of Homosexuality, 10,* 85–95.

Falk, P. J. (1989). Lesbian mothers: Psychosocial assumptions in family law. *American Psychologist, 44,* 941–947.

Fassinger, R. E., & Schlossberg, N. K. (in press). Understanding the adult years: Theoretical advances in lifespan development. In S. Brown & R. Lent (Eds.), *Handbook of counseling psychology* (2nd ed.). New York: Wiley.

Garcia, N., Kennedy, C., Pearlman, S., & Perez, J. (1987). The impact of race and cultural differences: Challenges to intimacy in lesbian relationships. In Boston Lesbian Psychologies Collective (Eds.), *Lesbian psychologies* (pp. 142–160). Chicago: University of Illinois Press.

Gerstel, C. J., Feraiso, A. J., & Herdt, G. (1989). Widening circles: An ethnographic profile of a youth group. *Journal of Homosexuality, 17,* 75–92.

Gibson, P. (1988, August). Gay male and lesbian youth suicide. In *Report of the secretary's [Department of Health and Human Services] task force on youth suicide* (pp. 3–110 to 3–142). Washington, DC: U.S. Government Printing Office.

Glaus, K. O. (1989). Alcoholism, chemical dependency and the lesbian client. *Women and Therapy, 8,* 131–144.

Griffin, C. W., Wirth, M. J., & Wirth, A. G. (1986). *Beyond acceptance: Parents of lesbians and gays talk about their experience.* Englewood Cliffs, NJ: Prentice-Hall.

Groves, P. (1985). Coming out: Issues for the therapist working with women in the process of lesbian identity formation. *Women and Therapy, 4,* 17–22.

Hall, M. (1987). Sex therapy with lesbian couples: A four-stage approach. *Journal of Homosexuality, 14,* 137–156.

Hart, B. (1986). Lesbian battering: An examination. In K. Loebel (Ed.), *Naming the violence: Speaking out about lesbian battering* (pp. 173–189). Seattle: Seal Press.

Hetherington, C., & Orzek, A. (1989). Career counseling and life planning with lesbian women. *Journal of Counseling and Development, 68,* 52–57.

Kassoff, E. (1989). Nonmonogamy in the lesbian community. *Women and Therapy, 8,* 167–182.

Kehoe, M. (1988). The present: Growing old (1950–1980). *Journal of Homosexuality, 16,* 53–62.

Kresten, J. A., & Bepko, C. S. (1980). The problem of fusion in the lesbian relationship. *Family Process, 19,* 277–289.

Loiacano, D. K. (1989). Gay identity issues among Black Americans: Racism, homophobia, and the need for validation. *Journal of Counseling and Development, 68,* 21–25.

Loulan, J. (1984). *Lesbian sex.* San Francisco: Spinsters Ink.

Loulan, J. (1987). *Lesbian passion: Loving ourselves and each other.* San Francisco: Spinsters/Aunt Lute.

McCandlish, B. (1982). Therapeutic issues with lesbian clients. *Journal of Homosexuality, 7,* 71–78.

Morrow, S. L., & Hawkhurst, D. M. (1989). Lesbian partner abuse: Implications for therapists. *Journal of Counseling and Development, 68,* 58–62.

Moses, A. E., & Buckner, J. A. (1986). The special problems of rural gay clients. In A. E. Moses & R. O. Hawkins (Eds.), *Counseling lesbian women and gay men: A life issues approach* (pp. 173–180). St. Louis, MO: C. V. Mosby.

Moses, A. E., & Hawkins, R. O. (1982). *Counseling lesbian women and gay men: A life issues approach.* St. Louis, MO: C. V. Mosby.

Murphy, B. C. (1989). Lesbian couples and their parents: The effects of perceived parental attitudes on the couple. *Journal of Counseling and Development, 68,* 46–51.

Neisen, J. (1988). Resources for families with a gay/lesbian member. In E. Coleman (Ed.), *Integrated identity for gay men and lesbians: Psychotherapeutic approaches for emotional well-being* (pp. 239–251). New York: Harrington Park.

Nicoloff, L. K., & Stiglitz, E. A. (1987). Lesbian alcoholism: Etiology, treatment and recovery. In Boston Lesbian Psychologies Collective (Ed.), *Lesbian psychologies* (pp. 283–293). Chicago: University of Illinois Press.

Pearlman, S. F. (1987). The saga of the continuing clash in the lesbian community, or will an army of ex-lovers fail? In Boston Lesbian Psychologies Collective (Eds.), *Lesbian psychologies* (pp. 313–326). Chicago: University of Illinois Press.

Pearlman, S. F. (1989). Distancing and connectedness: Impact on couple formation in lesbian relationships. *Women and Therapy, 8,* 77–88.

Peplau, L. A., Cochran, S., Rook, K., & Padesky, C. (1978). Loving women: Attachment and autonomy in lesbian relationships. *Journal of Social Issues, 34,* 7–27.

Pharr, S. (1988). *Homophobia—A weapon of sexism.* Little Rock, AR: Chardon.

Pies, C. (1985). *Considering parenthood: A workbook for lesbians.* San Francisco: Spinsters Ink.

Rainone, F. L. (1987). Beyond community: Politics and spirituality. In Boston Lesbian Psychologies Collective (Ed.), *Lesbian psychologies* (pp. 344-353). Chicago: University of Illinois Press.

Ritter, K. Y., & O'Neill, C. W. (1989). Moving through loss: The spiritual journey of gay men and lesbian women. *Journal of Counseling and Development, 68,* 9–15.

Roth, S. (1989). Psychotherapy with lesbian couples: Individual issues, female socialization and the social context. In M. McGoldrick, C. M. Anderson, & F. Walsh (Eds.), *Women in families* (pp. 286–307). New York: Norton.

Schneider, M. (1989). Sappho was a right-on adolescent: Growing up lesbian. *Journal of Homosexuality, 17,* 111–130.

Sophie, J. (1988). Internalized homophobia and lesbian identity. In E. Coleman (Ed.), *Integrated identity for gay men and lesbians: Psychotherapeutic approaches for emotional well-being* (pp. 53–66). New York: Harrington Park.

Toder, N. (1979). Lesbian couples: Special issues. In B. Berzon & R. Leighton (Eds.), *Positively gay* (pp. 41–55). Los Angeles: Mediamix.

Tully, C. T. (1989). Caregiving: What do midlife lesbians view as important? *Journal of Gay and Lesbian Psychotherapy, 1,* 87–104.

Vargo, S. (1987). The effects of women's socialization on lesbian couples. In Boston Lesbian Psychologies Collective (Eds.), *Lesbian psychologies* (pp. 161–174). Chicago: University of Illinois Press.

Welch, B. L. (1990, January). Statement made at a press conference on reparative therapies. (Available from the American Psychological Association, 1200 Seventeenth St., NW, Washington, DC 20036).

Wilcox-Matthew, L., & Minor, C. W. (1989). The dual career couples: Concerns, benefits, and counseling implications. *Journal of Counseling and Development, 68,* 194–198.

Zitter, S. (1987). Coming out to mom: Theoretical aspects of the mother–daughter process. In Boston Lesbian Psychologies Collective (Eds.), *Lesbian psychologies* (pp. 177–194). Chicago: University of Illinois Press.

17
Affirmative Psychotherapy for Gay Men

Joseph W. Shannon and William J. Woods

Gay men struggle with many of the same issues that confront other clients, but they also have to learn how to cope with problems that are unique to their life-styles and sexual orientation. Moreover, as Tievsky (1988) notes, gays must often come to terms with their concerns in the context of a "largely fearful and rejecting society." As counseling psychologists, we must be sensitive to the special issues gays will bring to therapy. We also need to avail ourselves of training in the theories, strategies, and techniques of effective psychotherapy with gay clients.

The purpose of this article is to present an overview of basic issues in counseling gay men. Our discussion will include sections on identity development, identity management, interpersonal issues, and special issues germane to counseling gay men, including the impact of aging, antigay violence, and acquired immune deficiency syndrome (AIDS). We will conclude with recommendations for treatment and research. Diversity within the male gay community will be addressed throughout the article, and case examples will be presented to illustrate more fully the issues being discussed.

Identity Development in Gay Men

Colgon (1987) defines identity as a "personal construct of self worth." Many current theorists (e.g., Colgon & Riebel, 1981; Isay, 1989; Johnson, 1985) suggest that optimal identity formation and development represents an ongoing dialogue between one's personal construct of self-worth and the responses of significant people (most notably parental figures) in the individual's life. If the responses are consistently negative, the individual's capacity for self-valuing is

From J. W. Shannon and W. J. Woods, "Affirmative Psychotherapy for Gay Men" in *The Counseling Psychologist, 19,* 197–215, 1991. Copyright © 1991. Reprinted by permission of Sage Publications, Inc., Newbury Park, CA.

diminished markedly. Identity development then becomes interrupted or disordered. An identity disorder will have a profoundly negative impact on the adult, especially with regard to self-esteem and the ability to develop satisfying interpersonal relationships. Conversely, if responses from others are largely positive or affirming, the individual will come to see himself as having positive self-worth. Ideally, as the individual grows and matures, he will rely more on his internalized sense of self and less on the reactions of others to determine self-perceptions and courses of action.

Although many gay clients do not present serious identity issues, it is important for the therapist to have a conceptual framework for understanding normal gay identity development so that he/she can assess how healthy the individual is. The therapist can calibrate the client's level of identity development by addressing a number of critical areas early in treatment, including (a) early relationships with parents (especially the father), siblings, and other significant caretakers; (b) ways in which tenderness/affection was or was not expressed in the family; (c) how conflict was handled within the family; (d) at what age he knew he was "different" from other boys and his understanding of this difference; (e) his first awareness of sexual/affectual feelings for other males; (f) a careful description of his process of "coming out"; (g) a history of significant romantic relationships (i.e., dating, boyfriends, and lover relationships); (h) a thorough sexual history, including a frank discussion of sexual fantasies and sexual preferences; and (i) gender-role conformity/nonconformity and the impact this had/has on the individual's process of coming out.

The importance of establishing a positive gay identity cannot be overstated. As Colgon (1987) notes, positive identity and intimacy interact to reinforce each other. Thus gay men with identity disorders will have significant difficulty in establishing and maintaining healthy relationships, romantic and otherwise, with others.

Colgon (1987) and others (e.g., Beattie, 1989) describe two specific intimacy issues that are directly related to poor identity development. Counterdependence (overseparation) involves forming and maintaining one's identity at the expense of emotionally satisfying relationships. The counterdependent person tends to repress or deny his emotional needs, has difficulty discriminating/labeling and expressing feelings, especially vulnerable feelings, and tends to create psychological distance by relating to others in an unemotional, detached, or superficial manner.

By contrast, the codependent (overattached) individual tends to feel insecure and anxious unless he is attached to others. He will have difficulty choosing healthy partners and will often tolerate extremely inappropriate and even abusive behavior from significant others. Like the counterdependent person, the codependent individual has difficulty attending to his feelings; however, he is usually inordinately attentive to the feelings of others. Codependent individuals invariably look to others for something that must ultimately come from within—self-validation (Beattie, 1989; Black, 1989).

Both the counterdependent and codependent client share characteristics of excessive needs for personal and interpersonal affect regulation (Colgon, 1987). In each case, control is exercised to prevent or create emotional involvement and thus reduce unmanageable anxiety. Both conditions are shame-based (Black, 1989) in that the counter- or codependent client feels that he is fundamentally flawed. These feelings result from lack of emotional support/affirmation early in life, which is later exacerbated by the shame of being different (i.e., homosexual) in a rejecting social context. It should also be noted that counter- and codependent clients may have other difficulties besides problems with interpersonal relationships per se. Compulsive (and addictive) patterns such as compulsive overeating, dieting, spending, sex, and drinking are often part of the symptom picture. All of these conditions have their origins in a shame-based upbringing, in which the gay child/adolescent is given a clear message from parents, siblings, peers, or others that he is somehow defective. The compulsive behaviors are developed to ward off feelings of anxiety and shame, to gain control of the environment, and to nurture the wounded self. Some of these behaviors may initially serve as a replacement for parental love and affirmation and later replace self-validation. This partially explains why a number of male gay clients will initially present with problems related to alcohol abuse or other compulsive behaviors (Fifield, 1975).

The case of Tim illustrates the phenomenon of identity disorder:

Tim is a 34-year-old computer programmer with 12 months of sobriety after a 20-year battle with alcohol. Despite regular attendance at Alcoholics Anonymous (AA) meetings and diligent efforts at 12-step work, Tim continued to feel depressed and anxious. Tim also reported frustration over his inability to develop a satisfying romantic relationship. From addressing the aforementioned critical areas in Tim's background, it became very apparent that he was suffering from a disorder of identity. Tim grew up in an extremely dysfunctional (shame-based) family. He also had difficulty making friends in the neighborhood and in school because he was very quiet and shy. Tim avoided competitive games and sports (non-gender-role conforming) and was quickly labeled a "sissy" by his peers. This label and others like it followed Tim throughout his primary and secondary education. He began drinking in high school, shortly after his first sexual encounter with another boy. Tim had always known he was different but had hoped he would change and be more like the other boys. As Tim's despair increased, so did his drinking. By the age of 24 he was a full-blown alcoholic. Sex by this time had also become compulsive. During his 20s and early 30s, Tim had a series of short-lived sexual relationships. In most cases, Tim found himself uncomfortable being with other men sexually (or otherwise) unless he was attending to their needs (codependency). With sexual encounters Tim would seldom allow his partner to reciprocate but would masturbate later when he was alone (counterdependent). Tim knew that he was oftentimes looking for affirmation from another person because he had no clear sense of who he was or of his inherent value as a human being. Before Tim could begin to develop healthier relationships, he clearly needed to address his lack of a positive identity as a gay male. Identity development thus became the primary focus of treatment.

Identity Management

Obstacles and Opportunities

As McDonald (1982) and Berube (1990) point out, gay men live in an antagonistic society, which can be experienced on many levels. Initial identity affirmation brings with it a certain peace of mind, even bliss, but ongoing confrontation with homophobia and heterosexist social policies, laws, institutions and organizations quickly challenges the individual's view of himself and the world and throws his sexual orientation into sharp relief. As the gay male client comes to grips with society's reaction to him, the therapist needs to assist him in identifying those issues that he feels compelled to fight and to support him in that fight, as well as to teach coping skills to deal with the issues that must be left for another time or for others to confront. These obstacles often present opportunities for gay men to develop further their positive gay identity and to integrate that identity within the larger context of their social/professional/familial lives. Therapists may work with gay men at any stage of development confronting these issues. As with similar issues among nongay clients, their task is to assist these men toward positive resolution of the conflict.

Coming Out

One very important step in identity development that fosters integration is coming out to family and friends. When gay men choose to come out, especially the first few times, caution and planning are worthwhile (Borhek, 1983). Therapists can assist clients to be sensitive to timing, needs, circumstances, and the identity of the recipient (e.g., fundamentalist Christian) first. Many recipients of the information will, in fact, experience initial grief at the loss of the person they thought they knew. Gay men should be aware of this possible reaction and be prepared to deal appropriately with it. Initial reactions, especially unfavorable ones, can change with some time and effort, and positive, stable relationships may flourish again.

Sometimes coming out ends a relationship with a friend or family member. In such cases, the gay man needs love and support as he (knowingly or unknowingly) passes through the various stages of grief and loss. Understandably, he may feel intense anger toward the rejecting friend or relative, or he may attempt to bargain with that person in a number of ways. He may also introject the anger and experience depression, despair, and even suicidal thoughts and feelings (Babuscio, 1976; Berzon, 1979c; Jay & Young, 1977; McDonald, 1982). Of course, the duration and intensity of these emotions depends on the significance of the relationship and the emotional maturity and ego strength of the gay man, as well as, to some degree, the kinds of ways that he was dependent on the rejecting person.

The case of Jim clarifies a number of the issues related to coming out:

Jim is a 33-year-old White male. He lives in an urban area with his lover of 5 years. Jim feels relatively comfortable with his gay identity, having been aware of his sexuality since his early teens, and out to his parents since his late teens. He came to therapy presenting concerns about his isolation and depression and his deteriorating relationship with his family. Jim came out to his parents in a fit of teenage anger. He needed something to hurt them and used his sexuality. His parents had always identified with their fundamentalist Christian church, and Jim's revelation, and the manner in which he revealed it, put additional stress on their already strained relationship.

In therapy, Jim began to consider the double standard he set for his family. He was strongly gay-identified and could not believe the teachings of his parents' church. Yet he expected them to deny their identity with that church and accept his sexuality fully. He realized that compromise was necessary. He had to allow his family their religious beliefs, but could ask them not to preach to him or to attempt to change him.

By the end of therapy, Jim had had a number of very positive experiences with several family members. Although tension with his family occurred from time to time, he saw these tensions as part of his family learning how to be with him as an adult, not as their rejecting him and his sexuality.

Gay men do, of course, come out to others besides friends and family. They can have similar experiences with colleagues at work or school, employers, clients, religious leaders, roommates, neighbors, and others with whom they have social and occupational associations. Depending on the state or city, one may have legal recourse to negative reactions (such as loss of job or housing), and the therapist can help the client in deciding whether and when to engage in such battles. The bottom line is that coming out is a matter of personal choice, and it will involve a certain degree of risk for most individuals. Clients must carefully prepare for the possible consequences of their choice to share or withhold information about their sexual orientation. Although sharing may result in some painful rejections, it may also lead to a deepening of relationships, less isolation, and a more integrated life-style.

Occupational/Career Issues

Given that the choice to live out an openly gay life-style may well lead to discrimination, ostracism, and even violence, career counseling and life-style planning represent special challenges to therapists working with gay individuals. Careful vocational/life-style planning might include, for example, preparing while still young for an occupation or profession in which there is a maximum of freedom from constraints imposed by other people. Or it might involve restructuring one's income-producing activity later in life to enable such freedom (Berzon, 1979b). Life-style planning might mean coming out to family and friends early in life so that deception does not have to become a painful habit to be broken later. Shifting one's values may also be necessary so that projects and goals would yield greater personal affirmation and freedom (versus material reward, for example). For clients who are exploring career/job choice per se, therapists need to be aware of special resources available to gays (Schmitz, 1988). These would include gay professional networks (e.g., National Lawyers Guild Gay Caucus, Association of Gay Social Workers, Gay Airline Pilots Association, and gay business and professional organizations in major cities); viable corporate climates (i.e., organizations recognized as possessing nondiscriminatory policies toward gays: see National Gay Task Force for listing); legal codes and statutes that protect the rights of gays in the job setting (i.e., legislation which prohibits discriminating practices based on sexual orientation); and printed materials that provide information relevant to the job search (e.g., *Gayellow Pages,* which provides an annual listing of gay networks, professional associations, and businesses, and can be purchased at gay bookstores). Therapists also need to educate their gay clients about careers that continue to discriminate based on sexual orientation (e.g., many federal government positions requiring a security clearance are not open to gays; Herek, 1990).

Race, Ethnicity, Class, Locale

We have described the general development and management of a gay male identity in the face of a homophobic and heterosexist society. For the most part, what has been studied and written about is based on a White male experience in a White, male-dominated culture. Obviously, men of other racial/ethnic groups are likely to have a different experience and to live within a subculture that has its own attitudes and beliefs about homosexuality (Moses & Hawkins, 1982). Therapists need to be aware of their own racism and prevailing cultural attitudes toward sexual and racial differences. Moreover, clients experiencing the "double whammy" of homophobia and racism will need special encouragement and support.

Class distinctions are also important. Across various racial and ethnic groups there can be more within-class similarity than within-race similarity in terms of how sexual diversity is viewed/tolerated (Atkinson & Hackett, 1988). It is clearly necessary to draw out a man's values and beliefs as related to his perceived social class and to assess how these may affect his identity as a gay man.

Finally, there are differences in locale. Regional differences across the country influence mores within the gay subcultures and the individuals who participate or choose not to participate in those subcultures (Clark, 1987). Within regions, there are also differences between rural and urban areas (Moses & Buckner, 1982). These differences include values and goals as well as resources and needs. Therapists need to be sensitive to the influence of locale on the developing gay identity. Generally speaking, the individual will fare better if he has the opportunity to develop in an urban, more psychologically sophisticated, and more tolerant setting. This is why so many gays emigrate to large urban settings that typically have large gay subcommunities. In these settings, the gay individual has greater opportunity to develop a network of supportive friends and an open life-style that will enhance his emerging identity.

Interpersonal Issues

Isolation, Marginality

Despite coming to terms with his sexuality and his own homophobia, each gay man will continue to live in a world of covert and obvious oppression. The temptation to isolate oneself will be constant, especially as one confronts new or renewed homophobia internally or in others. Sometimes isolation is complete aloneness in the comfort of one's closet; other times it manifests itself in token participation in relationships in which parts of oneself are continually and purposely hidden for fear of rejection. The isolation can also generalize beyond the gay issues and become part of a more general way of interacting with others (Clark, 1987).

Part of any successful therapy will be the enabling of fully interpersonal relationships with gay and nongay friends and relatives (Berzon, 1979b; Clark, 1987; McDonald, 1982). It will also entail encouraging the client to participate in the larger community. This may include gay and nongay interactions with social, political, religious, or other groups.

Gay Male Couples

There is very little descriptive or empirical research on gays seeking couples therapy. However, most writers (e.g., Berzon, 1988) point out that gay couples struggle with many of the same types of conflict and stress that nongay couples present in treatment; this conflict/stress may be exacerbated by living with oppression and the effects of same-sex socialization. Common issues include communication problems; sexual issues; money problems; intimacy issues with each other (e.g., the danger of fusion) and with others (e.g., the importance of developing supportive relationships outside the primary relationship); parenting issues, for a number of gay men do have at least partial custody of biological children from previous heterosexual unions and are choosing to parent (Cramer, 1986); and how to deal with differences (e.g., differences in background, values, and goals).

Clearly, as George and Behrendt (1987) note, all couples in a healthy relationship, whether gay or nongay, have similar characteristics: Partners are committed to each other, share feelings, respect each other, are intimate, and have the capacity to resolve conflicts. We would add to this list for male couples the following:

1. *Each partner is able to accept (and value) his homosexuality.* This acceptance is necessary for positive self-esteem and vital to the acceptance

of the sexuality of one's partner. Significant stress may occur in a gay relationship when there is a discrepancy between the two partners with regard to level of "outness." For example, one partner may be more closeted than the other. The less closeted person's openness about his sexuality will be potentially threatening to his partner, and conflict and stress could ensue. Therapists need to assess degree of outness with each partner in a male couple and determine whether there is a major discrepancy and how the latter may be affecting the relationship.

2. *Each partner has relinquished rigid male stereotypic roles.* The stereotypic male role in our culture is to be aggressive, competitive, unemotional, in control, always strong/competent, and independent. The problems that result are probably obvious: How do two men, behaving according to the rigid male stereotypic role, communicate (especially feelings of vulnerability) to each other? What kind of intimate, loving relationship can develop if both partners are constantly competing with each other? Therapists must assess the degree to which stereotypic male roles may be contributing to the couple's presenting problems and assist parties in expanding their behavioral and attitudinal repertoires.

3. *Each partner has relinquished stereotypic sexual roles.* As Zilbergeld (1978) notes, men are supposed to be sexually active, experienced, ready and able to perform at any time and under any circumstance. The gay male's self-esteem may be too dependent on his partner's perception of him as being masculine and as a good sex partner. The belief that he must always be desirous and capable of having sex may create considerable stress (George & Behrendt, 1987). There is also the danger of equating specific sex acts with masculinity and femininity. Most gay men prefer a variety of sexual positions and activities. Problems will occur when partners get locked into a specific sexual act because of a role that is being played. This limits the quality of sexual interactions and creates stressful expectations for both partners. Finally, the need to be always competent at sex, with the focus being on mutual orgasm and ejaculation (versus communion, intimacy, and playfulness), adds additional stress. This could ultimately result in sexual dysfunction for either partner.

4. *Each partner is committed to not abusing mood-altering chemicals or each other.* Although substance abuse and partner abuse are by no means unique to gay couples, they are clearly common issues in treatment. Both issues typically go hand in hand, in that it is rare to treat a case of partner abuse where neither partner has a serious problem with chemical abuse or dependency (Beattie, 1989). Moreover, a number of writers (e.g., Fifield, 1975) have suggested that substance abuse (particularly alcohol abuse or dependency) is a much more pervasive phenomenon in the gay community than in the general population. This is understandable in light of the previous discussion about the relationship between low self-esteem and

addictive behaviors. Also, gay bars continue to be the primary (and, in some settings, the only) social outlet for gay men. Therapists working with gay individuals or couples should have a solid foundation in assessment and treatment of chemical dependency, and the impact of chemical abuse/dependency on the individual and his partner should be assessed and addressed before other issues are dealt with in treatment, including partner abuse. With regard to the latter, firm guidelines regarding fair fighting (e.g., no physical violence, use of win-win conflict resolution model, "time-out") should be presented to the couple. Therapy would then involve helping the couple learn how to use a conflict resolution model to resolve sources of difficulty without resorting to physical or verbal abuse. A number of therapists (e.g., Berzon, 1979a, 1988) also recommend using a fair-fighting, conflict-resolution model to develop a relationship contract that clearly specifies boundaries, expectations, and values for the couple. If conflict cannot be resolved, or if abusive patterns persist, termination of the relationship will need to be presented as a viable option.

To illustrate some of the issues and interventions relevant to couples therapy, we will briefly discuss the case of Joe and Terry:

Joe is a 43-year-old florist who originally presented symptoms of a chronic, low-grade depression and alcohol dependence. Joe had also expressed concern about maintaining the stability of his 16-year relationship with Terry, a 36-year-old accountant. Joe completed an inpatient detox program, began a 12-step recovery program, was placed on an appropriate anti-depressant medication, and was seen for individual treatment for approximately 3 months before Terry was asked to come in for couples therapy. Many of the issues that Joe presented in his individual therapy were later discovered to have had a negative impact on his relationship with Terry. These included low self-esteem (to the extent that self-worth was equated with achievement), the need to be in control, a difficulty in accepting and sharing vulnerable feelings, a tendency to fear and avoid conflict with a corresponding tendency to internalize anger or express anger passive-aggressively, and intense performance anxiety during sexual encounters with Terry, which occasionally resulted in sexual dysfunction. Terry's level of self-esteem was significantly higher than Joe's, but he too was very fearful and avoidant of conflict. The initial task for the therapist was to help each party identify how they were contributing to the stress in the relationship. Once issues were identified, a constructive fighting model was presented to help Joe and Terry work through sources of distress as well as eliminate their fear of dealing with conflict directly. The process of conflict resolution enhanced intimacy for Joe and Terry and made it easier for them to approach and resolve future problems. Eventually, Terry was able to see how he had enabled Joe's drinking and reinforced Joe's unrealistic expectations about performance. Terry began attending Al-Anon meetings while Joe continued with AA. Both grew closer and reinforced each other's recovery and growth. Therapy had served as an effective catalyst for both individual and systemic change.

Special Issues

Impact of Aging

There has been little research done on older homosexual adults. The available research is primarily descriptive in nature and based on small samples of subjects. Much of this research has attempted to explore the validity of certain myths and stereotypes regarding the process of aging for homosexual persons (e.g., Almvig, 1982; Berger, 1980; Kimmel, 1977, 1978). This research would seem to suggest that older (i.e., age 55 and older) gay people have many of the assets and liabilities of older people in general. Aging is often seen as an equalizer of differences, in terms of social class, educational background, race, sex, and sexual orientation. The dominant issue for the aged person regardless of these variables is health status. Thus, as with nongays, older gays are concerned about maintaining good health and access to high quality medical care.

However, older gay men do have some unique issues. Being gay subjects one to special threats of exposure, loss of job (if still working), social stigma, arrest, or physical violence. Whether these threats are reality-based or not, they may exist in the mind of the older gay man because today's older gay men grew up in a more sexually repressive period; the fear of, and sense of vulnerability to, social oppression is often much stronger among older gays than among younger gays (Kimmel, 1977, 1978).

Older gay men are more likely to be angry at years of oppression. Generally, this anger may have been dealt with constructively via hard work in an occupation, developing a strong network of friends, and/or political activism. For others, anger was largely introjected, resulting in anxiety, depression, and self-esteem problems related to internalized homophobia.

Getting sexual/affectual needs met without being perceived as a "dirty old man" is another common issue. This may have less to do with being gay and more to do with society's negative views regarding sex among the elderly (one type of ageism). Also, as Kimmel (1977) notes, for many older gay men, the conquest-oriented, competitive, orgasm-focused emphasis of sex in youth often gives way during the second half of life to more concern with communion, companionship, and mutual sexual enjoyment.

Although all older individuals deal with issues of loss, older gays may receive less sympathy and attention when dealing with the loss of a long-term lover or close companions and friends. Legal issues, problems with family members, the reactions of health-care professionals, and the (oftentimes grossly) insensitive reactions of the bereaved's family can also complicate the grieving process (Kimmel, 1977).

Kimmel (1977, 1978) and others (e.g., Friend, 1987) have also elucidated some of the advantages of aging among gays, namely, that gays may be more prepared to live independently in older age, in that they do not have unrealistic expectations of relying on children or family to care for them as they grow older. There may also be greater continuity of life for gay men, who have not had to deal with children leaving home, who have not confined themselves to rigid male roles in the necessary tasks of living, and who may have already lived alone as adults. Gay men as a group are also more likely to develop a strong network of supportive friends apart from their primary relationships. Thus, as the gay man grows older, and as significant others die, he is less likely to feel completely isolated and lonely, unless he has led an extremely closeted existence.

Although the research discussed above may be helpful in understanding the issues of the older gay client, there is clearly a need for more extensive research (perhaps longitudinal studies of large samples) that would clarify the normal psychological changes and challenges that occur as gays grow older.

One related topic that has received virtually no attention in empirical research is the impact of AIDS on the generational structure of the gay male community. Thousands of gay men are dying or have died in their prime because of AIDS. How will this affect those who live? For example, how will gay men turning 55 in the next 20 years deal with the significant lack of men their age? Peers who die prematurely of AIDS in their 30s and 40s will not be there to provide support and continuity, nor will they be there to provide healthy role models for our gay youth. Our hope is that this and other topics related to aging will receive the attention they deserve in future research.

Antigay Violence

Antigay hate crimes can be defined as any action that is intended to harm or intimidate individuals who are gay or lesbian (Herek, 1989). Actions can include anything from slurs yelled by a passing motorist to torture and murder. Though prevalent throughout history (see Fassinger, this issue), antigay hate crimes are beginning to receive more attention, especially in the gay community. Some of this attention has been aimed at identifying the prevalence and severity of the problem. Despite the methodological flaws inherent in doing formal research on this issue (see Herek, 1989), several studies have clarified the epidemic proportions of hate crimes directed at gays. Because the problem of antigay violence occurs so frequently and is experienced by so many gay men, it is imperative that therapists be aware of the problem and assist their clients in confronting the reality of the hate crimes they experience. Obviously, these crimes can have insidious effects on self-esteem (Bohn, 1984), resulting in feelings of guilt, shame, depression, and isolation. Rage and anger toward society and the gay community can also ensue (Anderson, 1982). To the extent these crimes go largely unacknowledged by the criminal justice system and society, it is also likely that the victims of such crimes will give them inadequate attention, despite the long-term aversive effects (Finn & McNeil, 1987).

Therapists can play several vital roles in addressing antigay abuse. In treatment, the therapist can help the client acknowledge the problem and explore the potentially serious impact on the individual's sense of security and self-esteem. Helping the client to identify feelings about the experience and directing those feelings in positive channels facilitates a healthy recuperation from the encounter. As an advocate, the therapist can assist the client in identifying resources, such as legal and medical, for dealing with consequences of the crime. Furthermore, therapists can watch for suicidal ideation, particularly with rape-trauma victims. With the latter group, crisis intervention, advocacy, follow-up counseling, self-defense training, and community interventions (such as community education programs) could be legitimate functions of the therapist (Anderson, 1982; Herek, 1989; Miller & Humphreys, 1980).

AIDS

AIDS, though not a gay disease, is completely entwined with the gay experience in America, and perhaps throughout the world (Kübler-Ross, 1987). Even if a gay man has never known anyone who has had AIDS, he must still question any potential partner about previous sexual partners and experiences. Young gay men must face the issue in their already difficult struggle in coming to terms with their sexuality; not surprisingly, they wonder if a gay life-style is viable for them, given the potential consequences. Older gay men have had to accommodate major changes in their sexual practices, as well as confront the loss of friends and lovers. Grieving and death became a commonplace experience for many gay men of all ages during the 1980s and will increase in the 1990s. The other problems of gay men and the gay rights agenda have suffered serious setbacks as a result of a change of emphasis to the epidemic, draining the community of talent and resources.

The epidemic presents many areas of intervention for therapists. Most of these interventions have to do with coping with changes and making decisions. The spread of the virus compels all gay men to make changes in how they find partners and how they engage in sex with their partners (Silven & Caldarola, 1989). These changes require learning new behaviors, like how to use a condom, how to ask about previous partners, and how to insist on safe sex in highly charged sexual encounters. They also require examining values, such as monogamy and fidelity, and determining what kinds of risks one will take and not take, such as deep kissing (Stall, Coates, & Hoff, 1988). Gay men must accept that the old ways of being sexual are gone. Friends will die and the individual himself may get sick and progress through a series of stages of losing more and more physical independence. All these changes require letting go and coping with the losses.

Decisions are multiple for gay men in the era of AIDS. Many, if not most, gay men have reason to at least raise the question of whether they should take the HIV antibody test. This decision is extremely important and should never be minimized or taken lightly; the information obtained from testing can be psychologically devastating (Marks & Goldblum, 1989). One should take the test with an awareness of the consequences and some firm ideas about the direction to take if the results are positive (i.e., indicate that the individual is infected). Therapists can be very helpful in preparing an individual to make this decision and then to follow through and implement it. Obviously, this process requires directive and educational interventions, as well as support (Moskowitz, 1989). Other decisions include the degree to which the individual may want to take an aggressive approach to fighting the illness, and when such an approach might commence (Woods, 1989). These decisions will involve finding appropriate medical support (i.e., physicians who are willing to be as aggressive as the patient) and treatment information about alternative, nonmedical treatments. Other medical and legal decisions must be made, such as when life-sustaining efforts should be withheld and designating power of attorney.

The complexity of decisions and issues that arise in working with AIDS is evident in the case of Jack:

> Jack is a 50-year-old Black male who had recently stopped his successful career due to an AIDS diagnosis. Jack began therapy because of depression, loneliness, and isolation related to his illness and the recent loss of his lover, Tom. Apart from participating in therapy, Jack joined a support group and an activist group, the latter leading to several important relationships. He also took advantage of practical support services in the community. However, despite the success at breaking down the isolation, much of the loneliness and depression continued. Tom's death was not the only important loss in Jack's life. He had also lost many friends during the 1980s to the epidemic. The grieving process for one loss overlapped with that of so many others, to the point where Jack often felt completely overwhelmed with sadness and depression. Kaposi's sarcoma began to limit his mobility, and he soon noticed lesions growing on his face, a particularly scary and difficult development. Physicians had been treating the lesions topically, but a decision needed to be made concerning treating the lesions systemically, and by what means. The process of coming to terms with the decisions was agonizing for Jack. As with most things, there were no guarantees, and he was already feeling such loss and fear that decision making grew more and more difficult. The possible decision to stop fighting and let the disease take its course also existed. Jack continues to struggle with that question, as well as suicidal ideation that has plagued him since the loss of his lover. After all, for Jack, as for many persons living with AIDS (PLWAs), "death" holds promise and relief; it is the loss of bodily control and independence, the long-suffered pain before death, in a word, the "dying," that he fears.

Working with a client who has already been diagnosed with AIDS or an AIDS-related illness typically involves coordinating treatment with other professionals who are treating the client as well. For example, it is important for the therapist to maintain ongoing contact with the client's primary-care physician in order to ensure an integrated, holistic approach and to provide continuity of care. Therapists may find themselves acting as an advocate for the client, assisting him with obtaining vital resources (e.g., disability income, health insurance, hospice care) from public and private agencies. There may also be professional involvement with the client's significant others, for example, providing supportive counseling to the client's lover or family members as they struggle with issues of loss and grief. Finally, therapists who work with advanced cases of AIDS may find themselves providing increasing care and advocacy for the dying client as he finds it more difficult to interact directly with others providing care. Needless to say, working with clients diagnosed with AIDS is very demanding and draining. It is absolutely essential that the therapist examine his/her own issues about death and dying, explore his/her feelings of frustration and helplessness, and obtain emotional support from other colleagues and friends.

Spiritual/Existential Issues

Psychotherapy that does not address the existential/spiritual dimension is seriously lacking (Fortunato, 1982). Although many clients struggle with "meaning of life" questions, it is important for therapists to be sensitive to the existential issues commonly presented by gay clients. Many men, particularly in the early stages of coming out, struggle with the question of why they are gay. Some attempt to change their gayness in order to fit into the nongay world; the shame of being fundamentally different or flawed and the resulting fear of being despised, abused, and ultimately rejected by others make it difficult for gay men to see the positive meaning in their gayness.

One's confusion and internalized homophobia can be exacerbated further by religious teachings (McNaught, 1979; Nelson, 1982). Clients often have a difficult time reconciling their sexuality with the views of their religion and may detach completely from the organized religion. This can lead to feelings of isolation and alienation, or clients may repress their sexuality or live a double life in order to maintain ties with a religious institution that essentially does not support or affirm them (Nelson, 1982).

Therapists working with gay clients need to help them distinguish between spirituality and religiosity. One can believe in a deity or "higher power" or otherwise find meaning in life without participating in an organized religion that is antithetical to the individual's personhood. For those clients who wish to be involved with an organized religion, there are interdenominational groups (e.g., Metropolitan Community Church, Unity) that offer structure, community, and a gay-affirming theology. As McNaught (1979) notes, the spiritual search for meaning is ultimately a search for truth; the living of one's own truth can contribute to a sense of inner joy and wholeness.

Conclusions and Recommendations

Although therapeutic strategies have been discussed throughout this article, it is helpful to conclude with some general guidelines for treatment:

1. Therapists working with gay male clients need to adopt a nonhomophobic stance. In terms of practice, this translates into the therapist's being open to hear the client's story rather than jumping to conclusions about the client based on stereotyped pathological assumptions (Dillon, 1986).

2. Therapists working with gay male clients need to have a firm foundation of training and experience in conceptualizing and treating addictive disorders, including alcoholism and other substance abuse, sexual compulsiveness, and eating disorders. Although none of these disorders are unique to gay men, a number of gay clients will present symptoms of these disorders in treatment. Because of the painful process of coming to terms with one's homosexuality, there is a greater potential for narcissistic injury; this, in turn, fuels the development of compulsive coping responses.

3. Therapists providing couples therapy to gay clients need to educate themselves about issues unique to male couples (e.g., stereotypic male roles, stereotypic sexual roles) and how these may relate to the problems presented in treatment. It is often helpful for the therapist to teach the couple a win-win conflict resolution model so that they have a tool they can use to address issues as they arise. This facilitates problem resolution as well as enhancing the level of intimacy between the two partners.

4. Group therapy can often be a helpful adjunct to individual and couples treatment. Participants can address issues within a supportive, empathic environment, as well as learn vital information and interpersonal skills.

5. The smallness of gay communities sets the stage for unique ethical problems for gay psychologists. Even in large cities, the gay community is usually relatively small, or at least small enough that therapists and clients can find themselves interrelated through friendships, lovers, organizations, and social functions. Some gay therapists solve this problem by cutting themselves off from all but a small part of the community; others set limited boundaries between themselves and the community, whereas some, unfortunately, set no boundaries at all (the most extreme example, of course, would be therapists who engage in emotionally intimate or sexual relationships with their clients). These problems are not often addressed by gay-identified counselors and require more attention, discussion, and research.

6. Finally, it should be noted that, regardless of a therapist's theoretical orientation, there is a strong ethical obligation to inform gay men of safe-sex guidelines. It is especially urgent in this time of epidemic that we respond to the ignorance and denial of our clients. Although we must not promote sensationalism or a hysterical response, we also must not sit back and listen passively to material that includes the individual putting himself or others at risk for the transmission of HIV. A careful but direct, nonjudgmental inquiry into a client's knowledge, attitudes, and behaviors regarding safe sex is the best approach. Accurate information should also be given in a nonjudgmental manner. Also, therapists should keep in mind that behavior change is not rapid or easy and that clients need much reinforcement for their successes.

The demands of working with gay men can be a challenge to both gay and nongay therapists. Without question we must confront and work through our own homophobia and the many myths and stereotypes about gays. We also need to continue to educate ourselves about gay identity development and management, therapy issues unique to male gay clients, gay resources, and affirmative counseling models.

For those who conduct research in the area of counseling and development, there clearly needs to be continued effort at identifying "normal" developmental issues and tasks for the gay client, as well as special challenges he may face throughout his life span. Unique issues related to identity development and maintenance, career development, race/ethnicity/social class, coping with antigay violence, AIDS, same-sex coupling, and parenting also need further clarification and validation via longitudinal studies of large samples of subjects. Apart from further identification of these issues, challenges, and tasks, research must ultimately elucidate effective adaptive strategies. As counseling psychologists, we value preventive as well as ameliorative intervention efforts. For this reason, we must provide our gay clients with the necessary tools to cope with their special problems and concerns as well as with guidelines for developing a happy, healthy, and integrated life-style.

References

Almvig, C. (1982). *The invisible minority: Aging and lesbianism.* New York: Utica College of Syracuse University Press.

Anderson, C. L. (1982). Males as sexual assault victims: Multiple levels of trauma. *Journal of Homosexuality, 7,* 145–162.

Atkinson, D. R., & Hackett, G. (1988). *Counseling non-ethnic American minorities.* Springfield, IL: Charles C Thomas.

Babuscio, J. (1976). *We speak for ourselves.* Philadelphia: Fortress.

Beattie, M. (1989). *Beyond co-dependency.* New York: Harper/Hazelden.

Berger, R. M. (1980). Psychological adaptation of the older homosexual male. *Journal of Homosexuality, 5,* 161–175.

Berube, A. (1990). *Coming out under fire: The history of gay men and women in WW II.* New York: Free Press.

Berzon, B. (1979a). Achieving success as a gay couple. In B. Berzon (Ed.), *Positively gay: New approaches in gay and lesbian life* (pp. 30–40). Los Angeles: Mediamix.

Berzon, B. (1979b). Developing a positive gay identity. In B. Berzon (Ed.), *Positively gay: New approaches in gay and lesbian life* (pp. 1–14). Los Angeles: Mediamix.

Berzon, B. (1979c). Telling the family you're gay. In B. Berzon (Ed.), *Positively gay: New approaches in gay and lesbian life* (pp. 88–100). Los Angeles: Mediamix.

Berzon, B. (1988). *Permanent partners: Building gay and lesbian relationships that last.* New York: Dutton.

Black, C. (1989). *Shame* (Videocassette). Denver: MAC Publishing.

Bohn, T. R. (1984). Homophobic violence: Implications for social work practice. In R. Schoenberg & R. S. Goldberg (Eds.), *With compassion toward some: Homosexuality and social work in America* (pp. 91–112). New York: Harrington Park.

Borhek, M. V. (1983). *Coming out to parents: A two-way survival guide for lesbians and gay men and their parents.* New York: Pilgrim.

Clark, D. (1987). *The new loving someone gay.* Berkeley, CA: Celestial Arts.

Colgon, P. (1987). Treatment of identity and intimacy issues in gay males. *Journal of Homosexuality, 14,* 101–123.

Colgon, P., & Riebel, J. (1981). *Sexuality education for foster parents.* Minneapolis: University of Minnesota.

Cramer, D. (1986). Gay parents and their children: A review of research and practical implications. *Journal of Counseling and Development, 64,* 605–607.

Dillon, C. (1986). Preparing college health professionals to deliver gay-affirmative services. *Journal of American College Health, 34*(1), 36–40.

Fifield, L. (1975). *On my way to nowhere: Alienated, isolated, drunk.* Los Angeles: Gay Community Services Center and Department of Health Services.

Finn, P., & McNeil, T. (1987, October 7). *The response of the criminal justice system to bias crime: An exploratory review.* Washington, DC: U.S. Department of Justice, National Institute of Justice.

Fortunato, J. E. (1982). *Embracing the exile: Healing journeys for gay Christians.* New York: Harper & Row.

Friend, R. A. (1987). The individual and social psychology of aging: Clinical implications for lesbians and gay men. *Journal of Homosexuality, 14,* 307–331.

George, K. D., & Behrendt, A. E. (1987). Therapy for male couples experiencing relationship problems and sexual problems. *Journal of Homosexuality, 14,* 77–89.

Herek, G. M. (1989). Hate crimes against lesbians and gay men: Issues for research and policy. *American Psychologist, 44,* 948–955.

Herek, G. M. (1990). Gay people and government security clearances. *American Psychologist, 45,* 1035–1042.

Isay, R. A. (1989). *Being homosexual: Gay men and their development.* New York: Giroux.

Jay, K., & Young, A. (1977). *The gay report: Lesbians and gay men speak out about sexual experiences and lifestyles.* New York: Summitt.

Johnson, S. (1985). *Characterological transformation: The hard work miracle.* New York: Norton.

Kimmel, D. C. (1977). Psychotherapy and the older gay male. *Psychotherapy: Theory, research and practice, 14,* 386–393.

Kimmel, D. C. (1978). Adult development and aging: A gay perspective. *Journal of Social Issues, 34,* 113–130.

Kübler-Ross, E. (1987). *AIDS: The ultimate challenge.* New York: Macmillan.

Marks, R., & Goldblum, P. B. (1989). The decision to test: A personal choice. In J. W. Dilley, C. Pies, & M. Helquist (Eds.), *Face to face: A guide to AIDS counseling* (pp. 49–58). San Francisco: University of California.

McDonald, G. J. (1982). Individual differences in the coming out process for gay men: Implications for theoretical models. *Journal of Homosexuality, 8,* 47–60.

McNaught, B. (1979). Gay and Catholic. In B. Berzon (Ed.), *Positively gay: New approaches to gay and lesbian life* (pp. 56–64). Los Angeles: Mediamix.

Miller, B., & Humphreys, L. (1980). Lifestyles and violence: Homosexual victims of assault and murder. *Qualitative Sociology, 3*(3), 169–185.

Moses, A. E., & Buckner, J. A. (1982). The special problems of rural gay clients. In A. E. Moses & R. O. Hawkins (Eds.), *Counseling lesbian women and gay men: A life-issues approach* (pp. 173–180). St. Louis: C. V. Mosby.

Moses, A. E., & Hawkins, R. O. (Eds.). (1982). *Counseling lesbian women and gay men: A life-issues approach.* St. Louis: C. V. Mosby.

Moskowitz, R. D. (1989). Being seronegative in a seropositive world: A personal perspective. In J. W. Dilley, C. Pies, & M. Helquist (Eds.), *Face to face: A guide to AIDS counseling* (pp. 102–106). San Francisco: University of California.

Nelson, J. B. (1982). Religious and moral issues in working with homosexual clients. *Journal of Homosexuality, 7,* 163–176.

Raphael, S. M., & Robinson, M. K. (1980). The older lesbian. *Alternative Lifestyles, 3,* 207–229.

Schmitz, T. J. (1988). Career counseling implications with the gay and lesbian population. *Journal of Employment Counseling, 25,* 51–56.

Silven, D., & Caldarola, T. J. (1989). The HIV-positive client. In J. W. Dilley, C. Pies, & M. Helquist (Eds.), *Face to face: A guide to AIDS counseling* (pp. 307–310). San Francisco: University of California.

Stall, R., Coates, T., & Hoff, C. (1988). Behavioral risk reduction for HIV infection among gay and bisexual men: A review of results from the United States. *American Psychologist, 43,* 878–885.

Tievsky, D. L. (1988). Homosexual clients and homophobic social workers. *Journal of Independent Social Work, 2,* 51–62.

Woods, W. J. (1989). Experimental treatments and counseling issues. In J. W. Dilley, C. Pies, & M. Helquist (Eds.), *Face to face: A guide to AIDS counseling* (pp. 59–66). San Francisco: University of California.

Zilbergeld, B. (1978). *Male sexuality.* Boston: Little, Brown.

PART 6
Implications

18

Diversity Imperatives for Counseling Practice, Counselor Training, and Counseling Research

In chapter 1, we developed a rationale for viewing selected nonethnic groups as minorities, and we presented profiles of persons with disabilities, elders, women, and gay people. In chapters 2 through 5, the treatment of these four groups by society and psychology was placed in both a historical and contemporary context. Chapters 6 through 17 focused on the experiences and counseling related needs of individuals in each group. Chapters 6 through 17 also provided suggestions for counseling persons with disabilities, elders, women, and gay people from a human rights perspective, as well as a traditional counseling perspective. In this chapter, we highlight several aspects of counseling practice that we feel need special attention and we discuss changes that are needed in counselor training programs in order to adequately prepare counselors to work with nonethnic minorities and in counseling research in order to reduce research bias against nonethnic minorities.

Counseling Practice

In addition to the counseling practices specifically directed toward the four nonethnic minorities discussed in chapters 6 through 17, we feel it is important to draw attention to three practice topics that are relevant to all four groups. These topics are language, ethics, and advocacy.

Language

Professional counselors often unintentionally use imprecise and demeaning language that reinforces stereotypes of people with disabilities, older people, women, and gay people. Practicing counselors can help reduce discrimination against these groups and take a major step toward increasing their credibility and effectiveness with nonethnic minority clients by eliminating imprecise and demeaning language from their vocabulary and by sensitively and knowledgeably using the terminology employed by their clients. In general, it is best to respect the client's preference for self-reference and to accept the fact that this language changes over time.

Sometimes the counselor is in a situation where it is not possible to determine the client's preference for language of self-reference, as when the client is not present. In the following sections, we examine some general guidelines for the appropriate and inappropriate use of language with each of the four nonethnic minority groups on which this book is focused.

Persons with Disabilities

Perhaps no group has had more demeaning terms directed toward them *unintentionally* than do people with disabilities. Concern over the widespread use of inappropriate language in reference to persons with disabilities has been a theme in the rehabilitation counseling literature since about 1980.

Hadley and Brodwin (1988) reviewed the rehabilitation literature and developed four simple principles that they recommended rehabilitation counselors follow when discussing persons with disabilities:

1. *Precision:* Language should convey a speaker's or writer's intended meanings exactly and unambiguously.

2. *Objectivity:* One should avoid language that (a) implicitly expresses biases or unwanted surplus meanings or (b) treats opinions, interpretations, or impressions as facts.

3. *Perspective:* When one communicates about a person, the language chosen should emphasize the person and represent any disability in its proper perspective among his or her many other characteristics. This perspective is governed by the issues at hand; if disability is totally irrelevant to these issues, it may be omitted entirely.

4. *Portrayal:* People with disabilities should be portrayed as actively going about the business of living as other people do, *not* as passive victims, tragic figures, or superheroes. (p. 147)

Hadley and Brodwin (1988) point out that all professional counselors, not just rehabilitation counselors, should be concerned about the use of language, since people with disabilities often seek out counselors in other specialties to discuss problems with living that are unrelated to their disability. They go on to make several concrete suggestions about the use of language, although they qualify their suggestions by pointing out that the most appropriate use of language is often situation specific:

1. A form of the verb *to have* is usually the most effective way to express the link between a person and a disability.
   a. A person " has arthritis," *not* " is an arthritic"; "has diabetes" is preferable to "is a diabetic."
   b. One should scrupulously avoid words such as "victim" or "afflicted" to express this link. These words carry surplus emotional meaning.

c. The word "patient" correctly expresses a relationship with a medical service provider such as a physician or a hospital; it is a poor word choice for other uses. "Is a lupus patient" is an *imprecise* substitute for "has lupus."

d. To have a disability is not necessarily to "suffer from" it. Such gratuitous use of "suffer" conveys a stereotypical attitude. . . . If one wants to say a particular person is suffering, this point should be developed explicitly.

2. A disability should never be represented as causing (a) an individual's emotional or behavioral reactions to it or (b) sequelae to these reactions. We prefer to represent people as the causes of their own feelings and behavior, although disability often serves as a cue. For example:

a. It is neither precise nor objective to say that a disability or any other circumstance "makes" a person feel any particular way. "She feels depressed about her hearing loss" is better than "her hearing loss is making her depressed."

b. Neither blindness nor paraplegia has ever caused alcoholism. People have reacted to these conditions, however, with patterns of drinking that caused alcoholism.

3. A disability should not be represented, either explicitly or implicitly, as the sole cause of circumstances resulting from social reactions to it. For example, a person should not be described as unemployed because he or she has impaired vision, if the reason is employers' discriminatory hiring.

4. Wheelchairs, prostheses, and other assistive devices are tools that people use in their various activities; word choices should represent this fact. For example,

a. A client with paralyzed legs *uses* a wheelchair. The common expression, "confined to a wheelchair," is obviously imprecise and carries many of the same surplus meanings as "wheelchair-bound." Although "is in a wheelchair" is somewhat less offensive, . . . this expression . . . portrays the person as "passive."

b. It is preferable to say a person "walks with" crutches rather than "has to use" or "is on" crutches. (Hadley & Brodwin, 1988, pp. 148–149).

Similarly, Byrd, Crews, and Ebener (1991) identified the following points that should be taken into consideration when making written or verbal reference to persons with disabilities:

1. Only make reference to a person's disability when it is important to the context;

2. Avoid using adjectives as nouns;

3. Place persons or individuals before the disability;

4. Avoid value laden descriptions;

5. Do not sensationalize the effects of disability;

6. Avoid statements that qualify the person with a disability (e. g., he uses a wheelchair, but is very bright);

7. Avoid implying sickness when discussing disability conditions. (p. 40)

Researchers and academicians, as well as practitioners, need to be concerned about the terms they use in reference to people with disabilities. The

American Psychological Association's *Publication Manual* (APA, 1994) offers the following advice to authors of manuscripts submitted to APA journals for publication:

> The guiding principle for "nonhandicapping" language is to maintain the integrity of individuals as human beings. Avoid language that equates persons with their condition (e.g., *neurotics, the disabled*); that has superfluous, negative overtones (e.g., stroke *victim*); or that is regarded as a slur (e.g., *cripple*). . . . Use *disability* to refer to an attribute of a person and *handicap* to refer to the source of limitations, which may include attitudinal, legal, and architectural barriers as well as the disability itself (e.g., steps and curbs handicap people who require the use of a ramp). *Challenged* and *special* are often considered euphemistic and should be used only if the people in your study prefer those terms. As a general rule, "person with _____," "person living with _____," and "person who has _____" are neutral and preferred forms of description. (p. 53)

Elders

Cohen (1990) reviewed 60 issues of the *Gerontologist*, 30 issues of *Generations*, and a number of miscellaneous articles and monographs published by the federal government and reported having turned up:

> . . . an array of negative terms applied to or describing the elderly. . . . The following is a partial list of words and phrases that reinforce the elderly mystique from a variety of literatures, learned, policy, and legal. Elderly-at-risk, frail elderly, impaired elderly, institutionalized elderly, homebound elderly, chairbound elderly, bedridden elderly, wheelchairbound elderly, vulnerable elderly, dependent elderly, patient (rather than consumer), and "the Alzheimer" (referring to the person who has the disease). (p. 14)

Schaie (1993) has pointed out that ageist attitudes and language permeate both empirical research and psychological practice. With regard to research, he identified a number of language problems related to the description of the research topic, language used in describing study designs, descriptions of methodology and choice of participants, and language used in the analysis and interpretation of research findings. These problems and Schaie's recommendations for avoiding them are as follows:

I. Description of research topic
   A. Problems
      1. Focus of description of research topic on delineating a "problem of aging" rather than on building or extending an explanatory model.
      2. Reliance on biological models of decrement or decline.
      3. Neglect of research participants' health status.
      4. Age assumed to be the cause of differences or changes in behavior with little consideration of alternative explanations.

5. Undue focus on elders as care needing, instead of care providing; the emphasis is often on dependent aspects, ignoring sustaining aspects.
   B. Recommendation
      1. Recognize that older persons constitute a diverse population. Heterogeneity should be stressed and gender should always be considered.
      2. Recognize that ageism can apply to individuals at any age, not only to those who are old.
      3. Consider a life span context in formulating the research topic.
      4. Carefully reference existing literature on older persons, and in reviewing previous studies evaluate their possible age bias.
      5. Consider the impact of possible findings on public policy.
II. Design of the study
    A. Problems
       1. Failure to distinguish between normal age changes and disease.
       2. Reliance on chronological age.
       3. Lack of attention to age-sex-culture interaction; failure to describe other relevant demographic dimensions in which age groups in the population may differ, for example, culture/ethnicity, sexual orientation.
    B. Recommendations
       1. Examine the choice and definition of hypotheses. Is there a causal inference that involves age or aging? Is it influenced by age bias?
       2. Consider whether chronological age is the most relevant variable. Would classification by other variables, such as educational level, income, duration of marriage, retirement, duration of retirement, or generational membership, be more appropriate?
       3. Document that the constructs used in a study retain the same meaning at different ages. . . . Acknowledge that use of measures of such constructs developed for younger adults may introduce bias into a study of elders.
III. Methods
     A. Problems
        1. Inadequate operational definition of the age variable.
        2. Inappropriate or offensive research instruments.
     B. Recommendations
        1. Instruments should be evaluated to ensure that they do not contain explicitly or implicit age bias.
        2. Avoid uncalled-for assumptions.
        3. Beware of experimenter bias about how questions are asked of various age groups.
        4. Check measures for inappropriate questions.
        5. Consider use of alternative definitions for chronological age, such as subjective age or functional age.

IV. Description of data analysis and interpretation
   A. Problems
      1. Confusing age differences with age changes.
      2. Overlooking individual differences.
      3. Ignoring the magnitude of age change.
      4. Not reporting the absence of difference relevant to ageist stereotypes.
      5. Reporting age differences found accidentally (where age is included as a variable in the analysis without a clear rationale) as "findings."
   B. Recommendations
      1. Age-group differences should be characterized as such and not be labeled as *decline*. Often the term *age/cohort differences* is to be preferred.
      2. Age differences often can be explained by other variables and interactive effects; these should be discussed and ruled out before age is assumed to be the cause of differences in the dependent variable.
      3. In some instances it would be more desirable to use age as the dependent variable.
      4. Consider the practical significance of an age difference, especially when the data are relevant to public policy or might result in recommendations leading to important changes in an individual's life situation.
      5. Consider the impact of ageist assumptions and models applied to data analysis and interpretation. Formulate competing models that test for alternate interpretations.
      6. Use caution in generalizing results.
      7. Beware of interpreting trends or marginally significant findings, especially when they either fit or contradict social stereotypes about aging and older persons.
      8. Avoid value-laden language that implies negative characteristics for all study participants. (pp. 49–51)

The APA *Publication Manual* (APA, 1994) suggests that in scientific writing, it is best to give a specific age range for participants rather than referring to them with a label. The *Publication Manual* also indicates that "*elderly* is not acceptable as a noun and is considered pejorative by some as an adjective" (p. 53). In place of elderly the *Publication Manual* recommends use of *older person*. We feel that both *elder* and *older person* are acceptable terms and agree that elderly may be offensive to some older persons.

Women

Psychologists are also guilty of reinforcing sexism through the use of imprecise and derogatory language. The *Publication Manual of the American Psychological Association* first addressed this issue in 1974 in its second edition by suggesting that journal authors "be aware of the current move to avoid generic use of male nouns and pronouns when content refers to both sexes." This position was strengthened and elaborated upon in 1977 when the APA published the "Guidelines for Nonsexist Language in APA Journals" in the *American Psychologist*. In 1982, the APA Publications and Communications Board adopted a formal policy that requires authors who are submitting manuscripts to APA journals to use nonsexist language.

The current edition of the APA *Publication Manual* (APA, 1994) points out that by choosing the appropriate nouns, pronouns, and adjectives to describe the participants, an author can avoid ambiguity in sex identity and sex role and avoid sex bias:

> The unparallel nouns in the phrase *man and wife* may inappropriately prompt the reader to evaluate the roles of the individuals (i.e., the woman is defined only in terms of her relationship to the man) and the motives of the author. The phrase *husband and wife* or *man and woman* is parallel and undistracting. (p. 49)

> Sex bias can occur when pronouns are used carelessly: when the masculine pronoun *he* is used to refer to both sexes, or when the masculine or feminine pronoun is used exclusively to define roles by sex (e.g., "the nurse . . . *she*"). The use of *man* as a generic noun or as an ending for an occupational title (e. g., *policeman*) can be ambiguous and may imply incorrectly that all persons in the group are male. (p. 50)

Eichler (1988) suggests five questions to ask to ensure nonsexist language; a *yes* to any indicates the need for modifications:

1. Are any male (or female) terms used for generic purposes? [e.g., referring to all clients as "she"]

2. Are any generic terms employed when, in fact, the author(s) is(are) speaking about only one sex?

3. Are females and males in parallel situations described by nonparallel terms? [e.g., man and wife]

4. When both sexes are mentioned together in particular phrases, does one sex consistently precede the other? [e.g., "men and women"]

5. Are the two sexes consistently discussed in different grammatical modes? [e.g., using the passive voice when referring to women, but the active voice when referring to men] (p. 137)

Gay People

Issues of appropriate language usage are more complicated with gay men and lesbians than with the other three groups. Obviously, attention to the language issues raised in chapter 1 is a starting point. The terms *gay men* and *lesbians* are preferable to *homosexual* to distinguish gay identity from sexual behavior. The term *sexual orientation* rather than *sexual preference* reminds us that gay people do not choose their sexual orientation any more than nongays choose to be heterosexual. It is also extremely important that counselors not confuse sexual orientation with other descriptors, such as gender role, gender identity, transvestism, or transsexuality. Of course, counselors should not only refrain from using any of the vast array of derogatory labels for gay people in their professional roles, but must also extend this behavior to their personal lives, as such usage only serves to perpetuate the homophobia that is the primary source of oppression for gays. Beyond these basics, however, the issues become muddier.

When counseling gay men and lesbians, it is incumbent upon the counselor to understand the client's preferences for self-labels. There is often a considerable time gap (sometimes years) between a gay individual's first awareness of feelings for the same sex and their full acceptance of their gay identity (Dworkin & Gutierrez, 1992). In the earliest stages of the coming out process, clients may not accept that they are gay, and the counselor must, consequently, be careful in attaching labels to clients; however, neither should the counselor assume that homoerotic feelings are "just a phase." Understanding the coming out process is vital to gay affirmative counseling (Garnets, Hancock, Cochran, Goodchilds, & Peplau, 1991). Even clients who are fairly comfortable with being gay may prefer one self-descriptor over others, e.g., a woman who prefers to call herself gay rather than lesbian. Counselors must always recall that gay clients are no more immune from the effects of homophobia than nongay clients. Finally, some gay men and lesbians have reclaimed some of society's derogatory labels, e.g., queer or dyke, using them in a gay-affirmative manner. It is usually wise for the nongay counselor to refrain from such usage because of possible misinterpretations.

In all aspects of practice, counselors must scrupulously avoid heterosexist assumptions and language reflecting those assumptions. As we previously discussed, *heterosexist bias* is defined as "conceptualizing human experience in strictly heterosexual terms and consequently ignoring, invalidating, or derogating homosexual behaviors and sexual orientation, and lesbian, gay, and bisexual relationships and lifestyles" (Herek, Kimmel, Amaro, & Melton, 1991, p. 958). Even with nongay clients (or clients who are presumed to be nongay) counselors must take care to examine the ways the assumption that everyone is heterosexual can influence practice. A common example is assuming the sex of a client's significant other or partner (e.g., with a male client, assuming that the partner is female).

APA's Committee on Gay and Lesbian Concerns (1991) summarized the goals for reducing heterosexual bias in language:

1. *Reducing heterosexual bias and increasing visibility of lesbians, gay men, and bisexual persons.* Unless an author is referring specifically to heterosexual people, writing should be free of heterosexual bias. Ways to increase the visibility of lesbians, gay men, and bisexual persons include the following:
   a. Using examples of lesbians, gay men, and bisexual persons when referring to activities (e.g., parenting, athletic ability) that are erroneously associated only with heterosexual people by many readers.

b. Referring to lesbians, gay men, and bisexual persons in situations other than sexual relationships. . . .

c. Omitting discussion of marital status unless legal marital relationships are the subject of the writing. . . .

d. Referring to sexual and intimate emotional partners with both male and female terms (e.g., "the adolescent males were asked about the age at which they first had a male or female sexual partner").

e. Using sexual terminology that is relevant to lesbians and gay men as well as bisexual and heterosexual people (e.g., "when did you first engage in sexual activity" rather than "when did you first have sexual intercourse").

f. Avoiding the assumption that pregnancy may result from sexual activity. . . .

2. *Clarity of expression and avoidance of inaccurate stereotypes about lesbians, gay men, and bisexual persons.* . . . An example such as "Psychologists need training in working with special populations such as lesbians, drug abusers, and alcoholics" is stigmatizing in that it lists a status designation (lesbians) with designations of people being treated.

3. *Comparisons of lesbians and gay men with parallel groups.* . . . For example, contrasting lesbians with the "general public" or "normal women" portrays lesbians as marginal to society. More appropriate comparison groups might be "heterosexual women," "heterosexual men and women," or "gay men and heterosexual women and men." (p. 974)

Ethics and Ethical Issues

The American Psychological Association, American Counseling Association, and other professional mental health associations have made it clear that it is unethical to discriminate against clients with disabilities, older clients, women clients, and gay clients. The APA *Ethical Principles of Psychologists and Code of Conduct* (hereafter referred to as the APA *Ethics Code*) contains specific directives to psychologists regarding their treatment of diverse populations. Principle D (Respect for People's Rights and Dignity) states that:

Psychologists are aware of cultural, individual, and role differences, including those due to age, gender, race, ethnicity, national origin, religion, sexual orientation, disability, language, and socioeconomic status. Psychologists try to eliminate the effect on their work of biases based on those factors, and they do not knowingly participate in or condone unfair discriminatory practices. (APA, 1992, pp. 1599–1600)

Several of the standards that make up the APA *Ethics Code* make specific reference to psychologist behavior regarding diverse populations.

Standard 1.10 (Nondiscrimination): In their work-related activities, psychologists do not engage in unfair discrimination based on age, gender, race, ethnicity, national origin, religion, sexual orientation, disability, socioeconomic status, or any basis proscribed by law. (APA, 1992, p. 1601)

Standard 1.12 (Other Harassment): Psychologists do not knowingly engage in behavior that is harassing or demeaning to persons with whom they interact in their work based on factors such as those persons' age, gender, race, ethnicity, national origin, religion, sexual orientation, disability, language, or socioeconomic status. (APA, 1992, p. 1601)

In addition to the professional/ethical mandates prohibiting discrimination against diverse populations by psychologists, counselors should be aware of the ethical dilemmas they are likely to confront when working with people with disabilities, older people, women, and gay people. The ethical principles of autonomy, beneficence, nonmaleficence, justice, and fidelity identified by Kitchener (1984) as those "most critical for the evaluation of ethical concerns in psychology" (p. 46) along with the ethical principle of paternity will be used to highlight the nature of these dilemmas. Briefly, and in the context of a counseling relationship, autonomy refers to the client's freedom of action and freedom of choice. The principle of beneficence implies that the counselor should promote the client's welfare, while the principle of nonmaleficence mandates that the counselor should do no harm to the client. According to Kitchener (1984), justice in the broadest sense means "fairness" and "suggests that equal persons have the right to be treated equally and nonequal persons have a right to be treated differently if the inequality is relevant to the issue in question" (p. 49). Fidelity has to do with trustworthiness and in counseling requires the counselor to maintain confidentiality and obtain the client's informed consent to treatment. The principle of paternalism requires that counselors care for and safeguard the interests of their clients who can not do so themselves (Steininger, Newell, & Garcia, 1984).

Ethical dilemmas result when the mandates of ethical principles, codes of ethics, statutory law, common law, and/or the counselor's own moral standards conflict with each other. The thorniest of these potential conflicts may be when counselors hold certain religious beliefs that conflict with their professional role. For example, to act ethically, counselors must be accepting and affirming toward gay and lesbian clients. Whether that is possible when a counselor holds strongly to the conviction that homosexuality is a sin is highly questionable (see Nelson, 1985, for discussion of religious perspectives on homosexuality). There are an infinite number of specific ethical dilemmas that the counselor might confront when working with nonethnic minorities; even a thorough review of the dilemmas that can arise from conflicts between the ethical principles alone is beyond the scope of this text. A few conflicts between ethical principles will be cited as examples of dilemmas that the counselor may face when working with people with disabilities, older people, women, and gay people.

The ethical principle of justice is particularly relevant to clients who have been singled out for differential and inferior treatment but contains the basis for a counseling dilemma. In essence, the principle of justice places counselors in the position of deciding when they should provide unequal treatment because the inequality of the client's status is relevant to the counseling concern, or when they should provide equal treatment because the inequality of the client's status is not relevant to the counseling concern. An example of this dilemma might involve vocational placement of a person with a disability. Is the fact that the client has been released by three previous employers after a very brief tenure on the job evidence of disability discrimination (and thereby warranting of unequal treatment, perhaps in the form of counselor advocacy) or lack of effort (and thereby warranting treatment equal to that of a person without a disability)?

Conflicts between the principles of autonomy and paternalism frequently create dilemmas for counselors working with nonethnic minorities. The principle of autonomy (and treatment issues related to empowerment) dictate that the minority client should be allowed to exercise his or her freedom of choice and action. However, the counselor may feel that due to the client's limited cognitive functioning (as in the cases of some elders and most persons with developmental disabilities), the client is not in a position to exercise his or her autonomy in a beneficial way. This situation frequently arises when an elderly person must make a major life decision that affects not only him- or herself, but his or her family. Fitting (1986) has identified four types of clients/problems that frequently involve these types of decisions:

> (a) those who are coping with the developmental issues of aging (e.g., retirement, loss of spouse), (b) those who are coping with chronic illness common in late life (e.g., hearing and visual impairments, dementia), (c) those who have major mental illness (e.g., late onset schizophrenia, major depression), and (d) those who are suffering from terminal illnesses (e.g., cancer, end-stage renal disease).

With respect to the autonomy versus paternalism conflict when working with an older client, Fitting (1986) recommends that counselors become familiar with their professional code of ethics, knowledgeable about the health and medical status of their clients, and informed about the decision-making capability and psychological functioning of older adults. She recommends that the counselor first assess the decision-making capacity of the client, then assess the family relationships within the client's family, and finally weigh the choices in terms of the ethical principles of fidelity, beneficence, and autonomy.

Cayleff (1986) suggests that the paternalism inherent in the counselor-client relationship reinforces societal values that deny women a full measure of autonomy. "To discern the true autonomy of women, it may be necessary to establish women's own beliefs, as opposed to their socialized, sex-specific propensity to accommodate and attempt to please others" (Cayleff, 1986, p. 346). Counselors who neglect to examine the effects of gender-role socialization on their clients' attitudes and choices often unwittingly reinforce the status quo. Counseling that supports limited, sex-specific career and personal goals for women violates the ethical principles of beneficence and nonmaleficence, as well as the ethical principle of autonomy.

Paternalism, beneficence, and autonomy also can create ethical dilemmas for the counselor working with a gay or lesbian adolescent. Sobocinski (1990) points out that adolescence is a transitional period during which a young person moves from dependence to independence, a change that has special relevance for counseling clients around issues of emerging sexuality and acknowledging sexual orientation. After analyzing the competing ethical principles, Sobocinski (1990) concluded:

> There does not appear to be, a priori, reason to declare youth incompetent to consent to treatment dealing with issues of sexual orientation. Because of the inevitability of internalized negative stereotypes and stigma surrounding lesbians and gays in society, one cannot hope that the resolution of gay and lesbian adolescents' emerging sexuality will be facilitated in a manner in which their autonomy is respected until and unless these factors are addressed within therapy. Only when adolescents view their sexuality as acceptable and worthy can they be truly autonomous and free of the coercive, controlling influences of family, peers, and society. (p. 246)

Advocate and Change Agent Roles

A theme throughout this book is that many of the problems experienced by nonethnic minorities are the result of the oppression they experience and that counselors may need to assist their nonethnic minority clients to overcome the effects of oppression. This suggests the need for counselors to function as advocates and/or social change agents.

In the advocacy role, the counselor speaks on the client's behalf. This role is called for when the client is unable to speak for him- or herself. This might be the case when the client is an elder with limited English-speaking ability or a person with a disability that limits their ability to speak for themselves. In the change agent role, the counselor attempts to change the oppressive environment, either by directly or indirectly promoting the empowerment of the oppressed group.

According to Ruth and Blotzer (1995), "Psychotherapeutic work to empower people with disabilities is in its toddlerhood, a stage of hypothesis-generating and small-scale clinical experimentation" (p. 3). However, a number of authors have suggested how service providers can serve as advocates and change agents for people with disabilities. With respect to advocacy, the counselor's efforts may be as simple as calling attention to the language used in reference to a person with a disability. Bruce and Christiansen (1988) proposed that therapists "confront persons using pejorative language in their spoken and written communication by politely drawing attention to the negative effects of such language and suggesting preferred word alternatives" (p. 191). Advocacy also may involve extending rights to people with disabilities in the context of therapy. Brown (1995) developed a "Bill of Rights for People with Disabilities in Group Work" that helps identify rights that people with disabilities should be accorded in various groups (e. g., task groups, psychoeducational groups, counseling groups, psychotherapy groups). Sharing and implementing this "Bill of Rights" is another way counselors can advocate for people with disabilities.

On the other hand, advocacy may involve political action. Vargo (1989) proposed that counselors "encourage people who are interested to actively agitate for legislation which will ensure measures such as equal pay for equal work and barrier-free design of public buildings" (p. 283) on behalf of people with disabilities.

Fawcett et al. (1994) have developed a model of empowerment for people with disabilities based on the "personal and environmental factors that affect the behaviors and outcomes associated with empowerment" (p. 473). Personal factors that these authors include in their model are competence and experience (individual's or group's knowledge, skills, history of empowerment, and values/beliefs) and physical and biological capacity (individual's health, type of impairment, and degree of impairment). Environment factors included in the model are stressors and barriers (lack of opportunity, discrimination, punishment and behavioral requirements, environmental barriers and hazards, and poverty and deprivation) and support and resources (information and prompts, family and peer support, models and mentors, positive reinforcement, financial and material resources, policies and laws, and culture). Based on this model of empowerment, Fawcett et al. developed four strategies and 18 tactics for enhancing the empowerment of individuals (and groups representing individuals) with disabilities. The four strategies are (1) enhancing experience and competence, (2) protecting and maintaining physical and biological capacity, (3) removing stressors and barriers, and (4) enhancing support and resources. The reader is referred to Fawcett et al. for a discussion of the 18 tactics designed to enhance empowerment and examples of how they can be implemented.

A series of studies by Balcazar and his associates have examined the empowerment process for people with disabilities. Balcazar, Fawcett, and Seekins (1991) were able to train four college students with physical disabilities to approach their professors to request assistance in addressing personal goals. Balcazar, Seekins, Fawcett, and Hopkins (1990) documented that advocacy skills training for persons with physical disabilities resulted in an increase of disability-related issues they reported at monthly advocacy meetings, an increase of advocacy actions on the part of participants, and an increase in the number of targeted actions (i.e., changes in the environment, policy, budget allocations, and services). A subsequent study by Balcazar, Mathews, Francisco, Fawcett, and Seekins (1994) failed to replicate the training effect of the earlier study but did conclude that collective action and advocacy is required to make communities more responsive to the needs of people with disabilities.

Counselors can also serve as change agents by empowering families to act on behalf of a family member who has a disability. Munro (1991) has described a Step Approach Model to training families of persons with severe developmental, psychiatric, or neurological disabilities to be effective advocates. Eight commonsense rules define this model:

Rule 1. Never use a cannon where a pea-shooter will do! (p. 2) The advocate who is overly negative, aggressive or obnoxious may alienate potential supporters and problem solvers and may do more harm than good.

Rule 2. Get the big picture. (p. 2) By gathering facts about all the factors influencing the institutional decision-making process, the advocate is in a good position to establish realistic goals and to develop effective strategies.

Rule 3. Time your advocacy strategies carefully. (p. 3) To ensure proper timing, the advocate should do three things: first, make sure his or her own motivation and energy level is at its highest before raising a concern; second, present his or her case when the potential problem solver is most willing and able to listen to the concern; third, identify needs as early as possible and before a crises develops.

Rule 4. Use the cards you've been dealt. (p. 3) Assess your skills as an advocate and attempt to maximize those skills in the advocacy process. If you are better as a speaker than a writer, present the case verbally, and recruit someone else to present the case in writing.

Rule 5. Don't go it alone. (p. 3) Recruit other advocates; there is power, strength, and support in group advocacy.

Rule 6. Be willing to compromise. (p. 3) Politics are inherent in all social institutions. Negotiating a workable compromise can lay the groundwork for future successes.

Rule 7. Humanize the concern. (p. 3) A personal testimony from the client or the client's family can often be much more effective than a mountain of statistics.

Rule 8. Express appreciation and show support to helpful problem solvers. (p. 3) Failing to express appreciation to helpful decision makers ultimately may be self-defeating. A pat on the back may help ensure future cooperation.

Similarly, counselors can be advocates and change agents for older people. Crabtree (1988) has described an advocacy role for rehabilitation specialists that could be generalized to any counselors or psychologists who work with elders who live in a nursing home (or who work with the families of nursing home residents). Basically, the role involves educating elders, health care providers, third party payers, nursing home administrators, and nursing home staff as to what constitutes quality rehabilitation services and then following up to ensure that these services are provided.

Wolff (1987) has described the advocacy efforts of the Highland Valley Elder Service, Inc., an Area Agency on Aging/home care corporation in Northampton, Massachusetts, that was designed to empower elder citizens. The agency funded seven initiatives that we cite as examples of activities that can empower older people:

1. Conducting a marketing research survey on elder economic needs and interest in a membership system;

2. Establishing a Gray Panther organization to strengthen advocacy efforts;

3. Development of buying clubs for elders for cooperative buying of food;
4. Development of cooperative purchasing for home energy needs;
5. Development of a self-supporting membership newsletter offering economic benefit packages (coupons and discounts from member merchants) and advocacy tools (e.g., tear-out postcards);
6. Development of employment opportunities for elders in the child care field; and
7. Training elders to be leaders of self-help groups in their own communities.

These efforts by the Highland Valley Elder Service provide evidence that a group of advocates can bring about significant changes in community services for the elderly.

Netting and Hinds (1989) point out that the Comprehensive Older Americans Act Amendment of 1978 mandated that each state designate an ombudsman for the elderly at the state level. They describe the East Tennessee Advocates for Elders program as an example of a rural volunteer ombudsman program. The program is designed to meet the needs of elderly persons receiving long-term care. It has one paid professional director and a number of certified volunteers and is administratively responsible to the Area Agency on Aging. The volunteers are involved in community development, social planning, and social action:

> Community development emphasizes self-help and citizen participation. Individuals and groups work cooperatively to solve problems. . . . Social planning focuses on rational problem solving, which requires professionals to gather and analyze data to plan for community change. Consumers of service are usually relegated to client and recipient roles. . . . Social action attempts to restructure power relationships and to include consumers of service in the process of confronting difficulties. . . . social reform as a model mixes social planning and social action. (p. 423)

The community development strategy is implemented by having a volunteer ombudsman visit elderly nursing home residents and assist them with their needs. As an example of the social planning strategy, Netting and Hinds cite the use of volunteers who collect information for publication in a consumer guide to health care facilities in the 16-county area served by the program. As an example of social action efforts, they point to the work by volunteers who over two and a half years researched, studied, and drafted nursing home legislation that was introduced in the Tennessee State Assembly in 1986.

In making the case for gender aware or feminist approaches to counseling, we have already implicitly suggested a social advocacy approach to counseling women. Because so many of the concerns female clients present to counselors are heavily influenced by their gender, we argue that counselors perform a disservice to their female clients if the counselor is not sensitive to gender influences and gender inequities. However, a wide range of options remain as to the most effective ways of working with gender in counseling.

The earliest forms of feminist counseling were the grass roots consciousness raising (CR) groups of the early 1970s, which emerged out of the feminist movement. These were not originally conceptualized as "therapy" groups, but as a political force; participants came together to share their perceptions and discuss their experiences as women, with the common goal of social change (Enns, 1993). However, it soon became clear that CR participants often reported improvements akin to those we expect from counseling, for example, enhanced self-esteem, increased autonomy, and other personal changes, as well as modifications in interpersonal relationships.

> As the therapeutic benefits of CR groups became apparent to women, they were sometimes recommended as an adjunct to therapy. . . . Women therapists, who became members of CR groups, were changed and radicalized through their interactions with other women and expressed interest in using their skills to combat oppression in their professional work . . . [therapy] groups that were modeled after CR experiences . . . became the preferred modality for a substantial number of feminist therapists. . . . Groups were seen as an effective antidote to negative gender socialization in that women could gain power by practicing skills in a safe environment. (Enns, 1993, pp. 6–7)

Gradually, as the limitations of CR groups as the only form of feminist assistance to women became apparent, other methods of feminist and gender-aware therapy emerged focusing more on the personal issues and concerns of women. Today, there are a wide range of feminist approaches, some still intimately tied to political activism, others less overtly activist but retaining some of the basic principles of the earlier feminist CR groups.

Although feminism simply refers to the advocacy of equality between women and men, several feminist philosophies have been articulated. Each adopts a slightly different stance on the presumed reasons for gender inequality and, therefore, the manner in which inequalities and gender influences ought to be addressed. Feminist therapy, therefore, is not a monolithic entity; feminist *therapies* exist, corresponding to different feminist philosophies, each suggesting somewhat different strategies for effecting social change within and outside of counseling (Enns & Hackett, 1990; Hackett, Enns, & Zetzer, 1992). Some of the major traditions within feminist thought have been the liberal, radical, socialist, Marxist, cultural, and woman of color feminist philosophies. Of these, the liberal and radical feminist philosophies have been drawn from most heavily by feminist therapists:

> Liberal feminist writers emphasize current inequalities in educational opportunities and civil rights, focusing on the elimination of these inequalities, especially through legal and educational reform, as the mechanism for achieving a sex-fair society. . . . Consequently, the liberal feminist counselor focuses on expanding clients' awareness of gender role socialization, social barriers, and discrimination, in the context of exploring personal goals and options. Radical feminist theorists . . . see sexism as the fundamental oppression. Radical feminist

theorists all share the assumptions that historically women were the first oppressed group, that women's oppression is the most widespread and pervasive form of oppression, and that women's oppression is the hardest to eradicate and cannot be removed by other social changes such as legal or educational reform. (Enns & Hackett, 1990, p. 34)

One of the fundamental differences between the liberal and radical perspectives in counseling is that the radical feminist counselor will be much more active in assisting clients to identify social barriers and structural inequalities, and will be more likely to encourage (though not coerce) the client to engage in external change efforts and political action. The liberal feminist counselor will be more likely to support, but not necessarily actively encourage, clients' social change efforts. Although these philosophical distinctions are helpful in understanding the varieties of feminist approaches to counseling, we must also caution the readers that, in real life, the distinctions are often blurred.

What these approaches all have in common is an emphasis on empowering women: The social construction of gender [and feminist therapy] relocates women's problems from individual and internal to societal and external. The feminist construction of gender redefines the nature of women's and men's relationships in terms of the expression and maintenance of power. Emergent client populations were "discovered" where problems were never thought to exist [e.g., sexual abuse, sexual harassment, eating disorders]. The challenge of these new client populations stimulated the development of theories, research, and procedures to address their concerns. The combined efforts of women's groups in both the lay and professional communities have resulted in a new agenda for women's mental health. (Worell & Remer, 1992, p. 4)

In essence, counselors who address and explore gender socialization, gender-related beliefs and constraints, and structural influences on and barriers to women, by default engage in a form of social advocacy for all women.

Social advocacy for lesbians and gay men is also necessary and encouraged by the major professional associations:

In 1975, the American Psychological Association (APA) took a strong stance regarding bias toward lesbians and gay men, resolving that "homosexuality per se implies no impairment in judgment, reliability, or general social and vocational abilities. . . ." The APA urged psychologists "to take the lead in removing the stigma of mental illness long associated with homosexual orientations." (Garnets et al., 1991, p. 964)

Despite this exhortation, issued over 20 years ago, ongoing discrimination against gay people underscores the necessity of continuing efforts on the part of counselors and psychologists in educating ourselves, our clients, and the public at large. Our professional organizations have been involved in public policy debates on issues of concern to gay men and lesbians; for example, APA issued a review of the scientific research supporting lifting the ban on gays in the military and has also issued briefs on other civil rights issues of concern to gay people (Melton, 1989). However, therapists and counselors themselves have not universally surmounted the deeply ingrained negative attitudes toward gay people. Although 99 percent of service providers in a recent study reported having counseled at least one gay client (that they knew of), the majority (58 percent) were also personally aware of incidents of biased or inappropriate treatment of gay clients "including cases in which practitioners defined lesbians or gay men as 'sick' and in need of change, and instances where a client's sexual orientation distracted a therapist from treating a person's central problem" (Garnets et al., 1991, p. 970). Clearly, social change advocacy for gay clients must begin with each individual counselor. Our earlier review of language usage is a starting point, and the articles on gay affirmative counseling (chapters 16 and 17) contain many suggestions useful to the counselor attempting to grapple with antigay bias.

However, social advocacy must eventually extend beyond one's own attitudes and can take many forms. For example, Garnets et al. (1991), in their discussion of exemplary practice with gay clients, state that "a therapist is familiar with the needs and treatment issues of gay male and lesbian clients, and uses relevant mental health, educational, and gay male and lesbian community resources" (p. 970). This type of behavior with individual clients alone constitutes a form of advocacy: "A gay man, a client of mine, age 20, told me he particularly appreciated my willingness to gather information about coming out, including meeting with campus representatives, which he was not yet ready to do, having just concluded in therapy he was gay" (Garnets et al., 1991, p. 970). At some point, however, counselors must begin to engage in more visible advocacy efforts. Recommendations for exemplary practice with gay clients also include public advocacy:

> A therapist recognizes the importance of educating professionals, students, supervisees, and others about gay male and lesbian issues and actively counters misinformation or bias about lesbians and gay men: [for example] A colleague told me of how they changed the intake forms at the agency to include gay/lesbian and space for "significant other" identification instead of spouse. [And] I observed a colleague, at a case conference, ask the presenter if he had asked his single male patient about homosexual experience. The presenter had assumed that because he had never had a girlfriend or been married, he was asexual." (Garnets et al., 1991, p. 970)

Counselor Training

The justification for training counselors to work with nonethnic minority groups can be found in their representation among users of counseling and psychological services. As suggested in chapter 1, women alone make up the majority of clients being seen by counselors and psychologists. Elders also represent a significant (and growing) proportion of the population, as do gay people and persons with disabilities. It is imperative that future counselors receive training that prepares them to work with these populations.

Justification for training counselors and psychologists to work with special populations is also provided by the professional and ethical standards of the major professional counseling and psychology associations. For example, the APA *Ethics Code* makes it clear that psychologists are to seek training in order to ensure that they can work with diverse populations. Standard 1.08 states:

> Where differences of age, gender, race, ethnicity, national origin, religion, sexual orientation, disability, language, or socioeconomic status significantly affect psychologists' work concerning particular individuals or groups, *psychologists obtain the training* [italics added], experience, consultation, or supervision necessary to ensure the competence of their services, or they make appropriate referrals. (APA, 1992, p. 1601)

Also, the APA *Guidelines and Principles for Accreditation of Programs in Psychology* (APA, 1995) states that in order to be eligible for accreditation, a program must demonstrate it

> engages in actions that indicate respect for and understanding of cultural and individual diversity. . . . the phrase "cultural and individual diversity" refers to diversity with regard to personal and demographic characteristics. These include, but are not limited to, age, color, disabilities, ethnicity, gender, language, national origin, race, religion, sexual orientation, and social economic status. (p. 5)

> The program has and implements a thoughtful and coherent plan to *provide students with relevant knowledge and experiences* [italics added] about the role of cultural and individual diversity in psychological phenomena as they [are] related to the science and practice of professional psychology. (p. 10)

Furthermore, the APA *Guidelines and Principles for Accreditation of Programs in Professional Psychology* (APA, 1995) also mandate that programs not discriminate against diverse populations in their student and faculty recruitment, retention, and development processes:

> Respect for and understanding of cultural and individual diversity is reflected in the program's policies for the recruitment, retention, and development of faculty and students, and in its curriculum and field placements. The program has nondiscriminatory policies and operating conditions, and it avoids any actions that would restrict program access or completion on grounds that are irrelevant to success in graduate training or the profession. (p. 5)

Similar statements can be found in the *Code of Ethics and Standards of Practice of the American Counseling Association* and the accreditation requirements of the Council for Accreditation of Counseling and Related Activities (CACREP, 1990). It is clear from these statements that training counselors to work with nonethnic minorities is not only a desired function of counselor training programs, it is a mandated one.

We believe that in order to train counselors to work with nonethnic minorities, three components are needed: (1) a faculty sensitive to diversity issues; (2) a curriculum that is designed to train counselors to work with special populations; and (3) students who are receptive to training in the area of nonethnic minorities. All three are essential ingredients; the absence of any one of these components will seriously jeopardize the effectiveness of the training program.

Faculty Sensitivity to Diversity Issues

Although the major professional organizations require that counselors and psychologists recognize differences among people and that accredited training programs provide training in client diversity, they have not addressed the issue of faculty development and renewal in this area. Unfortunately, most professors in counselor and psychologist training programs were themselves trained before current professional and accreditation standards were in place mandating training for counseling of diverse populations. This places the responsibility for designing curricula related to client diversity in the hands of individuals who have no systematic training on the topic. It seems clear that faculty must actively seek out development and renewal activities to acquire both the attitudes and knowledge needed to train counselors and psychologists to work with diverse populations. Further, it is unreasonable to assume that graduate students will acquire the necessary sensitivity to and competency with client differences if the counselor training faculty cannot model these attributes.

A survey of psychologists on the practice and ethics of teaching exposes the failure of some of the teaching faculty to keep current in areas of diversity. Only 71 percent of the respondents regarded sexual involvement with a student as absolutely unethical; 30 percent of teaching faculty felt that telling a student "I'm sexually attracted to you" was either ethical, or ethical under certain circumstances (Tabachnik, Keith-Spiegel, & Pope, 1991). Although 64 percent of psychologists branded as unethical the teaching that homosexuality per se was pathological, 10 percent said it was ethical, 16 percent were unsure, and 8 percent said it was unethical under rare circumstances. Only 17 percent regarded teaching in buildings that did not accommodate physically challenged students as unethical (Tabachnik et al., 1991).

Although it is important for counseling professors trained over the past 50 years to develop sensitivity to minority issues through their own professional development and renewal, it is imperative that future faculty appointments include sensitivity to diversity issues as a selection criterion. Since faculty serve as professional models for the students with whom they work, we believe that sensitivity to diversity issues should be one of the top priorities in selecting a counselor educator. Faculty and administrators responsible for selecting new faculty should examine each candidate's background to determine familiarity with diversity issues and should include questions related to sensitivity in this area in any interviewing that is done.

In addition to selecting faculty who are sensitive to diversity issues, every effort should be made to ensure that people with disabilities, women, and gay people are represented among the faculty proportionate to their representation in the general population (most counselor training programs already include a diversity of ages). As indicated earlier, the APA *Guidelines and Principles for Accreditation of Programs in Professional Psychology* (APA, 1995) requires that accredited programs recruit, retain, and develop faculty as well as students from diverse populations. Although data on faculty members with disabilities and gay or lesbian faculty are generally not available, data on female representation among counselor education faculties is not encouraging.

Anderson and Rawlins (1985) report that although slightly over 50 percent of the new Ph.D.s and Ed.D.s in counselor education in 1983 were women; only 22.5 percent of the faculty in counselor education programs were women, and most of these were in the lower ranks. They suggest a concentrated effort is needed to recruit, select, and advance women in counselor education. We believe this recommendation applies to faculty members with disabilities and gay or lesbian faculty as well. In the area of recruitment for faculty positions, they suggest networking to identify qualified women applicants and including women on selection committees. In the area of selection, they suggest that screening committees be made familiar with discriminatory questions that are prohibited by law and that faculty discuss the "invisible discrimination of perceptual bias." In order to support the professional development of women faculty, these authors suggest research support groups, academic mentors, and selective committee involvement for female faculty. Each of these suggestions can be generalized to the recruitment, selection, and support of faculty with disabilities and gay or lesbian faculty as well.

Those university counseling centers, Veterans Administration centers, and mental health hospitals that participate in training counselors and psychologists through pre- and postdoctoral internships should also take steps to ensure that their training staff is sensitive to and knowledgeable about client diversity. Efforts should be made to expose all interns to the full range of client diversity seen at each agency.

Counselor Training Curriculum

Before examining suggestions for course content that addresses special populations, we will review the current status of counselor and psychologist training for work with people with disabilities, older people, women, and gay people and the training models that have been proposed for providing this training.

Training Currently Provided

In order to ensure that counselors are trained to effectively counsel clients from nonethnic minorities, counselor training programs need to focus attention on these groups as part of their curricula. To date, however, it appears that most counselor training programs do not require (or even offer) courses in counseling nonethnic minorities. In a survey of 285 counselor education programs, Scott and McMillian (1980) found that only 4 percent required counselor trainees to take a sex-fair counseling course, and only 33 percent offered a sex-fair counseling course as an elective.

With respect to training counselors to offering course work related to gerontological counseling, there is evidence that a trend toward offering such courses may have peaked and leveled off. Salisbury (1975) surveyed 304 counselor education programs and found that not one of them required their students to take a course in geriatric counseling, and only 6 percent offered an elective on the topic. Only eight years later, Myers (1983) determined that 37 percent of 306 responding counselor education programs offered courses to train counselors to work with the elderly, a substantial increase but still a clear minority of the programs surveyed. In a more recent survey, however, Myers, Loesch, and Sweeney (1991) found that only 31 percent of the 237 programs responding to their survey offered courses to train counselors to work with older persons. Assuming that programs offering such courses were overrepresented among respondents (responses were received from only 52 percent of the counselor education programs in the United States), it seems reasonable to conclude that the actual percentage of programs offering coursework in gerontological counseling is something less than 31 percent. Furthermore, 75 percent of the respondents to the Myers et al. (1991) survey indicated that they had no plans to offer additional coursework on gerontological counseling. Similar results were found in a study of psychology providers. Gatz, Karel, and Wolkenstein (1991) surveyed 74 psychologists who designated "aged" as a population they served and found that only 27 percent had any formal training in gerontological psychology. Gatz et al. (1991) concluded that "potential consumers might well be concerned about whether practitioners are adequately familiar with special problems of their age group" (p. 415). To help address the need for more psychologists who specialize in working with the elderly, a conference cosponsored by the APA Practice Directorate, the National Institute of Mental Health, and the Retirement Research Foundation recommended the development of standards for a specialization in clinical geropsychology (Moses, 1992).

Nonetheless, it should be acknowledged that some progress has been made with regard to gerontological counseling. Myers (1995) reviewed the 20-year history of the gerontological counseling specialty and cited the following five outcomes as evidence that "gerontological counseling is well established as a specialty within the counseling profession" (Myers, 1995, p. 146): (1) five national projects on aging sponsored by ACA, (2) an ACA division with a focus on the adult years (Association for Adult Development and Aging), (3) CACREP (ACA accrediting agency) accreditation of programs in community counseling that specialize in gerontological counseling, (4) NBCC (ACA certification agency) establishment of a national certification in gerontological counseling, and (5) identification of gerontological competencies for counselors

(Myers & Sweeney, 1990). However, she also acknowledged only about one-third of all counselor training programs now offer course work to prepare counselors to work with older people and that strong leadership at the national level and active advocacy at all levels will be needed if the specialty is to be maintained and enhanced.

Although rehabilitation counseling programs are specifically designed to train counselors to work with persons with disabilities, counselor training programs in general provide little training related to this population. Olkin (cited in Leigh, Corbett, Gutman, & Morere, 1996) reported that despite the passage of the American with Disabilities Act in 1990, only 44 APA accredited programs offer at least one course on disability, and most of these have to do with exceptional children, mental retardation, or learning disabilities. Leigh et al. point out that psychology programs appear to be ignoring deafness altogether, even though the ADA mandates that "anyone operating a business of any size or providing services, including psychological services in any setting (such as hospitals, clinics, and private or home offices) must anticipate providing accommodations for clients with disabilities, including those whose disability affects communication accessibility" (p. 364). Crespi (1988), addressing the lack of counselors trained to work with persons who have visual impairments, points out that as the population ages, the numbers of persons with a visual disability will increase. A similar observation applies to most other types of disabilities and suggests an urgent need for all counselors and psychologists to receive training to work with persons with disabilities.

There has been no research and, until recently, very little attention devoted to the coverage of gay issues in counselor preparation programs (Iasenza, 1989). However, Graham, Rawlings, Halpern, and Hermes (1984), in a study of practicing therapists' attitudes, knowledge, concerns, and counseling approaches with lesbians and gay men, reported a strong need for additional training in this area. Therapists were generally uninformed about the literature on gay lifestyles, many held inaccurate beliefs about gay people, and a significant minority (37 percent) stated that they would work with clients on the goal of changing sexual orientation (Graham et al., 1984). McDonald (1982) found misleading information and misrepresentation of data on gay people in a survey of introductory psychology textbooks, a finding that does not bode well for the undergraduate preparation of students entering graduate programs in mental health. Buhrke (1989a) found that almost one-third of female counseling psychology student reported no exposure to gay or lesbian issues during their graduate experience; 70 percent were in programs where no faculty were engaged in research on gay issues; and almost one-half of the respondents had not seen any gay or lesbian clients.

Although inclusion of training for competence with diverse populations is beginning to have an impact on counselor training programs, it seems clear that actual training of counselors in nonethnic minority issues still lags behind professional and accreditation standards that mandate such training.

Training Models

While there is general agreement that training must be provided, there is disagreement about the kind of training model that is most effective as a means of sensitizing counselors to work with special populations. Some authors have argued for specialized training related to specific groups, and others have argued for changes in the basic curriculum. Copeland (1982) identified four models for training counselors to work with special populations, the separate course model, area of concentration model, interdisciplinary model, and integrated model.

In the *separate* course approach, information about nonethnic minorities is provided in one course. Usually, this course would have as its goals the development of sensitivity to the experience of being a minority person, knowledge about each group discussed, and competency in adapting counseling strategies to the groups studied. The separate course can focus on only one minority, in which case a number of separate courses must be offered. The course also can focus on the effects of discrimination with an attempt to generalize the content to all minority groups (a human rights approach). In response to the need to increase student awareness, knowledge, and skills for counseling special populations, many counselor education programs have started to offer separate courses for each group. Margolis and Rungta (1986), addressing the issue of separate courses for ethnic groups, offer the following criticisms of this approach:

1. "Adding more and more special courses to an existing program may not be feasible because of budget constraints, the total number of courses that can be imposed on students, and availability of expert faculty." (p. 643)

2. A proliferation of separate courses for special groups may accent differences among them and lead to a separate set of standards and strategies for each group that, in turn, may lead to unequal treatment.

3. By focusing on one characteristic, we may fail to recognize the total person. If we focus on a person's ethnicity, sex, age, socioeconomic class, sexual orientation, or disability, we may fail to recognize other important characteristics or the unique combination of characteristics.

4. Another consequence of providing separate courses for each group is that it may limit the ability of counselor trainees to transfer their learning from one population to another. Margolis and Rungta argue that the common experiences of discrimination among minority groups suggests that some course content should be generalized across groups.

In the *area of concentration* model, students are offered several courses and perhaps a practicum that focus on special populations. These courses are either part of an elective concentration within a larger program or the entire program is identified as having a focus on a special population. In the former case, it is only helpful for some of the students, and in the latter case, only those students enrolled in programs that make the commitment to resources for this model benefit. Also, those programs that focus on one client population, say older clients, may fail to provide proper training in other types of diversity.

In the *interdisciplinary* model the program makes use of courses that are taught in other departments to provide an area of concentration. The interdisciplinary model appears to be inherent in the criteria for certification as a National Certified Gerontological Counselor. The National Board for Certified Counselors requires three graduate courses in gerontology (along with an internship in a gerontological setting and two years of professional gerontological counseling experience) for certification as a gerontological counselor (Myers, 1992). The interdisciplinary approach, assumes, of course, that such courses are available through other departments on the same campus. It also assumes the cooperation of other units on campus.

As applied to nonethnic minorities, the *integrated* model provides for integrating information about people with disabilities, older people, women, and gay people into all counselor training courses. For example, a human development course would address the sociopsychological development of people with disabilities, older people, women, and gay people. Similarly, a vocational psychology course would address the special vocational and avocational needs of women and people with disabilities and the employment problems experienced by all four groups. The integrated model was selected by the Council for Accreditation of Counseling and Related Educational Programs in developing recently adopted standards for training in gerontological counseling (Myers, 1992). This approach requires that all the faculty be familiar with diversity issues related to their courses and be willing to incorporate this content in their courses. Furthermore, the APA *Accreditation Guidelines* (APA, 1995) appear to mandate that training related to diverse populations be integrated into all courses in accredited programs.

Curriculum Content

Earlier authors have identified curriculum content needed to train counselors who will work with one of the four nonethnic minority groups discussed in this book. Most of these authors have recommended either an integrated or separate course approach. Some identify specific content that should be included in the curriculum; others focus on process more than content.

Most multicultural training models suggest that the first step toward become a multiculturally sensitive counselor is for counselors (or counselor trainees) to examine their own racial/ethnic biases (Atkinson, Morten, & Sue, in press). The same is true with regard to becoming more sensitive to the needs and experiences of all diverse populations. Hays (1996) created the acronym ADRESSING to emphasize the need for counselors and counselors-in-training to address their biases with respect to Age, Disability, Religion, Ethnicity, Social status, Sexual orientation, Indigenous heritage, National origin, and Gender diversity. The ADRESSING model described by Hays can be used to facilitate this process.

As we suggested earlier, another major step that counselors and psychologists can take toward becoming more credible and effective helpers is to eliminate imprecise and stereotypic language with respect to minorities from their vocabulary. However, can a course designed to teach the use of appropriate terminology have an impact? In order to determine if a course on language used in reference to people with disabilities could affect the language used by undergraduates in a special education class, Byrd et al. (1991) randomly assigned 107 students to hear either a lecture on appropriate language usage when referring to a person with disabilities or to a lecture on cultural divergence. Based on the results of a test administered one week after the examination, the authors concluded that "students do change their writing behavior, when making reference to persons with disabilities, if they receive a short training module on appropriate use of language" (Byrd et al., 1991, p. 41). Although it can be hypothesized that appropriate use of written language will generalize to oral language, the authors suggest that oral language may require consistent reinforcement to produce consistency in language usage.

Myers and Blake (1986) describe how course content related to counseling elders can be integrated into all counselor training courses, employing a model that could be generalized to other special populations as well. They suggest that the eight core areas of study and supervised experience included in the *Accreditation Manual* of the Council for the Accreditation of Counseling and Related Educational Program (CACREP) "provide an adequate and appropriate framework for the incorporation of specialized course work on counseling older persons into a counselor education curriculum" (Myers & Blake, p. 139). Myers and Blake provide a number of examples of aging-related content that could be included in the core areas of human growth and development, social and cultural foundations, the helping relationship, group dynamics, career development, appraisal of individuals, research, and professional orientation. Table 18.1 summarizes the course content these authors suggest for these eight CACREP core areas. They propose that an integrated model is the best means of ensuring that all students learn about aging and is most adaptable for a program training counselors for a variety of settings. Competencies that counselors should have who plan to specialize in working with older clients have been identified by Myers (1995). Myers recommends specialized courses taught on an interdisciplinary basis as the best approach to training counselors to work with older clients as a specialty.

Thomas and Martin (1992) cite efficiency and effectiveness as reasons why counselors should be trained to run groups for their elderly clients. They point out that to train counselors to run reality orientation, remotivation, psychotherapy, reminiscing, and other types of groups for elderly clients, counselor educators need to "bridge the training gaps by combining and connecting . . . three separate professional standards" (p. 57). The three training standards to which they refer are the standards for specialists in group work (Association for Specialists in Group Work, 1991), the standards for

Table 18.1

Course Content on Counseling Older People by Core Areas of Study from CACREP* Accreditation Standards

Core	Course Content
Human Growth and Development	Life span development Theories of aging
Social and Cultural Foundations	Older persons as a minority group Older women Changing population demography and increased numbers of older people Leisure and lifestyle of older people
The Helping Relationship	Impact of counselor and client age on interactions Ageist attitudes and beliefs Theories of personality and aging Techniques for use with older persons, such as life review therapy
Group Dynamics, Processes and Counseling	Pros and cons of groups for older people Structural versus unstructured groups Life review therapy groups Educational and guidance groups Support groups
Lifestyle and Career Development	Sources of occupational and educational information for older people Retirement adjustments Use of leisure time
Appraisal of Individuals	Validity of tests with older people Special techniques for testing older people Instruments for use with older people Renorming instruments for use with older people
Research and Evaluation	Obtaining access to older subjects Grant funding in aging Accommodating needs of older persons as research subjects
Professional Orientation	Professional associations in gerontology Gerontology certificate programs Roles of gerontological counselors Legal and ethical issues in gerontological counseling
Supervised Experiences	Aging network agencies Geriatric mental health hospitals and agencies Settings where older persons comprise a large segment of the clientele

Adapted from Myers & Blake (1986, pp. 139–140).
*CACREP = Council of Counseling and Related Activities

gerontological counselors (Myers & Sweeney, 1990), and the standards for counselors in general (CACREP, 1990). Agresti (1992) has provided a rationale for the inclusion of specialized training in ethics for gerontological counselors. He cites the variability among states concerning the reporting of elderly abuse, older adult ability to participate in decisions regarding his or her care, and the complex questions surrounding long-term care as examples of how counseling with older adults may present unique ethical issues.

Similarly, several authors (Buhrke, 1989b; Burhrke & Douce, 1991; Norton, 1982) have offered suggestions for integrating current information on gay people into the core counselor training curriculum. Beginning with the introductory course, counselor educators should ensure that if a course in psychology of sexuality is offered, it contain current, nonhomophobic information. Such a course should be not relied on as the sole training experience related to gay issues, however, and current issues on gays should be worked into all courses in counseling education. According to Norton (1982),

> There is not a course in counselor education in which gay issues are not appropriate. It is better that the topic appear as but a minor part of all courses, so that students get a feel for the pervasiveness of the gay group, but also a feel for the fact that this special population is really an integral part of the entire population. (p. 211)

Graham et al. (1984) offered a useful overview of the content on gay people that ought to be included in counselor preparation programs. Therapists and counselors need information about (1) lesbian/gay lifestyles and social networks; (2) homophobia and heterosexism; (3) self-esteem in lesbian and gay male clients, especially low self-esteem as a function of internalized homophobia; and (4) appropriate and inappropriate therapeutic goals, that is, gay-affirmative approaches. A book published by the American Counseling Association (Dworkin & Gutierrez, 1992) and the two special issues of major counseling journals devoted to counseling gay men and lesbians (*Journal of Counseling and Development*, September/October, 1989; *The Counseling Psychologist*, April, 1991) are also rich sources.

In terms of specific courses, introductory courses often include an overview of client concerns and populations. This is a good place to begin to introduce discussions of lesbians and gay men, for example, through case examples (Norton, 1982). Glenn and Russell (1986) suggest that training experiences that include ambiguous-sex clients can be used in existing courses to assess and confront subtle forms of heterosexual bias. Counseling theories must also be examined for heterosexist bias, e.g., Freud's views on heterosexual development (Buhrke, 1989b); heterosexual bias in assessment and diagnosis should also be an important aspect of any testing or measurement course. In group counseling courses, gay issues may be introduced in discussions of screening for group participation (e.g., a struggling gay adolescent in high school would probably not be a good candidate for a general counseling group), and gay support groups should be addressed (Buhrke & Douce, 1991). Gay men and lesbians experience unique career concerns that warrant coverage in career development course, e.g., occupational stereotypes, employment discrimination, dual career issues, and the work-nonwork interface (Buhrke, 1989b; Betz & Fitzgerald, 1993).

Gay issues should be incorporated into multicultural courses in two ways. First, counselors must be sensitive to the unique experiences and special needs of gay people of color, for example, the triple oppression experienced by lesbian African-Americans. Second, counselors need to develop an understanding of gay men and lesbians as minorities in this society (Buhrke, 1989b). Of course, gay issues should be well integrated into the practicum sequence. In prepracticum, students should be exposed to the range of issues experienced by gay and lesbian clients via roleplays (Buhrke & Douce, 1991). In practicum, attention to the effects of heterosexism on the counseling process and building gay affirmative counseling skills is vital (Buhrke & Douce, 1991). Buhrke and Douce (1991) also provide recommendations for incorporating gay issues into predoctoral internship training through training seminars and supervision.

The promotion of gender equity in counselor training and creating a program that will equip counselors with the skills to engage in gender-aware counseling, requires an in-depth knowledge of the literature on gender along with an examination of some fundamental beliefs about women (Good, Gilbert, & Scher, 1990). It may also require changes in almost all aspects of most training programs. The Division 17 guidelines for counseling/psychotherapy for women provide the basis for the content that must be integrated into counselor education programs (see chapter 12, Fitzgerald & Nutt, 1986). In addition, Worell and Remer (1992) offer a detailed overview of the literature on counseling women and provide recommendations for revamping training programs.

Introductory counseling courses might contain information about gender and gender-role issues in counseling; students can be introduced to the clinical concerns of special importance to women, for example, depression, eating disorders, sexual abuse, and sexual assault (Worell & Remer, 1992). Theory courses ought to include attention to feminist critiques of counseling theories, new developments in the psychology of women, and the current literature on counseling women (e.g., Brown & Gilligan, 1992; Kaschak, 1992; Laidlaw, Malmo, & Associates, 1990). Assessment courses should include an analysis of the sex bias literature; standardized tests should be critically examined for sex bias; and gender bias in clinical assessment and diagnosis can be introduced. Feminist alternatives to traditional assessment, for example, gender-role analysis, might be included (Hackett & Lonborg, 1993). Courses in career development ought to encompass sex bias in career development theories, gender-role stereotyping, the changing roles of men and women, and the special career counseling needs of women (e.g., dual career and multiple role counseling) (Walsh & Osipow, 1993). Practicum supervisors themselves must be conversant with the literature to be able to assist counselor trainees in addressing gender issues in the counseling process and to provide training in gender-aware and feminist approaches to counseling (Cook, 1993; Worell & Remer, 1992).

Lofaro (1982) suggests that although counselor education curricula may need to be modified in order to prepare counselors to work with disability-related concerns, new course work may not be the most desirable alternative. Rather, exercises and course content may be integrated into the existing curriculum. Lofaro (1982) goes on to describe a number of activities that could be included in basic counseling courses to generate sensitivity to disability-related issues and to develop competence in working with clients who have disabilities. Filer (1982) also describes a number of activities that could be integrated into existing counselor education courses to better prepare high school counselors for working with students with disabilities. These activities are designed to (1) motivate counselor trainees to work with children with disabilities, (2) teach counselor trainees the skills and resources needed to work with children with disabilities, (3) teach counselor trainees how to promote social interaction between students with disabilities and other students, and (4) teach counselor trainees how to help students with disabilities optimize their mainstreaming experience. There is some evidence that counseling trainees who receive training in disability issues develop a sensitivity to those issues. Kemp and Mallinckrodt (1996) found that counselors who received no training on disability issues were more likely than counselors who received such training to focus on extraneous issues and less likely to focus on appropriate themes for a sexual abuse survivor with a disability.

The outcomes of several court cases since the passage of the Americans with Disabilities Act suggest that counselors, psychologists, and other mental health workers may need to take courses in American Sign Language (ASL) in the future. Raifman and Vernon (1996) reviewed three state and federal court cases and concluded that "recent ADA court activity appears to have the consequence of requiring psychologists to become fluent in ASL before offering psychotherapy and psychodiagnostic services to deaf clients" (p. 377). They recommended that APA establish a subspecialty for service training and in-service training that will help psychologists learn ASL and recognize the special culture of deafness and its psychological implications.

Our Views on Training Models and Course Content

We believe that all counselors and other mental health providers should receive training to work with the four populations discussed in this book. Furthermore, we believe a combination of the integrated and separate course models is the most effective model for training counselors to work with nonethnic minorities. Ideally, issues related to people with disabilities, older people, women, and gay people should be integrated into all counselor training courses. As suggested earlier, however, this requires that each faculty member is sensitive to and knowledgeable about these special populations. Because most professors in counselor training programs were educated before training in diversity was mandated, we feel that a separate course will be needed to supplement attempts to integrate diversity issues into all counselor training courses for at least the next decade.

We also recognize that the resources available to a particular program will probably dictate which model is followed. Some programs, due to a unique mix of faculty, may find their faculty resources best suit an area of concentration model. It is important that the faculty of each program assess their resources and adopt an appropriate model for training counselors to work with nonethnic minorities. It is also important that the model adopted provide for training across the spectrum of client diversity.

We believe a counselor training program designed to prepare counselors to work with nonethnic minority clients will include three components: (1) experiences designed to confront students with their own biases and to sensitize them to the discrimination experienced by minority populations; (2) course content designed to familiarize students with the lifestyle and mental health needs of diverse populations; and (3) training in counseling strategies that are most effective with minority groups. As suggested earlier, we believe these components should be included in a separate class on nonethnic minorities, as well as integrated into all the courses in the counselor training program.

We suggest that each counselor training program develop a master plan for ensuring that content relevant to each non-ethnic minority group is included in all required courses. This plan could be based on accreditation requirements as Myers and Blake (1986) suggest, or it could be based on the program's own unique curriculum. In developing a plan, it is important to have direct input from representatives of the four groups discussed in this book. To the extent they are not represented on the faculty, the programs should seek out a consultant from nonrepresented groups who can help identify needed appropriate curriculum content and experiences.

The first step in developing a plan is to identify the knowledge and experiences counselors need vis-à-vis each minority group. The second step is to match knowledge and experiences with appropriate courses. We offer the following outline as an example of the kind of knowledge and experiences that should be integrated into the core counselor training program.

I. People with disabilities
   A. Counselor attitudes, values, biases
      1. Discussion of negative attitudes toward disability
      2. Methods of uncovering and addressing negative attitudes toward disabilities
      3. Promotion of positive attitudes toward persons with disabilities
   B. Summary of knowledge competencies
      1. Minimal medical information for counselors working with people with disabilities
      2. Knowledge of psychological aspects of physical disability

3. Knowledge of psychological aspects and adjustment to nonphysical disabilities
   a) Learning disabilities
   b) Mental retardation
   c) Knowledge of social conditions
   d) Discrimination
   e) Employment
   f) Health care
   g) Social services
   h) Laws
C. Counseling techniques
   1. Couples and family counseling
   2. Vocational counseling/rehabilitation
   3. Social change advocacy
   4. Environmental change focus

II. Older people
A. Counselor attitudes, values, biases
   1. Negative attitudes toward aging
   2. Geriophobia
   3. Positive perspectives on aging
B. Summary of knowledge competencies
   1. Definitions of aging
   2. Life span development and life transitions in old age
   3. Counseling needs
   4. Physical disabilities associated with aging
   5. Social conditions
      a) Discrimination
      b) Economics
      c) Health care
      d) Social services
      e) Victimization
      f) Laws
C. Counseling techniques
   1. Consciousness raising
   2. Group work
   3. Social change advocacy

III. Women
A. Counselor attitudes, values, biases
   1. Sexism
   2. Gender-role stereotyping
   3. Feminism
B. Summary of knowledge competencies
   1. Gender-fair models of mental health
   2. Biological sex differences

3. Sex bias in psychological theories
4. Psychology of women
5. Psychology of women of color
6. Knowledge of social conditions
   a) Discrimination
   b) Sexual harassment
   c) Women and work
   d) Multiple role conflicts and issues
   e) Health care
   f) Social services
   g) Laws
   h) Violence
C. Counseling techniques
   1. Gender-aware and feminist approaches to counseling
   2. Use of nonsexist psychological tests and interest inventories
   3. Feminist alternatives to traditional assessment (e. g., gender-role analysis)
   4. Career counseling for women
   5. Social change advocacy
IV. Gay men, lesbians, and bisexuals
A. Counselor attitudes, values, and biases
   1. Homophobia
   2. Heterosexist bias
   3. Appreciation vs. tolerance of gay men, lesbians, bisexuals
   4. Counselor' awareness of their own sexuality
B. Summary of knowledge competencies
   1. Past and current research on homosexuality
   2. Awareness of differences between being gay and nongay
   3. Awareness of differences between lesbians, gay men, and bisexuals
   4. Awareness of issues of gay men, lesbians, and bisexuals of color
   5. Theories of gay identify development
   6. The stages of the "coming out" process
   7. Internalized homophobia
   8. Gay relationships, lifestyles, and families
   9. Sources of societal oppression
      a) Discrimination
      b) Employment
      c) Health care
      d) Laws
      e) Violence
C. Counseling techniques
   1. Gay-affirmative counseling
   2. Gay support groups
   3. Gay lifestyle resources/referrals

4. HIV/AIDS counseling
5. Addictions counseling
6. Social change advocacy

Until such time as knowledge and experiences related to client diversity are integrated into all counseling classes, we feel there is a need to focus on diversity issues in a separate class. A separate class should examine the societal conditions that create oppression and discrimination. It should examine the mental health implications of oppression. It should also include a discussion of human rights counseling, with a focus on changing the environmental and social conditions that create client problems, rather than focusing on changing client attitudes and behaviors per se. A separate course of this type should teach skills that can be generalized to any minority group, ethnic or nonethnic.

Selection of Counselor Trainees

Assuming a faculty and curriculum sensitive to client diversity, a key component of preparing counselors competent to work with diverse clients is the raw material the program starts with, i.e., student receptiveness to client diversity. Because nonethnic minorities are discriminated against and because discriminatory attitudes are difficult to change, it is important for counselor training programs to include assessment of discriminatory attitudes in their student selection process. We believe a personal interview with questions that address ethnic and nonethnic minority issues is the best way to detect discriminatory attitudes. A background questionnaire also may be useful in the selection process; the purpose of the background questionnaire is to identify activities in which the applicant has been engaged that suggest discrimination against nonethnic minorities, or conversely, demonstrate interest and experience in working with special populations.

With respect to people with disabilities, women, and gay people, efforts should be made to ensure proportional representation. Selection of underrepresented populations for counselor training involves three phases: recruitment, admission, and support. A survey of counselor education programs indicated that only limited efforts were being made to recruit, admit, and support female students, students with disabilities, and gay students (Atkinson & Wampold, 1981). Because the possibility of bias in the selection process may exist for any one of these groups, every effort must be made to ensure they are given fair consideration. This should begin with a careful analysis of the selection process to determine if any built-in biases are operating. Another hedge against bias in the selection process is to have representatives of the minority group involved in all aspects of the selection process. A masked review of application materials, whenever appropriate, is another safeguard. Finally, counselor training programs must cultivate an environment of support for and affirmation of nonethnic diversity to enhance the success and satisfaction of all students.

Counseling Research

It is evident from psychology's treatment of nonethnic minorities, as reviewed in chapters 2 through 5, that past research has often been biased, usually based on a deficit model of the group being studied. This biased research, and the theories on which it has been based, has had a tragic impact on individuals and society alike. For example, disengagement theory and research have lead many elderly and elderly care providers to believe that after age 65 an individual's interest in social interaction should be expected to decline. We now know that elders will remain engaged in meaningful, productive interactions as long as social structures exist for their involvement and as long as their health allows for their involvement. Similarly, the variability hypothesis of sex differences was used as an argument in the early part of the twentieth century against admitting women to institutions of higher learning. Sex bias has been apparent in almost every area of psychological research and is still with us today (Enns, 1993). Psychological research has often denied the very existence of gay people; and when gays are studied, they are often stigmatized (Herek et al., 1991). Even in gay affirmative research, generalizations are problematic because of problems with the representativeness of the sample (Herek et al., 1991). Morin (1977), in a discussion of heterosexual bias in psychological research, pointed out that

> ". . . there is no such thing as a representative sample of lesbians or gay men. Researchers are sampling what is essentially a hidden or invisible population. Therefore, when homosexual samples are used, expanded subject descriptions that permit adequate replication are needed. (p. 636)

McHugh, Koeske, and Frieze (1986) have described three major types of barriers to sex-fair research that we believe can be expanded to research with any nonethnic minority group. The three barriers are (1) excessive confidence in traditional methods of research, (2) bias in explanatory systems, and (3) inappropriate conceptualization and operationalization.

Widely shared beliefs and biases may creep into the research process even though efforts are made to follow established research procedures (Denmark, Russo, Frieze, & Sechzer, 1988; McHugh et al., 1986). Excessive confidence in traditional methods of control is not warranted if these methods produce situations that are not reflective of "real-life" situations. "Context stripping" has been an ongoing problem in the study of gender issues (Gilbert, 1992). That is, many gender-related phenomena are manifest in specific social contexts; research that studies gender out of context may be seriously misleading. Further, excessive confidence in established (published) findings may cause them to be "cited repeatedly as evidence for a generalization when they are consistent with prevailing paradigms about human behavior, whereas important counterevidence may go unpublished or uncited" (McHugh et al., 1986, p. 881). In other words, studies may be (unintentionally) designed to confirm stereotypes of elders, people with disabilities, women, and gay people. Studies with results that support existing stereotypes are most likely to get published, and once published, are most likely to get cited.

Bias in explanatory systems refers to a model that is used to explain behavior for all members of the group when, in fact, the model applies to only a few members, if any at all. Biases that can affect explanatory systems include multiple and imprecise use of terminology (as when the term *handicapped* is applied to persons of differing ability regardless of situational factors), imprecision of explanatory model (as when simple biological, psychological, or sociocultural models are proposed to explain homosexual behavior), and "difference models" based on stereotypic assumptions (as when sex differences are proposed to explain differing performance levels between the sexes).

Inappropriate conceptualization and operationalization can occur when cultural ideologies about differences between groups of people influence psychological research and theory. For example, religious values play a prominent role in the deviance view of homosexuality that still underlies the thinking of many psychology researchers and practitioners. Any research that examines human behavior from the standpoint that behavior displayed by one group is inferior to or less desired than behavior displayed by another group may be conceptualizing differences in culturally biased terms rather than descriptive terms.

Other problems with research on nonethnic minority groups that can be generalized from the McHugh et al. (1986) concerns with sexist research include the fact that research topics are usually selected by researchers outside the group; minority group samples are often selected without concern for how representative they are of the entire group; tasks employed in an experimental setting may be familiar or salient for one group but not another; and identification of the experimenter as an outsider may affect how minorities respond to the study.

Although more recent studies have begun to dispel some of the myths generated by past research, caution needs to be exercised to ensure that potential biases are reduced in future research. While it is probably impossible to eliminate all bias in psychological research, we feel the most effective way to reduce research bias against any nonethnic group is to include members of the group in the research initiating and reviewing processes. Following are suggested procedures for involving nonethnic minorities in the research initiating and reviewing processes.

1. All members of research teams conducting studies on nonethnic minority groups should be informed about the special issues of these groups and should be committed to examining their own stereotypes and attitudes that might bias their research. Research questions should reflect the experiences and needs of the group, rather than be imposed from the outside.

2. Research that includes a nonethnic minority group (elderly, persons with disabilities, women, gay men, lesbians) as subject population should include a

member of that population on the research team. The nonethnic group representative should be involved in all phases of the research project, including the design, implementation, data collection, data analysis, and reported phases of the project. Publication credit should be assigned on the basis of the representative's contribution to the final product.

3. All research, whether funded by the federal government or not, should be reviewed by an independent human subjects' committee. Whenever a research project that includes a nonethnic minority group as a subject population is under review, the human subjects' committee should ensure that a member of the group is included in the reviewing process. In the case where the group to be studied is not represented by a standing member of the human subjects' committee, a representative should be added as a voting member for the purposes of reviewing the relevant proposal.

4. Similarly, research funding agencies should include a representative of a nonethnic minority group that is included as a subject population as part of their review team.

5. Editorial boards of professional journals should include representatives of nonethnic minorities at a parity with their representative in society. Every manuscript considered for publication should be reviewed by at least one board member who represents the nonethnic minority group included as a subject population.

Summary

Until counselor training and counseling research practices are brought in line with professional ethical and accreditation standards, direct services to nonethnic minority clients are likely to fall short of ideal practice. The suggestions offered here for changes in counselor training and counseling research should be viewed as a beginning point. At this point in the development of counseling as a profession, we have yet to determine the most effective ways of teaching and researching client diversity.

References

Agresti, A. A. (1992). Counselor training and ethical issues with older clients. *Counselor Education and Supervision, 32,* 43–50.

American Psychological Association. (1992). Ethical principles of psychologists and code of conduct. *American Psychologist, 47,* 1597–1611.

American Psychological Association. (1994). *Publication manual of the American Psychological Association* (4th ed.). Washington, DC: Author.

American Psychological Association Committee on Gay and Lesbian Concerns. (1991). Avoiding heterosexual bias in language. *American Psychologist, 46,* 973–974.

American Psychological Association. (1995). *Guidelines and principles for accreditation of programs in professional psychology.* Washington, DC: Author.

Anderson, J. A., & Rawlins, M. E. (1985). Availability and representation of women in counselor education with strategies for recruitment, selection, and advancement. *Counselor Education and Supervision, 25,* 56–65.

Association for Specialists in Group Work. (1991). Professional standards for the training of group workers. *Together, 20*(1), 9–24.

Atkinson, D. R., Morten, G., & Sue, D. W. (in press). *Counseling American minorities: A cross-cultural perspective* (5th ed.). Madison, WI: Brown & Benchmark.

Atkinson, D. R., & Wampold, B. (1981). Affirmative action efforts of counselor education programs. *Counselor Education and Supervision, 20,* 262–272.

Balcazar, F. E., Fawcett, S. B., & Seekins, T. (1991). Teaching people with disabilities to recruit help to attain personal goals. *Rehabilitation Psychology, 36,* 31–42.

Balcazar, F. E., Mathews, R. M., Francisco, V. T., Fawcett, S. B., & Seekins, T. (1994). The empowerment process in four advocacy organizations of people with disabilities. *Rehabilitation Psychology, 39,* 189–203.

Balcazar, F. E., Seekins, T., Fawcett, S. B., & Hopkins, B. L. (1990). Empowering people with physical disabilities through advocacy skills training. *American Journal of Community Psychology, 18,* 281–296.

Betz, N. E., & Fitzgerald, L. F. (1993). Individuality and diversity: Theory and research in counseling psychology. *Annual Review of Psychology, 44,* 343–381.

Brown, B. M. (1995). The process of inclusion and accommodation: A bill of rights for people with disabilities in group work. *The Journal for Specialists in Group Work, 20,* 71–75.

Brown, L. M., & Gilligan, C. (1992). *Meeting at the crossroads: Women's psychology and girls' development.* Cambridge, MA: Harvard University Press.

Bruce, M. A., & Christiansen, C. H. (1988). Advocacy in word as well as deed. *The American Journal of Occupational Therapy, 42,* 189–191.

Buhrke, R. A. (1989a). Female student perspectives on training in lesbian and gay issues. *The Counseling Psychologist, 17,* 629–636.

Buhrke, R. A. (1989b). Incorporating lesbian and gay issues into counselor training: A resource guide. *Journal of Counseling and Development, 68,* 77–80.

Buhrke, R. A., & Douce, L. A. (1991). Training issues for counseling psychologists in working with lesbian women and gay men. *The Counseling Psychologist, 19,* 216–234.

Byrd, K., Crews, B., & Ebener, D. (1991). A study of appropriate use of language when making reference to persons with disabilities. *Journal of Applied Rehabilitation Counseling, 22,* 40–41.

Cayleff, S. E. (1986). Ethical issues in counseling gender, race, and culturally distinct groups. *Journal of Counseling and Development, 64,* 345–347.

Cohen, E. S. (1990). The elderly mystique: Impediment to advocacy and empowerment. *Generations: The Journal of the Western Gerontological Society, 14* (Suppl), 13–16.

Cook, E. P. (Ed.). (1993). Women, relationships, and power: Implications for counseling. Alexandra, VA: American Counseling Association.

Copeland, E. J. (1982). Minority populations and traditional counseling programs: Some alternatives. *Counselor Education and Supervision, 21,* 187–193.

Council for Accreditation of Counseling and Related Educational Programs. (1990). *Standards for accreditation for graduate programs in counseling and student affairs practice.* Alexandria, VA: American Association for Counseling and Development.

Crabtree, J. L. (1988). Rehabilitation advocacy: A new role for therapists working with the elderly. *Physical and Occupational Therapy in Geriatrics, 6* (2), 3–12.

Crespi, T. D. (1988). Coping in the dark: Counseling adults with visual impairments. *Counselor Education and Supervision, 28,* 146–152.

Denmark, F., Russo, N. F., Frieze, I. H., & Sechzer, J. A. (1988). Guidelines for avoiding sexism in psychological research. *American Psychologist, 43,* 582–585.

Dworkin, S. H., & Gutierrez, F. J. (Eds.). (1992). *Counseling gay men and lesbians: Journey to the end of the rainbow.* Alexandria, VA: American Association for Counseling and Development.

Eichler, M. (1988). *Nonsexist research methods: A practical guide.* Winchester, MA: Allen & Unwin.

Enns, C. Z. (1993). Twenty years of feminist counseling and therapy: From naming biases to implementing mutifaceted practice. *The Counseling Psychologist, 21,* 3–87.

Enns, C. Z., & Hackett, G. (1990). Comparisons of feminist and nonfeminist women's reactions to variants of nonsexist and feminist counseling. *Journal of Counseling Psychology, 37,* 33–40.

Fawcett. S. B., White, G. W., Balcazar, F. E., Suarez-Belcazar, Y., Mathews, R. M., Paine, A. L., Seekins, T., & Smith, J. F. (1994). A contextual-behavioral model of empowerment: Case studies with people with disabilities. *American Journal of Community Psychology, 22,* 471–496.

Filer, P. S. (1982). Counselor trainees: Attitudes toward mainstreaming the handicapped. *Counselor Education and Supervision, 22,* 61–69.

Fitting, M. (1986). Ethical dilemmas in counseling elderly adults. *Journal of Counseling & Development, 64,* 325–327.

Fitzgerald, L. F., & Nutt, R. (1986). The Division 17 principles concerning the counseling/psychotherapy of women: Rationale and implementation. *The Counseling Psychologist, 14,* 180–216.

Garnets, L., Hancock, K. A., Cochran, S. D., Goodchilds, J., & Peplau, L. A. (1991). Issues in psychotherapy with lesbians and gay men. *American Psychologist, 46,* 964–972.

Gatz, M., Karel, M. J., & Wolkenstein, B. (1991). Survey of providers of psychological services to older adults. *Professional Psychology: Research and Practice, 22,* 413–415.

Gilbert, L. A. (1992). Gender and counseling psychology: Current knowledge and directions for research and social action. In S. D. Brown & R. W. Lent (Eds.), *Handbook of counseling psychology* (2nd ed.) (pp. 383-416). New York: John Wiley & Sons.

Glenn, A. A., & Russell, R. K. (1986). Heterosexual bias among counselor trainees. *Counseling Education and Supervision, 25,* 222–229.

Good, G. E., Gilbert, L. A., & Scher, M. (1990). Gender aware therapy: A synthesis of feminist therapy and knowledge about gender. *Journal of Counseling and Development, 68,* 376–380.

Graham, D. L. R., Rawlings, E. I., Halpern, H. S., & Hermes, J. (1984). Therapists' needs for training in counseling lesbians and gay men. *Professional Psychology, 15,* 482–496.

Hackett, G., Enns, C. Z., & Zetzer, H. A. (1992). Reactions of women to nonsexist and feminist counseling: Effects of counselor orientation and mode of information delivery. *Journal of Counseling Psychology, 39,* 321–330.

Hackett, G., & Lonborg, S. D. (1993). Career assessment and counseling for women. In W. B. Walsh & S. H. Osipow (Eds.), *Career counseling for women* (pp. 43–85). Hillsdale, NJ: Erlbaum.

Hadley, R. G., & Brodwin, M. G. (1988). Language about people with disabilities. *Journal of Counseling and Development, 67,* 147–149.

Hays, P. A. (1996). Addressing the complexities of culture and gender in counseling. *Journal of Counseling & Development, 74,* 332-338.

Herek, G. M., Kimmel, D. C., Amaro, H., & Melton, G. B. (1991). Avoiding heterosexual bias in psychological research. *American Psychologist, 46,* 957–963.

Iasenza, S. (1989). Some challenges of integrating sexual orientations into counselor training and research. *Journal of Counseling and Development, 68,* 73–76.

Kaschak, E. (1992). *Engendered lives: A new psychology of women's experience.* New York: Basic.

Kemp, N. T., & Mallinckrodt, B. (1996). Impact of professional training on case conceptualization of clients with a disability. *Professional Psychology: Research and Practice, 27,* 378–385.

Kitchener, K. S. (1984). Intuition, critical evaluation and ethical principles: The foundation for ethical decisions in counseling psychology. *The Counseling Psychologist, 12*(3), 43–55.

Laidlaw, T. A., Malmo, C., & Associates. (1990). *Healing voices: Feminist approaches to therapy with women.* San Francisco: Jossey–Bass.

Leigh, I. W., Corbett, C. A., Gutman, V., & Morere, D. A. (1996). Providing psychological services to deaf individuals: A response to new perceptions of diversity. *Professional Psychology: Research and Practice, 27,* 365–371.

Lofaro, G. A. (1982). Disability and counselor education. *Counselor Education and Supervision, 21,* 200–207.

Margolis, R. L., & Rungta, S. A. (1986). Training counselors for work with special populations. *Journal of Counseling and Development, 64,* 642–644.

McDonald, G. (1982). Misrepresentation, liberalism, and heterosexual bias in introductory psychology texts. *Journal of Homosexuality, 6,* 45–60.

McHugh, M. C., Koeske, R. D., & Frieze, I. H. (1986). Issues to consider in conducting nonsexist psychological research. *American Psychologist, 41,* 879–890.

Melton, G. B. (1989). Public policy and private prejudice: Psychology and the law on gay rights. *American Psychologist, 44,* 933–940.

Morin, S. F. (1977). Heterosexual bias in psychological research on lesbianism and male homosexuality. *American Psychologist, 32,* 629–637.

Moses, S. (1992). More clinicians needed to help a graying America. *APA Monitor, 23* (8), 34.

Munro, J. D. (1991). Training families in the "step approach model" for effective advocacy. *Canada's Mental Health, 39*(1), 1–6.

Myers, J. E. (1983). Gerontological counseling training: The state of the art. *Personnel and Guidance Journal, 61,* 398–401.

Myers, J. E. (1992). Competencies, credentialing, and standards for gerontological counselors: Implications for counselor education. *Counselor Education and Supervision, 32,* 34–42.

Myers, J. E. (1995). From "forgotten and ignored" to standards and certification: Gerontological counseling comes of age. *Journal of Counseling & Development, 74,* 143–149.

Myers, J. E., & Blake, R. H. (1986). Preparing counselors for work with older people. *Counselor Education and Supervision, 26,* 137–145.

Myers, J. E., Loesch, L. D., & Sweeney, T. J. (1991). Trends in gerontological counselor preparation. *Counselor Education and Supervision, 30,* 194–204.

Myers, J. E., & Sweeney, T. J. (1990). *Gerontological competencies for counselors and human development specialists.* Alexandria, VA: American Association for Counseling and Development.

Nelson, J. B. (1985). Religious and moral issues in working with homosexual clients. In J. C. Gonsiorek (Ed.), *A guide to psychotherapy with gay and lesbian clients* (pp. 163–175). New York: Harrington Park Press.

Netting, F. E., & Hinds, H. N. (1989). Rural volunteer ombudsman programs. *The Journal of Applied Gerontology, 8,* 419–431.

Norton, L. (1982). Integrating gay issues into counselor education. *Counselor Education and Supervision, 21,* 208–212.

Raifman, L. J., & Vernon, M. (1996). Important implications for psychologists of the Americans with Disabilities Act: Case in point, the patient who is deaf. *Professional Psychology: Research & Practice, 27,* 372–377.

Ruth, R., & Blotzer, M. A. (1995). Toward basic principles. In M. A. Blotzer & R. Ruth (Eds.), *Sometimes you just want to feel like a human being.* Baltimore: Paul H. Brookes Publishing.

Salisbury, H. (1975). Counseling the elderly: A neglected area in counselor education. *Counselor Education and Supervision, 14,* 237–238.

Schaie, K. W. (1993). Ageist language in psychological research. *American Psychologist, 48,* 49–51.

Scott, N. A., & McMillian, J. L. (1980). An investigation of training for sex–fair counseling. *Counselor Education and Supervision, 20,* 84–91.

Sobocinski, M. R. (1990). Ethical principles in the counseling of gay and lesbian adolescents: Issues of autonomy, competence, and confidentiality. Professional Psychology: *Research and Practice, 21,* 240–247.

Steininger, M., Newell, J. D., & Garcia, L. T. (1984). *Ethical issues in psychology.* Homewood, IL: The Dorsey Press.

Tabachnik, B. G., Keith–Spiegel, P., & Pope, K. S. (1991). Ethics of teaching. *American Psychologist, 47,* 506–515.

Thomas, M. C., & Martin, V. (1992). Training counselors to facilitate the transitions of aging through group work. *Counselor Education and Supervision, 32,* 51–60.

Vargo, J. W. (1989). "In the house of my friend": Dealing with disability. *International Journal for the Advancement of Counselling, 12,* 281–287.

Walsh, W. B., & Osipow, S. H. (Eds.). (1993). *Career counseling for women.* Hillsdale, NJ: Erlbaum.

Wolff, T. (1987). Community psychology and empowerment: An activist's insights. *American Journal of Community Psychology, 15,* 151–166.

Worell, J., & Remer, P. (1992). *Feminist perspectives in therapy: An empowerment model for women.* New York: Wiley.

AUTHOR INDEX

SUBJECT INDEX